W9-BGL-486

Advances in Image Analysis

Cover: The sequence shows (left to right) a segment of a commercial turbine blade, enhanced image, detected edges, and segmentation.

Advances in Image Analysis

Y. Mahdavieh
General Electric Aircraft Engines

R. C. Gonzalez
University of Tennessee, Knoxville

Editors

SPIE OPTICAL ENGINEERING PRESS

A Publication of SPIE—The International Society for Optical Engineering
Bellingham, Washington USA

Library of Congress Cataloging-in-Publication Data

Advances in image analysis / Y. Mahdavieh, R. C. Gonzalez, editors.
p. cm.
Includes bibliographical references and index.
ISBN 0-8194-1046-2. -- ISBN 0-8194-1047-0 (pbk.)
1. Image processing--Digital techniques. I. Mahdavieh, Y.
II. Gonzalez, Rafael C.
TA1632.A272 1992 92-25969
621.36'7--dc20 CIP

Published by
SPIE—The International Society for Optical Engineering
P.O. Box 10
Bellingham, Washington 98227-0010

Printed in the United States of America

Table of Contents

Contributors vii

Preface xi

Introduction

Chapter 0
Introduction
Y. Mahdavieh 3

Enhancement

Chapter 1
Adaptive Smoothing: Principles and Applications
J.-S. Chen, G. Medioni 13

Edge Detection

Chapter 2
Edge Detection from Severely Degraded Images
D. Lee 55

Chapter 3
Edge Detection with Gaussian Filters at Multiple Scales of Resolution
B. G. Schunck 75

Segmentation

Chapter 4
Hierarchical Segmentation Techniques with Applications to Magnetic Resonance Images
T. R. Jackson, D. M. Skyba, M. B. Merickel 109

Chapter 5
Color Image Segmentation
M. J. Daily 131

Chapter 6
Rewo's Filter and Image Segmentation
A. Niu, W. G. Wee 162

Feature Extraction

Chapter 7
Boundary Finding with Parametrically Deformable Models
L. H. Staib, J. S. Duncan 193

Chapter 8
Tracking Cells and Subcellular Features
L. M. Lifshitz 218

Chapter 9
Flaw Detection and Classification in Texture Materials
D. Brzakovic, H. Beck, N. Sufi 244

Morphology

Chapter 10
Introduction to Binary Morphology
R. C. Gonzalez, J. P. Basart 277

Chapter 11
Introduction to Gray-Scale Morphology
J. P. Basart, M. S. Chackalackal, R. C. Gonzalez 306

Chapter 12
Model-Based Morphology: The Opening Spectrum
R. M. Haralick, E. R. Dougherty, P. L. Katz 355

Motion

Chapter 13
Motion Analysis of Image Sequences
E. Salari 377

Chapter 14
Detection and Representation of Events in Motion Trajectories
K. Gould, K. Rangarajan, M. Shah 393

Applications

Chapter 15
Generating Structure Hypotheses in Cerebral Magnetic
Resonance Images Using Segment-Based Focusing and
Graph Theoretic Cycle Enumeration
K. L. Boyer, S. V. Raman, S. Sarkar 429

Chapter 16
Knowledge-Guided Boundary Detection for Medical Images
S. Tehrani, T. E. Weymouth 454

Chapter 17
Combining Edge Pixels into Parameterized Curve Segments
Using the MDL Principle and the Hough Transform
J. Sheinvald, B. Dom, W. Niblack, S. Banerjee 503

Chapter 18
Estimating Potato Acreage and Yield in the
Columbia Basin Using Landsat
G. R. Waddington, C.-F. Chen, L. Mann 537

Contributors

Saibal Banerjee
IBM Almaden Research Center
San Jose, CA 95120

John P. Basart
Iowa State University
Department of Electrical and Computer Engineering
Center for Nondestructive Evaluation
Ames, IA 50011

Hal Beck
University of Tennessee, Knoxville
Department of Electrical and Computer Engineering
Knoxville, TN 37996

Kim L. Boyer
The Ohio State University
Signal Analysis and Machine Perception Laboratory
Department of Electrical Engineering
Columbus, OH 43210

Dragana Brzakovic
University of Tennessee, Knoxville
Department of Electrical and Computer Engineering
Knoxville, TN 37996

Mathew S. Chackalackal
Iowa State University
Department of Electrical and Computer Engineering
Center for Nondestructive Evaluation
Ames, IA 50011

Chaur-Fong Chen
Oregon State University
Bioresource Engineering Department
Corvallis, OR 97331-3906

Jer-Sen Chen
Wright State University
Department of Computer Science and Engineering
Dayton, OH 45435

Michael J. Daily
Hughes Research Laboratories
3011 Malibu Canyon Road
Malibu, CA 90265

Byron Dom
IBM Almaden Research Center
San Jose, CA 95120

Edward R. Dougherty
Rochester Institute of Technology
Center for Imaging Science
Rochester, NY 14623

James S. Duncan
Yale University
Department of Electrical Engineering and Diagnostic Radiology
New Haven, CT 06510

Rafael C. Gonzalez
University of Tennessee, Knoxville
Department of Electrical and Computer Engineering
Knoxville, TN 37996-2100

Kristine Gould
University of Central Florida
Computer Science Department
Orlando, FL 32816

Robert M. Haralick
University of Washington
Department of Electrical Engineering, FT-10
Intelligent Systems Laboratory
Seattle, WA 98195

Theodore R. Jackson
University of Virginia
Biomedical Engineering
Box 377 Medical Center
Charlottesville, VA 22908

Philip L. Katz
University of Washington
Department of Electrical Engineering, FT-10
Applied Physics Laboratory
Seattle, WA 98195

David Lee
AT&T Bell Laboratories
Rm 2C-423
600 Mountain Avenue
Murray Hill, NJ 07974

Lawrence M. Lifshitz
University of Massachusetts
Biomedical Imaging Group
Medical Center
Worcester, MA 01655

Yaghoub Mahdavieh
General Electric Aircraft Engines
MD Q8
1 Neumann Way
Cincinnati, OH 45215

Lisa Mann
NASA Ames Research Center
MS 242-4
Moffett Field, CA 94035

Gerard Medioni
University of Southern California
Department of Electrical Engineering and Computer Science
Institute for Robotics and Intelligent Systems
Los Angeles, CA 90089-0273

Michael B. Merickel
University of Virginia
Biomedical Engineering
Box 377 Medical Center
Charlottesville, VA 22908

Wayne Niblack
IBM Almaden Research Center
San Jose, CA 95120

Aiqun Niu
University of Cincinnati
AI and Computer Vision Lab
Department of Electrical Engineering
Cincinnati, OH 45221

Subha V. Raman
The Ohio State University
Signal Analysis and Machine Perception Laboratory
Department of Electrical Engineering
Columbus, OH 43210

Krishnan Rangarajan
University of Central Florida
Computer Science Department
Orlando, FL 32816

Ezzatollah Salari
The University of Toledo
Department of Electrical Engineering
Toledo, OH 43606

Sudeep Sarkar
The Ohio State University
Signal Analysis and Machine Perception Laboratory
Department of Electrical Engineering
Columbus, OH 43210

Brian G. Schunck
University of Michigan
Department of Electrical Engineering and Computer Science
Artificial Intelligence Laboratory
Ann Arbor, MI 48109

Mubarak Shah
University of Central Florida
Computer Science Department
Orlando, FL 32816

Jacob Sheinvald
IBM Almaden Research Center
San Jose, CA 95120

Danny M. Skyba
University of Virginia
Biomedical Engineering
Box 377 Medical Center
Charlottesville, VA 22908

Lawrence H. Staib
Yale University
Department of Electrical Engineering and Diagnostic Radiology
New Haven, CT 06510

Nabeel Sufi
Aluminum Company of America
Equipment Development Division
Alcoa Center, PA 15069

Saeid Tehrani
Electronic Data Systems
5555 New King Street
Troy, MI 98007-7019

George R. Waddington
Cropix Inc.
Box 4180
Hermiston, OR 97838

William G. Wee
AI and Computer Vision Lab
Department of Electrical Engineering
Cincinnati, OH 45221

Terry E. Weymouth
University of Michigan
Department of Electrical Engineering and Computer Science
Artificial Intelligence Laboratory
Ann Arbor, MI 48109

Preface

Computerized image analysis is a field concerned principally with the automated extraction of information from data generated by two- and three-dimensional imaging sensors. This field has experienced significant growth in the past decade, motivated to a large degree by a wide variety of successful implementations based on processing platforms that range from inexpensive microcomputers to massively parallel systems capable of executing computationally complex algorithms operating on large volumes of image data.

Image analysis is a multidisciplinary field involving engineering, computer science, mathematics, physics, natural sciences, life sciences, and medicine. Today, it is not difficult to find commercial and scientific uses of image analysis in these and other fields. Typical applications include, to name a few, inspection of food products, dimensional and quality analysis of manufactured parts, character recognition for automated document processing, recognition of fingerprints, cell screening, analysis of earth resource satellite data, and a host of medical applications.

The level of activity in image analysis at university, government, and industrial research laboratories has kept pace with the increase in successful applications. Over the past decade, this level of activity has resulted in a virtual explosion of published information, causing the predictable difficulty of sorting through this material in a meaningful manner. As a consequence, there is a significant need for volumes such as this one, which attempts to bring together a selection of the latest results from researchers involved in state-of-the art work in image analysis.

This book is intended for scientists and engineers who are engaged in research and development in image analysis and who wish to extend their level of expertise in this field. It is also addressed to students following an advanced course of study in this area. The reader is assumed to have a general background in computer science, mathematics, and the fundamentals of image analysis. The book covers a wide range of timely topics organized into 19 chapters of comparable length.

Chapter 0 presents an introduction and overview of the book. The main areas covered are image enhancement (Chap. 1), edge detection (Chaps. 2, 3), image segmentation (Chaps. 4–6), feature extraction (Chaps. 7–9), morphology (Chaps. 10–12), motion analysis (Chaps. 13, 14), and medical (Chaps. 15, 16) and industrial (Chaps. 17, 18) applications of image analysis.

Acknowledgment

One of the editors (Y. M.) gratefully acknowledges General Electric Aircraft Engines for its support of this project.

Y. Mahdavieh
R. C. Gonzalez

September 1992

Introduction

Chapter 0

Introduction

Y. Mahdavieh

The subject of image analysis has been studied for more than 3 decades. Image analysis is about quantification and classification of images and of objects of interest within images. Here, we are dealing with the analysis of images performed by a computer. Recent interest in this subject has been motivated by the impressive advances in computer technology which have put within reach solutions to problems in a broad spectrum of areas of practical significance.

An image is a 2-dimensional distribution of energy, typically of light but it can also be X-ray, ultraviolet, infrared or other radiation, acoustic waves or nuclear imaging. In general, images generated from different sources can not be analyzed in the same way due to their characteristic differences. As an example, X-ray images may have a significantly lower and nonlinear contrast characteristics than images obtained from simple backlighting. Image analysis can vary from simple procedures (counting blobs) to complex operations (such as automated inspection of complex parts).

In the early 1960's image analysis generally was based on simple procedures for binary images. Analysis of binary images extended to gray-scale images during the 1970's as more main frame computers were introduced into the market. Applications of image analysis proliferated during 1980's as more high performance workstations became available. Improvements in cost/performance of personal computers have made image analysis a viable solution for applications that were previously dependent on the computing power of expensive main frames. The wide availability of large digital storage devices, more advanced integrated service digital networks (ISDN) and efficient data analysis algorithms will further stimulate the development of image analysis systems. The gap between theoretical and practical applications of image analysis is rapidly diminishing as the cost of imaging hardware and software continues to decrease. It is now possible to purchase a complete image analysis system for under $10K.

One of the problems with editing a book on image analysis is that there is little industry-wide acceptance of a common vocabulary, so that different terminology is frequently used by different authors for the same operations or elements of image analysis. The terms image analysis and image processing are often interpreted differently. Image processing often means simply improving an image in some way to make it easier for the human eye/computer to interpret, without any quantification or analysis taking place. Image analysis on the other hand quantifies as well as classifies objects of interest within the images.

Image analysis is a multifaceted subject that deals with sensors, data analysis algorithms, dedicated processing hardware and storage devices. This book is concerned only with the subject of data analysis algorithms. The purpose here is to cover the most important elements of data analysis tasks that one has to be aware of in order to successfully implement an image analysis system. The principal stages involved can be categorized as:

Image enhancement
Edge detection
Segmentation
Feature extraction and classification
Morphology
Motion analysis
Applications

This book will review recent developments related to the above topics. The intention here is not to have an exhaustive review but to include only selected material related to each topic. The chapters in the book follow the order in which an image analysis process takes place. As an example, segmentation of a given image into regions usually takes place before any features can be extracted and only after the image has been enhanced and edges have been detected. But this does not impose a rule in which all of the above modules are required for implementation of an image analysis system. The choice of integrating one or more of these modules is mostly application dependent.

The first four topics, namely: Image enhancement, Edge detection, Segmentation and Feature extraction are grouped together since they serve as a building block for most image analysis applications. However, each topic is covered in one or more chapters. The remaining topics: Morphology, Motion analysis, and Applications are treated as stand alone topics covered in separate chapters.

To further illustrate the concept of how the material in these chapters are related, consider the following example. Manufacturing of turbine blades includes complex interior passages and openings to the blade surface for blade cooling. These blades contain hundreds of holes (see Figure 1) drilled by a laser drilling machine. Any defects resulting from the drilling process can reduce the performance and life of the blades. This suggests 100% inspection of the blades which is performed by an X-ray inspection system. Images generated by the X-ray inspection system are currently interpreted manually by human operators. The cost of manual inspection combined with the inconsistency in accepting or rejecting blades has led to the development of an automated inspection system. The system reads X-ray images of blades, applies image enhancement tools to suppress noise and removes any nonlinear trends in the background. This is followed by detecting the edges of the cooling holes to be subsequently used for shape analysis and measurements. Images are then segmented into regions of interest and all other non-relevant regions are thresholded out. The system processes each region of interest and calculates several features that are input into a feature classifier from where a decision can be made about the status of the blades. The system incorporates morphological filters to remove certain kinds of noise and separates two or more regions of interests that are joined together as well as grouping those pixels that belong to one region. This example shows the flow of a typical image analysis process and the way in which the chapters are organized and related to each other. The following discussion considers each area in more detail.

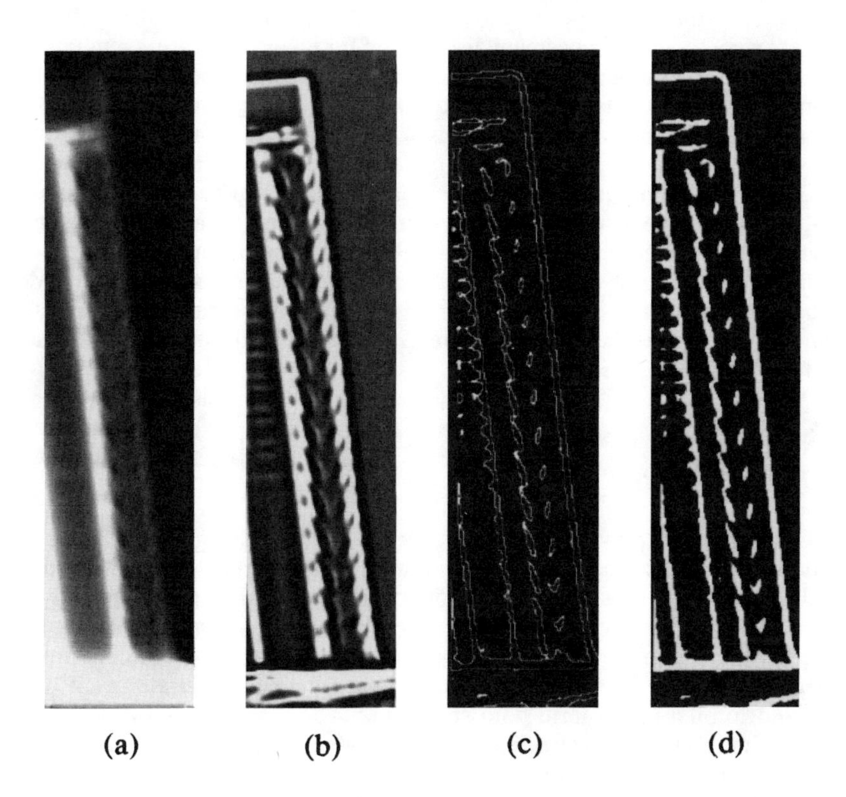

Figure 1: Leading edge section of a commercial turbine blade with laser drilled cooling holes (a), enhanced image of the blade (b), detected edges (c), and segmented regions of interest (d).

0.1 ENHANCEMENT

The purpose of image enhancement is to improve image quality by employing techniques that suppress noise, deblur objects boundaries and highlight some specific features within images. Image enhancement tools help simplify those operations (such as image segmentation, feature extraction and etc.) that normally follow the image enhancement step. Image enhancement also is used for image processing applications in order to enhance the image appearance for better visualization and image display. Histogram equalization, false coloring and sharpening are examples of enhancement techniques commonly used in image analysis.

Chapter 1 discusses an adaptive smoothing technique which is a nonlinear scheme that can achieve discontinuity preserving smoothing. The general idea behind this technique is to iteratively convolve a small mask with the signal to be smoothed. The coefficients of the mask are proportional to the gradient at each point and the degree of continuity of the signal. Adaptive smoothing sharpens the desired features in the image and removes noise at the same time. Several applications of this method are described in this chapter.

0.2 EDGE DETECTION

Edge detection plays an important role in almost all image analysis problems. Information content in the edges of an image can reveal important object characteristics such as shape and size. Most edge extraction techniques employ some type of gradient measure and often fail to provide satisfactory results for noisy images. The input image in most applications is often very noisy and subject to trade-offs between edge detail and noise suppression. Edge detection can be performed in single image resolution or multi image resolution using pyramid data structures. There is a trade off between the computation time and edge localization as the size of an image increases. Some of these issues are covered in chapters 2 and 3. Once the edges are detected, quantitative analysis can be performed. An example of this can be found in applications where objects are classified according to the irregularities of their boundaries or edges. In another example, edges can serve as a tool to register a reference image with an image to be analyzed. Edge detection techniques are application dependent and they vary from simple Sobel to more complex stochastic-based edge detection methods.

Chapter 2 describes a method of detecting edges from severely degraded images. The sources of degradation can be due to a defocused lens, long term exposure, and motion blur. In each case, an appropriate edge detector is explored in the context of invariant properties of edges. As a result, edge detection can be performed without dealing with computational intensive image restoration or blur identification.

Chapter 3 focuses on the subject of edge detection using multiple scales of resolution. The main part of this chapter is devoted to the description of an algorithm that detects step edges using Gaussian filters at multiple scales of resolution. The algorithm is designed in such a way that edges are localized and noise is removed. This technique eliminates the need for compiling a map of all edges detected at all scales and keeps only the most prominent edges. The chapter provides several practical applications and ends with a discussion and details of implementation issues.

0.3 SEGMENTATION

Image segmentation, the process of partitioning a digital image into regions, is important in nearly every application of image analysis. In particular, classification and description of the original images are usually carried out in terms of regions and properties of the segmented image. True image segmentation is important due to the fact that errors in the image segmentation process may propagate to measurement extraction and to the classification of the objects in the image and this may finally result in an erroneous image interpretation.

There are various segmentation algorithms that translate a group of pixels with similar image properties into simple and uniform regions. These can be grouped into three main categories as :

1) Thresholding
2) Edge detection
3) Region growing

Some of the above techniques are referred to as "bottom up" techniques in the sense that the image segmentation process relies on the individual gray values of pixels without using any knowledge of spatial relationships between various structures in the image. In contrast to "bottom up techniques", "top down" methods use information about the shape and position of regions of interest to guide the image segmentation process.

Chapter 4 describes a hierarchical segmentation technique and its application to medical imaging. The concept relies on an initial, approximate segmentation of the image from where the regions to be segmented are progressively refined. This technique is based on a "top down" approach which allows a priori constraints such as shape and location of regions of interest to be progressively used.

Chapter 5 focuses on the importance of color as a major attribute and its use in a segmentation algorithm. The chapter reviews various aspects of color image segmentation using variational energy-based approaches combined with the details of color transform formulation, color difference formulation, and multiple module formulation.

Chapter 6 studies the properties of Rewo's filter, its behavior, and capabilities in terms of segmenting concave or (convex) patterns. For images that can be modeled by a second order polynomial, the output of the Rewo's filter is proved to be a function of the sum of the second-order partial derivatives of the input image. The concept has been applied to detect and classify turbine engine water droplets resulting from heavy rain.

0.4 FEATURE EXTRACTION

Feature extraction is one of the essential steps that follow image segmentation. Typical features can be color, shape, area, texture, and several others. These features can be used to classify patterns, recognize shapes, or sort suspect parts from good parts. Features can be defined to be local, global, or both. Features based on only local image data can produce poor results due to image noise and poor image contrast. This problem has been recently investigated by using model-based image analysis techniques. Three chapters (7, 8 and 9) have been devoted to this important issue.

Chapter 7 describes a parametrically deformable model for finding object boundaries. The parametric model is based on the elliptic Fourier decomposition of the boundary. Since parametric representations use a small number of parameters, the computations needed for matching image and model data can be simplified.

Chapter 8 covers details of two algorithms for tracking cells and subcellular features. The first algorithm tracks the boundary of a slowly deforming 2-D object throughout a time series. The second algorithm is a model-based approach somewhat similar to one described in chapter 7.

Chapter 9 describes details of an expert system capable of detecting defects in surfaces that are generically characterized by complex texture patterns. Most of the techniques developed to date for feature extraction use a set of image features computed at a single level of image resolution. Chapter 9 includes a multi-resolution image representation scheme for extracting features to be used in texture analysis.

0.5 MORPHOLOGY

A rapidly evolving and promising field, mathematical morphology, provides tools that help to study and understand structure. The basic principle behind image morphology is to employ various shape structuring elements in order to implement image analysis tasks such as enhancement, edge detection, segmentation, and feature detection. Morphological functions are particularly attractive in image analysis applications with features that touch and are highly irregular in shape. Historically, practical implementations of image morphology have been limited due to extensive computational requirements. This is changing as new and dedicated image morphology hardware with good performance / cost characteristics becomes available. Image morphology is discussed in three chapters.

Chapter 10 starts with the introduction and basic principles of binary image morphology. This is followed by description and formulation of morphological filters ranging from simple operations such as erosion, dilation to more complex operations. This chapter ends with an illustration of binary morphology in a practical image analysis application.

Chapter 11 extends these concepts to gray-scale images and discusses various morphological processing tools applied to NDE of X-ray images. Some of the topics presented in this chapter include, gray-scale morphology, estimation of background trend and morphological edge detection. This chapter is extended to description of advanced tools such as the hit or miss transform, watershed segmentation, and image algebra.

Chapter 12 describes a morphological filtering model analogous to the classic Wiener filter. The model represents binary images in terms of an opening spectrum or opening basis for which the optimal restoration can be applied similar to a Wiener filtering method. The results of morphological filtering are compared to mean-square morphological filter estimation.

0.6 MOTION ANALYSIS

The subject of motion analysis refers to the task of estimating the movement of an object from a sequence of images as an object moves relative to a sensor. This movement results in an image flow field known as "optical flow" which carries information about the 3D structure, shape and boundaries of objects to be analyzed. Uses of motion analysis are found in medical, military, and industrial imaging applications.

Methods of motion analysis can generally be divided into two categories: feature matching and optical flow. The feature matching technique relies on the correspondences of extracted features between images in order to estimate the structure and shape of objects. Features can be simple, such as points, lines, curves, and surfaces, or complex features generated by combining simple features. Unlike the feature matching technique, the method of optical flow deals with the computation of velocity fields in an image and is more sensitive to noise.

Chapter 13 starts with an overview of some of recent work on motion analysis and describes a feature matching technique in detail. The emphasis is placed on the calculation of structure and motion from line correspondences.

Chapter 14 describes a method in which motion characteristics of moving objects are used without recovering the structure. This has the advantage of differentiating between objects that have the same structure and shape, but different motion. Included in this chapter is a multi-scale scheme for representing important events such as discontinuities in speed, direction, and acceleration of moving objects.

0.7 APPLICATIONS

The significant effort applied in the last three decades to image analysis has resulted in a number of applications ranging from military, space, commercial, medical and engineering uses of imaging. This book illustrates medical and industrial applications of image analysis. The challenges in medical image analysis are due to their complexity combined with a wide variety of detailed features and poor image contrast. These require more sophisticated segmentation and feature classification techniques. Industrial applications of image analysis are moving towards automation as more adaptive and robust data analysis algorithms are being developed.

Chapter 15 presents a method for the automatic generation of structure hypotheses and its application to the analysis of magnetic resonance images of the human brain. This method uses a segment-based edge focusing and detection scheme in order to obtain a set of primitives edge segments. The spatial relationships among the edge segments are stored in a proximity graph from where cycle enumeration methods are used to generate the structure hypothesis.

Chapter 16 discusses the difficulties associated with analyzing low contrast images of a moving non-rigid body such as cardiac X-ray images. This is further investigated by the development of a knowledge-based system that automatically extracts the left ventricular boundary using global and domain specific knowledge. This application can be useful as a diagnostic tool for assisting physicians during the manual interpretation of X-ray images.

Chapter 17 covers the principle of MDL (Minimum Description Length) and its applications to image analysis. This chapter includes details of using Hough transform in order to reduce a very large and irregular search space associated with MDL.

Chapter 18 concentrates on an application related to agriculture in which an accurate and timely monitoring of potato crops is valuable to growers and also for making marketing decisions. Neural networks combined with image analysis techniques are utilized as a tool for production management purposes. The results of using neural networks are compared to minimum distance and maximum likelihood classifiers.

Enhancement

Chapter 1

Adaptive Smoothing: Principles and Applications

J.-S. Chen, G. Medioni

1.1 Introduction

Feature extraction has long been considered as the first and necessary step in image understanding. Physical boundaries of objects are very important descriptors and are likely to generate edges during the imaging process. It is therefore reasonable to assume that the early stages in image analysis consist of detecting such discontinuities. Due to the complexity of the physical world and of the imaging apparatus, and to multiple sources of noise, the signal to be processed is complex, and the detection of such discontinuities is non trivial. Features detected locally can be validated only by considering a more global context. We begin by reviewing the major approaches chosen to tackle this challenging problem and classify them into three categories:

Optimal Operators: in this group, a single edge is considered. The goal is to find the optimal filter (in terms of signal to noise ratio) for the detection of such an edge. We only report the major ideas in this domain. Dickley *et al* [13] define an edge as a step discontinuity between regions of uniform intensity and show that the ideal filter is given by a prolate spherical wave function. Marr and Hildreth [25], extending the work of Marr and Poggio [26], convolve the signal with a rotationally symmetric Laplacian of Gaussian mask and locate zero-crossings of the resulting output. In their work, they mention that a multiple scale approach is necessary, pointing out the difficult problem of integration. Haralick [19] locates edges at the zero-crossings of the second directional derivative in the direction of the gradient where derivatives are computed by interpolating the data. In [20], his facet model is extended to the Topographic Primal Sketch. Canny [9] proposes to solve the problem by deriving, using variational methods, an optimal operator which turns out to be well approximated by a Derivative of Gaussian mask. Finally, Nalwa and Binford [30] propose an edge detector which fits, at each point, a set of surfaces within a window and accepts the best surface, in the least squares sense, which has the fewest parameters. They claim better results than those obtained using the Marr-Hildreth operator.

Since these methods ignore the occurrence of multiple interfering edges, they typically displace the true location of edges, or worse, fail to detect some of them. When the problem is displacement only, a nice method can recover the true location of the edges [10], but still leaves the problem of no-detection open.

Multiscale Approaches: as noted by several authors referring to the previous methods, automatic adjustment of the size (or scale) parameter is difficult, so using multiple scales should provide a reasonable answer. This idea is based on some physiological observations echoed in [24] for a few scales, but the integration of these discrete scales is an open problem. Instead of using discrete distant scales, Witkin [38] proposed a continuum of scales and showed that, at least in 1-D, the interpretation of the multiscale response made the important information explicit. In the case of more complex signals, the discretization of the formulation leads to the need for a large amount of memory allocation, such as in edge focusing [3], otherwise heuristics need to be applied to establish correspondence between scales. This was done with some success by Asada and Brady for 2-D curves [1] in their Curvature Primal Sketch, then by Ponce and Brady [33] and Fan *et al* [15] in the case of surfaces. In his paper [9], Canny defines a set of heuristic criteria for the integration of multiple size masks, and shows some promising results for two scales.

Adaptive Methods: the general idea behind adaptive smoothing is to apply a versatile operator which adapts itself to the local topography of the signal to smooth. Even though detailed overviews of some adaptive smoothing methods can be found in [11, 27] in which some evaluations are also provided, it is interesting to recall some ideas which form the basis of many of these methods, including the newest approaches.

One of the first interesting investigations in this field may be found in [23], in which Lev *et al* propose some iterative weighted averaging methods. In particular, they propose to apply at each point a weighted mask whose coefficients are based on an evaluation of the differences between the value at the center point and the values of its neighbors. A similar, but simpler approach, can be found in [37], in which the weighting coefficients are the normalized gradient-inverse between the current point and each neighbor. Another method consists in selecting the neighbor points which have the closest values from the value of the central point and replacing the latter by the average of these values [12]. More sophisticated methods are based upon local statistical studies of each point's neighborhood [27]. The major drawback of these iterated smoothing methods is that their convergence properties are unknown.

In more recent papers [6, 33], Brady *et al* prevent smoothing across previously detected discontinuities by using computational molecules proposed by Terzopolous [35]. This implies that they already have detected discontinuities, which is the problem we have to solve! Geman and Geman [17] propose to use simulated annealing, which is computationally very expensive. The results are impressive, but are shown only on images with very few gray levels. Blake and Zisserman [5] propose a different method which aims at overcoming the difficulty of local operator approaches by introducing weak continuity constraints to allow discontinuities in a piecewise continuous reconstruction of a noisy signal. Their results are very impressive, even though their method may require long computational times. A completely different approach, which makes use of the curvature of the underlying image surface, is proposed by Saint-Marc and Richetin [34], in which they apply a directional mask in the direction of least curvature in highly curved areas, or a standard averaging square mask otherwise. The results are very good, but this method is only applicable to the smoothing of surfaces, not to planar curves for instance. Parvin and Medioni [31] present a method to extract meaningful features from range images. Their strategy consists of automatically selecting an adequate kernel size for the detection and localization of such features. Although the method requires the non obvious setting of five parameters, it directly provides features at different scales and is applicable for curves. Finally, Perona and Malik [32] have proposed anisotropic diffusion in order to cast the problem in terms of the heat equation [22].

We propose a method, called *adaptive smoothing*, which turns out to be an implementation of anisotropic diffusion. The idea is to iteratively convolve the signal to be smoothed with a very small averaging mask whose coefficients reflect, at each point, the degree of continuity of the signal. After convergence, which may take an extremely large number of iterations, the resulting image consists of a set of constant intensity regions, separated by perfect step edges. Two effects can be observed during adaptive smoothing, one is the sharpening of those edges which would eventually become the boundaries the constant intensity regions, the other is the smoothing within each region. The smoothing effect is extremely slow and asymptotic, whereas the sharpening occurs after only a few iterations.

1.2 Adaptive Smoothing

1.2.1 Principle of the Algorithm

By far the most common filter used in smoothing is the Gaussian filter. As pointed out by many authors, such a filter has very desirable properties, in particular no new zero-crossings appear in the Laplacian of the smoothed signal as σ, the standard deviation of the Gaussian, increases [39]. In addition, Gaussian convolution can be computed efficiently by a cascade of convolutions with any finite averaging filter [8, 6, 9], using a small mask of equal weights for instance. In the case of a 1-D signal, we formulate this process as follows. Let $S^{(0)}(x)$ be the signal before smoothing, and the smoothed signal $S^{(t+1)}(x)$ at the $(t+1)^{th}$ iteration is simply:

$$S^{(t+1)}(x) = \frac{1}{N} \sum_{i=-1}^{+1} S^{(t)}(x+i) w^{(t)}(x+i) \tag{1.1}$$

with $N = \sum_{i=-1}^{+1} w^{(t)}(x+i)$ and $w^{(t)}(x) = 1$, $\forall x$ and $\forall t$

This filter smoothes the data everywhere, even across discontinuities. If we already knew the locations of these discontinuity points, then we could set the corresponding weights of the convolution mask $w^{(t)}(x)$ to zero, so that smoothing the signal near discontinuities would not take into account those points belonging to the discontinuities; and two points belonging to different regions separated by a discontinuity would not be averaged since we use a very small mask. For points belonging to discontinuities, the repeated averaging process would then force them to belong to one of the nearby regions, thereby enhancing the discontinuities.

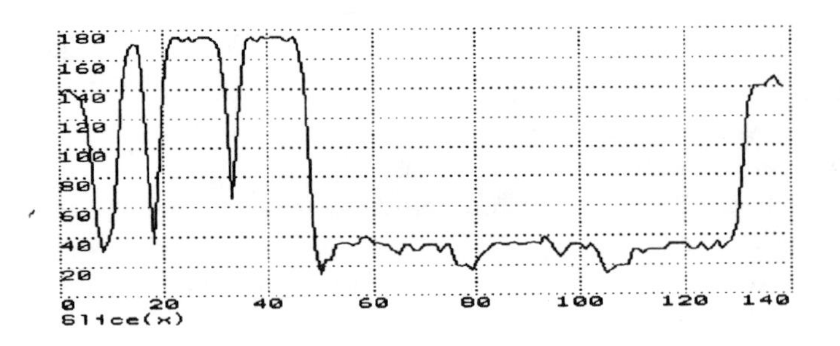

(a) Original 1-D Signal

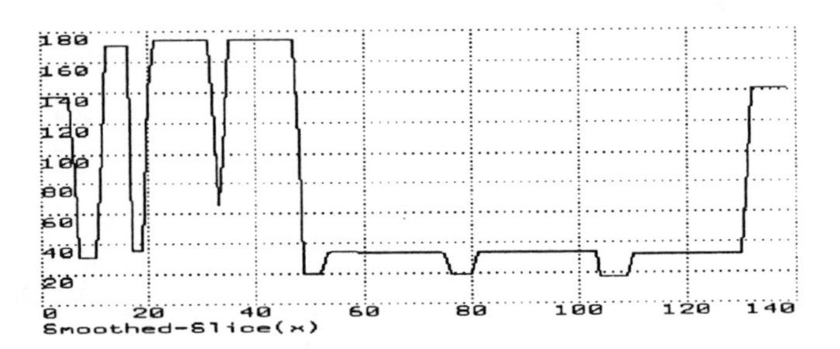

(b) After Adaptive Smoothing

Figure 1.1: Adaptive Smoothing of a 1-D Signal

Unfortunately, we do not know the locations of the discontinuities, otherwise our problem would be solved and we would not need any smoothing... Instead, we can formulate a guess by computing at each point of the signal a *continuity value* $w^{(t)}(x)$, using as in [32] any decreasing function $f(d^{(t)}(x))$ such that $f(0) = 1$ and $f(d^{(t)}(x)) \to 0$ as $d^{(t)}(x)$ increases, where $d^{(t)}(x)$ represents the amount of discontinuity at point x. An estimate of $d^{(t)}(x)$ can be computed simply by relating its value to the magnitude of the derivative at that point (if we assume that the original signal is approximatively piecewise constant) or it can be more elaborate as suggested in [32]. Hence a possible choice for the function f is:

$$w^{(t)}(x) = f(S'^{(t)}(x)) = e^{-\frac{|S'^{(t)}(x)|^2}{2k^2}} \tag{1.2}$$

where $S'^{(t)}(x)$ is the derivative of the signal $S^{(t)}(x)$, and k is a parameter controlling the degree of smoothing. Figure 1.1 illustrates the application of this algorithm on a 1-D signal which consists of a slice taken horizontally from a gray level image, as shown in figure 1.1(a) where the y-axis indicates the gray-level intensity and the x-axis the pixel positions along the extracted slice. As one can notice, this noisy signal contains several discontinuities of varying amplitude. The result of the application of adaptive smoothing to this signal after 250 iterations is shown in figure 1.1(b) with the value of k set to 2. Notice how smooth the signal is and how well the discontinuities have been preserved.

The parameter k determines the magnitude of the edges to be preserved during the smoothing process. The influence of this parameter is fully discussed in the next subsection, but we can summarize it as follows: If k is chosen to be large, all discontinuities disappear, and the result is the same as if Gaussian smoothing was used. If k is chosen to be small, then all the discontinuities are preserved, and no smoothing is performed. If we wait until the adaptive smoothing process converges, which may take an extremely large number of iterations, the resulting signal is piecewise constant. It is important to realize that there are two different operations affecting the signal as the iteration proceeds: one is the sharpening of the edges that will survive, the other is the smoothing within regions. The sharpening effect is obtained after just a few iterations, but the smoothing part is an extremely slow and asymptotic effect. It is therefore reasonable, for the purpose of edge detection, to stop the iterative process after only a few steps, since edges do not change afterwards, and to use a simple thresholding scheme in which the threshold is a simple function of the parameter k.

When the signal is a 2-D image $I^{(t)}(x, y)$, we define $d^{(t)}(x, y)$ as the magnitude of the gradient $(\frac{\partial I^{(t)}(x,y)}{\partial x}, \frac{\partial I^{(t)}(x,y)}{\partial y})^{\top} = (G_x, G_y)^{\top}$, computed in a 3×3 window. Therefore, the continuity value $w^{(t)}(x, y)$ is given by the following equations:

$$w^{(t)}(x, y) = f(d^{(t)}(x, y)) = e^{-\frac{|d^{(t)}(x,y)|^2}{2k^2}} \tag{1.3}$$

with

$$d^{(t)}(x, y) = \sqrt{G_x^2 + G_y^2}$$

The smoothed signal $I^{(t)}(x, y)$ is then defined at each point (x, y) by:

$$I^{(t+1)}(x, y) = \frac{1}{N^{(t)}} \sum_{i=-1}^{+1} \sum_{j=-1}^{+1} I^{(t)}(x + i, y + j) w^{(t)}(x + i, y + j) \tag{1.4}$$

with

$$N^{(t)} = \sum_{i=-1}^{+1} \sum_{j=-1}^{+1} w^{(t)}(x + i, y + j)$$

Figure 1.2 illustrates the application of the algorithm on the intensity image of an outdoor scene. Figure 1.2(a) shows the original image and figures 1.2(d) and (e) show the results after adaptive smoothing with k set to 6 and 10 respectively. The image has been smoothed while its discontinuities have been preserved. For comparison, we also show the results of Gaussian smoothing in figures 1.2(b) and (c) with the standard deviation (σ) of the Gaussian mask set to 2 and 4 respectively.

Figure 1.3(c) and (d) show the results of edge detection after adaptive smoothing of the intensity image of an outdoor scene (see section 2). The gradient maxima (in the direction of the gradient) above a given threshold τ were used. Notice that the location of the edges is not affected by the choice of the scale at which the smoothing was performed. For comparison, we also show the results of edge detection after Gaussian smoothing in figures 1.3(a) and (b) where, this time, the zero-crossings in the Laplacian were used. The edges are no longer localized correctly, hence the well-known coarse-to-fine correspondence problem.

(a) Original Image

(b) Gaussian Smoothing with $\sigma = 2$

(c) Gaussian Smoothing with $\sigma = 4$

(d) Adaptive Smoothing with $k = 6$

(e) Adaptive Smoothing with $k = 10$

Figure 1.2: Adaptive Smoothing of an Intensity Image

(a) Gaussian Smoothing with $\sigma = 2$

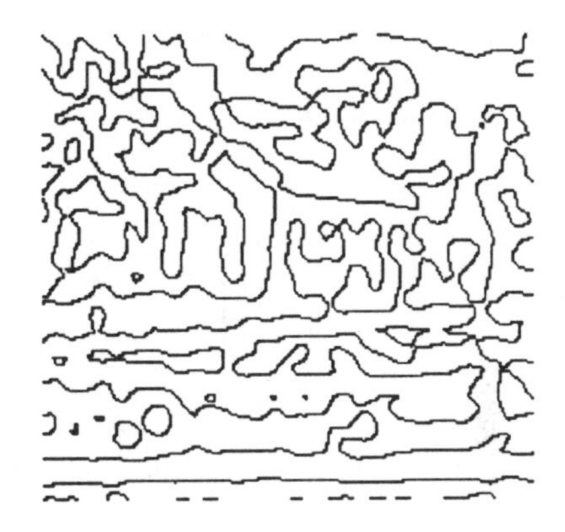

(b) Gaussian Smoothing with $\sigma = 4$

(c) Adaptive Smoothing with $k = 6$

(d) Adaptive Smoothing with $k = 10$

Figure 1.3: Results of Edge Detection

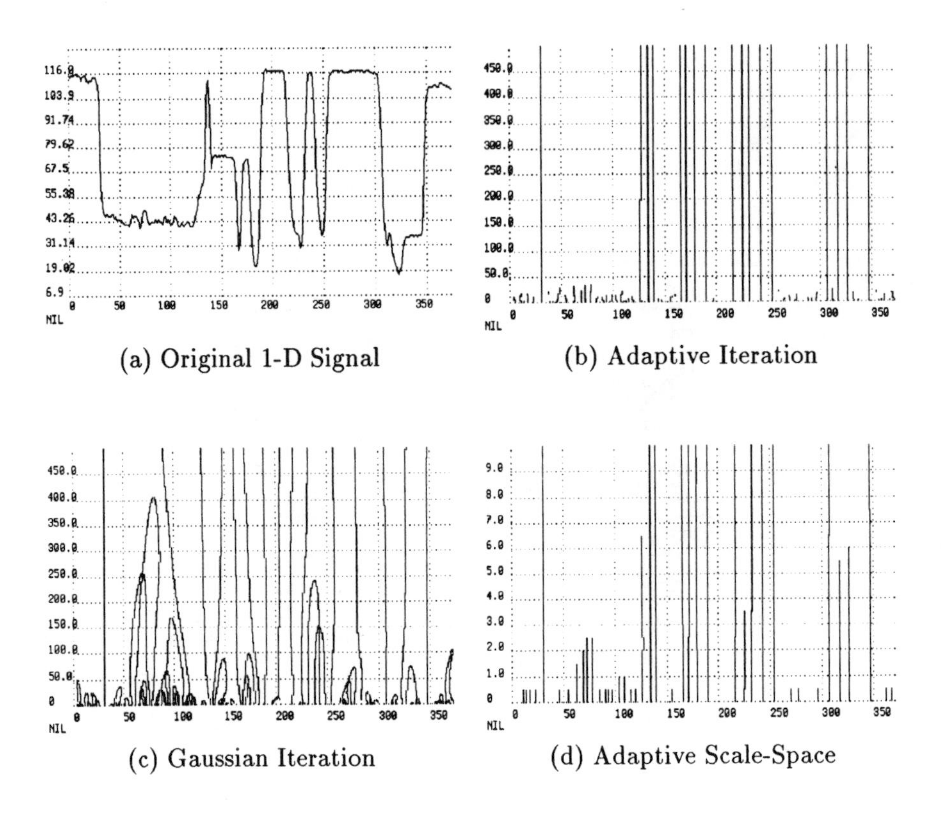

(a) Original 1-D Signal

(b) Adaptive Iteration

(c) Gaussian Iteration

(d) Adaptive Scale-Space

Figure 1.4: Scale-Space Representations

1.2.2 A New Scale-Space Representation

The purpose of multiscale signal processing is not only to identify the important features of a signal but also to construct a representation with different degrees of detail, which can be used for higher level vision tasks. Causality is a useful property for multiscale signal processing, i.e., features detected at a coarse scale are caused by features at the finer scales.

A scale-space representation of a 1-D signal can be visually displayed by a diagram which indicates the position of the discontinuities of the signal, computed at different scales (see figure 1.4(c)). The y-axis indicates the scale whereas the x-axis indicates the position of the discontinuities along the signal. Using adaptive smoothing, two different scale-space representations can be obtained.

The first approach, which is similar to Gaussian scale-space, is to fix k, the sensitivity or the threshold of the gradient magnitude, and then use the number of iterations to serve as scale (see figure 1.4(b)). Gaussian scale-space is a special case of this representation when k is set to infinity (see figure 1.4(c)). Note that in this case, the locations of the detected features do not change much as the iteration progresses (vertical axis). On the other hand, when Gaussian smoothing is used, the zero-crossings migrate and merge as the iteration progresses. Not surprisingly, discontinuities completely disappear after a certain number of iterations.

The other approach, which we call *adaptive scale-space*, is to use k as the scale while fixing the number of iterations. We prefer this approach because the iteration scale-space representation is useless in the case of adaptive smoothing since the location of the edges does not change along the scale (which avoids the tedious correspondence problem posed by traditional Gaussian smoothing). Having fixed the number of iterations to $n = 20$, adaptive smoothing has been applied to the signal of figure 1.4(a), with k varying from 0.5 to 10.5. The diagram of figure 1.4(d) shows for each value of k (vertical axis) the location of the zero-crossings along the smoothed 1-D signal. Because of the desirable properties of adaptive smoothing, it becomes feasible to represent a signal by just a few discrete scales, separated by an octave for instance.

1.2.3 Smoothing and Diffusion

We already pointed out that iterative averaging is commonly used for smoothing signals in early vision tasks. Iterative weighted averaging with constant weights is exactly implementing a linear filter by iteratively convolving with a very small mask. Considering the case of a 1-D signal, we can reformulate the iterative averaging process as follows:

$$I^{t+1}(x) = c_1 \times I^t(x-1) + c_2 \times I^t(x) + c_3 \times I^t(x+1) \tag{1.5}$$

with $c_1 + c_2 + c_3 = 1$ and $0 \leq c_1, c_2, c_3 \leq 1$ to guarantee the stability of the iterative process.

We can rewrite the above iteration scheme as follows:

$$I^{t+1}(x) - I^t(x) = c_1 \times (I^t(x-1) - I^t(x)) + c_3 \times (I^t(x+1) - I^t(x)) \tag{1.6}$$

In particular, when $c_1 = c_3$, it reduces to:

$$I^{t+1}(x) - I^t(x) = c_1 \times (I^t(x-1) - 2I^t(x) + I^t(x+1)) \tag{1.7}$$

which is a discrete approximation of the heat diffusion equation:

$$\frac{\partial I}{\partial t} = c\nabla^2 I \tag{1.8}$$

This formulation is therefore equivalent to Gaussian smoothing and the number of iterations is related to σ, the standard deviation of the Gaussian kernel. But we already saw that this filter smoothes the data everywhere, even across discontinuities.

When the weights are allowed to vary along spatial locations as well as time, we can rewrite the weighted averaging scheme as follows:

$$I^{t+1}(x) = c^t(x-1) \times I^t(x-1) + c^t(x) \times I^t(x) + c^t(x+1) \times I^t(x+1) \tag{1.9}$$

with

$$c^t(x-1) + c^t(x) + c^t(x+1) = 1 \quad \text{and} \quad 0 \leq c^t(x-1), c^t(x), c^t(x+1) \leq 1$$

It can be rearranged as:

$$I^{t+1}(x)-I^t(x) = c^t(x-1)\times(I^t(x-1)-I^t(x))+c^t(x+1)\times(I^t(x+1)-I^t(x)) \quad (1.10)$$

or

$$I^{t+1}(x)-I^t(x) = c^t(x+1)\times(I^t(x+1)-I^t(x))-c^t(x-1)\times(I^t(x)-I^t(x-1)) \quad (1.11)$$

which is implementing the anisotropic diffusion proposed by Perona and Malik [32]:

$$\frac{\partial I}{\partial t} = \nabla(c\nabla I) \quad (1.12)$$

1.2.4 Analysis of the Algorithm

Iterative Behavior

If we wait until the adaptive smoothing process converges, which may take an extremely large number of iterations, the resulting signal is piecewise constant. It is important to realize that there are two different operations affecting the image as the iteration proceeds: one is the sharpening of the edges that will survive, the other is the smoothing of regions. The sharpening effect is obtained after just a few iterations, but the smoothing part is an extremely slow and asymptotic effect. It is therefore reasonable, for the purpose of edge detection, to stop the iterative process after only a few steps, since edges do not change afterwards, and to use a simple thresholding scheme in which the threshold is a simple function of the parameter k. Note that, from these edges, it is also possible to predict the final convergence state for the entire image accurately, and therefore to reconstruct it (if necessary).

The stability problem concerns the unbounded growth or the controlled decay or boundness of the exact solution of the finite-difference equations, and therefore of all rounding errors introduced during the computation because the errors and exact solution are processed by the same arithmetic operations. The essential criterion defining stability is that this numerical process should limit the amplification of all components from the initial conditions.

A constant-coefficient iterative process, such as Gaussian smoothing (the solution to the diffusion partial differential equation), can be written as follows:

$$\mathbf{u}_{t+1} = \mathbf{A}u_t + \mathbf{b}_t \quad (1.13)$$

where $\mathbf{b}_t$ is a column vector of known boundary-values and zeroes, and matrix $\mathbf{A}$ is an $N \times N$ matrix of known elements and N is the number of data points. In order for the process to be stable, then, for some norm, $\mathbf{A}$ must satisfy $||\mathbf{A}|| \leq 1$.

The basic derivation of the above stability condition comes from the following famous equation of the norm:

$$||\mathbf{A}^n|| = ||\mathbf{A}\mathbf{A}^{n-1}|| \leq ||\mathbf{A}||||\mathbf{A}^{n-1}|| \leq ... \leq ||\mathbf{A}||^n \quad (1.14)$$

It follows that if $||\mathbf{A}|| \leq 1$ then $||\mathbf{A}^n|| \leq 1$, then the stability is guaranteed as the iteration progresses.

The same principle can be applied to a non-linear partial differential equation, more specifically, to the iterative process where the matrix $\mathbf{A}$ is actually time-dependent. Let us rewrite the iteration as follows:

$$\mathbf{u}_{t+1} = \mathbf{A}_t \mathbf{u}_t + \mathbf{b}_t \tag{1.15}$$

As a general property of the definition of a norm, it follows that:

$$||\mathbf{A}_{n-1}\mathbf{A}_{n-2}...\mathbf{A}_1\mathbf{A}_0|| \leq ||\mathbf{A}_{n-1}||||\mathbf{A}_{n-2}||...||\mathbf{A}_1||||\mathbf{A}_0|| \tag{1.16}$$

Therefore if we can guarantee that $||\mathbf{A}_k|| \leq 1$ for $k = 0, 1, ..., n-2, n-1$, we can guarantee the stability of the iterative process. We now show that the matrix A_t of the adaptive smoothing satisfies the stability requirement.

Let us consider the 1-D adaptive smoothing iteration equation:

$$u_x^{(t+1)} = \frac{1}{R^{(t)}} \sum_{i=-1}^{+1} u_{x+i}^{(t)} c_{x+i}^{(t)} \tag{1.17}$$

with

$$R^{(t)} = \sum_{i=-1}^{+1} c_{x+i}^{(t)}$$

We can rewrite the above equation in vector and matrix form as:

$$\mathbf{u}_{t+1} = \mathbf{A}_t \mathbf{u}_t \tag{1.18}$$

where $\mathbf{A}_t$ has the following form:

$$\begin{bmatrix} .... & .... & .... & .... & .... & .... & .... \\ .... & 0 & \frac{c_{x-2}}{c_{x-2}+c_{x-1}+c_x} & \frac{c_{x-1}}{c_{x-2}+c_{x-1}+c_x} & \frac{c_x}{c_{x-2}+c_{x-1}+c_x} & 0 & .... \\ .... & .... & 0 & \frac{c_{x-1}}{c_{x-1}+c_x+c_{x+1}} & \frac{c_x}{c_{x-1}+c_x+c_{x+1}} & \frac{c_{x+1}}{c_{x-1}+c_x+c_{x+1}} & 0 \\ .... & .... & .... & .... & .... & .... & .... \end{bmatrix}$$

The infinity norm of a matrix is simply the maximum sum of the moduli of the elements of the matrix. Since the continuity values are always positive, the infinity norm of our iteration matrix is unity, because

$$||\mathbf{A}_t||_\infty = \frac{c_{x-1}}{c_{x-1} + c_x + c_{x+1}} + \frac{c_x}{c_{x-1} + c_x + c_{x+1}} + \frac{c_{x+1}}{c_{x-1} + c_x + c_{x+1}} = 1 \tag{1.19}$$

Also, the largest of the moduli of the eigenvalues of the square matrix cannot exceed its infinity norm, i.e.

$$\rho(\mathbf{A}) \leq ||\mathbf{A}||_\infty \tag{1.20}$$

Therefore the 2-norm of the matrix $\mathbf{A}_t$ is also bounded by unity. And we derive the stability of the iteration of adaptive smoothing since $||\mathbf{A}_t|| \leq 1$ is always guaranteed during the iterative process.

The parameter k

In Gaussian smoothing, there is one parameter controlling the degree of smoothing, namely σ. Choosing a value for σ is equivalent to choosing the number of iterative convolutions with a small fixed averaging mask.

Adaptive smoothing, because it implements anisotropic diffusion, inherits the nice scaling behavior of the scale space of Gaussian smoothing when using the number of iterations as the scale parameter in the scale space. As stated earlier, the behavior of adaptive smoothing includes inter-region edge sharpening as well as intra-region edge smoothing. The locations of the inter-region edges will basically remain unchanged as the iteration progresses, while the locations of the intra-region edges will deviate along the iteration scale until they finally disappear. We choose the parameter k (in the computation of the continuity function c) to be the scale parameter of our new scale space. It has a stable interpretation at each scale when the iteration converges, and also the new scale space representation has the property of accurate edge detection at different scales, therefore removing the tedious correspondence problem encountered in the traditional scale space.

Let us consider a 1-D signal as shown in figure 1.5, and denote the signal as $f(x)$. At the neighborhood of the edge, $f(x)$ increases as x increases, i.e. $f_x > 0$. Also note that $f_{xxx} < 0$ in our example. Recall that the continuity function:

$$C(x,t) = e^{-\frac{f_x(x,t)^2}{2k^2}} \tag{1.21}$$

and the adaptive smoothing is the approximation of the following anisotropic diffusion:

$$\frac{df(x,t)}{dt} = \frac{d}{dx}(C(x,t)f_x(x,t)) \tag{1.22}$$

which can be expanded as:

$$\frac{df(x,t)}{dt} = f_{xx(x,t)}e^{-\frac{f_x(x,t)^2}{2k^2}}(1 - \frac{f_x(x,t)^2}{k^2}) \tag{1.23}$$

In order to observe the edge sharpening effect, we monitor the term $\frac{d}{dt}(\frac{df}{dx})$ which represents the change of the gradient or contrast $(\frac{df}{dx})$ along the time dimension, or as the iterations progress. Since $f(x,t)$ is a differentiable function, the order of differentiation (with respect to x and to t) is interchangeable, therefore:

$$\frac{d}{dt}(\frac{df}{dx}) = \frac{d}{dx}(\frac{df}{dt}) = f_{xxx}e^{-\frac{f_x^2}{2k^2}}(1 - \frac{f_x^2}{k^2}) + f_{xx}(\frac{d}{dx}(e^{-\frac{f_x(x,t)^2}{2k^2}}(1 - \frac{f_x(x,t)^2}{k^2}))) \tag{1.24}$$

Since $f_{xxx} < 0$, $f_{xx} = 0$ and the exponential term is always positive, the sign of $\frac{d}{dt}(\frac{df}{dx})$ is completely determined by the sign of $(1 - \frac{f_x^2}{k^2})$. In particular:

$$\frac{d}{dt}(\frac{df}{dx}) > 0 \; when \; f_x > k$$

and

$$\frac{d}{dt}(\frac{df}{dx}) < 0 \; when \; f_x < k$$

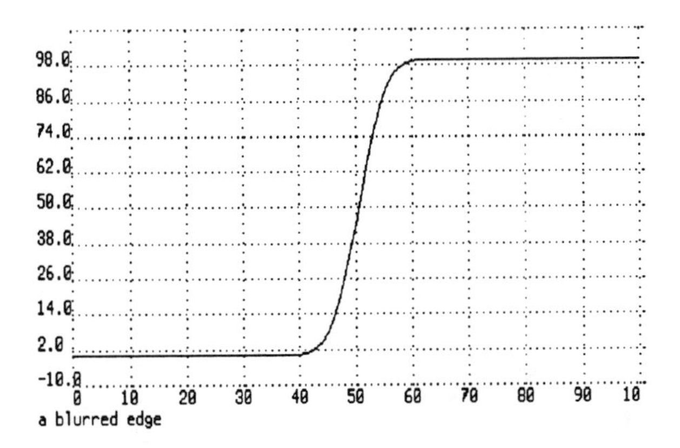

Figure 1.5: Profile of a blurred edge

Therefore we see that when the gradient is large enough ($f_x > k$), it will increase its magnitude as the iterations progress, achieving the edge sharpening effect. On the other hand, if the gradient is small ($f_x < k$), it will be smoothed eventually. The parameter k approximately sets the threshold to the gradient magnitude where discontinuities are preserved.

1.2.5 Preserving Higher Order Discontinuities

What happens if the original signal cannot be considered as approximatively piecewise constant? This question is of great importance if we wish to apply adaptive smoothing to the processing of range images for instance. Also, in range imagery, surface orientation discontinuities need to be preserved in addition to depth discontinuities. Figure 1.6(a) shows the $126 \times 131 \times 8$ bits range image of a toy chair, to which Gaussian noise ($\sigma = 10$) has been added. Here, depth is inversely encoded by gray-level. The higher the gray-level of a pixel, the closer it is to the sensor. We extracted from this image a vertical slice, which is displayed in figure 1.6(b), with the y-axis showing the range along that slice. We applied to this 1-D signal the same algorithm as for the 1-D signal of figure 1.1, leading, after 250 iterations, to the smoothed signal shown in figure 1.6(c). The depth discontinuities have obviously been preserved, but as the signal is not piecewise constant, areas with significant values of the derivative have been broken up into constant pieces. Furthermore, tangent orientation discontinuities have not been preserved.

There is an elegant solution that solves both of the above mentioned problems at the same time: instead of applying adaptive smoothing to the signal itself, the idea is to apply it to its first derivative. Figure 1.6(d) shows the result obtained with this method. Since we process the derivative only, the smoothed signal is not directly accessible. For the purpose of display only, we have performed a numerical integration of the smoothed derivative. The noise has been removed, while discontinuities, including tangent discontinuities, have been preserved.

We can now generalize this approach to the smoothing of a range image

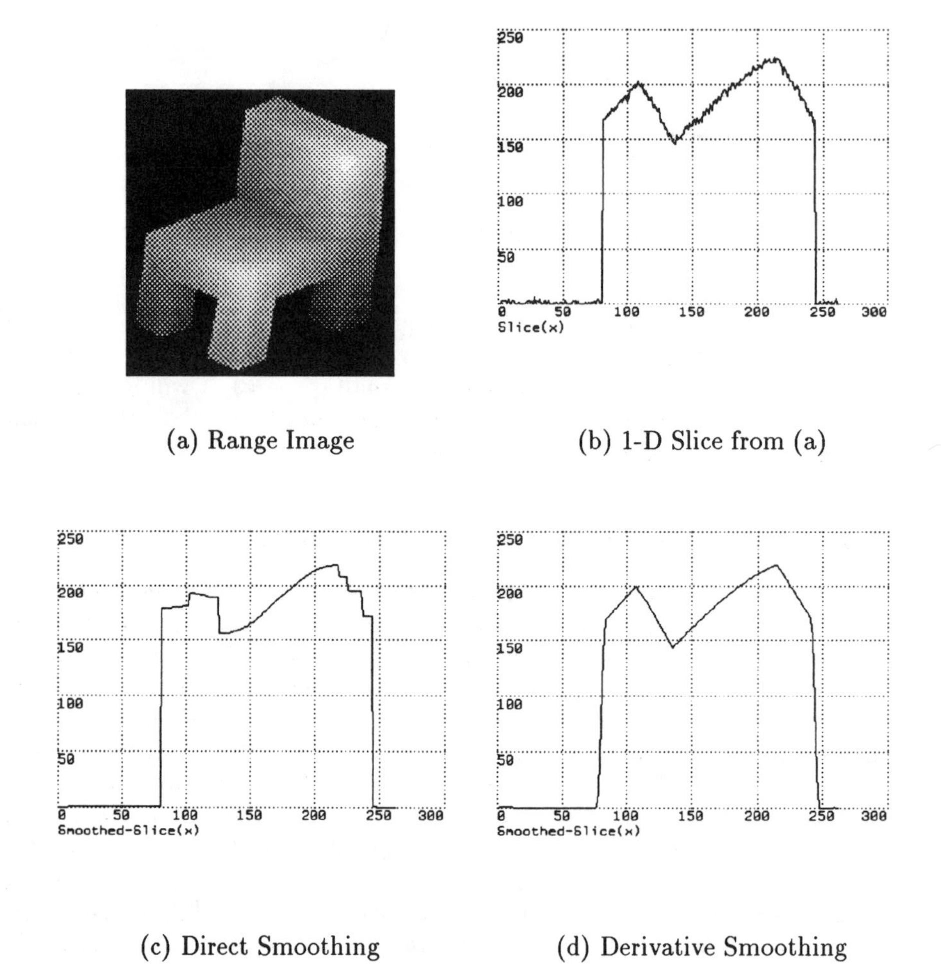

(a) Range Image

(b) 1-D Slice from (a)

(c) Direct Smoothing

(d) Derivative Smoothing

Figure 1.6: Preserving First Order Discontinuities.

$R^{(t)}(x,y)$. Let $P^{(t)}(x,y) = \frac{\partial R^{(t)}(x,y)}{\partial x}$ and $Q^{(t)}(x,y) = \frac{\partial R^{(t)}(x,y)}{\partial y}$ be the first derivative images of $R^{(t)}(x,y)$. The smoothed versions of $P^{(t)}(x,y)$ and $Q^{(t)}(x,y)$ are obtained according to the formula in equation 1.4, in which

$$d^{(t)}(x,y) = \Delta = \frac{\partial P^{(t)}(x,y)}{\partial x} + \frac{\partial Q^{(t)}(x,y)}{\partial y} \quad \text{(Laplacian)}$$

Note that here, $w^{(t)}(x,y)$ *simultaneously* reflects the continuity of both partial derivatives, so that the smoothing of $P^{(t)}(x,y)$ and $Q^{(t)}(x,y)$ cannot be performed independently, which is legitimate. The choice of the Laplacian is not unique but is the simplest. It would have been possible for instance to consider the quadratic variation or another measure of the local variation of the first derivatives. Furthermore, we do not attempt to impose the integrability constraint as it would lead to a much more complex expression (see [5], page 120 for a similar argument).

Even though the smoothed version of a given range image is not directly accessible using this scheme, one can compute values such as surface normals or principal curvatures from the available smoothed partial derivative images. For instance, it is possible to directly compute a shaded image of the smoothed range image using the smoothed partial derivatives [1]. Figure 1.7(a) shows the shaded image of the original range image of a complex object (a tooth) including jumps and creases. We applied the adaptive smoothing scheme to this range image, and the resulting shaded image after 10 iterations is shown in figure 1.7(b). The jumps and creases have been preserved while the curved surface has been smoothed in between, the irregularities present in the original range image having disappeared. Using the smoothed derivative images and eventually their derivatives, surface features such as jumps and creases can then be easily extracted using a simple thresholding scheme.

1.2.6 Range Image Segmentation

Surface curvature has been widely used recently by many researchers to achieve range image segmentation [4, 6, 15, 33]. Indeed, local curvature is an excellent tool to characterize a surface, especially because it captures *intrinsic* properties of the surface. The extraction of meaningful features from range images is thus possible by locally observing the behavior of the curvature. Zero-crossings and extrema of the maximal curvature are particularly interesting. Unfortunately, as curvature is very sensitive to noise, it is often difficult to both detect and localize *precisely* such events. Ponce and Brady [33] and Fan *et al* [16] both propose to solve this problem by integrating multiple scales, in effect *detecting* features at a coarser scale and *locating* them at a finer scale. Since there is, in general, no one-to-one correspondence, they use heuristics to resolve ambiguities.

As range image adaptive smoothing is applied to the first partial derivatives, the latter are directly available to compute the second partial derivatives, and hence the principal curvatures which we use to detect surface discontinuities. Figure 1.8 shows the result of the extraction of the surface orientation discontinuities from the range image of a toy chair. This extraction is performed as follows: we

[1] A shaded image of a range image is easily obtained by computing at each point the dot product of the surface normal unit vector with the unit vector pointing to an arbitrary light source.

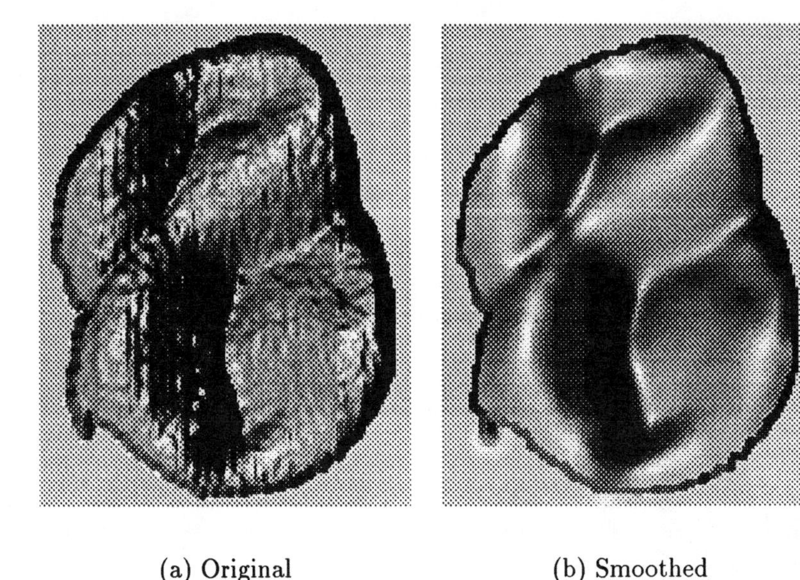

(a) Original (b) Smoothed

Figure 1.7: Adaptive Smoothing of a Range Image

first label all points in the image at which there is an extremum of the maximal curvature (in the direction of the maximal curvature). Then, starting from all points at which the maximal curvature is above a high threshold τ_1 (in absolute value), we follow the "contours" using hysteresis [9] until the maximal curvature becomes less than a low threshold τ_2. We use a similar scheme to extract zero-crossings of the maximal curvature.

Figure 1.8(a) and figure 1.8(b) show the results obtained after Gaussian smoothing with $\sigma = 2$ and $\sigma = 4$ respectively. The latter one is smoothed adequately, but the blurring effect causes the extrema to be detected away from their true locations. Figure 1.8(c) shows the result obtained after adaptive smoothing: the extrema are very well detected *and* localized. It is also important to note that since the discontinuities have also been enhanced during the smoothing process, the method is relatively insensitive to the choice of the thresholds τ_1 and τ_2.

1.3 Implementations

1.3.1 Serial Machine

We have already seen in the previous section some results of adaptive smoothing in the case of different types of signal: 1-D signal, intensity image, and range image. The different versions of the algorithm have been implemented on a Symbolics LISP machine. Typically, it takes 10 seconds per iteration to smooth a 128×128 intensity image. Since very few iterations are needed to achieve edge sharpening, feature extraction can be performed in a reasonable amount of time. If, however, a significant amount of smoothing is needed, then computational times may be much larger.

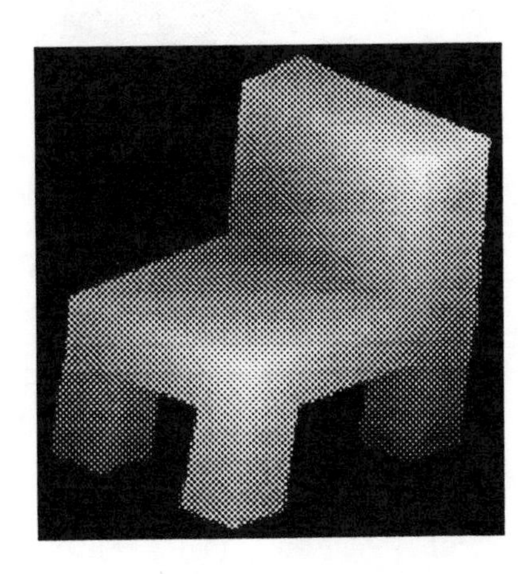

(a) Range Image

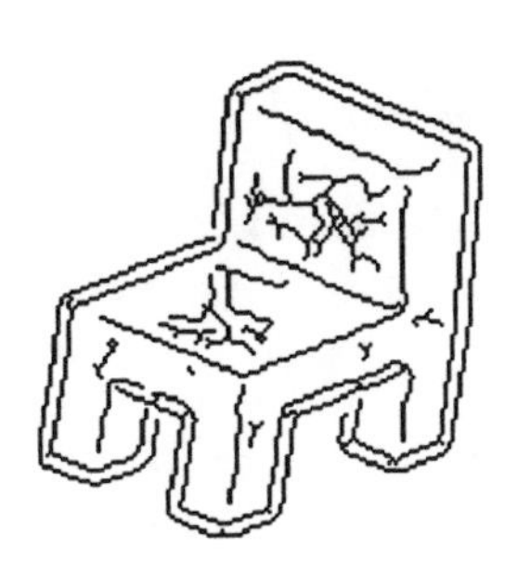

(b) Gaussian Smoothing with $\sigma = 2$

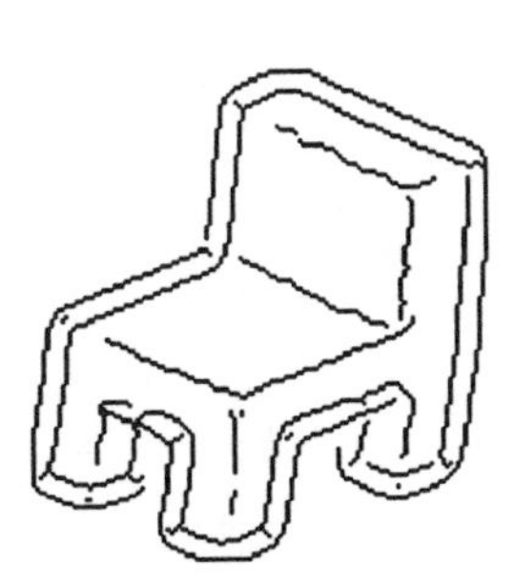

(c) Gaussian Smoothing with $\sigma = 4$

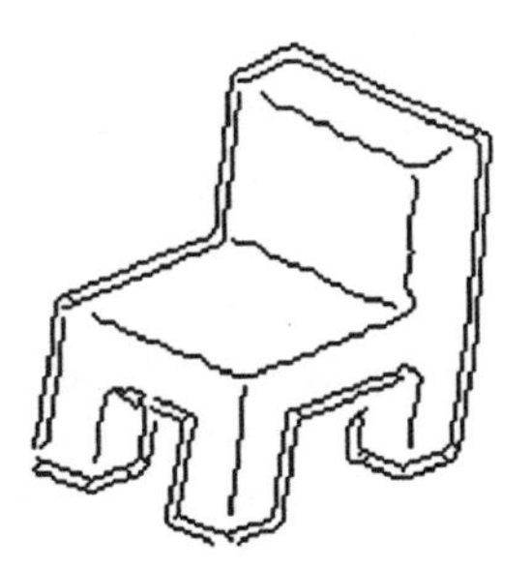

(d) Adaptive Smoothing

Figure 1.8: Range Image Feature Extraction

Multigrid Adaptive Smoothing

Multigrid methods were originally applied to simple boundary value problems which arise in many physical applications (see [7]). Many iterative methods for relaxation problems can be speeded up by multigrid algorithms. The basic idea behind multigrid methods is that the standard iterative methods are very effective at eliminating the high frequency or oscillatory components of the relaxation errors, while leaving the low-frequency or smooth components relatively unchanged. The coarser levels trade off spatial resolution for direct communication paths over larger distances. Hence, they effectively accelerate the global propagation of information to increase the overall efficiency of the relaxation process.

Principle of the Multigrid Algorithm We first briefly describe the multigrid algorithm. Consider a 2-level relaxation process: the original signal is relaxed at fine grid n_1 times to remove the high frequency components; that is followed by some decimation process to reduce the resolution to a coarser grid; we then perform the relaxation n_2 times at coarser grid for the decimated signal; the difference, which is called relaxation error, at coarser grid between the decimated signal before and after iteration is then interpolated back to the fine grid and subtracted from the signal at original resolution; finally, we relax the signal at fine grid n_3 times.

The algorithm described above has a recursive nature and we can therefore define an arbitrary level multigrid algorithm. The original signal at the finest grid level can use the relaxation error from the coarser grid level, while the coarser grid level can use the relaxation error from the next coarser grid level, and so on.

Multigrid Adaptive Smoothing Adaptive smoothing is basically a relaxation scheme and therefore inherently has the general property of faster converging speed for the high-frequency components than for the low-frequency ones. It not only removes the noise and undesired edges but also sharpens the desired features. Because of the inherent property of the relaxation scheme, as shown in the previous sections, the sharpening of the desired features is much faster than the smoothing of the noise and therefore we have proposed a simple thresholding scheme after a small number of iterations, to serve the purpose of feature extraction. We show in this section, however, a multigrid adaptive smoothing algorithm to achieve a more complete smoothing process in a reasonable computational time.

The assumption of the multigrid adaptive smoothing algorithm is that the edge sharpening effect should have been completed before entering the next coarser level, otherwise there will be some undesired overshoot produced at both ends of the edges. The overshoot, however, can be smoothed by some further iterations when the signal is interpolated back from the coarser resolution to finer resolution. Figure 1.9 shows a flowchart of the algorithm for a 2-level multigrid adaptive smoothing and it can be directly extended to more levels due to the recursive nature of the algorithm. The signal is first adaptively smoothed at full resolution, the smoothed signal is then decimated to half of its original resolution. The decimated signal is again adaptively smoothed and subtracted from the decimated signal to obtained the "relaxation error" at that resolution. This relaxation error is then interpolated back to original resolution to improve the relaxation at full resolution.

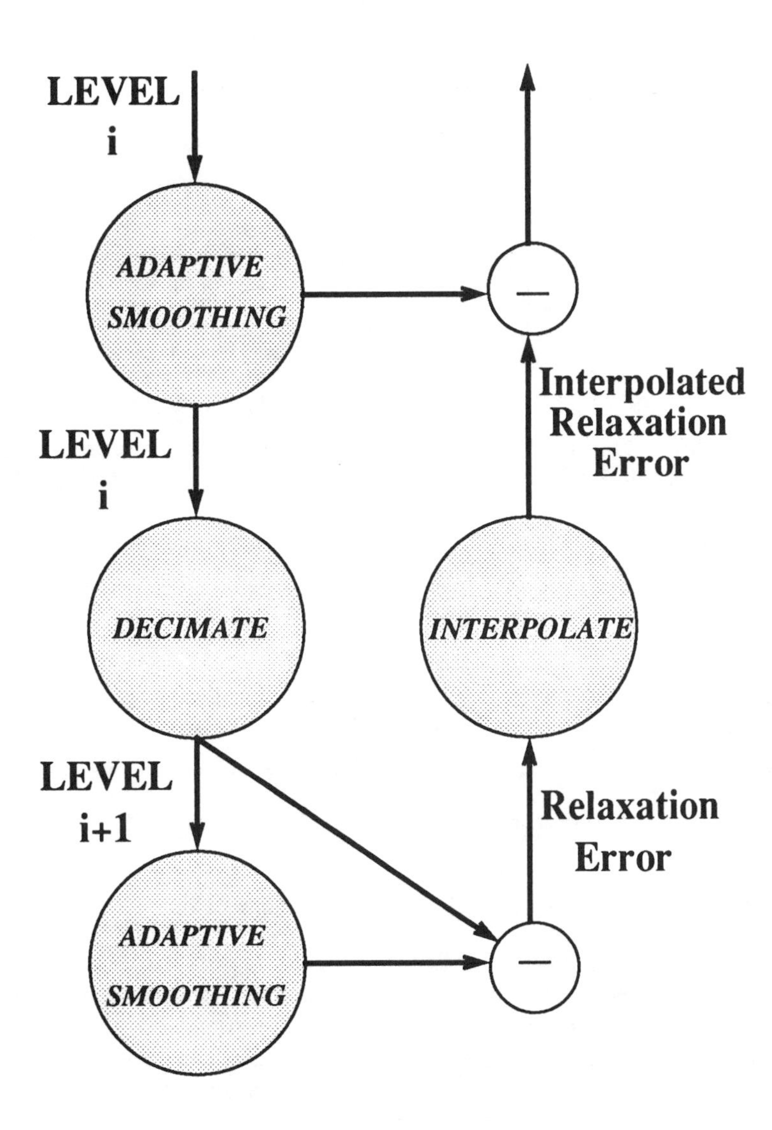

Figure 1.9: Flowchart of multigrid adaptive smoothing

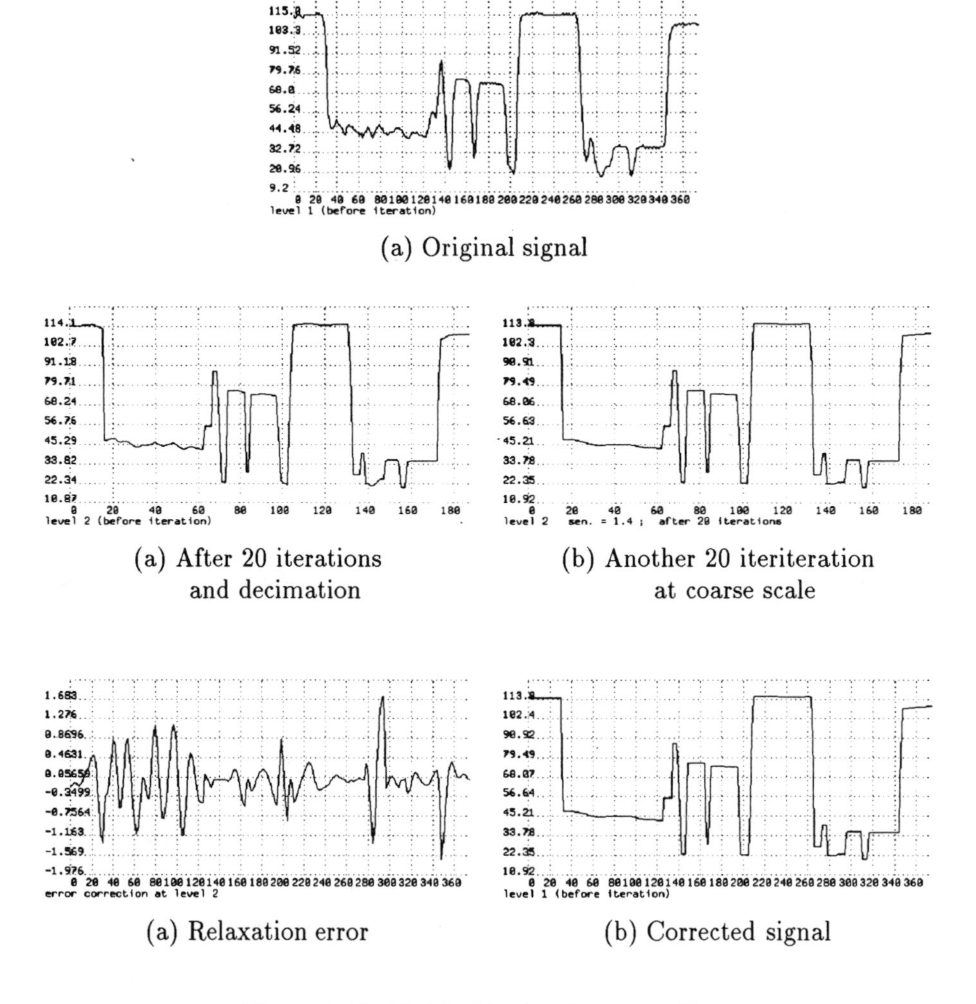

(a) Original signal

(a) After 20 iterations and decimation

(b) Another 20 iteriteration at coarse scale

(a) Relaxation error

(b) Corrected signal

Figure 1.10: Multigrid adaptive smoothing

Figure 1.10 illustrates the multigrid algorithm for adaptive smoothing. We show the original signal in figure 1.10(a). After 20 iterations at original resolution the signal is subsampled to a coarser resolution and is shown in figure 1.10(b). The signal at coarser grid is then relaxed for another 10 iterations, and we plot the signal and the relaxation error in figure 1.10(c) and (d) respectively. We then interpolate the relaxation error by a linear interpolation scheme back to the original full resolution and subtract it from the signal in figure 1.10(b) to get the result of figure 1.10(e). Finally, we relax the signal at full resolution.

The number of grid levels can be increased to achieve a significant degree of smoothing. The extra computation time, however, is only very small. We show in figure 1.11(a), with adaptive smoothing, the result of the signal in figure 1.10(a) after 40 iterations at full resolution, i.e. only using a single grid. We then show the results of multigrid adaptive smoothing with 2, 3 and 4 levels in figure 1.11(b), (c) and (d) respectively. The number of iterations for this example, i.e. the

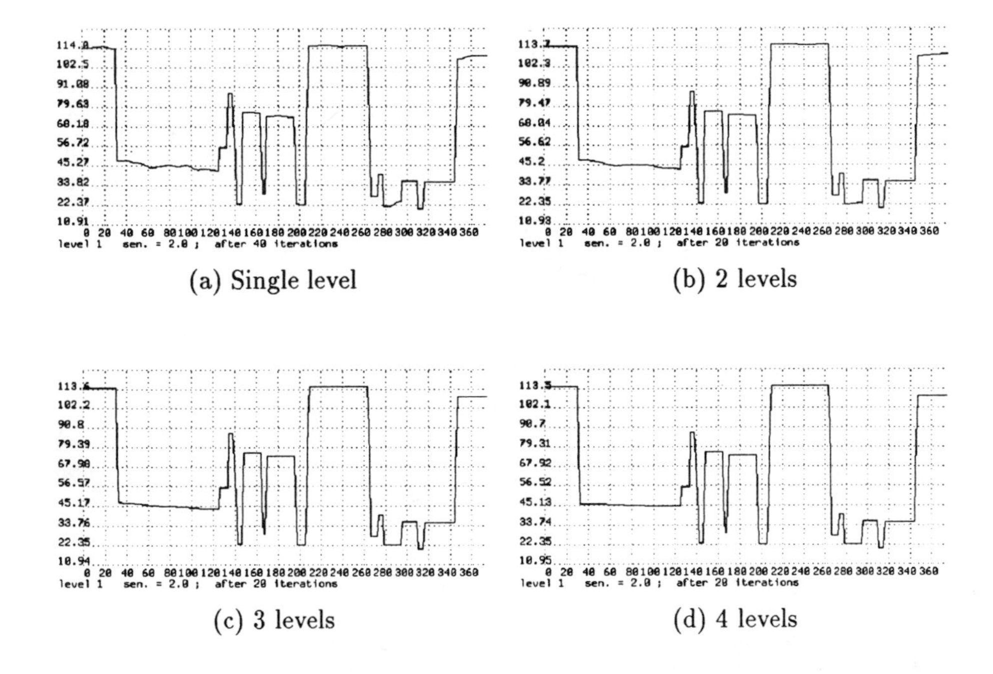

(a) Single level (b) 2 levels

(c) 3 levels (d) 4 levels

Figure 1.11: Multigrid adaptive smoothing with different levels

parameters n_1, n_2 and n_3 are all fixed at 20.

The number of iterations at each level, namely n_1, n_2 and n_3, can be fixed or dynamic. Dynamic schemes usually monitor the relaxation error to measure convergence rates. Although dynamic schemes tend to be more efficient, a fixed number of iterations is easier to implement on distributed locally interconnected machines since there is no need to compute the relaxation errors, which require global computations.

The speedup from the multigrid algorithm comes from two sources, one is the reduction in the number of iterations, and the other is the reduction in the number of data points because of the computation at a coarser resolution. There are overheads in multigrid algorithms, namely decimation and interpolation. We, however, implement the algorithm with direct subsampling for decimation and simple linear interpolation, and the overheads are therefore negligible.

For the multigrid algorithm described above, and assuming the parameters n_1, n_2 and n_3 are chosen to be the same constant, the computational time can be estimated as follows: for a 1-dimensional signal, each iteration takes half of the iteration time at the previous finer level since there are only half the number of data points at finer level, the total computation time for a limiting case, namely an infinite number of grid levels is twice the computation of the single grid adaptive smoothing ($\sum_{n=0}^{\infty} 2^{-n}$). For a 2-dimensional multigrid algorithm, since the number of data points at a coarser level is only $\frac{1}{4}$ of that at the next finer scale, the extra computation time for a limiting case is only one third of the total computation time by a single grid algorithm ($\sum_{n=0}^{\infty} 4^{-n}$).

We show in figure 1.12 an example of multigrid adaptive smoothing on a real image. We show the original $79 \times 114 \times 8bit$ image in figure 1.12(a), and the result of direct adaptive smoothing at the original image resolution with 220 iterations is shown in figure 1.12(b). We then apply the a 4-level multigrid algorithm on the image with the number of iterations at each level fixed at 10, and show the result in figure 1.12(c). To illustrate the degree of smoothing we extract a vertical slice from figure 1.12(b) and plot it in figure 1.12(d). We also extract the corresponding slice in figure 1.12(c) and plot it in figure 1.12(e).

The multigrid algorithm is implemented on the Symbolics Lisp Machine, and the computation for the direct single grid adaptive smoothing with 220 iterations takes 750 seconds. The computation for the result of figure 1.12(c) takes only 104 seconds. The major part of time consumed comes the iterations at full grid size, including 10 iterations before entering the next coarser grid level (113×104) and 10 iterations after coming back fro the coarser level. The degree of smoothing for figure 1.12(b) and (c) is approximately the same, the computation, however, is much faster for the multigrid algorithm.

1.3.2 Parallel Machine

The Connection Machine

The Connection Machine [21] is a Single Instruction Multiple Data (SIMD) machine having up to 64K processors. Most of the low-level vision tasks such as edge detection can be performed with a speed up of three orders of magnitude, depending on the degree of parallelism of the algorithms. Applications of the Connection Machine to various scientific research areas have also been developed, such as in VLSI design, fluid dynamics, neural networks and computer vision (see [36]).

The Connection Machine provides two modes of communication among processors. One of the communication mechanisms uses the topology of a boolean 16-cube and is called the router network. Long range communication is very efficient using the router. The other mechanism relies on a mesh of 128×512 grid (the so-called NEWS network since the connections are in the four cardinal directions), allowing fast direct communication between neighboring processors. This facilitates the processing of images, especially at the low level. To allow the machine to handle images larger than 64K (or 16K), the Connection Machine supports virtual processors: a single physical processor can be divided into several virtual processors, denoted as virtual-to-physical (VP) processor ratio, by serializing operations in time, and partitioning the memory in each processor.

Parallel Implementation

Given its local nature, adaptive smoothing is extremely suitable for the NEWS network of the Connection Machine. We summarize one iteration of the parallel adaptive smoothing of an image $I^{(t)}(x, y)$ as follows:

1. Compute the gradients $G_x(x, y)$ and $G_y(x, y)$:

$$G_x(x,y) = \frac{1}{2}(I^{(t)}(x+1,y) - I^{(t)}(x-1,y)) \tag{1.25}$$

$$G_y(x,y) = \frac{1}{2}(I^{(t)}(x,y+1) - I^{(t)}(x,y-1)) \tag{1.26}$$

(a) Original image

(b) Single level, 220 iterations

(c) 4 levels, 20 iterations each

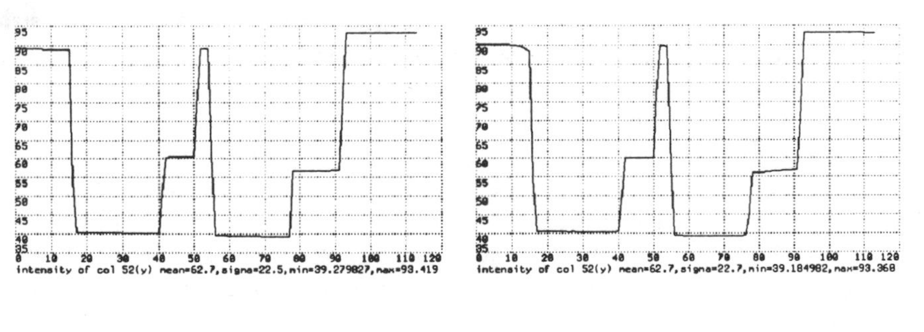

(d) A slice from (b)

(e) A slice from (c)

Figure 1.12: Multigrid adaptive smoothing on a 2-D image

VP	1	2	3
timing	11 ms	20 ms	36 ms
speedup	909	500	277

Table 1.1: Timing Statistics of Parallel Adaptive Smoothing

2. Compute the continuity coefficients $w(x,y)$:

$$w(x,y) = e^{-\frac{G_x^2(x,y)+G_y^2(x,y)}{2k^2}} \tag{1.27}$$

3. Perform weighted averaging to update $I^{(t)}(x,y)$:

$$I^{(t+1)}(x,y) = \frac{\sum_{i=-1}^{+1}\sum_{j=-1}^{+1} I^{(t)}(x+i,y+j)w^{(t)}(x+i,y+j)}{\sum_{i=-1}^{+1}\sum_{j=-1}^{+1} w^{(t)}(x+i,y+j)} \tag{1.28}$$

Note that elementary operations such additions, multiplications, exponentials, are applied simultaneously to each pixel of the image. Operations involving indexing, such as gradient computation or weighted averaging, need only very local neighboring information (direct neighbors of the pixel) and are efficiently performed through the NEWS network.

We have implemented the algorithm on a 16K Connection Machine, and it takes about 11 milliseconds for one iteration of adaptive smoothing in the case of one pixel per physical processor. Compared to the 10 seconds per iteration obtained on a serial machine (Symbolics 3645) for a 128×128 image, we obtain a speedup of three orders of magnitude. Table 1.1 summarizes the timing statistics of adaptive smoothing on the 16K Connection Machine for various virtual-to-physical (VP) processor ratios.

1.4 Multiscale Stereo Matching

Range or depth information has long been considered essential in the analysis of shape. High-resolution range information can be obtained directly when the range sensor is available. Binocular stereo has been widely used to extract the range information when such a high-resolution sensor is absent. Barnard and Fischler [2] define six steps necessary to stereo analysis: image acquisition, camera modeling, feature acquisition, image matching, depth reconstruction and interpolation. The mathematics of triangulation are very simple, but finding the corresponding points from two views is an important research topic in computer vision. The design of matching algorithms (image matching) is therefore necessary, and is clearly dependent on the selection of matching primitives (feature acquisition).

1.4.1 Matching Primitives

The correspondence problem between two images can be solved by matching specific features such as edges, or by matching small regions by the correlation of the

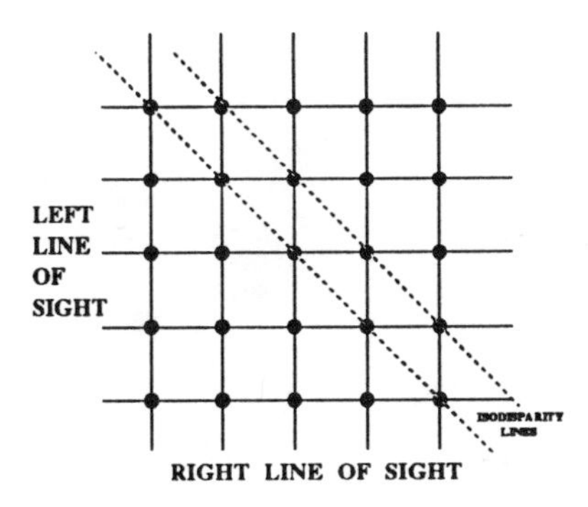

Figure 1.13: Potential matches

image intensities. Edgel-based stereo matching techniques usually use the edges characterized by the derivatives of a smoothed version of the signal, for instance the zero-crossings of a Laplacian-of-Gaussian convolved image. The correlation-based stereo matching measures the correlation of the image intensity patches centered around the matched pixels. Our multiscale stereo matching is edgel-based and the matching primitives are edgels extracted with the adaptive smoothing. Since adaptive smoothing provides accurate edge detection across different scales, it facilitates a straightforward multiscale stereo matching.

1.4.2 Matching Algorithm

To identify corresponding locations between two stereo images, or among a sequence of motion images, is difficult because of the *false target problem.* Consider the stereo matching in figure 1.13, there are 5 matching primitives from the left view and 5 from the right views, and therefore form 25 potential matches (marked by filled circles). The isodisparity line indicates the matches on the same line have the same disparity value. There are, however, at most 5 correct matches and the rest are called *false targets.* Certain constraints and assumptions have to be made in order to establish the correct matching results. The most widely used are listed below:

1. The *Uniqueness constraint* [24] is the most basic constraint for stereo matching. It states that there is at most one match from each line-of-sight since the depth value associated with each matching primitive, left or right, must be unique. The uniqueness constraint forces the number of correct matches to be at most 5 in figure 1.13.

2. The *Continuity constraint* [24] states that the depth map of an image should be mostly continuous, except at those points where depth discontinuities occur. Therefore neighboring potential matches having similar disparity values should support each other. With both the continuity and uniqueness constraints, the most probable matching result of figure 1.13 is shown in figure 1.14(a).

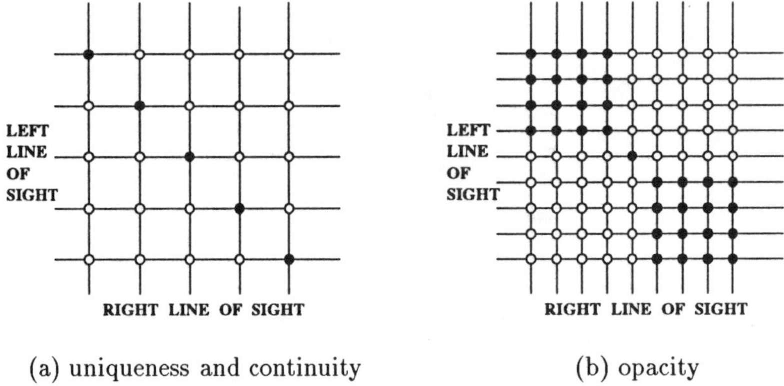

(a) uniqueness and continuity (b) opacity

Figure 1.14: Imposing matching constraints

3. The *Opacity constraint* further limits the occurrence of false targets. Consider figure 1.14(b) (similar to [14]), extending the uniqueness constraint which limits only one match at each line-of-sight, the opacity constraint states that there is at most one match in the hourglass-shape forbidden zone. Therefore if the center point in figure 1.14(b) is marked as a match, then all the potential matches in both the upper-right and lower-right quadrants are forbidden to be marked as a match (shown as circles).

4. The *Compatibility constraint* [24] limits the construction of potential matches from matching primitives, for example, the potential matches are allowed to occur only when two zero-crossings from the **LoG** convolved images have the same sign. Further restrictions can be made on the orientation and the gradient of the matching edgels.

1.4.3 Multiscale Stereo Matching

The stereo matching results are often presented in a so-called disparity map which shows the disparity between the matched features, and the depth information can be directly recovered from the disparity map with the knowledge of the camera geometry. It is often desirable to obtain a disparity map as dense as possible. A dense disparity map usually requires dense matching features which in return makes the false target problem worse. The false target problem can be alleviated either by reducing the range and resolution of the disparity or by reducing the density of the matching features in the image. One commonly used method to obtain both resolution and range of disparity information is to apply a multi-resolution algorithm. At coarse resolution, the density of the matching features is low, therefore reducing the probability of false targets. The information obtained from the matching at coarse resolution can be used to guide the matching at fine resolution to get the desired high density disparity information.

Marr and Grimson [24, 18] use Gaussian kernels as the scaling filters for multiscale stereo matching. The matches obtained at coarser scale establish a rough correspondence for the finer scales, thereby reducing the number of false matches.

Features at different scales are the zero crossings found by convolving the image with Laplacian of the Gaussian masks. Those zero crossings where the gradient is oriented vertically are ignored since the implicit camera model has the epipolar lines oriented horizontally. Masks of four different sizes are used, separated by one spatial octave, i.e. each mask is twice the size of the next smaller one.

The multiscale stereo matching first locates a zero crossing in one image, and the region surrounding the same location in the second image is then divided into three pools: a small zero disparity pool centered on the predicted match location and two larger "convergent" and "divergent" pools. The total size of the three pools is twice the width of the central positive region of the **LoG** convolution mask. Zero crossings from the pool of the second image can be matched to the ones in the first image if they have the same sign and approximately the same orientation.

A vergence control is necessary because of the poor accuracy of the **LoG** edge detection. Adaptive smoothing can overcome this disadvantage with its accuracy of edges over scales. The matching results at coarser scale with adaptive smoothing are therefore much more reliable and the propagation of the disparity information between scales is straightforward.

We have used our adaptive smoothing and implemented a multiscale stereo matching algorithm to extract the matching features. It is based on Drumheller and Poggio's [14] parallel stereo matching implementation on the Connection Machine. The parallel stereo matching, as in most stereo matching algorithms, utilizes the *uniqueness* the *continuity* constraint on the surface and therefore the values on the disparity map. It also imposes the *opacity* constraint on the surfaces and *compatibility* constraint on the matching of the edges.

We first extract edges at coarse scale for both images using adaptive smoothing. The stereo images are assumed to be epipolarly registered and the matching is performed scan-line by scan-line. A potential match is marked only when the corresponding edges from the two images have approximately the same orientation and gradient. Imposing the continuity constraint, the number of potential matches is counted over a flat uniformly-weighted square support (chosen for computational convenience) centered at each pixel. Enforcing the opacity and uniqueness constraints, there must be no more than one match in the forbidden zone, therefore a *winner-take-all* strategy is applied in the forbidden zone.

The matches at the edge locations from the coarse scale are then propagated to the intermediate scale. Each match at coarse scale generates a forbidden zone which forbids potential matches to be marked at intermediate scale. This greatly reduces the number of potential matches at intermediate scale and therefore facilitates producing more reliable matching results. After potential matches are formed at intermediate scale, the same continuity, opacity and uniqueness constraints are employed to produce the mathes which are then propagated to the fine scale. Figure 1.15 shows the flowchart of our multiscale stereo matching algorithm.

The multiscale stereo matching algorithm is implemented on the Connection Machine and takes only a matter of few seconds depending on the range and the resolution of the disparity. The accurate edge detection by adaptive smoothing provides a very simple control mechanism for multiscale processing, and the simplicity is essential when considering parallel implementation.

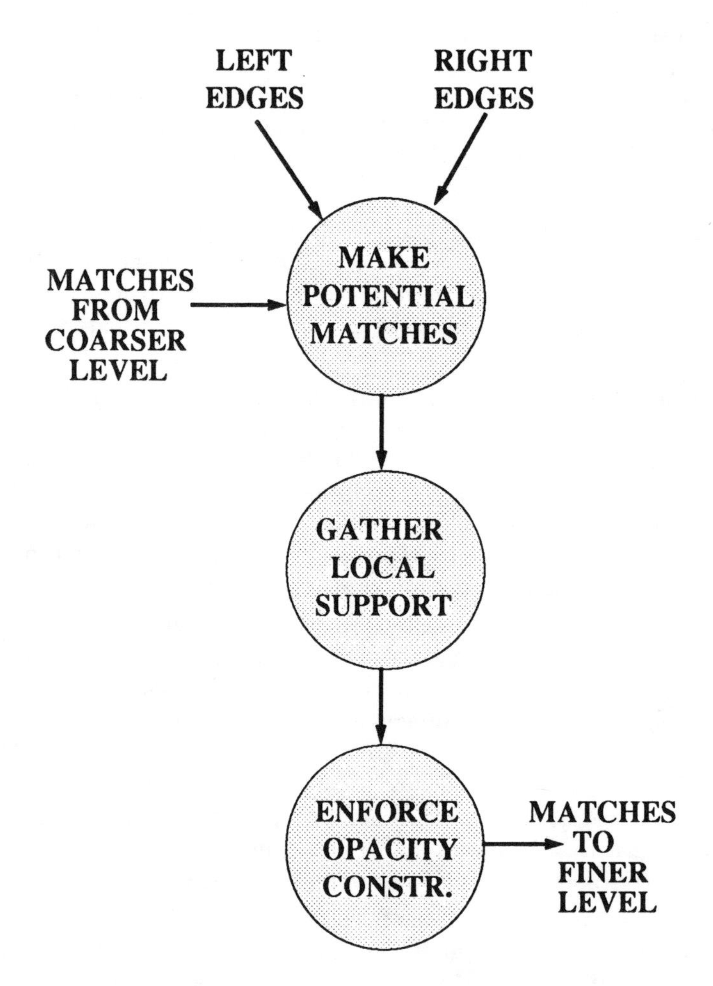

Figure 1.15: Flowchart of multiscale stereo matching

	Pentagon			Fruit		
	coarse	inter.	fine	coarse	inter.	fine
singlescale	22670	28892	33323	36885	80045	120026
multiscale	22670	11372	11279	36885	37588	35676

Table 1.2: Number of potential matches

1.4.4 Results

We first show in figure 1.16 a pair of stereo images of the aerial view of Pentagon ($256 \times 256 \times 8bits$, courtesy of Dr. W. Hoff). The pair is epipolarly registered, i.e. the two images correspond to each other scan-line by scan-line. We show in figure 1.17, figure 1.18 and figure 1.19, the results of multiscale matching at the coarse, intermediate and fine levels respectively. In each figure, part (a) and (b) show the edges extracted by the adaptive smoothing for left and right images at that level and part (c) shows the matched disparity map at edge locations. The scaling parameter k is set to 8, 4 and 0 (no smoothing) for the coarse, intermediate and fine scales respectively. We also show in figure 1.16(d) the disparity map of the result of single scale (fine scale) stereo matching. Finally, figure 1.20 shows a 3-dimensional plot of the disparity map viewed from the upper-left corner of the image. The range of disparity for this example is -5 (farther) to 5 (nearer) pixels, and the brighter gray level values indicate a position closer to the viewer.

We also show in figure 1.21, 1.22, 1.23 and 1.24 another example of a fruit scene ($256 \times 256 \times 8bits$, courtesy of Professor T. Kanade, Carnegie-Mellon University). The scaling parameter k is set to 8, 4 and 0 for coarse, intermediate and fine scales respectively. Figure 1.24(d) shows the result of single scale stereo matching. Figure 1.25 shows the 3-dimensional plot viewed from the bottom-right corner of the image. The range of disparity is -15 to 22 pixels.

Table 1.2 summarizes the statistics of the number of potential matches for the stereo matching. The row "multiscale" stands for multiscale stereo matching and row "single scale" stands for stereo matching at each scale individually. Since the matches at coarser scale are used to form the forbidden zones when constructing potential matches at finer scale, the number of potential matches is greatly reduced at the finer scales as we can observe from the table.

1.5 Conclusion

Adaptive smoothing is a non-linear filtering scheme that can achieve discontinuity-preserving smoothing. It is a weighted averaging algorithm which turns out to be an implementation of anisotropic diffusion. The weights vary at each pixel and at each iteration, being computed as a function of the gradient at each pixel. This function depends on a single parameter k controlling the amplitude of the discontinuities to be preserved during the smoothing process. Using this parameter k, we form an adaptive scale-space in which the accuracy of edge detection at different scales is guaranteed. We also propose a scheme to process signals involving higher order discontinuities, range images for instance.

Since very few iterations are needed to achieve edge sharpening, feature extraction can be performed in a reasonable computational time on a serial machine. However, when a significant amount of smoothing is needed, we propose a multigrid implementation which speeds up the smoothing effect significantly. Since adaptive smoothing uses at each pixel a very small neighborhood, it is straightforward to implement on a massively parallel computer such as the Connection Machine and we have obtained a speedup factor of three orders of magnitude over the direct implementation on a serial machine.

We have presented several applications of adaptive smoothing: edge detection, range image feature extraction, corner detection. We have also shown a multiscale coarse-to-fine hierarchical approach for extracting matching primitives in a stereo image pair. The number of matching primitives at coarse scale is small, therefore reducing the number of potential matches, which in return increases the reliability of the matching results. A dense disparity can be obtained at a fine scale where the density of edgels is very high. The control strategy is very simple compared to other multiscale approaches such as the ones using Gaussian scale space, this results from the accuracy of edges detected by adaptive smoothing at different scales. The simplicity of control strategy is especially important for low-level processing, and it is therefore straightforward for a parallel implementation and even direct hardware realization.

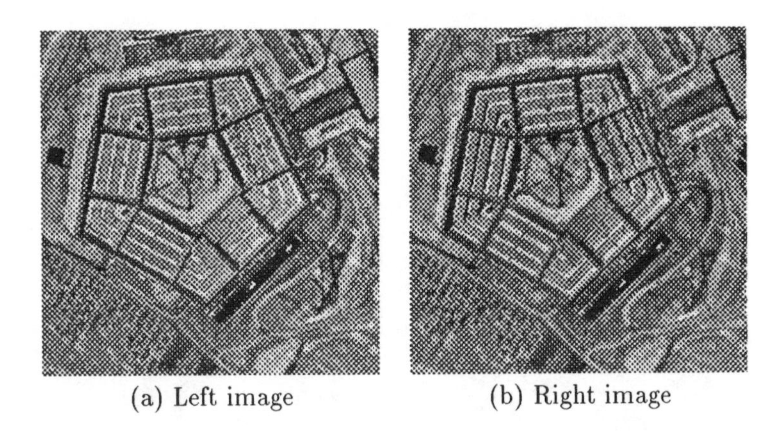

(a) Left image (b) Right image

Figure 1.16: Stereo image pair of the Pentagon

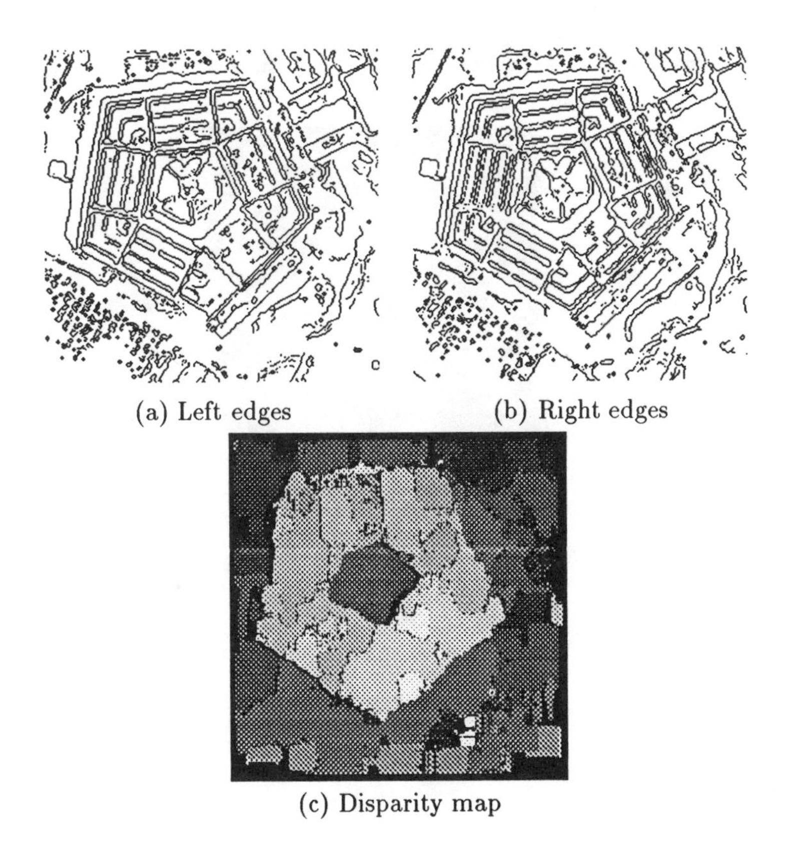

(a) Left edges (b) Right edges

(c) Disparity map

Figure 1.17: Matches of the Pentagon at coarse scale

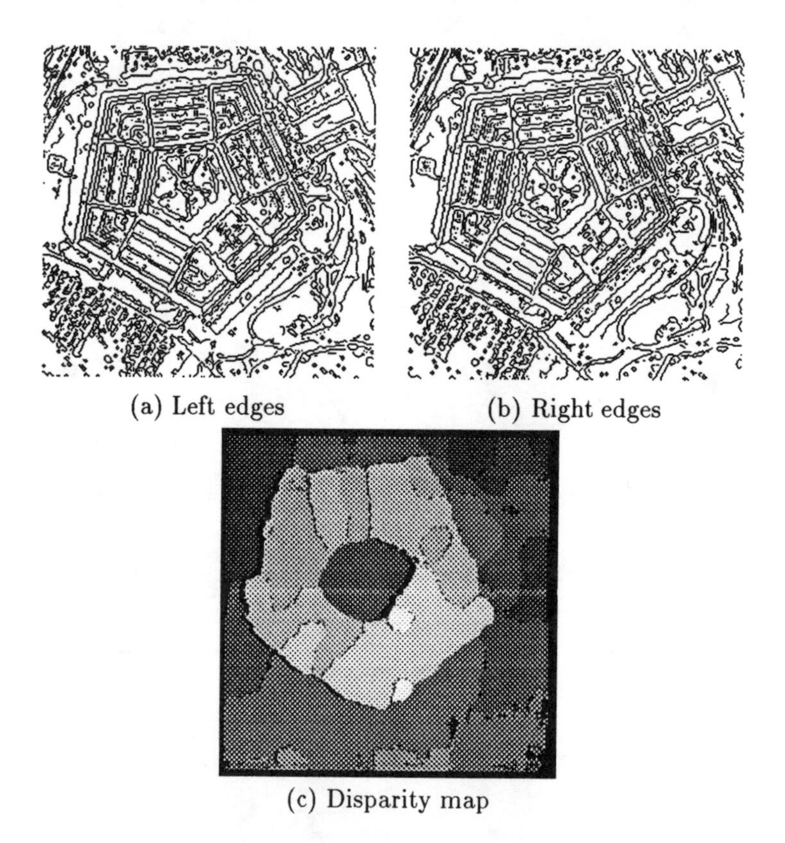

(a) Left edges (b) Right edges

(c) Disparity map

Figure 1.18: Matches of the Pentagon at intermediate scale

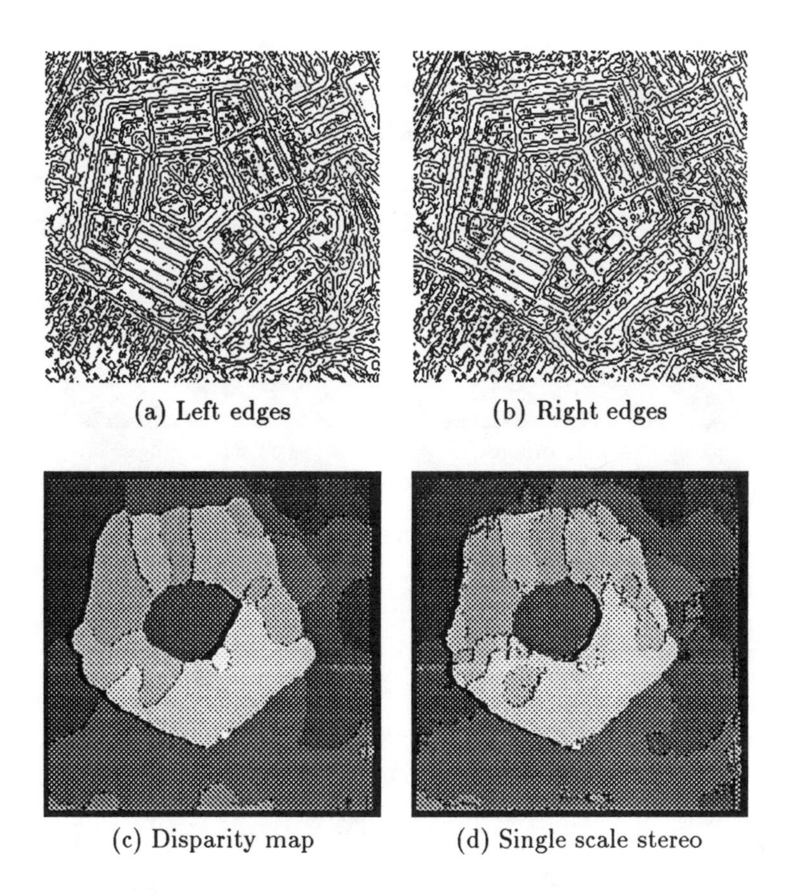

(a) Left edges (b) Right edges

(c) Disparity map (d) Single scale stereo

Figure 1.19: Matches of the Pentagon at fine scale

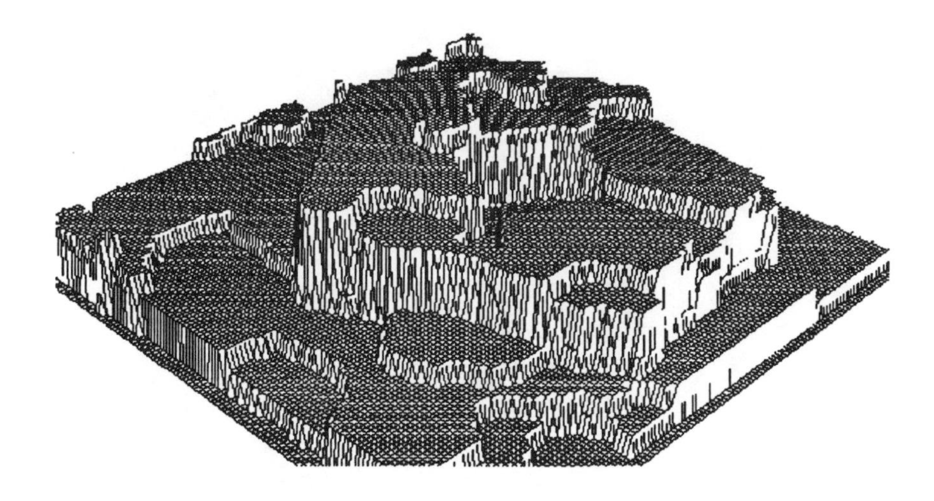

Figure 1.20: 3-D plot of disparity map of the Pentagon

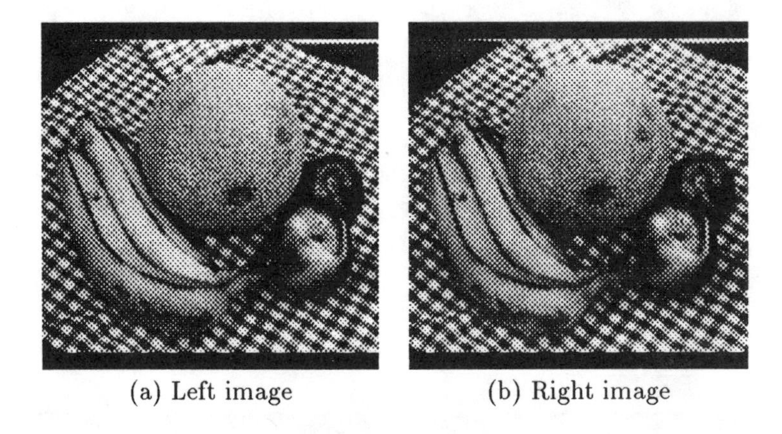

(a) Left image (b) Right image

Figure 1.21: Stereo image pair of a fruit Scene

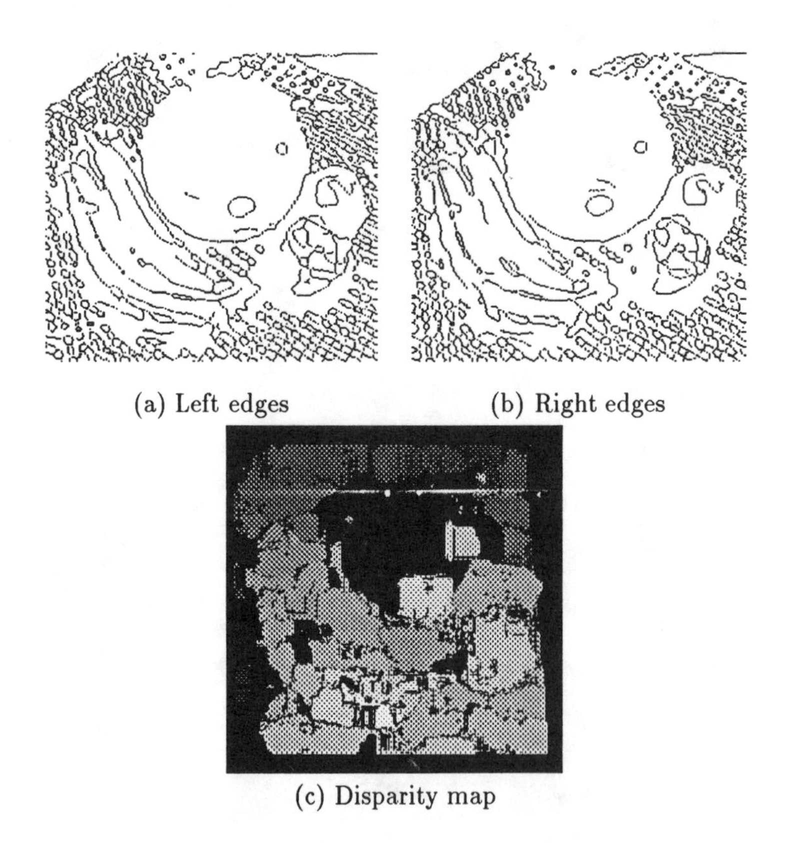

(a) Left edges (b) Right edges

(c) Disparity map

Figure 1.22: Matches of the fruit scene at coarse scale

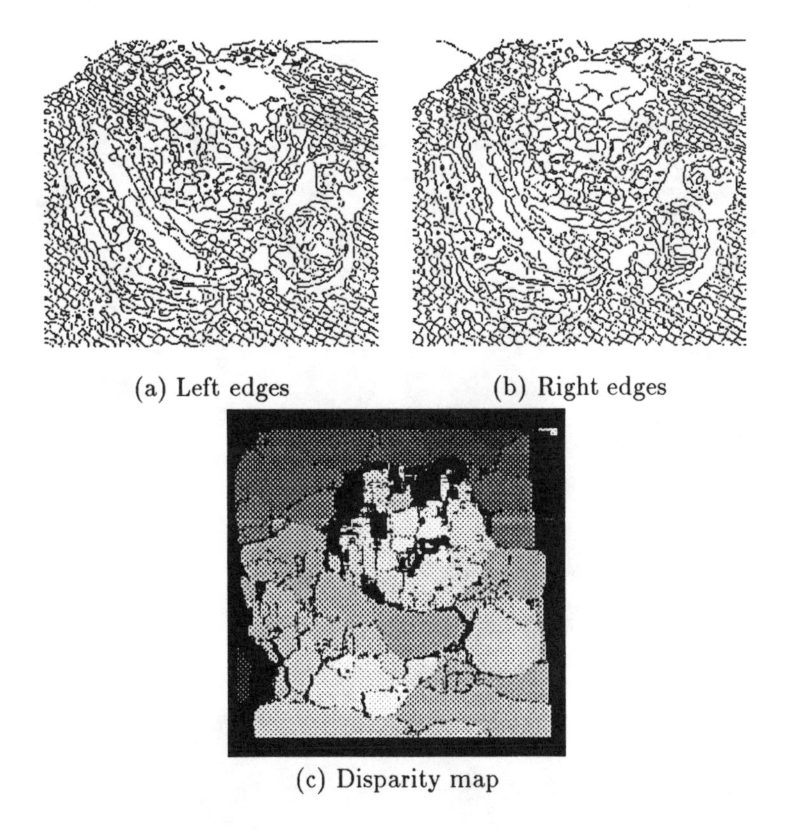

(a) Left edges

(b) Right edges

(c) Disparity map

Figure 1.23: Matches of the fruit scene at intermediate scale

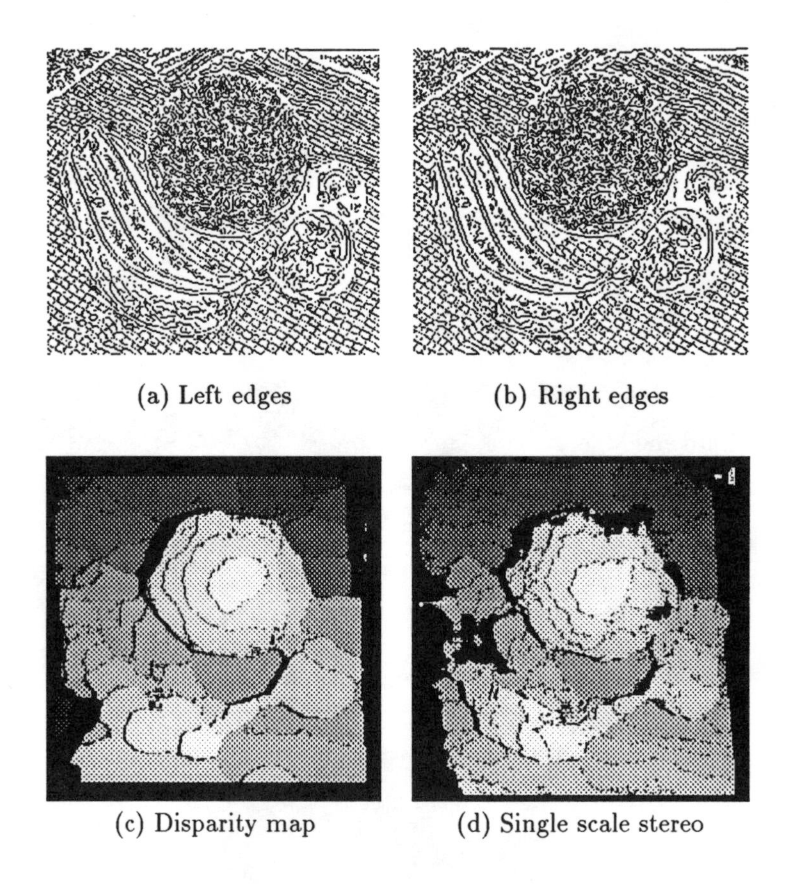

(a) Left edges

(b) Right edges

(c) Disparity map

(d) Single scale stereo

Figure 1.24: Matches of the fruit scene at fine scale

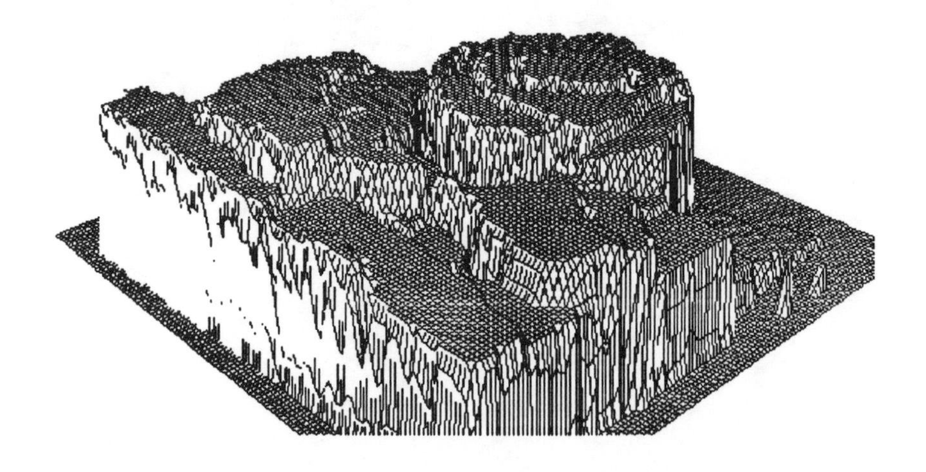

Figure 1.25: 3-D plot of disparity map of fruit scene

References

[1] H. Asada and M. Brady. The curvature primal sketch. *IEEE Transactions on Pattern Analysis and Machine Intelligence*, PAMI-8:2–14, January 1986.

[2] S. Barnard and M. Fischler, Computational Stereo. *ACM Computing Surveys*, Vol. 14, No. 4, December 1982, pp 553-572.

[3] F. Bergholm. Edge focusing. *IEEE Transactions on Pattern Analysis and Machine Intelligence*, PAMI-9:726–741, 1987.

[4] P. J. Besl and R. C. Jain. Segmentation through symbolic surface descriptions. In *Proceedings of the Conference on Computer Vision and Pattern Recognition*, pages 77–85, Miami, 1986.

[5] A. Blake and A. Zisserman. *Visual Reconstruction.* MIT Press, Cambridge, MA, 1987.

[6] J. Brady, J. Ponce, A. Yuille, and H. Asada. Describing surfaces. *Computer Vision, Graphics, and Image Processing*, (32):1–28, October 1985.

[7] K. Brand. Multigrid methods. In W. Hackbush and U. Trottenberg, editors, *Lecture Notes in Mathematics*, pages 631–650. Springer-Verlag, New-York, 1982. Volume 960.

[8] J. P. Burt. Fast algorithms for estimating local image properties. *Computer Graphics and Image Processing*, (21):368–382, 1983.

[9] J. F. Canny. A computational approach to edge detection. *IEEE Transactions on Pattern Analysis and Machine Intelligence*, PAMI-8(6):679–698, 1986.

[10] J. S. Chen and G. Medioni. Detection, localization and estimation of edges. In *Proceedings of the IEEE Workshop on Computer Vision*, pages 215–217, Miami, November 1987.

[11] R. T. Chin and C. L. Yeh. Quantitative evaluation of some edge preserving noise smoothing techniques. *Computer Vision, Graphics, and Image Processing*, (23):67–91, 1983.

[12] L. S. Davis and A. Rosenfeld. Noise cleaning by iterated local averaging. *IEEE Transactions on Systems, Man and Cybernetics*, SMC-8:705–710, 1978.

[13] F.M. Dickley and K.M. Shanmugan. An optimal frequency domain filter for edge detection in digital pictures. *IEEE Transactions on Pattern Analysis and Machine Intelligence*, PAMI-1(1):37–49, 1977.

[14] M. Drumheller and T. Poggio. On parallel stereo. In *Proceedings of the IEEE International Conference on Robotics and Automation*, pages 1439–1448, Cambridge, Massachusetts, April 1986.

[15] T.-J. Fan, G. Medioni, and R. Nevatia. Segmented description of 3-D surfaces. *IEEE Journal of Robotics and Automation*, pages 527–538, December 1987.

[16] T.-J. Fan, G. Medioni, and R. Nevatia. 3-D object recognition using surface description. In *Proceedings of the DARPA Image Understanding Workshop*, pages 383–397, Cambridge, Massachusetts, 1988.

[17] S. Geman and D. Geman. Stochastic relaxation, gibbs distributions, and the bayesian restoration of images. *IEEE Transactions on Pattern Analysis and Machine Intelligence*, PAMI-6:721–741, 1984.

[18] W. E. L. Grimson. *From Images to Surfaces.* MIT Press, Cambridge, MA, 1981.

[19] R. M. Haralick. Digital step edge from zero-crossings of second directional derivatives. *IEEE Transactions on Pattern Analysis and Machine Intelligence*, PAMI-6(1):58–68, 1984.

[20] R. M. Haralick, L. T. Watson, and T. J. Laffey. The topographic primal sketch. *International Journal of Robotics Research*, 2(1):50–72, 1983.

[21] D. Hillis. *The Connection Machine.* MIT Press, 1985.

[22] R. A. Hummel. Representations based on zero-crossings in scale-space. In *Proceedings of the Conference on Computer Vision and Pattern Recognition*, pages 204–209, Miami, 1986.

[23] A. Lev, S. W. Zucker, and A. Rosenfeld. Iterative enhancement of noisy images. *IEEE Transactions on Systems, Man and Cybernetics*, SMC-7:435–441, 1977.

[24] D. Marr. *Vision: A Computational Investigation into the Human Representation and Processing of Visual Information.* W.H. Freeman and Co., San-Fransisco, CA, 1982.

[25] D. Marr and H. Hildreth. Theory of edge detection. *Proceedings of the Royal Society of London*, B(207):187–217, 1980.

[26] D. Marr and T. Poggio. A computational theory of human stereo vision. *Proceedings of the Royal Society of London*, B(204):301–328, 1979.

[27] G. A. Mastin. Adaptive filters for digital image noise smoothing: An evaluation. *Computer Vision, Graphics, and Image Processing*, (31):103–121, 1985.

[28] G. Medioni and Y. Yasumoto. Corner detection and curve representation using cubic B-splines. *Computer Vision, Graphics, and Image Processing*, (39):267–278, 1987.

[29] F. Mokhtarian and A. Mackworth. Scaled-based description and recognition of planar curves and two-dimensional shapes. *IEEE Transactions on Pattern Analysis and Machine Intelligence*, 1986.

[30] V. S. Nalwa and T. O. Binford. On detecting edges. *IEEE Transactions on Pattern Analysis and Machine Intelligence*, PAMI-8(6):699–714, 1986.

[31] B. Parvin and G. Medioni. Adaptive multiscale feature extraction from range data. In *Proceedings of the IEEE Workshop on Computer Vision*, pages 23–28, Miami, 1987.

[32] P. Perona and J. Malik. Scale space and edge detection using anisotropic diffusion. In *Proceedings of the IEEE Workshop on Computer Vision*, pages 16–22, Miami, 1987.

[33] J. Ponce and M. Brady. Toward a surface primal sketch. In *Proceedings of the IEEE International Conference on Robotics and Automation*, pages 420–425, St-Louis, March 1985.

[34] P. Saint-Marc and M. Richetin. Structural filtering from curvature information. In *Proceedings of the Conference on Computer Vision and Pattern Recognition*, pages 338–343, Miami, 1986.

[35] D. Terzopoulos. The role of constraints and discontinuities in visible surface reconstruction. In *Proceedings of the International Joint Conference on Artificial Intelligence*, pages 1019–1022, Karlsruhe, 1983.

[36] L.W. Tucker and G.G. Robertson. Architecture and applications of the connection machine. *IEEE Computer Magazine*, 21(8):26–38, August 1988.

[37] D. C. C. Wang, A. H. Vagnucci, and C. C. Li. Gradient inverse weighted smoothing scheme and the evaluation of its performance. *Computer Graphics and Image Processing*, (15):167–181, 1981.

[38] A. P. Witkin. Scale-space filtering. In *Proceedings of the International Joint Conference on Artificial Intelligence*, pages 1019–1022, Karlsruhe, 1983.

[39] A. L. Yuille and T. A. Poggio. Scaling theorems for zero-crossings. *IEEE Transactions on Pattern Analysis and Machine Intelligence*, PAMI-8:15–25, June 1986.

Edge Detection

Chapter 2

Edge Detection from Severely Degraded Images

D. Lee

2.1. Introduction

An edge in an image corresponds to a discontinuity in the intensity surface of the underlying scene. It may result from a depth discontinuity, a surface normal discontinuity, a reflectance discontinuity, or an illumination discontinuity in the scene. Edge detection is a fundamental problem in image analysis; edges represent a major fraction of information content in an image [16]. Edge detectors have been an important part of many computer vision systems. Because of its importance, much work has been done on edge detection. There are Marr-Hildreth type detectors, detectors using regularization, methods based on Markov Random Field models, detectors from residual analysis, Wiener type detectors, detectors based on statistical pattern matching, and a number of other detectors. Interested readers are referred to [7, 11] and recent issues of CVPR, ICCV, and PAMI, among others.

A serious problem edge detectors often encounter in practice is: intensity images are degraded; the performance of edge detectors is severely hampered by image degradation, and commonly used detectors may fail under such circumstances. On the other hand, only degraded images are available for many practical vision systems, such as for the analysis of satellite data, for autonomous vehicle navigation, etc.

Image degradation is a complicated process [8]. There is a variety of sources of image blurring, such as severely defocused lens, long-term exposure of atmospheric turbulence, and motion blur. To detect edges from a blurred image, one could first *deblur* it and then apply usual edge detectors to the restored image. While image deblurring is a complicated and time consuming process itself, it is an ill-conditioned problem at best and a singular problem at worst [2, 8]. Therefore, a reliable and real time vision system can not depend on such approaches.

In this work, we study edge detection directly from degraded images without any deblurring. We explore the invariance properties of edges with respect to image blurring. For different types of blurred images, we discuss corresponding detectors. After a brief discussion of image degradation, we study edge detection of degraded images from rotationally invariant blurring, which includes defocused lens and long-term exposure blurring among others. We show that edges are invariant with respect to such blurring, given an appropriate detector. We then discuss edge detection of motion blurred images. We explore the invariance of edges and discuss detectors.

2.2. Image Degradation

A spatially invariant image degradation can be modeled by [2, 8]

$$I(x, y) = (f * H)(x, y) = \int_{-\infty}^{\infty}\int_{-\infty}^{\infty} f(x - \xi, y - \eta)H(\xi, \eta)\, d\xi d\eta \qquad (2.1)$$

where f is the original image, H is the *point spread function (psf)*, * is the convolution operator, and I is the degraded image. The psf represents the process of degradation.

An image degradation is *rotationally invariant* if the psf H in (2.1) is rotationally invariant, i.e., $H(x, y) = g(r)$ where $r = \sqrt{x^2 + y^2}$. Otherwise, it is *rotationally variant.*

Three commonly encountered cases of image degradation are [8]:

Case (i) Severely defocused lens with circular aperture stop [9].

When a three-dimensional scene is imaged by a camera onto a two-dimensional image field, some parts or all of the scene may not be in focus. The psf

$$H(x, y) = \begin{cases} \dfrac{1}{\pi r^2}, & r = \sqrt{x^2 + y^2} \le \rho \\ 0, & \textit{elsewhere} \end{cases} \qquad (2.2)$$

where $\rho > 0$ is the radius of the circle of confusion.

Figure 2.1 is a 300×600 digitized image of characters. Figure 2.2 is a defocused image of Fig. 2.1 with $\rho = 16$ *pixels*.

Fig. 2.1. a 300×600 digitized image of characters

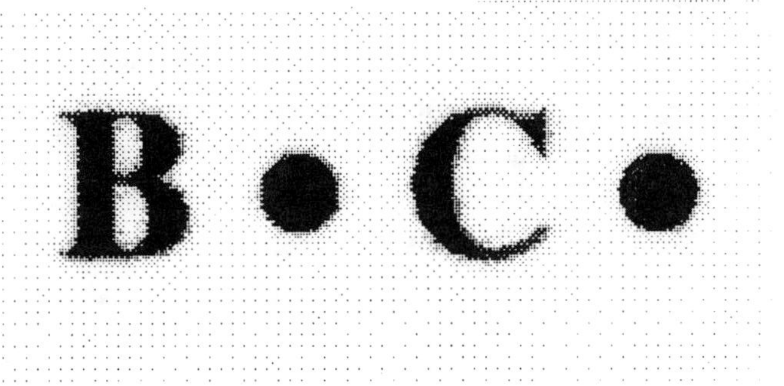

Fig. 2.2. a defocused image of Fig. 2.1. with ρ = 16 pixels

Case (ii) Long-term exposure of atmospheric turbulence [17].

Under certain circumstances, a long-term exposure of the camera is necessary to obtain useful information in the scene. The psf

$$H(x, y) = e^{-\frac{r^2}{\sigma^2}} , \quad r = \sqrt{x^2 + y^2} \tag{2.3}$$

where the constant $\sigma^2 > 0$ is the variance of a *Gaussian*.

Figure 2.3 is a long-term exposed image of Fig. 2.1 with $\sigma = 0.1$.

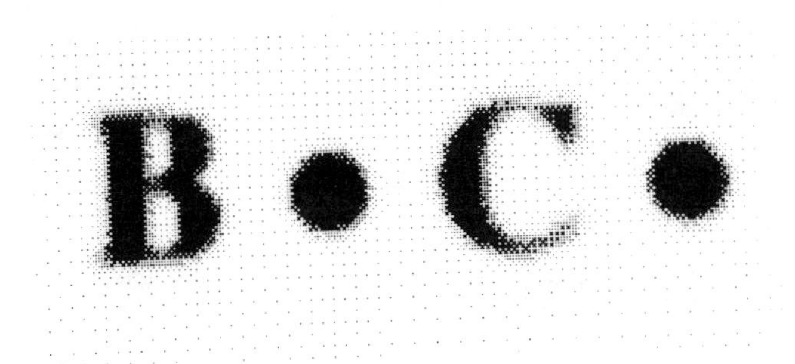

Fig. 2.3. a long-term exposed image of Fig. 2.1. with $\sigma = 0.1$

Case (iii) Uniform motion blur [18].

Motion blurring is due to the relative motion between the camera and the object in the scene during the exposure period. We only consider uniform motion blurring, which is due to a translation of the camera or the object. For simplicity, assume that the relative motion is along the direction of the x-axis of the camera coordinate system [(1)]. Then the blurring process becomes

$$I(x, y) = \int_{-\infty}^{\infty} f(x - \xi, y) H(\xi) \, d\xi$$

where the psf

$$H(x) = \begin{cases} 1, & |x| \leq T \\ 0, & |x| > T \end{cases} \tag{2.4}$$

where T is a constant, which is proportional to the camera or object moving distance.

(1) In general, the psf H is complex. However, if we know the motion direction, we can always choose a coordinate system to satisfy the above assumption.

Figure 2.4 is a motion blurred image of Fig. 2.1 with $T = 32$ *pixels*.

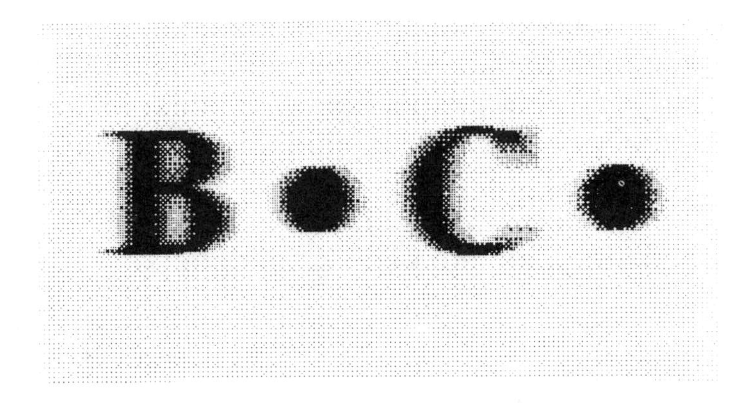

Fig. 2.4. a motion blurred image of Fig. 2.1. with $T = 32$ pixels

Obviously, Case (i) and (ii) are rotationally invariant blurring and Case (iii) is not.

Our goal is to detect edges of the original image f from the blurred image I in (2.1). One might want to restore the original image first and then detect edges. While image restoration is not a trivial task itself it may also introduce additional errors to the process. We shall show that for rotationally invariant blurring edges are invariant with respect to image degradation, given appropriate detectors. As a result, we can apply edge detectors directly to the blurred images and obtain the same edges as if we apply them to the original (unblurred) images. Consequently, there is no need for image deblurring and not even for blur identification. On the other hand, for rotationally variant blurring such as motion blurring, the invariance property is more subtle and the problem is more complex.

2.3. Rotationally Invariant Blurring

We want to detect edges of images from rotationally invariant blurring, such as defocused and long-term exposed images. An image from such a blurring can be represented by $I = f * H$, where f is the original image and H is a rotationally invariant psf. We want to detect edges of the original image f from the blurred image I. We show that edges are invariant with respect to a rotationally invariant edge detector. More specifically, if we were able to apply such an edge detector to the original image to find edges then we would find the same edges by applying the detector to the blurred image. We do not need any information of the psf of the blurring process so long as it is rotationally invariant. Therefore, there is no need for image restoration or blur identification for edge detection of this type of blurred images.

We first discuss briefly edge detection of unblurred images. Based on the analysis, we derive the invariance of edges with respect to rotationally invariant blurring.

We want to detect the discontinuities of an input function f. For simplicity, we only consider function value discontinuities (jumps). We apply a linear filter ψ to the input function f, and the filter response is

$$Z = f * \psi \ . \tag{2.5}$$

We want to design a filter ψ such that discontinuities of the input function f are represented by the feature points in the filter response Z. By locating the feature points in Z, we identify the discontinuities of f. There are different choices of feature points, such as zero-crossings, extrema, and others. We choose zero-crossing's due to their desirable properties [1].

It has been shown in [14] that if an input function f has a discontinuity at a point then the filter response in (2.5) has a corresponding zero-crossing at the same point. This provides justifications for zero-crossing-based linear filters. However, it only applies to unblurred images. We now show that edges detected from such filters are invariant with respect to rotationally invariant blurring. The first part of the derivation is similar to that in [14] and we omit the details.

Let D be a compact and connected set in R^2 where R is the set of real numbers. We assume that D is partitioned into n regions: $D_1, \cdots, D_n$, with boundaries $\Gamma_1, \cdots, \Gamma_n$, respectively. Assume that the input function f has discontinuities only on the boundaries $\Gamma = \bigcup_{i=1}^{n} \Gamma_i$. Furthermore, f has uniformly bounded first and second order partial derivatives within each region D_i. Denote the Euclidean distance of a point (x, y) from the boundaries Γ by $dist((x, y), \Gamma)$.

Lemma 2.1. Assume that ψ supports on a disc $B(0, h)$ of radius h, is rotationally invariant with $\int_{B(0,h)} \psi = 0$, and is normalized: $\int_{B(0,h)} |\psi| \, du \, dv = 1$. Then (i) If (x, y) is away from any possible discontinuities, i.e., $dist((x, y), \Gamma) \geq h$, then the filter response has small absolute values: $Z(x, y) = O(h^2)$. (ii) If (x, y) is close to the boundaries, i.e., $dist((x, y), \Gamma) < h$, then the filter response

$$Z(x, y) = \sum_{i=1}^{p-1} H_{k_i} \cdot L_{k_i}(x, y) + R \ , \tag{2.6}$$

where $D_{k_i}, i = 1, \cdots, p$, are the regions intersecting $B((x, y), h)$,

$$H_{k_i} = f_{k_i}(x_{k_i^*}, y_{k_i^*}) - f_{k_p}(x_{k_p^*}, y_{k_p^*}) ,$$

where $(x_{k_i^*}, y_{k_i^*})$ is an arbitrary point in $D_{k_i} \cap B((x, y), h)$, term $R \leq 4\sqrt{2}K \cdot h$ and $K > 0$ is the bound of the first and second order partial derivatives of f within each region D_i, and

$$L_{k_i}(x, y) = \int_{D_{k_i}} \psi(x - u, y - v)\, du\, dv .$$

□

For a chosen filter ψ, term $L_{k_i}(x, y)$ is irrelevant to the input function f. However, it depends on Γ, H, and $dist((x, y), \Gamma)$. Furthermore, term R is negligible unless the differences H_{k_i} in (2.6) are very small (weak discontinuities) or $\Gamma \cap B((x, y), h)$ is highly irregular. Therefore, the filter response Z depends on the differences H_{k_i}.

To explain the situation, consider the special case when $p = 2$. Assume that the boundary between D_{k_1} and D_{k_2} is almost a straight line or forms an angle which is not too acute and that there is a jump of size J at (x^*, y^*). Taking $(x_{k_1^*}, y_{k_1^*}) = (x_{k_2^*}, y_{k_2^*}) = (x^*, y^*)$, since $J = f_{k_1}(x^*, y^*) - f_{k_2}(x^*, y^*)$, the filter response becomes

$$Z(x, y) = J \cdot \int_{D_{k_1}} \psi(x - u, y - v)\, du\, dv + R . \tag{2.7}$$

Furthermore, it can be shown that if $(x_1, y_1) \in D_{k_1}$ and $(x_2, y_2) \in D_{k_2}$ are close to the boundaries and are mirror images of each other with respect to the boundary then $\int \psi(x_1 - u, y_1 - v)\, du\, dv \approx - \int \psi(x_2 - u, y_2 - v)\, du\, dv \approx O(dist((x, y), \Gamma)/h)$. Therefore, when (x, y) moves from D_{k_1} to D_{k_2} across the boundaries Γ, if there are discontinuities (jumps) at Γ, then there is a sign change (zero-crossing). Furthermore, when $h^2 << dist((x, y), \Gamma) < h$, term R is small comparing with L_{k_1}, and $Z(x_i, y_i), i = 1, 2$, have relatively large values of different signs across the boundaries Γ. We summarize:

Corollary 2.1. In general, if the input function f has a discontinuity (jump) at a point, then the filter response Z in (2.5) has a corresponding zero-crossing at the same point.

□

Corollary 2.1 provides justifications for almost all the zero-crossing-based linear filters published in the literature, including Marr-Hildreth detector, differences of Gaussians, residual detectors, and others, see [14].

So far the results apply only to unblurred images. We now proceed to show that edges detected from such filters are invariant with respect to rotationally invariant blurring.

Suppose that we apply a filter ψ to a blurred image $I = f * H$ where ψ satisfies conditions in Lemma 2.1. with a support $B(0, h_1)$ and H is a rotationally invariant psf with a support $B(0, h_2)$. Then the filter response

$$Z = I * \psi = (f * H) * \psi = f * (H * \psi) \ . \tag{2.8}$$

One checks that $H * \psi$ is still rotationally invariant and supports on $B(0, h)$ with $\int_{B(0,\,h)} (H * \psi) = 0$ where $h = h_1 + h_2$. Therefore,

Theorem 2.1. Suppose that we apply a rotationally invariant filter ψ to an image $I = f * H$ from a rotationally invariant blurring with a filter response:

$$Z = I * \psi. \tag{2.9}$$

In general, if the original image f has an edge point, then the filter response Z from the blurred image has a corresponding zero-crossing at the same point. □

Due to the invariance of edges with respect to rotationally invariant blurring, for edge detection of such degraded images we can simply apply a rotationally invariant edge detector directly to the blurred image. There is a variety of rotationally invariant edge detectors available, and we shall not digress by discussing them here.

For an image degradation $I = f * H$, usually there is another factor involved, i.e., the psf of the recording system G, which is typically a Gaussian [5]. The blurred image can be represented as $I = f * (H * G)$. It can be shown that, taken into consideration of the psf of the recording system, edges remain invariant.

We have discussed edge detection of images from a rotationally invariant blurring, such as defocused and long-term exposed images. In practice, a degraded image could be the result of blurrings from multiple sources. If all the degradations are rotationally invariant then their combination is still rotationally invariant, since their convolution is still rotationally invariant. Consequently, the edges are still invariant with respect to the combined blurring. Therefore, we can still apply an appropriate detector to the blurred images to obtain edges.

2.4. Motion Blurring

We have discussed edge detection of degraded images from rotationally invariant blurring. We show that for appropriately chosen detectors edges are invariant with respect to such blurring. Consequently, edge detectors can be applied directly to degraded images and there is no need for image restoration or blur identification. However, for degraded images from rotationally *variant* blurring, the edges are in general not invariant and the problem is more difficult. We have no general edge detection procedure, which is invariant with respect to such blurring.

We only discuss a commonly encountered problem here: motion blurred images. We believe that certain information of motion has to be available. Imagine that we have a 1"x1" black square against a while background. We move it to the right by 1" and obtain a 1"x2" grey image against a white background. If there is no information of motion, we can never tell the image is from a stable 1"x2" rectangle or a moving 1"x1" square. To identify the direction and extent of translation is a nontrivial problem, known as blur identification. We want to avoid image restoration or complete blur identification and conduct edge detection directly on blurred images, using as little information of motion as possible.

We show that edges are still invariant so long as they are not in the direction of motion. As a result, we can use appropriately designed one-dimensional detectors along the direction of motion. Consequently, we only need to know the direction of motion; such information could often be available [8, 18].

We first study edge detection of motion blurred images, assuming that we know the direction of motion. Then we discuss a procedure to find the motion direction.

2.4.1. Motion Blurred Images

Uniform motion blurring is due to a translation of the camera or the object. For simplicity, assume that the relative motion is along the horizontal direction (the direction of the x-axis of the camera coordinate system). Then the blurring process is modeled by (2.4).

Our approach detects edges along the direction of motion. More specifically, we apply a one-dimensional detector in the horizontal direction. We show that edges are still invariant with respect to motion so long as they are *not* in the horizontal direction.

We need some results of one-dimensional edge detection. The proof is similar to that of Corollary 2.1 and we omit it.

Lemma 2.2. Let $f: R \to R$ be a function with discontinuities. Let ψ be a symmetric function, which supports on interval $[-h, h]$ with $\int_{-h}^{h} \psi = 0$ and is normalized: $\int_{-h}^{h} |\psi| = 1$. Let $Z = f * \psi$. If the input function f has a discontinuity (jump) at a point then the filter response Z has a corresponding zero-crossing at the same point.

□

For a motion blur psf in (2.4), it can be easily shown that function $H * \psi$ still satisfies the property in Lemma 2.2 except for a normalization constant. Therefore,

Theorem 2.2. Assume that the original image f has an edge at a point p. Let $I = f * H$ be a motion blurred image. Let $Z = I * \psi$ be the filter response, where ψ satisfies the conditions in Lemma 2.2. Then the filter response from the blurred image Z has a corresponding zero-crossing at the same point p.

□

Theorem 2.2 is a result for symmetric filters. The following observation is for antisymmetric filters.

Lemma 2.3. Let $f: R \to R$ be a function with discontinuities. Let ϕ be an antisymmetric function, which supports on interval $[-h, h]$ with $\int_{-h}^{h} \phi' = 0$ and is normalized: $\int_{-h}^{h} |\phi'| = 1$. Let $Z = f * \phi$. If the input function f has a discontinuity (jump) at a point then the filter response Z has a corresponding extremum at the same point.

□

For a motion blur psf in (2.4), it can be easily shown that function $H * \phi$ still satisfies the property in Lemma 2.3 except for a normalization constant. Therefore,

Theorem 2.3. Assume that the original image f has an edge at a point p. Let $I = f * H$ be a motion blurred image. Let $Z = I * \phi$ be the filter response, where ϕ satisfies the conditions in Lemma 2.3. Then the filter response from the blurred image Z has a corresponding extremum at the same point p.

□

Informally, if the filter ψ is symmetric then the feature points in the filter response are zero-crossings, which correspond to edges; if the filter ϕ is antisymmetric then the feature points are extrema. Both types of filters have been reported in edge detection literature, and we state results for both of them. We shall specify the filter ψ and ϕ in Subsection 2.5.

The theorems shows that edges are still invariant so long as we apply an appropriate one-dimensional edge detector in the direction of motion.

2.4.2. Motion Blur Identification

We have discussed an edge detection procedure for motion blurred images with the assumption that we know the motion direction. Motion blur identification is a complex and well studied problem [8, 18] and is not a main topic of this work. Here we describe briefly a motion blur identification procedure.

Assume that an object is moving with a constant (image) flow velocity (u, v). Then the motion blurred image has intensity [18]:

$$I(x, y) = \int_0^T f(x - ut, y - vt)\, dt \tag{2.10}$$

where $f(x, y)$ is the image that would result if there were no motion, and T is the exposure time.

The Fourier transform of I is

$$G(\xi, \eta) = \left\{ F(\xi, \eta) e^{-i[(\xi Tu + \eta Tv)/2]} \right\} \frac{\sin\,[(\xi Tu + \eta Tv)/2]}{(\xi u + \eta v)/2}$$

where F is the Fourier transform of f. Therefore, the Fourier transform of the blurred image has value zero on a family of parallel lines:

$$\xi Tu + \eta Tv = 2n\pi, \quad n = \pm 1, \pm 2, \cdots \tag{2.11}$$

Here Tu and Tv are the motion distance in the horizontal and vertical directions, respectively. Formula (2.4) is a special case of (2.10) with $v = 0$ and $u = 1$.

To estimate the motion distance (uT, vT) from the Fourier transform of a motion blurred image is a well-studied problem for image restoration [2, 3, 8, 18]. We can easily determine motion direction from their ratio.

For a fixed value η, $G(\xi,\eta)$ has equi-spaced zeros ξ_n, $n = \pm 1, \pm 2, \cdots$. The distance between two consecutive zeros $\Delta\xi$ determines Tu:

$$Tu = \frac{2\pi}{\Delta\xi} \tag{2.12a}$$

Similarly,

$$Tv = \frac{2\pi}{\Delta\eta} \tag{2.12b}$$

Due to noise, etc, $\Delta\xi$ and $\Delta\eta$ are difficult to estimate. From our experience, the following method is simple and efficient. We first compute $\log |G(\xi, \eta)|$. It has large negative spikes along zero-crossings of $G(\xi, \eta)$. Their presence indicates the presence of motion and their positions indicate the extent. Averaging out the image dependent part could be applied [2]. From our experimental results, the accurate location of the negative peaks is the most important issue. To avoid unnecessary deviation, we do not use averaging. We propose the following algorithm. For the details, see [15]. Note that essentially we are detecting periodic zero-crossings in one dimension.

Algorithm 2.1. Detecting zeros of $G(t)$:

(i) Compute $r = \log |G(t)|$ and mean m;

(ii) Compute the autocorrelation of r: $A = [r(\tau) - m] * [r(-\tau) - m]$;

(iii) Find the maxima of A;

(iv) Compute the variance of distance between two consecutive maxima;

(v) If the variance is small, accept the location of the maxima as the zeros of $G(t)$.

Note that our approach is different than Cepstrum, which is to detect echoes and is computationally more expensive [(2)].

(2) Cepstrum is used to detect echoes with the following procedure: (i) Compute $s = \log F[I]$; (ii) Compute the autocovariance of s; (iii) Take the Fourier Transform; (iv) Search for peaks. The purposes and the procedures are different, even Step (i). On the other hand, for motion detection, after Step (i), we could use cepstrum to detect negative peaks of $\log |G[I]|$ which correspond to zeros of $G[I]$. This approach does not provide satisfactory results, and slows down the process.

2.5. Experiments

Our approach is implemented in the ANSI C language and is tested on a $SGI4D-480$[(3)] machine running the $IRIX-UNIX$ operating system.

The original image f is a 300×600 digitized characters in Fig. 2.1. We blur it by computer simulation and use our method to detect edges. When choosing the filters there is a variety of filters available, which satisfy our constraints. In our experiment we only use one for each blurring. We would like to admit that the choice is subjective and depends on availability of software. Our goal is to indicate and test the invariance of edges. We do not intend to compare all the existing filters, even though such a comparison would be insightful. One might suggest to compare our results with that from deblurred images. We would like to emphasize that our purpose is to detect edges *without* deblurring. We do compare our results with that from applying detectors to the original (*unblurred*) images.

I. Severely defocused lens with circular aperture stop.

It is a rotationally invariant blurring, modeled by (2.2). A degraded image from computer simulation is in Fig. 2.2 with $\rho = 16$ pixels.

From Theorem 2.1, a variety of rotationally invariant filters can be used. We choose the following:

$$\psi = \begin{cases} \dfrac{4}{h^2}\left[\ln\dfrac{x^2+y^2}{h^2}+1\right] & \text{for } x^2+y^2 \le h^2 \\ 0 & \textit{otherwise}\ . \end{cases} \tag{2.13}$$

Among other desirable properties, this filter maximizes the signal-to-noise ratio. It was first reported in [13].

The zero-crossings from filter response is inevitably noisy and thresholding is indispensable. We apply a dynamic thresholding technique proposed in [14]. The edges detected are in Fig. 2.6.

As a comparison, we apply the same filter and thresholding to the original image and obtain edges in Fig. 2.5. The results in Fig. 2.6 are more or less that same as that in Fig. 2.5.

(3) Only one processor is engaged in the computation.

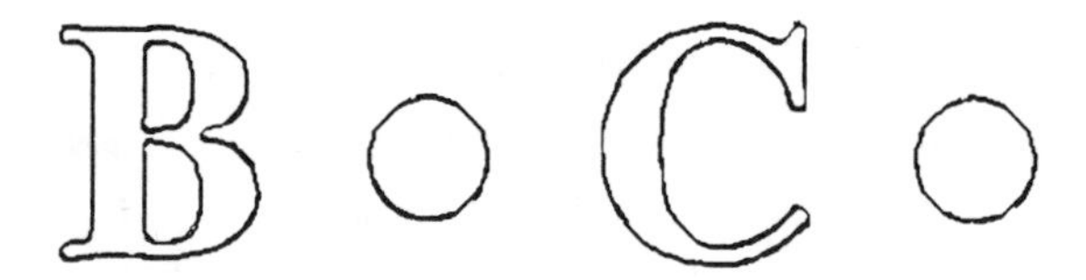

Fig. 2.5. edges from the original (unblurred) image
from a filter with $h = 16$ pixels

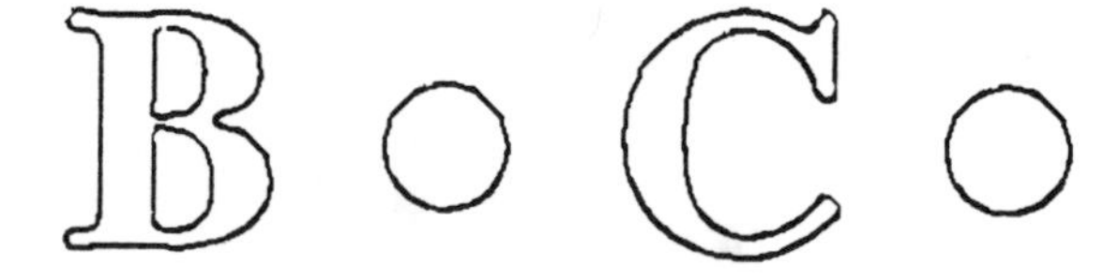

Fig. 2.6. edges from degraded image in Fig. 2.2.

II. Long-term exposure of atmospheric turbulence.

It is a rotationally invariant blurring, modeled by (2.3). A degraded image from computer simulation is in Fig. 2.3 with $\sigma = 0.1$.

From Theorem 2.1, a variety of rotationally invariant filters can be used. We choose (2.13) for the same reason as before and use the same thresholding method. The edges detected are in Fig. 2.7. They are comparable to that in Fig. 2.5.

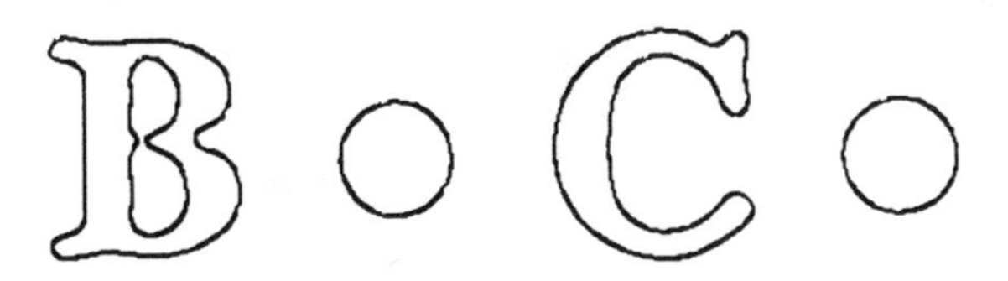

Fig. 2.7. edges from degraded image in Fig. 2.3.

One might notice that edges in Fig. 2.7 do not have as good locality as that in Fig. 2.5. When we apply filter in (2.13) with $h = 16$ pixels to the blurred image, it is the same as applying a filter with $h = 32$ pixels to the original image, since the "virtual" filter $H * \psi$ is a convolution of H and ψ, and each of them has $h = 16$ pixels. It is well known in edge detection research that as filter support increases locality decreases [4, 6, 10, 12]. As a comparison, we apply filter in (2.13) to the *original* image but with $h = 32$ pixels, and obtain edges in Fig. 2.8. They are comparable to that in Fig. 2.7.

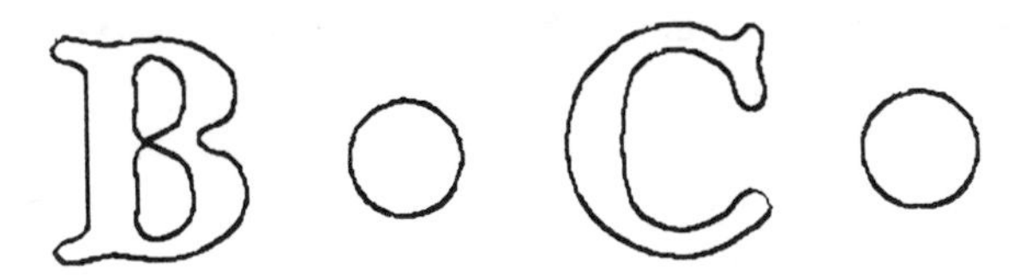

Fig. 2.8. edges from the original (unblurred) image from a filter with $h = 32$ pixels

III. Uniform motion blur.

It is a rotationally variant blurring, modeled by (2.4). A degraded image from computer simulation is in Fig. 2.4 with $T = 32$ pixels.

We cannot simply apply a rotationally invariant filter to the blurred image, see Fig. 2.9. As discussed in Subsection 2.4, we need a one-dimensional filter. From Theorem 2.2 and 2.3, a variety of filters can be used. We choose the following anti-symmetric filter:

$$\phi(t) = \begin{cases} -\dfrac{6t(t+h)}{h^3}, & -h \le t \le 0 \\ \dfrac{6t(t-h)}{h^3}, & 0 < t \le h \\ 0, & \textit{otherwise} \end{cases} \tag{2.14}$$

This filter was proposed in [12] with a discussion of its optimality properties. The edges detected are in Fig. 2.10. Comparing with Fig. 2.9, the results are improved, especially for edges orthogonal to the motion direction (vertical edges). Note that the motion distance is 32 pixels. Still we have good locality, and this is due to the invariance of edges with respect to motion, see Fig. 2.11. On the other hand, the detector does not perform well near corners. Also, edges in the horizontal direction are missing, since the detector is direction sensitive. We could apply another one-dimensional detector along the vertical direction. But the results are not good since edges are no longer invariant in that direction.

It is a challenging problem to do edge detection of motion blurred images without deblurring. We are unable to find a robust detection procedure yet.

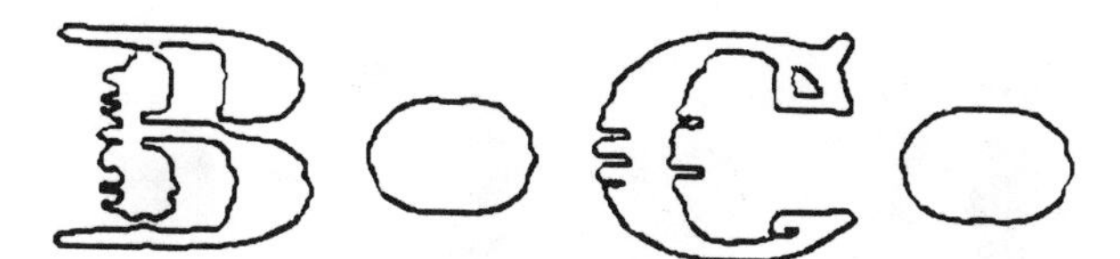

Fig. 2.9. edges from applying a rotationally invariant filter to motion blurred image in Fig. 2.4.

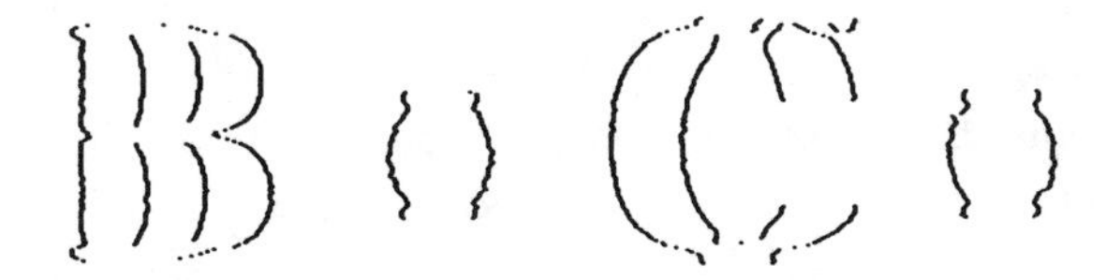

Fig. 2.10. edges from applying a direction sensitive filter to motion blurred image in Fig. 2.4.

Fig. 2.11. edges in Fig. 5.6 superimposed on image in Fig. 2.1.

2.6. Conclusion.

We study edge detection of images, which are degraded by defocused lens, long-term exposure, motion, among others. We explore invariance of edges with respect to blurring and propose detectors without image restoration.

Edge detection of high-quality images itself is a complex task, because of noise, quantization errors, intensity irregularity, and other effects. Image blurring further complicates the issue, and edge detection of severely degraded images is a difficult problem. On the other hand, one has to face this problem in the design and implementations of practical vision systems. This work is an attempt to understand the problem. A number of issues remain to be resolved, and we only mention some of them here.

To model image degradation, the space invariant point spread function model may not be appropriate under certain circumstances. Consequently, the invariance property becomes more subtle.

Image degradation in practice can be caused by different sources of blurring other than what we have discussed, such as blurring from a non-uniform motion or motion along a curve. These and many other sources introduce additional errors to the edge detection process.

We have to cope with missing or false edges, also we have to deal with detected edges that deviate from the corresponding edges in the scene, as blurring degenerates locality of edge detectors.

Reliable and real time blur identification is a difficult task. Our detection procedure from motion blurred images depends on an estimation of motion direction and is sensitive to the parameters from blur identification.

In spite of all the difficulties of edge detection for degraded images, the analysis and experiments give us feeling that the problem is not totally intractable. Furthermore, to make edge detection a useful process for practical vision systems, we believe it is worth further investigation.

Acknowledgements. Valuable comments from Chinmoy Bose and Theo Pavlidis are deeply appreciated.

References.

[1] R. Abraham and J. Robbin, *Transversal Mappings and Flows,* Benjamin, New York, 1967.

[2] H. C. Andrews and B. R. Hunt, *Digital Image Restoration*, Prentice-Hall, Englewood Cliffs, New Jersey, 1977.

[3] J. Biemond and R. L. Lagendijk, "Iterative Methods for Image Deblurring," to appear in *IEEE Proceedings.*

[4] J. Canny, "A Computational Approach to Edge Detection," in *IEEE Trans. on Pattern Analysis and Machine Intelligence,* Vol. 8, 1986, pp. 679-698.

[5] K. R. Castleman, *Digital Image Processing,* Prentice-Hall, Inc., Englewood Clifs, New Jersey, 1979.

[6] J. S. Chen and G. Medioni, "Detection, Localization, and Estimation of Edges", in *IEEE Trans. on Pattern Analysis and Machine Intelligence,* Vol. 11, 1989, pp. 191-198.

[7] L. S. Davis, "A Survey of Edge Detection Techniques," in *Computer Graphics and Image Processing,* Vol. 4, No. 3, 1975, pp. 248-270.

[8] R. C. Gonzalez and P. Wintz, *Digital Image Processing,* Addison-Wesley, 1977.

[9] J. W. Goodman, *Introduction to Fourier Optics,* McGraw-Hill, New York, 1968.

[10] R. M. Haralick, "Digital Step Edges from Zero Crossings of Second Directional Derivatives," in *IEEE Trans. on Pattern Analysis and Machine Intelligence,* Vol. 1, 1984, pp. 58-68.

[11] B. K. P. Horn, *Robot Vision,* MIT Press, Cambridge, 1986.

[12] D. Lee, *Coping with discontinuities in computer vision: their detection, classification, and measurement,* in *IEEE Trans. on Pattern Analysis and Machine*

Intelligence, Vol. 12, 1990, pp. 321-344.

[13] D. Lee, R. Mehrotra, and G. W. Wasilkowski, "An Optimal Zero-crossing-based Discontinuity Detector," in *Proc. of the 7th Scandinavian Conference on Image Analysis*.

[14] D. Lee and G. W. Wasilkowski, "Discontinuity Detection and Thresholding - a Stochastic Approach," in *Proc. IEEE Conference on Computer Vision and Pattern Recognition*, Hawaii, 1991.

[15] D. Lee and Y. Vardi, "Maximum Likelihood Motion Deblurring", in preparation.

[16] D. Marr, *Vision*, Freeman, San Francisco, 1982.

[17] B. L. McGlamery, "Restoration of Turbulence Degraded Images," *JOSA*, Vol. 57, No. 3, 1967, pp. 293-297.

[18] D. Slepian, "Restoration of Photographs Blurred by Image Motion," in *The Bell Sys. Tech. Journal*, Dec. 1967, pp. 2353-2362.

[19] W. L. G. van Warmerdam and V. R. Algazi, "Describing 1-D Intensity Transitions with Gaussian Derivatives at the Resolutions Matching the Transition Widths," in *IEEE Trans. on Pattern Analysis and Machine Intelligence*, Vol. 11, 1989, pp. 973-977.

Chapter 3

Edge Detection with Gaussian Filters at Multiple Scales of Resolution

B. G. Schunck

3.1 Introduction

A new algorithm for the detection of step edges using Gaussian filters at multiple scales of resolution is presented. By combining edge information at multiple scales, the algorithm achieves the noise immunity of the larger scale filters while retaining the edge fidelity from the smaller ones. Over a hundred experiments with the algorithm have been performed on more than a dozen real images. Experimental results that show its performance on real images are presented along with theoretical analysis that justifies the algorithm formulation. The algorithm can be implemented very efficiently since Gaussian filters are separable and multiple smoothed images at different scales can be computed by repeated Gaussian convolutions.

This chapter presents an algorithm for combining edge information across multiple scales of resolution. The algorithm can be implemented efficiently since it is based on edge detection with separable filters and the multiple smoothed images can be computed by repeated convolution with a small Gaussian filter. The algorithm was not designed from an optimization criterion so there is no claim that it is the best, but the algorithm combines edge information across multiple scales using a simple technique that can be used in practical applications. The results show that a simple algorithm for combining edge information across multiple scales can produce excellent results and provide a constructive demonstration of the power of scale-space algorithms relative to edge algorithms that work at a single level of resolution.

Edge detection with Gaussian filters suffers from two tradeoffs: (1) the choice of the scale of resolution for smoothing creates a tradeoff between retaining the detail in the edges and suppressing unwanted edges due to noise and fine texture and (2) the choice of the threshold for separating true edges from false edges creates a tradoff between retaining all of the edges that comprise a contour regardless of the edge strengths and eliminating edges that represent excessive clutter. These tradeoffs are fundamental to edge detection algorithms based on Gaussian filtering at a single scale. Gaussian filters have many desirable properties and it would be desirable to develop new approaches to using Gaussian filters for edge detection that avoid difficult tradeoffs. The objective of this research is to develop an edge detection algorithm that is based on Gaussian filtering and uses edge information from multiple scales to avoid compromising edge fidelity for noise suppression.

Section 3.2 describes the properties of Gaussian filters that justify their use in this work, summarizes related edge detection algorithms, describes prior work on scale-space, and presents the experimental observations that led to the new algorithm. Section 3.3 presents the algorithm and section 3.4 describes the implementation in sufficient detail to allow other researchers to duplicate the experiments. The algorithm has been tested with over a hundred experiments on more than a dozen real images. Selected experimental results are presented in section 3.5. Additional analysis that justifies the algorithm and explains its properties is provided in section 3.6. Conclusions and supplementary discussion are provided in section 3.7.

3.2 Background

The early stages of vision processing identify features in images that are relevant to estimating the structure and properties of objects in a scene [1, 2, 3]. Different edge types and the surface features that may correspond to different kinds of edges are discussed by Horn [4] and Binford [5].

This chapter will deal almost exclusively with step edges although many of the ideas can be adapted to other types of image intensity discontinuities. An edge is a significant local change in the image intensity. Intensity changes due to noise are not edges even though the changes are local, because the changes are not significant. Intensity changes due to variations in illumination across the scene are not edges even though the changes are significant, because the changes are not local. It is difficult to develop an edge detection operator that reliably detects step edges, accurately estimates edge location, and is immune to noise.

The essential idea in detecting step edges is to find points in the sampled image that have locally large gradient magnitudes. Much of the research work in step edge detection is devoted to finding numerical approximations to the gradient that are suitable for use with real images. The step edges in real images are not perfectly sharp since the edges are smoothed by the low-pass filtering inherent in the optics of the camera lens and the bandwidth limitations in the camera electronics. The images are also severely corrupted by noise from the camera and unwanted detail in the scene. An approximation to the image gradient must be able to satisfy two conflicting requirements: (1) the approximation must suppress the effects of noise and (2) the approximation must locate the edge as accurately as possible. There is a tradeoff between noise suppression and localization [6]. An edge detection operator can reduce noise by smoothing the image, but this will add uncertainty to the location of the edge; or the operator can have greater sensitivity to the presence of edges, but this will increase the sensitivity of the operator to noise.

3.2.1 Gaussian Smoothing Filters

The impulse response of the Gaussian smoothing filter is

$$g(x, y) = e^{-(x^2+y^2)/2\sigma^2}, \tag{3.1}$$

where the spread σ determines the width of the Gaussian and the amount of smoothing. The level of resolution, also called the scale, of the filter is the value of σ. This definition of scale and resolution extends to any edge detection algorithm derived from Gaussian filtering at a single scale.

Gaussian filters are rotationally symmetric so the amount of smoothing is the same in all directions. The Gaussian filter has a single lobe which decreases monotonically from the center. Since the Fourier transform of a Gaussian is itself a Gaussian [7], the filter has a single lobe in the frequency domain. Large Gaussian filters can be implemented efficiently because Gaussian functions are separable. Two dimensional Gaussian convolution can be performed by convolving the image with a one-dimensional Gaussian and then convolving the result with the same one-dimensional filter oriented orthogonal to the Gaussian used in the first stage. The amount of computation required for a 2D Gaussian filter grows linearly with the width of the filter mask instead of growing quadratically. The Gaussian is the only function that is both rotationally symmetric and separable [8]. Gaussian convolutions can be cascaded to produce the effect of filtering with a larger filter [9, 10]. This is important for edge detection at multiple scales since the image must be smoothed multiple times. With Gaussian cascading, smoothed images at successive levels of resolution can be obtained by repeated convolution with a small Gaussian filter. This reduces computation time by eliminating redundant computations between levels and simplifies the implementation in hardware.

3.2.2 Gaussian Edge Detection

Gaussian filters have been shown to play an important role in edge detection in human vision [11]. Canny [6] showed for the one-dimensional case that the type of linear operator that provided the best compromise between noise immunity and localization, while retaining the advantages of Gaussian filtering, was the first derivative of a Gaussian. This operator corresponds to smoothing an image with a Gaussian function and then computing the gradient. The results of the Canny operator and the optimal operator are indistinguishable and the Canny operator has a more efficient implementation since it is based on Gaussian filtering; consequently, the Canny operator is informally called the optimal edge detection filter.

The stages of the Canny edge detection algorithm which constitute Gaussian edge detection at a single scale are summarized by the following notation. This version of the algorithm omits noise estimation and edge masking across scales which will be discussed in section 3.2.3. Let $E(x, y)$ denote the image and let $E(x_i, y_j)$ denote the sampled image. The location of the (i, j) grid point is (x_i, y_j), but the precise sampling scheme is not specified. For most of the concepts presented in this chapter, the sampling scheme could be rectangular or hexagonal or could even be an irregular grid pattern or a set of sparse data points. The result from convolving the image with a Gaussian smoothing function is an array of smoothed data, $F(x_i, y_j) = G(x_i, y_j; \sigma) \star E(x_i, y_j)$, where σ is the spread of the Gaussian and controls the degree of smoothing. The gradient of the smoothed array $F(x_i, y_j)$ can be computed using 2 by 2 first difference approximations for the partial derivatives in the x and y directions to produce two arrays for the x and y partial derivatives: $F_x(x_i, y_j)$ and $F_y(x_i, y_j)$. The formulas are presented in section 3.4. The magnitude $\rho(x_i, y_j)$ and orientation $\theta(x_i, y_j)$ are computed using the formulas for rectangular-to-polar conversion. The magnitude image array will have large values where the image gradient is large, but this is not sufficient to identify the edges since the problem of finding points in the image array where there is rapid change has merely been transformed into the problem of finding points in the magnitude array that have locally large values. To identify edges, the broad ridges in the magnitude array must be thinned so that only the magnitudes at the points of greatest local change remain. The gradient angle is reduced to one of four possible orientations of a line through the center of a 3 by 3 window, $\zeta(x_i, y_j) = \text{Sector}(\theta(x_i, y_j))$ as described in section 3.4.4. The gradient ridges are thinned with non-maxima suppression [12, pp. 275], $\mu(x_i, y_j) = \text{nms}(\rho(x_i, y_j), \zeta(x_i, y_j))$. Finally, the thinned gradient magnitude is thresholded to produce the edge map, $\mu_\tau(x_i, y_j) = \mathcal{T}_\tau\left(\mu(x_i, y_j)\right)$. Canny [13, 6] described a double thresholding scheme that was not used in this chapter. The steps in the algorithm for Gaussian edge detection adapted from the work of Canny [6] are summarized in algorithm A. This algorithm forms the foundation for the multiresolution Gaussian edge detection algorithm presented in this chapter.

Daugman [14] provides additional analysis on Gaussian filter and related functions and the general subject of rotationally symmetric operators is discussed by Brady and Horn [8]. Torre and Poggio [15, 16] analyze edge detection as an ill-posed problem that can be solved by regularization [17] and show the relationship between the regularizing parameter and filter scale. Poggio, Voorhees, and Yuille [18] show the relationship between edge detection and cubic spline interpolation. Canny [13] discusses the relationship between edge detection based on convolution with an operator like the gradient of Gaussian and the surface fitting approach to edge detection advocated by Haralick [19].

Marr and Hildreth [11, 20] introduced the Laplacian of Gaussian as an edge detection operator. This operator is interesting for several reasons: (1) the edge location corresponds to a zero in the operator output as opposed to a maxima in the output of the gradient of Gaussian [6] and (2) the zeros in the output of the Laplacian of Gaussian operator for different choices of the Gaussian spread σ define scale-space [21] which is a key representation in modern approaches to the issue of edge representations at multiple scales of resolution which are discussed in the next section. The scheme for combining the outputs of edge operators at multiple scales that is presented in this chapter depends on the property that the edge location is indicated by a local maximum in the output of the gradient of Gaussian operator. This is why the multiresolution Gaussian edge detection algorithm is based on the results of Canny [13, 6]. The algorithm presented in this chapter implements edge

Algorithm A The steps in Gaussian edge detection adapted from Canny [6] are summarized. The algorithm omits noise estimation and edge marking across scales.

[1] Smooth the image using Gaussian convolution, $F(x_i, y_j) = G(x_i, y_j; \sigma) \star E(x_i, y_j)$.

[2] Compute finite-difference approximations to the partial derivatives of the smoothed image, $F_x(x_i, y_j)$ and $F_y(x_i, y_j)$, using the formulas presented in section 3.4.

[3] Compute the gradient magnitude, $\rho(x_i, y_j) = \sqrt{F_x^2(x_i, y_j) + F_y^2(x_i, y_j)}$.

[4] Compute the gradient angle, $\theta(x_i, y_j) = \arctan(F_y(x_i, y_j), F_x(x_i, y_j))$.

[5] Reduce the gradient angle to one of 4 sectors.

[6] Suppress non-maxima by setting all elements to zero that are not local maxima along the line perpendicular to the gradient ridge in a 3 by 3 window.

[7] Threshold the result to eliminate edges due to noise.

detection in scale-space [21], except that the edge locations at different scales are defined by the locations of maxima rather than zeros in the edge operator output.

3.2.3 Multiple Scales

Theories of vision processing are incorporating the idea of multiple scales of resolution [22]. Vision processes such as edge detection can be performed at multiple scales. The largest scale extracts the major contours of an object, while the smaller scales extract finer image features. Unfortunately, when a Gaussian filter is scaled to fit the major contours of an object, the fine detail in the contours is lost. This effect is clearly seen in the results presented in section 3.2.4. In many practical applications, it is necessary to estimate the major edges (contours) without distortion while suppressing minor edges (scene noise).

Witkin introduced the notion of scale space in the analysis of edge images obtained with Gaussian filtering [21]. Considerable theoretical work has been performed in this area [23, 24, 25]. Yuille and Poggio [24] proved that the zeros of the Laplacian of Gaussian edge operator, and more generally any linear operator applied to the result of Gaussian filtering, have nice scaling behavior: edges are not created as scale increases. Yuille and Poggio were not able to prove similar results for nonlinear edge detection operators such as the magnitude of the gradient of Gaussian. Because of the nice scaling properties of the zeros in the output of the Laplacian of Gaussian and the theoretical completeness of zero-crossings as a representation for image structure [26, 23], most research in scale-space has concentrated on the multilevel representations derived from the zeros in the output of the Laplacian of Gaussian operator. This chapter shows that the local peaks in the output of the gradient of Gaussian operator can lead to a very simple algorithm for combining edge information across multiple scales which suggests that loci of the maxima in an operator based on Gaussian filtering can also lead to a useful scale-space representation.

Rosenfeld [27] described an algorithm for edge detection that computed measurements of edge strength at several scales and multiplied the edge strength measurements to produce sharper edge estimates. The computation did not use Gaussian smoothing, the edge strength measurement was not the magnitude of the gradient, and no experiments on real images were cited in the chapter. Rosenfeld and Thurston [28] described a technique similar to the non-maxima suppression scheme over large neighborhoods used in this work, but the technique was not combined with Gaussian filtering or multiple scales of resolution. The combination of Gaussian filtering over multiple scales, computation of the gradient magnitude and orientation, and non-maxima suppression over large neighborhoods is unique to this work.

The Canny edge detection algorithm [13, 6] incorporated a scheme called edge marking for building an edge map from the edge information available at different scales. Edge marking builds the edge map by using the output from the smallest operator subject to the restriction that the noise level in the output of the operator is below a threshold. The Canny algorithm computes the gradient of Gaussian at different scales and measures the noise level present in each operator. Since larger operators perform more smoothing, they exhibit a lower noise level at the expense of fidelity in edge location. If the output of one edge operator must be chosen, then it is reasonable to choose the operator with greatest localization (the smallest operator) that has sufficient noise suppression. This is the motivation behind edge marking in the Canny algorithm. The algorithm presented in this chapter combines edge information from multiple scales rather than choosing the edge operator output at a single scale. The result is better localization than using only the smallest filter with better noise suppression than using only the largest filter.

3.2.4 Experimental Observations

Many experiments with the Gaussian edge detection algorithm have been performed by the author on real images. Two problems have been observed: (1) it is impossible to choose a single resolution that simultaneously suppresses noise and retains the detail in the major contours and (2) images occur in practice where it is impossible to choose one threshold that is suitable for all areas of the image. Figure 3.1 shows the image of a connecting rod. Figures 3.2 and 3.3 present the results of applying the edge detection algorithm summarized in this section to the test image in figure 3.1. In figure 3.2, a 7 by 7 Gaussian filter was used to smooth the image before computing the gradient; in figure 3.3, a 31 by 31 Gaussian filter was used. The non-maxima suppressed gradient magnitude for the smaller filter exhibits excellent fine detail in the edges, but suffers from excessive unwanted edge fragments due to noise and fine texture. For the larger filter size, there are fewer unwanted edge fragments but much of the detail in the edges has been lost. This illustrates the tradeoff between edge localization and noise immunity and shows that no choice for the Gaussian spread σ would suppress the undesirable edges due to noise and the internal texture of the object without eliminating the desirable detail in the major contours.

Figure 3.4 is an image of a gear. The right side of the gear has good contrast and the contours corresponding to the large gear teeth (the boundary of the gear) would map into high ridges in gradient magnitude; but the lower side of the gear has poor contrast: the ridges in gradient magnitude would be low. The interior gear teeth have low contrast. It is not possible to set a threshold on gradient magnitude such that all of the outer gear teeth are above the threshold while most of the interior gear teeth are below the threshold. The need for thresholding is shown by the plots in figures 3.2b and 3.3b. Common practice displays the output of gradient-based edge operators encoded as gray levels, but this transfers the edge identification problem to the human viewer. A fair method of display is to map all non-zero output values (edge candidates) to white and map all zero output values (non-edge candidates) to black.

In summary, the problem with Gaussian edge detection at a single scale is that two parameters, the Gaussian spread σ and the threshold τ, must be chosen by the user, the parameters are very difficult to choose, and in many practical situations no parameter values are adequate.

3.3 Edge Detection with Multiple Scales

In this section, an algorithm for combining several edge images at different scales into a single edge image will be described. The combined edge image has fewer

Figure 3.1: A test image of a connecting rod is shown. The image was acquired by a Reticon 256 by 256 area CCD array camera. The image was processed before halftoning to improve the range of image intensities.

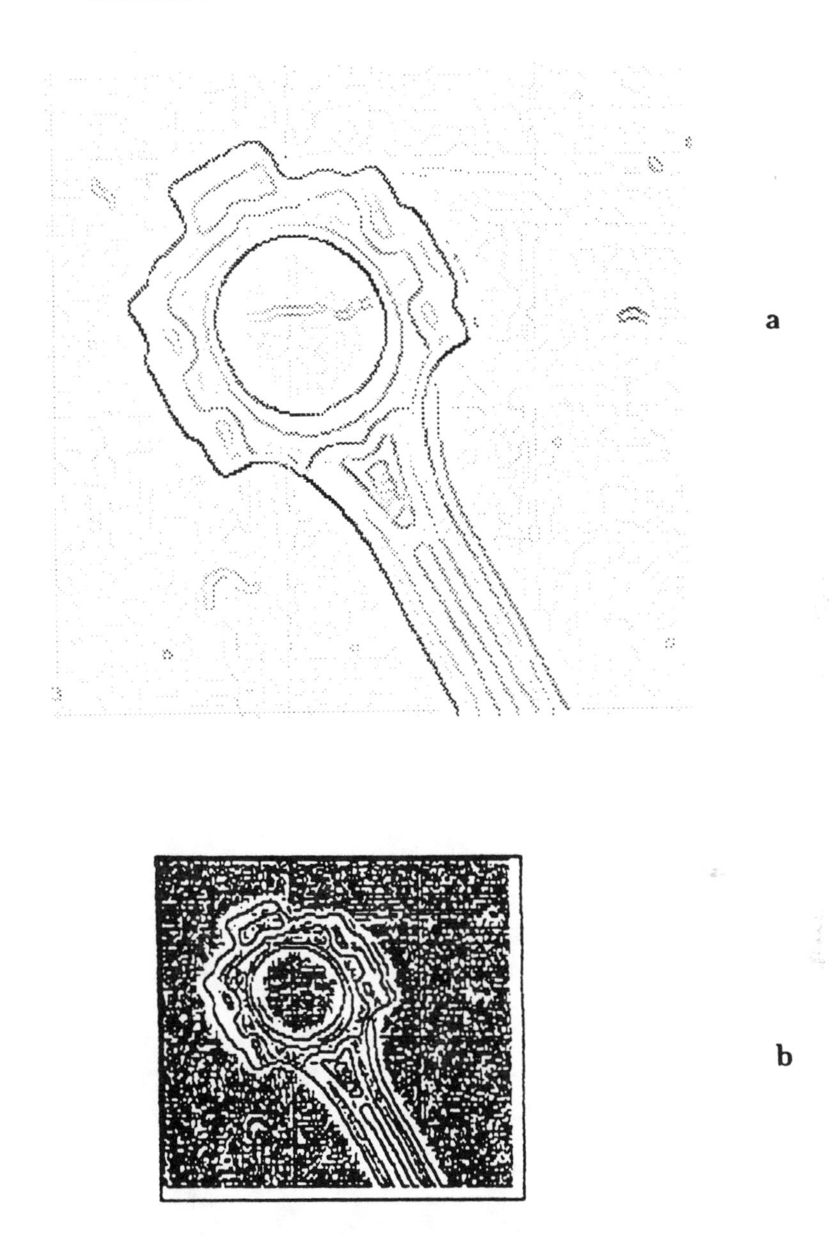

Figure 3.2: The result of edge detection applied to the test image from figure 3.1 with a 7 by 7 Gaussian smoothing filter is displayed. The picture in part **a** is an inverted gray level image of the result after smoothing with a Gaussian smoothing filter, computing the gradient approximation, and suppressing non-maxima. The weak edge fragments due to noise and fine texture do not show up clearly. Part **b** is a plot of the image from part **a** with every pixel that was greater than zero drawn in black. This plot shows the large number of weak edge fragments that are present in the result of edge detection but do not show up clearly in a gray level display of the results.

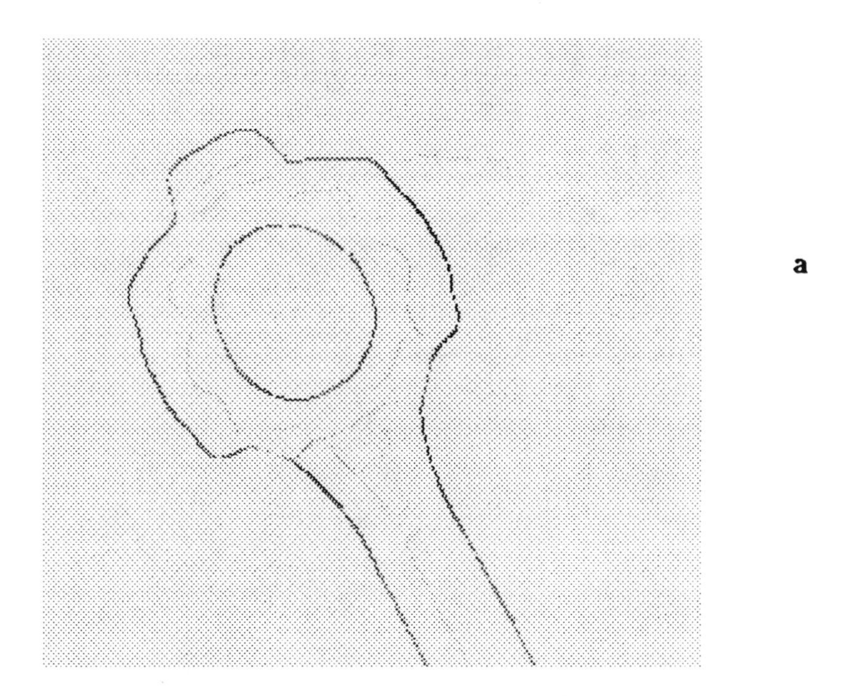

a

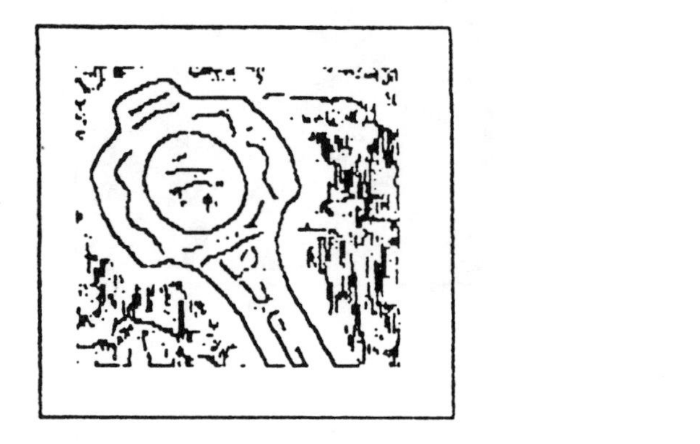

b

Figure 3.3: The result of edge detection applied to the test image from figure 3.1 are shown. A 31 by 31 Gaussian filter was used to smooth the image followed by computation of the gradient approximation and then non-maxima suppression. Part **a** displays the non-maxima suppressed result as an inverted gray level image. The weak edge fragments due to noise and fine texture are not easily seen. Part **b** plots the results to show all of the edge fragments.

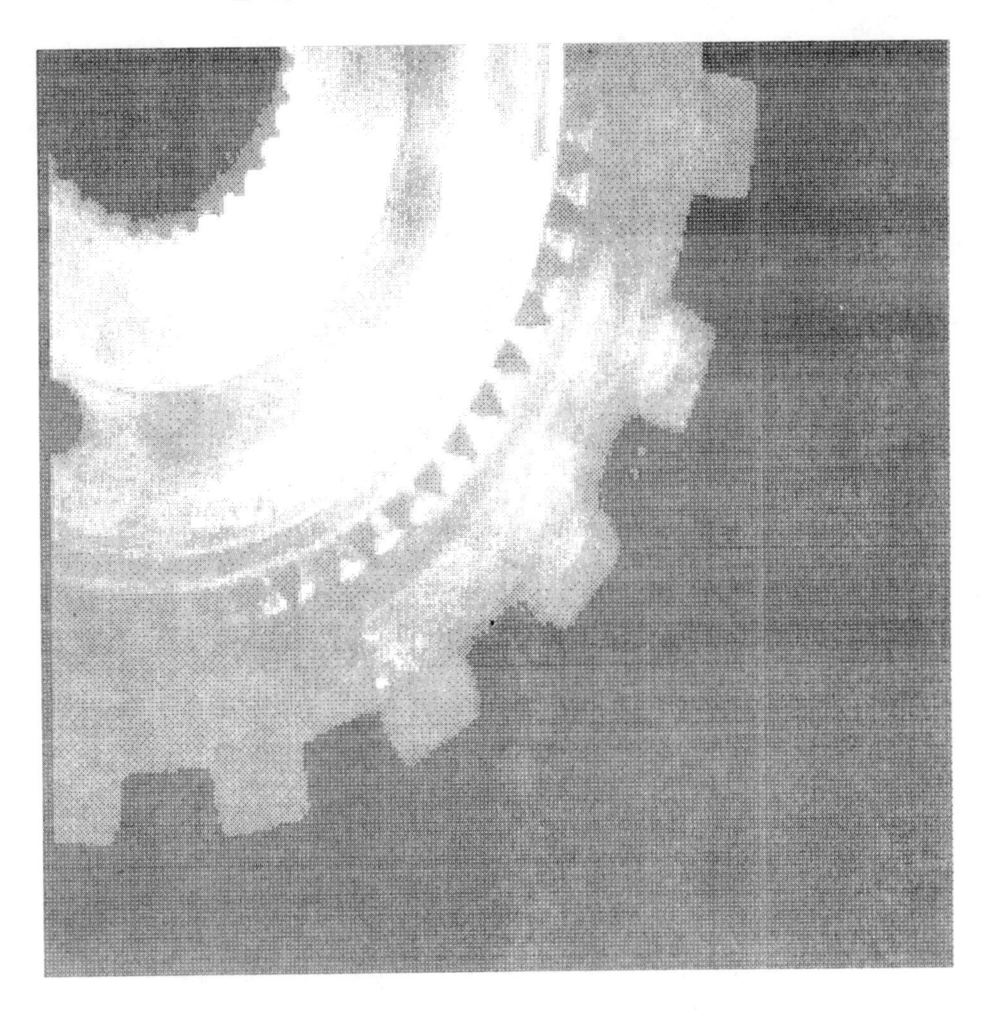

Figure 3.4: The figure shows a closeup image of a gear with three rings of teeth. This test case is particularly demanding since the sharp corners in the large gear teeth should be retained in the edge image, but the contrast near the bottom of the image is very poor. The image was processed before halftoning to improve the range of image intensities.

undesirable edges caused by noise and unwanted fine texture and better fine detail in the major edges. There are two key ideas in the algorithm: (1) the gradient magnitudes are multiplied so that magnitude ridges at different scales are reinforced and (2) non-maxima suppression over large neighborhoods can eliminate ridges that do not correspond to major edges.

The result of convolving a Gaussian filter with spread σ over an image $E(x, y)$ is

$$F(x, y; \sigma) = G(x, y; \sigma) \star E(x, y). \tag{3.2}$$

Assume that the edge detection algorithm approximates the magnitude and orientation of the gradient of the smoothed image:

$$\begin{aligned} \rho(x, y; \sigma) &= |\nabla F(x, y; \sigma)| && (3.3) \\ \theta(x, y; \sigma) &= \arctan(F_x(x, y; \sigma), F_y(x, y; \sigma)). && (3.4) \end{aligned}$$

The edge image is obtained from the magnitude and orientation of the gradient by non-maxima suppression [6],

$$\mu(x, y; \sigma) = \mathrm{nms}(\rho(x, y; \sigma), \theta(x, y; \sigma)). \tag{3.5}$$

3.3.1 Combining Gradient Magnitudes

Multiresolution Gaussian edge detection begins by computing smoothed versions of the image $E(x, y)$ at several scales $\{\sigma_1, \sigma_2, \ldots, \sigma_n\}$. Without loss of generality, the simple case of two scales σ_1 and σ_2, with $\sigma_1 < \sigma_2$, will be explained. The general case will be covered in section 3.3.3. The gradient magnitudes and orientations can be computed at both scales:

$$\begin{aligned} \rho(x, y; \sigma_1) &= |\nabla F(x, y; \sigma_1)| && (3.6) \\ \theta(x, y; \sigma_1) &= \arctan(F_x(x, y; \sigma_1), F_y(x, y; \sigma_1)) && (3.7) \end{aligned}$$

$$\begin{aligned} \rho(x, y; \sigma_2) &= |\nabla F(x, y; \sigma_2)| && (3.8) \\ \theta(x, y; \sigma_2) &= \arctan(F_x(x, y; \sigma_2), F_y(x, y; \sigma_2)) && (3.9) \end{aligned}$$

The gradient magnitude for the larger scale σ_2 will contain a few large ridges corresponding to the major edges in the image. The gradient magnitude for the smaller scale σ_1 will contain numerous ridges, large and small, some of which correspond to major edges, some of which correspond to the edges of finer detail, and the rest are due to noise and unwanted texture. The gradient magnitudes are multiplied to produce a composite magnitude image,

$$M(x, y; \sigma_1, \sigma_2) = \rho(x, y; \sigma_1) \cdot \rho(x, y; \sigma_2). \tag{3.10}$$

The small ridges in $\rho(x, y; \sigma_1)$ that correspond to major edges will be reinforced by the ridges in $\rho(x, y; \sigma_2)$ and the small ridges in $\rho(x, y; \sigma_1)$ that do not correspond to major edges will be attenuated by the absence of a ridge nearby in $\rho(x, y; \sigma_2)$. These ideas are illustrated for the one-dimensional case in figure 3.5. Note how the position of the minor edge is displaced in the two magnitude plots in figure 3.5**b**. In the magnitude at the larger scale, the major edge affects the estimate of the position of the minor edge more than the minor edge affects the estimate of the position of the major edge. When the gradient magnitudes are multiplied, the major edge is enhanced because the locations of the major edge at the two scales coincide; the minor is attenuated because the locations of the minor edge do not coincide at the two scales. This kind of asymmetry is one of the reasons why multiplying the gradient magnitudes works so well.

3.3.2 Suppression of Unwanted Detail

Non-maxima suppression is usually applied over only a 3 by 3 neighborhood [12, p. 275], but there is no reason why the technique cannot be applied over larger neighborhoods. The combined magnitude image $M(x,y;\sigma_1,\sigma_2)$ will contain all of the ridges in $\rho(x,y;\sigma_1)$, but the ridges from $\rho(x,y;\sigma_1)$ that were within the support of the ridges in $\rho(x,y;\sigma_2)$ will be amplified and the ridges from $\rho(x,y;\sigma_1)$ outside the support of the ridges in $\rho(x,y;\sigma_2)$ will be attenuated. The ridges in $M(x,y;\sigma_1,\sigma_2)$ that correspond to major edges are much higher than the ridges that do not correspond to major edges. If non-maxima suppression with a 3 by 3 neighborhood were applied to $M(x,y;\sigma_1,\sigma_2)$, both the major and minor ridges would be retained; but if the neighborhood size for non-maxima suppression were comparable to the distance between major edges, then non-maxima suppression would eliminate the minor edges between the major edges. The width w_2 of the larger filter can be selected so that it corresponds to the distance between major features. In terms of σ_2, $w_2 \approx 4\sigma_2$. The width ν of the neighborhood for non-maxima suppression should be about the same as the distance between major features, which is the width w_2 of the larger filter. The edge image obtained by applying non-maxima suppression over a large neighborhood to the combined gradient magnitude is

$$\mu(x,y;\sigma_1,\sigma_2) = \text{nms}_\nu(\rho(x,y;\sigma_1)\cdot\rho(x,y;\sigma_2), \text{Sector}(\theta(x,y;\sigma_2))). \tag{3.11}$$

The gradient orientation used for non-maxima suppression over a neighborhood of size $\nu = 4\sigma_2$ is the gradient orientation computed at the larger scale. The same four sector partitions as used for ordinary non-maxima suppression (shown in figure 3.6) are used for non-maxima suppression with a large neighborhood size. The only difference in implementation is that the search along the horizontal, vertical, or diagonal line extends for a greater distance.

3.3.3 Generalization to Several Scales

The algorithm can be generalized to several scales $\sigma_1,\sigma_2,\ldots,\sigma_n$. Assume that $\sigma_i < \sigma_{i+1}$. For several scales, the edge detection algorithm is

$$\mu(x,y;\sigma_1,\sigma_2,\ldots,\sigma_n) = \text{nms}_\nu(\prod_{i=1}^{n}\rho(x,y;\sigma_i), \text{Sector}(\theta(x,y;\sigma_n))), \tag{3.12}$$

where the neighborhood size for non-maxima suppression is $\nu \approx 4\sigma_n$.

Empirical evidence from neurophysiology suggests that the scales may differ by approximately a factor of 2 in primate visual systems [11], though it has been suggested that a factor of $\sqrt{2}$ may be better from the standpoint of computational efficiency [10]. Because of the cascading property of Gaussian filters, it is best

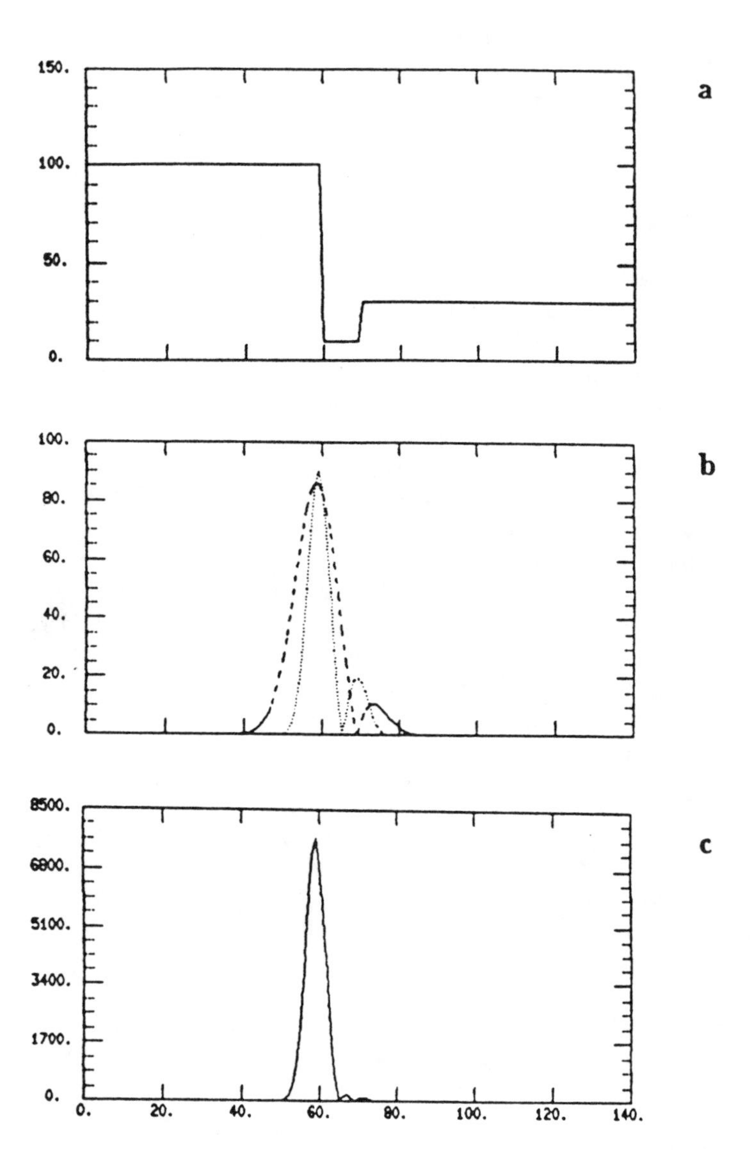

Figure 3.5: The profile of two ideal step edges is shown in part **a**. There is a major step edge and a minor step edge in the profile. The two edges are separated by 10 pixels. The result of computing the first derivative after smoothing with Gaussians at two scales is shown in part **b**. The dashed curve is the magnitude of the first derivative after smoothing with a Gaussian filter of size $n = 23$. The dotted curve is the magnitude of the first derivative after smoothing with a Gaussian filter of size $n = 11$. Note how the peaks that correspond to the major step edge are aligned, while the peaks that correspond to the minor step edge are separated. The product of the two first derivative estimates is shown in part **c**. Note how multiplying the derivative estimates reinforces the major step edge while suppressing the minor step edge.

to choose filter widths n that differ by about a factor of two. Since very small Gaussian filters will be too small to retain the properties of Gaussians, the smallest filter width should be around $n = 7$. The cascading property should be used to select the larger filters, so given a filter of size n, the next filter size would be $n' = 2n - 1$. Experiments performed as part of this research indicate that the difference in the results between, for example, a 13 point filter and the next smaller and larger odd filter sizes, for example $n = 11$ or $n = 15$, is small. There is no reason to abandon the computational advantages of the cascading property; filter sizes should be selected to fit the sizes dictated by cascading.

The size of the largest scale σ_n should be chosen so that the distance between major features in the image is approximately $4\sigma_n$. For a wide range of applications, the variation in the distance between major features will be less that the width of the largest filter. As mentioned above, empirical observations show little difference in the results of edge detection when the filter width is changed by a small fraction of its width. In other words, the width of the largest filter can be set to the average distance between major features in typical images and the variations in the distances between major features will not matter.

An implementation of the algorithm can work with a fixed set of filter sizes starting with a filter width of 5 or 7 and progressing through the sizes dicated by cascading up to a size similar to the average distance between major features. This means that the filter sizes do not have to be chosen by the user. Realize that the distance between major features is determined by the optics and imaging geometry of the camera and the scene and it is reasonable to assume that the user will always choose (for reasons apart from the needs of this algorithm) the lens and distance from the camera to the objects in the scene so that the distance between major features is the same within the large tolerance provided by the insensitivity of the algorithm to variations in filter size.

Multiresolution Gaussian edge detection should be done with a set of filter widths that roughly double since empirical observations indicate that the filter width must nearly double to produce a significant difference in output. Cascading Gaussian convolutions by repeatedly convolving with a single filter is an efficient way to generate a sequence of smoothed images with roughly twice as much smoothing; but extra smoothed images are produced. The issue is generating a sequence of smoothed images where the effective filter size is a power of two times the fundamental size, $\sigma_k = 2^{k-1}\sigma_1$, versus generating a sequence of smoothed images where the effective filter size is a multiple of the fundamental size, $\sigma_k = k\sigma_1$. There are two choices: (1) ignore the extra smoothed images and only compute the gradient magnitudes for the smoothed images at scales corresponding to doubling the filter width or (2) use gradient magnitudes from all of the smoothed images. There is no evidence that indicates a preferance for one choice over the other, but using all smoothed images leads to a slight increase in computation.

3.3.4 Multiple Outputs

The algorithm presented in this chapter can be easily modified to produce multiple edge operator outputs at different scales. Suppose that there are n scales, σ_1, σ_2, ..., σ_n, with $\sigma_i < \sigma_{i+1}$ and suppose that edge output at each of the scales is desired to accommodate the need to retain features across a variety of scales. The product of the gradient magnitudes can be computed over successive ranges of scales to produce a sequence of edge outputs $\{\mu_k(x,y)\}$ corresponding to different levels of resolution,

$$\mu_k(x,y) = \text{nms}_{4\sigma_k}(\prod_{i=1}^{k} \rho(x,y;\sigma_i), \text{Sector}(\theta(x,y;\sigma_k))). \tag{3.13}$$

This provides a set of outputs that retain features at a range of separations while retaining the detail from the finest scale and greater noise suppression. The higher numbered edge outputs in the sequence have fewer edge fragments and may be useful for algorithms such as binocular stereo [29] that need edge information in separate channels with fewer edge fragments in the larger channels.

If for some reason it is desirable to blur the details in the outputs at higher scales, then the output can be computed from overlapping intervals that always include the largest scale:

$$\mu_k(x,y) = \text{nms}_{4\sigma_n}(\prod_{i=n-k+1}^{n} \rho(x,y;\sigma_i), \text{Sector}(\theta(x,y;\sigma_n))). \tag{3.14}$$

The set of edge outputs will exhibit variation in the amount of detail ranging from the coarsest output at $k = 1$ to the output with greatest fidelity at $k = n$. In this situation, variation in detail means variation in the amount of blurring in the detail in the contours as opposed to variation in the amount of edge fragments. Because all of the outputs use the largest scale σ_n with non-maximum supression over the largest neighborhood size $\nu = 4\sigma_n$, there will be few edge fragments in any output; but the amount of detail in the contours will vary. This configuration of outputs at different scales could be useful for contour analysis at multiple scales where it is required that contours be successively blurred. For example, this strategy could be used to produce contours with successively greater blurring, without needing to smooth the contours with one-dimensional filters, prior to the computation of curvature primitives [30, 31] or smoothed local symmetries [32].

The ideas in this section can be generalized to produce a two-dimensional array of outputs representing different tradeoffs in the dimensions of feature separation and detail suppression:

$$\mu_{k,l}(x,y) = \text{nms}_{4\sigma_l}(\prod_{i=l-k+1}^{l} \rho(x,y;\sigma_i), \text{Sector}(\theta(x,y;\sigma_l))), \tag{3.15}$$

for $1 \leq k,l \leq n$. These ideas for producing sets of edge outputs have not been explored in this work since the objective was to produce a single edge output that combines the detail from the smallest filter with the noise suppression of the largest filter.

3.3.5 Elimination of Thresholding

Besides providing edge images of excellent quality, the algorithm has the special advantage of not requiring the selection of a threshold. Most edge detection algorithms require the user to select a threshold for the thinned edge magnitude $\mu(x,y;\sigma)$ to eliminate insignificant edges, but non-maxima suppression with a large neighborhood size in effect automatically performs local thresholding based on the strength of major edges in a local neighborhood. Most spurious edges due to noise and unwanted texture are cancelled either by major edges or by other spurious edges. In effect, threshold selection has been replaced with neighborhood size selection. The advantage is that the threshold depends on illumination and noise, which can vary, and is hard to choose analytically; whereas, the neighborhood size depends on the imaging geometry and the distance between edges in the scene, which can easily be determined in advance.

Another explanation is that multiplying the gradient magnitudes enhances the contrast of the major edges so that the range between the peaks of major edges in gradient magnitude and the peaks due to noise is beyond the dynamic range typically provided by the number of bits per pixel.

3.4 Experimental Methods

This section describes the details of the implementation of Gaussian edge detection at single and multiple scales with sufficient detail so that other researchers can implement the algorithms and perform their own experiments. The multiresolution Gaussian edge detection algorithm is summarized in algorithm B. The following sections describe the detail of the implementation and explain the problems with the current implementation.

3.4.1 Gaussian Filter Design

The coefficients of the Gaussian filters were chosen by sampling the Gaussian function

$$g(x) = Ae^{-x^2/2\sigma^2} \tag{3.16}$$

and rounding to the nearest integer. Although floating-point arithmetic could be used in a research setting, integer arithmetic was used in this work to conform to the constraints on industrial applications. The mask size n must be an odd integer and is selected before selecting the filter coefficients. The filter amplitude should be as large as possible to provide more resolution for the filter coefficients; but if the filter amplitude is too large, then integer overflow occurs too frequently. Once the mask size n and the filter amplitude A are chosen, the strategy that makes good use of the available mask width and maximum amplitude is to set the center mask coefficient to A and the coefficient at the mask end point to 1. Assume that n is odd, $n = 2m + 1$. The coefficients of the sampled Gaussian filter are given by

$$g[k] = Ae^{-k^2\Delta^2/2\sigma^2}, \qquad k = -m, -m+1, \ldots, m-1, m, \tag{3.17}$$

for some sampling distance Δ. If the coefficient at the end of the mask, $g[m] = g[-m]$, is to be 1, then

$$Ae^{-m^2\Delta^2/2\sigma^2} = 1. \tag{3.18}$$

Algorithm B An algorithm for combining the results of Gaussian edge detection at multiple scales of resolution which has the noise suppression of the largest filter with the fidelity to detail provided by the smallest filter. Assume that $E(x_i, y_j)$ is the input image and a set of scales $\{\sigma_1, \sigma_2, \ldots, \sigma_n\}$ with $\sigma_i < \sigma_{i+1}$ has been selected. The scales should be chosen as explained in section 3.3.3 so that the Gaussian filters can be cascaded.

[1] Filter the image $E(x_i, y_j)$ with each of the filters.

[2] Compute the gradient magnitude for each filtered image.

[3] Compute the product of the gradient magnitudes.

[4] Compute the gradient orientation for the largest filter and reduce the orientation to one of the four sectors as described in 3.4.4.

[5] Perform non-maxima suppression on the product of the gradient magnitudes with a neighborhood size of $\nu = 4\sigma_n$.

Algorithm C The algorithm designs an n point Gaussian filter given an odd filter size n and an initial guess for the filter amplitude A. The filter amplitude must be chosen to insure that the filter calculations will not overflow while smoothing typical images. For simplicity, unit sample spacing is assumed, so that $\Delta = 1$. The value of σ is chosen so that the smallest filter coefficient is 1.

[1] Calculate the filter half-width m such that $n = 2m + 1$.

[2] The Gaussian spread σ must be chosen so that the filter fills the given mask size n efficiently. Calculate σ from the filter half-width and amplitude, $\sigma = \sqrt{\frac{m^2}{2 \ln A}}$.

[3] Choose the integers closest to $Ae^{-k^2/2\sigma^2}$, for $k = 0, 1, \ldots, m$ as the filter coefficients. Since the Gaussian is symmetric, only one side of the coefficients need to be computed and stored.

[4] Try the filter on typical images. If the smoothing operation overflows, then choose a smaller filter amplitude A and go back to step 2.

From this, the optimum spread σ, relative to the spacing Δ, that scales the filter width so that it efficiently fits into the n point mask is given by

$$\sigma^2/\Delta^2 = \frac{m^2}{2 \ln A}, \tag{3.19}$$

for any positive integer m where $n = 2m + 1$ is the filter size. The steps of the algorithm are listed in algorithm C. This technique has been used to generate coefficients for Gaussian masks from $n = 3$ up to $n = 63$ and these masks have been used in all of the experiments presented in this chapter. Note that the smallest filter $n = 3$ provided by algorithm C is not a good smoothing filter since it is too close to a δ-function, but that filter size was not used in the experiments reported in this chapter. Better methods for filter design that properly scale the amplitude are discussed by Schunck [33], Canny [13], and Horn [34]. The filter coefficients calculated with algorithm C were sufficient for testing the ideas presented in this paper.

3.4.2 Gaussian Convolution

The implementation of Gaussian convolution used for the examples in this paper used the composition of two horizontal convolutions. The input was convolved with a horizontal Gaussian and the result was placed in a temporary array in its transposed position. The temporary array was then used as input to the same convolution code so that the vertical convolution was performed by horizontal convolution. The output data from the second convolution was transposed as the convolution was performed so the data was restored to its proper (original) orientation.

3.4.3 Computing the Gradient

The gradient of the smoothed array $F(x_i, y_j)$ can be computed using the 2 by 2 first difference approximation to the partial derivatives in the x and y directions to produce two arrays for the x and y partial derivatives:

$$\begin{aligned} F_x(x_i, y_j) &\approx (F(x_{i+1}, y_j) - F(x_i, y_j) \\ &\quad + F(x_{i+1}, y_{j+1}) - F(x_i, y_{j+1}))/2 \end{aligned} \tag{3.20}$$

$$\begin{aligned} F_y(x_i, y_j) &\approx (F(x_i, y_j) - F(x_i, y_{j-1}) \\ &\quad + F(x_{i+1}, y_j) - F(x_{i+1}, y_{j-1}))/2. \end{aligned} \tag{3.21}$$

The formulas can be displayed as computational molecules in the style of numerical analysis,

$$\frac{\partial}{\partial x} \approx \begin{bmatrix} -1 & 1 \\ -1 & 1 \end{bmatrix} \quad \frac{\partial}{\partial y} \approx \begin{bmatrix} 1 & 1 \\ -1 & -1 \end{bmatrix}. \tag{3.22}$$

The finite differences are averaged over the 2 by 2 square so that the x and y partial derivatives are computed at the same point in the image. The magnitude and orientation of the gradient can be computed from the standard formulas for rectangular-to-polar conversion:

$$\rho(x_i, y_j) = \sqrt{F_x^2(x_i, y_j) + F_y^2(x_i, y_j)} \tag{3.23}$$

$$\theta(x_i, y_j) = \arctan(F_y(x_i, y_j), F_x(x_i, y_j)), \tag{3.24}$$

where the arctan function takes two arguments and generates an angle over the entire circle of possible directions. These functions must be computed efficiently, preferrably without using floating-point arithmetic. It is possible to compute the gradient magnitude and orientation from the partial derivatives by table lookup. It is also possible to compute the magnitude of the gradient using an integer version of the algorithms developed by Dubrulle [35] and Moler and Morrison [36] for computing Pythagorean sums without using square roots. The arctangent can be computed using mostly fixed-point arithmetic[1] with a few essential floating-point calculations performed in software using integer and fixed-point arithmetic [37, chap. 11]. Since the only use for the gradient orientation in this algorithm is to compute the sector for non-maxima suppression, the inverse tangent function of one argument could be used to compute the orientation in the range $[-\pi/2, \pi/2)$.

3.4.4 Non-Maxima Suppression

Non-maximum suppression thins the ridges of gradient magnitude in $\rho(x_i, y_j)$ by suppressing all values along the line of the gradient that are not peak values of a

[1] In this context, fixed-point arithmetic is like integer arithmetic except that the number carries an implicit scale factor that assumes that the binary point is to the left of the number. Fixed-point arithmetic can be implemented using integer arithmetic on many machines.

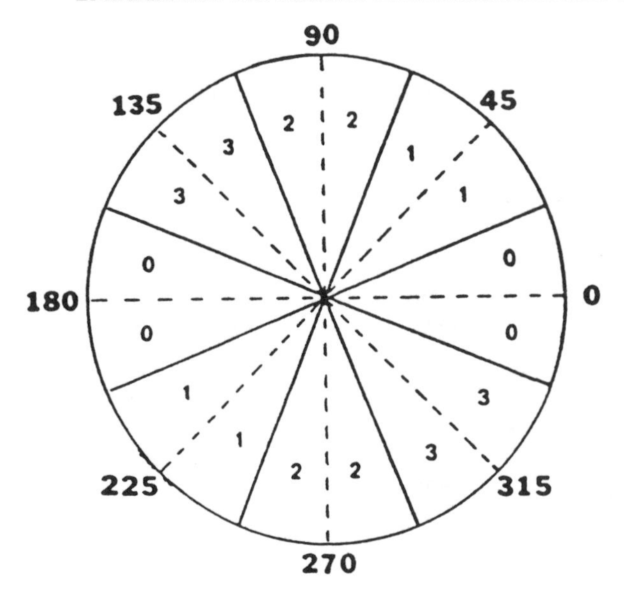

Figure 3.6: The partition of the possible gradient orientations into sectors for non-maxima suppression is shown. There are four sectors, numbered 0 to 3, corresponding to the four possible combinations of elements in a 3 by 3 neighborhood that a line must pass through if it passes through the center of the neighborhood. The divisions of the circle of possible gradient line orientations are labeled in degrees.

ridge. The algorithm begins by reducing the angle of the gradient $\theta(x_i, y_j)$ to one of the four sectors shown in figure 3.6. The non-maxima suppression algorithm passes a square neighborhood across the magnitude array $\rho(x_i, y_j)$. The width of the neighborhood is approximately equal to the width of the largest Gaussian filter used to compute the smoothed images. At each point, the center element $\rho(x_i, y_j)$ of the neighborhood is compared with all of its neighbors along the line of the gradient given by the sector value $\zeta(x_i, y_j)$ at the center of the neighborhood. If the magnitude array value $\rho(x_i, y_j)$ at the center is not greater than all of the neighbor magnitudes along the gradient line, then $\rho(x_i, y_j)$ is set to zero. This process thins the broad ridges of gradient magnitude in $\rho(x_i, y_j)$ into ridges that are only one pixel wide. The values for the height of the ridge are retained in the non-maxima suppressed magnitude.

The non-maxima suppression algorithm used in this work compares the center element with the elements along one of the four possible horizontal, vertical, or diagonal lines passing through three elements in a 3 by 3 neighborhood. The comparison of elements along the line can extend beyond the 3 by 3 neighborhood that defines the line orientation. The line along which non-maxima suppression is performed may be a poor approximation to the true line of the gradient. Canny [13] implements non-maxima suppression by interpolating the values along the line of the gradient in a 3 by 3 neighborhood and claims that this gives better results than using values from the neighboring cells. It would clearly improve non-maxima suppression over large neighborhoods if the values for comparison were computed by interpolation along the true line of the gradient, but this scheme was not used for the experiments presented in this paper due to the complexity of the implementation.

3.5 Experimental Results

Several experiments were performed to test the multiresolution Gaussian edge detection algorithm presented in this section. One of the experiments is documented in figure 3.7, which shows the result of applying multiresolution Gaussian edge detection to the test image in figure 3.1. Notice how the corners are very sharp and the edge image is very clean given that no thresholding has been performed. The small dislocation in the bounding contour on the right side of the shaft of the connecting rod is due to a shadow effect that is barely visible in the image of the connecting rod shown in figure 3.1 and is not due to an error in the algorithm. There is no way for multiresolution Gaussian edge detection to differentiate between shadow boundaries and the bounding contours of objects. The comparison between the plot of the edges obtained with multiresolution Gaussian edge detection shown in figure 3.7 and the plots of the results of conventional Gaussian edge detection shown in figures 3.2 and 3.3 show the dramatic reduction in the number of false edge fragments due to noise and fine texture. Examine the sharp corners of the bounding contour of the connecting rod in figure 3.7 with the corners of the bounding contour shown in the plots in figures 3.2 and 3.3. This demonstration shows that multiresolution Gaussian filtering retains the detail from the output of the finest scale while providing better noise suppression that the output of the coarsest scale. The analysis presented in section 3.6 shows that the effective localization of multiresolution Gaussian edge detection is even greater than the localization of the smallest filter.

The result of another experiment with multiresolution Gaussian edge detection is displayed in figure 3.9. The input image is displayed in figure 3.4 and for comparison plots of the results of ordinary Gaussian edge detection with 5 and 21 point filters are displayed in figure 3.8. The result of multiresolution Gaussian edge detection applied to the gear tooth image in figure 3.4 shows that multiresolution Gaussian edge detection is able to preserve faint edges such as the large gear tooth in the bounding contour at the bottom of the gear which would be erased by edge detection algorithms that were forced to threshold the output. The comparison between the result of multiresolution Gaussian edge detection shown in figure 3.9 and the edge plots for conventional Gaussian edge detection shown in figure 3.8 shows that it is possible to simultaneously achieve sensitivity to weak edges, suppression of unwanted edges due to noise and fine texture, and excellent edge localization.

The result of multiresolution Gaussian filtering shown in figure 3.9 is good, but some of the edges in the middle ring of gear teeth have been lost. The problem is that the strong edges that outline the small teeth in the middle ring of the gear are very close together. Either the neighborhood size for non-maxima suppression can be large enough to eliminate most false edges in the image or the neighborhood size can be small enough so that the edges that outline the middle gear teeth do not eliminate each other. It is probably asking too much to expect that non-maxima suppression over a large neighborhood would eliminate false edges near major edges and at the same time retain major edges that happen to be very close to other major edges.

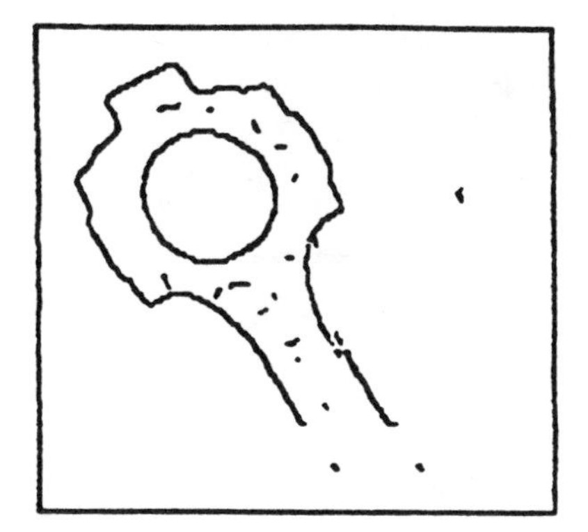

Figure 3.7: The figure shows a plot of the result of applying the multiresolution Gaussian edge detection algorithm presented in this paper to the test image in figure 3.1. The image was smoothed with Gaussian filters at sizes $n = 7$, $n = 15$, and $n = 31$. Non-maxima suppression was performed over a neighborhood width of $\nu = 29$. Every pixel in the edge image that is greater than zero is plotted as a black dot. Compare this result with the results shown in figures 3.2 and 3.3. Note how the detail in the major contours is retained while the minor edges are suppressed. Multiresolution Gaussian edge detection retains the detail from the smallest scale of resolution, but suppresses noise and unwanted texture better than the largest Gaussian filter.

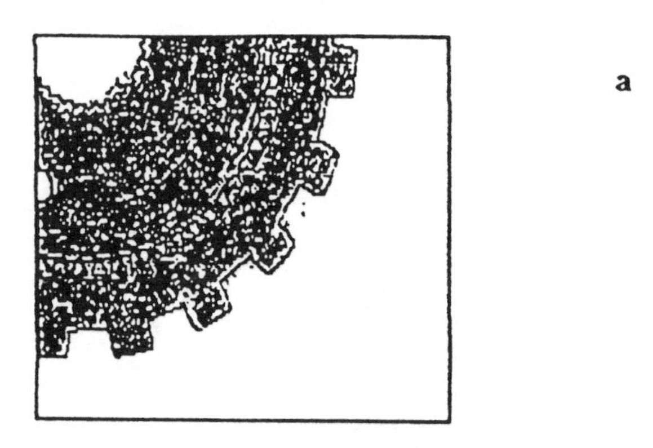

a

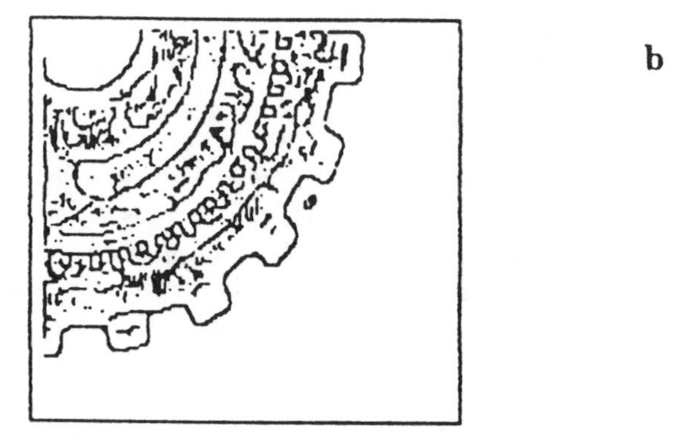

b

Figure 3.8: The result of Gaussian filtering and edge detection at two scales is shown. The plot in part **a** displays the result after non-maxima suppression of Gaussian edge detection with a smoothing filter of size 5. The plot in part **b** displays the result after non-maxima suppression of Gaussian edge detection with a smoothing of size 21. Even at the larger filter size, there is excessive clutter in the edge image. The gear teeth in the middle gear ring are not well-defined.

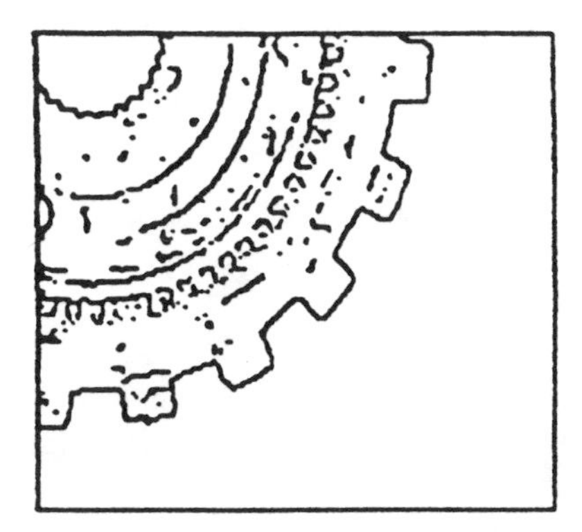

Figure 3.9: The result of applying multiresolution Gaussian edge detection to the test image from figure 3.4 is plotted. The result was obtained by filtering the image in figure 3.4 with two Gaussians of size $n = 7$ and $n = 15$, computing the gradient for each smoothed image, multiplying the gradient magnitudes, and performing non-maxima suppression with a neighborhood size of $\nu = 11$.

3.6 Analysis of Multiresolution Edge Detection

In this section, some analysis that explains properties of the multiresolution Gaussian edge detection algorithm is presented. The performance of the algorithm is also analyzed.

3.6.1 Effective Localization

Consider the profile of an ideal step edge. The result of applying a Gaussian smoothing filter with spread σ to an ideal step edge and then computing the magnitude of the first derivative is the Gaussian smoothing function itself. This is because a step function is the integral of an impulse function and the first derivative cancels the integral leaving the convolution of an impulse function with the Gaussian function. Suppose that edge detection is performed on the profile of an ideal step edge at two scales of resolution with Gaussian spreads σ_1 and σ_2. The profiles of the magnitude images will be two Gaussians with spreads σ_1 and σ_2 described by the equations

$$\rho(x;\sigma_1) = e^{-x^2/2\sigma_1^2} \tag{3.25}$$

$$\rho(x;\sigma_2) = e^{-x^2/2\sigma_2^2}. \tag{3.26}$$

The product of the two magnitude images is

$$\rho(x;\sigma_1)\cdot\rho(x;\sigma_2) = e^{-x^2/2\sigma_1^2}e^{-x^2/2\sigma_2^2} \tag{3.27}$$

$$= e^{-\left(x^2/2\sigma_1^2 + x^2/2\sigma_2^2\right)} \tag{3.28}$$

$$= e^{-x^2/2\sigma^2}, \tag{3.29}$$

where the spread of the product Gaussian is given by

$$\frac{1}{\sigma^2} = \frac{1}{\sigma_1^2} + \frac{1}{\sigma_2^2}. \tag{3.30}$$

If $\sigma_2^2 = 2\sigma_1^2$, then the spread of the product Gaussian is

$$\sigma^2 = \frac{2}{3}\sigma_1^2. \tag{3.31}$$

This means that the localization of the product is better than the localization of the smaller Gaussian since the effective Gaussian filter width is smaller. Experiments documented in previous sections show that the product is more immune to noise. The multiresolution edge detection algorithm provides improvement in both localization and noise immunity.

3.6.2 Effect of Displacement in Edge Location

In real images, the two Gaussians that correspond to the edge magnitudes at two different scales may be slightly displaced since the two Gaussian smoothing filters will be affected differently by noise and nearby image features. With respect to each magnitude image, the location of the step edge is estimated by finding the location of the peak of the Gaussian. The location of the peak in the magnitude for the smaller scale is a better estimate of the edge location than the location of the peak at the larger scale. In the product of the magnitudes, the location of the edge is estimated by the location of the peak in the product. The following analysis determines the relationship between the location of the peak in the product and the locations of the peaks in the derivative magnitudes. The product of two Gaussians with spreads σ_1 and σ_2, offset by δ, is

$$\rho(x;\sigma_1)\cdot\rho(x-\delta;\sigma_2) = e^{-\left(x^2/2\sigma_1^2 + (x-\delta)^2/2\sigma_2^2\right)}. \tag{3.32}$$

The location of the peak in the product is found by differentiating the equation above, setting it equal to zero, and solving for x. The peak location is given by

$$x = \delta\frac{\sigma_1^2}{\sigma_1^2+\sigma_2^2}. \tag{3.33}$$

The peak in the product of the magnitudes is between the peaks in the individual magnitudes. If $\sigma_2^2 = 4\sigma_1^2$, then the location of the peak in the products is $x = \delta/5$. This means that if the Gaussian smoothing functions differ in width by a factor of 2 and if for any reason the edge locations in the magnitudes are separated, then the edge location in the product will always be closer to the more accurate edge location. The edge location in the product will respond to the detailed variations in the edge location at the smaller scale. The edge contour at the larger scale will exhibit very little variation (wiggle) from the detail in the object contour, but the detail in the contour at the smaller scale will be transmitted to the edge contour in the product through the relationship in equation 3.33.

3.6.3 Performance Analysis

Suppose that there are n scales and that the filter sizes for the scales have been chosen so that the successive Gaussian filter convolutions can be cascaded. As a worst case, assume that all of the intermediate scales produced by Gaussian cascading will be used rather than using only scales corresponding to filter sizes that double. This adds a small amount of additional computation since the gradient magnitude must be computed for each of the intermediate scales and the additional gradient magnitudes must be multiplied into the composite magnitude. Each successive smoothed image is obtained from the last by filtering with a Gaussian filter of size m by m, where m would typicaly be given as $m = 5$ or $m = 7$ for reasons discussed in section 3.3.3. Assuming a straightforward convolution algorithm, the total number of multiplies and adds for each output point is given by $G(m) = 4nm$ since each convolution is separable and requires $4m$ multiplies and adds (n multiples and n adds for each of two applications of the one dimensional filter) and the filter will be applied n times. It takes 4 more addition/subtraction operations at each scale to compute the partial derivatives which brings the total number of multiplies and adds to $4n(m + 1)$ for each output point. The gradient magnitude will have to be computed for each scale and the sector orientation must be computed for the largest scale. These computations could be done by table lookup. The gradient magnitudes must be multiplied together which requires n multiplies per output point. Non-maximum suppression will require at worst roughly w comparisons per output point where w is the length of the diagonal of the support of the largest effective filter.

3.7 Conclusions

A new algorithm for edge detection with Gaussian filters at multiple scales of resolution has been presented. The results of computational experiments in which the new algorithm was applied to real images were presented. The methods used in the experiments were clearly presented so that the algorithm can be tested by other researchers. Theoretical analysis of some aspects of the algorithm was presented to provide additional justification for the statements about the power of multiresolution Gaussian edge detection relative to edge detection at a single scale.

The multiresolution Gaussian edge detection algorithm is a constructive proof of the power of edge detection at multiple scales of resolution. The algorithm was not developed through a problem formulation using optimization theory, hence no statement can be made regarding the optimality of this algorithm; but the algorithm is extremely simple and effective as demonstrated by the experimental results and theoretical analysis. The results presented in this paper suggest an alternative to scale-space representations based on the zeros of an edge operator since the multiresolution Gaussian edge detection algorithm is based on the scaling behavior of local maxima in the output of the gradient of Gaussian operator. In addition to using local maxima rather than zeros in the output of an operator based on Gaussian filtering, the edge operator at each scale is nonlinear. This is a departure from the class of linear operators based on Gaussian filtering that have been shown to have nice scaling properties [23] since no proof exists for nice scaling behavior for the magnitude of the gradient of a Gaussian smoothed image. Hopefully, the results obtained in this research for combining the outputs across scales of a nonlinear operator based on Gaussian smoothing will encourage further research on the scaling behavior of nonlinear edge operators.

Acknowledgements

I would also like to thank Robert Tilove, Mary Pickett, John Boyse, and Richard Young in the Computer Science Department at General Motors Research Laboratory for their help in revising early drafts of this paper and would like to extend special thanks to Ramesh Jain for his advice and encouragement.

References

[1] D. Marr, "Early processing of visual information," *Phil. Trans. R. Soc. Lond.* B, vol. 275, pp. 483–524, 1976.

[2] D. Marr, "Representing visual information," in *Computer Vision Systems* (A. R. Hanson and E. M. Riseman, eds.), pp. 61–80, New York: Academic Press, 1979.

[3] D. Marr, *Vision: A Computational Investigation into the Human Representation and Processing of Visual Information.* San Francisco: W. H. Freeman and Company, 1982.

[4] B. K. P. Horn, "Image intensity understanding," *Artificial Intelligence*, vol. 8, pp. 201–231, 1977.

[5] T. O. Binford, "Inferring surfaces from images," *Artificial Intelligence*, vol. 17, pp. 205–244, 1981.

[6] J. F. Canny, "A computational approach to edge detection," *IEEE Trans. Pattern Analysis and Machine Intelligence*, vol. 8, pp. 679–698, November 1986.

[7] W. Feller, *An Introduction to Probability Theory and Its Applications*, vol. 2. New York: John Wiley & Sons, 2nd ed., 1971.

[8] M. Brady and B. K. P. Horn, "Rotationally symmetric operators for surface interpolation," Memo 654, Artificial Intelligence Laboratory, M. I. T., November 1981.

[9] P. J. Burt, "Fast algorithms for estimating local image properties," *Computer Vision, Graphics and Image Processing*, vol. 21, pp. 368–382, 1983.

[10] J. L. Crowley and R. Stern, "Fast computation of the difference of low-pass transform," *IEEE Trans. Pattern Analysis and Machine Intelligence*, vol. 6, pp. 212–222, March 1984.

[11] D. Marr and E. C. Hildreth, "Theory of edge detection," *Proc. R. Soc. Lond.* B, vol. 207, pp. 187–217, 1980.

[12] A. Rosenfeld and A. C. Kak, *Digital Picture Processing.* New York: Academic Press, 1976.

[13] J. F. Canny, "Finding edges and lines in images," Technical Report 720, Artificial Intelligence Laboratory, M. I. T., June 1983.

[14] J. G. Daugman, "Six formal properties of two-dimensional anisotropic visual filters: Structural principles and frequency/orientation selectivity," *IEEE Trans. Systems, Man, and Cybernetics*, vol. 13, no. 5, 1983.

[15] T. Poggio and V. Torre, "Ill-posed problems and regularization analysis in early vision," Memo 773, Artificial Intelligence Laboratory, M. I. T., April 1984.

[16] V. Torre and T. Poggio, "On edge detection," *IEEE Trans. Pattern Analysis and Machine Intelligence*, vol. 8, pp. 147–163, March 1986.

[17] T. Poggio, V. Torre, and C. Koch, "Computational vision and regularization theory," *Nature*, vol. 317, pp. 314–319, 1985.

[18] T. Poggio, H. Voorhees, and A. Yuille, "Regularized solution to edge detection," Memo 833, Artificial Intelligence Laboratory, M. I. T., May 1985.

[19] R. M. Haralick, "Zero-crossing of second directional derivative edge operator," in *SPIE Proceedings on Robot Vision*, (Arlington, Virginia), 1982.

[20] E. C. Hildreth, "The detection of intensity changes by computer and biological vision systems," *Computer Vision, Graphics and Image Processing*, vol. 22, pp. 1–12, 1983.

[21] A. P. Witkin, "Scale-space filtering," in *Int. Joint. Conf. Artificial Intelligence*, pp. 1019–1022, August 1983.

[22] D. Terzopoulos, "Multilevel computational processes for visual surface reconstruction," *Computer Vision, Graphics and Image Processing*, vol. 24, pp. 52–96, 1983.

[23] A. L. Yuille and T. Poggio, "Fingerprint theorems for zero crossings," *J. Opt. Soc. Am. A*, vol. 2, pp. 683–692, May 1985.

[24] A. L. Yuille and T. Poggio, "Scaling theorems for zero-crossings," *IEEE Trans. Pattern Analysis and Machine Intelligence*, vol. 8, pp. 15–25, January 1986.

[25] R. A. Hummel, "Representations based on zero-crossings in scale-space," in *Proc. Conf. Computer Vision and Pattern Recognition*, pp. 204–209, 1986.

[26] B. F. Logan, "Information in the zero crossings of bandpass signals," *Bell System Technical Journal*, vol. 56, pp. 487–510, April 1977.

[27] A. Rosenfeld, "A nonlinear edge detection technique," *Proceedings of the IEEE*, vol. 58, pp. 814–816, May 1970.

[28] A. Rosenfeld and M. Thurston, "Edge and curve detection for visual scene analysis," *IEEE Trans. Computers*, vol. 20, pp. 562–569, May 1971.

[29] W. E. L. Grimson, *From Images to Surfaces: A Computational Study of the Human Early Vision System*. Cambridge: M. I. T. Press, 1981.

[30] H. Asada and M. Brady, "The curvature primal sketch," *IEEE Trans. Pattern Analysis and Machine Intelligence*, vol. 8, pp. 2–14, January 1986.

[31] F. Mokhtarian and A. Mackworth, "Scale-based description and recognition of planar curves and two-dimensional shapes," *IEEE Trans. Pattern Analysis and Machine Intelligence*, vol. 8, pp. 34–43, January 1986.

[32] J. M. Brady and H. Asada, "Smoothed local symmetries and their implementation," *Int. J. Robotics Research*, vol. 3, pp. 36–61, 1984.

[33] B. G. Schunck, "Gaussian filters and edge detection," Research Publication GMR-5586, Computer Science Department, General Motors Research Laboratories, October 1986.

[34] B. K. P. Horn, *Robot Vision.* New York: McGraw-Hill, 1986.

[35] A. A. Dubrulle, "A class of numerical methods for the computation of Pythagorean sums," *IBM J. Res. Develop.*, vol. 27, pp. 582–589, 1983.

[36] C. Moler and D. Morrison, "Replacing square roots by Pythagorean sums," *IBM J. Res. Develop.*, vol. 27, pp. 577–581, 1983.

[37] W. J. Cody and W. Waite, *Software Manual for the Elementary Functions.* Englewood Cliffs, New Jersey: Prentice-Hall, 1980.

Segmentation

Chapter 4

Hierarchical Segmentation Techniques with Applications to Magnetic Resonance Images

T. R. Jackson, D. M. Skyba, M. B. Merickel

Segmentation of complex images is difficult using general purpose methods. Region-based techniques often fail to yield the desired structure due to the difficulty of choosing a reasonable starting "seed" point, an appropriate growing rule or a suitable stopping rule. Similarly, edge-based techniques may fail due to the similarity of objects within the scene or indistinct boundaries between image objects. All of these techniques suffer from the problem of being based on individual gray level values, and are hence "bottom up" techniques.

Due to these problems, it is necessary to develop more robust approaches for segmenting complex images. One approach to this problem is to acquire multi-modal images of a scene and apply multispectral analysis to differentiate various objects in the scene.[1,2] A second approach involves utilizing information from different imaging modalities to guide a region growing algorithm in an image pyramid.[3] However, there are a number of cases in which it is desirable to segment an object from a scene using only a single type of image. These cases include, first, those in which multi-modal imaging is not practical, second, those in which multi-modal images are not necessary for further scene analysis, and, third, cases in which it may not be possible to extract different structural information from each image as in highly correlated imaging modalities.

The approach we have developed is a hierarchical "top down" technique[4,5] which permits *a priori* constraints regarding the location and shape of the region of interest to be progressively employed. The concept is to initially roughly segment the scene to localize the region, and then progressively refine the resulting estimate of the region boundary (see Figure 4.1). Typically, the centroid of a region found using an edge-based algorithm can be used as a "seed" point for a region-based algorithm. Similarly, statistics from a rough region segmentation can be used to estimate an appropriate growing rule for a region-based algorithm and the initial region boundary can provide a stopping rule for the algorithm. The preliminary region can be refined by growing the region of interest using the seed point, growing rule, and stopping rule determined from the results of an edge-based algorithm. The estimates of the seed point, growing rule, and stopping rule can be iteratively refined using the results of a region growing algorithm.

The combination of region-based and edge-based techniques in a progressive fashion means that the decision making process regarding the region of interest is spread out over many steps. More traditional edge and region based approaches are typically "bottom up" (i.e. pixel based) and rely on the success of a single, or small number of criteria. In our procedure, the steps are arranged in a "top down" hierarchical fashion permitting information regarding spatial localization and shape to be incorporated as shown in Figure 4.1. Incorporating multiple criteria means that the success of the procedure is not completely dependant on a single step and that any minor errors can be detected and corrected to provide a progressive approach which is more robust than traditional

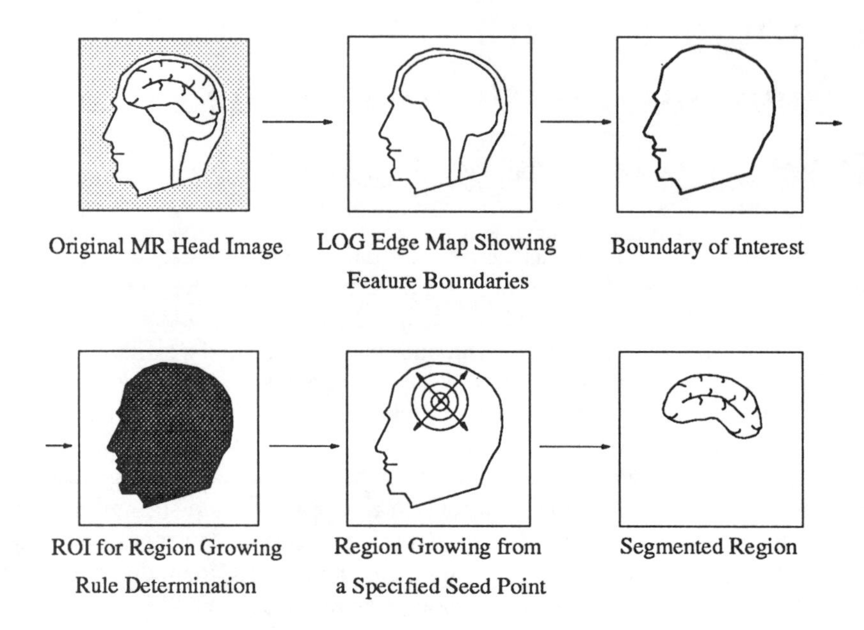

Figure 4.1 Flow diagram depicting hierarchical "top down" segmentation technique as applied to the brain as a general region of interest: (a) sagittal MR image through the head, (b) edge map showing rough feature boundaries, (c) utilization of the outer boundary as a stopping rule for a region-growing procedure, (d) determination of growing rule from characteristics of preliminary region of interest, (e) choice of a seed point based on spatial position within the region, and (f) final segmented region.

approaches. This approach has been applied to two segmentation problems using examples from Magnetic Resonance (MR) imaging: (1) segmentation of the abdominal aorta from transverse MR images for the purpose of quantifying atherosclerosis and (2) segmentation of breast lesions for identification of malignant versus benign lesions. This chapter explores these two examples of complex image segmentation in detail.

4.2 Aorta Segmentation

The first application of this hierarchical segmentation technique has been segmentation of the aorta from a sequence of transverse MR images through the abdomen. Each slice in the sequence has a T_1, Pd, and T_2 weighted image associated with it (see

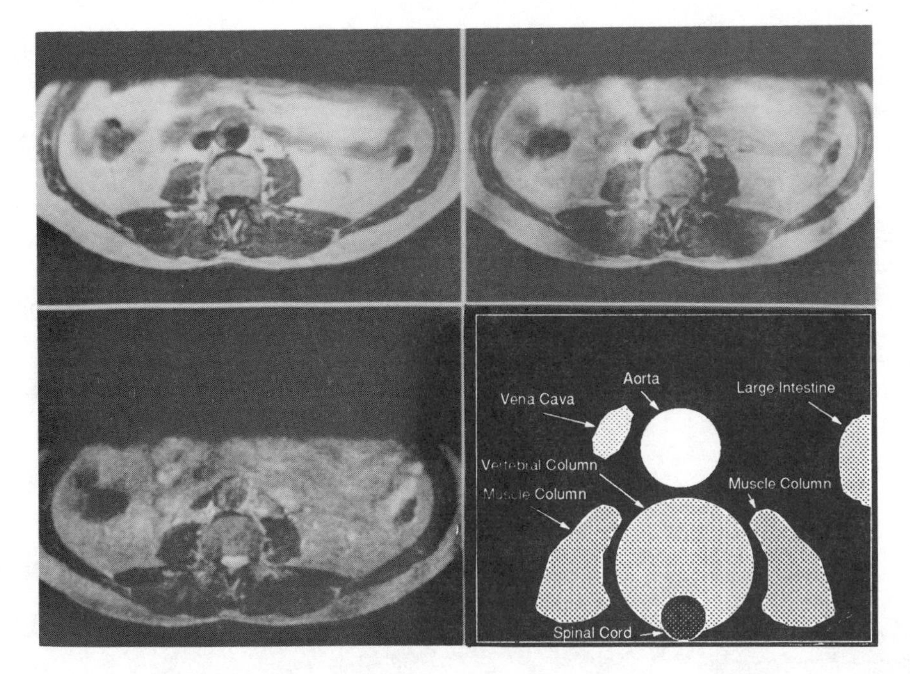

Figure 4.2 **An example of a typical set of transverse MR images of the abdomen.** The images were obtained on a 1.5 Tesla Siemens Magnetom Imager using standard spin-echo pulse sequences with the addition of spatial presaturation pulses to reduce breathing and flow artifacts. The pulse sequence parameters for this patient are: (a) T_1 = SE 650/17, (b) Pd = SE 2200/30, (c) T_2 = SE 2200/80; x-y resolution = 1.37 mm/pixel; slice thickness = 4mm; slice gap = 4mm. A schematic diagram of the abdominal aorta and neighboring structures is shown in (d).

Figure 4.2). The T_1 weighted sequence is utilized for segmentation since it provides good structural information regarding the vessel boundary as well as a relatively small amount of noise. The hierarchical aorta segmentation procedure combines region-based and edge-based techniques to successively refine the estimate of the aorta region.

The aorta segmentation procedure involves three distinct steps: aorta detection, aorta extraction, and estimation of the aorta boundary. Aorta detection uses a modified edge detection technique combined with spatial information to locate the aorta. Next, aorta extraction uses region-based and morphological techniques to refine this estimate of the aorta position. This position is used to extract a sub-image surrounding the aorta from the original image. Finally, this sub-image is used to estimate the outer wall of the aorta. This boundary estimation procedure uses region-based techniques to roughly segment the aorta and shape information to improve this segmentation.

4.2.1 Aorta Detection

The first procedure, aorta detection, is used to grossly estimate the position of the aorta. The procedure relies on the appearance and spatial position of the aorta being consistent throughout the sequence of images acquired at different slice positions. This introduces two problems immediately. The first problem is that the intensity of the aorta lumen depends on the time in the cardiac cycle the image is acquired. These artifacts may be reduced using cardiac gating[6] or spatial presaturation.[7,8] The second problem, inconsistent spatial position of the aorta between slices, is primarily a result of the abdominal aorta curvature; however, because the variation of the aorta position is small in the section of interest, this inconsistency does not affect the aorta detection procedure enough to be a consideration.

The procedure to detect the aorta first implements a number of *preprocessing* steps to reduce the size and noise of the image. Second, a *spot detector* is used to find circular structures within the image. Thirdly, the *aorta location* is estimated using a combination of the spot detector results and spatial information. Finally, a sub-image is extracted from the original image based on this position.

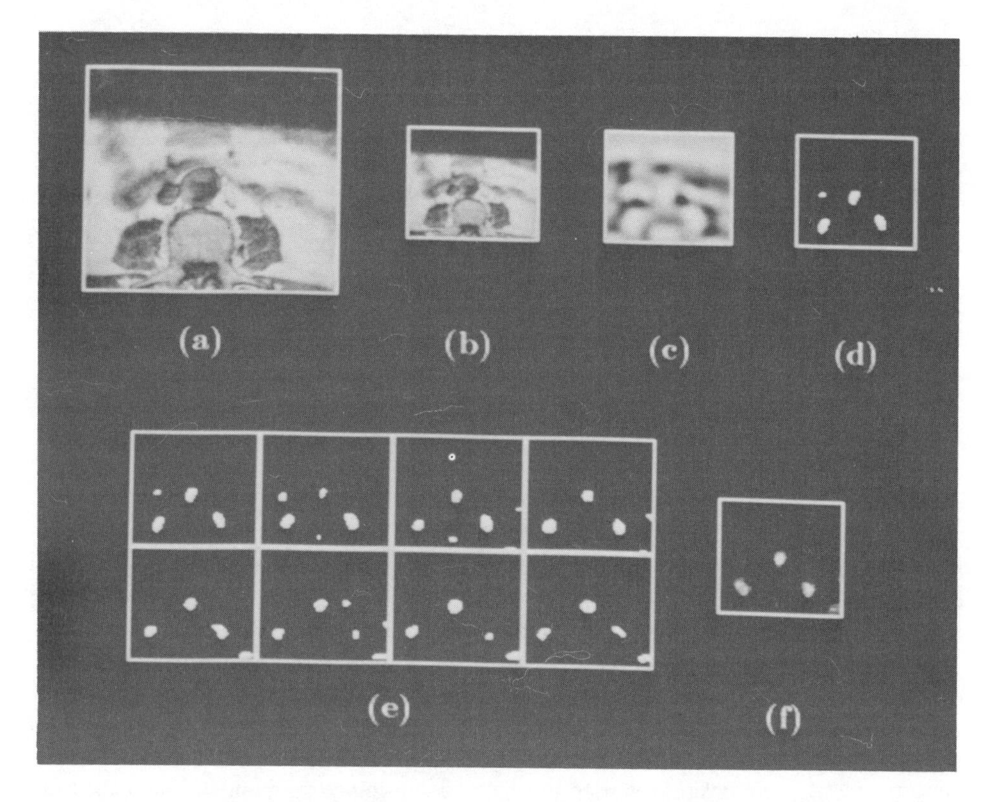

Figure 4.3 Detection of the aorta: (a) 128 × 128 extraction form the original T_1-weighted image, (b) reduction by non-overlapping averaging to 64 × 64 pixels, (c) convolution with LOG to detect spots in the image, (d) thresholding to locate peaks in the convolved image, (e) sequence of peak detected images from 8 slice positions, and (f) cross-correlation of peaks using an inter-slice average.

Preprocessing

As an initial step, a gross extraction of half the image dimensions about the center of each image in the sequence is performed (see Figure 4.3(a)). This extraction is used to eliminate some of the extraneous structures that could confuse the spot detector. An additional benefit of this extraction is the factor of four reduction in processing time resulting from dividing the image dimensions by two. This extraction can be used because the body is centered in the field of view and the probability of the aorta appearing near the edges of the image is very low.

The following step, spot detection, uses a band-pass spatial filter that can amplify any image noise and, therefore, requires some form of noise reduction as a final preprocessing step. The noise in the extracted image is reduced by a 2×2 non-overlapping averaging process (see Figure 4.3(b)). This averaging process has the secondary benefit of further decreasing the processing time by an additional factor of four. The spot detector is then used to estimate the position of the aorta.

Spot Detection

This spot detector is a modification of the Laplacian of a Gaussian (LOG) operator.[9] The Laplacian operator is a non-directional, linear approximation to the second order derivative and emphasizes high spatial frequencies in the image. Therefore, the Laplacian will amplify any noise in the image. The Gaussian operator has the opposite effect on high spatial frequencies, reducing any high frequency noise. As a result, the LOG emphasizes structures with a similar size and shape (see Figure 4.3(c)). Because of this, the LOG used for a particular segmentation depends on the image resolution and the size of the aorta.

Aorta Location

Bright spots in the convolved image correspond to the aorta, vena cava, and various other circular structures approximately the size of the LOG. These bright spots are located using a threshold operation with a threshold of 98% of the cumulative distribution function of the histogram (see Figure 4.3(c-d)). In general, the aorta is the only structure emphasized by the LOG that has a consistent size, shape, and position between slices. As a result, an inter-slice average of the LOG images after this threshold operation (see Figure 4.3(e)) should have the highest value at the aorta position. In practice, the positions of other structures such as the vena cava, the large intestine, and the muscle columns supporting the spine may also have a high value in the inter-slice peak average depending on the structure size with respect to the size of the aorta. This problem is aggravated by a poor choice of LOG size. In some data sets the inter-slice average of peaks corresponding to one of these structures may be greater than the average of the peaks corresponding to the aorta.

Spatial information has been incorporated to handle cases in which the LOG peak does not locate the aorta. The two positions with highest inter-slice average are chosen as candidates for the aorta position (see Figure 4.4(a)). A region growing operation is performed around these two positions. That is, any non-zero pixel in the inter-slice average that is eight-connected to one of these positions is included in a region. This

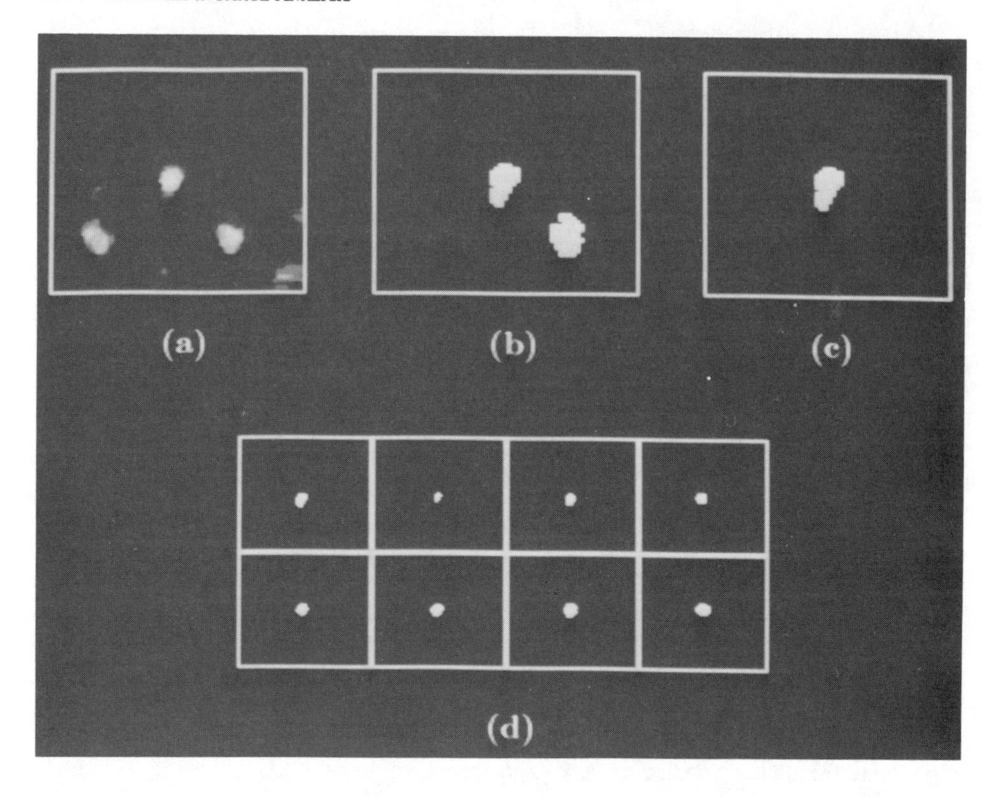

Figure 4.4 Locating the aorta: (a) cross-correlation of peaks using an inter-slice average, (b) two regions with the highest inter-slice correlation chosen as candidate regions for average aorta position, (c) selection of region corresponding to the average aorta position using heuristic based on spatial information, (d) region corresponding to the average aorta position used to determine aorta position in each slice.

procedure may yield either one region or two regions. In the first case, the two positions are eight-connected, causing the regions to merge. The resulting region is then used as an intermediate aorta position, corresponding to both the aorta and vena cava. In the second case, the two regions are distinct and spatial information is employed to distinguish the region corresponding to the aorta from the other. The criteria for selecting the aorta region is based on the distance between the two peaks. If the resulting regions are far apart, the region with x position nearest the center of the image corresponds to the aorta (see Figure 4.4(b)). This is used because the aorta has a higher probability of being in the center of the image than at the border. This eliminates regions that may appear at positions near the edges of the image such as those corresponding to the position of the large intestine or the muscle columns supporting the spine. Otherwise, the two regions are assumed to be near each other. In this case, the region with the greatest x position should correspond to the average aorta position. The other region will generally correspond to the position of the vena cava (see Figure 4.5).

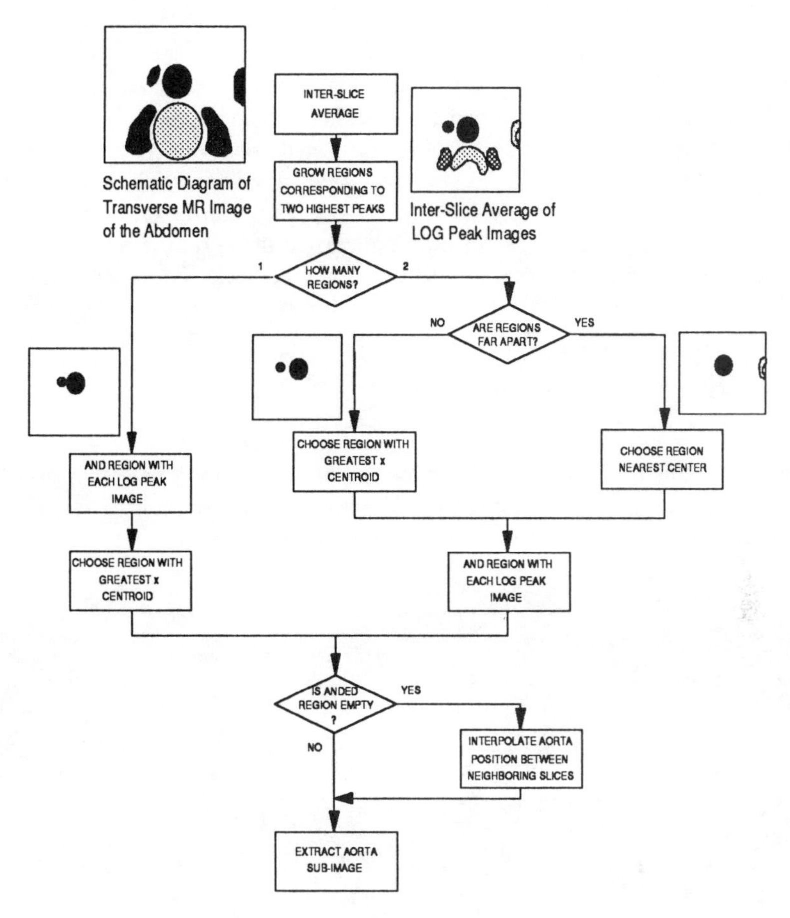

Figure 4.5 Flowchart of heuristics to estimate the aorta position from among many similar structures utilizing spatial information.

The resulting region is used to determine the position of the aorta in each slice. If this region corresponds to only the average position of the aorta, a pixel by pixel logical AND is performed between the global aorta region and each LOG peak image to give a slice specific region corresponding to the aorta position (see Figure 4.4(c-d)). Otherwise the region corresponds to the average position of both the aorta and vena cava. A pixel by pixel logical AND is performed between this average region and each LOG peak image, giving two slice specific regions, corresponding to the aorta and the vena cava. The region corresponding to the aorta is then determined using spatial information. Because the aorta and vena cava are spatially consistent with respect to each other, the region with largest x position corresponds to the position of the aorta. Occasionally, the image resulting from the pixel by pixel logical AND is empty for a particular slice. The average aorta region is then substituted for this slice specific region.

A preliminary extraction of the aorta is performed about the center of the resulting region. This eliminates some of the structures that may confuse the remainder of the segmentation procedure, effectively providing a stopping rule for future region growing operations, and reduces the amount of information that the aorta extraction routine must process. However, the aorta detection procedure generally does not locate the center of the aorta well. These preliminary extractions of the sequence are used to determine the center of the aorta.

4.2.2 Aorta Extraction

The aorta extraction routine builds upon the results of aorta detection to refine the estimation of the aorta center. A small sub-image around the aorta is extracted from the original image. The purpose of this step is two-fold; (1) to remove structures that may

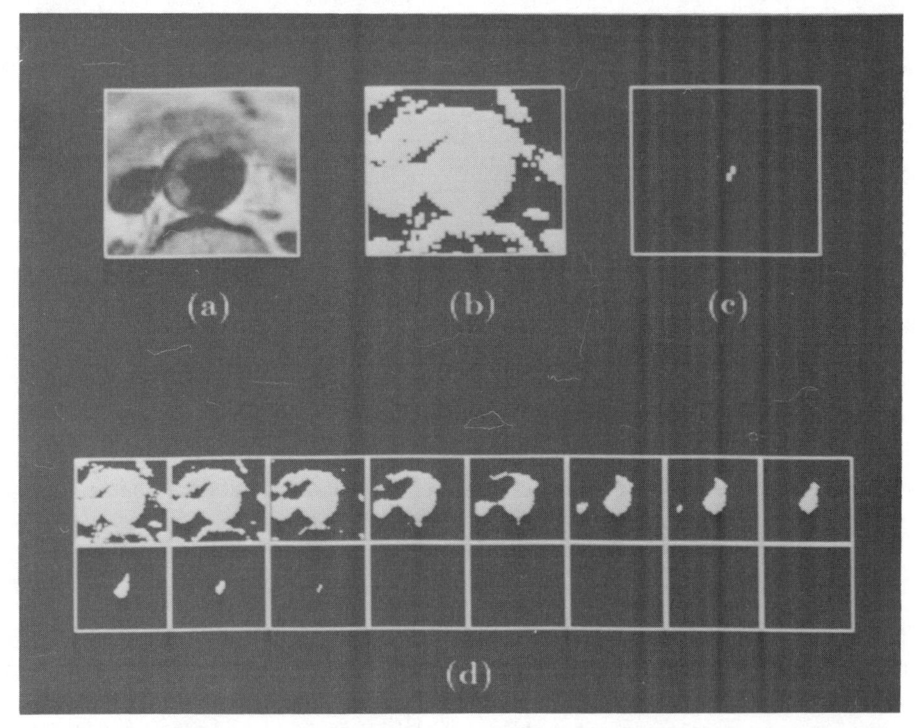

Figure 4.6 Determination of the center of the aorta: (a) results of aorta detection, (b) Otsu's discriminant function used to perform gross segmentation of the aorta from surrounding tissues, (c) results of erosion granulometry to determine the center of the aorta, and (d) an example of the granulometry operation. Erosion of the binary image by successively larger circular elements ranging from radius 1 pixel to 16 pixels.

confuse the routine to estimate the aorta boundary, and (2) to better locate the center of the aorta. The size of this sub-image should be large enough to contain the entire aorta wall. The procedure is divided into three steps: a threshold operation, granulometry, and estimation of the aorta center. A *threshold* operation is used to roughly segment the aorta from the sub-image, *granulometry* then attempts to determine the center of the aorta, and finally, a check of the *estimation of the aorta center* ensures that it is reasonable.

Threshold Operation on the Aorta Sub-Image

The aorta extraction procedure first roughly segments the aorta from the surrounding tissue. This done by automatically determining a threshold for the sub-image resulting from aorta detection (see Figure 4.6(b)). This threshold is determined using the discriminant function developed by Otsu.[10] The discriminant function evaluates the choice

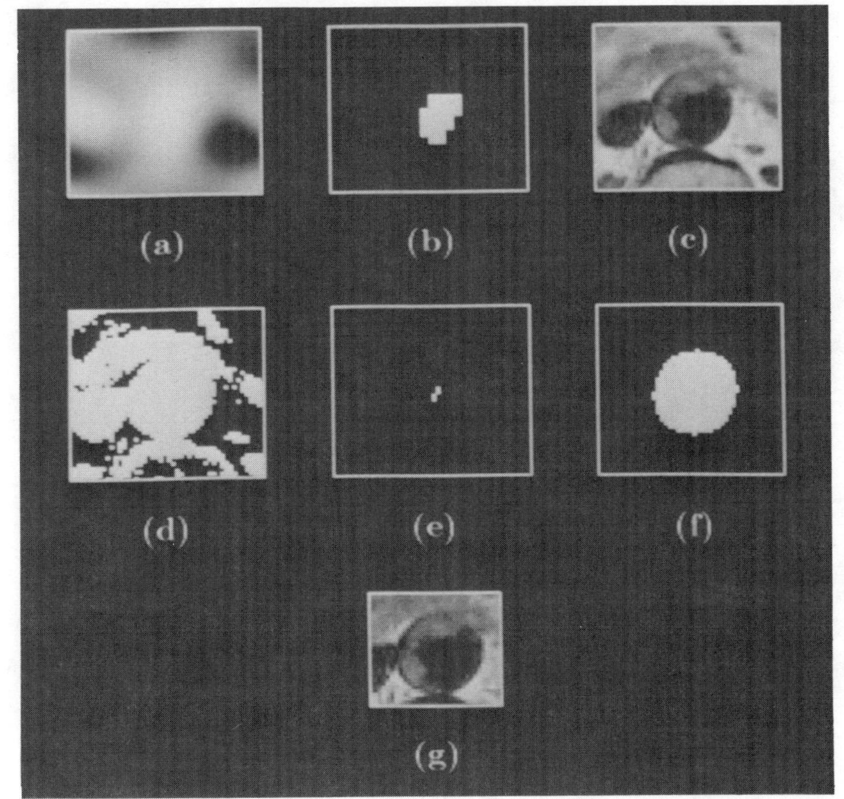

Figure 4.7 Aorta extraction: (a) extraction of the LOG image at position corresponding to the aorta, (b) peak of the LOG image, (c) results of aorta detection, (d) Otsu's discriminant function used to perform a gross segmentation of the aorta from the surrounding tissues, (e) center of the aorta located using an erosion granulometry, (f) dilation of the center of the aorta, and (g) aorta centered in the final extraction (24 × 24 pixels).

of threshold using a measure of "goodness" based on maximization of the between class variance. The discriminant function is able to find a good threshold even in images that do not have a bimodal distribution. The resulting binary image is used as a primitive to find the center of the aorta.

Granulometry

The goal of the granulometry[11] procedure is to locate the aorta center by removing structures from the binary region that do not correspond to the aorta. Using two assumptions, first, that the aorta is approximately cylindrical and second, that the aorta is the largest convex structure in the binary region, the generating structure is chosen as a circle with radius of one pixel. The radius of the circular structuring element is

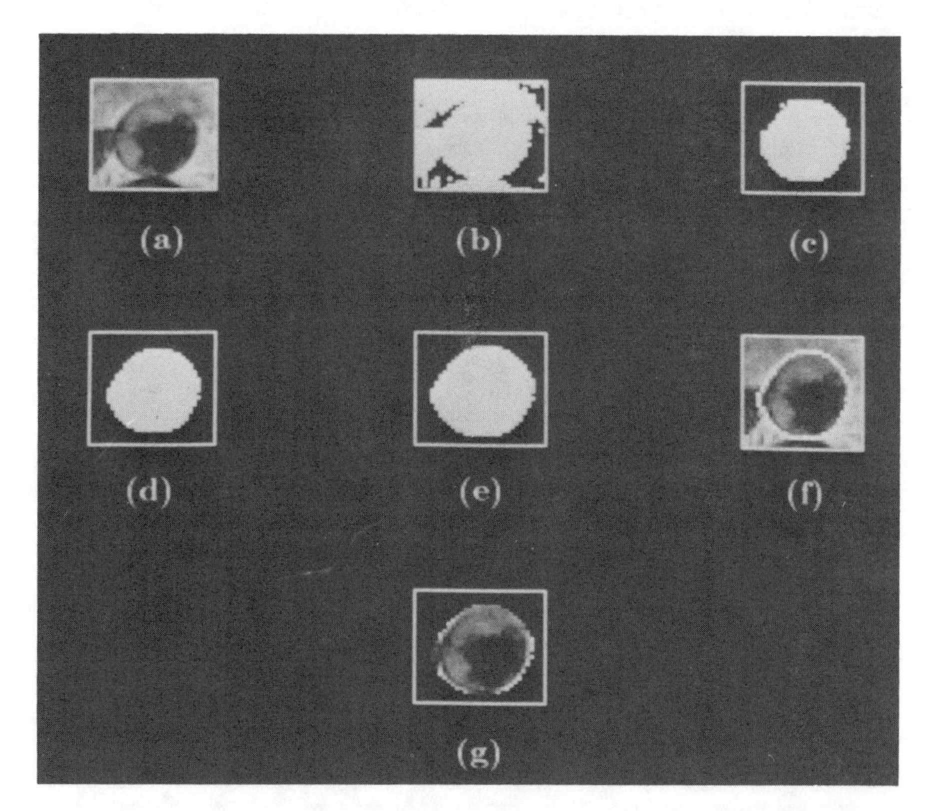

Figure 4.8 Estimation of the aorta boundary: (a) final extraction of the aorta, (b) Otsu's discriminant function used to perform gross segmentation of the aorta, (c) removal of exterior structures using a radial threshold, (d) smoothing of region boundary by morphological opening with a circular structuring element of radius 3 pixels, (e) dilation of the region of interest by a circular element of radius 1 pixel to include adventitial fat in the segmentation, and (f) the segmented aorta.

parameterized and the largest circle that will fit into the binary image is assumed to correspond to the largest circle that will fit into the aorta region. Theoretically, the granulometry builds the size distribution of the binary image eroded with this family of circular structuring elements with increasing radius (see Figure 4.6(d)). Since erosion is decreasing in the sense that $E(\mathbf{A},t'\mathbf{E}) \subseteq E(\mathbf{A},t\mathbf{E})$ for $t' \geq t$, the size distribution of the granulometry will also be decreasing. Thus, the cardinality (area of the binary region in pixels) of the eroded region will be zero for sufficiently large radius. The size distribution of the transformed image is analyzed to find the largest radius that results in non-zero cardinality (see Figure 4.6(c)). This should correspond to the radius of the largest structuring element that will fit into the binary region.

The resulting binary image is analyzed to determine the number of regions that remain (see Figure 4.7(f)). If there are more than one region in the eroded binary image, the region nearest the aorta region in the peak LOG image (see Figure 4.7(c)) corresponds to the aorta. Any other regions in the eroded binary image are eliminated. The remaining region is dilated and the center of the resulting region should be a close approximation to the aorta center.

Estimation of the Aorta Center

Occasionally, the granulometry fails, yielding coordinates that do not correspond to the center of the aorta. To ensure that these coordinates correspond to the aorta center, the estimation of the center of the aorta in each slice is compared to those of the previous and next slices. Any position that is more than 10 pixels (about 1 cm. in the patient) from its neighbors is assumed to be in error. These stray coordinates are replaced by the value of the neighboring slice for end slices and a value linearly interpolated between the previous and next slices for all other slices.

A sub-image around the coordinates found above is extracted (see Figure 4.7(g)). This removes structures that may confuse the boundary estimation procedure. Since the aorta is now centered within the extracted sub-image, a table of the aorta position in each slice must be maintained in order to reconstruct the aorta in three dimensions. The sequence of final aorta extractions is used to estimate the boundary of the aorta.

4.2.3 Estimation of the Aorta Boundary

Once the aorta has been extracted, the segmentation procedure estimates the aorta boundary. This procedure is divided into four steps: rough segmentation of the aorta, removal of any structures that appear to be attached to the aorta region, smoothing of the aorta region boundary, and enlargement of the region to include all pixels in the aorta wall and a small amount of adventitial fat.

The first step is to roughly segment the aorta from the surrounding tissue. To accomplish this, an automatic threshold operation is applied to the extracted aorta using the discriminant criterion described above (see Figure 4.8(b)). The resulting region corresponds to the aorta and various other structures in the sub-image.

These other structures appear as regions attached to or surrounding the aorta. Since the aorta is somewhat circular, shape information can be employed to remove these extraneous regions. The criteria used to determine the aorta region is the maximum radius of the aorta. A radial histogram of the binary image is calculated whose maximum is then found by a d-peak algorithm. This algorithm uses a sliding window to iteratively

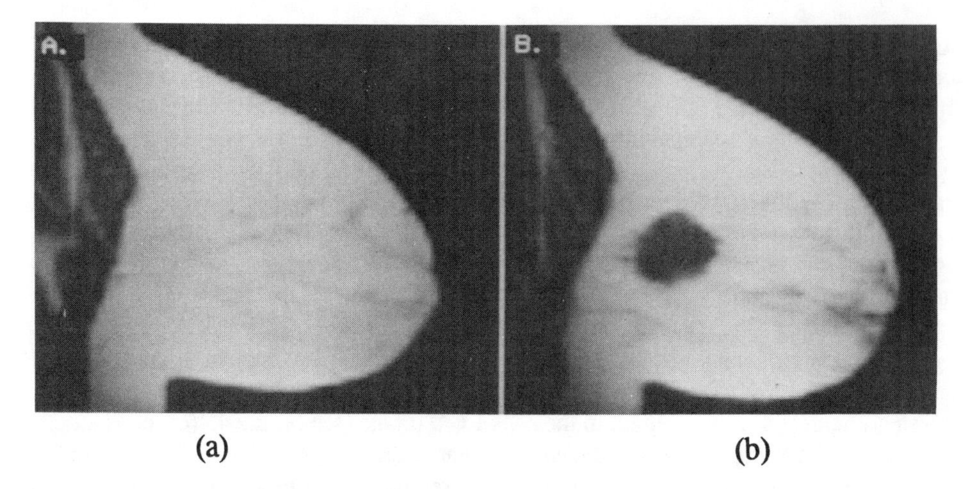

(a) (b)

Figure 4.9 T_1-weighted images of two slices through the breast. The images were acquired using a Siemens Magnetom Imaging System at field strength of 1.0 Telsa. The pulse sequence parameters for these images are TR = 500ms, TE = 17ms. A two-turn Siemens breast coil (10cm depth by 14cm diameter was also used as a MR receiver coil to improve the S/N ratio.

search the radial histogram for peaks and valleys. A peak is found when the window is centered over a radius with the maximum number of non-zero pixels within the window. Valleys in the table are found in an analogous manner. The smallest radius corresponding to a valley lying between two peaks is the maximum radius of the aorta. If the d-peak algorithm is unable to find a valley in the radius table, the Otsu discriminant function is used to determine the maximum radius of the aorta. Any regions that are outside of the maximum radius are removed (see Figure 4.8(c)). The resulting region corresponds to the aorta shape and position.

The boundary of the resulting region is smoothed using a morphological opening[11,12] as a two-dimensional, spatial, low-pass filter (see Figure 4.8(d)). The radius of the structuring element used to filter the image is 3 pixels. Next, the region is enlarged to ensure that the entire wall of the aorta and a portion of the adventitial fat is included in the segmented region (see Figure 4.8(e)). This enlargement is a morphological dilation using a circular structuring element of radius one pixel.

Finally, the sequence of regions found above is used to segment the T_1, Pd, and T_2 weighted images in the sequence of slices. This sequence can then be processed further by a pattern recognition procedure to classify tissues in the aorta wall.

4.3 Breast Lesion Segmentation

Hierarchical segmentation techniques similar to those applied to the abdominal aorta have also been applied to the detection and characterization of lesions in MR images of the human breast. Like the aorta segmentation procedure, the segmentation of breast lesions relies only on T_1-weighted images. The T_1-weighted image alone provides sufficient information about the extent and nature of the lesion to adequately segment it from the breast (see Figure 4.9). In addition, the hierarchical breast segmentation procedure combines edge-based and region-based techniques to successively refine the estimate of the lesion.

The breast lesion segmentation procedure involves two distinct steps: lesion detection and lesion growing. Lesion detection employs the use of an edge detector to find a preliminary lesion boundary. Lesion growing uses both statistical and morphological techniques in order to choose which pixels in the neighborhood of the preliminary boundary actually are part of the lesion. The result is a statistical lesion segmentation at a predetermined confidence level.

It is important that carcinomas which have spread throughout the breast or into the muscle wall typically require mastectomy. Early detection is crucial to the treatment of any form of cancer. This hierarchical procedure intends to aid physicians in the detection and classification of lesions in the early to intermediate stages, where the extent and position of the lesion are less likely to hinder the segmentation. The procedure may be used as an adjunct to mammography to significantly reduce the need for biopsy. In many cases, early detection of small lesions may allow aspiration or removal thorough lumpectomy, sparing the breast.

4.3.1 Lesion Detection

The first portion of the breast lesion segmentation procedure involves a gross detection of the lesion. Lesion detection relies heavily on the quality and contrast of the original image, as well as on the size and position of the lesion within the breast. To ensure good quality and contrast of the images to be segmented, some pre-processing is needed. Pre-processing ensures that noise and/or gradients which appear on the images due to the MR acquisition process are minimized. The size and position of the lesion is

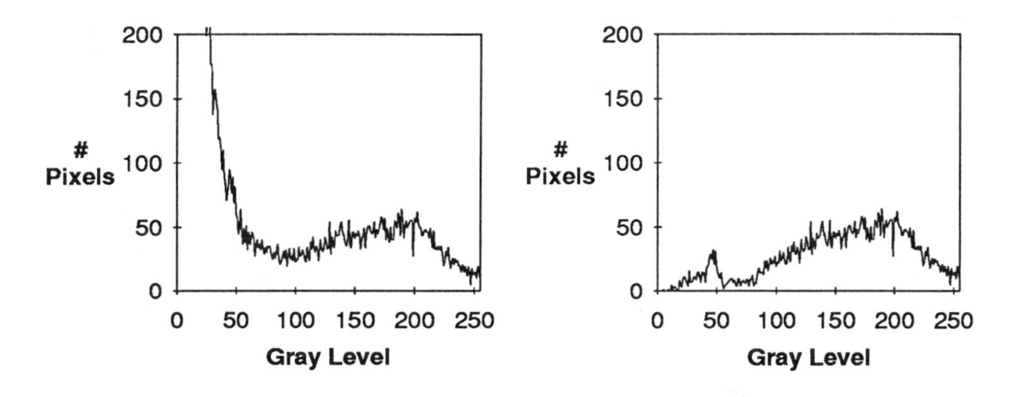

Figure 4.10 Histogram thresholding: (a) histogram of the diseased breast image where the large first mode in the histogram corresponds to background pixels, and (b) removal of this mode by establishing a local minima between the first and second modes is an effective method of separating the background from pixels of interest.

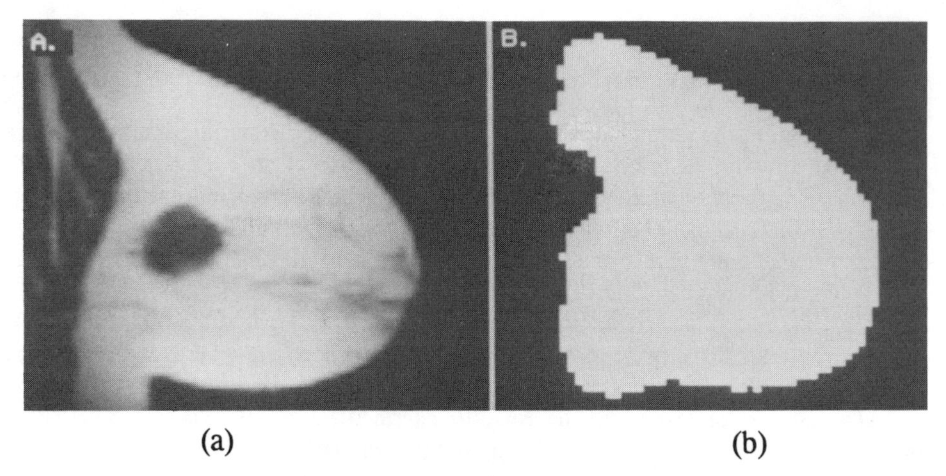

(a) (b)

Figure 4.11 Creating a breast mask from (a) the original diseased breast image by separating the background pixels from pixels of interest through histogram thresholding, and (b) creating a binary image from the remaining bins to isolate the breast in all subsequent processing operations.

also important. Very large lesions or lesions which are very near the pectoral wall will cause region growing to fail. It is important to note that the procedure was designed to detect lesions in the early to intermediate stages.

The major steps in lesion detection involve first creating a mask for the entire breast to remove background pixels of non-interest. Second, a Laplacian of a Gaussian (LOG) mask is convolved with the image to approximately locate the edges of structures within the image. A zero-crossing algorithm is applied next to detect the transitions from dark-to-light and light-to-dark pixels which approximate the edges of the breast, lesion, and pectoral wall. Next, an enhancement operation is performed to reduce noise and gradients, and improve the overall image quality. Finally, a histogram of the improved image is used to increase the contrast between the normal breast and the lesion.

Preprocessing

To save computational time and storage space, the first preprocessing step involves reducing the original images from their 256 × 256 pixel size down to 64 × 64 pixels. This can be done by extracting the breast from the surrounding image, and then reducing the image by one-half. An added benefit is that image reduction is also accompanied by a reduction in image noise.

A threshold algorithm is used next to separate any remaining background pixels from pixels of interest (see Figure 4.10). The histogram of the extracted image is examined, and the first true histogram mode is isolated. It is a safe assumption that the pixels which comprise the lowest mode are associated with the background of the image. The isolated mode is set to zero using a threshold operation in order to separate these background pixels from the rest of the image.[13]

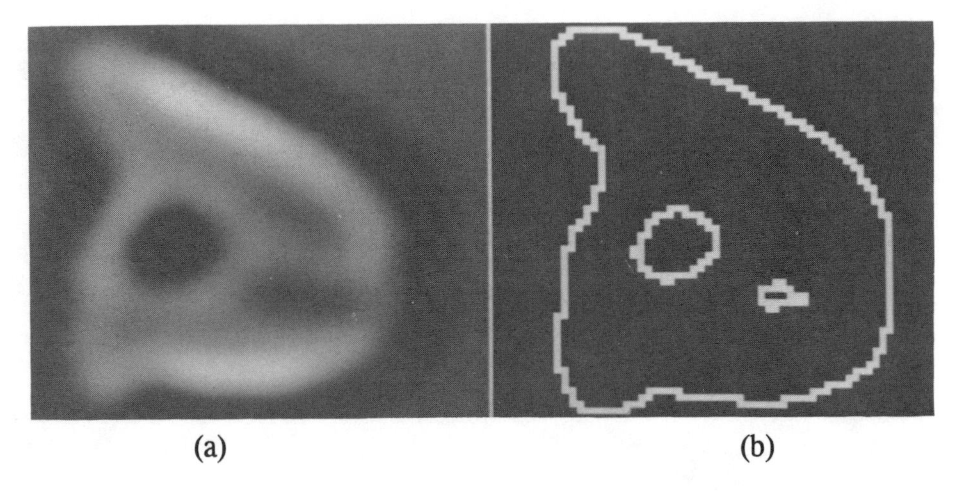

(a) (b)

Figure 4.12 The two major steps in the detection of lesions are: (a) convolution of the image with a non-directional, second derivative LOG operator to determine the edges of the breast and any internal structures, and (b) using a zero-crossing algorithm to locate these edges. The LOG mask size of 21 x 21 pixels was found to be adequate for locating regions of interest in the breast.

The remaining pixels in the image correspond to breast tissue, and are set to a gray level of 255. The result of these operations is a binary "breast mask" which can be used to isolate the breast from the background in all future operations. A morphological close and open using a circular structuring element are performed to smooth the mask, ensure the entire breast is included under the mask, and to remove any stray noise pixels (see Figure 4.11).

Edge Detection

Now that the breast has been isolated, a modified Laplacian of a Gaussian (LOG)operator[9] is applied as an edge detector (see Figure 4.12(a)). The LOG operator, as explained in the previous section on aorta segmentation, is a two-dimensional, non-directional, linear approximation to the second order derivative which can be used to emphasize transitions from dark-to-light and light-to-dark regions. When convolved with the breast image, the LOG emphasizes the transitions between background, normal and diseased tissue.

The application of the LOG mask is followed by an operator which marks the zero-crossings, hence the edges, found by the edge detector. This "edge map" typically defines the outside border of the breast and any lesions within the breast. The edge map can be superimposed on the original image so that the edge detected structures can be visualized (see Figure 4.12(b)).

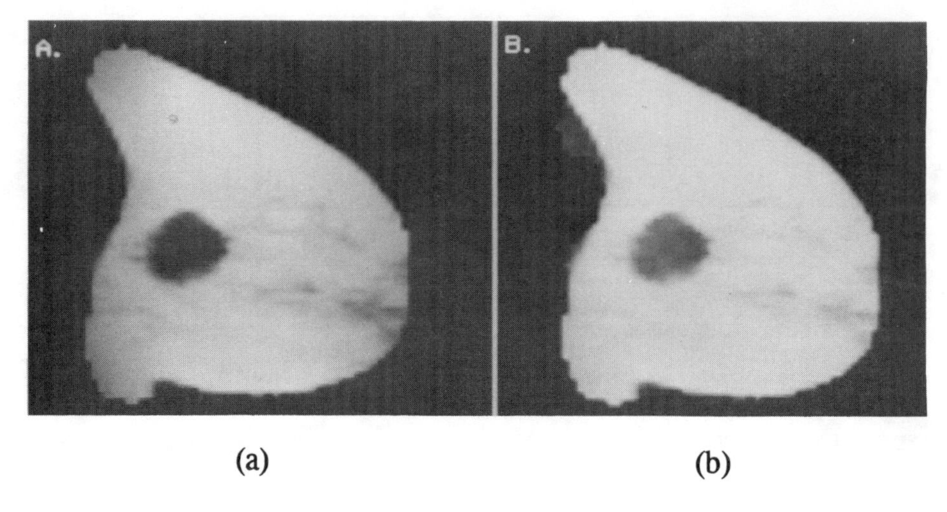

(a) (b)

Figure 4.13 Demonstration of the gradient removal technique: (a) original T_1-weighted breast image exhibiting gradient artifacts near the outside edges, and (b) the same image after a divide by median filter and histogram contrast stretching. A median filter window size of 17 × 17 proved to attenuate the artifact without edge effects or severe gray level intensity changes.

Image Enhancement

At this stage, more processing is done on the original images before the next major step of region growing. A major problem with MR images of the breast are gradients superimposed on the image due to the surface receiving coil (see Figure 4.13(a)). Surface coils increase the signal to noise ratio, thereby improving the contrast of the resulting images. However, increased image signal-to-noise occurs at a cost of image homogeneity.[14] Surface coil gradients distort the gray level intensity values and must be attenuated before automatic region growing is attempted.

Several approaches have been used to attenuate surface coil artifacts. Among these are high-pass filtering, dividing by a phantom image, and dividing by a Fourier low-passed or smoothed image.[15] The approach used in this work involved median filtering the original image and then dividing the original image by this median filtered image on a pixel by pixel basis. Due to the variation in lesion size from slice to slice, and more importantly, from patient to patient, a median filter size must be chosen carefully. The window size of the filter should be approximately the size of the lesion, so that the gradient intensity is attenuated, while the lesion interior is not significantly enhanced. A median filter window size of 17 × 17 was chosen by trial. The result is an image with good surface coil artifact attenuation, good edge retention, and relatively unchanged tumor interior gray level intensity values (see Figure 4.13(b)).

As a final step, the divide by median image histogram is examined, and the high valued peaks corresponding to the normal breast fat are mapped to the highest gray level intensities. Similar in principle to that of background pixel remapping, the contrast between the lesion and the normal tissue is additionally enhanced.

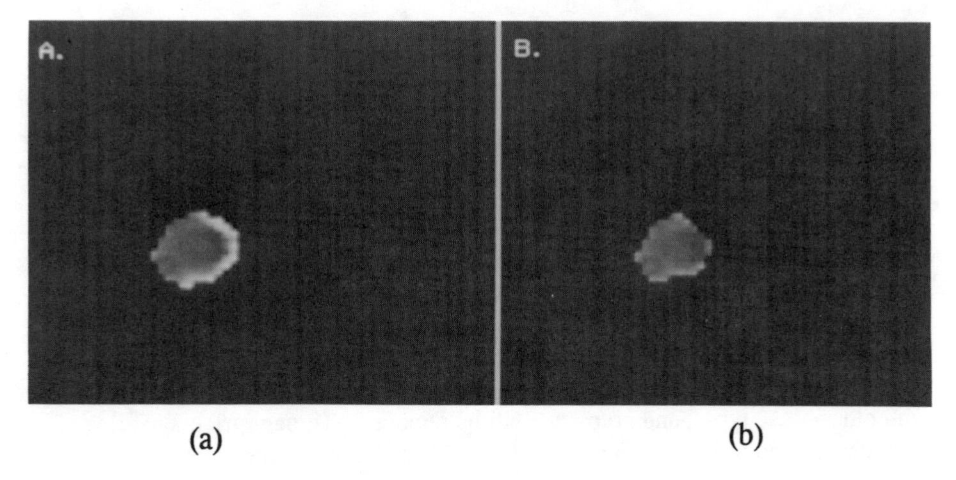

(a) (b)

Figure 4.14 **Thresholding of the extracted lesion to improve lesion segmentation: (a) gross segmentation of the image using the chain coded edge map created by edge detection, and (b) the same lesion after the application of a localized histogram thresholding operation to remove any fat pixels or chemical shift artifacts.**

4.3.2 Lesion Growing

The second major step in breast lesion segmentation is the process of region growing. The edge maps depicting the major regions in the breast are converted to chain code. An operator can then select one of the regions most likely to be a lesion. Once a region is specified, the progressive segmentation can proceed. First, a histogram of the gross lesion region is examined, and the highest valued peaks are discarded. Statistical information of this modified region such as mean pixel intensity and variance is calculated. The region is then morphologically eroded to a seed point. From this seed point the lesion growing proceeds, using the previously collected statistical information and a operator specified confidence level as a growing rule.

Chain Coding

A simple method of representing and working with the edge detected elements is through the use of chain code. Only the starting pixel must be represented by its specific location. The other pixels on the same curve need only be represented by their successive displacements from the previous pixel.[16] Chain code connectivity indicates the number of directions from which pixel displacement can occur given a starting element. Four connectivity only allows displacement in the north, south, east and west directions; eight connectivity also allows diagonal displacement. All of the edges detected in the above procedures are converted to chain code using eight neighbor connectivity. A chain code "wild-point" filter has also been added to ensure that chains which are comprised of fewer than five elements are excluded. An operator then sets the region growing portion of the lesion segmentation into motion by selecting a chain which most likely corresponds to a lesion.

Lesion Threshold Operation

The selected chain is filled in to create a binary mask of the preliminary lesion region. A logical AND operation is then performed between the mask and the enhanced image in order to segment out the actual gray level intensity values of the region. Edge detection extracts only a gross area about the lesion, leaving many pixels which correspond to the neighboring normal tissue still present in the extracted image. The first refinement of the lesion once again involves a localized histogram thresholding (see Figure 4.14). The iterative procedure attempts to remove the n highest peaks in the histogram of the region (where n may be operator specified). If n peaks cannot be removed, the procedure attempts to remove only the n-1 highest peaks, and so forth. If only one smooth peak exists, the operation concludes that the region is not contaminated with other tissue types, and no pixels will be removed. Through trial, a n value of 2 has been determined to be sufficient for all of the cases thus far encountered.

Region of Interest Statistics

Important statistical information regarding the modified region is then collected. This information is directly pertinent to the development of a growing rule for the region grow. The mean pixel value and variance are calculated. Using these values, the univariate normality of each pixel can be evaluated and compared to a prescribed χ^2 confidence level.

Seed Point Selection for Region Growing

The region growing process depends on a starting point or seed point, as well as on a growing rule. In the least, the seed point must lie within the lesion. In many cases, the centroid of the modified region could be used as a seed. There is no guarantee, however, that the centroid of a region must fall within the region itself, i.e. in the case of a crescent, or "*L*" shaped object. In order to ensure a seed point within the breast lesion, a morphological erosion is performed on the modified region. The coordinates of the resulting pixel are used as the seed point to initiate region growing.

Region Growing by Pixel Aggregation

Region growing by pixel aggregation is a process by which pixels or subregions are grouped into larger regions. A "seed" or initial point is chosen, and regions are grown by appending to the seed those neighboring pixels with similar properties.[13] Region growing may be conducted in a four-connected, or eight-connected fashion. In four-connected region growing, only the four pixels which share an immediate boundary with a seed pixel can be considered for assignment. In eight-connected growing, the four immediate neighbors as well as the four closest diagonal neighbors are considered for assignment. The difference is that eight-connected region growing considers two subregions connected by one diagonally adjoining pixel element to be of the same region, whereas four connected region growing would not. MR images of the breast typically contain physiologic structures such as cuprous ligaments and muscle which may lie adjacent to the lesion and have similar gray level intensity. To prevent overgrowth of the

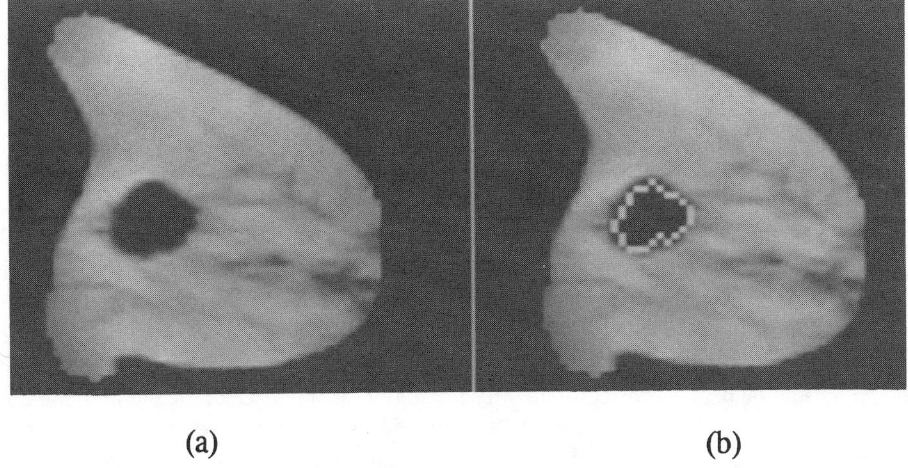

(a) (b)

Figure 4.15 Medullary carcinoma segmented from the diseased breast image: (a) original T_1-weighted breast image and (b) the results of the hierarchical segmentation procedure.

lesion into these adjacent structures, a four-connected region growing rule was used for breast lesion segmentation.

Two immediate problems associated with region growing are the choice of initial seeds that properly represent a region and the formulation of a stopping rule.[13] The previous sections have described the choice of seed point by a progressive refinement of the lesion region and finally by erosion to ensure the seed lies within the region of interest. The stopping rule incorporated in breast lesion segmentation is a simple one: region growing is halted when no more adjoining pixels satisfy the criteria for inclusion, or the region reaches the breast/background boundary as defined by the breast mask. The criteria for inclusion, as mentioned previously, involves using the statistical information collected from the preliminary lesion region, and a χ^2 value. A pixel is included in the lesion if the following inequality is true:

$$\frac{(adjacent\ pixel\ -\ region\ mean)^2}{(region\ variance)} < \chi^2\ Value \qquad (4.1)$$

where 3.84 is the χ^2 value chosen, corresponding to 95% of the univariate normal distribution. In other words, one can be 95% confident that a pixel which meets the criteria set forth by the preliminary extraction belongs to the lesion.

Once the lesion has been grown (see Figure 4.15), statistical information such as area, perimeter, mean gray level intensity, and variance can again be collected. The lesion mask created by region growing using the T_1- weighted image can also be applied to collect information from the T_2, Pd, and Dixon opposed images. Using all of the statistical and multispectral information available in MR images, further processing by pattern recognition procedures may allow the various types of lesions of the breast to be classified.

4.4 Conclusions

By developing hierarchical, application specific segmentation procedures in which segmented regions are successively refined, specific objects have been successfully segmented from complex images. This approach has solved many of the problems associated with traditional, single-step methods and has important applications to additional segmentation problems.

Of particular importance, knowledge of spatial relationships of various structures in the image can be used to correctly identify the region of interest. In the hierarchical aorta segmentation procedure this means that spatial information can be incorporated into a heuristic to identify the aorta from among structures such as the vena cava, muscle columns supporting the spine, and large intestine. This is a significant improvement over methods based on a single step spot detector[17] which may fail if the aorta is not the only spatially consistent structure between slices. Also, the progressive aorta segmentation procedure implements a second method to extract the aorta if the peak LOG image does not locate the aorta in a particular slice. For breast lesion segmentation, spatial information can be used in many cases to distinguish the lesion from the pectoral wall.

Secondly, the use of edge-based methods combined with spatial information have been used to automatically determine seed points, growing rules, and stopping rules for region-growing algorithms used in both aorta and breast lesion segmentation procedures. This reduces the three limitations of general region-growing procedures. For the aorta segmentation procedure, granulometry is used to determine a seed point, a simple threshold is used as the growing rule, and a preliminary extraction determines the stopping rule. Similarly, the progressive breast lesion segmentation procedure uses erosion to find a seed point, statistical information representing the lesion region to determine a region growing rule, and breast extraction to provide a stopping rule.

Thirdly, spatial information can be used to eliminate structures with gray levels similar to the region of interest from a preliminary segmentation of the image. This has improved aorta boundary estimation compared to procedures using either Fourier descriptor transformations, Hough transformations, or edge linking techniques. The resulting estimation of the boundary will be similar in size, shape and position to that perceived by the observer.

Finally, progressive segmentation techniques can be applied to many other problems. Other applications, which we have been exploring, include the extension of the aorta segmentation method into the aorta/iliac artery bifurcation, segmentation of tumors from MR images of the liver, segmentation of cranial tissues and tumors, and segmentation of ventricles from images of the heart. The segmentation problems addressed in these MR images are similar to the segmentation problems encountered in other complex "real world" imagery. It is believed that the hierarchical "top down" approach we have developed can be applied to these other "real world" images.

Acknowledgements--This research was supported in part by The Virginia Center for Innovative Technology, DuPont Merck Pharmaceutical (Wilmington, DE), Dynatech Computer Systems (Sunnyvale, CA), The Dana Trust Foundation, AMVEST Corp. (Charlottesville, VA), and The University of Virginia School of Medicine Pratt Foundation. The authors wish to acknowledge the assistance of Drs. J. Brookeman, S. Berr, and J. P. Mugler of the Department of Radiology for acquisition of images and Drs C. Ayers of Department of Cardiology and E. deParedes for providing access to patient data. The work on aorta segmentation has been submitted to *Computerized Medical Imaging and Graphics* as an original paper.

References

1. R. Ohlander, K. Price, and D. Raj Reddy, "Picture Segmentation Using a Recursive Region Splitting Method", *Computer Graphics and Image Processing* , 313-333 (1978).

2. M.W. Vannier, R.L. Butterfield, D. Jordan, W.A. Murphy, R.G. Levitt, and M. Gado, "Multispectral Analysis of Magnetic Resonance", *Radiology* **154**, 221-224 (1985).

3. H. Asar, N. Nandhakumar, and J.K. Aggarwal, "Pyramid-Based Image Segmentation using Multisensory Data", *Pattern Recognition* **23(6)**, 583-593 (1990).

4. T.R. Jackson and M.B. Merickel, "Applications of Hierarchical Image Segmentation Techniques: Aorta Segmentation", *Computerized Medical Imaging and Graphics* **In Print**, (1991).

5. A.P. Dhawan and L. Arata, "Knowledge-Based 3D Analysis from 2D Medical Images", *IEEE EMBS* **10(4)**, 30-37 (1991).

6. P. Lanzer, E.H. Botvinick, and N.B. Shiller, "Cardiac Imaging using Gated Magnetic Resonance", *Radiology* **150**, 121-127 (1984).

7. R.R. Edelman, D.J. Atkinson, M.S. Silver, F.L. Loaiza, and W.S. Warren, "FRODO Pulse Sequences: A New Means of Eliminating Motion, Flow, and Wraparound Artifacts", *Radiology* **166**, 231-236 (1988).

8. J.P. Felmlee and R.L. Ehman, "Spatial Presaturation: A Method for Suppressing Flow Artifacts and Improving Depiction of Vascular Anatomy in MR Imaging", *Radiology* **164**, 559-564 (1987).

9. D. Marr and E. Hildreth, "Theory of Edge Detection", *Proceedings of the Royal Society of London* **275**, 187-217 (1980).

10. N. Otsu, "A Threshold Selection Method from Gray-Level Histogram", *IEEE Trans. SMC* **9**, 62-66 (1979).

11. E.R. Dougherty and C.R. Giardina, *Image Processing-Continuous to Discrete, Volume 1: Geometric, Transform, and Statistical Methods*, Prentice-Hall, Englewood Cliffs, NJ (1987).

12. R.M. Haralick, S.R. Sternberg, and X. Zhuang, "Image Analysis Using Mathematical Morphology", *IEEE Trans. PAMI* **9**, 532-550 (1987).

13. G.C. Gonzalez and P. Wintz, *Digital Image Processing*, Addison-Wesley, Reading, MASS (1987).

14. L. Axel, J. Costantini, and J. Listerud, "Intensity correction in surface coil MR Imaging", *American Journal of Radiology*, **148** 418-20 (1987).

15. A. Adams, J.R. Brookeman, and M.B. Merickel, "Pattern Recognition of Breast Lesions using Magnetic Resonance Imaging", *Computerized Medical Imaging and Graphics,* In Press, (1991).

16. D.H. Ballard and C.M. Brown, *Computer Vision* 1st Edition, Prentice-Hall, Englewood Cliffs, New Jersey (1982).

17. T. Jiang and M.B. Merickel, "Identification and Boundary Extraction of Blobs in Complex Imagery", *Comp. Med. Imaging and Graphics* **13**, 369-382 (1989).

Chapter 5

Color Image Segmentation

M. J. Daily

5.1 INTRODUCTION

The process of segmentation in digital images represents a critical step in most computer vision systems. The goal of segmentation is to locate regions with constant attributes and the associated edges or discontinuities. Raw or filtered data from sensors must be converted to labelled regions and discontinuities for later stages of recognition to proceed.

A major attribute that is useful in segmentation, especially for the purpose of object recognition, is color. In the digital image domain, color imagery is typically composed of three separate planes obtained by digitizing a scene from a video camera using filters sensitive in the red, green, and blue wavelengths. These three-color RGB image sets contain all the information, together with knowledge of sensor characteristics, necessary to accurately reconstruct the spectral content of the incoming light. The role of color in segmentation is often limited in practical systems by the constraints of computation and memory. However, color communicates the existence of salient objects better than single plane intensity images and is largely invariant under geometric transformations, making it an ideal feature for object recognition.

This chapter focusses on several aspects of color image segmentation using variational energy-based approaches. Variational approaches to early vision have become popular due to their elegant mathematical formulation and inherently parallel and local computation. These approaches use an energy functional embodying known constraints about the problem which can be minimized using standard optimization techniques. Deterministic formulations for the energy functionals relate the elastic potential energy of thin plates or membranes to the energy surface. Energy function methods for color segmentation and detection of salient objects are reviewed in Section 2.

Central to the capability of color image segmentation is the method for computing color differences. A large body of research has accurately defined the human perceptual ability for color differencing, yet complete understanding of color perception is still lacking. In color difference theory, a number of transformations have

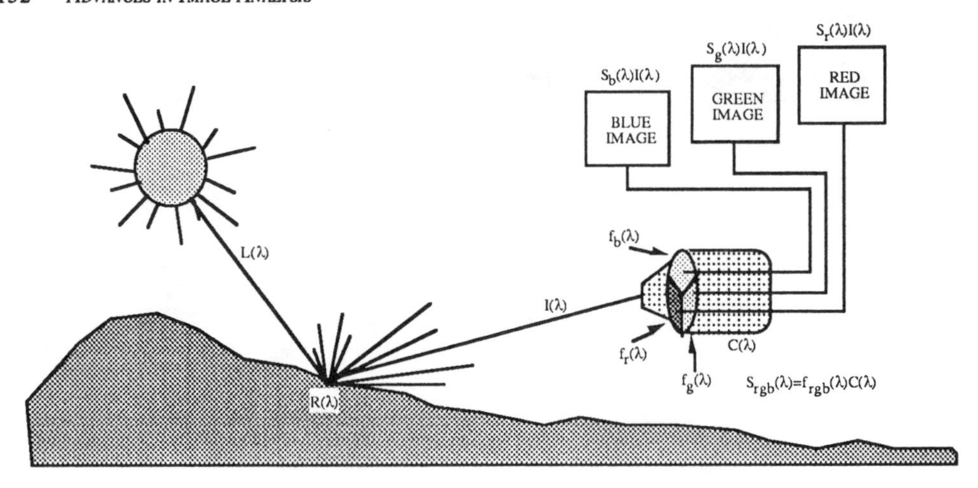

Figure 5.1: Sensor model for color imaging. $L(\lambda)$ is the incident light. $R(\lambda)$ is the surface reflectance function. $S(\lambda)$ is the sensor response, while $C(\lambda)$ is the response of the camera and $f(\lambda)$ is the filter transmission. The sensor output is then D.

been devised to separate various aspects of multi-dimensional spectral content from one-dimensional intensity information. Several of these transformations and their effect on color segmentation are described in Section 3.

Section 4 discusses three formulations for color segmentation: the color transform approach, the color difference formulation, and the multiple module formulation. We present energy functional results from real color imagery showing smooth regions and explicitly marked discontinuities obtained using several color difference techniques implemented on a 4K node mesh-connected SIMD machine, the AMT DAP. Finally, in Section 5 we analyze the interrelationships between critical parameters and describe efforts to automatically set the parameters using interparameter constraints.

5.1.1 Background for Color Perception

The physiological and pyschophysical aspects of human color perception are not completely understood. Psychophysical models typically explain color perception in terms of the activity elicited in chromatic and achromatic channels. Physiological models describe numerous types of color sensitive opponent and nonopponent cells, while psychophysiologic models assume a one to one correspondence between the physiologic cell types and the psychophysical channels. At the photoreceptor cell layer of the retina there are both rod and cone photoreceptors. Rod photoreceptors have peak sensitivity at one wavelength and are primarily used in low light conditions. Three types of cone pigment sensitive in the short-, middle-, and long-wavelength regions of the visible spectrum are responsible for color sensing. Beyond early vision, color perception has a major role in the recognition pathway in the visual cortex, and has a weak link to motion perception and stereo depth perception (see [29, 50] for more details).

We can model color CCD cameras using a similar three-color (or multi-spectral) sensing strategy (see Figure 5.1). These sensors measure the irradiance of the incident light across the plane of the CCD imaging chip. The spectral response of a color sensor for wavelength λ is defined at each image point as

$$S_i(\lambda) = f_i(\lambda)C(\lambda) \tag{5.1}$$

where$f_i(\lambda)$ is the i-th filter transmission function and $C(\lambda)$ is the spectral response of the camera. The sensor output D at each image point is

$$D_i = \int_{\lambda_{min}}^{\lambda_{max}} S_i(\lambda)I(\lambda) \tag{5.2}$$

where $I(\lambda)$ is the image irradiance and is defined as the product of the spectral power distribution of the light $L(\lambda)$ and the surface reflectance function $R(\lambda)$. λ_{min} and λ_{max} are normally the limits of the visible spectrum, although most CCD cameras are sensitive in the near infrared. Any number of color filters may be used to improve color discrimination capability, and for each filter, a digitized image is produced. Filters sensitive in the red, green, and blue wavelengths are typically employed, producing an RGB image set, as follows:

$$\begin{aligned} R &= \int_{\lambda_{min}}^{\lambda_{max}} S_r(\lambda)I(\lambda) \\ G &= \int_{\lambda_{min}}^{\lambda_{max}} S_g(\lambda)I(\lambda) \\ B &= \int_{\lambda_{min}}^{\lambda_{max}} S_b(\lambda)I(\lambda) \end{aligned} \tag{5.3}$$

The addition of color information holds promise for improving segmentation results in several important ways. Several studies indicate that the color of imaged surfaces is more stable under geometric changes than the image irradiance, and color is typically less dependent on image resolution [18, 41]. Other studies have shown the usefulness of chromatic information in improving stereo matching algorithms [23] and in color indexing into large databases of objects for object identification in an active vision system [41]. In the later, some success at object identification and location using histograms was achieved. Methods for low-level segmentation of color imagery are numerous. Techniques using recursive region splitting with histogram analysis [34, 35] and edge and boundary formation [16] have been applied to natural color imagery with some success. While histogram-based methods offer invariance to image rotation and translation under some circumstances, they lack adequate means to represent spatial adjacency and form and often depend on global thresholds. Statistical methods, such as classical Bayes decision theory, which are based on previous observation have also been quite popular [6, 43]. These methods depend on global *a priori* knowledge about the image content and organization. Sophisticated hierarchical clustering techniques have also been applied to the color segmentation problem with some success [48].

Recent methods using underlying physical models of the color image formation process in developing color difference metrics are promising. Physically-based algorithms have produced excellent segmentations separating highlight reflections and matte regions in color imagery obtained under controlled conditions [26]. In addition, a large body of literature has addressed the related problem of color constancy, i.e. the recovery of an illuminant invariant surface spectral reflectance (see [7, 28]).

5.1.2 MRF Background

Recent developments in the use of regularization theory and MRFs have established a unifying mathematical framework for many vision problems. These methods can be traced to the late 70's when Ullman attempted to solve the correspondence problem (motion) by minimizing a cost [47]. Horn and Schunk defined a convex energy function to minimize for the components of optical flow [22]. Hildreth [19], Grimson [13], and Terzopoulos [42] applied similar methods to motion analysis and surface interpolation. Poggio and Torre formally cast the problem of early vision in terms of regularization theory and presented solutions for edge detection, optical flow, surface reconstruction, color, shape from shading, and stereo [40]. To avoid limitations of regularization theory, Blake and Zisserman proposed the idea of weak constraints, which allow a surface to break when the tension is too large [2], and they developed a graduated non-convexity algorithm to minimize the non-convex functionals.

Similar early vision problems ranging from image and surface reconstruction to fusion of multiple low-level vision modules have been addressed using the more general, statistically derived formulation of MRFs. Geman and Geman [11] have used the MRF approach on simple synthetic intensity images for image reconstruction. They added a useful twist to the standard approach by coupling two MRFs, one for the intensity process, and one for a binary line process. The binary line process explicitly marks the location of discontinuities in the intensity surface, making the energy non-convex and requiring sophisticated minimization techniques. They perform the non-convex energy minimization using a simulated annealing algorithm with an annealing schedule that theoretically guarantees locating the global minimum; however, practically the schedule is sub-optimal.

Marroquin [31] was the first to apply coupled MRFs with line processes to the problem of surface reconstruction from sparse depth data. More recently, Poggio and colleagues [38] have used coupled MRFs for fusing low-level visual information. The formation of line process discontinuities and smoothing of processes in depth and motion data, color, and texture are coupled through separate lattices of MRFs to the intensity edges, which guide their formation. Following Marroquin, they chose sub-optimal deterministic procedures to minimize the energy functionals. Another method for surface reconstruction using sparse synthetic depth and intensity data is due to Chou and Brown [3]. Using MRFs and a technique called Highest Confidence First (HCF) to minimize the energy, they chose to update sites with the least stability (highest confidence for changing states) with respect to the current state before updating sites which were more stable. Koch, Marroquin, and Yuille [27] have used the coupled MRF approach to perform surface reconstruction from sparse depth data as well. They used a neural network to minimize the energy functional, based on the work of Hopfield and Tank [20]. This method lends itself more readily to implementation in analog VLSI [17, 27]. Other neural network formulations were also developed by Zhou and colleagues for image restoration, stereo, and optic flow [51]. Other researchers have developed regularization/MRF techniques for stereo, image preprocessing, shape from shading, and boundary completion [14, 36].

Recent efforts have addressed the problem of integration of different early vision modules within the MRF and regularization frameworks [1, 8, 45]. Work in the field of analog VLSI implementations has produced promising results toward development of fast specialized analog chips for early vision [17, 33]. In addition, further advancements of the MRF framework have applied mean field theory to generalize and explain many complex interactions and to describe classes of solutions for similar values of MRF parameters [10]. Continuous formulations for discontinuity space as a scalar field are theoretically advantageous for removing vertical and horizontal biases in discrete lattices.

Markov random fields possess several characteristics which make them useful in color image segmentation. Properties such as smoothness and continuity of color regions over an entire image can be enforced using only dependencies among local neighbors. Discontinuities which separate regions of constant color may be computed while smooth regions are being found. In addition, the inclusion of both the prior and posterior distributions (through Bayes' rule) establishes a relationship between noisy observed imagery and the color segmentation results.

Functional optimization has been applied to the problem of color segmentation in several different ways. In the Gamble/Poggio system, color discontinuities are heavily weighted to occur at the location of previously detected intensity edges [8]. They apply a simple difference between red and green images as a measure of color. Wright applied coupled MRFs to the problem of color segmentation of simple synthetic images by treating the three RGB planes as separately sensed images and adding an inter-image coupling function [49]. The coupling function increases when a discontinuity site in one image is not in agreement with the other two, forcing it to become more like the other two images. This approach effectively treats the color segmentation problem as a data fusion problem. Daily used coupled MRFs to segment color imagery similar to previous surface reconstruction methods with the exception that there are multiple surfaces representing each spectral component of the color imagery [4]. Color difference techniques were used in a general framework to reduce the multi-dimensional color space, simplify segmentation, and produce maximal color separation. Hexagonal lattice structures also proved to more naturally segment difficult scenes. Perez and Koch have used weak continuity constraints and modulo operators in hue space to segment color imagery [37]. In their method, smoothing occurs at low confidence regions in hue space (places where singularities in hue occur, i.e. low saturation or intensity) while discontinuities form where significant color changes are detected away from unstable values.

5.2 MRFS AND REGULARIZATION THEORY

The wide variety of early vision problems that have been addressed within the framework of MRFs and regularization theory demonstrate the adaptability of these methods. In this section we present a more precise overview of the regularization and MRF frameworks and show how the problem of color segmentation can be defined using coupled MRFs. We also discuss the use of Hopfield networks for minimizing the energy functionals.

5.2.1 Regularization Theory

A primary objective of early vision is the recovery of 3-D surface properties from sparse, noisy 2-D images. Most early vision problems are difficult because the 2-D image does not provide sufficient information to constrain the solution. For example, with surface reconstruction, we are given a sparse set of depth points and must determine the entire surface by interpolation. However, without additional information it is impossible to find a unique solution. Another example problem, and the one considered throughout this paper, is color segmentation. Given 2-D color images, the objective is to identify boundaries of the 3-D surfaces from changes in color or components of color. Simple methods that attempt to locally detect color changes using the numeric gradient in color space are inherently unstable because numerical differentiation amplifies noise.

In general, most early vision problems suffer from the symptoms alluded to above: either solutions do not exist, are not unique, or do not vary continuously with the data. These properties are characteristic of *ill-posed* problems as defined by Hadamard [15]. The main objective of regularization theory is to convert ill-posed problems into well-posed problems by restricting the number of admissible solutions and insuring that solutions vary smoothly with the data. Tikhonov [44] suggested several ways of converting an ill-posed problem into a well-posed problem by introducing additional constraints derived from assumptions about the physical system. One method finds a solution by minimizing:

$$E(u) = ||Au - d||^2 + \lambda||Pu||^2 \tag{5.4}$$

where d is the image data, λ is the regularizing parameter that controls the impact of the current solution,u, versus the physical constraints represented by P, $|| \bullet ||$ is the quadratic norm and $||Pu||$ is called the stabilizing functional [32, 39]. This last term, Pu, embeds whatever constraints are necessary to change the problem from ill-posed to well-posed. Note that quadratic functionals are especially appealing because their convexity generally means a unique solution exists.

Unfortunately, this formulation has serious limitations [27]. The main problem is that the degree of smoothness required for the function is unknown. As a result, edge discontinuities may be lost by over-smoothing, an undesirable property since discontinuities often correspond to the most significant features.

Several approaches have been used to reduce or eliminate the problem of over-smoothing in standard regularization. For example, perhaps the simplest method is to explictly account for discontinuities using a separate binary variable l that marks gradients in the intensity that exceed some threshold. This approach is used by Blake and Zisserman's *weak continuity constraint* method [2] and is similar to the *line processes* defined by Geman and Geman's stochastic model [11]. Equation 5.4 can be modified to incorporate line processes by adding a coupling term to the smoothing term and a line process penalty term. In discrete form in one dimension the new equation would be:

$$E(u) = \alpha \sum (u_i - d_i)^2 + \lambda \sum (u_i - u_{i+1})^2 (1 - l_i) + \beta \sum l_i \tag{5.5}$$

where u is the solution and d the data. When the change in intensity is above the threshold, β, the smoothing term gets very large and it becomes cheaper to set a line process and incur the penalty β. A good analogy is to imagine an elastic membrane being stretched over a bunch of stakes. The more the membrane is stretched the greater its elastic potential energy. If the membrane is stretched too far it tears, and the locations of the tear represent discontinuities in the membrane. With the addition of the line process variable l, Equation 5.5 is nonquadratic. As a result, we have to use iterative methods of nonconvex optimization to find an approximate solution.

5.2.2 MRF Formulation

Regularization can be viewed as a special case of the stochastic MRF formulation for early vision problems. In this section we show how regularization and MRFs may be viewed in terms of minimizing energy functionals composed of data and constraint terms. Additional details of MRF theory can be found in [11, 31]. MRFs provide an elegant means of specifying a local energy function which embodies the expected dependencies of neighboring pixels and includes both the prior and posterior probabilistic distributions. This local, neighborhood-based specification of dependencies avoids *ad hoc*, brittle methods using global knowledge.

Suppose we have a 2-D array of pixels, $d_{i,j}$, representing a set of sparse and noisy image data. The objective is to find the "best" estimate of values for the entire image given this input data. In probabilistic terms, we want to maximize the probability of the global estimate $u_{i,j}$ given the observed data:

$$max \; [P(u_{i,j} | d_{i,j})] \;\; \forall u_{i,j} \tag{5.6}$$

Using Bayes rule the problem can be rewritten as:

$$max \; [\frac{P(d_{i,j} | u_{i,j}) P(u_{i,j})}{P(d_{i,j})}] \;\; \forall u_{i,j} \tag{5.7}$$

However, since the probability of observing the data $d_{i,j}$ is independent of the estimate $u_{i,j}$ the $P(d_{i,j})$ term may be factored out to give an equivalent form of the problem (also called the *maximum a posteriori* or MAP estimate):

$$max[P(d_{i,j} | u_{i,j}) P(u_{i,j})] \;\; \forall u_{i,j} \tag{5.8}$$

In general it is very difficult to determine the probability distributions for these terms. Fortunately, the nature of the problem allows us to define the array of pixels as a discrete Markov random field. A discrete MRF on a finite lattice is defined as a collection of random variables, which correspond to the sites of the lattice, whose probability distribution for any given site is only a function of the values in a small neighborhood of the given site. In other words, the conditional probability of a particular pixel having a certain value is only a function of the neighboring pixels, not of the entire image (i.e. pixels have only local interactions). The Hammersley-Clifford theorem establishes the equivalence between the conditional probabilities of the local characteristics in the MRF and local energy potentials in a Gibbs distribution:

$$P(u_{i,j}) = \frac{e^{\frac{-E(u_{i,j})}{T}}}{Z} \tag{5.9}$$

Where Z is a normalizing factor, $E(u_{i,j})$ is an energy function containing all assumptions and constraints about the physical system, and T is a temperature parameter controlling the peakedness of the probability distribution. Making some assumptions about noise in the data, the conditional probability $P(d_{i,j}|u_{i,j})$ can also be written as a Gibbs distribution that is proportional to:

$$P(d_{i,j}|u_{i,j}) = e^{-(d_{i,j}-u_{i,j})^2} \tag{5.10}$$

The combined probability is proportional to:

$$P(d_{i,j}|u_{i,j})P(u_{i,j}) = e^{-[E(u_{i,j})+(d_{i,j}-u_{i,j})^2]} \tag{5.11}$$

In order to maximize this probability we need to minimize the quantity inside the brackets. So the problem can be restated:

$$min[E(u_{i,j}) + (d_{i,j} - u_{i,j})^2] \quad \forall u_{i,j} \tag{5.12}$$

Notice that this form is very similar to standard regularization where the least square estimator is combined with a regularizer, $E(u_{i,j})$. However, in this case, we have not made any restrictions on the functional form of $E(u_{i,j})$. The exact form of this energy function depends on the assumptions and constraints of the problem. Consequently, regularization can be viewed as a special case of the stochastic MRF formulation.

Therefore, the Gibbs distribution energy function consists of two parts, one describing the interaction potential between neighbors, and the other associated with the difference between the predicted image and the actual observed data. Several methods of minimizing the energy function over the image (i.e. maximizing the probability) can be used, among them simulated annealing, deterministic procedures, and network solutions.

The behavior of piecewise smooth surfaces (i.e. color images, optic flow, etc.) may be modeled using two coupled MRFs [11]. One field is used for a continuous-valued smooth process, while the other is binary with "line process" variables denoting edge discontinuities between sites of the smooth process. MRF lattices are coupled to reflect the interdependencies between the physical processes (smoothness, positivity, bounds) and discontinuity. To completely define the energy function E we need to define additional variables used in constructing the smooth estimate, $u_{i,j}$. In addition to $u_{i,j}$, vertical and horizontal line process variables $v_{i,j}$, $h_{i,j}$ are defined at sites between the smooth $u_{i,j}$. These line process variables don't actually appear in the image but simply mark places in the image where a discontinuity is detected. The energy function for a single two-dimensional surface (for example, intensity segmentation) on a rectangular grid may be written as the sum of three parts:

$$\begin{aligned} E_I &= \lambda \sum_{i,j} (u_{i,j+1} - u_{i,j})^2 (1 - v_{i,j}) + (u_{i+1,j} - u_{i,j})^2 (1 - h_{i,j}) \\ E_D &= \alpha \sum_{i,j} (u_{i,j} - d_{i,j})^2 \\ E_L &= \beta \sum_{i,j} (v_{i,j} + h_{i,j}) \end{aligned} \tag{5.13}$$

E_I is the smoothing term. As long as the difference in intensity between neighboring pixels is not too large, E_I is small and the line process variables are set to zero. However, if the intensity difference grows greater than a threshold (set by the line process term E_L), then a line process variable is set to represent an intensity discontinuity. E_D is the data term which establishes the influence of the input data, $d_{i,j}$. The parameter α is used to weigh the importance or reliability of the sparse, sampled data. The third term, E_L represents the cost of introducing a line process discontinuity. The parameter β controls the threshold for discontinuity detection. If β is too low, many discontinuities will form and over-segment the image. Likewise, setting β too high results in a very coarse segmentation with few discontinuities. In contrast with gradient-based operators (such as for edge detection), this formulation displays both noise suppression and hysteresis in the line process resulting in contour completion.

Many methods for minimizing the nonconvex functional energy exist, including simulated annealing, graduated non-convexity, and steepest descent (for an overview see [30]). In this paper, we chose to minimize the energy functionals using a Hopfield network [20, 27]. In this minimization, we use the following fourth energy term, called the gain term, to force the line process to 0 or 1 values:

$$E_g = \sum_{i,j} \left(\int_0^{v_{i,j}} g^{-1}(v)\, dv + \int_0^{h_{i,j}} g^{-1}(h)\, dh \right) \tag{5.14}$$

where $g()$ is a sigmoid function defined as

$$g(x) = \frac{1 + tanh(kx)}{2} \tag{5.15}$$

and k controls the steepness of the sigmoid. State update equations are formed similar to Hopfield in that changes are equal to the negative gradient of the energy. Since the gradient of the energy is always positive, the system will tend to a minimum (not necessarily the global minimum):

$$\frac{du_{i,j}}{dt} = -\frac{\partial E}{\partial u_{i,j}} \tag{5.16}$$

$$\frac{dm_{i,j}}{dt} = -\frac{\partial E}{\partial h_{i,j}} \tag{5.17}$$

$$\frac{dn_{i,j}}{dt} = -\frac{\partial E}{\partial v_{i,j}} \tag{5.18}$$

where the total energy E is simply the sum of the component energies defined in Equations 5.13 and 5.14. Taking the derivatives and solving for the state variables at equilibrium we obtain the following update equations:

$$u_{i,j} = \frac{\lambda(L^v_{i,j}u_{i,j+1} + L^v_{i,j-1}u_{i,j-1} + L^h_{i,j}u_{i+1,j} + L^h_{i-1,j}u_{i-1,j}) + \alpha d_{i,j}}{\lambda(L^v_{i,j} + L^v_{i,j-1} + L^h_{i,j} + L^h_{i-1,j}) + \alpha} \tag{5.19}$$

$$m_{i,j} = \lambda(u_{i,j+1} - u_{i,j})^2 - \beta \tag{5.20}$$

$$n_{i,j} = \lambda(u_{i+1,j} - u_{i,j})^2 - \beta \tag{5.21}$$

where $L^x_{i,j} = 1 - x_{i,j}$, and the sigmoid function determines the value of the vertical and horizontal line process variables according to $v_{i,j} = g(m_{i,j})$, and $h_{i,j} = g(n_{i,j})$, where $m_{i,j}$ and $n_{i,j}$ are internal state variables. Since the energy function is not convex, the system is not guaranteed to reach a global minimum. Several methods have been suggested for bumping the system out of local minima and hopefully towards the global solution [2, 25]. In these experiments the line process gain function is used to deterministically "anneal" the system into lower energy states. Initially, the line process gain is set low so that values are continuously distributed in [0,1]. Each time the system reaches equilibrium, the gain parameter k in Equation 5.15 is increased. This procedure continues until the high gain limit is reached where all line processes are set to either 0 or 1. The use of "annealing" schedules for the gain of the non-linear sigmoid performs a similar function to decreasing convexity in the graduated non-convexity algorithm of Blake and Zisserman or to temperature in simulated annealing. The effect of increasing the gain (e.g. from nearly linear in the low gain end to a step edge in the high gain limit) helps to force the solution out of local minima during the iterative minimization of the energy.

5.3 COLOR TRANSFORMATIONS

Of primary importance to the process of color segmentation is the use of color differencing methods. The manner in which significant changes in color are detected plays an important role in the formation of color change boundaries. As described in Section 5.1, a color image is composed of three spectral components obtained using filters with different sensitivities in the red, green, and blue wavelengths. In many cases, it is desirable to transform from the resulting red, green, and blue (RGB) images to other color spaces which separate intensity from color (hue). This is because the RGB images have a strong intensity factor and are highly correlated, resulting in duplication of information content.

Kender's [24] discussion of color transformations points out that linear transformations from RGB data (e.g. YIQ) are preferable to non-linear transformations such as intensity, hue, and saturation (IHS) and normalized color since they suffer from non-removable singularities and spurious gaps in the color distribution. The IHS transformation from RGB is defined as follows [1]:

$$I = \frac{R+G+B}{3} \tag{5.22}$$

[1] Other definitions of the IHS system exist, but are functionally equivalent.

$$H = arctan(\frac{\sqrt{3}(G-B)}{2R-G-B} \tag{5.23}$$

$$S = \frac{max(R,G,B) - min(R,G,B)}{max(R,G,B) + min(R,G,B)} \tag{5.24}$$

Saturation is unstable when $R+G+B$ is small and undefined for $R+G+B=0$. Hue is unstable when saturation is low and has a nonremovable singularity when $R = G = B$ (i.e. for gray intensities). The IHS transformation also has the drawback that it is computationally expensive. However, the IHS system has advantages for segmentation as long as other transforms are used when hue and saturation are unstable. The IHS transform separates intensity, hue, and saturation information allowing emphasis to be placed on whichever component is most salient. No other transformation produces a separate measure for hue alone. In addition, hue has both multiplicative and additive scale invariance [37]. That is, $hue(R,G,B) = hue(\gamma R, \gamma G, \gamma B)$ and $hue(R,G,B) = hue(R+\delta, G+\delta, B+\delta)$. Additive scale invariance is beneficial for eliminating shadows or constant values within one component of the RGB image, while multiplicative scale invariance cancels effects of a constant multiplier to each component.

A second non-linear transformation from RGB, normalized color, is defined as:

$$\begin{aligned} r &= \frac{R}{R+G+B} \\ g &= \frac{G}{R+G+B} \\ b &= \frac{B}{R+G+B} \end{aligned} \tag{5.25}$$

Normalized color produces a space that is independent of luminance because it possesses multiplicative scale invariance. Since only two components of normalized color are necessary to define the color, we can plot perceived color in two dimensions, producing a chromaticity diagram which, for a given intensity, contains nearly all realizable colors. Assuming r and g are the color axes in the normalized color space, luminance may be written as:

$$Y = c_1 R + c_2 G + c_3 B \tag{5.26}$$

where $c_1 + c_2 + c_3 = 1$. Once again, normalized color is unstable for low intensities. The two components r and g define orthogonal, arbitrary axes in a hue and saturation space, and together are similar to hue and saturation. However, they do not separate hue and saturation.

Ohta, Kanade, and Sakai developed a set of color feature vectors by examining the optimal feature vectors obtained using the Karhunen-Loeve transformation of RGB data from eight natural scenes [35]. The Karhunen-Loeve components are derived using the orthogonal Karhunen-Loeve expansion which minimizes the mean-square error in basis functions as well as a measure of dispersion (entropy function) for the three RGB components [46]. A simple transformation that closely matched the KL vectors was:

$$I_1 = \frac{R+G+B}{3}$$

$$
\begin{aligned}
I_2 &= \frac{R-B}{2} \\
I_3 &= \frac{2G-R-B}{4}
\end{aligned} \tag{5.27}
$$

I_1 is the feature vector along the axis with greatest variance and corresponds to intensity, suggesting that most of the information content is present in the intensity dimension. I_2 and I_3 contain the color and saturation information similar to the normalized color space. The *Commission Internationale de l'Eclairage* (CIE) has established several standard colorimetric transformations with the chief aim being to produce uniform color spaces where color differences a human perceives as equal correspond to equal Euclidean distances [50]. Two such transformations are the CIELUV and CIELAB transformations. In each system the RGB color stimulus is transformed to three components; L,U, and V, and L, A, and B. The first component, L, corresponds to lightness or intensity. UV and AB are different measures of combined color and saturation. In each case, color difference formulae that quantify the amount of perceived change between two colors can be used.

More recent work attempting to quantify the significance of a color change in an image is based on physical models of the sensors and environment [18]. Using the color imaging model from Section 5.1, the image irradiance at a point, $I(\lambda)$, may be approximated by using an orthogonal set of basis functions and the sensor output, as in [18]. Color differences between points are then computed by normalizing and calculating a distance between basis functions integrated over the entire visible spectrum, which gives more reliable results than measures operating at only one spectral wavelength. Of course, this method is also computationally expensive. For additional information on color transforms, see [35, 50].

By comparing color differences computed using several transformations, we have found that measuring differences in hue consistently produces larger relative changes than other corresponding color and intensity measures normalized to the same range. The fact that hue tends to produce the difference with highest magnitude suggests the usefulness of color as a means of segmenting. However, in many instances, hue is also more susceptible to variation from noise, and, in practice, may not yield significantly better results. Figure 5.2 shows an example of the usefulness of each measure in computing color differences for a typical natural color image. The graphs were obtained by normalizing and comparing the magnitude of the difference of each measure from the following set: *Euclidean RGB, intensity, hue, saturation, Maximum IHS, CIELAB, CIELAB hue, CIELAB chroma, CIELAB intensity, Karhunen-Loeve components, and normalized color.* Differences were computed between neighbors along the overlayed line. For the Maximum IHS technique, the maximum difference in each component in IHS space is used as long as the intensity is above 10% (25 where 255 is the maximum). When the intensity is below 10%, only the intensity difference is considered.

5.4 MRFS FOR COLOR SEGMENTATION

For intensity contour detection or surface reconstruction as defined in Equation 5.13 in Section 5.2, the continuous process and input data are only one-

(a) Original image

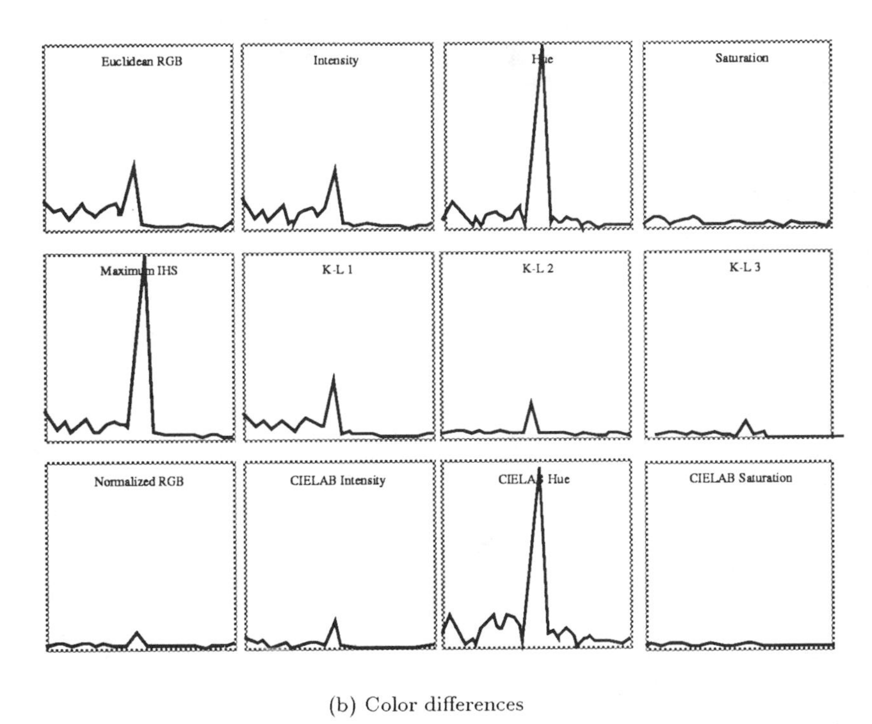

(b) Color differences

Figure 5.2: Color differences in (b) were computed between neighboring pixels along the line in (a). In (b), the horizontal axis corresponds to distance along the line, while the vertical axis signifies the magnitude of the color difference.

Figure 5.3: Original 256 by 256 pixel color image for subsequent results. The red plane is upper left; the green plane is upper right; the blue plane is bottom. The image contains both bright, highly saturated colors (the sails and buoy) and dull gray areas (the sky and ocean).

dimensional. However, we must now deal with the multidimensional nature of the color data. We describe three basic formulations using MRFs for color segmentation. In the first formulation, we transform from the original RGB data to a new color space such as the intensity, hue, saturation space and then choose a single component image from the new space (for example, hue). This converts the problem to a one dimensional space and the energy functionals from Equation 5.13 can be used. The second formulation, which we call a color difference-based approach, treats the energy functionals as an adiabatic system, i.e. the different processes have different convergence rates. The interpolation and data terms require three dimensional color vectors and are iterated separately from the line process update, which is still one dimensional. The two sets of equations are coupled through the line process discontinuities. The third approach allows any number of separate color component modules (e.g. intensity, hue, saturation, red green, blue, etc.), with each module treated as a one dimensional problem, and couples the line processes of each module together using additional energy terms. In this way, a line process discontinuity in one module (e.g. hue) effects the formation of a line process discontinuity in another module (e.g. saturation).

5.4.1 Color Transform Formulation

The simplest application of color in an MRF color segmentation framework

(a) Smoothed intensity

(b) Intensity edges

Figure 5.4: Color transform method. Images (a) and (b) show intensity regions and edges for Figure 5.3. All images processed were 256 by 256 pixels.

is to transform from the three dimensional RGB color space of the input data to a one dimensional space that contains the desired color information. Equation 5.13 describes the necessary constraints, and using the Hopfield update equations, we can solve for the state update equations as in Equations 5.19 through 5.21. This method has the advantage of being computationally simpler, although it has limited flexibility. In addition, use of hue requires modulo computation of differences between neighboring pixels since hue is measured as an angle (see [37]). Other color transforms do not separate hue from intensity or saturation, resulting in an ambiguous space for color segmentation. Figures 5.4 and 5.5 show the result for independent segmentations from intensity, hue, and saturation for the original 256 by 256 pixel image in Figure 5.3.

5.4.2 Color Difference Formulation

This section describes an MRF formulation for color segmentation that uses color difference techniques to break the surface at discontinuity sites. We treat the energy equations as an adiabatic system by first iterating one set until an equilibrium state is reached, then updating the second set, and repeating the process for a higher gain. The smooth color surface is defined by the terms E_i and E_d which are as follows:

$$E_I = \lambda \sum_{i,j} ((\mathbf{f}_{i,j+1} - \mathbf{f}_{i,j})^2 (1 - v_{i,j}) + (\mathbf{f}_{i+1,j} - \mathbf{f}_{i,j})^2 (1 - h_{i,j})) \qquad (5.28)$$

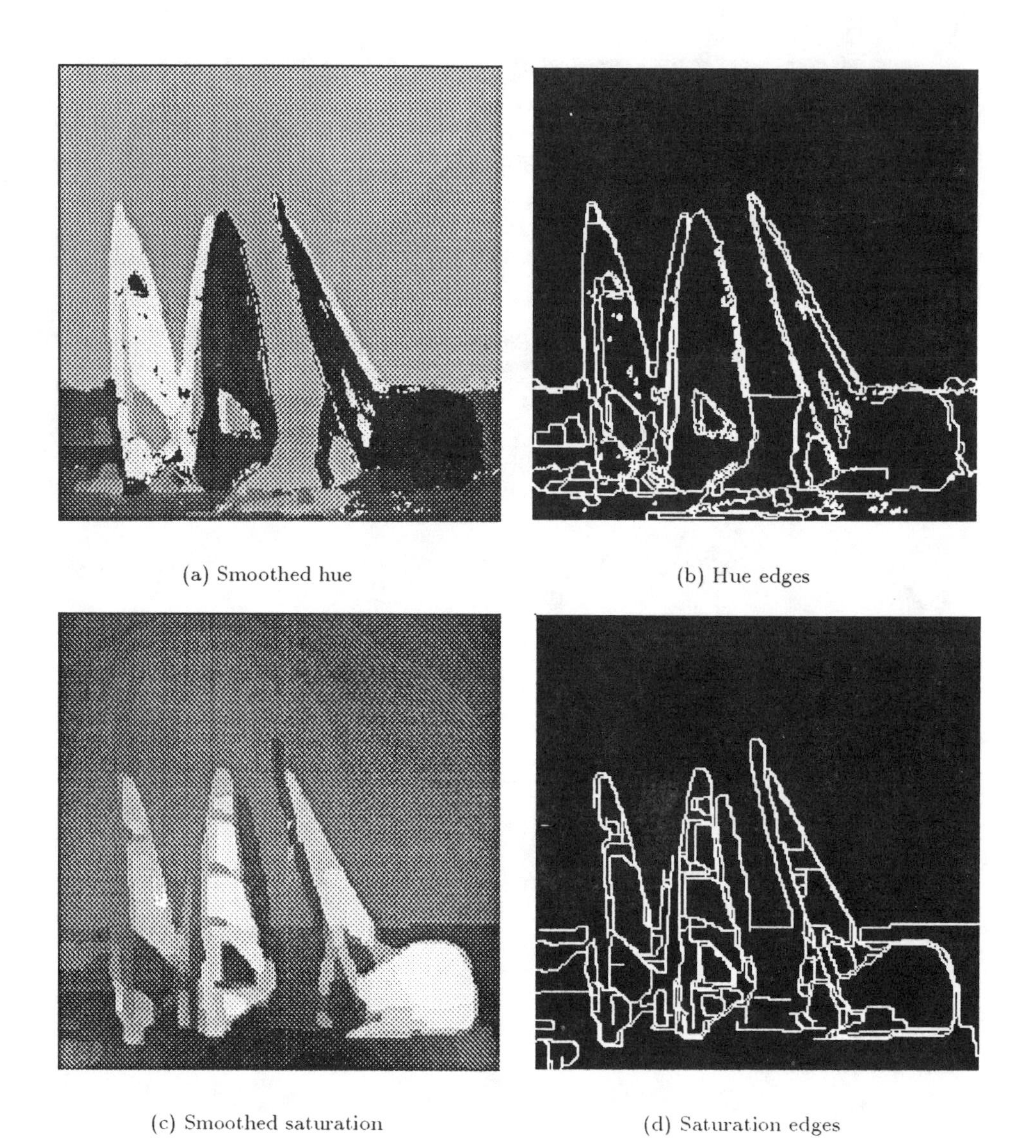

(a) Smoothed hue

(b) Hue edges

(c) Smoothed saturation

(d) Saturation edges

Figure 5.5: Color transform method showing hue and saturation regions and edges. Hue is displayed as an intensity, but is measured as an angle modulo 2π. White and black correspond to reddish hues, dark gray to greenish hues, and light gray to bluish hues. Saturation is also displayed as an intensity where brighter corresponds to higher saturation.

where E_I is the interpolation or smoothing energy and λ controls the degree of smoothness in the solution. The vector $\mathbf{f}$ represents the continuous-valued color process and is typically composed of red, green, and blue color components, and v and h correspond to the vertical and horizontal line processes respectively and vary continuously between 0 and 1. E_I contributes when the line process variables v and h are less than one (i.e. a discontinuity has not yet formed). The data term is defined as

$$E_D = \alpha \sum_{i,j} (\mathbf{f}_{i,j} - \mathbf{d}_{i,j})^2 \tag{5.29}$$

where the α parameter weights the importance of the input data, and $\mathbf{d}$ is a color process vector representing the observed color (RGB) input image. This term ties the resulting segmentation to the original input. For given constant values of v and h, these equations are minimized for $\mathbf{f}$ using a Hopfield network. The Hopfield update rule is:

$$\frac{d\mathbf{f}_{i,j}}{dt} = -\frac{\partial E}{\partial \mathbf{f}_{i,j}} \tag{5.30}$$

where $E = E_I + E_D$. Taking the derivatives and solving for the state variable $\mathbf{f}_{i,j}$ at equilibrium we obtain the following update equation:

$$\mathbf{f}_{i,j} = \frac{\lambda(L^v_{i,j}\mathbf{f}_{i,j+1} + L^v_{i,j-1}\mathbf{f}_{i,j-1} + L^h_{i,j}\mathbf{f}_{i+1,j} + L^h_{i-1,j}\mathbf{f}_{i-1,j}) + \alpha\mathbf{d}_{i,j}}{\lambda(L^v_{i,j} + L^v_{i,j-1} + L^h_{i,j} + L^h_{i-1,j}) + \alpha} \tag{5.31}$$

where $L^v_{i,j} = (1 - v_{i,j})$ and $L^h_{i,j} = (1 - h_{i,j})$. After equilibrium is reached, the following three equations are used to determine the values of v and h for the next step:

$$E_{Ic} = \lambda \sum_{i,j} ((\mathbf{f}_{i,j+1} \ominus \mathbf{f}_{i,j})^2(1 - v_{i,j}) + (\mathbf{f}_{i+1,j} \ominus \mathbf{f}_{i,j})^2(1 - h_{i,j})) \tag{5.32}$$

$$E_L = \beta \sum_{i,j} (v_{i,j} + h_{i,j}) \tag{5.33}$$

$$E_G = \sum_{i,j} \left(\int_0^{v_{i,j}} g^{-1}(v)\, dv + \int_0^{h_{i,j}} g^{-1}(h)\, dh \right) \tag{5.34}$$

In Equation 5.32, the symbol $\ominus$ represents a color difference scheme. Equation 5.33 is the cost for introducing a new line process discontinuity, where β represents the penalty for formation of a line process discontinuity. When the difference terms in E_{Ic} become larger than the line process penalty β, it becomes cheaper to add a discontinuity than to continue smoothing. Equation 5.34 forces the line processes to on (1) or off (0) states. g^{-1} is a sigmoid function, defined in Equation 5.15, for the line processes. The initial gain is nearly linear from 0 to 1 and, as the gain is increased, eventually becomes a step edge, at which time the discontinuities are driven to their final states. Once again, choosing the Hopfield update rule to minimize $E = E_{Ic} + E_L + E_G$,

$$\frac{dm_{i,j}}{dt} = -\frac{\partial E}{\partial v_{i,j}} \tag{5.35}$$

(a) Smoothed Maximum IHS

(b) Maximum IHS edges

Figure 5.6: Maximum IHS color difference method applied to Figure 5.3.

(a) Smoothed Euclidean RGB

(b) Euclidean RGB edges

Figure 5.7: Euclidean RGB color difference method applied to Figure 5.3.

$$\frac{dn_{i,j}}{dt} = -\frac{\partial E}{\partial h_{i,j}} \tag{5.36}$$

where m and n are internal state variables corresponding to the vertical and horizontal line processes respectively (i.e. $v_{i,j} = g(m_{i,j})$, and $h_{i,j} = g(n_{i,j})$). Taking the derivatives and solving for the state variables $m_{i,j}$ and $n_{i,j}$ at equilibrium we obtain the following update equations for the line process variables:

$$m_{i,j} = \lambda(\mathbf{f}_{i,j+1} \ominus \mathbf{f}_{i,j})^2 - \beta \tag{5.37}$$

$$n_{i,j} = \lambda(\mathbf{f}_{i+1,j} \ominus \mathbf{f}_{i,j})^2 - \beta \tag{5.38}$$

Since m and n (and thus v and h) are only dependent on the value of $\mathbf{f}$, the line process update occurs in one iteration. The new values of v and h are then used in the minimization of Equations 5.28 and 5.29 for a higher gain until the line process variables are forced to 0 or 1 states. Note that the color difference metric is applied only in the computation of the discontinuities, allowing a general framework to test many color differencing techniques and their effect on segmentation. The particular color difference chosen may also be a combination of several differencing techniques in some normalized coordinate space. This also has the effect of enhancing the discrimination capability available with a particular color differencing scheme at discontinuity sites. Breaks in the color surface $\mathbf{f}$ are applied equally to each of the RGB components of $\mathbf{f}$ since there is only one line process. Figures 5.6 and 5.7 show the results when the maximum IHS and Euclidean RGB color difference methods are used on the image from Figure 5.3. Since hue is a more sensitive measure than intensity, saturation, or Euclidean RGB, the edges tend to form thicker around large color differences due to the bleeding of color across physical color boundaries in the original image.

5.4.3 Multiple Module Formulations

A third approach treats color segmentation as a data fusion problem. Each component of a color image is treated as a separate coupled MRF with continuous and line process fields. The separate coupled MRFs are linked by coupling terms through the line process discontinuities [45]. For the k-th MRF, the following coupling term (added to Equation 5.13) defines the interaction between the k-th and l-th MRFs with line process variables v_k and h_k:

$$+\sum_{i,j}\sum_{l} C_{kl}[(1 - v_{k,i,j})v_{l,i,j} + (1 - h_{k,i,j})h_{l,i,j}] \tag{5.39}$$

where l varies over all modules interacting with the k-th module. Each term acts to increase the cost of a horizontal or vertical line process (v_k or h_k) remaining off when the corresponding line process in the other MRF module (v_l or h_l, $l \neq k$) is on. The coupling weight C_{kl} scales the influence of the l-th module on the k-th module. The line process update equations for the k-th module then become

$$m_{k,i,j} = \lambda(f_{k,i,j+1} - f_{k,i,j})^2 - \beta + \sum_{l} C_{kl} v_{l,i,j} \tag{5.40}$$

$$n_{k,i,j} = \lambda(f_{k,i+1,j} - f_{k,i,j})^2 - \beta + \sum_{l} C_{kl} h_{l,i,j} \tag{5.41}$$

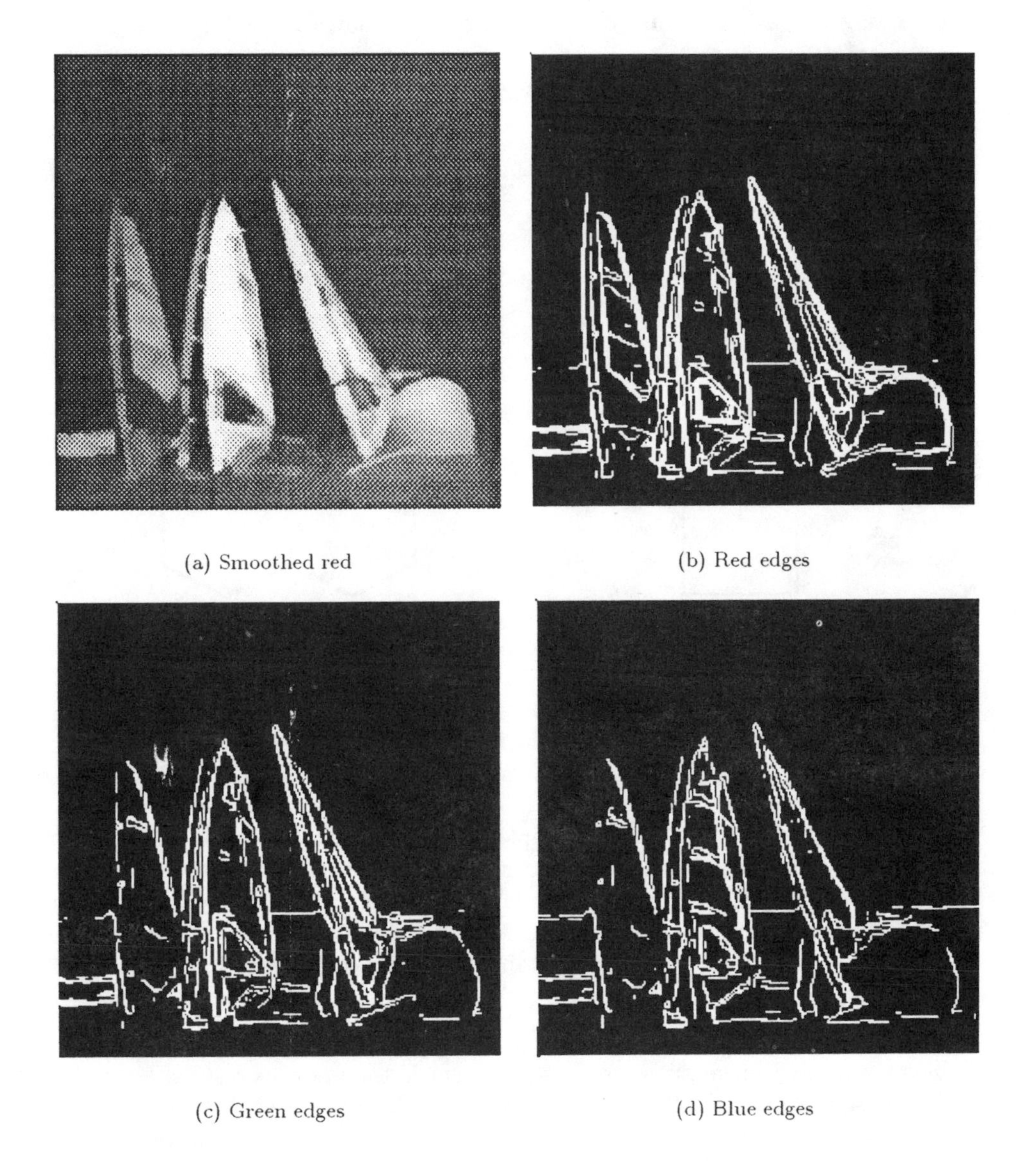

(a) Smoothed red

(b) Red edges

(c) Green edges

(d) Blue edges

Figure 5.8: Multiple module formulation applied to Figure 5.3. The upper left image shows smooth regions in the red plane (green and blue are similar). The remaining images show the corresponding edges for the red, green, and blue planes.

In its simplest form, one dominant module influences the formation of discontinuities in all other modules [8]. For example, discontinuities in intensity strongly influence formation of discontinuities in hue and saturation by setting the coupling weights so $C_{intensity} << C_{hue}$ or $C_{saturation}$. Figure 5.8 shows the results when the red, green, and blue image planes are coupled unbiased for Figure 5.3.

5.4.4 Hexagonal Lattices

The underlying lattice structure for the color and line processes plays an im-

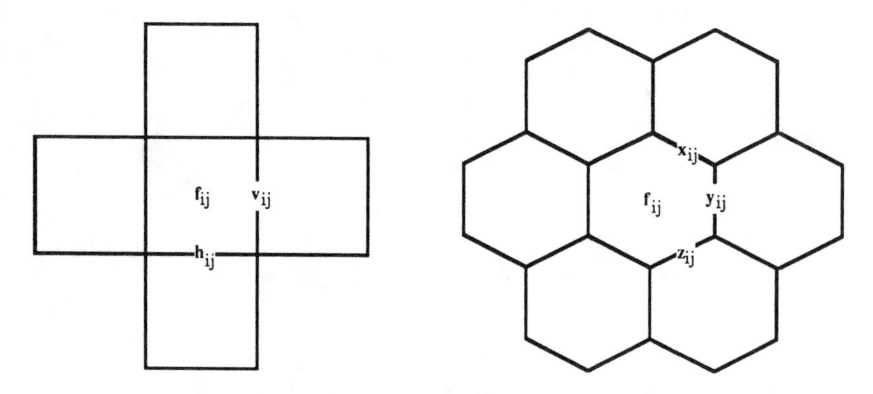

Figure 5.9: Lattice and line process locations for rectangular and hexagonal cases.

portant role in the quality and structure of the segmentation. The simplest lattice structure is a rectangular grid, and the line processes are defined over some neighborhood of a pixel. By adjusting the energy function, larger cliques (neighbors of a site) encompassing additional directional and topographical structures can be heuristically added [8, 11]. For example, line process energies which penalize the formation of adjacent parallel discontinuities may be added. For the rectangular case, as we have seen, the line process can be broken into two components, horizontal and vertical, corresponding to the nearest neighbor, 4-connected system. Each of the four neighbors is of equal distance from the central pixel and is weighted identically.

Vertical and horizontal line processes on a rectangular lattice suffer from a bias toward rectilinear structures, as is evident in the previous results. For natural terrain imagery where 90° angles are rare, the effects are especially noticeable. In his book, *Robot Vision*, Horn gives three important advantages of hexagonal grids for computer vision [21]. Hexagonal grids allow improved sampling and quantization during the image formation process, markedly improve the understanding of connectivity (since all neighbors touch a center pixel), and allow easy use of edge detection masks (e.g. Laplacian masks). For our purposes, hexagonal lattices in an MRF allow increased resolution of the line process and replace the unnatural rectilinear bias with a hexagonal and triangular bias much more suitable to natural imagery. A given site in the hexagonal lattice has six equally distant neighbors and three different line process directions, each at 120° angles, as shown in Figure 5.9. In addition, modifying the energy terms used in the rectangular case is straightforward, as discussed below. The major disadvantage to using a hexagonal lattice is the reduction in resolution required to simulate hexagonal sampling from a rectangularly sampled image [2]. Increased accuracy in the hexagonal sampling can be achieved by increasing the size of the hexagons in the lattice and thus decreasing the effect of the digitization bias of the rectangular grid.

The energy terms for the hexagonal case are similar to those for the rectangular lattice discussed earlier, with the exception that three line processes must be used, and special indexing for even and odd rows must be included. The new energy terms for the simple color transform formulation are:

$$\begin{aligned} E_I &= \lambda \sum_{i,j} ((\mathbf{f}_{i-1,k} - \mathbf{f}_{i,j})^2 (1 - x_{i,j}) + (\mathbf{f}_{i,j+1} - \mathbf{f}_{i,j})^2 (1 - y_{i,j}) \\ &\quad + (\mathbf{f}_{i+1,k} - \mathbf{f}_{i,j})^2 (1 - z_{i,j})) \qquad (5.42) \\ E_D &= \alpha \sum_{i,j} (\mathbf{f}_{i,j} - \mathbf{d}_{i,j})^2 \qquad (5.43) \\ E_L &= \beta \sum_{i,j} (x_{i,j} + y_{i,j} + z_{i,j}) \qquad (5.44) \\ E_G &= \sum_{i,j} (\int_0^{x_{i,j}} g^{-1}(x)\, dx + \int_0^{y_{i,j}} g^{-1}(y)\, dy + \int_0^{z_{i,j}} g^{-1}(z)\, dz) \qquad (5.45) \end{aligned}$$

where x, y, and z are the line processes labelled in Figure 5.9. The subscript k is set based on whether the current site is on an even or odd row as follows:

$$k = j + 1 \quad (i \text{ even})$$

$$k = j \quad (i \text{ odd})$$

As in the rectangular case, using Hopfield's update rule $d\mathbf{f}_{i,j}/dt = -\partial E/\partial \mathbf{f}_{i,j}$, $da_{i,j}/dt = -\partial E/\partial x_{i,j}$, $db_{i,j}/dt = -\partial E/\partial y_{i,j}$, and $dc_{i,j}/dt = -\partial E/\partial z_{i,j}$, we can solve for the values of $a_{i,j}$, $b_{i,j}$, $c_{i,j}$, and $\mathbf{f}_{i,j}$, which correspond to the three line processes, $x_{i,j}$, $y_{i,j}$, and $z_{i,j}$ and the color process, respectively. Let $L^x_{i,j} = (1 - x_{i,j})$, $L^y_{i,j} = (1 - y_{i,j})$, and $L^z_{i,j} = (1 - z_{i,j})$. Then the update rule for $\mathbf{f}_{i,j}$ is

$$\begin{aligned} \mathbf{f}_{i,j} &= \frac{\lambda(Lx + Ly + Lz) + \alpha d_{i,j}}{\lambda(L^x_{i,j} + L^x_{i+1,s2} + L^y_{i,j} + L^y_{i,j-1} + L^z_{i,j} + L^z_{i-1,s2}) + \alpha} \qquad (5.46) \\ a_{i,j} &= \lambda(\mathbf{f}_{i-1,k} - \mathbf{f}_{i,j})^2 - \beta \qquad (5.47) \\ b_{i,j} &= \lambda(\mathbf{f}_{i,j+1} - \mathbf{f}_{i,j})^2 - \beta \qquad (5.48) \\ c_{i,j} &= \lambda(\mathbf{f}_{i+1,k} - \mathbf{f}_{i,j})^2 - \beta \qquad (5.49) \end{aligned}$$

with

$$Lx = L^x_{i,j}\mathbf{f}_{i-1,s1} + L^x_{i+1,s2}\mathbf{f}_{i+1,s2}$$

$$Ly = L^y_{i,j}\mathbf{f}_{i,j+1} + L^y_{i,j-1}\mathbf{f}_{i,j-1}$$

[2]This problem is purely an artifact of the rectangular grid CCD cameras used. A camera properly designed for computer vision research would use a hexagonal tesselation of photoreceptors.

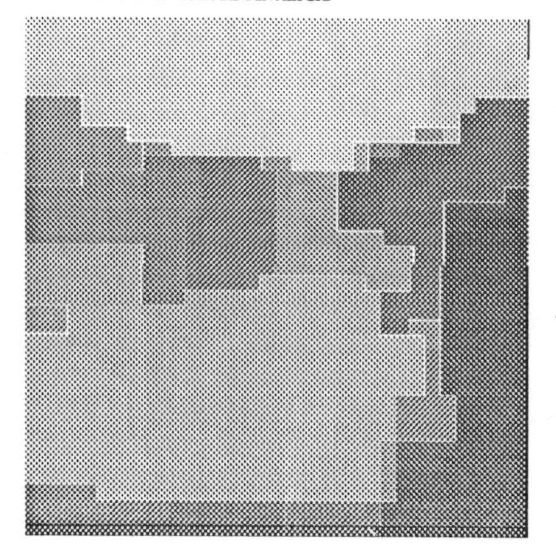

(a) Rectangular result

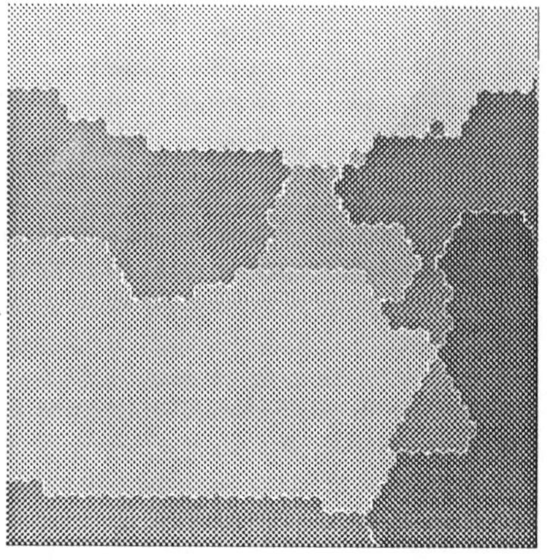

(b) Hexagonal result

Figure 5.10: Comparison of rectangular and hexagonal lattice effects on line process formation (35x40 pixel lattice).

$$Lz = L^z_{i,j}\mathbf{f}_{i+1,s1} + L^z_{i-1,s2}\mathbf{f}_{i-1,s2}$$

where s1 and s2 are defined as

$$s1 = j + 1,\ s2 = j \quad (i \text{ even})$$

$$s1 = j,\ s2 = j - 1 \quad (i \text{ odd})$$

and k is defined as above. Figure 5.10 shows a comparison of the results for the rectangular and hexagonal grids applied to a natural terrain image with identical line process penalty values and using the maximum IHS difference, as mentioned in Section 5.3. Both MRFs were computed on 35x40 lattices (so hexagons have approximately 14 pixel width) sub-sampled from an original 512x512 image.

5.5 PARAMETER SELECTION

As in most early vision algorithms, coupled MRF methods require a number of parameters. In this section we analyze the significance of three parameters: the line process penalty β, the smoothness weight λ, and the data weight α.

Recall from Equation 5.13 that parameter λ controls the degree of smoothing in the interpolation term. Higher values of λ increase the amount of smoothing. The data weighting term, α, controls the importance of the input data. Higher values of α place more confidence in the validity of the input data, while lower values are desirable for noisy data. The line process penalty, β, penalizes the formation of discontinuities. Higher values of β will restrict the formation of line process discontinuities and thereby allow increased smoothing. Each of these parameters may be set locally depending on characteristics of the problem.

Coupling of the input data d to the smooth intensity process u is controlled by α. When the noise model for the input data is known, α may be set accordingly. For example, when the random noise is assumed to have a Gaussian distribution, $\alpha = \frac{1}{\sigma^2}$ where σ is the standard deviation [31]. As $\alpha \rightarrow \infty$, the data is assumed noiseless and the result will equal the input data. For $\alpha = 0$, no coupling occurs between u and d. The ratio of λ to α may be used to control the amount of confidence in the input as well as the degree of smoothing (i.e. either λ or α may be one), thus reducing the number of explicit parameters. In the absence of discontinuities, this ratio has a physical interpretation in analog resistive grids [17].

Understanding of the line process parameter β is far more elusive and tends to be data dependent. There are clear critical ranges for selection of β across a broad range of inputs. An inverse logarithmic relation between β and the discontinuity of the smooth process has been observed [4]. As β increases beyond the elbow of the inverse log curve, smoothness takes over. As β approaches zero, discontinuities prevail, and at zero, all line process values will be set, allowing no smoothness (analogous to $\alpha \rightarrow \infty$). The value of β may be chosen automatically from the data by analyzing the discontinuity inherent in the data, however, this assumes at least an estimate of knowledge we are trying to extract. When λ is set to one and α chosen to embody the noise constraints of the input and the amount of smoothness desired, the ratio of β to α is significant. By increasing this ratio, more discontinuities will form, while lowering the ratio produces fewer discontinuities and increases smoothing. By analyzing the ratios of the different parameters, fewer explicit parameters are needed at the expense of decreased control.

Blake and Zisserman have analyzed the relationship between λ and β in simple cases where an isolated step discontinuity and adjacent step discontinuities occur [2]. Their analysis sets bounds on the magnitude of a step which will be detected for given values of λ and β (or equivalently, when a step of known magnitude should be detected, what values of λ and β should be). In their discussion, λ is described as a length or scale parameter since its effect on the formation of discontinuities is to decrease the length of edges as the parameter decreases. This analysis may be applied similarly to the line process penalty β. For example, the line process penalty β will tend to cause a decrease in the length of discontinuities as the parameter increases, making it harder for discontinuities to form.

Letting $\gamma = \sqrt{\lambda}$, when adjacent discontinuities exist, a step of magnitude h_1 will be detected if $h_1 > \sqrt{\frac{\beta}{\gamma}}$, a relationship they call the contrast ratio. This analysis holds for simple steps and does not allow for complex interaction of multiple discontinuities. They describe a method for adaptively setting the contrast ratio at local pixels by computing a proportional measure of the average such that $h_1(x,y) = \eta I_{av}(x,y)$. To avoid double edges in the output, $\eta > \sqrt{\frac{2}{\gamma}}$. For two interacting discontinuities (in one dimension) a distance d apart such that $d << \gamma$, a discontinuity of magnitude h_2 will be found only when $h_2 > h_1\sqrt{\frac{\gamma}{d}}$ where h_1 is the contrast ratio. Therefore, when two discontinuities interact in one dimension, the minimum step magnitude must be greater for equal parameter values in order to locate the discontinuities. They have also defined a limit on the gradient of the intensity surface above which spurious discontinuities will form, $g_l = \frac{h_1}{2\gamma}$. If the surface is too steep over longer scale, multiple breaks in the surface will result.

Several researchers have suggested varying parameters in MRF formulations to obtain generalized scale space descriptions of the data [2, 9]. Geiger and Yuille propose tracking a path through parameter space by watching solutions vary as the parameters change. By differentiating the energy equations (in their case the mean field equations) with respect to the parameters, they obtain first-order equations describing how the solution varies relative to the parameters. They also point out that tracking solutions in parameter space by repeatedly minimizing the energy functionals for different parameter values may be more robust than by computing explicit partial derivatives with respect to the parameters.

5.5.1 Experimental Analysis of λ, β, and α

Due to the difficulty of analytically determining values for three interrelated parameters with two dimensional images and real data, experimental analysis may provide clues to methods for setting parameters. In previous work [5], we used constraints on the values the parameters could assume in order to force the energy to be minimal at the extremes of the parameter range. In their paper on objective function optimization, Yuille and Gennert describe several constraints on parameters so that the total energy of the solution for different parameter values reaches a maximum between the minimal extremes [12]. They claim that the maximum energy solution of many minimum energy solutions represents a balance between the different components that ensures each will be adequately represented in the solution. The simplest constraint applies to λ and α for a fixed value of β such that $\lambda + \alpha = 1.0$. The value of λ is varied from 0.0 to 1.0 (so $\alpha = 1.0 - \lambda$), producing a typical energy plot as in Figure 5.11. When $\lambda = 0.0$, the solution equals the data, while for $\lambda = 1.0$ the solution is completely smooth. This method of setting λ and α is not adequate for dealing with the line process term, and tends to produce fragmented edges.

A better constraint for multiple energy terms is to force the parameter values to lie on a sphere, that is $\lambda^2 + \alpha^2 + \beta^2 = 1.0$. In order to choose values for the parameters that are meaningful, we may force a ratio between two of the parameters and vary the third from 0.0 to 1.0 while satifying the constraint. For example, if $\frac{\beta}{\alpha} = k$, then as λ increases from 0.0 to 1.0, $\alpha = \sqrt{\frac{(1-\lambda^2)}{(k^2+1)}}$ and $\beta = k\alpha$. This does not yield good results because α is too large for most of the range (i.e. a large ratio of λ and β to α is important). On the other hand, the resulting solutions for constant λ to α and β to α are reasonable (see [5] for details). Figure 5.12 shows the energy plot for constant $\frac{\lambda}{\alpha} = 100.0$. This approach holds promise for selecting parameters, but additional research is required.

5.6 CONCLUSION

This paper has presented a review of the basic energy-based approach to early vision processing, with emphasis on the topic of color segmentation. We described several techniques for computing color differences which are central to the problem of color segmentation. These were then incorporated in three formulations for color segmentation which addressed the color difference problem at different

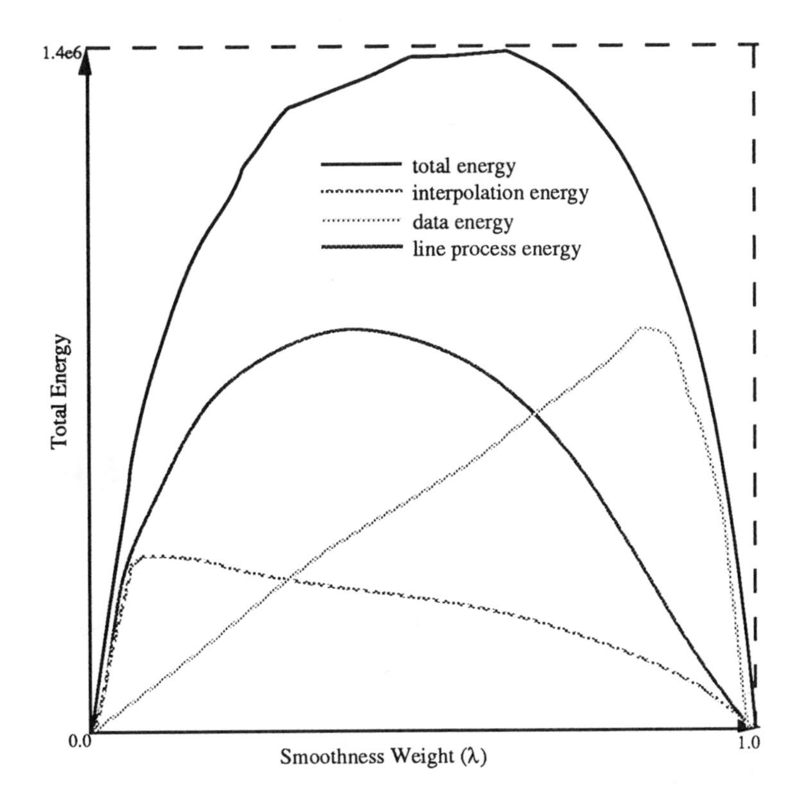

Figure 5.11: The total energy of each component plotted against values of the smoothness weight λ for a typical image. The maximum peak near the center should represent a reasonable set of parameter values, excluding the line process.

stages. In the color transform case, a color transformation was computed in advance and a one-dimensional smooth surface segmented in the transform space. In the color difference case, the energy equations were treated as an adiabatic system by first iterating to produce a smooth surface, recomputing discontinuities, and then repeating the process for a higher gain until convergence. This approach had the advantage of directly applying a color difference formulae to a single line process while smoothing the original RGB color vector. In the multiple module case, the color segmentation problem was treated as a data fusion problem by coupling multiple color planes and discontinuity planes. This approach offered flexibility but added several new coupling parameters. Finally, we reviewed details concerning the meaning and appropriate values of important parameters. A method of analyzing the effect of parameters on segmentation results by constraining the ratios of certain parameters while varying another parameter was presented.

The wide variety of early vision problems that have been addressed within the framework of MRFs demonstrate the power and flexibility of these methods. Applied to the problem of color segmentation, the MRF energy formulation offers a useful method for smoothing color regions without destroying important information at discontinuities.

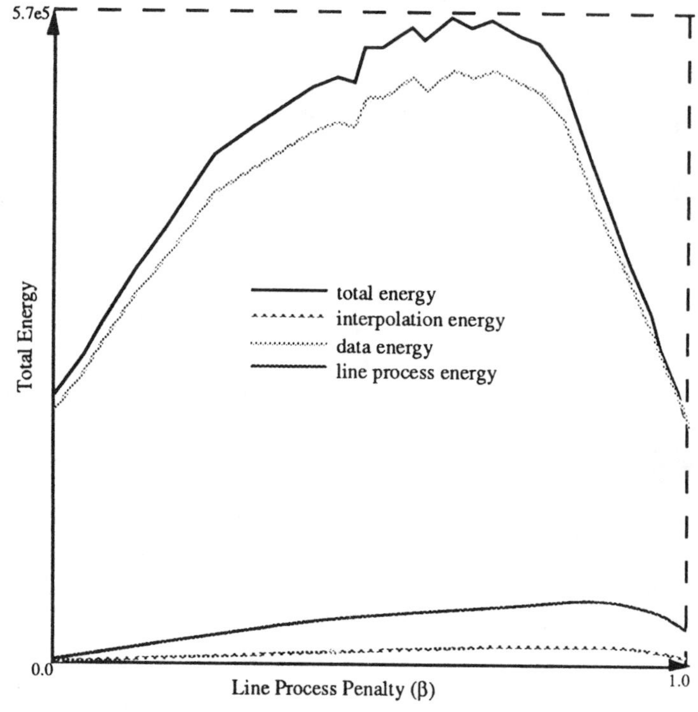

Figure 5.12: The total energy of each component plotted against values of the line process penalty β for a typical image using a spherical constraint. The maximum peak near the center represents a reasonable set of parameter values.

Acknowledgements

The author thanks the Hughes Artificial Intelligence Center staff, directed by David Tseng, for continued support. In addition, Scott Toborg provided insight into the theory of MRFs and regularization.

References

[1] J.Y. Aloimonos and D. Shulman. *Integration of Visual Modules.* Academic Press, 1989.

[2] A. Blake and A. Zisserman. *Visual Reconstruction.* MIT Press, 1987.

[3] P. Chou and C. Brown. Multimodal reconstruction and segmentation with markov random fields and hcf optimization. In *Proceedings of the DARPA Image Understanding Workshop*, pages 214–221, Cambridge, MA, April 1988.

[4] M.J. Daily. Color image segmentation using markov random fields. In *Computer Vision and Pattern Recognition*, June 4 1989.

[5] M.J. Daily. Parameter studies for markov random field models of early vision. In *Visual Information Processing: From Neurons to Chips*, volume 1473, pages 138–152. SPIE, April 1991.

[6] M.J. Daily, J.G. Harris, K.E. Olin, K. Reiser, D.Y. Tseng, and F.M. Vilnrotter. Knowledge-based vision techniques annual technical report. Technical report, U.S. Army ETL, October 1987.

[7] D.A. Forsythe. A novel approach to colour constancy. In *IEEE International Conference on Computer Vision*, pages 9–18, 1988.

[8] E. Gamble and T. Poggio. Visual integration and the detection of discontinuities: the key role of intensity edges. AI Memo 970, MIT Artificial Intelligence Laboratory, October 1987.

[9] D. Geiger and F. Girosi. Mean field theory for surface reconstruction. In *Image Understanding Workshop*, pages 617–630, 1989.

[10] D. Geiger and A. Yuille. A common framework for image segmentation. AI Memo 89-7, Harvard University, 1989.

[11] S. Geman and D. Geman. Stochastic relaxation, gibbs distributions, and the bayesian restoration of images. *IEEE Transactions on Pattern Analysis and Machine Intelligence*, PAMI-6:721–741, June 1984.

[12] M. A. Gennert and A. Yuille. Determining the optimal weights in multiple objective function optimization. In *IEEE ICCV 2*, pages 87–89, 1988.

[13] W.E.L. Grimson. *From Images to Surfaces: A computational study of the human early visual system.* MIT Press, Cambridge, MA, 1981.

[14] S. Grossberg and M. Kuperstein. *Neural Dynamics of Adaptive Sensor-Motor Control.* Pergamon Press, 1989.

[15] J. Hadamard. *Lectures on the Cauchy Problem in Linear Differential Equations.* Yale University Press, 1923.

[16] A.R. Hanson and E.M. Riseman. *Segmentation of Natural Scenes*, pages 129–163. Academic Press, Orlando, FL, 1978.

[17] J.G. Harris, C. Koch, J. Luo, and J. Wyatt. *Resistive Fuses: Analog Hardware for Detecting Discontinuities in Early Vision*, chapter 3, page 80. Klumer, Norewell, MA, 1989.

[18] G. Healey and T. Binford. A color metric for computer vision. In *DARPA Image Understanding Workshop*, pages 854–861, Cambridge, MA, April 1988.

[19] E.C. Hildreth. *The Measurement of Visual Motion.* MIT Press, Cambridge, MA, 1984.

[20] J.J. Hopfield and D.W. Tank. "neural" computation of decision in optimization problems. *Biological Cybernetics*, 52:141–152, 1985.

[21] B.K.P. Horn. *Robot Vision.* MIT Press, Cambridge, MA, 1986.

[22] B.K.P. Horn and B.G. Schunck. Determining optic flow. *Artificial Intelligence*, 17:185–203, 1981.

[23] J.R. Jordan and A.C. Bovik. Computational stereo vision using color. *IEEE Control Systems Magazine*, pages 31–36, June 1988.

[24] J. Kender. Saturation, hue, and normalized color: Calculation, digitization effects, and use. Technical report, Department of Computer Science, Carnegie Mellon University, 1976.

[25] S. Kirkpatrik, C.D. Gelatt, and M.P. Vecchi. Optimization by simulated annealing. *Science*, 220(4598):671–680, May 13 1983.

[26] G.J. Klinker, S.A. Shafer, and T. Kanade. The measurement of highlights in color images. *International Journal of Computer Vision*, 2(1):7–32, June 1988.

[27] C. Koch, J. Marroquin, and A. Yuille. Analog "neuronal" networks in early vision. AI Memo 751, MIT Artificial Intelligence Laboratory, June 1985.

[28] E.H. Land. Recent advances in retinex theory. *Vision Research*, 26(7), 1986.

[29] P. Lennie and M. D'Zmura. Mechanisms of color vision. *CRC Critical Reviews in Neurobiology*, 3:333–400, 1988.

[30] D.G. Luenberger. *Linear and Nonlinear Programming.* Addison-Wesley, 1984.

[31] J.L. Marroquin. Probablistic solutions of inverse problems. Technical Report 860, MIT Artificial Intelligence Laboratory, September 1985.

[32] J.L. Marroquin, S. Mitter, and T. Poggio. Probabilistic solution of ill-posed problems in computational vision. AI Memo 897, MIT Artificial Intelligence Laboratory, March 1987.

[33] C. Mead and M. Ismail (eds.). *Analog VLSI Implementation of Neural Systems.* Klumer, 1989.

[34] R. Ohlander, K. Price, and D.R. Reddy. Picture segmentation using a recursive region splitting method. *Computer Graphics and Image Processing*, 8:313–333, 1978.

[35] Y. Ohta, T. Kanade, and T. Sakai. Color information for region segmentation. *Computer Graphics and Image Processing*, 13:222–231, 1980.

[36] A. Pentland. A possible neural mechanism for computing shape from shading. *Neural Computation*, 1:208–217, 1989.

[37] F. Perez and C. Koch. Color segmentation in hue space. Tr, California Institute of Technology, 1990.

[38] T. Poggio, E. Gamble, and J.J. Little. Parallel integration of vision modules. *Science*, 242:436–440, October 1988.

[39] T. Poggio and C. Koch. Ill-posed problems in early vison : from computational theory to analogue networks. *Proceedings of the Royal Society of London*, B 266:303–323, 1985.

[40] T. Poggio and V. Torre. Ill-posed problems and regularization analysis in early vision. AI Memo 773, MIT Artificial Intelligence Laboratory, 1984.

[41] M.J. Swain. Color indexing. technical report 360, University of Rochester, November 1990.

[42] D. Terzopoulos. Multilevel computational processes for visual surface reconstruction. *Computer Vision, Graphics, and Image Processing*, 24:52–96, 1983.

[43] C. Thorpe, S. Shafer, and T. Kanade. Vision and navigation for the carnegie mellon navlab. In *DARPA Image Understanding Workshop*, pages 143–152, Los Angeles, CA, February 1987.

[44] A.N. Tikhonov and V.Y. Arsenin / translated by F.John. *Solutions of Ill-Posed Problems.* V.H. Winston and Sons, Washington, D.C., 1977.

[45] S.T. Toborg and K. Huang. Cooperative vision integration through data-parallel neural computations. *IEEE Transactions on Computers*, 40(12):1368–1379, December 1991.

[46] J.T. Tou and R.C. Gonzalez. *Pattern Recognition Principles.* Addison-Wesley, 1982.

[47] S. Ullman. Relaxation and constrained optimization by local processes. *Computer Graphics and Image Processing*, 10:115–125, 1979.

[48] R.S. Wallace and T. Kanade. Finding hierarchical clusters by entropy minimization. In *DARPA Image Understanding Workshop*, pages 1105–1116, Palo Alto, CA, May 1989.

[49] W.A. Wright. A markov random field approach to data fusion and colour segmentation. *Image and Vision Computing*, 7(2):144–150, 1989.

[50] G. Wyszecki and W.S. Stiles. *Color Science: Concepts and Methods, Quantitative Data and Formulae.* John Wiley and Sons, New York, NY, 1982.

[51] Y.T. Zhou, R.Chellappa, A. Vaid, and B.K. Jenkins. Image restoration using a neural network. *IEEE Transactions on Acoustics, Speech, and Signal Processing*, 36(7):1141–1151, July 1988.

Chapter 6

Rewo's Filter and Image Segmentation

A. Niu, W. G. Wee

6.1 Introduction

Segmentation is one of the most important steps in automated image analysis. According to Pratt,[1] "Segmentation of an image entails the division or separation of the image into regions of similar attribute." Many attributes can be utilized to segment objects from their background. In this chapter, the boundary sharpness is taken as the similar attribute.

In the chapter, we first briefly review Rewo's filter[2] and analyze its behavior, then discuss its potential for practical applications. It turns out that under certain conditions, the output of the filter is proportional to the sum of the second-order partial derivatives of the image surface at the processed point. Taking the advantage of this property of Rewo's filter, we can use it not only to detect concave (or convex) patterns in an image for segmentation, but also to classify these patterns. Since a convex surface will look like a concave surface if we look at it in the opposite direction, hereafter we use only the term concave to indicate both convex and concave surface unless mentioned otherwise.

As an example of application of this image segmentation method, the detection and classification of water droplets in a two-dimentional image is given in detail. The effects of water droplet ingestion into turbine engines resulting from heavy rain and wheel spray generated on a wet runway is of importance.[3] The effects of water ingestion in engine performance have been investigated by Murthy et. al[4] and a probe for stagnation pressure measurement in a droplet laden airflow was developed.[5] The adverse effects of large quantities of water ingestion can include the compressor stall and combustor flame-out. Even smaller quantities of ingested water may affect engine matching, trimming and controls[4]. Engine certification requirement as set forth in FAA regulations[6] call for continued engine operation at takeoff and flight idle conditions while ingesting water at four percent by weight of airflow, generated by a spray of simulated rain. There is also a certification requirement on the entire aircraft system which dictates that the system must be designed to prevent hazardous quantities of water from being ingested into the engine during takeoff, landing, and taxing operations.[7] There are several mechanical, electrical and optical methods available for droplet size determination in fuel sprays as surveyed by Jones[8] and McCreath and Beer.[9] Parikh et al[3] have developed a non-intrusive optical technique for the determination of drop sizes, spatial distribution of drops at the nacelle inlet plane and instantaneous mass flow rate of liquid water entering the nacelle. A simple thresholding criterion was used to detect the droplet region based on the observation that the contrast between the images of droplets within the light sheet and the background is very sharp. In this chapter, the Rewo's filter is utilized to deal with water droplet segmentation and identification problem. The experimental results obtained are very satisfactory.

6.2 Review of Rewo's Enhancement and Detection Approaches

Originally, the enhancement and detection approaches developed by Rewo,[2] were used to evaluate aerial photographs of forest, i.e., to carry out an automatic tree counting operation. We call these approaches Rewo's filter. Since the approaches are applicable for processing concave objects in the image, it is expected that these approaches would be suitable to analyzing any blobs that have concave graylevel images.

6.2.1 Image model

An object is said to be convex (concave) if its image graylevel distribution f(x,y) is a convex (concave) function, possibly corrupted by noise. The image of a tree can be modeled by a convex intensity function f(x, y), and this function may be described by a second order polynomial as

$$z(x, y) = f(x, y) = b_1x^2 + b_2y^2 + b_3xy + b_4x + b_5y + b_6 \tag{6.1}$$

where (x, y): the coordinates of a pixel; z: the greylevel of pixel (x, y); and b_i (i = 1, 2, ..., 6): unknown parameters. We call this image model Model 1.

6.2.2 Regression model and the least squares method

Consider a process with n input-output pairs (observations): $(\mathbf{u}_1, z_1), ..., (\mathbf{u}_n, z_n)$ and assume that the process may be described by the model

$$\hat{z}_j = b_1h_1(\mathbf{u}_j) + b_2h_2(\mathbf{u}_j) + ... + b_kh_k(\mathbf{u}_j) \tag{6.2}$$

where $\mathbf{u}_j$ (j = 1, 2, ..., n) is the input vector of the process; $h_i(\mathbf{u}_j)$ (i = 1, 2, ..., k) the function of $\mathbf{u}_j$; k the number of parameters; and $\hat{z}_j$ the estimated value of z_j. Hereafter we call this model Model 2. Going still further, we define the vector of process outputs

$$\mathbf{Z} = [\, z_1 \ z_2 \ ... \ z_n]^T \tag{6.3}$$

and an n×k matrix of function $h_i(\mathbf{u}_j)$:

$$\mathbf{U} = \begin{bmatrix} h_1(\mathbf{u}_1) & ... & h_k(\mathbf{u}_1) \\ ... & & ... \ ... \\ h_1(\mathbf{u}_n) & ... & h_k(\mathbf{u}_n) \end{bmatrix} \tag{6.4}$$

By using Model 2 and assigning the coordinates for each pixel within predefined neighborhood (window), the elements of **U** can be easily calculated. Then Model 2 can be rewritten in matrix form as

$$\hat{\mathbf{Z}} = \mathbf{Ub}; \tag{6.5}$$

where $\hat{\mathbf{Z}} = [\ \hat{z}_1\ \ \hat{z}_2\ \ldots\ \hat{z}_n]^T$ and $\mathbf{b} = [\ b_1\ \ b_2\ \ldots\ b_k]^T$. At this point, the sum of squares of differences $(\hat{z}_j - z_j)$, j = 1, 2, ..., n may now be written as

$$\mathbf{S} = (\mathbf{Z} - \mathbf{Ub})^T(\mathbf{Z} - \mathbf{Ub}) \tag{6.6}$$

The least square method requires that the value of **S** be minimum. When $\frac{d\mathbf{S}}{d\mathbf{b}} = \mathbf{0}$, we obtain

$$\hat{\mathbf{b}} = [\mathbf{U}^T\mathbf{U}]^{-1}\mathbf{U}^T\mathbf{Z} \tag{6.7}$$

where $\hat{\mathbf{b}} = [\ \hat{b}_1\ \hat{b}_2\ \ldots\ \hat{b}_k]^T$ is so called the least estimate of the parameters **b**. Expression 6.7 shows that $\hat{\mathbf{b}}$ is the function of both coordinates (represented by **U**) and graylevles (represented by **Z**) of the pixels within a given window. By substituting $\hat{\mathbf{b}}$ for **b** in Expression 6.5, the predicted value of **Z** can be given by

$$\hat{\mathbf{Z}} = \mathbf{U}\hat{\mathbf{b}} \tag{6.8}$$

6.2.3 Rewo's mask and detector

Suppose the domain under consideration is a square window with size being W×W. If we let the central pixel, $Z_{0,0}$, have coordinates (0,0), then the predicted value for the central pixel can be derived as

$$\hat{Z}_{0,0} = \hat{b}_6 \tag{6.9}$$

This is because that for the central pixel the middle row of **U** in Expression 6.8 is always structured as [0 0 0 0 0 1]. It is worth to note that the value of $\hat{b}_6$ is the linear combination of the pixel graylevels within the window. Thus, the calculation of $\hat{Z}_{0,0}$ is equivalent to applying a fixed mask to the processed image.

$$E(7)=\frac{1}{147}\begin{bmatrix} -7 & -2 & 1 & 2 & 1 & -2 & -7 \\ -2 & 3 & 6 & 7 & 6 & 3 & -2 \\ 1 & 6 & 9 & 10 & 9 & 6 & 1 \\ 2 & 7 & 10 & 11 & 10 & 7 & 2 \\ 1 & 6 & 9 & 10 & 9 & 6 & 1 \\ -2 & 3 & 6 & 7 & 6 & 3 & -2 \\ -7 & -2 & 1 & 2 & 1 & -2 & -7 \end{bmatrix} \qquad (6.10)$$

When W = 7, we have a 7×7 fixed mask, E(7), as shown above. Rewo called Regression Mask like E(7) enhancement mask, for it can enhance all second order surfaces, convex as well as concave. From mask E(7), a concave object detector, D(7) as given by Expression 6.11, has been derived by subtracting $\frac{1}{7\times 7}$ from each element of

$$D(7)=\frac{1}{147}\begin{bmatrix} -10 & -5 & -2 & -1 & -2 & -5 & -10 \\ -5 & 0 & 3 & 4 & 3 & 0 & -5 \\ -2 & 3 & 6 & 7 & 6 & 3 & -2 \\ -1 & 4 & 7 & 8 & 7 & 4 & -1 \\ -2 & 3 & 6 & 7 & 6 & 3 & -2 \\ -5 & 0 & 3 & 4 & 3 & 0 & -5 \\ -10 & -5 & -2 & -1 & -2 & -5 & -10 \end{bmatrix} \qquad (6.11)$$

E(7) to force the zero sum of all elements. Detector D(7) is also a fixed mask. Rewo[2] has pointed out that this detector yields a zero output when applied to an image with constant graylevel or planar graylevel. That is

$$\text{(a)}\ O_D=\sum_{i=1}^{W^2}(d_iC)=C\sum_{i=1}^{W^2}d_i=0;$$

$$\text{(b)}\ O_D=\sum_{i=1}^{W^2}d_i(Ax_i+By_i+C)=0, \qquad (6.12)$$

$$W_h = \text{INT}(W/2),$$
$$x_i = \text{MOD}(i, W) - 1 - W_h, \text{ and}$$
$$y_i = -\text{INT}((i-1)/W) + W_h;$$

where O_D is the output of the detector; d_i is the ith element of this detector with row-major order (for example, d_8 = -5 is the first element of Row 2 in D(7)); A, B and C are constant; x_i and y_i are coordinates of the ith pixel within a given window (in the formula, MOD is a remainder taking operator, and INT is a truncating operator); and W is the size of the window (W=7 in our case). According to the value of the output of this detector, different objects in the image can be detected as shown by Expression 6.13:

$$O_D \begin{cases} > 0; & \text{if the central pixel belongs to a convex object;} \\ = 0; & \text{if the central pixel belongs to a planar object;} \\ < 0; & \text{if the central pixel belongs to a concave object.} \end{cases} \tag{6.13}$$

However, the reason why this detector can detect convex or concave object is not mentioned in Rewo's paper.[2]

In his paper,[2] Rewo has given enhancement masks and detectors for 3×3 and 5×5 neighborhood as well. Mask E(3) and Detector D(3) for 3×3 neighborhood are copied here for later use.

$$E(3) = \frac{1}{9}\begin{bmatrix} -1 & 2 & -1 \\ 2 & 5 & 2 \\ -1 & 2 & -1 \end{bmatrix} \tag{6.14}$$

$$D(3) = \frac{1}{9}\begin{bmatrix} -2 & 1 & -2 \\ 1 & 4 & 1 \\ -2 & 1 & -2 \end{bmatrix} \tag{6.15}$$

It is possible to obtain masks with size being larger than seven. The perspective plots of E(7) and E(15) are shown in Figure 6.1 where planes indicates zero level. The shape of each corresponding detector is the same as enhancement mask except the position of zero level. Generally speaking, Rewo's detector, D(7), will give best results in practical applications.

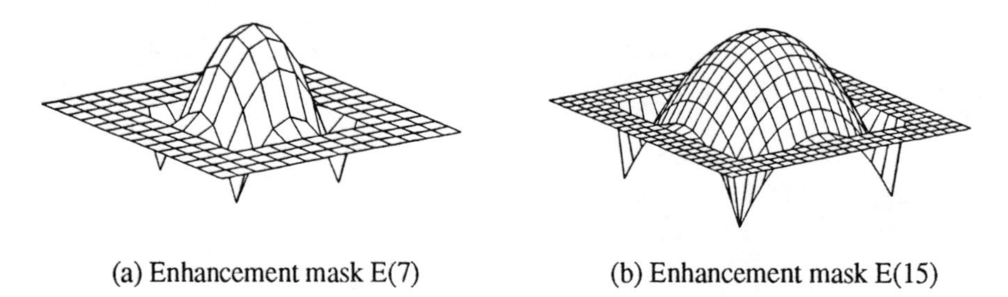

(a) Enhancement mask E(7) (b) Enhancement mask E(15)

Figure 6.1 Perspective plots of Rewo's filters

6.3 The Properties of Rewo's Mask and Detector

In order to apply Rewo's mask and detector to eliminate noise, detect blob patterns and classify the blobs (determine the boundary sharpness of the blobs), we need to study the properties of these mask and detector.

6.3.1 Property of Rewo's mask

Rewo's regression mask can be used to enhance the second order features in the image. If the mask is applied repeatedly, the noise in the image can be eliminated to the full extent. In other words, the filtering process is guaranteed convergent. To show this, we describe the process by

$$\hat{Z}_{0,0} = \mathbf{EZ} \tag{6.16}$$

where $\hat{Z}_{0,0}$ is the estimated value of the central pixel $Z_{0,0}$; $\mathbf{Z} = [\, z_1 \;\; z_2 \;\; \ldots \;\; z_n]^T$, $n = W^2$, is a vector of the graylevels of the pixels within the window whose size is W; and $\mathbf{E} = [\, (\mathrm{row}_1 \;\; \mathrm{row}_2 \;\; \ldots \;\; \mathrm{row}_W)$ of E(W)] is a vector that consists of elements of mask E(W) with the row-major order (if W = 3, then $\mathbf{E} = [\, -\frac{1}{9} \; \frac{2}{9} \; -\frac{1}{9} \; \frac{2}{9} \; \frac{5}{9} \; \frac{2}{9} \; -\frac{1}{9} \; \frac{2}{9} \; -\frac{1}{9}]$). When Model 1 holds within the window and there is no noise, $\hat{Z}_{0,0} = \mathbf{EZ} = Z_{0,0}$, namely, nothing is changed. Now, suppose the central pixel is corrupted by noise whose value is ΔZ, then the graylevel of this pixel is $Z_{0,0} + \Delta Z$. After applying E(W) once we obtain

$$\hat{Z}^{1}_{0,0} = \mathbf{EZ} + \Delta Z*E_{0,0} = Z_{0,0} + \Delta Z*E_{0,0} \tag{6.17a}$$

where $E_{0,0}$ is the central element of E(W), for instance, $E_{0,0} = \frac{5}{9}$ if W=3, and $E_{0,0} = \frac{11}{147}$ if W = 7; and "*" denotes multiplication. If we apply E(W) twice, the new estimated value of $\hat{Z}_{0,0}$ is

$$\hat{Z}^{2}_{0,0} = \mathbf{EZ} + \Delta Z*E_{0,0}*E_{0,0} = Z_{0,0} + \Delta Z*(E_{0,0})^2 \tag{6.17b}$$

It is clear that applying K times of E(W) yields

$$\hat{Z}^{K}_{0,0} = Z_{0,0} + \Delta Z*(E_{0,0})^K. \tag{6.17c}$$

Since $E_{0,0} < 1$, $\hat{Z}^{K}_{0,0} = \hat{Z}_{0,0} = Z_{0,0}$ when $K \to \infty$. This shows the convergency of E(W).

6.3.2 Properties of Rewo's detector

The discussion of the properties of Rewo's detector starts with studying an example. Consider two edges with different slopes as input patterns, as shown in Figure 6.2a. The output of Rewo's detector D(7) for these two patterns are plotted in Figure 6.2b. Comparing Figure 6.2a and 2b, we find that the edges are located at the place where the output curves pass through the pixel-axis. This implies that there might be some relation between the output and the derivative of the input pattern.

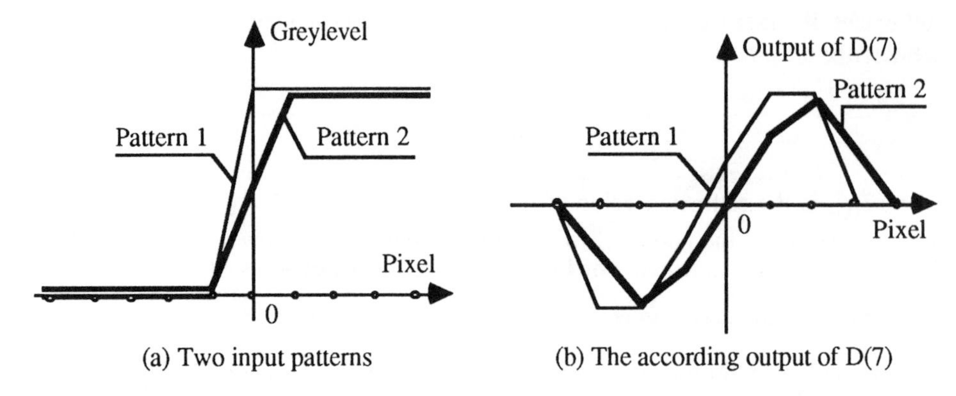

(a) Two input patterns (b) The according output of D(7)

Figure 6.2 The output of Rewo's detector for edges

For a two-variable function $z = f(x,y)$, the partial derivatives, $z_{xx} = \frac{\partial^2 z}{\partial x^2}$ and $z_{yy} = \frac{\partial^2 z}{\partial y^2}$, can numerically be approximated as[10]

$$\frac{\partial^2 z_{0,0}}{\partial x^2} \approx \frac{1}{3h^2}(z_{1,1} - 2z_{0,1} + z_{-1,1} + z_{1,0} - 2z_{0,0} + z_{-1,0} - z_{1,-1} + 2z_{0,-1} + z_{-1,-1}) \tag{6.18a}$$

$$\frac{\partial^2 z_{0,0}}{\partial y^2} \approx \frac{1}{3h^2}(z_{1,1} - 2z_{1,0} + z_{1,-1} + z_{0,1} - 2z_{0,0} + z_{0,-1} - z_{-1,1} + 2z_{-1,0} + z_{-1,-1}) \tag{6.18b}$$

$$\begin{bmatrix} z_{-1,1} & z_{0,1} & z_{1,1} \\ z_{-1,0} & z_{0,0} & z_{1,0} \\ z_{-1,-1} & z_{0,-1} & z_{1,-1} \end{bmatrix} \tag{6.18c}$$

where $z_{i,j}$ denotes the digitized function value (graylevel) of each point (pixel) within a 3×3 window as illustrated by 16c, and subscripts (i, j) are the coordinates of the pixel, for instance, $z_{0,0}$ is the graylevel of the central pixel with coordinates being (0,0); and h is the grid size in x and y direction (here h = 1). Expression 6.18a and 18b are equivalent to applying masks 6.19a and 19b to window 6.16c, respectively.

$$W(z_{xx}) = \frac{1}{3}\begin{bmatrix} 1 & -2 & 1 \\ 1 & -2 & 1 \\ 1 & -2 & 1 \end{bmatrix} \tag{6.19a}$$

$$W(z_{yy}) = \frac{1}{3}\begin{bmatrix} 1 & 1 & 1 \\ -2 & -2 & -2 \\ 1 & 1 & 1 \end{bmatrix} \tag{6.19b}$$

Because masks 6.19a and 19b are applied to the same neighborhood, the total effect is the sum of these two mask operations and can be represented by one mask operation, defined as:

$$W(z_{xx} + z_{yy}) = W(z_{xx}) + W(z_{yy}) = -\frac{1}{3}\begin{bmatrix} -2 & 1 & -2 \\ 1 & 4 & 1 \\ -2 & 1 & -2 \end{bmatrix} \tag{6.20}$$

Comparing (6.20) with (6.15), we have

$$W(z_{xx} + z_{yy}) = -3D(3) \tag{6.21}$$

Expression 6.21 implies that the output of D(3) is related to the sum of the second-order partial derivatives. Please note that there is no assumption made about the form of function f(x,y) for obtaining Expression 6.21.

When the size of a neighborhood is larger than 3×3, it is very difficult to derive the approximate expressions like (6.18a) and (18b). In order to find the relation between the derivatives and the output of Rewo's detector, we need to employ different calculation strategy. Assume Model 1 holds when the image graylevel is fitted by function f(x,y), i.e.,

$$z(x, y) = f(x, y) = b_1x^2 + b_2y^2 + b_3xy + b_4x + b_5y + b_6 \tag{6.22}$$

then the sum of the second-order partial derivatives of z(x, y) is

$$z_{xx} + z_{yy} = 2(b_1 + b_2) \tag{6.23}$$

Assume again that the neighborhood is defined by 6.18c (without loss of generality, the coordinate increments both in the x-direction and y-direction are considered to be 1), thus the output of detector D(3), $O_{D(3)}$, can be calculated as

$$\begin{aligned} O_{D(3)} &= \sum_{i=1}^{9}[d_i(3)f(x_i, y_i)] \\ &= \sum_{i=1}^{9}[d_i(3)(b_1x_i^2 + b_2y_i^2 + b_3x_iy_i + b_4x_i + b_5y_i + b_6)] \end{aligned} \tag{6.24}$$

where x_i and y_i are defined as in (6.12). Because of symetry of the detector and the coordinates, $\sum_{i=1}^{9} b_3x_iy_i = 0$. Considering Expression 6.12, we have

$$O_{D(3)} = \sum_{i=1}^{9} [d_i(3)(b_1 x_i^2 + b_2 y_i^2)]$$

$$= 2\,[1^2(-2 + 1 - 2)b_1 + 1^2(-2 + 1 - 2)b_2]/9 \qquad (6.25)$$

$$= -\frac{1}{3}\,[2(b_1 + b_2)]$$

In general, the output of Rewo's detector, D(W) can be given as

$$O_{D(W)} = \{2b_1 \sum_{j=1}^{W_h} [j^2 * d_{xj}(W)]\} + \{2b_2 \sum_{j=1}^{W_h} [j^2 * d_{yj}(W)]\} \qquad (6.26)$$

where $d_{xj}(W)$ is the sum of the $(W_h + 1 - j)$th column of D(W), and $d_{yj}(W)$ is the sum of the $(W_h + 1 - j)$th row of D(W). Using Expression 6.26, we are able to obtain

$$O_{D(5)} = -1[2(b_1 + b_2)], \text{ and}$$
$$O_{D(7)} = -2[2(b_1 + b_2)] \qquad (6.27)$$

In other words, the output of Rewo's detector is related to the sum of the second-order partial derivatives in the discrete case by (6.28):

$$O_{D(3)} = -\frac{1}{3}\left(\frac{\partial^2 z}{\partial x^2} + \frac{\partial^2 z}{\partial y^2}\right)$$
$$O_{D(5)} = -1\left(\frac{\partial^2 z}{\partial x^2} + \frac{\partial^2 z}{\partial y^2}\right) \qquad (6.28)$$
$$O_{D(7)} = -2\left(\frac{\partial^2 z}{\partial x^2} + \frac{\partial^2 z}{\partial y^2}\right)$$

The relationships shown in (6.28) are not surprizing. Recall that we have assumed that Model 1 holds and the central pixel has coordinates (0, 0). This gives rise to Expression 6.26. Whenever the detector is circularly symmetric, i.e., $d_{xj}(W) = d_{yj}(W)$, then (6.28) holds true. Actually, we can obtain similar results for output of Rewo's detector with any size due to symmetry of the detector and the coordinates within the neighborhood under consideration.

We know that for a curve g(x), if $\frac{d^2g}{dx^2} < 0$, then g is convex; if $\frac{d^2g}{dx^2} > 0$, then g is concave. Roughly speaking, the second-order partial derivatives can be used to indicate the convexity of a surface f. $O_D > 0$ means that either two partial derivatives are negative or at least one is negative and it is dominant. This guarantees that at least one of the intersected curves made by surface f and plane x = 0 and y = 0 is convex. In other words, the surface is most likely convex.

6.3.3 Gaussian curvature at any point on a surface

The Gaussian curvature[11] K at a point P of a surface f(x,y) is the product of the principal normal curvatures of f(x,y), $\frac{1}{R_1}$ and $\frac{1}{R_2}$, at P, is given by (6.29):

$$K = \frac{1}{R_1}\frac{1}{R_2} = \frac{1}{H^2}(LN - M^2) \tag{6.29}$$

where $H = \sqrt{1 + z_x^2 + z_y^2}$, $z_x = \frac{\partial z}{\partial x}$, $z_y = \frac{\partial z}{\partial y}$, $L = \frac{1}{H}\frac{\partial^2 z}{\partial x^2}$, $N = \frac{1}{H}\frac{\partial^2 z}{\partial y^2}$, and $M = \frac{1}{H}\frac{\partial^2 z}{\partial x \partial y} = \frac{1}{H} z_{xy}$. Substituting these back into (6.29), we have

$$K = \frac{1}{H^4}(z_{xx}z_{yy} - z_{xy}^2) \tag{6.30}$$

The Gaussian curvature is one of two curvatures (the other is mean curvature) which are frequently used in studying the shape of the surface in the neighborhood of point P. At all elliptic points the Gaussian curvature is positive, at parabolic ones it vanishes, and at hyperbolic ones it is negative.[12] If $K > 0$ at the point P, then the principal radii, R_1 and R_2, of normal curvature of the surface f(x,y) at the point P have the same sign.[11] Since all the other radii of normal curvature of f(x,y) at P lie between R_1 and R_2, these also have the same sigh. Therefore all the centers of of normal curvature are on one side of the tangent plane of f(x,y) at P, and so the surface in the neighborhood of the point P lies entirely on one side of its tangent plane at P. In other words, the surface is convex within this neighborhood.

If the surface is fitted by Model 1 and the central pixel whose coordinates are (0,0) is selected as point P, then

$$z_x = b_4,\ z_y = b_5,\ z_{xy} = b_3,\ z_{xx} = 2b_1,\ z_{yy} = 2b_2,$$

$$H = \sqrt{1 + b_4^2 + b_5^2}\text{, and}$$

$$K = \frac{1}{H^2}(4b_1b_2 - b_3^2) \tag{6.31}$$

Expression 6.31 tells us that if K is greater than zero, then b_1 and b_2 must have the same sign. Recall that the output of Rewo's detector is for the central pixel within the window, and is proportional to the value of $(b_1 + b_2)$. In a certain degree, this value is related to the value of (b_1b_2) because of the Inequality 6.32

$$\frac{1}{2}|b_1 + b_2| \geq \sqrt{b_1b_2},\ b_1b_2 > 0 \tag{6.32}$$

and b_1 and b_2 will close to each other if the convex object is symmetrical. Thus the output of Rewo's detector is somehow related to the Gaussian curvature. When $b_1 + b_2$ exceed a certain threshold, $(4b_1b_2 - b_3^2)$ could be greater than zero, i.e. $K > 0$. Hence, the Rewo's detector can be used to detect the convex object in an image.

In summary, when Model 1 holds, we have the following comments:

(a) Only x_i^2 and y_i^2 will make contribution to the output of Rewo's detector, i.e.

$$O_D = \sum_i [d_i(b_1 x_i^2 + b_2 y_i^2)] \tag{6.33}$$

(b) The output of Rewo's detector is proportional to the sum of the second-order partial derivatives, i.e.

$$O_D = - c \left(\frac{\partial^2 z}{\partial x^2} + \frac{\partial^2 z}{\partial y^2}\right) \tag{6.34}$$

where c is a positive constant.

(c) Expression 6.34 implies that Rewo's detector is a gradient operator (or high pass filter) in nature. Therefore it may be used as an edge detector like Laplacian operator.

(d) Because Rewo's detector involves only the second-order derivatives, it is an isotropic operator.[13] It can be used to enhance or detect the edges running in any direction in an image.

(e) Based on Expressions 6.31, 32 and 34, the reason why Rewo's detector is able to identify concave object can be explained.

(f) The larger the mask size, the smoother the filtered image. It has a low-pass filtering effect.

6.3.4 Comparison with Gaussian-Laplacian operator

Zero-crossing edge detection is one of the popular methods for localizing edges in images. It associates edges with the zero-crossings of the second-order derivative of a smoothed version of the image.[14] Gaussian-Laplacian operation is a good representative of this method. In this process, the Gaussian serves as a low-pass filter, where variance σ^2 controls spatial range of the filter, and the Laplacian is a second-order differential operator. The Gaussian is commonly used for a number of properties, for example, it is symmetric and strictly decreasing about the mean, its Fourier transform is still a Gaussian, and so on. However, Gaussian convolving function is infinite and it must be approximated by a finite mask size. The mask size is determined by σ^2. Although the scale space concept can be used to fine tune edge elements, the process of selecting a specific Gaussian-Laplacian mask for a particular image is still an open problem.[15]

Unlike the Gaussian operation in the Gaussian-Laplacian operator, the smoothing process in Rewo's filter is implicit, and is done by the model fitting with a second order polynomial. The optimization (least-mean-square error minimization) is defined and derived from a given finite mask size, and consequently it is a local optimization operator. The degree of smoothness is determined by the size of the mask, i.e., the larger the mask, the smoother is the resulting image. Since it involves a model fitting as mentioned above, the filter gives a natural interpretation of concavity. Other polynomial functions can also be used in the least-mean-square minimizing process. Finally, the filter is derived from a numerical analysis concept, and no frequency concept is applied.

6.4 Boundary Sharpness Determination

In Section 6.3, we showed that the output of Rewo's detector is proportional to the sum of the second-order partial derivatives within a given window. Therefore, Rewo's detector operates as both a concave object detector and an edge detector. It is known that second-order derivative edge detection methods are often able to eliminate smeared ramp edge markings.[1] In some applications, it is needed to determine the sharpness of the boundary of detected concave object. We discuss the classification (segmentation) approach based on boundary sharpness in this section.

6.4.1 The basic idea

Suppose we have 3 edges with different slopes as shown in Figure 6.3a, then apply a Rewo's detector, say D(3) for simplicity, to these edges, and obtain the outputs shown in Figure 6.3b. As expected, these edges result in a positive impulse followed by a negative impulse for the Rewo's detector, like Laplacian operator, can differentiate the edges. The edge is located between the two impulse at the point where there is a zero crossing of the second derivative. If the width of an edge is longer than the size of the edge detector, there will not be a zero-crossing. For example, in Edge 3 there is no zero-crossing point in Figure 6.3b, as its width is 4 pixels. Let us denote the distance between the positive peak and the negative peak by δ measured in pixels, as indicated by Figure 6.3b, then we can see that the sharper the edge, the shorter the distance δ. Therefore distance δ can be used as a measurement of the edge sharpness in our problem.

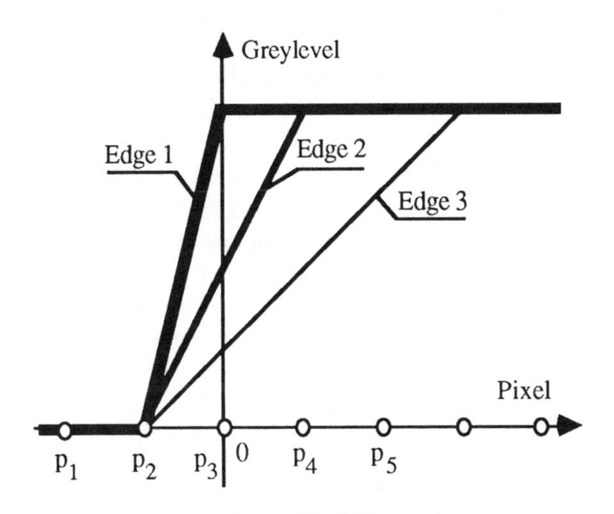

(a) Three edges with different slopes

Figure 6.3

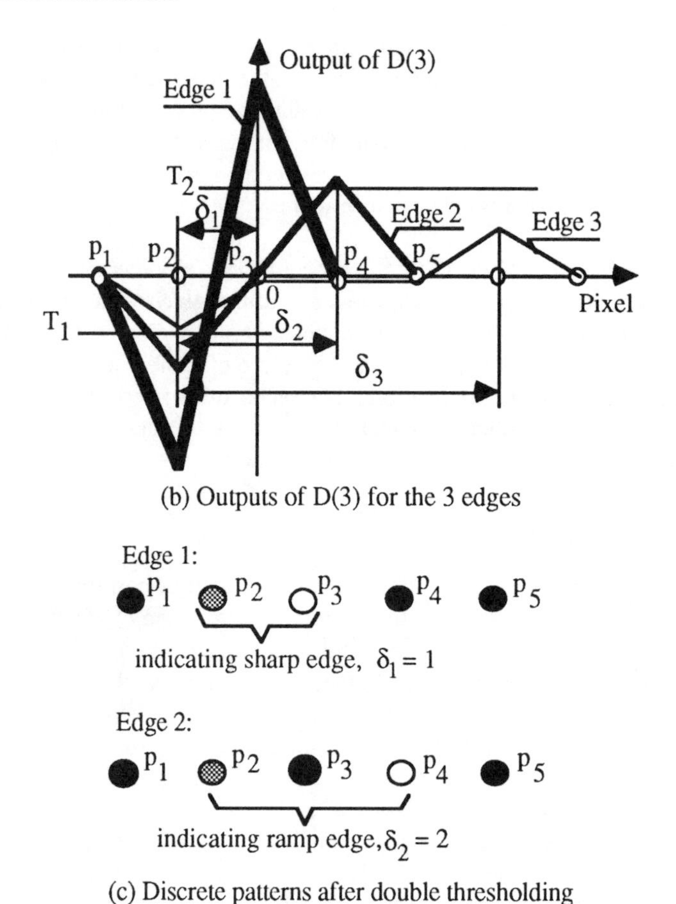

(b) Outputs of D(3) for the 3 edges

(c) Discrete patterns after double thresholding

Figure 6.3 Illustration of classification approach

To determine distance δ and find the sharpness of an edge, we use a double thresholding defined by Expression 6.35, where d(x,y) denotes the image obtained by applying Rewo's detector; T_1 and T_2 are negative and positive thresholding values, respectively; G_1 , G_2, and G_3 are three different graylevels; and g(x,y) is the image after thresholding. Thus g(x,y) is a triple image, and can be called the gradient image. After thresholding of the outputs in Figure 6.3b, we obtain patterns plotted in Figure 6.3c. In Figure 6.3c, the white pixels represent pixels with positive derivatives, the gray pixels represent pixels with negative derivatives; and the black pixels represent the background. It can be seen clearly that the output patterns in Figure 6.3b or equivalently in Figure 6.3c reflect the sharpness of the corresponding input edges. Although the discussion thus far has been limited to one-dimensional edges, a similar argument applies to an edge of any orientation in an image.

$$g(x,y) = \begin{cases} G_1 \text{ — } \odot & \text{if } d(x,y) < T_1 \\ G_2 \text{ — } \circ & \text{if } d(x,y) \geq T_2 \\ G_3 \text{ — } \bullet & \text{otherwise} \end{cases} \qquad (6.35)$$

For the problem of detection and classification of concave blobs, the gray pixels may belong to the detected blobs and indicate negative second derivatives, the white pixels represent positive second derivatives, and black pixels represent background. If the gray pixels are clustered the cluster is considered to be a blob. Furthermore, if each boundary pixel of the detected blob has a white pixel as its neighbor, the boundary is considered very sharp. Thus the detected blobs can be classified based on their boundary sharpness with the aid of distance δ. The greylevel image of a typical blob (here is a water droplet) and its gradient image are illustrated in Figure 6.4a and 4b, respectively. Whenever there exists a boundary in the graylevel image, there is always an annulus formed by white pixels alternating with an annulus formed by gray pixels in the gradient image corresponding to this boundary. The gap γ, i. e., the number of black pixels between these two annulus, takes the value of 0, 1, 2 and so forth. The value of γ indicates the value of distance δ -- the wider the γ, the larger the δ. Since γ can be obtained more easily than δ, we use γ instead of δ in implementation. For the purpose of classification, only external boundary is of interest.

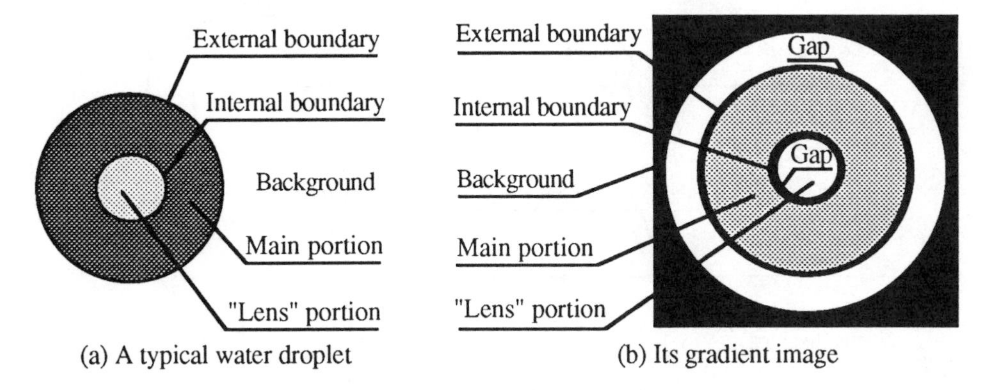

(a) A typical water droplet (b) Its gradient image

Figure 6.4 The gradient image of a typical droplet obtained after double thresholding

6.4.2 Boundary sharpness determination approach

In implementation, we isolate each blob first, then find the external boundary for a particular blob, finally count the total number of boundary pixels, N_B, and the number of boundary pixels, N_P, which have white pixel (indicating positive derivatives) neighbors with gap $\leq \gamma$. If the ratio of N_B to N_P, R (called zero-crossing ratio), is greater than a threshold value, T_g, then the blob is classified as a blob of sharp boundary. As will be mentioned in Section 6.5, we can calculate ratio R for different gap widths, and set different threshold accordingly. Thus, the classification criteria can be expressed as

$$R_j \geq T_{gj}, \quad j = 0, 1, 2, \ldots \quad \text{or} \tag{6.36a}$$

$$(R_0 \geq T_{g0}) \cap (R_1 \geq T_{g1}) \cap (R_2 - R_1 \leq T_{RD}) \tag{6.36b}$$

where j in (6.36a) and the numbers in subscript in (6.36b) indicate the gap width γ, and T_{RD} is a threshold. Criterion expressed by (6.29b) will give better classification results.

6.5 An Example of Application

The power of Rewo's approach lies in that it can enhance and detect concave blobs in digitized images. In addition, based on the same results obtained from applying Rewo's detector the boundary and its sharpness can be identified. Besides the original application of the approach, i. e., evaluating aerial photographs of forest, other potential applications may be found in the industry. for instance, the Rewo's detector can be employed to detect and classify the water droplets as described below.

6.5.1 The problem and testing data set

To estimate the volume of water droplets ingested into turbine engines resulting from heavy rain and wheel spray generated on a wet runway, we may divide the whole engine into a number of thin planer layers, then estimate and sum up the volumes of droplets

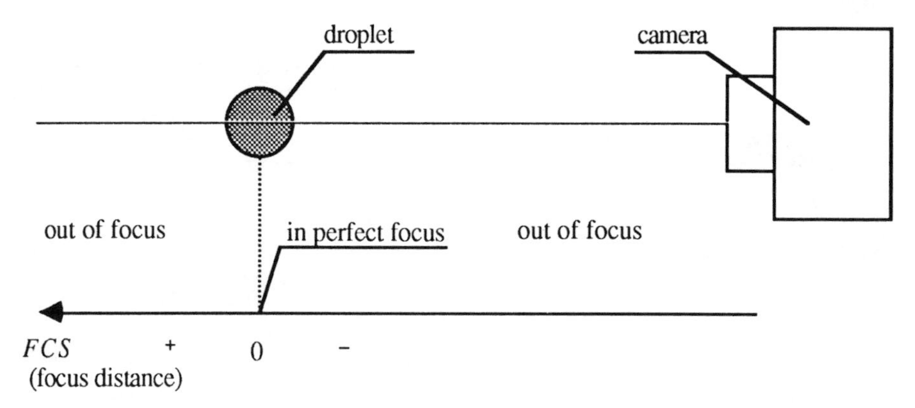

Figure 6.5 A scanning system

fallen into these layers. Therefore how to estimate the water volume for a single layer is the core of the problem to be solved. One solution for this problem is as follows. First we take picture for each layer, then detect all potential droplets in the picture, next determine which droplet is within the layer (in-focus droplet), and finally calculate the equivalent diameter for each in-focus droplet (see Figure 6.5).

The data set used in this chapter consists of 11 testing images of size 512×512. They were captured at focus distance (*FCS*) of 0, 1, 2, 3, 4, 5, 6, 7, 9 , 11, and 13 mm, and denoted by F0.P, F1.P, ..., and F13.P, respectively. Each image contains same group of 10 droplets lying on a glass plate and some noise. Hence, the major difference among theses images is the degree of focus-out of the entire image. The testing images are not exactly the same as rain droplet images captured in the real situation, but are close to them.

6.5.2 The profile of water droplets

We examine the profile of water droplets through four droplets at the tips of bars captured at focus distances 0, 2, 6 and -15mm and denoted by C0, C2, C6 and C-15, respectively. The graylevels of transverse sections through the central portion of each droplets are accordingly plotted in Figure 6.6.

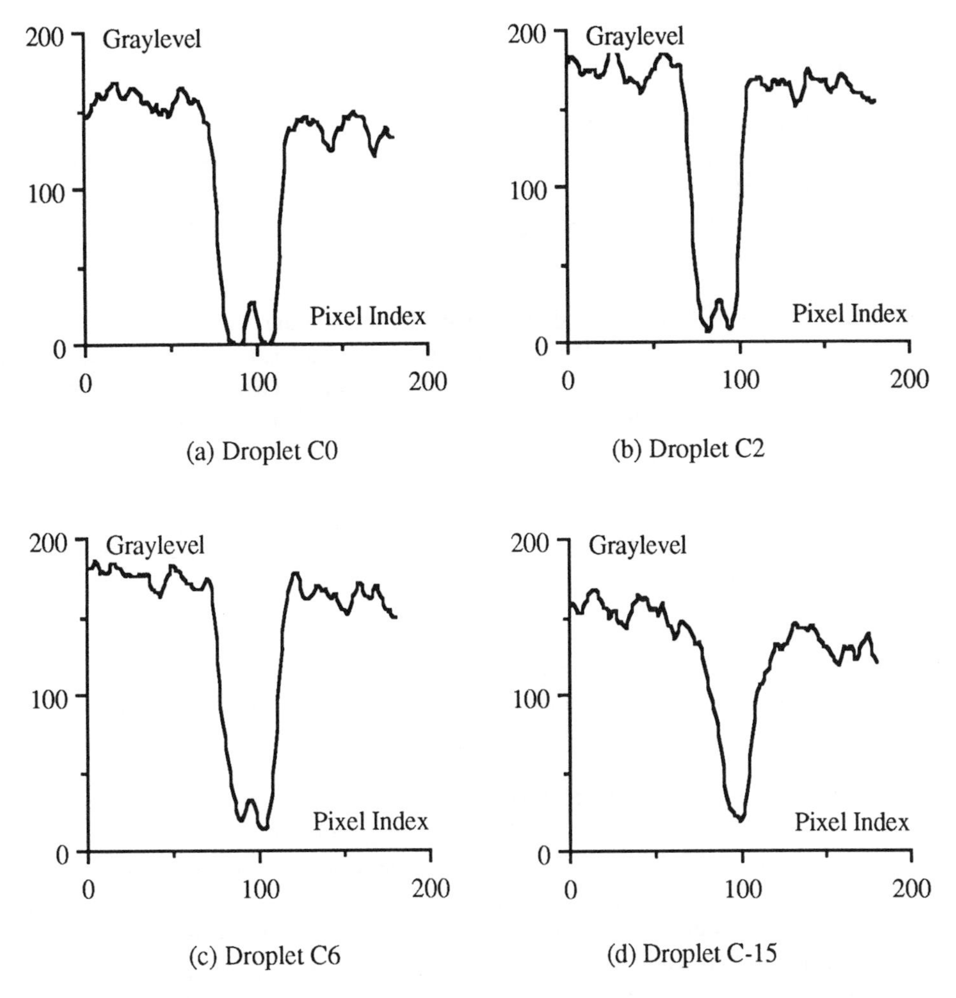

Figure 6.6 Profiles of water droplets

Based on Figure 6.6, the following observations can be made:

(a) Generally speaking, the image of an in-focus droplet has a sharp boundary and a clear lens portion (the bright portion located at the center of the droplet).

(b) As the degree of focus-out increases, the droplet boundary becomes blurred, the lens portion gets darker, and the size of the lens portion reduces or disappears. The more the droplet out of focus, the more blurred the external boundary, and the less the lens portion.

(c) The droplet image is darker than the background. If the surface of a second order polynomial is used to fit the graylevel of a droplet, this surface should be concave. In other words, it is natural to assume the droplet model to be a concave image graylevel function.

It should be pointed out that since not all in-focus droplets have the lens portion, the features related to this portion were not used in classification.

6.5.3 Processing procedures

Detection and classification system based on the above mentioned approach has been developed. The processing procedure consists of the following steps:

Step 1 -- Concave Feature Enhancement

The input image can be enhanced by applying Rewo's enhancement mask, for example E(7). This step is optional, depending on the quality of the image: either applying repeatedly until a satisfied enhanced image is achieved if the input image is noisy, or skipped if otherwise.

Step 2 -- Concave Object Detection and Double Thresholding

At this stage the input is either the original image or the filtered image obtained from Step 1. The output of this step is a triple image g(x,y). There are three parameters, detector size, threshold T_1 and T_2, which should be selected during execution.

Step 3 -- Gap Filling and Image Cleaning

A program is needed to fill gaps by converting black pixels into white pixels according to the given gape size γ. Then any white pixel that does not have any immediate gray pixel within γ as its neighbor will be deleted. After this procedure, all potential droplets are isolated.

Step 4 -- Droplet Position Determination

This step is to mark every droplet remained after Step 3 with square boxes.

Step 5 -- Droplet Classification and Area Calculation

In order to classify droplets based on gape size γ, we need to find the external boundary of each droplet and count the total number of boundary pixels, N_B, and the number of those boundary pixels, N_P, which have positive value of second partial derivatives. Since not all droplets have a perfect circular shape, scanning in both x-direction and y-direction is made. The larger number of N_P will be chosen as the counting result. There are two parameters, minimum droplet size and threshold for zero-crossing ratio, should be given in this step. In the mean time the areas of each droplet are calculated.

To check the accuracy of boundary detection, the detected external boundaries will be superposed on each classified in-focus droplets in the original input image.

6.5.4 Experimental results

In Section 6.4.2, we have presented two criteria, 6.36a and 36b, for determination of boundary sharpness. We call 36a the simple determination approach, and 6.36b the modified determination approach. The experimental results are given in this subsection according to the determination approach applied.

6.5.4.1 Simple determination approach

The approach used here is essentially the combination of Rewo's approach and zero-crossing detection. The processing procedure is illustrated step by step in Figure 6.7.

Figure 6.7a is the original input image. After applying Rewo's detector and double thresholding, we have the image shown in 6.7b, and this is so called gradient image. The highest graylevel (white) represents pixels with positive second-order derivative; the medium (grey) graylevel negative derivative; the lowest graylevel (black) background. The gaps between white pixels and gray pixels, where edges are located, are filled according to the given gap size $\gamma = 1$. Then internal and external boundaries of each detected droplet is extracted, and the resulting image is 6.7c. Next, positions of each droplets are determined and marked by white boxes as shown in 6.7d. The final result of processing image F0.P is shown in 6.7e where the resulting boundaries are overlaid on each corresponding droplet. This picture visualizes how accurate the boundary detection is. The droplets with detected white boundaries are classified as in-focus ones.

Figures through 6.8 to 6.11 are original input images, F1.P, F2.P, F3.P and F4.P, and their corresponding results. Since no in-focus droplets were detected for F4.P, the intermediate result is shown in Figure 6.11b instead. All the processing conditions are the same as those for Image F0.P, namely, the detector size is 7×7; thresholds are T_1=-5.0, T_2=3.0; the value of γ is 1 for gap filling; the minimum size of droplet is set to 2×2; and the zero-crossing ratio (the ratio of the number of white pixel to the number of the total pixels on the external boundary), which is used as the classification threshold, is set to 0.85. The processed results are summarized in Figure 6.12a-c. Figure 6.12a gives the index for each droplet, 6.12b the detailed results, and 6.12c the curve of the number of detected droplets versus focus distance. The figure shows that all droplets with focus distance longer than 3mm can be classified as out-of-focus droplets. This classification result is very encouraging. We can also note that Droplet 7 (refer to Figure 6.12a), which is actually a noise pattern, is partially detected because of its abnormal shape.

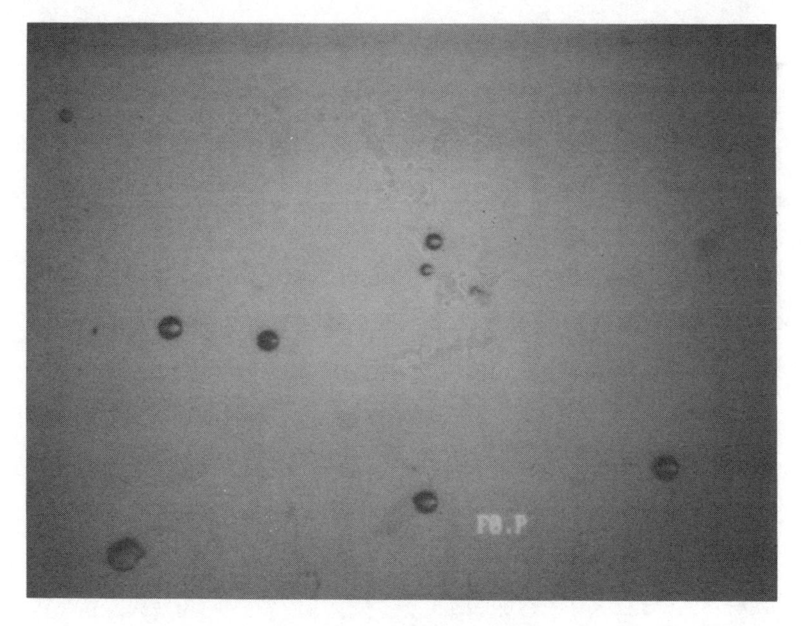

(a) The original image

Figure 6.7 The processing procedures for Image F0.P

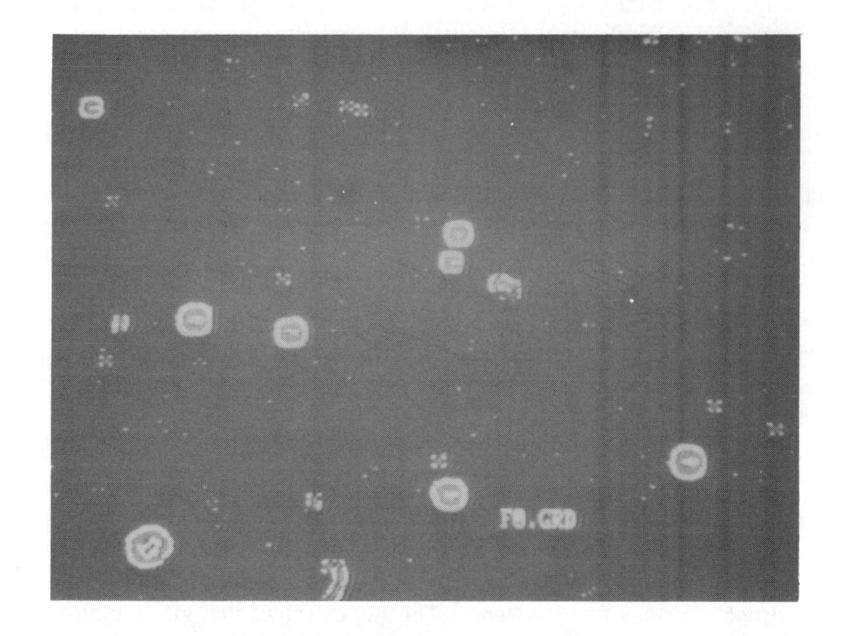

(b) The result obtained by using Rewo's detector and double thresholding
(Detector size: 7×7; Thresholds: T_1=-5.0, T_2=3.0)

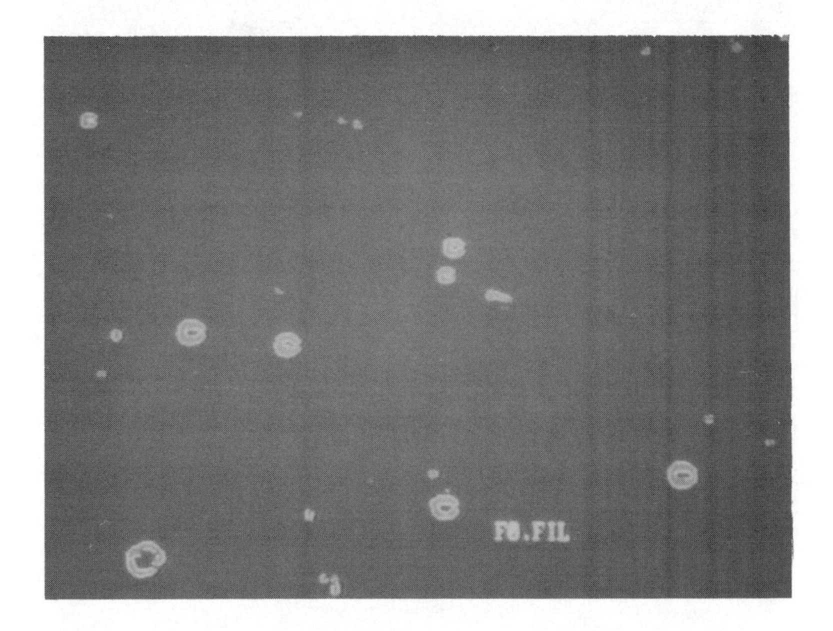

(c) The gradient image obtained after gap (γ = 1) filling and boundary extraction

Figure 6.7 continued

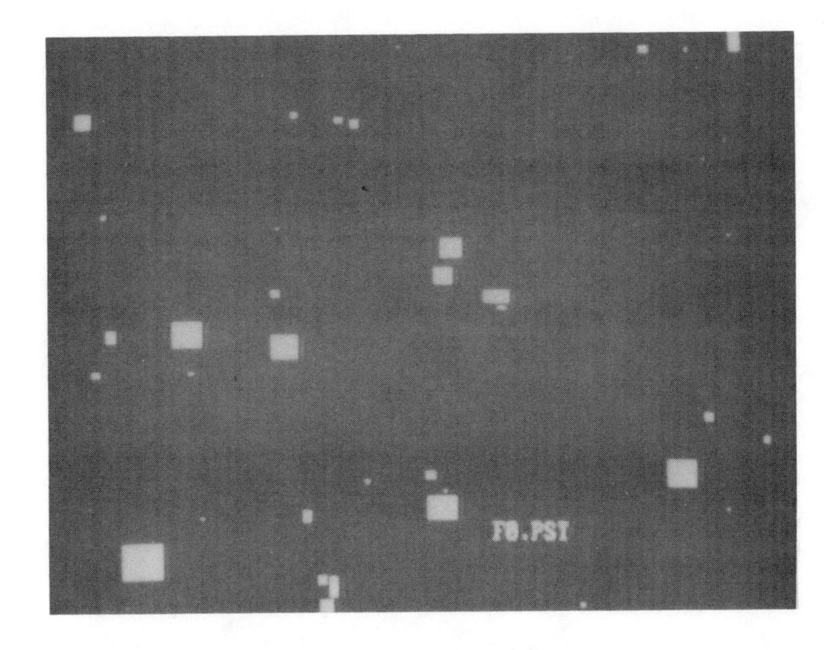

(d) The positions of detected droplets

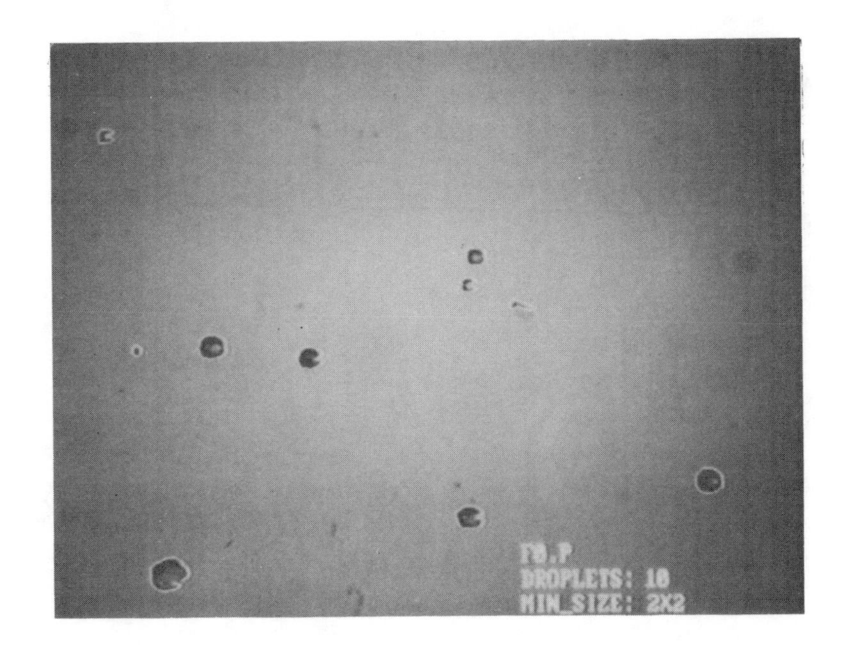

(e) The final result (zero-crossing ratio R=0.85; minimum size=2×2)

Figure 6.7 continued

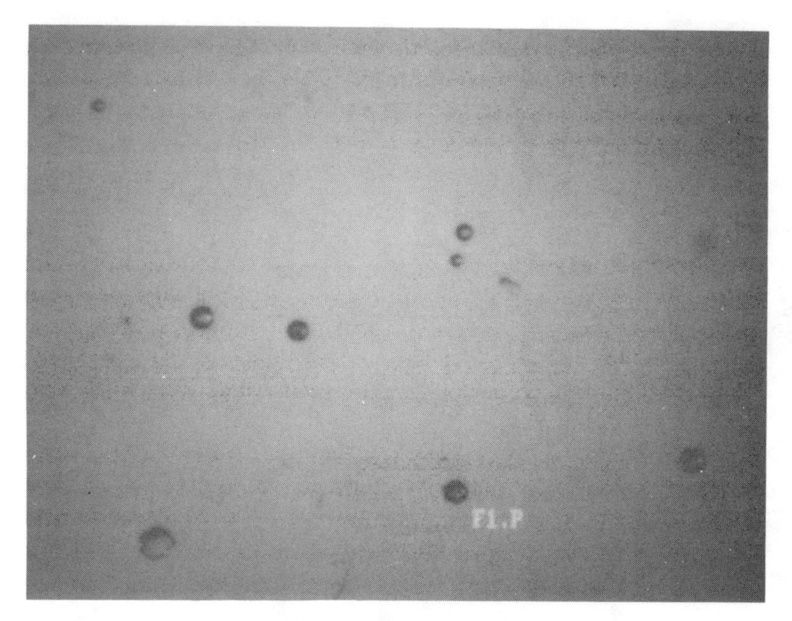

(a) The original image

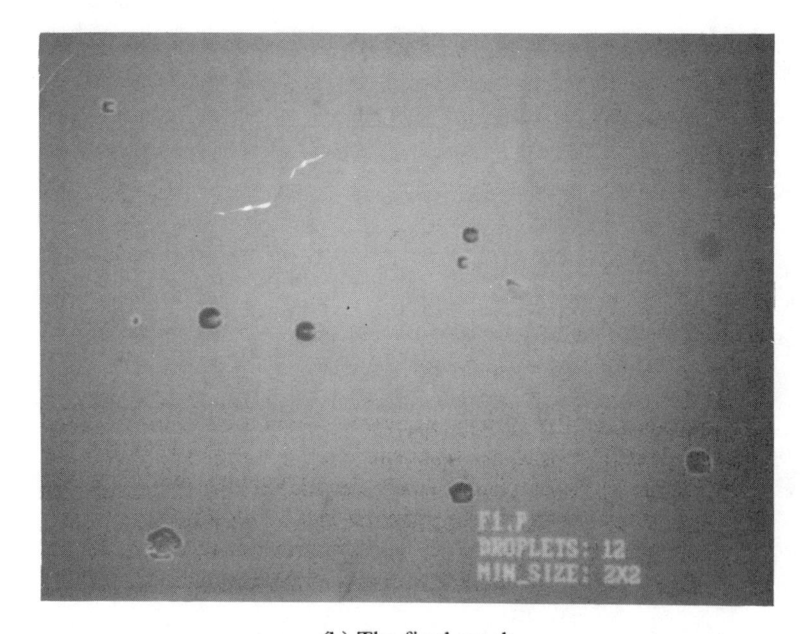

(b) The final result

Figure 6.8 The original and processed images of F1.P

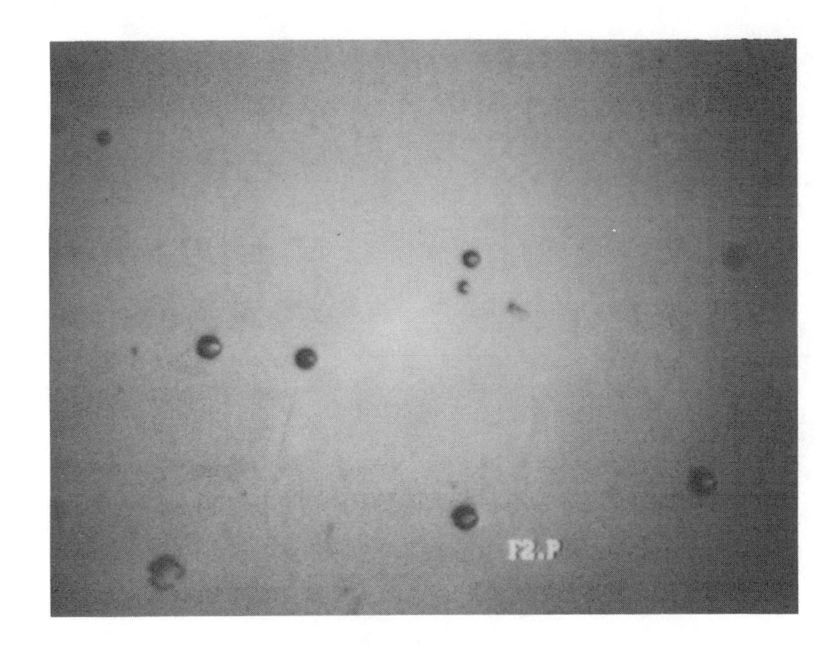

(a) The original image

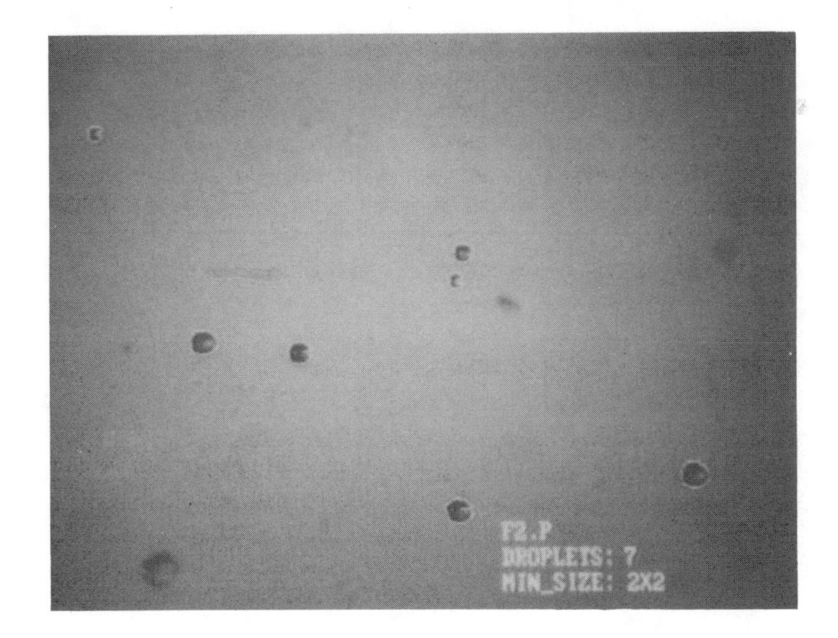

(b) The final result

Figure 6.9 The original and processed images of F2.P

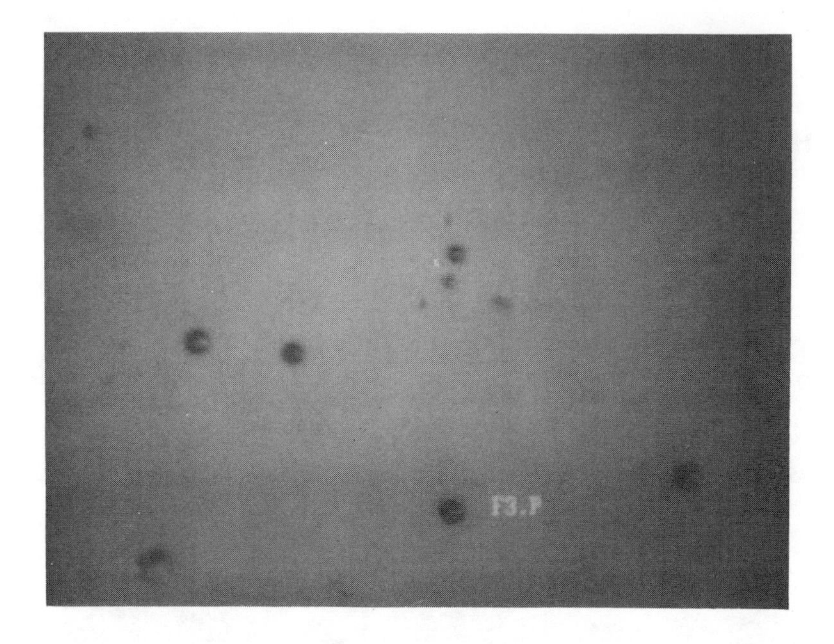

(a) The original image

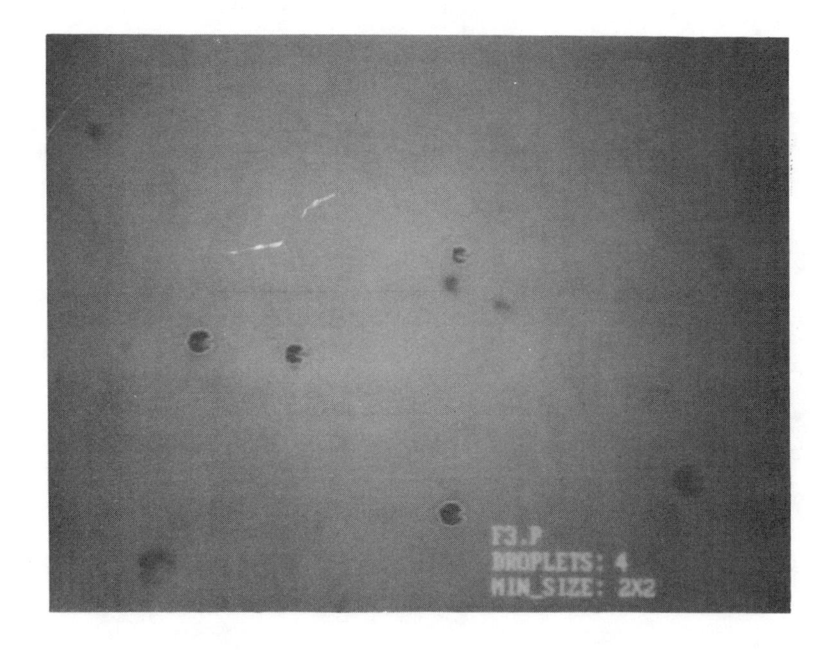

(b) The final result

Figure 6.10 The original and processed images of F3.P

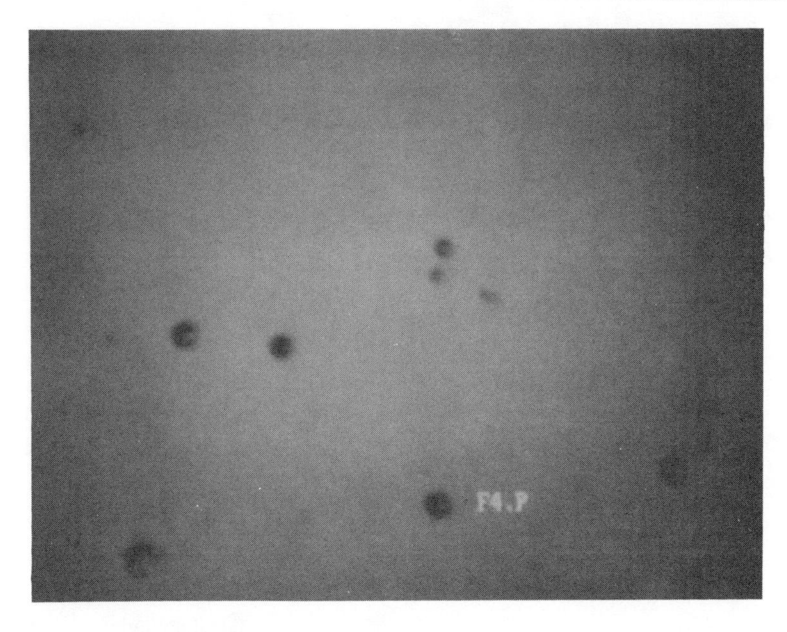

(a) The original image

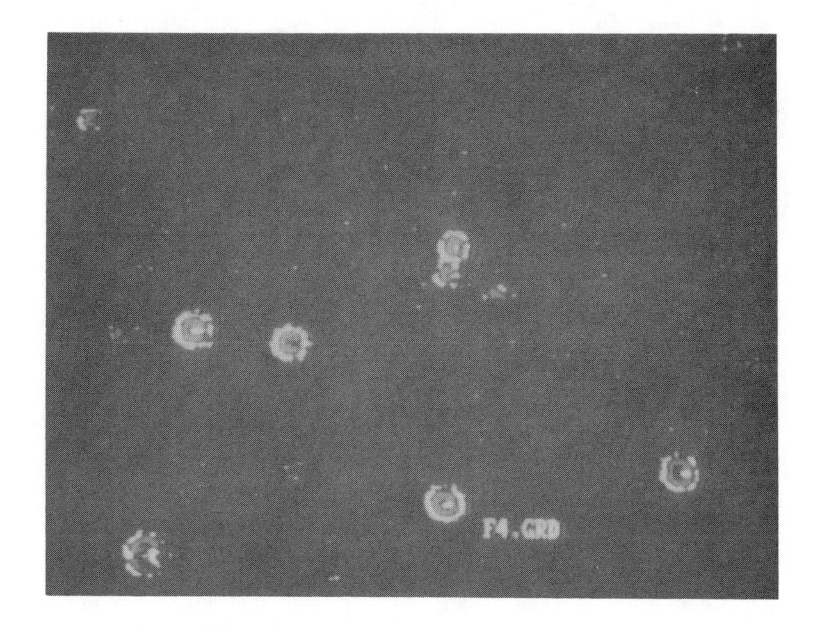

(b) The result obtained by using Rewo's detector and double thresholding

Figure 6.11 The original and processed images of F4.P

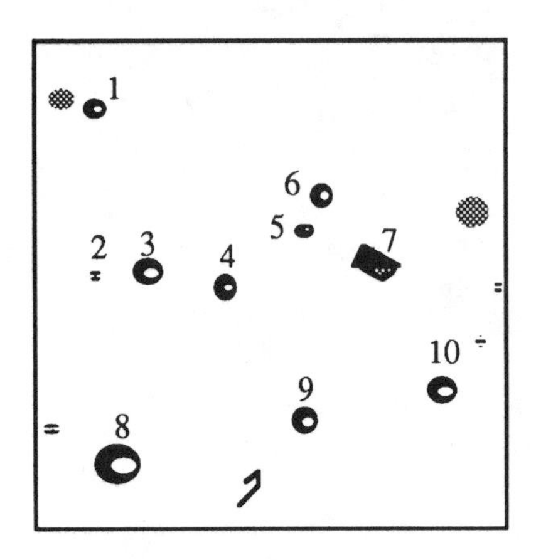

(a) The distribution of large-sized droplets in data set F#.P (GE:FRM#.PIX)

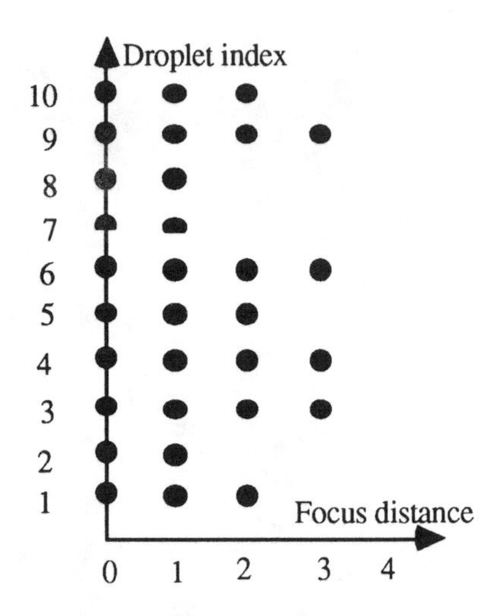

(b) Detected large-sized infocus droplets for images with different focus distances

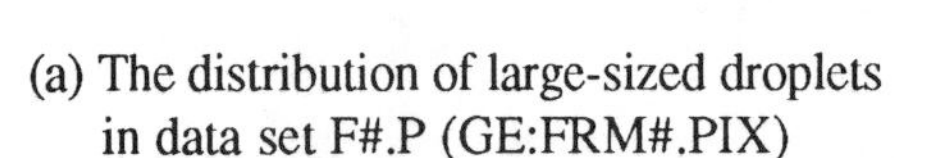

●: detected as one droplet;
⊖: detected as two droplets;
◓: partially detected.

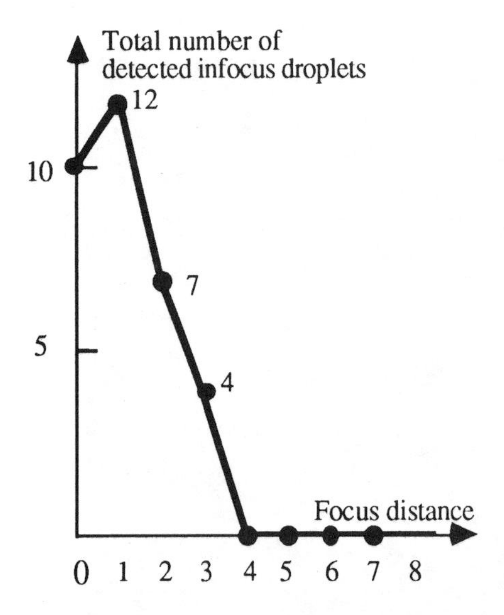

(c) Detected all-sized infocus droplets for images with different focus distances

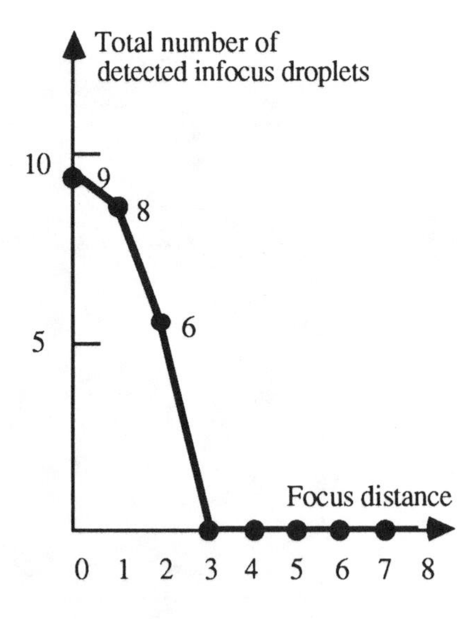

(d) Detected all-sized infocus droplets for images with different focus distances

Figure 6.12 The results of processing data set (F#.P) with AICV Infocus Droplet Detection and Classification System

(Rewo's regression mask: not applied; REWO's detector size:7×7; Thresholds: T_1=-5.0, T_2= 3.0; Gap size: 1 pixel; Minimum drop size 2×2; Classification threshold=0.85.)

6.5.4.2 Modified determination approach

Comparing Figures 6.11b with 6.7b, we are able to see some clear differences between them. One of the differences is the white annuli, and the other is the gap size. The white annuli are broken in 6.11b, and the gaps are wider than those in 6.7b. In order to see the differences more visually, we arbitrarily chose droplet 4 and plotted three-dimentional mesh drawings for this droplet in image F0.P and F4.P. The drawings for the original image, the output of Rewo's filter, and the double thresholding results for droplet 4 in F0.P are shown in Figure 6.13a, b, and c, respectively. Figure 6.14a, b, and c are drawings for the same droplet in F4.P. Since the images were taken at different focus distance (*FCS* = 0mm, for F0.P; *FCS* = 4mm, for F4.P), the differences of boundary

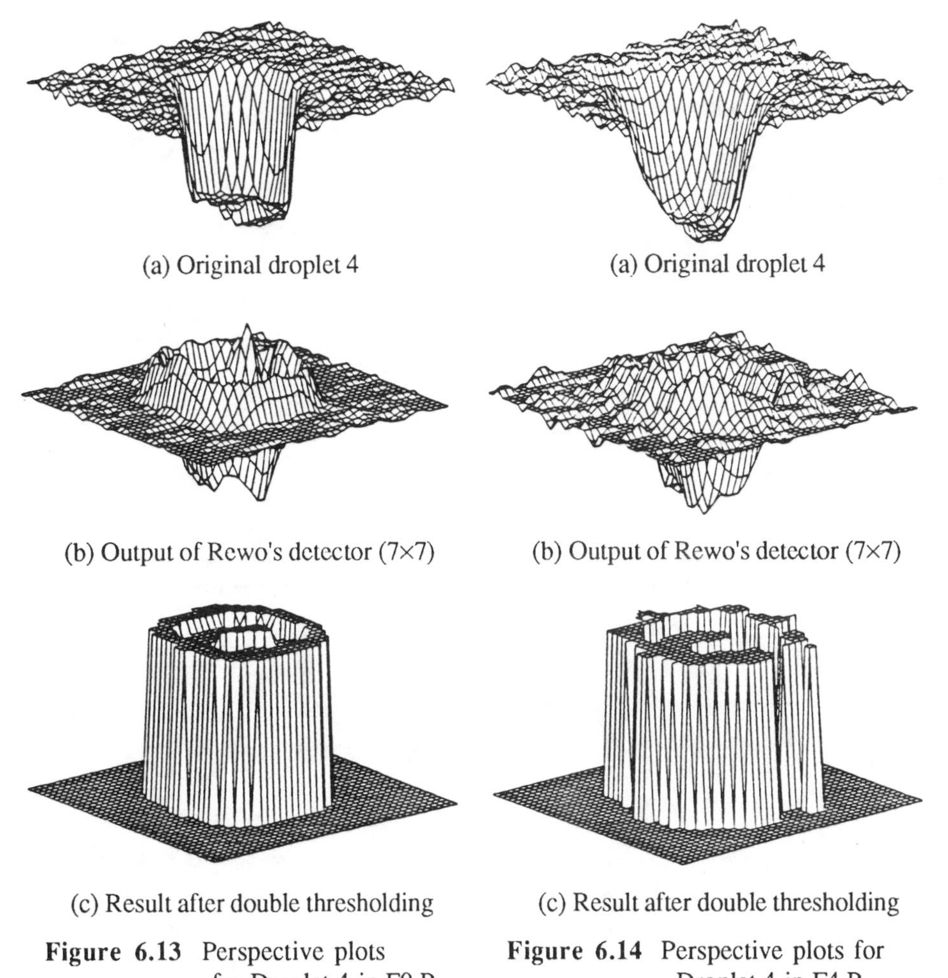

(a) Original droplet 4 — (a) Original droplet 4

(b) Output of Rewo's detector (7×7) — (b) Output of Rewo's detector (7×7)

(c) Result after double thresholding — (c) Result after double thresholding

Figure 6.13 Perspective plots for Droplet 4 in F0.P

Figure 6.14 Perspective plots for Droplet 4 in F4.P

sharpness, the distribution of positive and negative values of the outputs of Rewo's detector, and the gaps in the thresholded images can be seen clearly in these pictures. Again, these pictures suggest that the gap size can be used to measure the sharpness of boundaries.

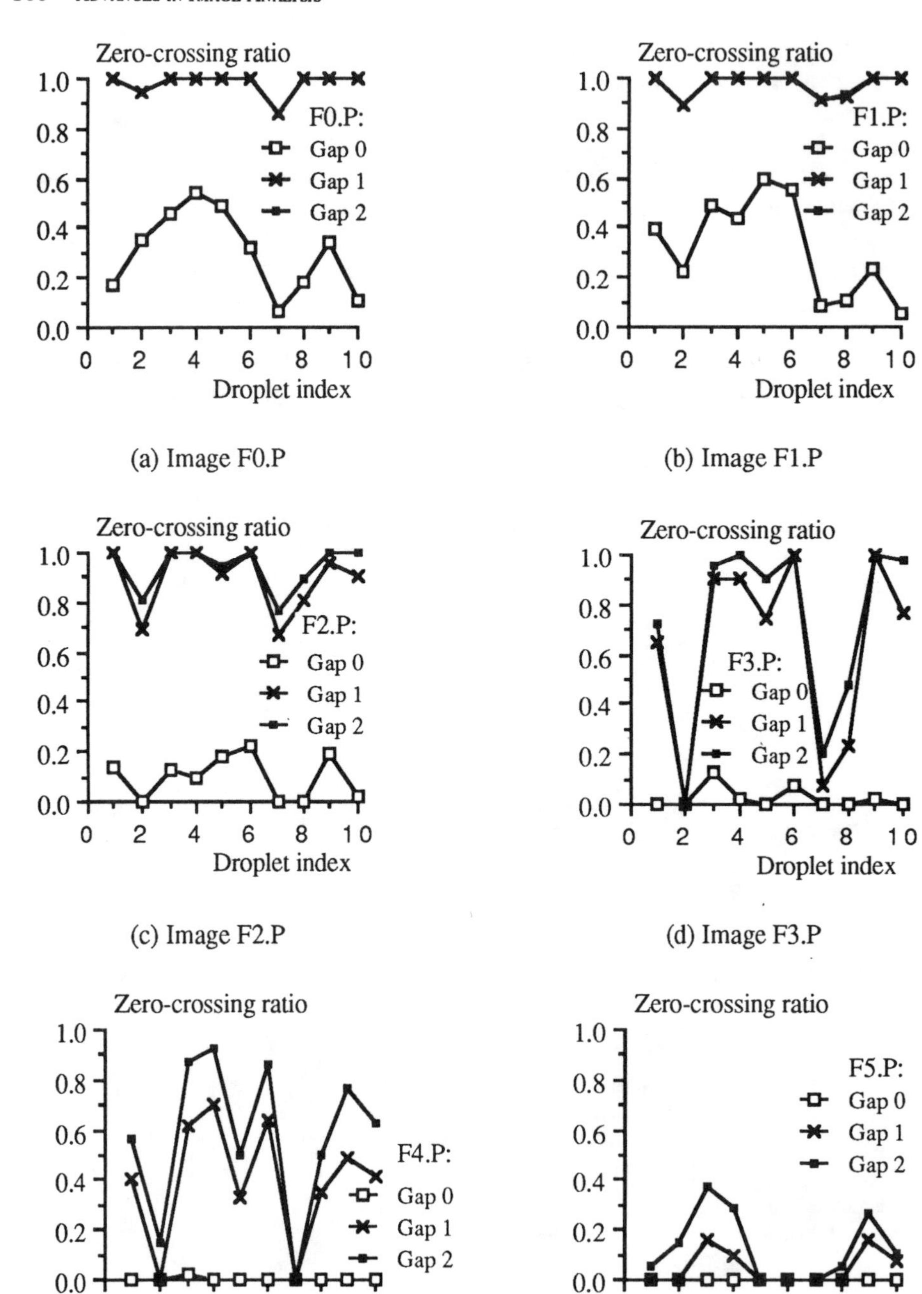

(a) Image F0.P

(b) Image F1.P

(c) Image F2.P

(d) Image F3.P

(e) Image F4.P

(f) Image F5.P

Figure 6.15 Ratio R versus gap size γ for droplets in different degree of focus-out

To achieve more reliable and accurate classification results, we need to take the gap sizes into account. Filling gaps according to different values of γ, we can obtain a family of curves that represent the relations between zero-crossing ratio, R, and gap sizes, γ, for a particular droplet. The relations for each droplet in different degree of focus-out in Images F0.P -- F5.P are given in Figure 6.15. For each plot in this figure, the horizontal axis indicates the droplet index (refer to Figure 6.12a), and the vertical axis the zero-crossing ratio. The higher the ratio, the clearer the boundary. If a droplet maintains high value of R for different values of γ, it must have a sharp boundary. Let's take curves with gap $\gamma = 1$, called curve 1's (all curves marked "Gap 1" in Figure 6.15), as an example. Since droplets 3, 4, 6, and 9 have high value of zero-crossing ratio, they are always classified as in-focus ones when focus distance is less than 4mm. These results have been shown in Figure 6.12b and 12c, and can be obtained by simple thresholding of curve 1's, i.e. by applying (6.36a). If we set $T_{g0} = 0.10$, $T_{g1} = 0.85$, and $T_{RD} = 0.05$, and apply determination criterion 6.36b:

$$(R_0 \geq T_{g0}) \cap (R_1 \geq T_{g1}) \cap (R_2 - R_1 \leq T_{RD}) \tag{6.37}$$

to curve 0's ($\gamma = 0$), curve 1's and the differences of curve 1's and curve 2's ($\gamma = 2$), we will obtain results shown in Figure 6.12d. Thus, all droplets with focus distance being shorter than 3mm may be classified as in-focus ones. In other wards, if a droplet is classified as out-of-focus one, it must have been captured at a distance not less than 3mm for the testing data.

The major difference between the results obtained by using simple and modified approaches is the classification range of focus distance (3mm versus 2mm). Droplet 7 was classified as out-of focus one in latter case mainly because of its special shape.

6.6 Conclusion Remarks

The properties of Rewo's enhancement mask and concave object detector have been studied in this chapter. It can be proved that the output of this detector is proportional to the sum of the second-order partial derivatives of the input image if it can be modeled by a second order polynomial. By taking the advantage of this property of the detector, the concave blobs in a given image can be detected and classified. As an application example, a system for detection, classification and size estimation of in-focus water droplets has been developed. The system finds water droplets by applying Rewo's detector because the profile of a water droplet is of concave shape. The system classifies isolated droplets into two groups, in focus one and out-of focus one, by identifying sharpness of their boundaries. Based on the same results obtained by applying Rewo's detector, the boundaries of each droplet are extracted and the corresponding area (or diameter) is estimated. The experimental results show that the system has the following features:

(a) Reliable droplet detection -- All potential in-focus droplets can be isolated;

(b) High droplet detection and classification rate -- All droplets that are exactly in focus are identified and counted;

(c) Accurate boundary extraction; and

(d) Simple and fast algorithms -- The major computation consists of 7×7 window operation.

The experimental results achieved so far for the testing data set used show that all droplets captured at a focus distance longer than 2mm can be classified as out-of-focus ones. The future work should concentrate on thresholding value determination, and system testing by using real data.

References

[1] W. K. Pratt, *Digital Image Processing*, A Wiley-Interscience Publication, John Wiley & Sons, Inc., New York, Second edition, 536 (1991).

[2] L. Rewo, "Enhancement and detection of convex objects using regression models", *Computer Vision, Graphics, and Image Processing* **25**, 257-269 (1984).

[3] P. Parikh, M. Hernan and V. Sarohia, "Quantitative determination of engine water ingestion", DOT/FAA/CT-86/10 (1986).

[4] Murthy, S. N. B. and C. M. Ehresman, "Effects of water ingestion into jet engine", AIAA paper No. **84-0542** presented at the Airbreathing Propulsion Session of the 22nd Aerospace Sciences Meeting (January 1984).

[5] Murthy, S. N. B. et. al., "A stagnation pressure probe for droplet-laden air flow", AIAA paper No. **85-0330** presented at the Airbreathing Propulsion Session of the 23rd Aerospace Sciences Meeting (January 1985).

[6] Code of Federal Regulations, Title 14-Aeronautics and Space, Chapter 1-Federal Aviation Administration, Article **33.77**, Paragraphs (c) and (f), (January 1980).

[7] Code of Federal Regulations, Title 14-Aeronautics and Space, Chapter 1-Federal Aviation Administration, Article **25.1091**, Paragraphs (d) (2), (January 1980).

[8] A. R. Jones, "A review of drop size measurement - the application of techniques to dense fuel sprays", *Progress in energy and combustion science* **3**, (1977).

[9] McCreath, C. G. and J. M. Beer, "A review of drop size measurement in fuel sprays", *Progress Applied Energy* **2**, (1976).

[10] Editors of the mathematical handbook, *mathematical handbook*, People Education Press, Beijing, P. R. China, 208-209 (1979).

[11] E. P. Lane, *Metric differential geometry of curves and surfaces*, The University of Chicago Press, Chicago, Illinois, 161-163 (1940).

[12] B. Kreyszig, *Differential Geometry*, University of Toronto Press, Toronto, 131 (1959).

[13] L. J. Galbiati, Jr., *Machine Vision and Digital Image Processing Fundamentals*, Prentice Hall, Englewood Cliffs, New Jersey 07632, 114-115 (1990).

[14] Y. Lu and R. C. Jain, "Behavior of Edges in Scale Space", *IEEE Trans. Pattern Analysis and Machine Intelligence* **11**(4), 337 - 356 (April 1989).

[15] D. Marr and E. C. Hildreth, "Theory of edge detection", Proc. Roy. Soc. London, Ser. B **207**, 187-217 (1980).

Feature Extraction

Chapter 7

Boundary Finding with Parametrically Deformable Models

L. H. Staib, J. S. Duncan

7.1 Introduction

This work describes an approach to finding objects in images based on deformable shape models. Boundary finding in two and three dimensional images is enhanced both by considering the bounding contour or surface as a whole and by using model-based shape information.

Boundary finding using only local information has often been frustrated by poor-contrast boundary regions due to occluding and occluded objects, adverse viewing conditions and noise. Imperfect image data can be augmented with the extrinsic information that a geometric shape model provides. In order to exploit model-based information to the fullest extent, it should be incorporated explicitly, specifically, and early in the analysis. In addition, the bounding curve or surface can be profitably considered as a whole, rather than as curve or surface segments, because it tends to result in a more consistent solution overall.

These models are best suited for objects whose diversity and irregularity of shape make them poorly represented in terms of fixed features or parts. Smoothly deformable objects do not necessarily have an obvious decomposition that can be exploited. A uniform shape representation that describes the entire shape is therefore needed and it should describe a relatively broad class of shapes.

For a representation to be useful for modeling it should be concise. Methods based on explicitly listing points or patches on the surface are verbose because of the implicit redundancy. Parametric representations capture the overall shape in a small number of parameters. This means that the optimization of a match measure between data and a model can occur in a lower dimensional space.

Boundary finding is formulated as a optimization problem using parametric Fourier models which are developed for both curves and surfaces. The model is matched to the image by optimizing in the parameter space the match between the model and a boundary measure applied to the image. Probability distributions on the parameters of the representation can be incorporated to bias the model to a particular overall shape while allowing for deformations. This leads to a maximum *a posteriori* objective function.

7.2 Related Work in Boundary Finding

Local edge detectors applied to real images produce spurious edges and gaps. These problems can only be overcome by the incorporation of information from higher scale organization of the image and models of the objects sought. Contextual information has been used for boundary determination via grouping [1], relaxation labeling [2] and scale-space methods [3]. These methods, by themselves, will not necessarily find complete boundaries. Pixel search methods associate edge elements by finding an optimal path through a two-dimensional image, based on criteria designed to find boundaries. The typical objective function combines boundary strength and low overall curvature [4]. Pixel search does not generalize obviously to three dimensions because there is no natural ordering of voxels in a surface.

An alternative method for boundary analysis is the Hough transform [5]. The Hough approach is similar to the current method in that it finds shapes by looking for maxima in a parameter space. However, the storage and computational complexity of the Hough method are a great disadvantage, especially if deformations are envisaged.

Other investigators have considered whole-boundary methods that adjust a tentative curve or surface mesh in order to match to the image. By considering the boundary as a whole, a structure is imposed on the problem that bridges gaps and results in overall consistency.

For curve finding, Gritton and Parrish [6] used a flexible bead chain, where the beads are putative boundary points. The beads are attracted towards pixels that have a higher gradient magnitude. Cooper [7] formulated boundary estimation using maximum likelihood. A boundary adjustment scheme similar to the bead chain algorithm [6] is presented to perform the optimization. Kass *et al.* [8] used energy-minimizing snakes that are attracted to image features such as lines and edges while internal spline forces impose a smoothness constraint. The weights of the smoothness and image force terms in the energy functional can be adjusted for different behavior. The solution is found using variational methods.

For surface finding, Terzopoulos *et al.* [9] used energy-minimizing meshes that are attracted to image features such as lines and edges while internal spline forces impose a smoothness constraint. The goal was to find surfaces implied by silhouettes in two-dimensional images. This idea has also been used for finding symmetry surfaces from scale space stacks of two-dimensional images [10], surfaces in range images [11, 12] and surfaces in three-dimensional images [13].

Other whole-boundary methods optimize in a parameter space. Parametric representations are useful for modeling because they capture the overall shape concisely. This means that the optimization of a match measure between data and a model can occur in a lower dimensional space. Widrow [14] used parametrized templates called rubber masks to model objects. The parameters are sizes and relationships between subparts. Yuille *et al.* [15] used a similar method for finding features in images of faces. Both of these methods describe the overall shape of the structure using very few parameters. However, the object must have sufficient structure to be represented in terms of parts and a new model must be developed for each new object. Work has also been done developing deformable templates based on Markov models of two-dimensional boundaries incorporating knowledge of shape from statistical features [16]. In the next section we will discuss parametrizations for surfaces in more detail.

Pentland and his group have developed a physically-based method for analyzing shape [17, 18]. Shapes are represented by the low-order frequency displacement eigenvectors corresponding to the free vibration modes of the object. Thus, it is similar to a Fourier representation. The shape is recovered using the finite element method.

7.3 Curve and Surface Representations

Implicit equations are a traditional and natural representation which define a relationship between coordinates such that all points that satisfy this relationship belong to the structure. Such representations are ideal for determining whether specific points belong to the object but there is no general way for generating such points. Because such operations will be crucial for this work, only explicit parametric representations will be considered further.

An arbitrary curve can be represented explicitly by two functions of one parameter: $x(s)$ and $y(s)$. A surface can be represented explicitly by three function of two parameters: $x(u,v)$, $y(u,v)$ and $z(u,v)$. A surface is indexed or parametrized by the two parameters (u,v). While a curve's points are naturally ordered (by arclength), there is no natural ordering of points on an arbitrary surface. Certain classes of curves and surfaces can be represented as a single function. For example, curves expressible as a single function of one parameter, $r(\theta)$, are radial deformations of a circle. Similarly, surfaces expressible as a function of two angles, $r(\theta,\phi)$, are radial deformations of a sphere and are parametrized by (θ,ϕ). Surfaces expressible as a single function of two coordinates, $z(x,y)$, are perpendicular deformations of a plane and thus the points in the plane, (x,y), provide the parametrization.

The main approaches to parametric modeling in computer vision have been polynomials [19], superquadrics [17, 20], spherical harmonics [5, 21] and generalized cylinders [22]. All of these parametrizations are restricted to a limited class of objects.

7.3.1 Polynomials

Second degree algebraic surfaces have been used extensively because of their simplicity and conciseness. Conics are second degree curves including ellipses, parabolas and hyperbolas. Quadrics are second degree surfaces which include spheres, ellipsoids, cones, cylinders, planes, paraboloids and hyperboloids. Their conciseness, however, greatly limits their expressiveness. Higher order polynomial surfaces are expressed using implicit representations.

7.3.2 Superquadrics

Superquadrics are an extension of quadrics using an exponent that allows the shape to vary from an ellipsoid to a rectangular parallelepiped. The two-dimensional analog is the superellipse. Superquadrics can be expressed parametrically by:

$$\begin{aligned} x(u,v) &= x_0 + a_1 \mathrm{sign}(\cos v \cos u)|\cos u|^{\epsilon_1}\,|\cos v|^{\epsilon_2} \\ y(u,v) &= y_0 + a_2 \mathrm{sign}(\sin v \cos u)|\cos u|^{\epsilon_1}\,|\sin v|^{\epsilon_2} \\ z(u,v) &= z_0 + a_3 \mathrm{sign}(\sin u)|\sin u|^{\epsilon_1} \end{aligned} \qquad (1)$$

The surface parameters u and v represent latitude and longitude. The exponent ϵ_1 controls the squareness in the u plane and ϵ_2 controls the squareness in the v plane. The parameters a_1, a_2 and a_3 control the size in the x, y and z directions.

The basic shape can be altered by such operations as twisting, bending and tapering [23], as can any explicit representation. The main disadvantage of superquadrics is that even with these altering operations, superquadrics are limited by their doubly symmetric cross-section and thus still only represent a very limited family of shapes (without resorting to composition). Superquadrics have been augmented by deformations according to spline models [9] and strain modes [17] in order to increase their expressiveness. Hyperquadrics [24] are a generalization of superquadrics that allow smooth deformations from shapes with convex polyhedral bounds, although no explicit parametrized form is possible.

7.3.3 Generalized Cylinders

Generalized cylinders (or cones) are a way of representing elongated objects. They are defined by a one-dimensional curve representing the spine of the object and a two-dimensional cross-section that is swept along the spine to define the surface. This cross-section may vary along the spine. The actual properties of this representation depend on the choices of spine (sweeping rule) and cross-section.

Practical choices usually limit the class of object that is representable. The most common restriction is to straight, homogeneous generalized cylinders (SHGCs) where the spine is straight and the cross-section shape is constant (allowing scaling). These can be defined by [25]:

$$\begin{aligned} x(u,v) &= r(u)x(v) + pz(u) \\ y(u,v) &= r(u)y(v) + qz(u) \\ z(u,v) &= z(u) \end{aligned} \quad (2)$$

where u varies along the spine, v varies along the cross-section, $r(u)$ defines the scaling, $x(t)$ and $y(t)$ define the cross-section shape and $z(u)$, p and q define the spine. If the spine is allowed to bend, the cross-section is usually taken to be perpendicular to the axis. The cylinder radius must therefore be greater than the radius of curvature or else the boundary will cross itself. If the spine and cross-section are represented parametrically, as opposed to directly as an explicit list of coordinates or segments, generalized cylinders can be completely parametric.

An object can be represented by a generalized cylinder only if there exists an axis that a cross-section can sweep along in order to define the surface. The choices for the form of the spine and the cross-section further limit the expressibility of the representation.

7.3.4 Spherical Harmonics

Spherical harmonics have been used as a type of surface representation for radial or stellar surfaces ($r(\theta,\phi)$). The surface is represented as a weighted sum of spherical harmonics which are orthogonal over the sphere. A surface is represented in polar coordinates by:

$$r(\theta,\phi) = \sum_{m=0}^{M}\sum_{n=0}^{N}(A_{mn}\cos n\theta + B_{mn}\sin n\theta)\sin^n\phi\, P(m,n,\cos\phi) \quad (3)$$

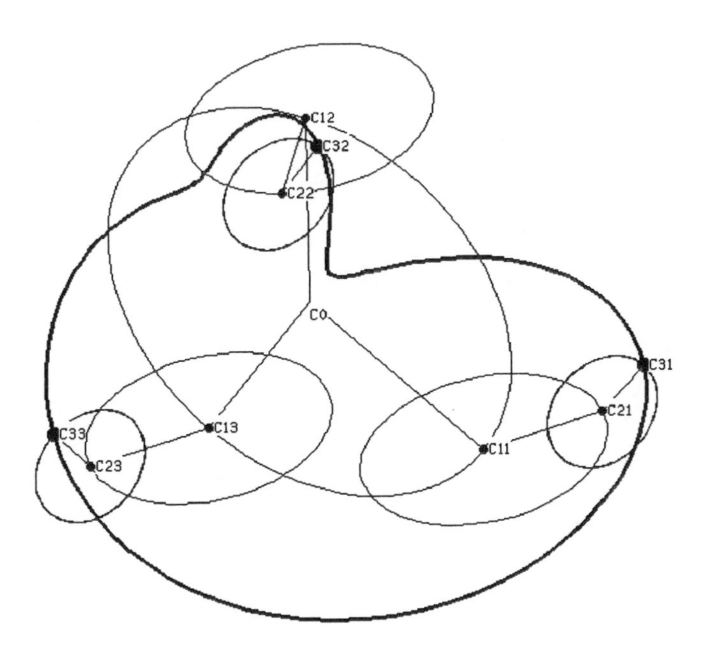

Figure 1: The contour (dark line) at the left is constructed from three component ellipses shown at three different times.

where P(m,n,x) is the nth derivative of the mth Legendre polynomial as a function of x. The parameters of the representation are the weights A_{mn} and B_{mn}.

This is a type of Fourier representation, as defined below, but restricted to stellar surfaces. Stellar surfaces are obtained by deforming a sphere by moving points only in the radial direction. This means that all surface points must be seen from one point in the interior. Thus, spherical harmonics model a somewhat limited class of objects.

7.4 Fourier Models

Smoothly deformable objects do not necessarily have an obvious decomposition that can be exploited. A uniform shape representation that describes the entire shape is therefore needed and it should describe a relatively broad class of shapes.

Fourier representations are those that express the function in terms of an orthonormal basis. The motivation for a basis representation is that it allows us to express any object as a weighted sum of a set of known functions. An orthonormal set is desirable because it makes the parameters (weights) distinct.

For example, to express the one-dimensional function $f(t)$ on the interval (a, b) in terms of the basis $\phi_k(t)$, we write:

$$f(t) = \sum_{k=1}^{\infty} p_k \phi_k(t) \qquad \text{where} \quad p_k = \int_a^b f(t)\phi_k(t)\,dt \tag{4}$$

The coefficients p, the projections of the function onto the k basis functions, are the parameters of the representation. In order to use this representation the sum is truncated. In most such representations, the higher indexed basis functions represent higher spatial variation. Therefore, if the function to be represented is expected to have limited spatial variation, as is the case for most real object boundaries, the series can be truncated and still accurately represent the function. The usual basis functions are the sinusoids [26], although others, such as orthogonal polynomials or spherical harmonics in two dimensions, are possible. The sinusoids have the advantage of representing the familiar notion of frequency.

7.5 Fourier Curves

This one-dimensional decomposition can be used as a representation for curves in two (or more) dimensions. A closed curve can be represented by two periodic functions of t, where t varies along the curve from 0 to 2π, $x(t)$ and $y(t)$. A Fourier representation for closed curves can be based on the Fourier decomposition of these two functions using the sinusoidal basis

$$\phi = \frac{1}{2\pi}, \frac{\cos x}{\pi}, \frac{\sin x}{\pi}, \frac{\cos 2x}{\pi}, \frac{\sin 2x}{\pi}, \ldots \tag{5}$$

If we write the resulting equations in matrix form, we get the elliptic Fourier representation [27], [28], [29]:

$$\begin{bmatrix} x(t) \\ y(t) \end{bmatrix} = \begin{bmatrix} a_0 \\ c_0 \end{bmatrix} + \sum_{k=1}^{\infty} \begin{bmatrix} a_k & b_k \\ c_k & d_k \end{bmatrix} \begin{bmatrix} \cos kt \\ \sin kt \end{bmatrix} \tag{6}$$

where:

$$a_0 = \frac{1}{2\pi}\int_0^{2\pi} x(t)dt \qquad c_0 = \frac{1}{2\pi}\int_0^{2\pi} y(t)dt$$

$$a_k = \frac{1}{\pi}\int_0^{2\pi} x(t)\cos kt\, dt \qquad b_k = \frac{1}{\pi}\int_0^{2\pi} x(t)\sin kt\, dt$$

$$c_k = \frac{1}{\pi}\int_0^{2\pi} y(t)\cos kt\, dt \qquad d_k = \frac{1}{\pi}\int_0^{2\pi} y(t)\sin kt\, dt$$

The closed curve is thus represented by $\mathbf{p}_{\text{raw}} = (a_0, c_0, a_1, b_1, c_1, d_1, \ldots)$ which will be referred to as the raw parameter vector. This particular version of Fourier boundary representation has a number of advantages. A geometric interpretation, in terms of ellipses, can be developed from this decomposition. The geometric interpretation will allow for better visualization of the effect of the parameters and invariance to starting point, scale and two-dimensional rotation and translation. Invariance to rotation, scale and translation is important because these parameters are determined not by the object but by the view of the object, which often cannot be held constant.

In Equation 6, the first two coefficients, a_0 and c_0, determine the overall translation of the shape. Each term in the summation is the parametric form for an ellipse. In the degenerate case $a_k d_k - b_k c_k = 0$ and the parametric form defines a straight line (a degenerate ellipse). In each term, the matrix determines the characteristics of the ellipse. The contour can be viewed as being decomposed into a sum of rotating phasors, each individually defining an ellipse, and rotating with a speed proportional to their harmonic number, k. This can be seen in Figure 1 where a contour is shown constructed from three component ellipses forming a sort of planetary system. The straight lines represent the phasors for each ellipse shown at three different times. Thus, the point C_{ij} traces out the ith ellipse at time j. Each point is the center of the next higher ellipse. C_0 is the center of the first ellipse. Points C_{31}, C_{32} and C_{33} are three different points on the final curve.

It is important that the curve representation that is decomposed into Fourier components be both continuous and periodic. Discontinuities slow the convergence because of the high frequencies inherent in a step jump. In this representation, both $x(t)$ and $y(t)$ are periodic because the contour is closed, and both $x(t)$ and $y(t)$ are continuous because the contour is continuous.

The geometric properties of each of the component ellipses can be derived from the raw elements of each ellipse matrix. Each ellipse can be described by four geometric properties: semi-major axis length, semi-minor axis length, rotation and phase shift. The rotation is the angle from the x-axis to the major axis of the ellipse, defined from $-\pi/2$ to $\pi/2$. The phase shift is the difference in phase from the major axis to the position of $t = 0$ (the ellipse starting position), defined from $-\pi$ to π.

These ellipse properties can be derived as follows. First consider the general form for an ellipse, which is the product of the raw ellipse matrix and the trigonometric basis function vector:

$$\begin{bmatrix} a & b \\ c & d \end{bmatrix} \begin{bmatrix} \cos kt \\ \sin kt \end{bmatrix} \tag{7}$$

In order to determine the ellipse parameters, consider the matrix for an ellipse with its major axis aligned with the x-axis and with no phase shift where A and B are the major and minor semi-axis lengths, respectively. The phasor moves counterclockwise for B positive, clockwise for B negative. The ellipse can be rotated simply by pre-multiplying the ellipse matrix by a rotation matrix. A phase shift of the ellipse by ϕ_0 means replacing t by $t + \phi_0$. This is the same as a pre-multiplication of the basis function vector by a rotation matrix, or equivalently, a post-multiplication of the ellipse matrix. Thus, a rotation of this ellipse by θ and shift by ϕ can be written as a pre-multiplication and a post-multiplication by rotation matrices:

$$\begin{bmatrix} \cos\theta & -\sin\theta \\ \sin\theta & \cos\theta \end{bmatrix} \begin{bmatrix} A & 0 \\ 0 & B \end{bmatrix} \begin{bmatrix} \cos\phi & -\sin\phi \\ \sin\phi & \cos\phi \end{bmatrix} \tag{8}$$

This represents a general ellipse and is thus equivalent to the raw ellipse matrix in Equation 7. Therefore, to find the ellipse parameters given the values of these matrix elements, solve the following four equations that come from identifying corresponding matrix elements for A, B, θ and ϕ.

$$\begin{aligned} a &= +A\cos\theta\cos\phi - B\sin\theta\sin\phi \qquad b = -A\cos\theta\sin\phi - B\sin\theta\cos\phi \\ c &= +A\sin\theta\cos\phi + B\cos\theta\sin\phi \qquad d = -A\sin\theta\sin\phi + B\cos\theta\cos\phi \end{aligned} \tag{9}$$

This results in:

$$\begin{aligned} A^2 &= \frac{\alpha + \sqrt{\alpha^2 - 4\beta^2}}{2} \qquad B^2 = \frac{2\beta^2}{\alpha + \sqrt{\alpha^2 - 4\beta^2}} \\ \theta &= \tan^{-1}\frac{Ac + Bb}{Aa - Bd} \qquad \phi = \tan^{-1}\frac{Ba - Ad}{Ac + Bb} \end{aligned} \tag{10}$$

where:

$$\alpha = a^2 + b^2 + c^2 + d^2, \qquad \beta = ad - bc$$

By taking A to be positive and B to agree in sign with j, we get a consistent sign convention. These parameters, $\mathbf{p}_{\text{ref}} = (a_0, c_0, A_1, B_1, \theta_1, \phi_1, \ldots)$, represent the shape in terms of the ellipse properties and will be referred to as the refined parameters.

A further conversion can improve this set by converting the rotation and shift parameters from absolute quantities to values relative to the preceding harmonic and by normalizing the axes' lengths [30]. This conversion to relative quantities will allow the isolation of an overall rotation parameter and the removal of the overall phase shift, ϕ_1, which is arbitrary. Normalizing the axes' lengths creates an overall scale parameter.

Open Curves

Open curves can be represented by having the parameter t start at one end of the line, trace along the contour to the other end, and then retrace the curve in the opposite direction to create a closed path. That is, $x(t) = x(2\pi - t)$ and $y(t) = y(2\pi - t)$ [26]. The resulting functions are even and thus they can be represented by the even sinusoidal basis functions

$$\phi_{\text{even}} = \left\{ \frac{1}{2\pi}, \frac{\cos x}{\pi}, \frac{\cos 2x}{\pi}, \frac{\cos 3x}{\pi}, \ldots \right\} \tag{11}$$

This representation can be thought of as decomposing the curve into degenerate ellipses (flattened down to two coincident lines). The equations for the corresponding ellipse parameters are simplified because the sine terms, b_k and d_k, are zero:

$$A^2 = a^2 + c^2 \qquad B^2 = 0 \qquad \theta = \tan^{-1}\frac{c}{a} \qquad \phi = 0 \tag{12}$$

The ellipses are all degenerate with a fixed starting point at one end, thus forcing both the minor semi-axis length, B, and the starting point, ϕ, to be zero.

7.5 Fourier Surfaces

In order to represent surfaces, a function of two variables is needed. Because the parity of the functions will be important, a useful two-dimensional basis is [31]:

$$\begin{aligned} \phi = \{ & 1, \cos 2\pi mu, \sin 2\pi mu, \cos 2\pi lv, \sin 2\pi lv, \ldots, \\ & \cos 2\pi mu \cos 2\pi lv, \sin 2\pi mu \cos 2\pi lv, \\ & \cos 2\pi mu \sin 2\pi lv, \sin 2\pi mu \sin 2\pi lv, \ldots \qquad (m = 1, 2, \ldots; l = 1, 2, \ldots) \ \} \end{aligned} \tag{13}$$

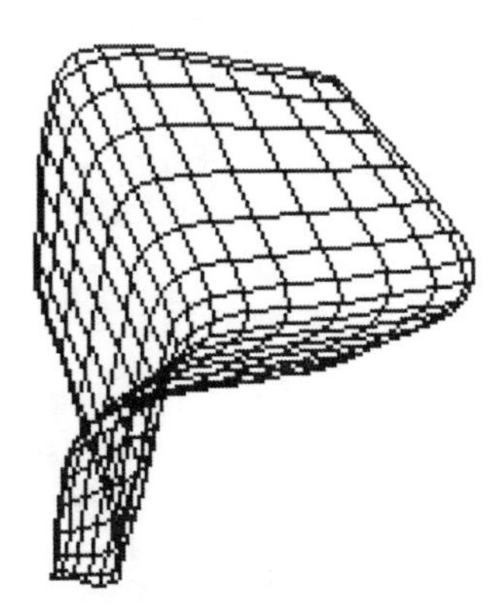

Figure 2: An example torus surface (left) using up to second order harmonics and an example open surface (right) using up to fourth.

The function is then represented by:

$$f(u,v) = \sum_{m=0}^{2K} \sum_{l=0}^{2K} \lambda_{m,l} \; [\; a_{m,l} \cos 2\pi mu \cos 2\pi lv + b_{m,l} \sin 2\pi mu \cos 2\pi lv + c_{m,l} \cos 2\pi mu \sin 2\pi lv + d_{m,l} \sin 2\pi mu \sin 2\pi lv] \quad (14)$$

where:

$$\lambda_{m,l} = \begin{cases} 1 & \text{for} \quad m=0,\ l=0 \\ 2 & \text{for} \quad m>0,\ l=0 \text{ or } m=0,\ l>0 \\ 4 & \text{for} \quad m>0,\ l>0 \end{cases}$$

This allows the specification of even functions (using the cosine terms) and odd functions (using the sine terms). The complex basis is useful for computational purposes because the parameters can be computed in a single transform:

$$\phi = \{1, e^{2\pi i(mu+lv)}, \ldots \quad (m = \pm1, \pm2, \ldots; l = \pm1, \pm2, \ldots) \ \} \quad (15)$$

Using Euler's formula, $e^{ix} = \cos x + i \sin x$, we can derive the conversion between the sine-cosine basis parameters and the complex basis parameters.

The bases presented can be used for parametrizing surfaces in three dimensions. Such surfaces can be described explicitly by three functions of two surface parameters:

$$\mathbf{x}(u,v) = (x(u,v), y(u,v), z(u,v)) \quad (16)$$

where u and v vary over the surface and x, y, and z are the associated Cartesian coordinates. This surface representation imposes no restriction on the class of surfaces representable. There are three corresponding sets of parameters: a_x, b_x, c_x, d_x, a_y, b_y, c_y, d_y, a_z, b_z, c_z, d_z. While the choice of u and v is obvious for simple surfaces such as spheres (use latitude and longitude) or cylinders (use longitude and height), very complicated surfaces will require some further analysis to determine the appropriate surface parametrization. Axis transforms [10] may provide a way of determining the overall structure on which to base the surface parametrization.

There are four classes of simple surfaces in three dimensions that will be described: tori (closed tubes), open surfaces (with one edge), tubes (open surfaces with two edges) and closed surfaces (no edges). The torus is formed using the entire basis shown in Equation 14. The result is a torus because both surface parameters are forced to be periodic. An example torus surfaces using this parametrization is shown in Figure 2. The other three types of surfaces can be described using subsets of the above basis which flatten out or constrain the torus in different ways.

7.5.1 Open Surfaces

Representing open surfaces with the basis in Equation 14 is complicated by the periodicity property. Since the surface is open, a straightforward representation of the surface would result in discontinuities at the boundary. Thus, these discontinuities can be avoided by having the two surface parameters start at one side of the surface, trace along the surface to the other end, and then retrace the surface in the opposite direction to create a closed path.

This results in a function $x(u,v)$ that is even and thus only the purely even terms, $a_{x,0,0}$, $a_{x,m,0}$, $a_{x,0,l}$ and $a_{x,m,l}$ are nonzero. This also holds for $y(u,v)$ and $z(u,v)$. The converse is also true; that is, any expansion with only those terms nonzero for all l and m results in an even function and thus describes an open surface. We are therefore effectively restricting the basis to include only even functions of both u and v.

$$\begin{aligned} \phi_{\text{open}} &= \{1, \cos mu, \cos lv, \ldots, \\ &\quad \cos mu \cos lv, \ldots \qquad (m = 1, 2, \ldots; l = 1, 2, \ldots)\} \end{aligned} \tag{17}$$

Open surfaces are useful for a wide variety of structures including objects with one prominent opening, the bounding surface between two touching objects and flat objects. An example open surfaces using this parametrization is shown in Figure 2.

7.5.2 Tube Surfaces

Tubes require the open representation along one of the surface parameters and the closed representation along the other. This results in the following basis which is even in v and unrestricted in u:

$$\begin{aligned} \phi_{\text{tube}} &= \{1, \cos lv, \sin mu, \cos mu, \ldots, \\ &\quad \cos mu \cos lv, \sin mu \cos lv, \ldots \qquad (m = 1, 2, \ldots; l = 1, 2, \ldots)\} \end{aligned} \tag{18}$$

Thus the only nonzero terms are $a_{x,0,0}$, $a_{x,0,l}$, $a_{x,m,0}$, $b_{x,m,0}$, $a_{x,m,l}$ and $b_{x,m,l}$ and the corresponding y and z terms. Tubes are an extension of generalized cylinders where the cross-section is no longer constrained to be planar. This allows for a wider range of shapes to be represented. All of the standard types of generalized cylinders can be represented in a Fourier representation as well. For example, the SHGC defined in Equation 2 can be represented by decomposing the cross-section function ($x(v)$ and $y(v)$) using the closed curve representation, and decomposing the scaling function ($r(u)$) and the spine ($z(u)$) using the open curve representation described above.

Tubes are useful for elongated hollow objects and elongated objects with flat ends. They are also useful for temporal sequences of planar images, where the third

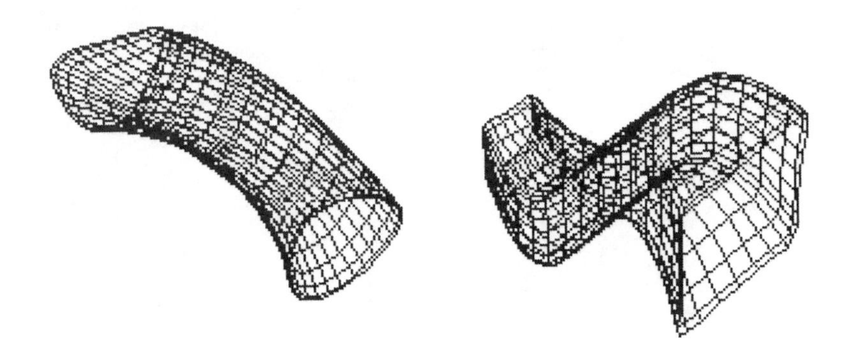

Figure 3: Two tube surface examples using up to fourth order harmonics.

dimension is time, and multimodal images, where the third dimension is modality. In this case a simplified tube model would be used where the third dimension was independent of the two surface parameters, for example, $z(u, v) = t$. Two example tube surfaces using this parametrization are shown in Figure 3.

7.5.3 Closed Surfaces

Closed surfaces are the most difficult to represent because they are most dissimilar to tori. One way to represent closed surfaces is by considering tubes whose ends close up to a point at both ends instead of being open. This is done by expressing x and y using the following basis:

$$\begin{aligned}\phi_{\text{closed-xy}} &= \{1, \sin lv, \ldots, \\ &\qquad \cos mu \sin lv, \sin mu \sin lv, \ldots \qquad (m = 1, 2, \ldots; l = 1, 2, \ldots)\}\end{aligned} \tag{19}$$

thus forcing both functions to constants at $v = 0, \pi, 2\pi$. This means that z must be expressed using only the cosines:

$$\phi_{\text{closed-z}} = \{1, \cos lv, \ldots, \qquad (l = 1, 2, \ldots)\} \tag{20}$$

This requires that the values for v be repeated as for a open curve but negated for x and y because they are both odd functions. The values for v are just repeated for z because it is an even function. That is:

$$\begin{aligned}x(u, v) &= -x(u, 2\pi - v) \\ y(u, v) &= -y(u, 2\pi - v) \\ z(u, v) &= z(u, 2\pi - v)\end{aligned} \tag{21}$$

This representation is limited in that the axis along z is straight because $z(u, v) = z(v)$. Because the axis is aligned along z, an additional general rotation is necessary to allow for all orientations. Two example closed surfaces using this parametrization are shown in Figure 4, with terms up to fourth order on the left and eighth order on the right.

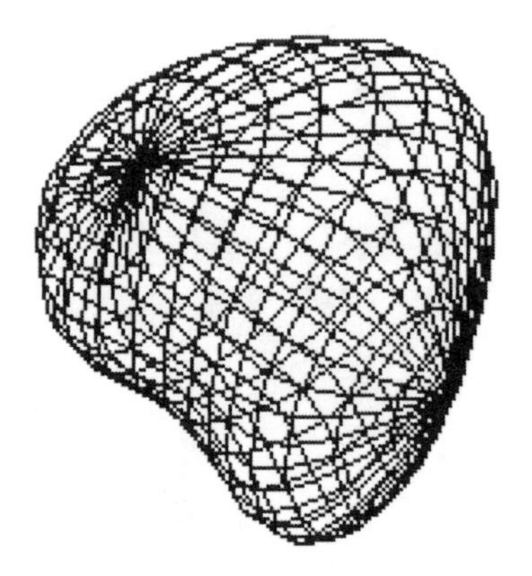
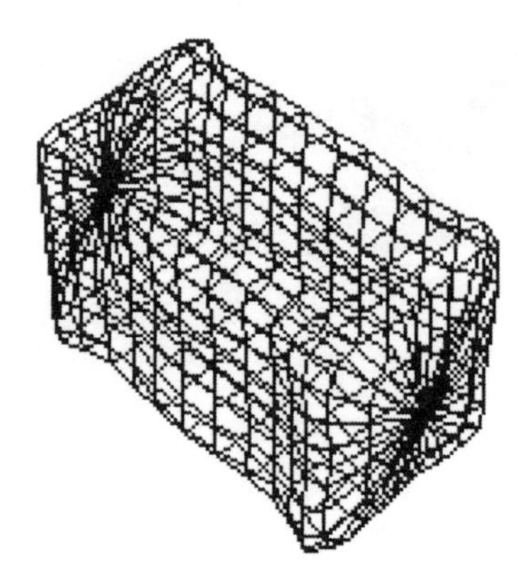

Figure 4: Two closed surface examples using up to fourth order harmonics on the left and eighth order on the right.

7.5.4 Surface geometry

The Fourier surface description makes the calculation of geometric surface properties straightforward because a continuous description of the surface is known. Without an analytic description of the surface, curvature can be calculated based on the computation of derivatives from a local surface patch fit, or from a discrete approximation of the derivatives at each point. These methods are dependent on the proper choice of the size of the patch or neighborhood. For Fourier surfaces, partial derivatives of the surface functions can be calculated from the functional description. Curvature is then calculated directly from these partial derivatives [19]. Surface curvature properties have been used to classify and characterize shape. For example, surface regions can be classified by the sign of the surface curvatures as peaks, ridges, saddles, valleys, pits and flats.

7.6 Boundary Finding Objective Function

In order to fit one of these models to the image data, a measure of fit is optimized by varying the model parameters. The surface is expected to be distinguishable by some measure of boundary strength (direction can also be used) computed from the image. The sum or integral of the boundary strength image over a given surface indicates the degree of correspondence between them, and this can be used as the measure of fit.

Any measure that indicates a change in some property that distinguishes the object from the background could be used as a boundary measure. A natural candidate for many images is the gray-level gradient. The magnitude is the strength of the boundary and the direction is the normal to the boundary. The gray level gradient can be calculated by first smoothing with a Gaussian to reduce the effect of noise. This is followed by a finite difference approximation to the partial derivatives in order to control smoothing independently. The smoothed boundary response will also help in the optimization by attracting the surface from further away. For two-dimensional images, 2×2 or 3×3 finite differences are used. For three-dimensional images, $2 \times 2 \times 2$ or $3 \times 3 \times 3$ finite differences are used.

The measure of fit for curves can be written as follows, here using only boundary strength:

$$M(b, \mathbf{p}) = \int_0^S |b(x(\mathbf{p}, s), y(\mathbf{p}, s), z(\mathbf{p}, s))| ds \tag{22}$$

where $\mathbf{p}$ is the vector consisting of the basis function parameters. Although this implies fixing the highest order harmonic used, an iterative method for determining the best K using a trade-off between conciseness and fit could be devised. The equivalent measure for surfaces is:

$$M(b, \mathbf{p}) = \iint_{\mathcal{A}} |b(x(\mathbf{p}, u, v), y(\mathbf{p}, u, v), z(\mathbf{p}, u, v))| dA \tag{23}$$

Equation 23 can be evaluated by numerical integration. The boundary strength array, $|b|$ can be evaluated at each point on the surface using linear interpolation.

The length element on the curve is given by:

$$ds = \left|\frac{d\mathbf{x}}{dt}\right| dt = \sqrt{\left(\frac{dx}{dt}\right)^2 + \left(\frac{dy}{dt}\right)^2} dt \tag{24}$$

The area element on the surface $\mathcal{A}$ is given by:

$$dA = \left|\frac{\partial \mathbf{x}}{\partial u} \times \frac{\partial \mathbf{x}}{\partial v}\right| dudv \tag{25}$$

The gradient of the objective is necessary for optimization. The derivative of the curve objective with respect to the parameters governing x is:

$$\frac{\partial M}{\partial \mathbf{p}_x} = \int_0^S \left[|b(x, y)| \frac{\partial}{\partial \mathbf{p}_x} \left|\frac{d\mathbf{x}}{dt}\right| + \frac{\partial |b(x, y)|}{\partial x} \frac{\partial x(\mathbf{p}, s)}{\partial \mathbf{p}_x} \left|\frac{d\mathbf{x}}{dt}\right| \right] ds \tag{26}$$

The corresponding derivative for the surface objective is:

$$\frac{\partial M}{\partial \mathbf{p}_x} = \iint_{\mathcal{A}} \left[|b(x, y, z)| \frac{\partial}{\partial \mathbf{p}_x} \left|\frac{\partial \mathbf{x}}{\partial u} \times \frac{\partial \mathbf{x}}{\partial v}\right| + \frac{\partial |b(x, y, z)|}{\partial x} \frac{\partial x(\mathbf{p}, u, v)}{\partial \mathbf{p}_x} \left|\frac{\partial \mathbf{x}}{\partial u} \times \frac{\partial \mathbf{x}}{\partial v}\right| \right] dudv \tag{27}$$

and similarly for y and z. This expression can also be evaluated by numerical integration. Expressions such as $\frac{\partial |b|}{\partial x}$ can be determined by discrete derivative calculations at each point on the curve or surface, again using linear interpolation.

The expressions such as $\frac{\partial x}{\partial \mathbf{p}_x}$ can be calculated from the expressions for x, y, and z (shown in Equation 6 or Equation 14).

The partials $\frac{\partial \mathbf{x}}{\partial u}$ and $\frac{\partial \mathbf{x}}{\partial v}$ can be evaluated either analytically or from discrete approximation. The expressions $\frac{\partial}{\partial \mathbf{p}_x}|\frac{\partial \mathbf{x}}{\partial u} \times \frac{\partial \mathbf{x}}{\partial v}|$ and $|\frac{d\mathbf{x}}{dt}|$ can be calculated by expanding and evaluating expressions such as $\frac{\partial}{\partial \mathbf{p}_x}(\frac{dx}{dv})$ by discrete approximation. The above follows similarly for $\frac{\partial}{\partial \mathbf{p}_y}$ and $\frac{\partial}{\partial \mathbf{p}_z}$.

7.6.1 Probabilistic Formulation

In order to incorporate probabilistic information into the measure of fit, consider the problem of boundary determination as one in which the data is a two or three dimensional image, $b(\mathbf{x})$, which could be depicting the boundary of any object in the parametric representation and $t_{\mathbf{p}}(\mathbf{x})$ is an image template corresponding to a particular value of the parameter vector $\mathbf{p}$. In terms of probabilities, if we want to decide which template, $t_{\mathbf{p}}$, an image, b, corresponds to, we need to evaluate the probability of the template given the image, $\Pr(t_{\mathbf{p}}|b)$, and find the maximum over $\mathbf{p}$. This can be expressed using Bayes rule, where:

$$\Pr(t_{\mathrm{map}}|b) = \max_{\mathbf{p}} \Pr(t_{\mathbf{p}}|b) = \max_{\mathbf{p}} \frac{\Pr(b|t_{\mathbf{p}})\Pr(t_{\mathbf{p}})}{\Pr(b)} \tag{28}$$

Here, t_{map} is the maximum *a posteriori* solution, $\Pr(t_{\mathbf{p}})$ is the prior probability of template $t_{\mathbf{p}}$ and $\Pr(b|t_{\mathbf{p}})$ is the conditional probability, or likelihood, of the image given the template. This expression can be simplified by taking the logarithm and eliminating $\Pr(b)$, the prior probability of the image data, which is equal for all $\mathbf{p}$:

$$M(b, t_{\mathrm{map}}) = \max_{\mathbf{p}} M(b, t_{\mathbf{p}}) = \max_{\mathbf{p}} \left[\ln \Pr(t_{\mathbf{p}}) + \ln \Pr(b|t_{\mathbf{p}})\right] \tag{29}$$

This maximum *a posteriori* objective function shows the tradeoff or compromise that is made between prior information, $\Pr(t_{\mathbf{p}})$, and image-derived information, $\Pr(b|t_{\mathbf{p}})$. For a uniform prior, this formulation reduces to the maximum likelihood solution.

In order to derive the expression for the likelihood, consider the image b to be a noise-corrupted version of one of these templates with noise that is independent and additive: $b = t_{\mathbf{p}} + n$. This assumption avoids an excessive increase in complexity. Furthermore, Cooper [7] showed, for a related problem, that this assumption did not alter the performance significantly. Then, the likelihood, $\Pr(b|t_{\mathbf{p}})$, is equivalent to $\Pr(n = b - t_{\mathbf{p}})$. The noise at each image point, $n(\mathbf{x})$, equals $b(\mathbf{x}) - t_{\mathbf{p}}(\mathbf{x})$ and is governed by the probability density $\Pr(n)$. These events are independent for each point, so the probability for the noise over the entire region $\mathcal{A}$ is just the product of the individual probabilities. The noise is the combined effect of many factors such as signal degradation, occlusion and boundary measurement which are difficult to model explicitly. We make the assumption that the noise is Gaussian with zero mean and standard deviation σ_n.

The object template, $t_{\mathbf{p}}(\mathbf{x})$, represents the boundary of the object. The boundary can be embedded into the image template by making $t_{\mathbf{p}}(\mathbf{x})$ constant along the boundary of the object it represents and zero everywhere else. In order to match this template with the image, consider $b(\mathbf{x})$ to be a boundary measure applied to the raw image data, $b(\mathbf{x}) = b(i(\mathbf{x}))$. Both $t_{\mathbf{p}}$ and b are image functions that represent boundaries that are summed (or integrated), only along the boundary.

Because the template has support only along the boundary, it is not necessary to sum over the entire image for terms involving the template, but only where the template has support. In addition, the magnitude of $t_{\mathbf{p}}(\mathbf{x})$ is taken to be constant (k), over the boundary that it defines. The function M can be simplified further by removing the terms that do not depend on $\mathbf{p}$.

The continuous version of this for a curve is:

$$M(b, \mathbf{p}) = \ln \Pr(\mathbf{p}) + \frac{k}{2\sigma_n^2} \int_0^S [b(x(\mathbf{p}, s), y(\mathbf{p}, s)) - k]ds \tag{30}$$

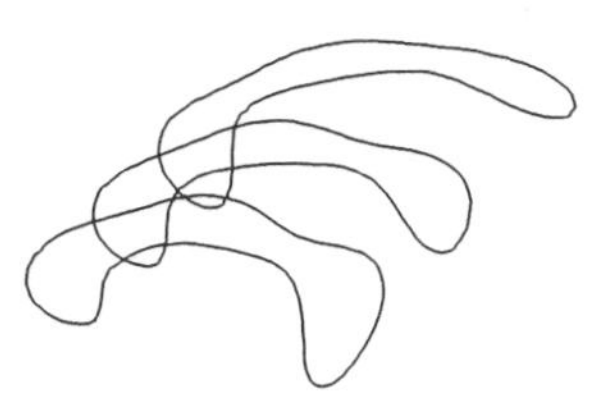

Figure 5: Example mean curve, shown with curves corresponding to parameters plus and minus one standard deviation.

where s is arclength. For a surface, it is:

$$M(b,\mathbf{p}) = \ln \Pr(\mathbf{p}) + \frac{k}{2\sigma_n^2}\iint_{\mathcal{A}} [b(x(\mathbf{p},u,v), y(\mathbf{p},u,v), z(\mathbf{p},u,v)) - k]dA \qquad (31)$$

where dA is an area element on the surface $\mathcal{A}$.

Equations 30 and 31 are the maximum *a posteriori* objective functions for curve and surface finding. In both, the first term is the contribution of the prior probability of the parameter vector. The greater the variance of the prior, the smaller the influence of this term. The second term is equivalent to the objectives in Equations 22 and 23.

The probability distributions associated with the parameters are intended to bias the model towards a particular range of shapes. This prior knowledge comes from experience with a sample of images of the object being delineated, when such a sample is available. When prior information is not available, uniform distributions are used for the prior probabilities of the parameters and an initial estimate of the boundary must be supplied. The images in a sample will differ due to variability in the object shape and the view of the object. The prior probability distributions can then be estimated from the shapes determined from the sample by decomposing the boundaries into their model parameters and collecting statistics. The boundaries of the sample objects are determined either by manual segmentation or, alternatively, this method can go through a training phase on a set of images with manual initialization and uniform distributions. This has been done only for the curve models so far because invariance to the surface parametrization has not been established for the surface models.

An independent, multivariate Gaussian can be used for the parameters. An example distribution is shown in Figure 5. The middle curve corresponds to the mean parameter values. Above and below it are the curves corresponding to the mean parameter values plus and minus one standard deviation.

7.7 Boundary Parameter Optimization

The problem to be solved is that of maximizing the objective function $M(\mathbf{p})$. The objective function we are solving is not in general convex, but depends ultimately on the gray-level surface shape of the image. If the starting point of the optimization is good enough, the global optimum can be found by a local optimization. Thus, an initial position for the surface must be supplied by the user or some initial processing step. Continuous gradient ascent [32] was used to optimize the objective function. This method takes small steps in the direction of the gradient (the direction of greatest increase) until an optimal point is found.

The problem to be solved is that of maximizing the objective function $M(\mathbf{p})$. The objective function we are solving is not in general convex, but depends ultimately on the gray-level surface shape of the image. However, the prior probability term in the objective function is quadratic and it dominates on the tails of the distributions, making distant points in the space non-optimal. The starting point for the optimization will be taken to be the maximum of the prior distributions. The global optimum probably will be near the starting point and thus a local optimum is likely to be a global optimum. The degree to which this is true depends on the width of the distributions. Since a local optimization method is likely to be sufficient, although there is still the possibility of converging to a poor local maximum, the excessive computation involved in finding a global optimum is deemed not necessary. Poor convergence can be identified by a corresponding low objective function value and verified visually. Smoothing can also be used to avoid getting trapped in a local maximum.

7.8 Experiments

From experiments varying the amount of noise added to a synthetic image, this method has been shown to be relatively insensitive to noise [33]. The effect of the initial values of the parameters on the performance was investigated by examining the results of running the same problem from different starting points. Each parameter was found to have a range within which the solution was found reliably [33]. Once the parameters are varied beyond that range, the result will converge to false local minima corresponding to nearby features. This region of success or capture about the true boundary depends on the quality of the image, the degree of smoothing and the particular problem. False minima can be distinguished, however, both visually and by the relative value of the objective function.

The deformable object boundary finding method has been applied to a variety of objects from real images, with an emphasis on heart and brain images using primarily magnetic resonance images. The results of the method applied to the problem of delineating the corpus callosum in the human brain from magnetic resonance images are shown in Figure 6. In these images, the corpus callosum is separated from the rest of the brain by a dark line. In this case, we used the positive magnitude of the Laplacian of the Gaussian as a line detector. The final contour succeeds in delineating the structure properly.

Magnetic resonance is becoming more and more important for cardiac imaging as acquisition rates increase into the range required for imaging the moving heart. In Figure 7, a transaxial cardiac image shows a section through the left ventricular wall. Here, the endocardial (inner) and epicardial (outer) walls of the left ventricle are objects to be delineated. The results of the two separate optimizations are shown.

In Figure 8, a transaxial slice of one frame of a cardiac image of a dog from the Dynamic Spatial Reconstructor (DSR) is analyzed. The DSR is a dynamic, three-dimensional imaging device based on high-speed x-ray computed tomography

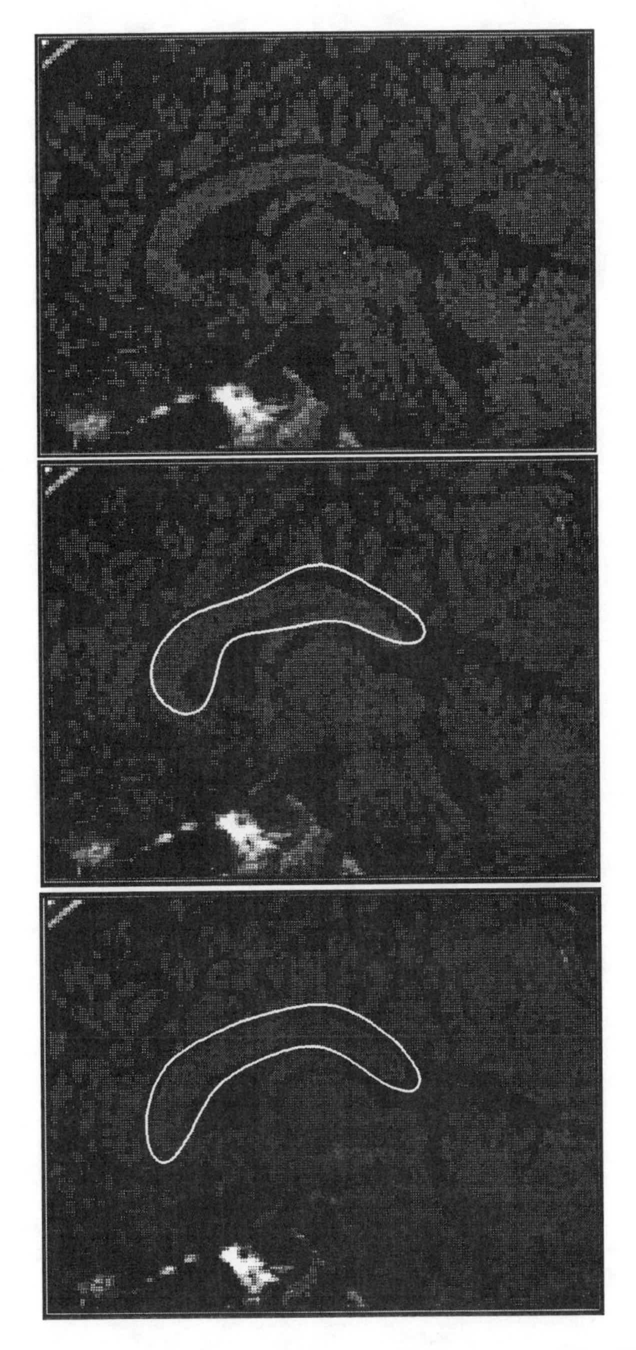

Figure 6: Magnetic resonance mid-brain sagittal image example. Top: Magnetic resonance image (146 × 106). Middle: Initial contour (6 harmonics). Bottom: Final contour on the corpus callosum of the brain.

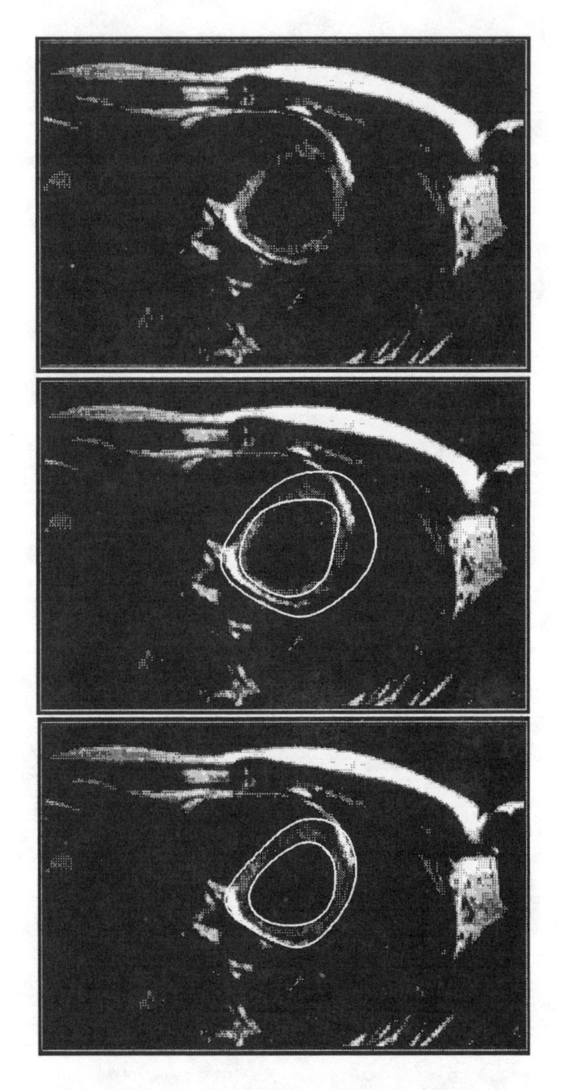

Figure 7: Magnetic resonance transaxial cardiac image example. Top: Magnetic resonance image (256×156). Middle: Initial contour on the endocardium and epicardium (4 harmonics). Bottom: Final contour on the endocardium and epicardium of the left ventricle.

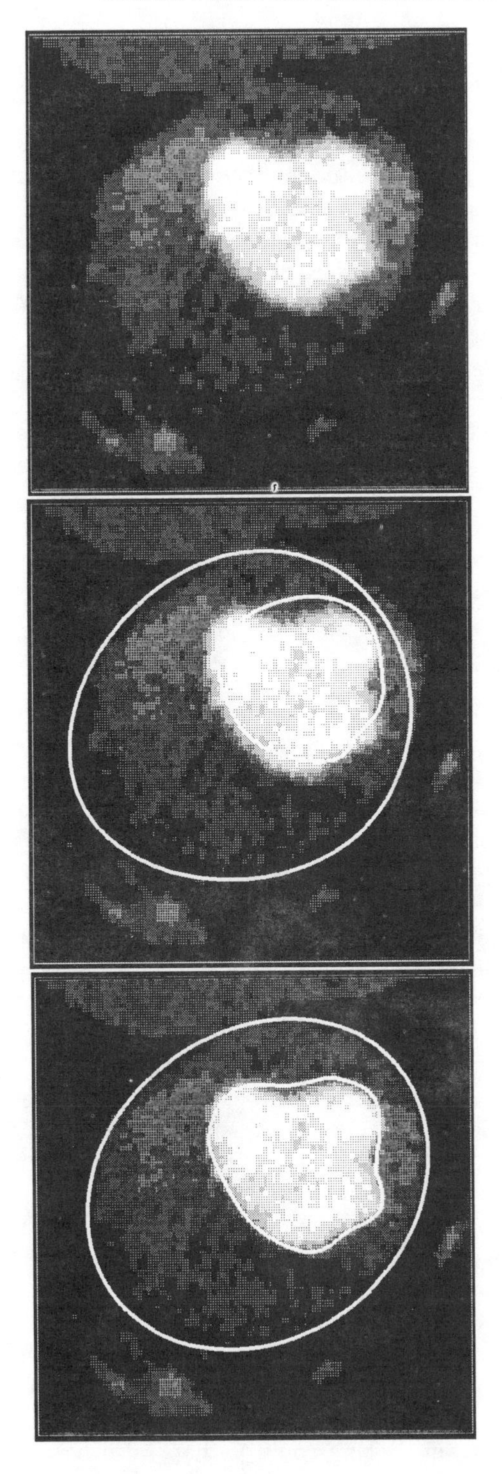

Figure 8: Dynamic Spatial Reconstructor (DSR) transaxial cardiac image example. Top: Original transaxial view of left ventricle. Middle: initial contour for epicardium and endocardium. Bottom: Converged result of boundary detection algorithm on epicardium and endocardium.

capable of imaging the moving heart [34]. Both the endocardial (inner) and epicardial (outer) walls of the left ventricle are delineated as the result of two separate optimizations.

Surface finding in three-dimensional images is becoming more important due to the availability of range images and true three-dimensional images from magnetic resonance imaging (MRI), computed tomography (CT), single photon emission computed tomography (SPECT), positron emission tomography (PET) and confocal microscopy. Results of the surface finding method applied to the problem of delineating the upper portion of the cerebrum of the human brain from a three-dimensional magnetic resonance image are shown in Figure 9. The surface was matched to the gradient magnitude calculated from the image. The final boundary succeeds in delineating the structure properly.

In Figure 10, a three-dimensional cardiac image of a dog's heart from the Dynamic Spatial Reconstructor (DSR) is analyzed. The DSR is a dynamic, three-dimensional imaging device based on high-speed x-ray computed tomography capable of imaging the moving heart [34]. As before, the surface was matched to the gradient magnitude calculated from the image. The endocardial (inner) wall of the left ventricle is successfully delineated.

7.9 Summary

This work presents a general boundary finding system for both two-dimensional and three-dimensional images of simple natural objects. The goal of this work was to incorporate model-based information about global shape into boundary finding for continuously deformable objects. In addition, the shape parametrization can be augmented with probabilistic information. From testing on real and synthetic, the system was found to perform well at delineating structures and to be relatively insensitive to the problems of broken boundaries and spurious edges from nearby objects. The flexibility of the model make this an attractive method for boundary finding. In addition, a new global shape parametrization for surfaces useful as a representation for computer vision and modeling has been described. This parametrization extends the expressibility of previous parametrizations. Although the current formulation is for three-dimensional images, these surface models also could be used to model $2\frac{1}{2}$-D range data where the model would include the hidden surface.

There are, of course, areas of potential improvement for this work. The surface shape parametrization needs invariance to view and choice of surface parametrization u, v. Because the initial estimates of the view parameters may not be very good, an additional process to determine them could be added. This could involve an initial exhaustive coarse search over just those parameters. If this were done at a low resolution, the computation might not be excessive. Additional information, such as other low-level features or constraints between objects, might also help to guide the initial placement.

The framework presented here could perhaps also be used with other shape parametrizations better suited to man-made objects with straight sides and corners. The method could also be extended to object recognition where an image is fit to each of the models for different objects in a database. The correct model will result in the best fit because it will be the closest in the parameter space. The boundary

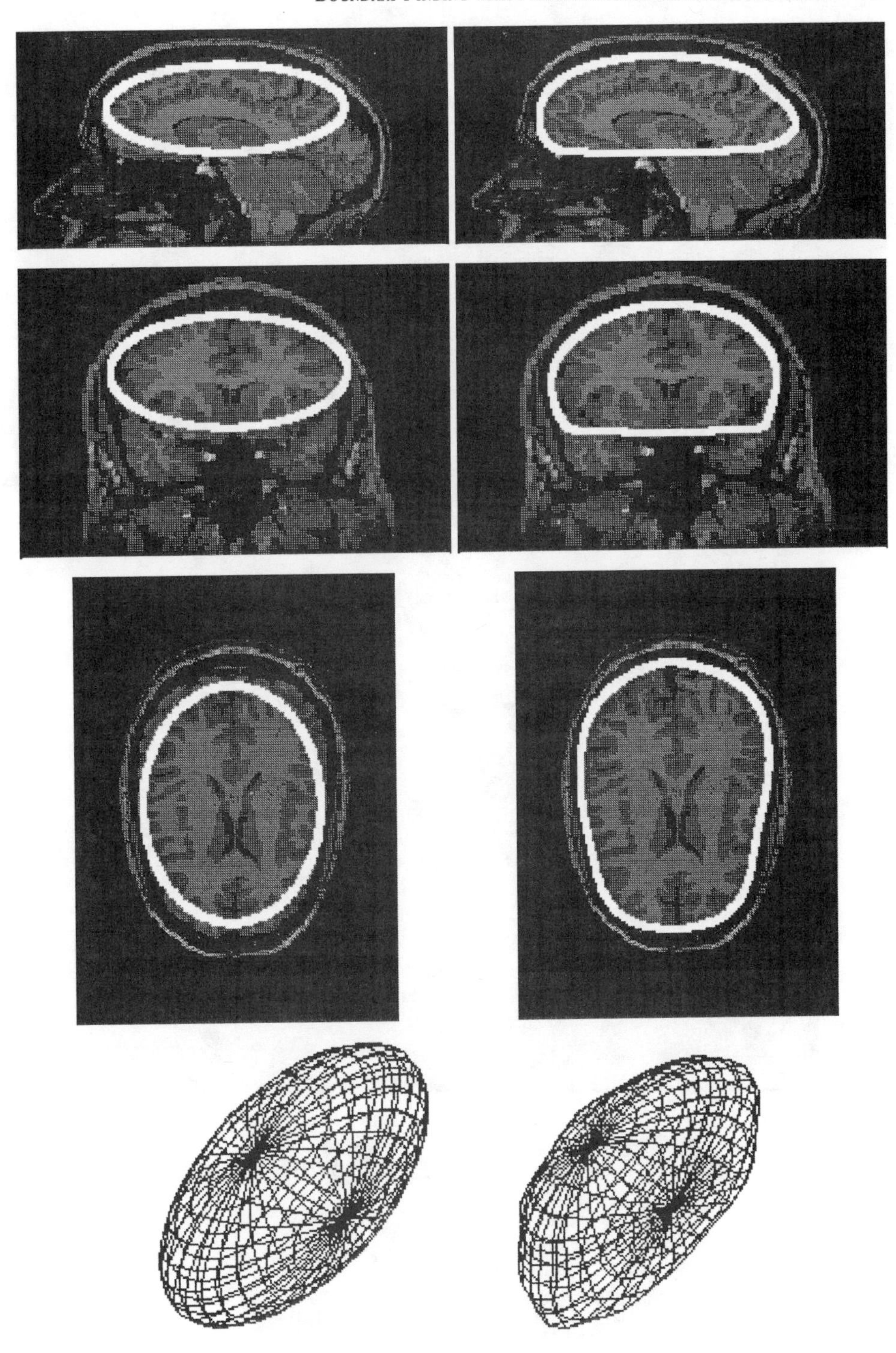

Figure 9: Magnetic resonance brain image example. Left: Three perpendicular slices through the three-dimensional image ($120 \times 160 \times 78$) are shown with the initial surface. Right: The same slices shown with final surface indicating the upper portion of the cerebrum. Bottom: Wire frame of initial (left) and final (right) surface.

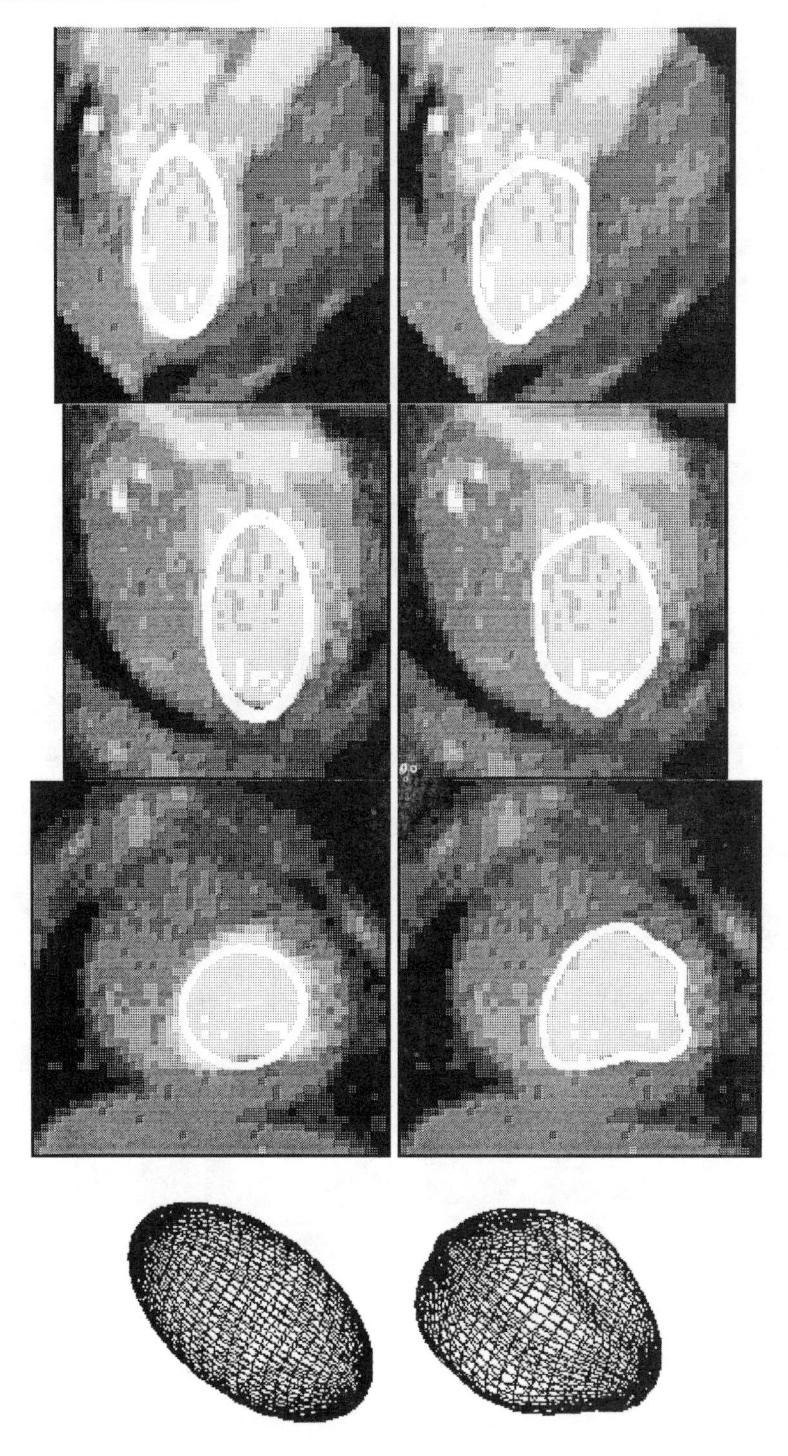

Figure 10: Dynamic Spatial Reconstructor (DSR) cardiac image example. Left: Three perpendicular slices through the three-dimensional image ($49 \times 50 \times 55$) are shown with the initial surface. Right: The same slices shown with final surface at the endocardium. Bottom: Wire frame of initial (left) and final (right) surface.

finder and some of the ideas from this work have also been applied to the problem of contour-based deformable object motion [35].

Spatiotemporal models can be developed and used to measure motion. For two-dimensional objects, the motion can be characterized by the spatiotemporal surface corresponding to the object's moving boundary. The motion of surfaces could be modeled by a manifold in four dimensions. These spatiotemporal surfaces would be parametrized using basis functions. Note that if the correspondence between points on successive boundaries can be determined, this represents an approach to general, non-rigid object motion.

7.10 Acknowledgements

The dynamic spatial reconstructor data was obtained from Richard Robb of the Mayo Clinic. The code for the 3-D image gradient calculation was written by John Mceachen. This work was supported in part by the National Institutes of Health under Grants T15LM07056 and F36LM00007 from the National Library of Medicine and Grant R29HL38333 from the National Heart Lung and Blood Institute.

References

[1] R. Mohan and R. Nevatia. Segmentation and description based on perceptual organization. In *Proc. IEEE Conf. Computer Vision and Pattern Recognition*, pages 333–341, June 1989.

[2] P. T. Sander and S. W. Zucker. Inferring surface trace and differential structure from 3-D images. *IEEE Trans. Pattern Anal. Machine Intell.*, 12(9):833–854, September 1990.

[3] F. Bergholm. Edge focusing. *IEEE Trans. Pattern Anal. Machine Intell.*, 9(6):726–741, November 1987.

[4] A. Martelli. An application of heuristic search methods to edge and contour detection. *Communications of the ACM*, 19(2):73–83, February 1976.

[5] D. H. Ballard and C. M. Brown. *Computer Vision.* Prentice-Hall, Englewood Cliffs, 1982.

[6] C. W. K. Gritton and E. A. Parrish, Jr. Boundary location from an initial plan: The bead chain algorithm. *IEEE Trans. Pattern Anal. Machine Intell.*, 5(1):8–13, January 1983.

[7] D. B. Cooper. Maximum likelihood estimation of Markov-process blob boundaries in noisy images. *IEEE Trans. Pattern Anal. Machine Intell.*, 1(4):372–384, October 1979.

[8] M. Kass, A. Witkin, and D. Terzopoulos. Snakes: Active contour models. *Int. J. Computer Vision*, 1(4):321–331, 1988.

[9] D. Terzopoulos, A. Witkin, and M. Kass. Symmetry-seeking models and 3D object reconstruction. *Int. J. Computer Vision*, 1:211–221, 1987.

[10] J. M. Gauch and S. M. Pizer. Image description via the multiresolution intensity axis of symmetry. In *Proc. Second Int. Conf. Computer Vision*, pages 269–274, 1988.

[11] H. Delingette, M. Hebert, and K. Ikeuchi. Shape representation and image segmentation using deformable surfaces. In *Proc. IEEE Conf. Computer Vision and Pattern Recognition*, pages 467–472, June 1991.

[12] Y. F. Wang and J. F. Wang. Surface reconstruction using deformable models with interior and boundary constraints. In *Proc. Third Conf. Computer Vision*, pages 300–303, December 1990.

[13] I. Cohen, L. D. Cohen, and N. Ayache. Introducing new deformable surfaces to segment 3D images. In *Proc. IEEE Conf. Computer Vision and Pattern Recognition*, pages 738–739, June 1991.

[14] B. Widrow. The "rubber mask" technique. *Pattern Recognition*, 5:175–211, 1973.

[15] A. L. Yuille, D. S. Cohen, and P. W. Hallinan. Feature extraction from faces using deformable templates. In *Proc. IEEE Conf. Computer Vision and Pattern Recognition*, pages 104–109, June 1989.

[16] Y. Chow, U. Grenander, and D. M. Keenan. Hands: A pattern theoretic study of biological shapes. Monograph, Division of Applied Mathematics, Brown University, Providence, Rhode Island, 1989.

[17] A. P. Pentland. Automatic extraction of deformable part models. *Int. J. Computer Vision*, 4:107–126, 1990.

[18] A. Pentland and S. Sclaroff. Closed-form solutions for physically based shape modeling and recognition. *IEEE Trans. Pattern Anal. Machine Intell.*, 13(7):715–729, July 1991.

[19] P. J. Besl. Geometric modeling and computer vision. *Proc. of the IEEE*, 76(8):936–958, August 1988.

[20] F. Solina and R. Bajcsy. Recovery of parametric models from range images: The case for superquadrics with global deformations. *IEEE Trans. Pattern Anal. Machine Intell.*, 12(2):131–147, February 1990.

[21] R. B. Schudy. Harmonic surfaces and parametric image operators: Their use in locating the moving endocardial surface from three-dimensional cardiac ultrasound data. Computer Science Technical Report 112, University of Rochester, Rochester, New York, March 1981.

[22] K. Rao and R. Nevatia. Computing volume descriptions from sparse 3-D data. *Int. J. Computer Vision*, 2(1):33–50, 1988.

[23] A. H. Barr. Global and local deformations of solid primitives. *Computer Graphics*, 18(3):21–30, July 1984.

[24] A. J. Hanson. Hyperquadrics: Smoothly deformable shapes with convex polyhedral bounds. *Computer Vision, Graphics and Image Processing*, 44:191–210, 1988.

[25] J. Ponce. Straight homogeneous generalized cylinders: Differential geometry and uniqueness results. *Int. J. Computer Vision*, 4(1):79–100, 1990.

[26] E. Persoon and K. S. Fu. Shape discrimination using Fourier descriptors. *IEEE Trans. Pattern Anal. Machine Intell.*, 8(3):388–397, May 1986.

[27] C. R. Giardina and F. P. Kuhl. Accuracy of curve approximation by harmonically related vectors with elliptical loci. *Computer Graphics and Image Processing*, 6:277–285, 1977.

[28] F. P. Kuhl and C. R. Giardina. Elliptic Fourier features of a closed contour. *Computer Graphics and Image Processing*, 18:236–258, 1982.

[29] C. S. Lin and C. L. Hwang. New forms of shape invariants from elliptic Fourier descriptors. *Pattern Recognition*, 20(5):535–545, 1987.

[30] L. H. Staib and J. S. Duncan. Boundary finding with parametrically deformable models. *IEEE Trans. Pattern Anal. Machine Intell.*, 1992. (to appear).

[31] G. P. Tolstov. *Fourier Series.* Prentice-Hall, Englewood Cliffs, 1962.

[32] D. A. Pierre. *Optimization Theory with Applications.* Dover, New York, 1986.

[33] L. H. Staib. *Parametrically Deformable Contour Models for Image Analysis.* PhD thesis, Yale University, New Haven, CT, 1990.

[34] R. A. Robb. High speed three-dimensional x-ray computed tomography: The dynamic spatial reconstructor. *Proc. of the IEEE*, 71:308–319, 1983.

[35] J. S. Duncan, R. L. Owen, L. H. Staib, and P. Anandan. Measurement of non-rigid motion in images using contour shape descriptors. In *Proc. IEEE Conf. Computer Vision and Pattern Recognition*, June 1991.

Chapter 8

Tracking Cells and Subcellular Features

L. M. Lifshitz

8.1 Introduction

This chapter discusses research directions and results from a multidisciplinary effort, at the University of Massachusetts Medical School, to develop feature extraction tools for analysis of the changes in molecular distribution during cell movement. This work is part of a broader effort directed at developing hardware for a new digital imaging microscope[1], as well as image restoration algorithms[2] which precede the extraction steps, making them simpler. New voxel based display techniques[3] are also being developed for improved visualization of the two and three dimensional data sets.

Two feature extraction algorithms will be described in this chapter. The first tracks the boundary of a slowly deforming two dimensional object throughout a time series[4]. This algorithm has been used to analyze a time sequence of two-dimensional phase contrast images of a white blood cell moving on a microscope slide. It tracks the moving cell and also identifies the lamellipodia of the cell. This allows the extraction of quantitative information relating cell motility to lamellipod formation.

The second algorithm is a model-based technique which tracks fluorescently labelled microtubules (long, intracellular filaments) through a time series of two dimensional images of a moving cell[5]. The images are acquired via a light microscope. The tracking algorithm is designed to be general enough to follow any bright, slowly deforming filaments through a series of two dimensional, greyscale images. The images can have both structured and unstructured background noise. Tens of filaments can exist in each image; the filaments can cross each other and need not be uniformly bright along their lengths. The images of fluorescently labelled moving cells have all of these characteristics.

8.2 The Physiological Test Problems

This research represents the application of computer vision paradigms to the biological problem of analyzing changes in shape and the intracellular molecular distribution in a single cell during cell movement. White blood cells are motile cells of the immune system that form part of the body's defense mechanism against parasitic infections. They exhibit chemotaxis, that is, they move towards a source of chemoattractant. Newt white blood cells are several times larger than their mammalian counterparts and are very active at room temperature. This makes them ideal specimens for physiological studies on the mechanisms that underlie the chemotactic response, namely signal transduction, polarization (i.e., elongation and orientation) and motility. As these cells move and turn they extend and retract lamellipodia. They also reorganize their microtubules.

Microtubules are long filament-like structures which join together at a microtubule organizing center (MTOC). It is believed by cell physiologists that these structures play a role in intracellular transport and cell motility. Specifically, since microtubules are essential as intracellular transport mechanisms, and the integrity of this system is essential for the ability of the cell to polarize and move, there should be a strong correlation between microtubule location/orientation and the direction of cell motion[6]. We would like to discover if such a correlation in fact exists, and to quantify it. The physiologists would also like to quantify how the distance from the microtubule end to the cell membrane correlates with the activity level in that region of the cell. The activity level is related to the velocity of the cell, so cell motion should affect microtubule proximity to the membrane.

8.2.1 Image acquisition and characteristics

In order to answer such questions, the physiologists in our lab can acquire either fluorescently labelled cells or phase contrast images of cells.

8.2.1.1 Fluorescent Images

Fluorescent images are obtained by injecting cells with fluorescent probes and then acquiring images of these cells via a normal light microscope. Microtubules are dynamic polymers of the protein tubulin, which can be isolated and chemically conjugated with a fluorophore. The fluorescent tubulin is then microinjected into a living cell and the cell uses it along with its own tubulin to make microtubules. When imaged, these fluorescent microtubules are seen against the background of unincorporated fluorescent tubulin monomers. The monomers are distributed throughout most of the cell, but are excluded from the nucleus and the granules.

A two dimensional time series is obtained by placing a living, fluorescently labelled, cell on a microscope slide, upon which it is permitted to move. Motion in specific directions can be induced by using a pipette to introduce a chemical attractant onto the slide at the location the cell should move towards. As the cell moves it is illuminated and two dimensional images are acquired every two seconds. A one minute sequence of images may include 600 microtubules (approximately 20 microtubules per image and one image every two seconds).

These time series images of microtubules have several challenging characteristics (see figure 1). Some of the most significant are as follows.

1. Each microtubule can change shape, size, and position during an image sequence.
2. Microtubules can move in and out of the plane of focus (and hence seem to appear or disappear from the image).
3. The fluorescent label also exists in the cytoplasm, but is excluded from the ball-like granules which are in the cytoplasm, thus producing a structured background of a honeycomb nature.
4. Microtubules may not be uniformly stained along their length. Microtubules (and background) may be significantly brighter in some regions of the cell than others.
5. Microtubules can be in close proximity to other microtubules. In the image they may even appear to cross one another.

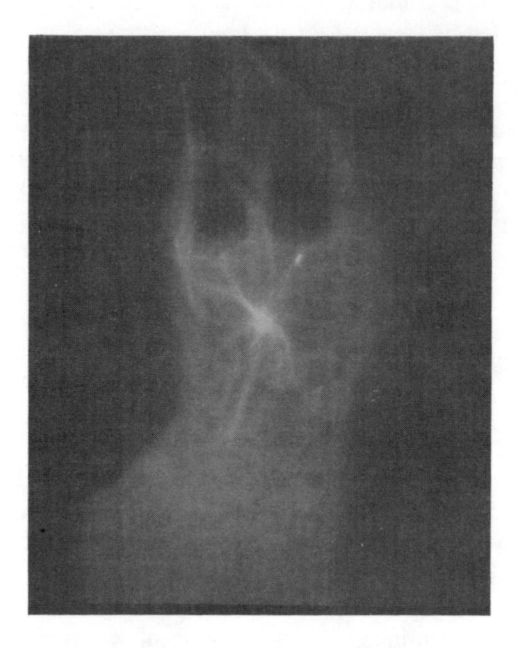

Figure 1a. Microtubules fluorescently stained in a white blood cell. The microtubules are the long filament-like structures. The brightest region is the microtubule organizing center. The granules appear as dark disks.

8.2.1.2 Phase Contrast Images

A phase contrast image of a white blood cell is shown in figure 1. We have chosen to analyze phase contrast images with our cell tracking algorithm because phase contrast images can be obtained at the same time as a fluorescent image with very little extra effort. Thus it is a modality that many researchers may easily employ if computer analysis of their data is desired. Phase contrast images are formed by recording the interference pattern between a reference light beam, which only passes through a one-quarter wavelength retarder, and a beam passing through the cell. As light passes through different structures in the cell its phase will shift by varying amounts. The interference pattern recorded measures the amount of phase shift of the light. Of course, due to the periodic nature of light, a phase shift can only be determined modulo 360 degrees. Parts of the cell which do not retard the light at all appear gray in the image (due to the retarder); other parts appear lighter or darker. Thus, the granule containing region of the newt cell appears as a black and white mottle, while the very thin lamellipodia look gray.

The imaging characteristics determine the visibility of cellular components. Microtubules are not visible in phase contrast images. The nucleus and granule containing regions typically are visible. The position of the MTOC can be identified sometimes. Phase contrast images can theoretically be acquired at video rates (30 images per second) if digitization of the image takes place after image acquisition. Cells move with a maximum speed of 30 microns per minute and can complete turns of 90 degrees in under one minute. It takes them less than three minutes to reform from maximum elongation (at which time they are approximately 60 microns long and 20 microns wide) to a spherical shape. With a numerical aperture lens of .75 our images have a resolution of .25 microns per pixel. **Given these biological constraints, we image the cell at a frame every two seconds so that the position of any boundary pixel does not change by more than three pixels between frames. This motion constraint is a significant component of the cell tracking algorithm.**

A time series of phase contrast images has the following characteristics (see figure 1).

1. Pixels inside the cell can be significantly brighter or darker than the background pixel intensities (these bright and dark regions are intracellular structures, granules).
2. Pixels in the lamellipod regions can have intensities which are the same as the background intensity.
3. The phase contrast microscope introduces a bright phase halo around the main cell (i.e., the part excluding the lamellipodia, henceforth "mcell") and also a dimmer one around the lamellipod regions (the mcell plus the lamellipodia will be called the "cellam").
4. The background itself has small phase dark objects in it and also varies in intensity (i.e., has structured noise in it).
5. The area of the cell and its shape change significantly as it moves but it cannot change quickly (relative to the image acquisition rate of a frame every two seconds).
6. The image of the nucleus region has a different texture from that of the granule containing region.

8.3 Related Research in Motion Analysis and Tracking

Research in motion analysis spans a wide range of issues and applications[7,8,9]. Many people have addressed the basic task of locating and tracking one or more objects through a sequence of images. The exact definition of the objects (e.g., points, lines, cells) and the order in which the analysis is done (i.e., are the objects first found in each slice and then matched, or are both performed concurrently) varies from application to application.

Considerable effort has been expended on correctly matching objects in each frame of a time series. Several researchers have attempted to match a set of points over time[10]. Rigid motion is often assumed. For instance, Leung[11] automatically extracts points of interest (from a stereo time series) using the zero crossings of a Laplacian operator. Points are then matched both between stereo pairs and between different frames in the time series.

Cell tracking and analysis has been performed by several researchers. The segmentation step used by these researchers to identify the cell is simpler than is possible with our data. Levine[12] tracks multiple cells moving in two dimensions by modelling the motion of the centroid of each cell as a Markov chain. The segmentation step is done via simple thresholding. In[13] Levine uses a rule based system to understand the morphological changes a cell undergoes (relating pseudopod formation and cell motion). But again, all that is required to locate the cell is a threshold based upon the intensity histogram followed by simple filtering of the binary image. Ferrie[14] tracks cells undergoing morphological change (with states such as growth, mitosis, contact with other cells, death). Cells are manually identified and a threshold is used to segment them from the background.

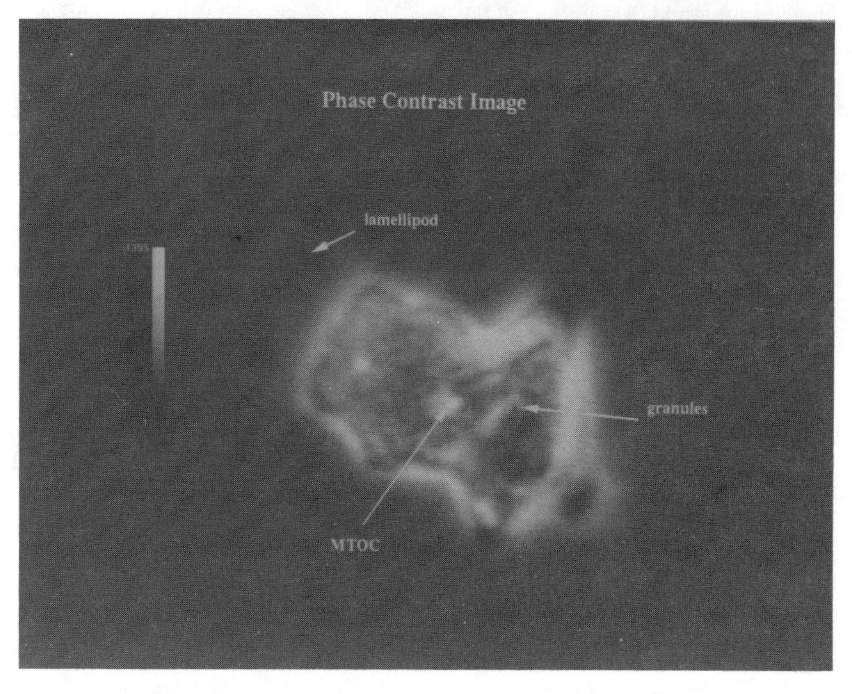

Figure 1b. A phase contrast image of a Newt white blood cell.

Both Zucker[15] and Kass[16] use energy minimizing splines to find curves in an image. Zucker creates a discrete tangent field from the original image. He then dynamically fits small splines to the potential field created from the discrete tangent field. The small splines grow and merge, eventually forming long continuous curves. Kass starts with a long spline positioned near its correct location in the image. The potential energy field includes components from the image (related to the positions of lines, edges, and line termination points) and from outside constraints (e.g., a spring force between a point on the spline and a point in the image). Both Zucker and Kass model their splines with internal tension (first derivative) and rigidity (second derivative) energy components. Thus, when absent or ambiguous data does not uniquely determine an optimal spline, internal forces produce a unique solution.

Similarly, Duncan and Staib[17] use a deformable global model to describe the object of interest. Duncan models the outline of the left ventricle of a heart (in a 2D image) by modelling the curve which describes the ventricular outline using fourier descriptors. An initial, approximate, boundary is deformed towards a best fit boundary by moving along a gradient of a goodness of fit function. The goodness of fit is a function of the fourier descriptors and the edge strengths in the image.

All three methods (Kass', Zucker's, and Duncan's) can be applied to tracking either open curves (e.g., microtubules) or closed curves (e.g., a cell boundary). They all would have difficulty tracking microtubules for several reasons. Due to the nature of the structured honeycomb patterned noise in our images, the splines would most likely move towards the honeycomb structure instead of the true microtubules. When the curve moves it goes to the nearest local minimum of the potential energy field. It is unable to find the globally best curve which fits the data. It will only track a curve well if movement between frames is very small and noise is small enough so that no local minima get introduced between the starting position of the spline and its correct new position. Because of the honeycomb nature of our background noise, our images would tend to produce many local minima. It would also be difficult to modify the algorithms so that the best possible fits were found for all the microtubules simultaneously. It would not be desirable if several curves ended up fitting to data from the same microtubule.

Much of what we are proposing for tracking microtubules is philosophically related to the approaches of Kass and Duncan. A deformable model (composed of all of the microtubules) *is* used. We do, however, differ significantly in many respects. Most significantly, since we need to identify many closely spaced objects, we include constraints based upon how the model also matches the other microtubules in the image. We also do not employ a gradient descent search since structured noise may cause the process to get stuck in a local minimum. In addition, the goodness of fit measure employed is different since it is based upon the output of an AVS detector.

The algorithm we are using to track the cell boundary bears little resemblance to any of the above approaches. The main similarity is that we too use topological constraints (i.e., that a boundary must be a *closed* curve) and geometrical relationships (i.e., the spatial relationship between parts of the curve) to guide the tracking process*.

8.4 The Cell Tracking Algorithm

8.4.1 Overview

We decided to use a boundary based algorithm for tracking phase-contrast images of a cell since pixel intensities and image textures inside the cellam are not significantly different than those outside the cell. We determined that for an algorithm to successfully deal with all the noise and variation between images it would have to make strong use of information from the previous image in the sequence, i.e. the constraint that the cellam does not change too quickly. The phase halo around the mcell and the cellam would be used to help locate the cell boundary. What emerged is a boundary based algorithm with strong prior spatial constraints based upon the previous image.

The boundary tracking algorithm finds the cell by finding those pixels in the image which belong to the boundary of the cell. Potential boundary pixels are identified by locating intensity changes due to the phase contrast halo surrounding the cell. While most boundary based image segmentation algorithms form a closed boundary by moving from a starting boundary pixel along a path which locally or globally optimizes a cost function our algorithm does not trace a path from a

*We have also been experimenting with a 3D surface version of Kass' algorithm as an alternative (to the method described in this chapter) for tracking the cell boundary. Results seem promising for it too.

starting point and does not minimize a cost function. Instead, we close the boundary by examining the geometrical and topological relationships among potential boundary pixels. Gaps in the boundary are closed by connecting gap points to the "closest" boundary point. "Close" is determined by a distance metric which combines Euclidean and other types of geometric information about the boundary pixels already found. The position of the cell in the previous image is used both to constrain the location of the cell in the image being examined and to insure that the boundary eventually found is indeed closed.

The algorithm which has been developed will track the mcell and cellam boundaries. Once this is done it identifies those pixels which belong to lamellipodia. After this, any calculations relating lamellipod location to the position and velocity of the cell can be performed simply. As the algorithm exists now, no other structures in the cell are identified. The plan is to extend the algorithm to track the microtubule organizing center and the nucleus. Currently the mcell boundary and the cellam boundary are found in completely separate passes of the algorithm. Once they are found, pixels which belong to the cellam but not to the mcell are determined to be lamellipod pixels. A concise overview of the steps in the algorithm for each pass follows.

Step 1. The user outlines the mcell (or the cellam) in the first image of the time series and specifies a threshold intensity (which will be applied to edge strength pixels on subsequent images).

For all succeeding images the computer does the following:

Step 2. Edge pixels are identified by calculating edge strengths for all the pixels in the image. Edge strength is a measure of how likely it is that a pixel is at a phase halo edge (see figure 2). All pixels below the user specified threshold are ignored. All those above are marked as candidate boundary pixels.

Step 3. All pixels in the image which are exactly three pixels inside the boundary found on the previous image are also marked as candidate boundary pixels. These boundary pixels constitute the "central region" of the cell.

Step 4. Connected sequences of candidate boundary pixels ("strings") are identified (a connected sequence is the set of boundary pixels such that a path consisting solely of boundary pixels exists between any two pixels in the set).

Step 5. Strings which are very close to each other are connected.

Step 6. Strings which at least partly cross the cell's location in the previous image are connected, all other strings are removed. There now exists just one connected string, which is guaranteed to completely enclose a central region (step 3), but still has some "dangling" parts (i.e., pieces of the string which do not completely surround any pixels, see figure 3).

Step 7. These dangling pieces have their free end connected up to the central region (thus adding a new completely enclosed region to the central region) when it is appropriate to do so. If it is not appropriate to connect the end, all the string pixels along the dangling piece are removed.

Step 8. The union of all enclosed regions is the mcell (or cellam) for this image.

8.4.2 Details of the cell tracking algorithm

The principle steps of the cell tracking algorithm are presented below. Some of the implementation details and a few of the less significant criteria applied are not presented to aid in the clarity of the explanation.

8.4.2.1 Edge strength calculation - step 2

Phase contrast images of newt cells exhibit large variations in intensity inside the mcell. The background in the images is also noisy. For these reasons conventional edge filtering algorithms create many strong edges at locations other than the boundary of the cell. Several of the most common edge filters were tested, with poor results. Therefore an edge filter was created which was specifically tuned to look for the phase halo around the cell (instead of looking for an intensity *step* like most edge filters). This was possible because the phase halo has a reasonably characteristic intensity profile. Therefore, "edge strength" at a pixel is a measure of how similar the intensities near the pixel are to the generic phase halo intensity profile. The generic phase halo profile looks very similar to that produced by taking a difference of Gaussians. Therefore, the search for pixels along the phase halo is conducted by convolving the image with a two-dimensional difference of Gaussian function (a Gaussian with a standard deviation of two pixels minus a Gaussian with a standard deviation of four pixels works well, when the microscope is set-up as described above). This convolution can be considered as an approximation to a matched filter detector. Such a detector produces a maximum output when it is positioned over a signal that is the same shape as it (assuming proper normalization). All of the pixels in the resultant image are then checked to see if they have a larger intensity than both of their neighbors in any one of four directions (i.e., than their neighbors above and below, left and right, upper left and lower right, or lower left and upper right). If a pixel is such a "one-dimensional maximum", it is considered an edge pixel. Its strength is the average of the intensity difference between it and its two neighboring pixels (in the direction of the one-dimensional maximum). This measure of edge strength compensates for changes in region intensity throughout the image and also produces thin edges. It also tends to correct for the use of a two-dimensional filter when theoretically a one-dimensional filter oriented perpendicular to the boundary of the cell should be used. A typical edge strength image is shown in figure 2 (intensities have been increased in this image for visualization purposes).

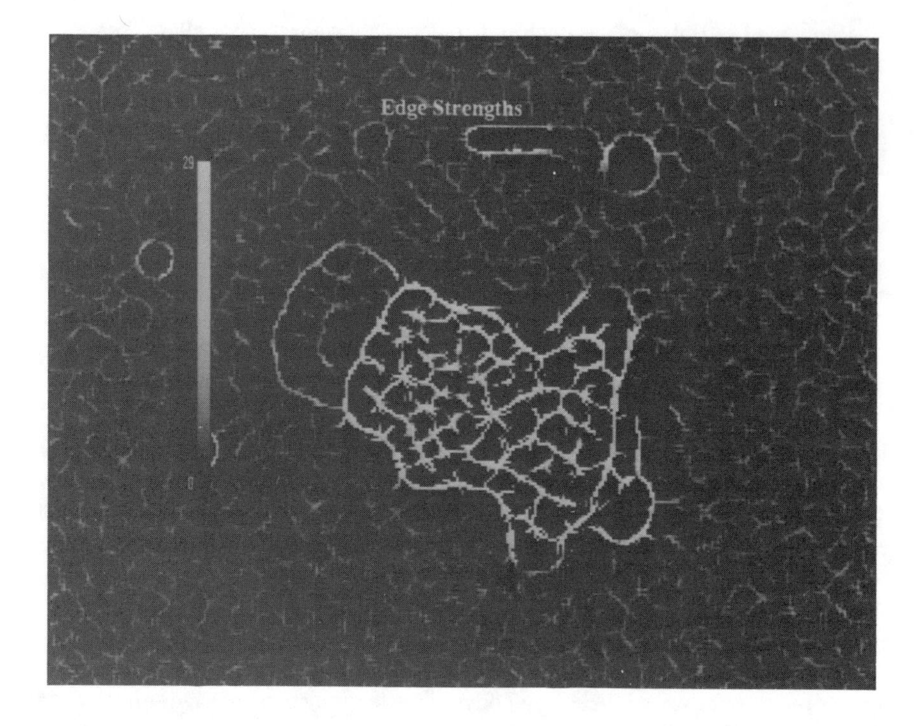

Figure 2. An edge strength image produced from figure 1b.

This filter still produces strong edge pixels at locations other than the phase halo (and weak edge pixels in the background). But it is better than the traditional edge filters that we tried. In addition, strong edges interior to the cell do not confuse the algorithm nearly as much as they would if they were in the exterior. This is because, in later stages (steps 3 and 7), the algorithm finds many candidate "boundary pixels". After all the candidate boundary pixels are found (including boundary pixels added to close gaps) there is an outer boundary and, perhaps, some inner boundary pieces. Only those "boundary pixels" which are truly on the boundary between the cell and the background make up the final boundary for an image.

8.4.2.2 A priori location constraint - step 3

Given the aforementioned optics and image acquisition rate, it is fairly certain that no point on the cell boundary will move more than three pixels between frames. But each part of the boundary can move in any direction. Therefore, all that is really known is that all those pixels at least three pixels inside the boundary found on the previous image must still be inside the cell. Therefore, this stage of the analysis marks all pixels in the image which are exactly three pixels inside the previous boundary as candidate boundary pixels. This also guarantees that the boundary that eventually will be formed will be topologically closed which is, of course, a necessary property for any boundary based algorithm.

8.4.2.3 String identification and connection - steps 4, 5, and 6

More topological information is added to the algorithm by identifying groups of connected candidate boundary pixels. Each connected group is called a "string" since it is one-dimensional (but it can certainly branch and/or completely surround some pixels) and tends to curve. Strings which are very close to one another (within three pixels) are connected. The assumption justifying this action is that due to noise or thresholding boundary pixels have been missed.

Next, all strings which might be part of the cell boundary are identified. Any string which contains a pixel which could conceivably be part of the cell is considered to be such a string. Pixels which could be part of the cell are all those pixels enclosed by the boundary which is three pixels *outside* the boundary found on the previous image. All strings which could not be part of the cell are deleted. All the remaining strings are connected by joining them with straight lines at their closest pixels. This results in just one big connected string which is guaranteed to enclose at least some pixels. The string usually will still have some pieces which simply "dangle" (i.e., that do not completely enclose any region, see figure 3).

As just described, the algorithm first identifies groups of connected pixels as strings and then deletes entire *strings*. This is done instead of first removing *individual* candidate boundary pixels which could not possibly be part of the cell and then identifying strings. The latter approach would only be possible if the constraints based upon the boundary location in the previous image always held. This is not the case. The primary exception to this rule occurs during the formation of lamellipodia. In their initial stages the lamellipodia are small and typically form very weak phase contrast edges or edges that are so close to the main cell that they are not well differentiated from the main cell. These lamellipod edges, and hence the lamellipod itself, may be (mistakenly) missed for several frames. If edge pixels further out from a previous boundary than three pixels were never examined, this mistake could never be corrected even after the edge strength of the pixels bounding the lamellipod became quite strong. But, once the edge surrounding the lamellipod is strong it will create a string of candidate boundary pixels which probably extends back to the main cell. Therefore, the algorithm operates on strings rather than individual candidate boundary pixels. Working with strings rather than individual pixels makes the algorithm more robust because it becomes more global.

8.4.2.4 Connection of dangling pieces of string - step 7

Dangling string pieces have several causes. They may be part of boundary of the main part of the cell (mcell). Sometimes they are simply due to structured noise in the background or bits of debris on the slide. Much more frequently they partially surround a lamellipod. The task at this stage is to determine if a dangling piece of string should be kept and, if so, where to connect it to the main boundary.

The first step is to identify the end points of these dangling string pieces (see figure 3). This is done by giving each pixel in the string topological knowledge about the nature of its connection in the string. Pixels are classified into one of three types: a normal pixel, a branch pixel, and an end point pixel. Branch pixels exist at places where the string branches, e.g., where a dangling string connects to the closed part of the boundary. An end point pixel is at the "unconnected" end of a dangling piece of string (it is connected to the string, but not in the "other direction"). All other pixels are normal pixels. Pixel type can be identified by noting how many times the string is crossed when traversing a small path surrounding the pixel of interest. A path surrounding a normal pixel will cross the string twice. A path around a branch pixel will cross the string three or more times. A path surrounding an end point will cross the string only once.

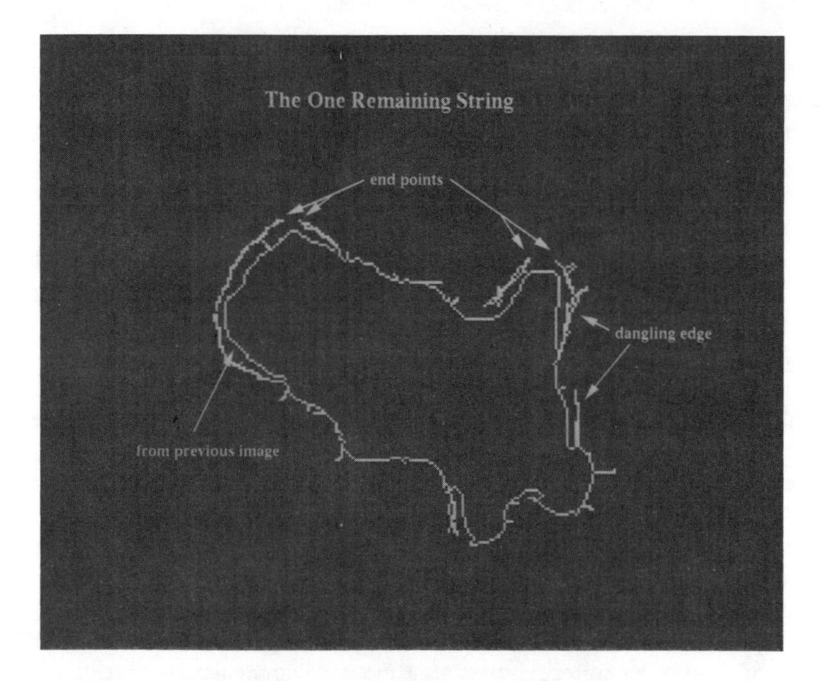

Figure 3. The one remaining string with dangling edges.

The next step is to identify a likely pixel on the boundary to which the end point should be connected. This is something which a person does so easily it is difficult to imagine that it is a complicated procedure for a computer. One reason a person can handle this easily is because he or she sees the *entire* string at once and can recognize which parts are close to each other. To emulate this, the algorithm must be able to manipulate some geometric knowledge, information describing the distances between its pixels. There are two basic distances of interest. The first is the straight line or Euclidean distance between any two pixels in the string. This is simply calculated since we know the x and y coordinates of every pixel in the string. The second distance may be called the "string" distance. It is the distance between two points on the string if the path taken between the two points is the shortest path along the string. The string distance between an end point and all other pixels along the string can be calculated quite simply. The essence of the algorithm is to make repeated passes. At the start of the first pass the end point pixel of interest is marked as the "current" pixel. On each pass string pixels neighboring the "current" pixels are marked with the pass number (if they have not been marked on a previous pass). They become the "current" pixels. The pass number is then incremented. This process is continued until all string pixels are marked. Pass number can be replaced by a more accurate distance measure taking into account whether a pixel is a diagonal neighbor or a 4-connected neighbor, if desired. This is a very simple and quick algorithm which requires no backtracking or complicated logic, yet it finds the shortest path between the end point of interest and all other pixels along the string.

Once the Euclidean distance and string distance between an end point and all the other string pixels are known, the algorithm calculates the ratio of the Euclidean distance to the string distance for each pixel. The pixel which has the minimum ratio is identified as the most likely candidate for the end point to connect with. People usually perceive the dangling string to be curling back towards this pixel.

This measure is used because several other obvious methods fail to work. End points do not, for instance, always join up with other end points, but sometimes they do. Similarly, the "direction" the dangling part of the string is heading in, even if that could defined and determined accurately, is not necessarily the direction the string should be extended to connect it correctly.

The straight line between the end point pixel and the candidate connection pixel is examined. If this line goes outside the region of possible pixels (based upon the boundary from the previous image), the connection is not allowed. If the connection is not allowed, the algorithm considers connecting to the *end point* which has the smallest distance ratio among all the *end points*. If this connection is not allowed, no connection is made for this end point (and the piece of dangling string which it terminates is eventually removed). If a connection is allowed, it is created. This extension of the dangling string back to the main part of the cell causes new pixels to be completely surrounded by the string. This new region is now part of the cell.

During development we tried examining the intensity distribution of the pixels in this new region to help determine if the connection was being made to the appropriate boundary pixel. Unfortunately, the intensity distribution of pixels in a lamellipod region have no characteristics which distinguish them from background pixels. Similarly, there was no apparent measure of the size or shape of the new region which was able to accurately discriminate between correct and incorrect connections. It is possible that an appropriate measure will be found. If so, it will most likely be for those regions which should be added because they are part of the main cell, and not for lamellipod regions.

8.4.2.5 The final cell boundary - step 8

The final cell boundary consists of those string pixels along the outside of all the regions which have been enclosed (i.e., along the boundary between pixels in the cell and pixels in the background). Cell pixels can be found very simply by doing a flood fill of the image starting from a pixel known to be definitely outside the cell. If the flooding algorithm is not allowed to cross string pixels, only those pixels outside the desired boundary are filled. All other pixels are cell pixels. This boundary is then used as the "previous boundary" for the next image in the time series.

8.4.3 Results of the cell tracking algorithm

This cell tracking algorithm has been implemented on a Silicon Graphics Personal Iris 4D/20. This is roughly a 10 Mips, 2 Mflop machine. Currently it takes about 4-8 minutes to analyze each image in the time series (depending upon the complexity of the image). A time series typically takes between one and two hours to analyze. We believe the time per image can be reduced to under two minutes fairly easily, since the current version is a research version which has undergone extensive modification since its initial design. It should be stressed that the amount of time a user must actually spend interacting with the program is only about 5 minutes (to outline the initial boundaries and set the edge strength thresholds). We have written programs which take the mcell and cellam boundaries for the image sequence and play a "movie" on the workstation. Programs are also available which automatically calculate cell velocity, lamellipod position and velocity, and the sizes of the lamellipodia. All this information can be graphically superimposed on the movie of the moving cell.

The algorithm seems to perform fairly well (see figure 4). It will often find exactly the same boundary a trained physiologist would find. Sometimes it finds a lamellipod when a physiologist misses it (until it is pointed out and the image is examined closer). On the other hand, sometimes the algorithm will miss a lamellipod for a few images, although it will almost always correct its error eventually. Lamellipodia which are most likely to be missed are small, forming lamellipodia (which have very weak halos).

Whether the algorithm is currently good enough to be used on a routine basis to answer the physiologists' questions is not yet certain. Since the algorithm does err occasionally, we must determine if its errors are significant. If they turn out to be significant, we plan to improve the algorithm. The issue arises, what is a significant error? The answer to this clearly depends upon the questions that are being asked of the data. The errors may be insignificant if the questions pertain to the average amount of lamellipod on either side of a turning cell, but may be significant if one wants to know the exact time of lamellipod formation. To test the accuracy, we have applied the algorithm to time series data which was also outlined interactively[18]. When the centroids of the automated and manual cell outlines were compared they were found to be within about 5 pixels of one another throughout the time series. This represents about 10 percent of the total distance moved during the time series (but the absolute distance between the centroids of the two versions remained fairly constant, i.e., given an initial offset the cell was tracked reasonably well). Further tests are necessary to completely characterize the algorithm's performance.

There are two major improvements which we plan to add to the cell tracking algorithm, if it is necessary. The first improvement will permit very weak edges, which currently are below threshold and therefore ignored, to be used when there is enough corroborating evidence for their inclusion from strong edges nearby. The second improvement will use both a priori and a posteriori boundary information. In other words, both the image preceding the image being analyzed and the image following it will be used for boundary information.

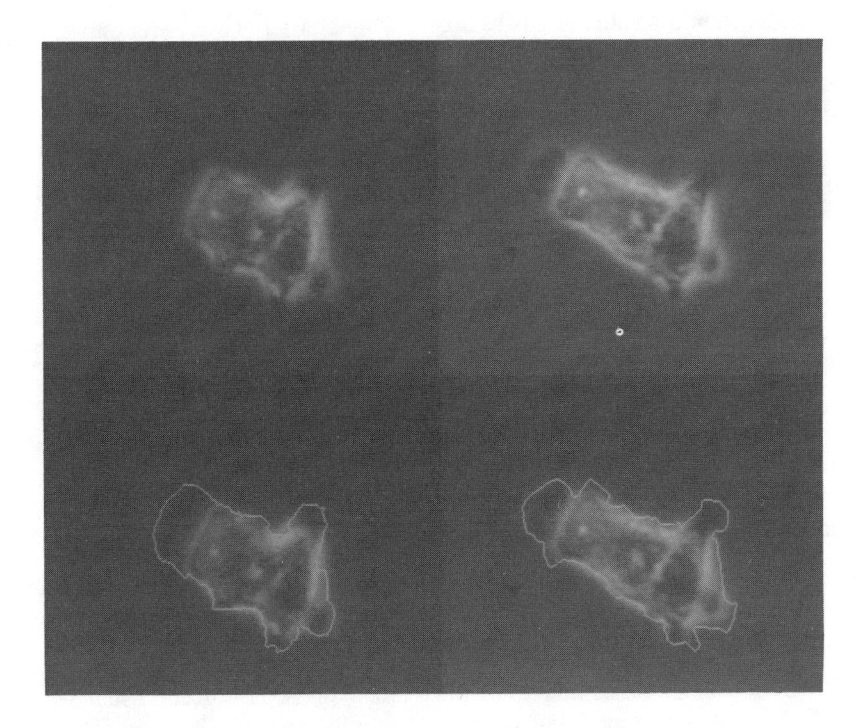

Figure 4. Results from tracking a phase contrast image of a cell. Top: images without the boundaries drawn. Left: initial image. Right: cell 8 seconds (4 frames) later. The boundary found by the algorithm is presented in white. Although it is substantially correct, there is a small region which is included in the cell which should not be.

8.5 Tracking Deformable Filaments

8.5.1 Design Criteria

As described in the introduction and background sections, the imaging characteristics of our driving problem create a challenging situation. Aspects which make it difficult are: flexible thin structures of large extent (microtubule filaments), nonuniform staining and background, structured honeycomb noise, limited depth of focus (so microtubules can get dimmer or brighter over time), and minimal knowledge of microtubule dynamics with which to constrain the search space. The solution we have implemented is based upon several design decisions. They are as follows.

1. A tracking algorithm which contains **models** of the microtubules present is necessary. The models should have the following characteristics.
   a. The model should be a **spatially global one** to allow the best possible fit to the data to be found without becoming mislead by locally structured noise.

b. The model should be able to **easily incorporate spatial constraints** that apply to microtubule motion. The primary constraint available being that motion cannot be too large between frames.
c. The model must be **flexible** enough to accurately model a microtubule.

2. The detection of microtubules in the data must be **insensitive to the nonuniform illumination and fluorescent staining** which causes some areas of the image to be significantly brighter than others.

3. The search algorithm which matches the model to the data should find the match which is the **global optimum**, not a local optimum. The fit of the model to the data should not be too computationally expensive to calculate.

4. **All the microtubules in an image should be fit simultaneously** to maximize the probability of a correct fit by including global information about the entire image. This will prevent several model microtubules from fitting the identical well imaged microtubule in an image.

8.5.2 The Filament Tracking Algorithm

The microtubule tracking algorithm which we have developed has three basic steps. The first step identifies individual microtubule parts. The second step matches these parts with a model of microtubules in the image. (Microtubules are interactively identified in the first image of the time series. These microtubules are used as the initial model to which parts found in the second image of the series are matched.) The third step chooses a subset of the matched parts and interpolates between neighboring parts matched to the same model microtubule, thereby producing a new model for each microtubule in the image. This model is used in the following image as the model to which microtubule parts are matched. The steps are described in more detail below.

Step 1: The AVS detection algorithm

Microtubule parts are found by applying a detection algorithm to the microtubule image. The detection algorithm is an Artificial Visual System (AVS) designed to detect very short line segments. The AVS detector used is a two dimensional version of the one described in Coggins.[19] The detector consists of four overlapping cone-shaped sectors of a disc of a given radius (see figure 5). The four sectors (filters) are centered around lines at 0, 45, 90, and 135 degrees. They each take on their maximum value at the orientation at which they are centered. Each filter's intensity decreases linearly as a function of angle, falling to zero at the center of both adjacent filters. Thus, summing all the filters would produce a disc of uniform maximum intensity.

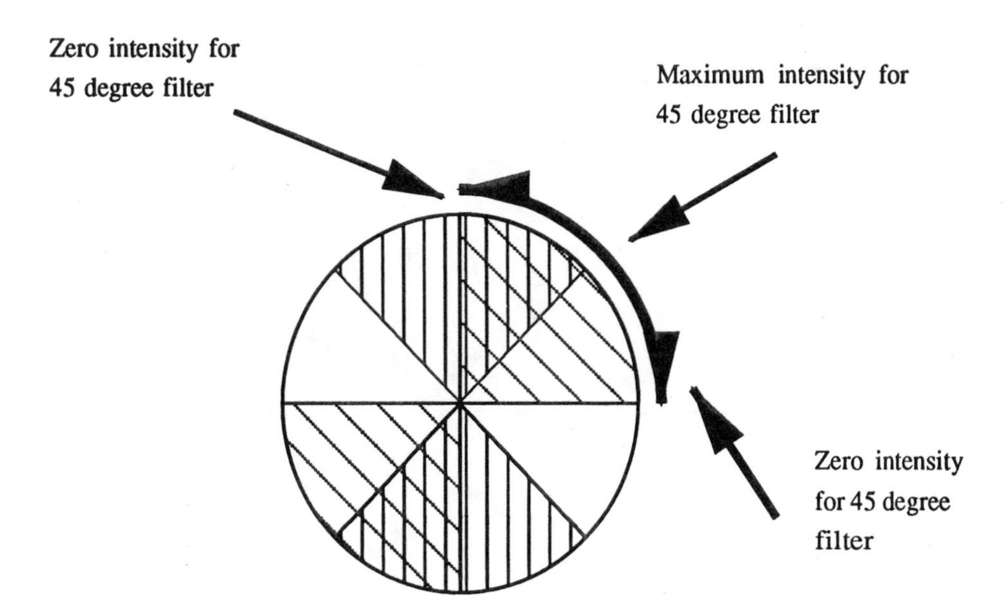

Figure 5. Schematic of the 4 overlapping filters used in the AVS system. The diagonal lines represent the extent of the 45° filter, the vertical lines the 90° filter extent.

Each filter kernel is convolved with the microtubule image. The response of each filter at each pixel is interpreted as representing a vector. The vector magnitude is the magnitude of the filter response (divided by the total response of the four filters). The orientation of the vector is at twice the angle of its filter kernel (see figure 6). The vector originates at the origin. The four vectors (from the responses of the four filters) are added, and the resulting vector is rotated to one-half of its angle. This final angle is the estimate of the orientation of a line centered at the pixel in question. The length of the resulting vector is the measure of certainty that a line actually exists at this pixel.

In the ideal situation, the filter responses will be largest along a ridge down the center of a microtubule. These ridge responses are identified as those responses which are a local maximum along at least one of four directions (up-down, left-right, or one of the 2 diagonals). Unfortunately, a small, bright pixel may cause a locally maximum response to occur, even though the AVS filter is not centered on the pixel. To minimize such spurious responses, two separate AVS filters are applied. The first one which is applied has a radius of 3 pixels. This size is fairly sensitive to microtubules since a microtubule has a width of approximately 3 pixels. The second filter has a radius of 2 pixels, this smaller size makes it less likely to include bright, off-center pixels. A pixel is only considered if it produces a locally maximum response to both AVS filters. In addition, only the strongest 20 percent of the maxima are kept as truly indicating the presence of a line segment.

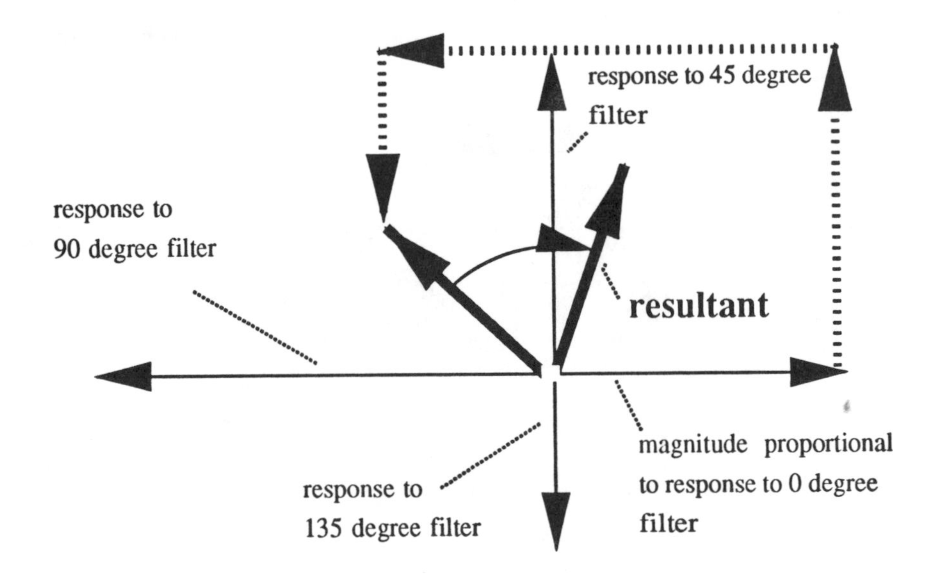

Figure 6. The addition of 4 AVS vectors and subsequent halving of the resultant angle.

This detection and recombination system possesses several desirable properties. The doubling of the vectors' angles, and then the final halving of the angle, insures that a constant uniform intensity image will produce a vector of zero magnitude. Therefore the detector is insensitive to any dc shift in image intensity, as well as to spatially randomly distributed noise. The accuracy of this detector given an ideal signal and no noise is quite high (within 2 degrees for 4 filters). It is difficult to analytically characterize its performance under structured noise, since it is a nonlinear estimator. However, its performance seems to be robust in practice. We have also tried Hough[20] and MAP[21] (maximum a posteriori) detectors designed to find straight line segments. They do not appear to be as robust when applied to our image data.

A new, binary image is created by drawing a small (approximately 3 pixel) line segment (at the estimated orientation) at those locations which produce a high confidence measure. Once this is done for the entire image, connected regions of pixels are identified and thinned. After thinning all branch points are deleted (resulting in several connected groups of pixels where there was one). This insures that all connected groups of pixels are nonintersecting space curves (and can therefore be matched to a model microtubule). Each resulting group of connected pixels is marked as a **microtubule part** (see figure 7).

Figure 7. The fragments (after thinning and branch points are removed) produced by the AVS filter.

Step 2: Matching microtubule parts to the model microtubules

Microtubule parts are matched to a model of the microtubules that exist in the image. In the first image of the time series, this model is created by having the user interactively draw curves which represent each microtubule in the image. In subsequent images, the model consists of the microtubules found in the immediately preceding image (translated by the amount the MTOC has moved between images). Each microtubule curve is represented as an ordered list of connected pixels.

An interpretation tree[22] is used to match each part to the globally best microtubule in the model (see figure 8). To start the matching process, the root node (level 0) of the interpretation is created. Microtubule parts are then examined one at a time, the longest ones first. Each part could conceivably match to any of the microtubules in the model, or it could merely be due to noise. Each of these possible matches is represented by a different branch from the root node. So, if there were N microtubules in the model, there would be N+1 branches coming from the root node. The ith node on level 1 represents the possibility that the first part matches the ith microtubule. One level of the tree gets created for each node part, so if there are M parts M levels of the tree get created. Any given node in the tree represents a set of matches of parts to microtubules, i.e., those matches represented by the ancestor nodes of the given node. In other words, **each path in the interpretation tree represents a specific match of parts to microtubules.** The best path through the interpretation tree represents the globally best assignment of parts to microtubules.

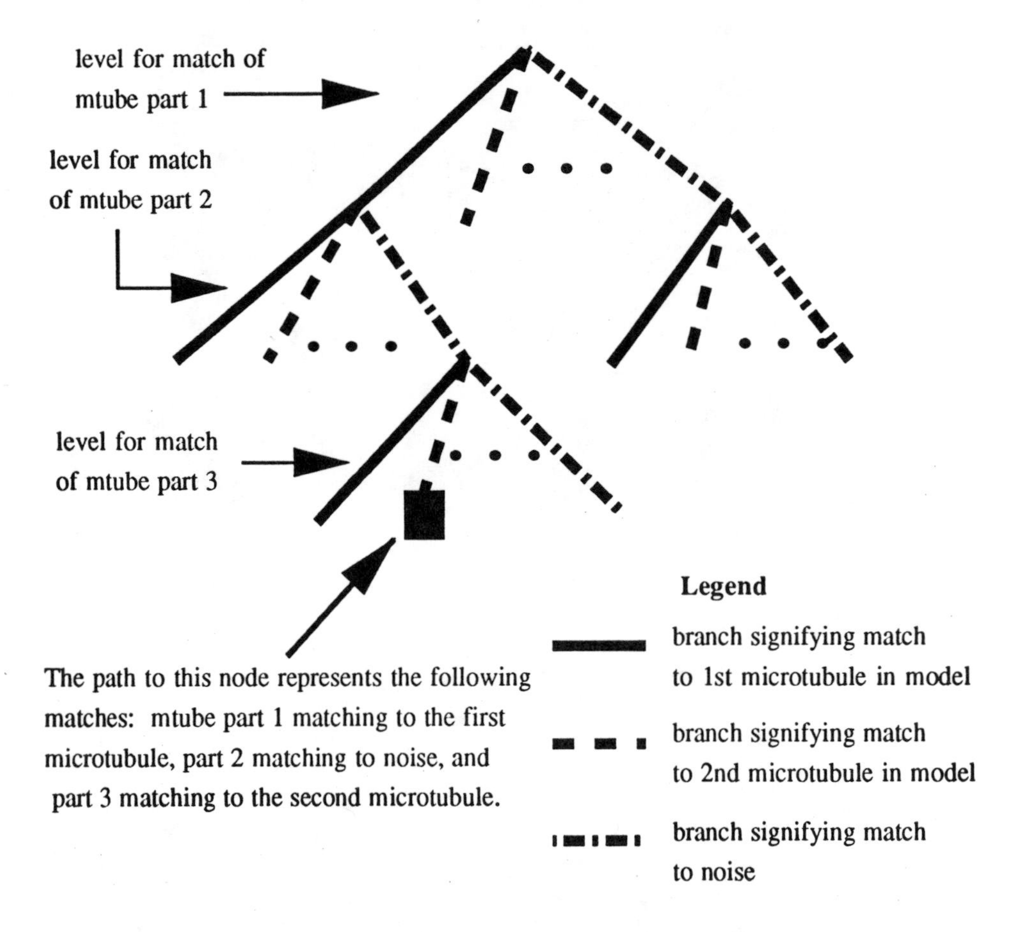

Figure 8. A schematic of an interpretation tree.

Since there are potentially $O(N^M)$ nodes in the interpretation tree, an efficient method of searching the tree is necessary. The minimum cost path through the tree is obtained via a best first search, A*[23]. The cost of a node in the tree (say at level l and branch b) is related to how well the position and orientation of its microtubule part (part l) agrees with that of the microtubule model to which it is being matched (microtubule b). In addition, a microtubule part is not allowed to match to a microtubule (i.e., incurs an extremely high cost) if it would overlap with another part which has already matched to that microtubule. This overlap constraint helps prune the tree significantly. A part is matched to a microtubule by matching each pixel in the part to the closest pixel in the microtubule. This then defines a continuous interval along the microtubule which is associated with that part.

The cost of a node (i.e., of matching a specific microtubule part to a specific model microtubule or to noise) is a combination of several factors. The cost of matching a part to noise is 10 times the length of the part. Thus, the larger the part, the less likely it is to be labelled as noise. A microtubule part is not allowed to match to a microtubule if it is too far away from the microtubule. We define this to be the case when at least 90% of the pixels in the part are not within 30 pixels of the microtubule or when the median distance is greater than 20 pixels away from the microtubule. This constraint is imposed since we do not believe it is physiologically possible for a microtubule to move more than this distance (1.25 microns) in the time between images in the time series[24].

If a part is allowed to match to a particular microtubule, the cost of the match is $C = D + (M - D) * (1 - |\cos(A)|)$, where D is the average distance of the part to the microtubule, M is some maximum cost (30) and A is the angle between a vector approximation of the part and a vector approximation of the piece of the microtubule to which the part is matching. This is a cost function which goes linearly (in cos(A)) from D to M.

The A^* algorithm requires two costs for a path to a node: the cost of the path to the node (which is known since it is just the sum of the costs of the nodes from the root to the node in question) and an estimate of the cost of the best path from the node to a leaf. If this estimate is less than the true cost then A^* is guaranteed to eventually find the best path. The more accurately this estimate approximates the correct remaining path cost, the fewer the number of nodes in the tree which will have to be examined. The estimate used was the sum of the costs of the best matches for all remaining parts (with no overlap constraints). Since constraints between parts are ignored, the cost is easy to calculate and will always be less than or equal to the true cost once constraints are imposed.

The node costs and overlap constraints, combined with the A^* best first search strategy, define a procedure which only has to examine a very small percentage of the nodes which would be present in a full interpretation tree. The search procedure can be stopped as soon as the last part is matched to a microtubule in a consistent manner. The path back from this last node to the root defines the lowest cost, consistent matching of parts to microtubules.

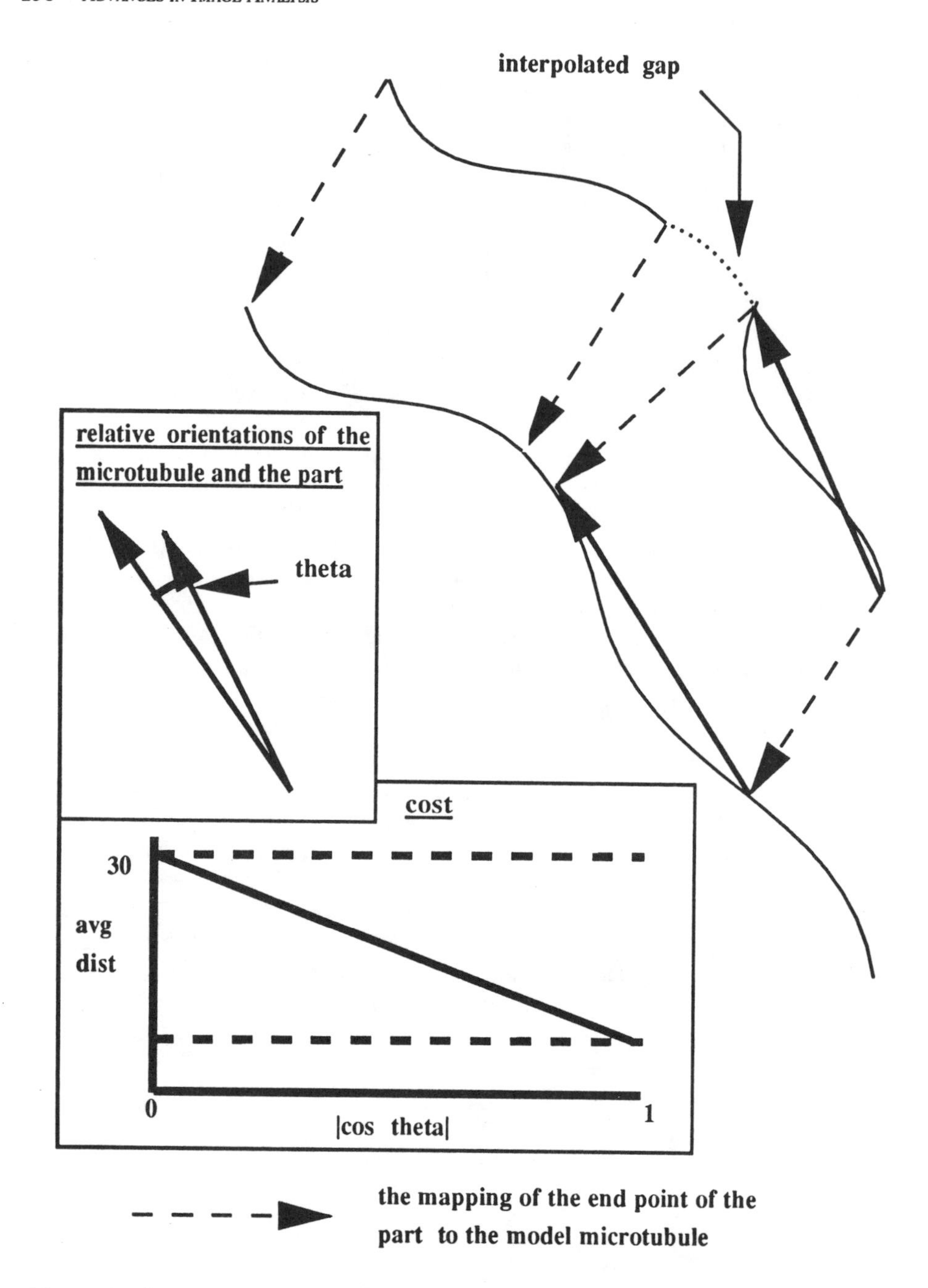

Figure 9. Schematic of parts matching to a model microtubule.

Step 3: Linking a subset of matched parts to create a new model

Fragments which match to the same microtubule are linked together to form the new model of that microtubule. This is done by associating each pixel in the microtubule with that pixel among the parts which is closest to it. Since the pixels along the microtubule have a clearly defined order to them, the pixels in the matching parts will now have an order imposed upon them by virtue of their association with the pixels in the microtubule. The matched part pixels constitute part of the new model of the microtubule.

There will still be gaps between microtubule parts which must be filled appropriately. These gaps are simple to identify since the part pixels are now ordered. The gaps are interpolated by essentially following the shape of the model microtubule (which is the position of the microtubule from the previous image), with offsets added to insure continuity (see figure 9). In addition, the microtubule part closest to the microtubule organizing center (or MTOC, which is the beginning of the microtubule) is connected to it. The MTOC is easily found since it is very bright. Similarly, the part which matches furthest away from the MTOC is extended so that the resulting microtubule does not shrink inappropriately. This linking procedure is performed for each microtubule in the image. The algorithm is then ready to be applied to the next image in the time series.

Actually, only the *best subset* of the parts which match to the same microtubule are linked together to form the new model of that microtubule. The subset chosen is the one which has the largest percentage of its pixels represented by parts (i.e., the ratio of interpolated data pixels to total pixels in the microtubule is smallest). This measure is meant to be somewhat of a smoothness constraint. A part will tend not to be included in the best subset if it is not long relative to the extra length added to the microtubule in order to include it. It would not be necessary to find a subset if a similar cost could be included in the nodes of the interpretation tree. Unfortunately, since the microtubule parts are not evaluated in the same order that they map to microtubules, the shape of the resulting microtubule is not known until the entire tree is traversed.

8.5.3 Microtubule Tracking Results

The system is just beginning to produce its first results. Initial indications are promising. Figures 10 and 11 the results for a typical time series. Most of the microtubules are tracked well. In general, the system seems to track most of the microtubules well through 5 or 10 frames. The fundamental difficulty remaining is that once a significant error is made in one image, it is difficult to recover. Small errors, however, can be corrected in the next image. How readily an error is corrected depends upon image quality and the spatial relationship between microtubules. If microtubules are sparse in one area of an image, the algorithm will be less likely to persist in incorrectly matching a data part to the wrong microtubule.

Total computation time for the analysis of one image of the time series was roughly 5 minutes. An optimized version could probably run at least twice as fast. This performance was achieved on a Silicon Graphics Iris Personal Workstation. This computer operates at approximately 30 mips and 4 mflops. Processing time is clearly image dependent, since the greater the number of parts and the more microtubules there are in the model, the larger the possible interpretation tree. A typical cell image may contain 12 microtubules. From this about 150 parts will be produced. Perhaps one-half of these will be labelled as noise immediately due to their extreme distance from any microtubule. The search of the interpretation tree will only cause an extremely small subset of the possible nodes to be examined.

Typically only 250 nodes in the entire tree will be examined (of the approximately 12^{75} nodes in the full tree).

It is difficult to derive a precise expression for the relationship of the number of microtubules and parts to the number of nodes examined in the tree (and hence the time). The number of nodes examined is highly dependent upon how quickly the overlap constraint binds and the distribution of node costs. The earlier in the search process a constraint can be applied, the greater the number of potential nodes which can be pruned from the tree. But how quickly the constraints will bind depends upon characteristics of the specific image (e.g., the spatial separation between the microtubules, and the amount of overlap when matching parts to microtubules).

8.5.4 Future Directions

There are several improvements which we intend to make to the current algorithm. Some of the improvements are as follows. First, tracking performance could probably be improved if several images in the time series were analyzed simultaneously. This would permit weak (e.g., out of focus) data in one image to be buttressed by stronger information in the following images. Second, the criterion for choosing a best subset of matched parts in step 3 of the algorithm could be changed to use a more sophisticated measure of shape (e.g., smoothness or total curvature) than the one currently used (which is the percentage of microtubule described by the data).

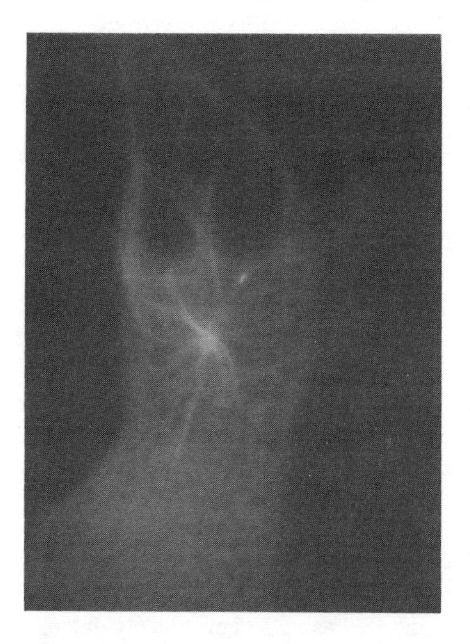

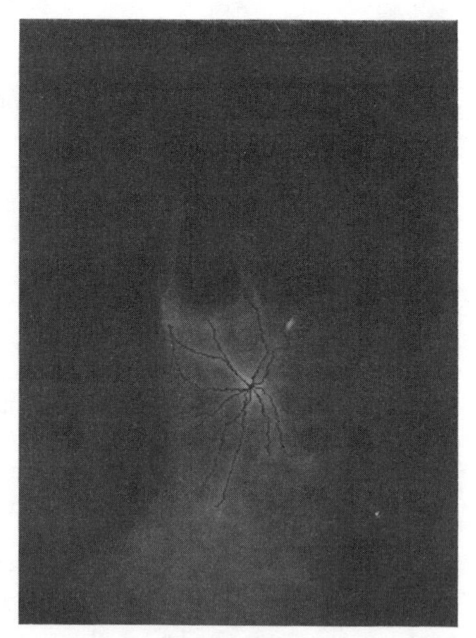

Figure 10. Left: initial image in a time series. Right: same image with initial microtubules shown in black.

8.5.5 Conclusions

The combination of a robust line detector (the AVS detector) and a globally optimum match of image data to a microtubule model has produced an algorithm which is able to track multiple deforming filaments fairly well. Rejection of microtubule parts due to noise and the assignment of parts to the appropriate microtubule are usually correct. Difficulties exist when very little image data exists for a microtubule, eventually resulting in incorrect positioning of the microtubule. We believe, however, that initial results are promising and that the current formalism is powerful and flexible enough to permit the extensions necessary to significantly improve the results. These extensions are currently being implemented.

8.6 Acknowledgements

This research was partially supported by NSF grant #DIR-8720188. Programming support was provided by Jeffrey A. Collins and the time series data of fluorescently labelled cells were provided by Fredric S. Fay. Susan Gilbert provided the phase contrast time series data.

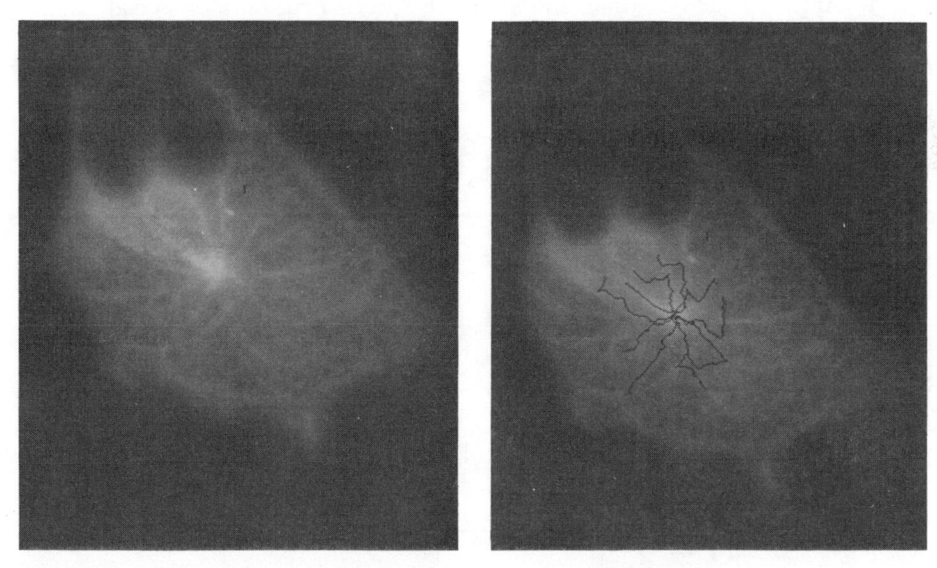

Figure 11. Left: final image in a time series (20 frames later). Right: same image, resulting microtubules shown in black.

8.7 References

1. W. Carrington, R. A. Tuft, and F. S. Fay, "High-speed 3-D fluorescence microscope using image restoration", *SPIE Proceedings*, vol. 1660, 1992.

2. W. Carrington, K. E. Fogarty, and F. S. Fay, "3D Fluorescence Imaging of Single Cells Using Image Restoration", Non-invasive Techniques in Cell Biology, K. Foster, ed., Wiley-Liss, 1990, pp. 53-72.

3. K.C. Carter, D. Bowman, W. Carrington, K. Fogarty, F. Fay, and J. B. Lawrence, "3-D Distribution of Poly A-mRNA in Eukaryotic Nuclei", submitted to *Science*, 1991.

4. L. M. Lifshitz, F. S. Fay, S. Gilbert, K. Fogarty, and W. Carrington, "Tracking Cellular Features using Motion Constraints and Global Information", *SPIE Proceedings*, vol. 1205, pp. 93-103, 1990.

5. L. M. Lifshitz, "Model-based Tracking of Deformable Filaments", *SPIE Proceedings*, vol. 1609, pp. 185-191, 1991.

6. G. Albrecht-Buehler, "The orientation of centrioles in migrating 3T3 cells", *Journal of Experimental Cell Research*, vol. 120:1, pp. 111-118, 1979.

7. J. K. Aggarwal and N. I. Badler (guest eds.), Special Issue on Motion and Time Varying Imagery, *IEEE Transactions on Pattern Analysis and Machine Intelligence*, vol. 2:6, 1980.

8. J. K. Aggarwal (guest ed.), Special Issues on Motion, *Computer Graphics, Vision, and Image Processing*, vol. 21:1 and 21:2, 1983.

9. B. G. Schunk (chair), Proceedings of the Workshop on Visual Motion, IEEE Computer Society, March, 1989.

10. H. Shariat and K. E. Price, "Motion Estimation with more than Two Frames", *IEEE Transactions on Pattern Analysis and Machine Intelligence*, vol. 12:5, pp. 417-434, 1987.

11. M. K. Leung, A. N. Choudhary, J. H. Patel, and T. S. Huang, "Point Matching in a Time Sequence of Stereo Image Pairs and Its Parallel Implementation on a Multiprocessor", Proceedings: Workshop on Visual Motion, Computer Society Press, Washington, D. C., 1989.

12. M. D. Levine, Y. M. Youssef, P. B. Noble, and A. Boyarsky, "The Quantification of Blood Cell Motion by a Method of Automatic Digital Picture Processing", *IEEE Transactions on Pattern Analysis and Machine Intelligence*, vol. 2:5, pp. 444-450, Sept. 1980.

13. M. D. Levine, P. B. Nobel, and Y. M. Youssef, "Understanding Blood Cell Motion", *Computer Graphics, Vision, and Image Processing*, vol. 21, pp. 58-84, 1983.

14. F. P. Ferrie, M. D. Levine, and S. W. Zucker, "Cell Tracking: A Modeling and Minimization Approach", *IEEE Transactions on Pattern Analysis and Machine Intelligence*, vol. 4:3, pp. 277-290, May 1982.

15. S. W. Zucker, C. David, A. Dobbins, and L. Iverson, "The Organization of Curve Detection: Coarse tangent fields and fine spline coverings", *Technical report*, McGill University, 1985.

16. M. Kass, A. Witkin, and D. Terzopoulos, "Snakes: Active Contour Models", *International Journal of Computer Vision*, pp. 321-331, 1988.

17. J. S. Duncan, and L. H. Staib, "Left Ventricular Analysis from Cardiac Images Using Deformable Models", *Proceedings: Computers in Cardiology-1988*, pp. 427-430, IEEE Computer Society Press, Washington, D. C., 1989 (see also this volume).

18. S. Gilbert, L. Lifshitz, and F.S. Fay, "Feature Analysis of Phase Contrast Images on Newt Eosinophil Chemotaxis", *Physiologist*, vol. 32:211a, 1989.

19. J.M. Coggins, K.E. Fogarty, and F.S. Fay, "Interfacing Image Processing and Computer Graphics Systems using an Artificial Visual System",Proceedings: Graphics Interface '86, pp. 229-234.

20. D. H. Ballard and C. M. Brown, Computer Vision, Prentice-Hall, Inc., 1982.

21. H. L. Van Trees, Detection, Estimation, and Modulation Theory - Part I, John Wiley and Sons, Inc., 1968.

22. W.E.L. Grimson, "On the Recognition of Curved Objects", IEEE Transactions on Pattern Analysis and Machine Intelligence, vol. 11:6, pp. 632-642, June 1989.

23. N.J. Nilsson, Principles of Artificial Intelligence, Tioga Publishing Co., Palo Alto, CA, 1980.

24. F.S. Fay, K. Fogarty, W. Carrington, and L. Lifshitz, "Extraction of Information from Biological Systems using the Digital Imaging Microscope: Analysis of White Blood Cell Chemotaxis", Optical Microscopy for Biology, by Herman and Jacobson (eds.), pp. 419-435, Wiley-Liss Publishers, New York, 1990.

Chapter 9

Flaw Detection and Classification in Texture Materials

D. Brzakovic, H. Beck, N. Sufi

9.1 Introduction

Product reliability is an integral component in today's highly competitive world of industrial manufacturing. The time, energy, and money dedicated to quality control often make it the single most costly part of the production process. This drain in resources stems from the necessity of utilizing highly skilled human inspectors to visually examine materials, parts, subassemblies, and finished products. While this has often been necessary in the past due to the immaturity of automated inspection systems, current technology can provide on-line computer-based systems that are capable of performing these tasks and performing them more efficiently than human inspectors. One reason for this is that the computer-based inspection systems do not fatigue as human inspectors often do. Quality control remains consistent. A second reason is that the computer-based inspection systems operate at the same high speeds as the production lines. Thus, on-line computer-based inspection provides a means of removing defective components from the assembly line before they can be included in the final product. In short, utilizing modern computer technology makes it possible to reduce production costs and maintain high quality standards. The resultant savings in labor and materials make efficiency a by-product of quality control.

While, in general, different sensors may be utilized as inputs to an inspection system, particular interest has been with the development of automated systems for visual inspection, e.g., [3,4,9,13]. This paper describes an automated system, called TEXIS (TEXture Inspection System), which identifies visual flaws in texture surfaces. Such surfaces may contain complex patterns that are visually regular and homogeneous on a global scale. Locally, however, the texture elements often exhibit a large variability in terms of intensity distribution, pattern size, and pattern shape. These local variations complicate the inspection process. TEXIS circumvents some of the related complications by utilizing multiresolution image analysis to locate discrepancies in the texture of a sample and labels these discrepancies as potential flaws. Potential flaws are subjected to flaw verification and classification.

Presently, TEXIS is used for detecting flaws in parquet samples placed on a background surface. Potential flaws are detected in two steps: first, individual parquet samples are isolated from the background surface, and, second, flaws are isolated within individual samples. In the first step, isolating individual samples, it is assumed that the samples are of rectangular shape, that there is information about the intensity of the background on which the samples are laying, and that the average width of the samples is known. In the second step, isolating flaws within the samples, each sample is partitioned into flaw and generic texture regions by a fuzzy pyramid linking method that capitalizes on texture homogeneity retained at different resolutions.

The flaw classification method employs a hierarchical scheme that utilizes Bayesian and deterministic classifiers and measurements pertaining to flaw shape, size, texture characteristics, and background texture characteristics. The classification process steps through the hierarchy only when the decision regarding the class of the flaw cannot be made with certainty. The hierarchy is organized in such a way that the simplest measurements are utilized at the highest level in order to minimize (on the average) the classification computation time.

Detection of potential flaws is described in Section 2. In particular, Section 2.1 describes isolating individual texture samples, Section 2.2 details a novel pyramid-based image segmentation method, and Section 2.3 describes post processing needed to extract very thin, long flaws. The second part of the paper, Section 3, describes a flaw classification method developed for inspecting wood. Both sections contain examples of the results obtained when using the system for identification of flaws in parquet samples. Section 4 discusses the overall performance of the system.

9.2 Texture Image Segmentation

TEXIS detects flaws in images that contain texture samples placed on a background surface. The samples may appear in various arrangements; however, it is assumed that they do not overlap. Flaw detection is carried out in two steps: first, individual samples are isolated and, second, flaws within the individual samples are isolated. TEXIS employs various parameters and threshold values when segmenting texture images. These parameters and threshold values are determined experimentally and are generally a function of the material being inspected and the digitization conditions. Specific values currently used by TEXIS for inspecting parquet are listed in Table 1.

TABLE 1

Parameters and threshold values utilized in parquet inspection.

Isolation of individual samples

D_w = 40pixels
I_b=17
e_c = 25
e_{min} = 19
D_{min} = 2.99pixels
n = 15
ϵ_w = 7pixels

Defect detection

α = 5.0
τ = 0.5
γ =mean intensity value of the image
W_m = 3pixels
L_w = 25pixels
σ = 1.

Defect classification

L = 4
P_t = .85
W_{max} = 4pixels
T_{thresh} = 250-with $f_\tau(x,y)$ [Equation (8)] scaled to 0-255
$m = n = 1$
M_{lin} = .5-with $f_\tau(x,y)$ [Equation (8)] scaled to 0-255
A_{max} = 60pixels
M_{cir} = .5-with $f_\tau(x,y)$ [Equation (8)] scaled to 0-255
B_{th} = 3

9.2.1 Isolation of Individual Samples

The isolation of individual texture samples is accomplished by first separating the texture from the background by utilizing the known intensity characteristics of the background and performing image thresholding. Following this, individual texture samples are extracted from the thresholded image by grouping the samples' edges. The method for isolating individual samples assumes that samples are rectangular and of known average width, D_w. Utilizing these assumptions, the isolation of individual samples involves:

(i) extracting edge pixels, (ii) grouping edge pixels that constitute individual edges and computing the coefficients of the corresponding lines, and (iii) grouping the parallel and perpendicular edges that bound individual samples. Processing is done sequentially by scanning the image top to bottom and left to right.

The process of isolating individual samples begins with separating the texture regions of the image array from a background of known characteristics, e.g., a conveyer belt, by image thresholding. The process assumes that the background is of a lesser intensity, I_b, than the samples. The thresholded image, $f_t(x, y)$, is obtained from the digitized image, $f(x, y)$, by

$$\begin{aligned} f_t(x,y) &= 0 && \text{if } f(x,y) \leq I_b, \\ f_t(x,y) &= f(x,y) && \text{if } f(x,y) > I_b. \end{aligned}$$

The next step is to label all edge pixels of the texture samples. It should be noted that in some cases small regions within a sample may be labeled as background. However, through the analysis that follows, these regions are rejected as possible edges of the sample. Edge pixels are defined in the thresholded image, as any $f_t(x, y) > 0$ for which there exists at least one

$$f_t(x+i, y+j) = 0, \qquad \text{for any } i, j = -1, 0, 1.$$

These pixels form the boundaries of the samples and are grouped according to the common boundary to which they belong. From this grouping, the edges of each sample are defined. Each edge is represented by a corresponding line $l_k : y - a_k x - b_k = 0,\ k = 1, 2, \ldots$. TEXIS calculates the coefficients of these lines and utilizes them to group the lines representing the edges of a single sample. With the camera set-up used in this work, the maximum possible number of edges enclosing a single sample is three and the least number of edges is one.

The grouping of edge pixels begins with the determination of an initial edge pixel from which to begin the grouping process. The initial edge pixel is the first pixel located in the scan of the image array (performed in a top to bottom, left to right manner) that is connected (with 8-connectivity) to a chain at least e_c edge pixels. The value of e_c is determined experimentally to provide accurate calculations of line parameters. Once a starting pixel is determined, TEXIS uses a least squares method to fit a line to the e_c connected pixels. If e_{min} of the e_c edge pixels are within a distance D_{min} from the fitted line l_k, the coefficients a_k and b_k are considered to accurately represent one edge of the sample. The image array is scanned for other edge pixels within a distance D_{min} of line l_k. The coefficients a_k and b_k

are updated for each subsequent group of e_{min} connected pixels within a distance D_{min} from l_k.

The digitization process often introduces distortion that results in slightly irregular and jagged edges. As a result, some pixels along an edge can be farther than distance D_{min} from line l_k. These pixels are not grouped as pixels along an edge but are treated as noise and rejected. In addition, a group of less than e_{min} connected pixels is treated as noise. The grouping process continues until all the labeled edge pixels have either been grouped into lines or have been rejected.

The obtained edge equations are used as linear decision boundaries when grouping texture pixels into common samples. A line l_k corresponds to a decision boundary defined by

$$d_k(\mathbf{X}) = \mathbf{W}_k'\mathbf{X} + b_k, \tag{1}$$

where $\mathbf{W}_k' = (1\ a_k)$ and $\mathbf{X}' = (y\ x)$. The side of the decision boundary corresponding to texture is determined by substituting the coordinates of a representative texture pixel into Equation (1) and noting the sign of the results. This is established by projecting a line, l_p, perpendicular to l_k at a particular pixel, i.e., the nth edge pixel, P_r. (Given the equation of l_k and the coefficient $a_p = tan(tan^{-1}(a_k) - \pi/2)$, b_p is determined using the known coordinates of pixel P_r.) The line l_p is searched along both sides of line l_k for the closest texture pixel. The (y, x) location of that pixel is substituted into Equation (1) and the sign of the decision surface corresponding to the texture region is determined.

Extracting an individual texture sample involves grouping texture pixels under the constraints of all the decision boundaries defining the edges of the particular sample. Since the texture samples in this implementation are restricted to rectangular shapes, the decision boundaries of a sample are defined by parallel and perpendicular lines. The borders of the image array provide the only other possible edges for the samples. Taking into account digitization effects, two lines, $l_c : y - a_c x - b_c = 0$ and $l_d : y - a_d x - b_d = 0$, are determined to be parallel if $|tan^{-1}(a_c) - tan^{-1}(a_d)| \leq \theta_a$. Two lines l_c and l_d are determined to be perpendicular if $|\pi/2 - |(tan^{-1}(a_c) - tan^{-1}(a_d)|| \leq \theta_e$. The decision boundaries defining a single sample are determined by a sequential grouping of lines under the following conditions.

Given two parallel lines l_c and l_d, if the sign of $d_c(\mathbf{X})$ defining the texture side of the decision surface is the opposite of the sign of $d_d(\mathbf{X})$, the lines are included in an initial grouping. A final grouping is based on two conditions. First, the representative pixel P_r (i.e., the nth pixel) on l_d is within a distance

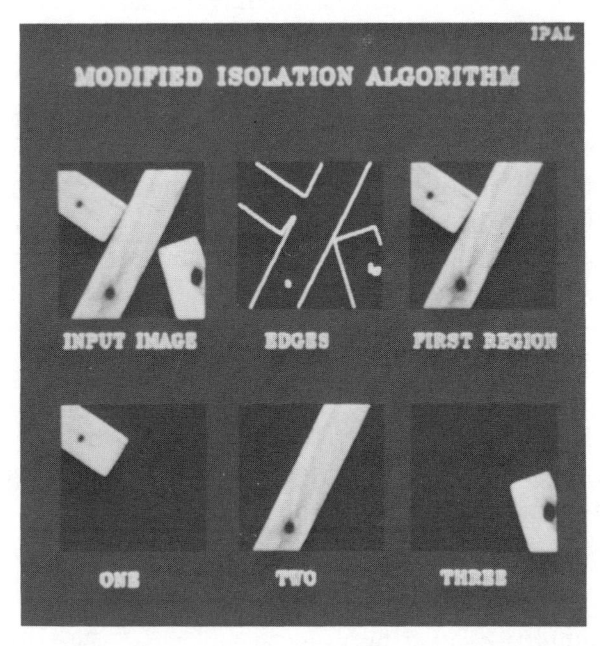

Figure 1: An examples of a typical configuration of samples and the corresponding isolated samples.

$D_w \pm \epsilon_w$ from l_c, where D_w is the average sample width. Second, a pixel, $P_m(x_o, y_o)$, along a line projected from P_r on l_c to P_r on l_d and midway between the two lines, must be texture (i.e., $f_t(x_o, y_o) > 0$) and must satisfy the sign conditions of the decision boundaries, $d_c(\mathbf{X})$ and $d_d(\mathbf{X})$.

Similar conditions provide grouping rules for perpendicular lines. The coordinates of the pixel at the midpoint of a line projected from P_r on l_c to P_r on l_d (l_c is perpendicular to l_d) must be texture and must satisfy the sign conditions of the decision boundaries, $d_c(\mathbf{X})$ and $d_d(\mathbf{X})$. Single edges which intersect an image border and which can not be grouped with other edges are utilized to isolate the remaining samples. In the case of an ambiguous configuration of edges, e.g., two samples orthogonal to each other, TEXIS considers all possible arrangements of the samples and decides on the proper arrangement by testing for background pixels along the samples' borders.

The individual samples are extracted from the image array in a sequential manner starting with the samples with the largest number of edges. This strategy minimizes the ambiguity in the assignment of texture pixels to the appropriate individual samples. Texture pixels that satisfy all sign conditions established by the decision boundaries marking boundaries of an individual sample are grouped together. Figure 1 shows isolated samples in an image.

9.2.2 Flaw Detection

Ideally, the segmentation of images for determining surface quality will yield two primary regions, flaws and background. When the surfaces are characterized by complex textural patterns, the segmentation often results in the misinterpretation of a textural pattern as a flaw. Conventional approaches to image segmentation, such as edge detection and standard region growing, can not accomplish this task when the material to be segmented is characterized by complex texture patterns. In this work we use a fuzzy pyramid linking method for segmentation. In essence, this is a multiresolution, flexible region growing method. The term "fuzzy" is used since a membership function from fuzzy set theory [15] is used in this algorithm. Basic concepts of pyramids, fuzzy pyramid linking, and its performance in comparison to other pyramid linking methods is discussed in the following.

9.2.2.1 Pyramids

An image pyramid is created by using an array I_0 $[I_0(x,y) = f_t(x,y)]$ of dimensions $2^n \times 2^n$, representing the original image, as the base of the pyramid. Each subsequent level of the pyramid, $I_1 \ldots I_n$, is a square array which is half the dimensions of its predecessor. These arrays are lower resolution representations of the original image. The top level I_n of the pyramid is a 1×1 array. An element (node) of the array I_l $(l > 0)$ is obtained by a weighted average of I_{l-1} nodes within a 4×4 neighborhood. A convenient approach to choosing weights is to use a Gaussian weighted averaging technique, as is done in this work. The image pyramid thus created is known as a Gaussian pyramid and is shown in Figure 2. The Gaussian pyramid was initially proposed by Burt [6] and has been investigated by various authors, e.g., [1]. The creation of each level in the pyramid is obtained by convolving the image created one level below with a 4×4 Gaussian mask $w(m,n)$, and is described by

$$I_l(i,j) = \sum_{m=-2}^{2} \sum_{k=-2}^{2} w(m,k) I_{l-1}(2i+m-\frac{m}{2|m|}+\frac{1}{2}, 2j+k+\frac{1}{2}-\frac{k}{2|k|}) \ for \ m,k \neq 0, \quad (2)$$

where the 4×4 generating kernel $w(m,k)$ is separable, normalized, and symmetric (see [6]).

9.2.2.2 Fuzzy Pyramid Linking

Linking is the process by which the nodes belonging to a given level of the pyramid are connected with nodes at adjacent levels. Since each level is created by convolving the 4×4 weight kernel with the preceding level of the pyramid, there exists a spatial relationship between nodes in two adjacent

Figure 2: Example of a Gaussian pyramid where each subsequent level of the pyramid is a square array which is the half of dimensions of its predecessor. Each element at level I_l is obtained by a Gaussian weighted average of I_{l-1} nodes within a 4×4 neighborhood.

levels. From Equation (2) it follows that each node at level l, $l > 0$, has a 4×4 array of candidate son nodes at level $l - 1$. Conversely, for each node at level l, $l < n - 1$, there exists a 2×2 array of candidate father nodes at level $l + 1$. Based on the linking scheme, links are established for all son nodes in the pyramid starting with the base of the pyramid. The pyramid is then redefined and new links are determined. Once the linking arrangement within the pyramid has stabilized, image segmentation can be achieved by mapping the lower resolution image at the apex of the pyramid onto the original image at the base of the pyramid by following the linking paths through the intermediate levels. This form of segmentation by hierarchical region growing results in a number of regions equal or less than the number of nodes at the apex of the pyramid, provided that there are no constraints limiting the propagation of the apex nodes to the base of the pyramid.

Various schemes can be used for linking nodes at adjacent levels of the pyramid; the most obvious scheme being one where a son node is linked to the father node that is the most similar based on a chosen property, e.g., intensity. This scheme was originally proposed by Burt [6], and will be referred to in the following as hard linking. In our approach, a son node is linked to all four candidate father nodes. The strength of the link is a function of the absolute difference between the value of a son node and its candidate father node. The value of the node is iteratively updated based on the weighted sum of the node's children, where the strengths of the links are used as the weights. New link strengths are calculated as the value of the node is updated.

In this work the following variables are defined for linking and the ensuing iterative process:

- $t_l(i,j)$: the local image property (in this paper intensity);
- $p_l(i,j)$: a pointer to the node's father one level above having the strongest link strength;
- $s_l(i,j)$: the strength value of the link between the father and the son nodes.

The iterations proceed in the following manner:

1. For level $l = 0$ set

$$s_0(i,j) = 1 \quad \text{and } t_0(i,j) = I_0(i,j).$$

2. For each level l from 1 to $n - 1$ set

$$s_l(i,j) = \sum_{i'j'} s_{l-1}(i',j')\phi_{i,j,i',j'},$$

where $\phi_{i,j,i',j'}$ denotes the strength of the link between the node (i,j) at level l and it's son (i',j') at level $l-1$,

and

$$t_l(i,j) = \sum_{i'j'} t_{l-1}(i',j')\phi_{i,j,i',j'},$$

with summations performed over all sons of the node.

3. For each node at level l, for $0 \leq l < n-2$, the pointer $p_l(i,j)$ points to the father node at level $l+1$ that has the strongest link strength among the four candidate father nodes. If two or more fathers have the same link strength, a link is chosen randomly; however, if either link existed in the previous iteration, the link remains unchanged.

4. Once the links have propagated to the top of the pyramid the value of every node, except those at level 0, is recomputed in the following manner:
$$I_l(i,j) = t_l(i,j)/s_l(i,j) \quad for\ s_l(i,j) > 0.$$

5. If no link is reassigned during the current iteration, it is assumed that a steady state has been reached. If any number of links have been reassigned during the current iteration, the procedure is repeated starting from step 2.

Upon reaching steady state, image partitioning is achieved in one top-down pass beginning from level $n-1$. In this pass, a son node at level l is replaced by the father node pointed at by $p_l(i,j)$ if the link between the two exceeds a threshold τ.

The choice of the function ϕ, representing the strength of the link, determines the flexibility of the pyramid segmentation. In this work we choose

$$\phi_{i,j,i',j'}(u;\alpha,\beta,\gamma) = 1 - S(u;\alpha,\beta,\gamma), \tag{3}$$

where

$$S(u;\alpha,\beta,\gamma) = \begin{cases} 0 & \text{for } u \leq \alpha \\ 2\left(\frac{u-\alpha}{\gamma-\alpha}\right)^2 & \text{for } \alpha \leq u \leq \beta \\ 1-2\left(\frac{u-\gamma}{\gamma-\alpha}\right)^2 & \text{for } \beta \leq u \leq \gamma \\ 1 & \text{for } u \geq \gamma \end{cases} \tag{4}$$

and $u = |I_l(i,j) - I_{l-1}(i',j')|$. This function, shown in Figure 3, is widely used in various applications based on fuzzy set theory (e.g., [7]). The parameter α determines the difference between pixels at different levels below which the link strength assigned is 1; γ is the difference above which

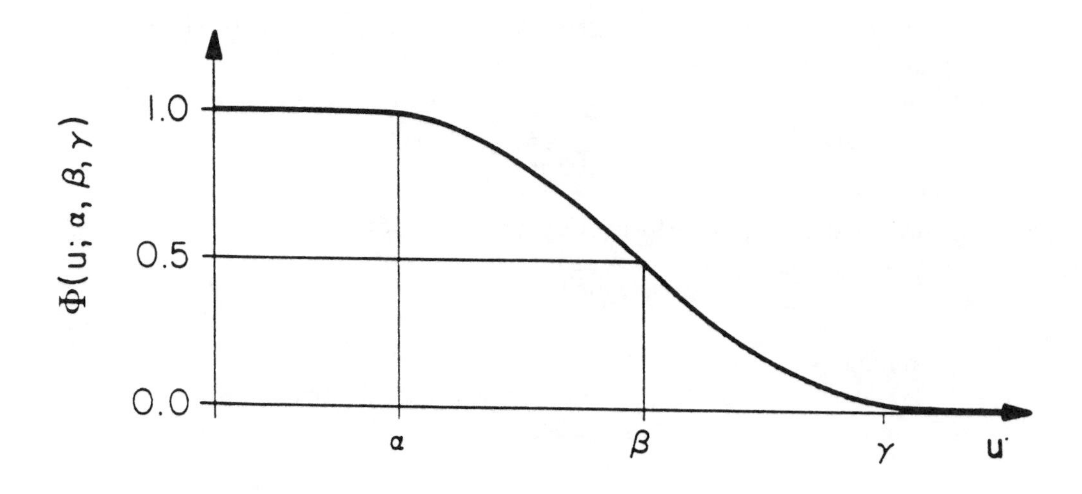

Figure 3: Function ϕ representing the strength of the link between the father and the son nodes. Parameters α, β, and γ are indicated on the graph.

the link strength assigned is 0; $\beta = \frac{\alpha+\gamma}{2}$ is the crossover point at which $\phi_{i,j,i',j'}(u;\alpha,\beta,\gamma) = 0.5$.

Besides the membership function described by Equations (3) and (4), three other monotonically decreasing functions (linear-like, sigmoid-like, and step function) were investigated. Considering Fisher ratios and false detections, the membership function described by Equations (3) and (4) was selected [14].

The function $\phi_{i,j,i',j'}$, described by Equations (3) and (4), makes the proposed pyramid linking method a special case of the fuzzy isodata clustering [11]. Consequently, based on the convergence of the fuzzy isodata clustering [2], the proposed pyramid linking is convergent [14]. (The relationship between pyramid linking and isodata clustering is discussed by Kasif and Rosenfeld [11].)

9.2.2.3 Performance

In this section the quality of segmentation achieved using the fuzzy pyramid linking algorithm is discussed and compared to hard pyramid linking. It should be noted that the fuzzy pyramid linking algorithm requires more memory, as well as numerical operations, than hard pyramid linking.

The inputs to both pyramid linking procedures are the Gaussian image pyramid, the maximum number of iterations allowed (for practical purposes), and the level from which the segmentation is to begin. Three additional parameters α, γ and τ are required for fuzzy pyramid linking.

Parameters α and γ define the critical points in the subjectively chosen membership function shown in Figure 3. The third parameter, τ, is used to decide whether a son node can be replaced by a father node in the segmentation procedure. This parameter determines the number of segments in the segmented image, since links with a strength value below the minimum threshold strength do not propagate down to the base of the pyramid.

We have found experimentally that the method is particularly sensitive to the values of α and τ. Experiments have been conducted with $2.0 \leq \alpha \leq 20.0$ and $0.3 \leq \tau \leq 0.9$. Generally, low values of α, e.g., $\alpha = 2.0$, give the best results. When the objective is to isolate the more prominent features in an image, $\tau = 0.5$ is appropriate; this value needs to be increased when isolating the less prominent features. Finally, the best results are obtained with parameter γ chosen as the mean intensity value. Sufi [14] discusses in detail the effects of parameters α, γ, and τ on the performance of this method. Examples of effects of the three parameters on the segmentation results are shown in Figure 4.

Comparison between hard and fuzzy pyramid linking reveals that the hard pyramid linking successfully identifies prominent features, but fails when textural detail and smaller features are present (see also Figure 5). The fuzzy pyramid linking, in comparison, successfully handles textural detail, Figure 5.

We have experimentally determined the parameters' values, Table 1, useful for analyzing wood images. (It should be noted that the parameters in Table 1 are a function of the material and the chosen resolution.) The results of segmenting two wood images using these parameters are shown in Figure 6. In the case of parquet samples, for computational efficiency, each parquet sample is divided into overlapping nxn ($n = 32$) subregions and each of these subregions is independently analyzed by the pyramid linking method. The number of subregions is determined by the length of the longest edge of the sample and its slope relative to the rectangular coordinate system with the origin located in the upper left corner of the image.

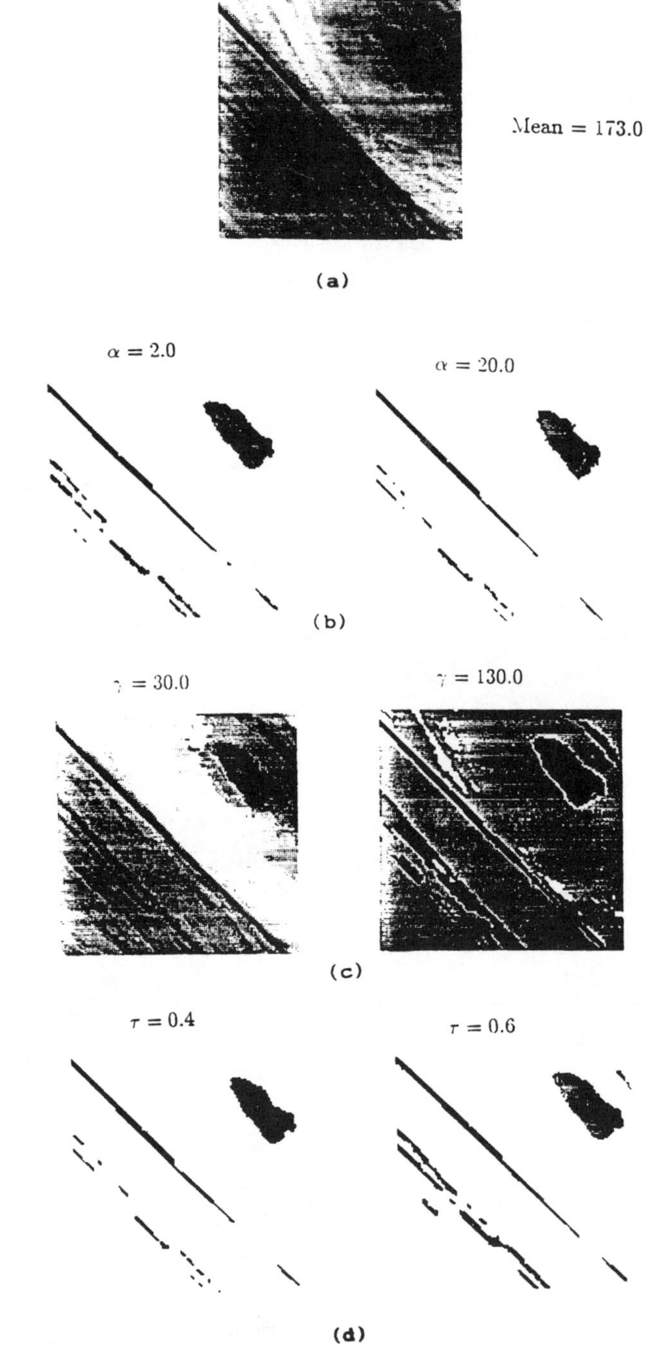

Figure 4: Effects of parameters α, γ and τ on results of fuzzy pyramid segmentation: (a) test image, (b) effects of parameter α ($2.0 \leq \alpha \leq 20.0$, $\gamma = 170.0$, $\tau = .5$), (c)effects of parameter γ ($30. \leq \gamma \leq 130.$, $\alpha = 5.0$, $\tau = .5$), (d) effects of parameter τ ($.4 \leq \tau \leq .6$, $\alpha = 5.$, $\gamma = 170.$).

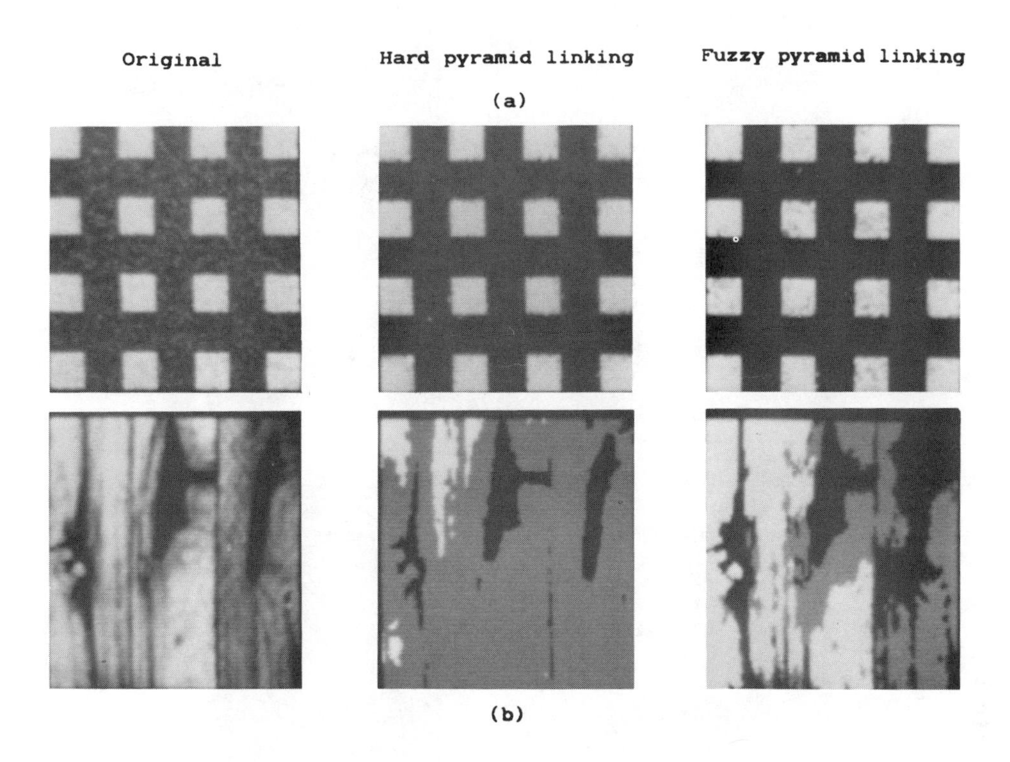

Figure 5: Comparison between the hard and fuzzy pyramid linking algorithms: (a) noisy binary image (parameters used by the fuzzy pyramid linking $\alpha = 5.0$, $\gamma = 120.$, $\tau = .5$), (b) texture image (parameters used by the fuzzy pyramid linking $\alpha = 5.0$, $\gamma = 170.$, $\tau = .6$).

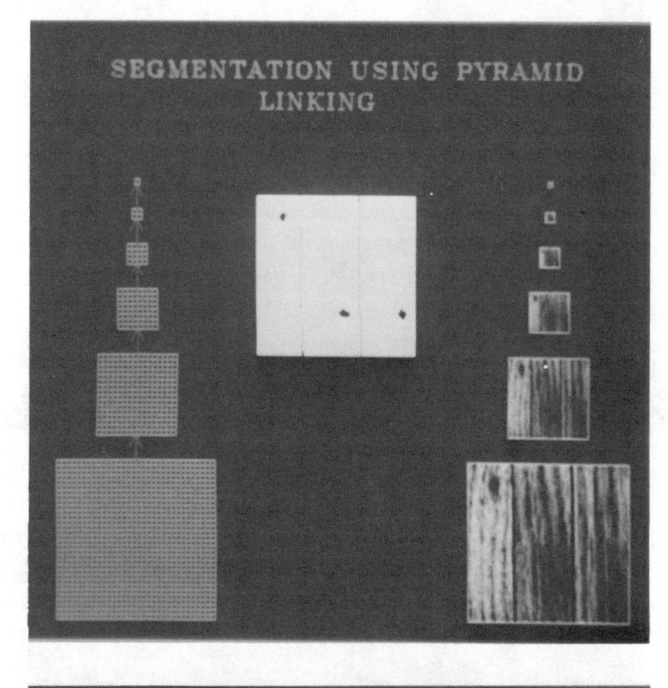

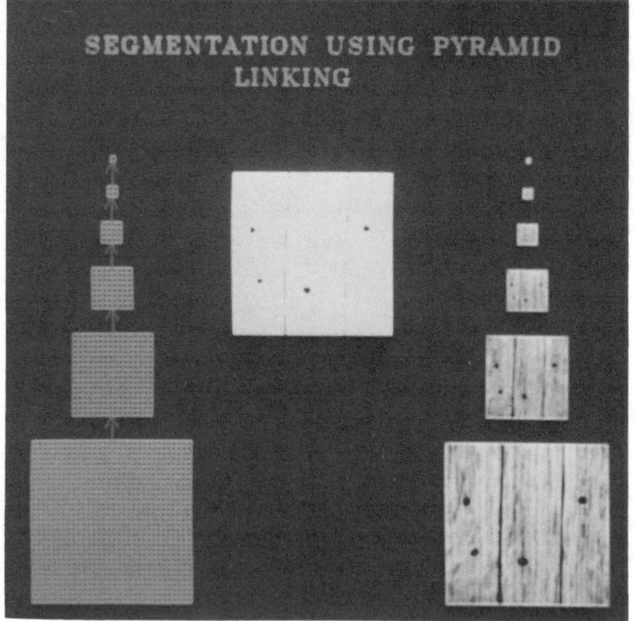

Figure 6: Two examples of images processed by the fuzzy pyramid linking method. The result is shown in the center.

9.2.2.4 Post Processing

Due to the resolution of the camera, very thin linear flaws, such as cracks, may become discontinuous when extracted by the pyramid segmentation method (see also Figure 6). Consequently, prior to performing recognition, TEXIS connects discontinuous linear flaws.

The edge of an isolated flaw is checked for continuity if its width is at most W_m and its length is at least L_w (see Table 1 for particular values employed by TEXIS). Linear flaw tracking utilizes the Marr-Hildreth operator [12] which guarantees edge continuity. Thus, the image array is convolved with

$$\nabla^2 G(x,y) = \frac{1}{2\pi\sigma^4}(-2 + \frac{x^2+y^2}{\sigma^2})e^{\frac{-(x^2+y^2)}{2\sigma^2}}. \tag{5}$$

The relationship between the edges of the extracted flaw and the zero-crossings of the convolved image is established by taking into account possible shifts of the edges by a few pixels. The tracking process involves tracking the appropriate zero-crossings in the convolved image by considering the eight neighbor connectivity until the extent of the edge is completely defined.

Once the potential flaws are identified, the output of the fuzzy pyramid linking and post processing is turned into a binary image by assigning a value of 0 to regions pertaining to possible flaws and assigning a value of 255 to regions corresponding to the background. This binary image together with the original image is the input to the flaw classification process.

9.3 Flaw Classification

The method of texture image segmentation, described in Section 2, is general and applicable to various segmentation tasks. In contrast, the method of flaw classification is dependent on the type of material being inspected. Consequently, the method employed in flaw classification is designed specifically for a particular material. This section details the classification method employed in analyzing wood images. Various flaws found in wood are discussed by Conners et al. [9]. In this section we describe flaw classification for four flaw classes: cracks, mineral streaks, worm holes, and knots; typical representatives of three of these classes are shown in Figure 7.

Classification is performed in a hierarchical fashion. In order to minimize classification time, the computational complexity of the measurements is minimal at the top of the hierarchy and increases towards the bottom. Classification is attempted at each level of the hierarchy and the process continues through the hierarchy only when the decision regarding the class of a flaw

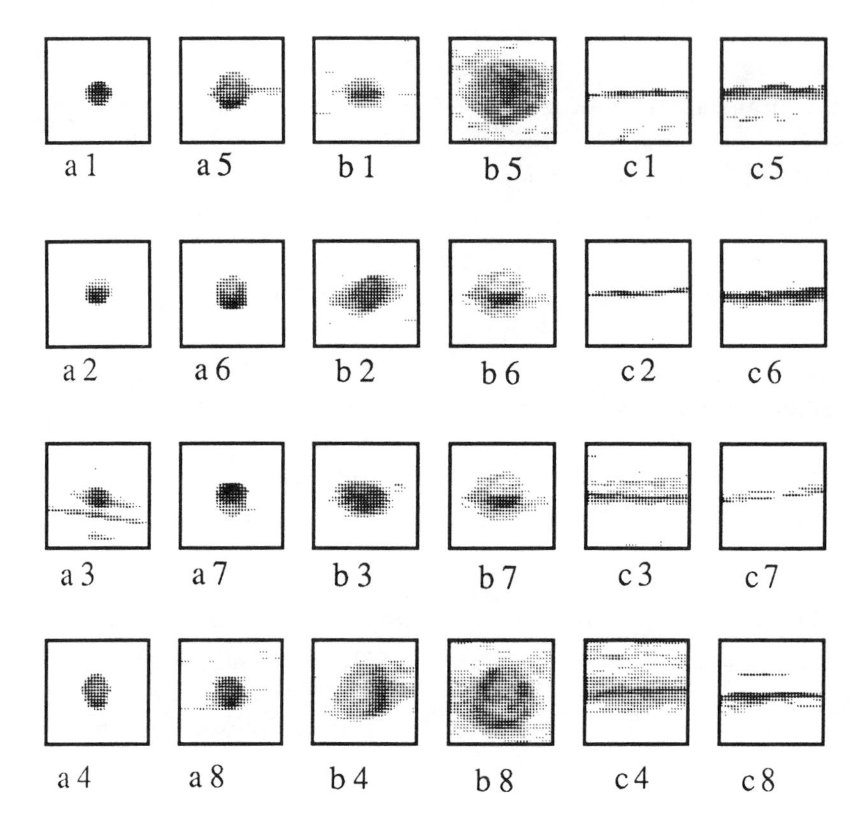

Figure 7: Typical examples of flaws used for training the classifiers: a1-a8 worm holes, b1-b8 knots, c1-c8 cracks.

cannot be made with certainty. The classification uses a four-level hierarchy (Figure 8). At the first level, TEXIS uses a Bayes classifier; at subsequent levels, decision making is performed using deterministic classifiers.

The classification hierarchy uses the following measurements:

- Shape descriptor
- Area/width
- Flaw texture descriptor
- Background texture descriptor

Section 3.1 describes the flaw classification procedure, Section 3.2 details the measurement procedures, and Section 3.3 concentrates on learning issues.

9.3.1 Classification

This section first describes the classifiers used and, then, describes the decision making process.

9.3.1.1 Bayes Classifier

The first level of the classification hierarchy uses a Bayes classifier and a shape descriptor, C (Section 3.2.1). This descriptor forms a one-dimensional pattern vector x. The classifier assumes that: (i) all classes are equally likely, (ii) the loss L_{ij} incurred when misclassifying a flaw that belongs to class i as a flaw belonging to class j is $L_{ij} = 1 - \delta_{ij}$ (where δ_{ij} is the Kronecker delta function), and (iii) each class ω_j is characterized by a normal conditional probability density

$$p(x|\omega_j) = \frac{1}{\sqrt{2\pi}\sigma_j} e^{\frac{-1}{2}\left(\frac{x-m_j}{\sigma_j}\right)^2}, \tag{6}$$

where m_j and σ_j are the mean and the standard deviation for the jth class. Under these assumptions, for an N class problem, the Bayes classifier assigns a pattern vector x to class ω_i if

$$p(x|\omega_i) > p(x|\omega_j), \quad j = 1, 2, ..., N \ (j \neq i). \tag{7}$$

9.3.1.2 Deterministic Classifier

Flaws are classified at levels 2-4 using deterministic classifiers and one-dimensional pattern vectors. At each of these levels a flaw may be classified as a member of a particular class, ω_i, or its classification remains unknown.

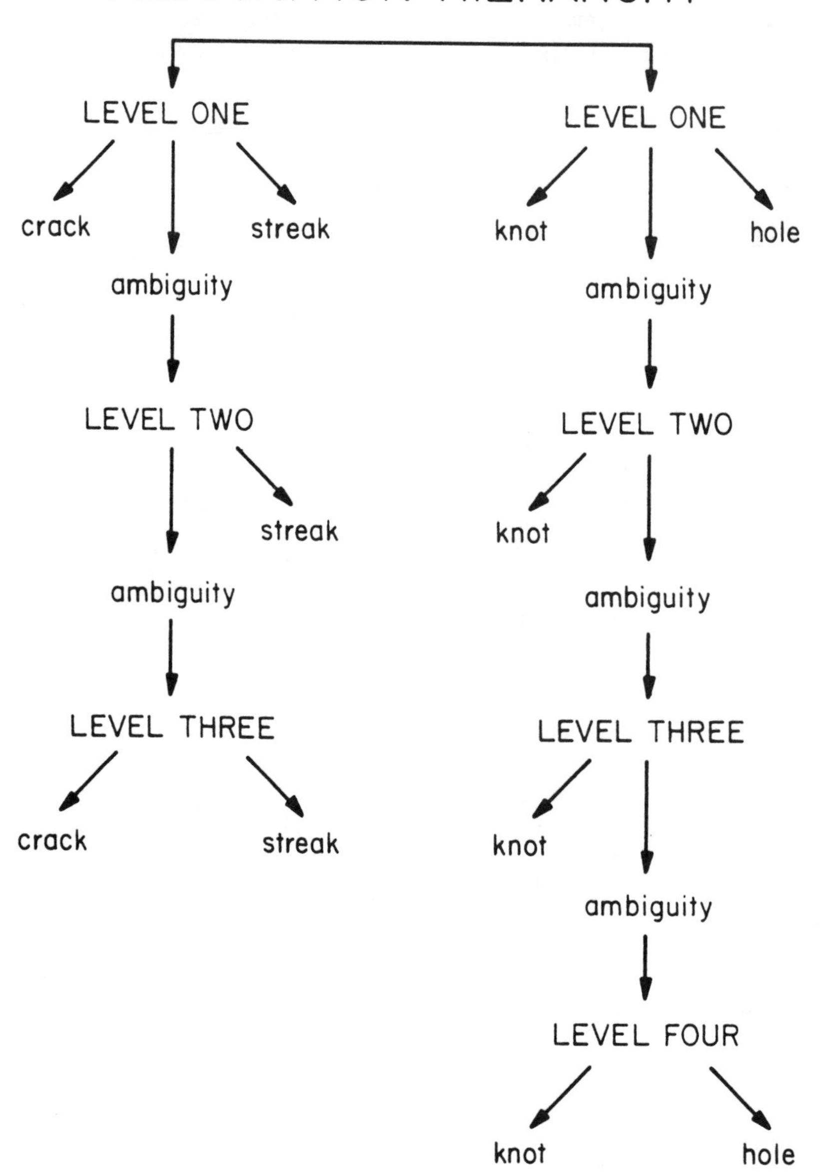

Figure 8: Hierarchical classification scheme utilized by TEXIS for classifying four types of flaws (cracks, mineral streaks, knots and worm holes) found in wood. Level one utilizes the measure of compactness; level two utilizes the flaw's area in the case of knots and worm holes and the flaw's width in the case of cracks and mineral streaks; level three utilizes textural characteristics of the flaws; level four utilizes textural characteristics of the background.

Consequently, the deterministic classifiers are acting on two-class problems, a known class and an unknown class. In practical implementations, a particular measurement, e.g., μ, is compared to a threshold value T_μ and a flaw is classified as member of ω_i if $\mu \leq T_\mu$ (or alternatively if $\mu \geq T_\mu$).

9.3.1.3 Classification Hierarchy

The objective of the first level of classification is to differentiate between round flaws (worm holes and knots) and elongated flaws (cracks and mineral streaks). Levels 2-4 differentiate between flaws within these two classes. Specific values used by the classifier are summarized in Table 1. Details of the classification procedure are as follows:

- Level 1— This level uses a Bayes classifier and a shape descriptor (measure of compactness, C, Section 3.2.1). A flaw is assigned to a particular class based on Equation (7); however, the overlap of conditional probability density functions for similar flaws (knots-worm holes, cracks-mineral streaks) is generally significant and in only some cases is it possible to classify a flaw at this level. Specifically, when the a posteriori probability is sufficiently high for one of the classes, i.e., if $p(\omega_i|x) \geq P_t$, then the flaw is classified as ω_i and no further processing is needed. The physical meaning of P_t is described in Section 3.3. In other cases, classification proceeds by following one of the two classification paths (Figure 8).
- Level 2—At this level the deterministic classifier and the measurements pertaining to width (cracks-mineral streaks) and area (knots-worm holes) are used.
  - Level 2 cracks-mineral streaks—Based on our experimentation we have found that the width of a crack never exceeds a specific width W_{max}. Therefore, a flaw is classified as a mineral streak if the average width of the flaw $W_a > W_{max}$. If the width of the flaw is less than W_{max} classification proceeds to level 3.
  - Level 2 knots-worm holes—Similarly, worm holes and knots are distinguished based on the area, A. A flaw is considered to be a knot if $A > A_{max}$; otherwise, classification proceeds to the next level.
- Level 3—This level uses a deterministic classifier and a flaw texture descriptor M_{tex} (Section 3.2.4) in both classification paths. Generally, cosmetic flaws such as knots and mineral streaks are characterized by textural changes generic to wood, in contrast to flaws generated by outside forces, such as worm holes and cracks which have no texture.

Consequently, a flaw is classified as a mineral streak if $M_{tex} > M_{lin}$; otherwise, a flaw is classified as a crack. A flaw is classified as a knot if $M_{tex} > M_{cir}$; otherwise classification proceeds to level 4. Specific threshold values are listed in Table 1.

- Level 4—This level uses a deterministic classifier and a descriptor of background texture to differentiate between small round knots and worm holes. The background texture descriptor, B, establishes if the grain pattern follows a flaw and is described in Section 3.2.5 and Appendix. A flaw is classifed as a knot if $B > B_{th}$; otherwise, it is classified as a worm hole.

9.3.2 Measurements

The present system differentiates between four classes of flaws based on their shape and intensity variations. The primary objective of the shape descriptor is to differentiate between round flaws (worm holes and knots) and elongated flaws (cracks and mineral streaks). The intensity variations pertain to textural properties of the flaws and the background. Specific measurements are described in the following.

9.3.2.1 Shape Descriptor

The shape descriptor is determined using the output of fuzzy pyramid linking and thresholding, in which possible flaws are assigned intensity 0 and background 255. Measure of compactness, C, is chosen as a shape descriptor and is defined as $C = P^2/A$, where P denotes the perimeter and A denotes the area of a binary flaw under consideration.

9.3.2.2 Area Measurement

The flaw area is determined using the thresholded output of fuzzy pyramid linking. The area is obtained by counting the number of pixels in each possible flaws (region with intensity 0), scanning from left to right, top to bottom. It should be noted that the area is already calculated when measuring compactness.

9.3.2.3 Flaw Width

This measure uses the average width of a flaw, and is used to differentiate between cracks (generally narrow) and mineral streaks (generally wide). The width is determined by analyzing the thresholded output of fuzzy pyramid linking (same as in area) and the width of the flaw is determined pixel by pixel along the major axis of symmetry (determined using the method of moments [10]).

9.3.2.4 Flaw Texture Descriptor

A flaw texture descriptor is used to differentiate between flaws characterized by texture (knots, mineral streaks) and those that have no textural characteristics (worm holes, cracks). The texture descriptor is

$$M_{tex} = f_{count}/A, \tag{8}$$

where A is the area of the flaw and f_{count} is the number of pixels (in the flaw area) with $f_T(x, y) > T_{thresh}$, where

$$f_T(x, y) = \sum_{i=-m}^{m} \sum_{j=-n}^{n} [f_t(x, y) - f_t(x + i, y + j)]^2, \tag{9}$$

and f_t is as in Section 2.1. Equation (9) measures pixel typicality relative to its neighbors. In cases of small intensity variations within the flaw f_T takes small values. In highly textured regions containing many pixels f_T becomes very large. In such cases, the value of f_T is larger than the deterministic threshold value T_{thresh}; therefore, f_{count} becomes large and M_{tex} approaches one.

9.3.2.5 Background Texture Descriptor

This descriptor is used to differentiate between worm holes and knots, that in many cases are very similar. It is based on the observation that the directionality of wood grain follows the basic shape of knots, while it's pattern directionality remains undisturbed by worm holes. The descriptor (B in Section 3.1.3) counts the number of grain patterns following the potential flaw. Since the wood images and, in particular, the grain patterns show variability in intensity changes, directions, and generic patterns this descriptor is obtained by using a transform that simplifies the counting procedure. A gray level image is transformed in such a way that the outer edge of a flaw maps into a vertical line. The grain pattern that follows a flaw maps into parallel lines that can be easily extracted and counted when combining directional filtering with edge detection. The transformation is detailed in the Appendix. The input to this step is the thresholded original image (Section 2.1). The region for processing is chosen by identifying the center of gravity of the potential flaw (thresholded output of the fuzzy pyramid linking) as the center of the window for processing. The window dimensions are determined by the physical dimensions of a particular parquet sample.

9.3.3 Learning

Flaw classification requires a learning phase for the Bayes classifier. Using the assumptions stated in this paper (Gaussian distribution and equal likelihood), learning involves obtaining the mean and standard deviation for each

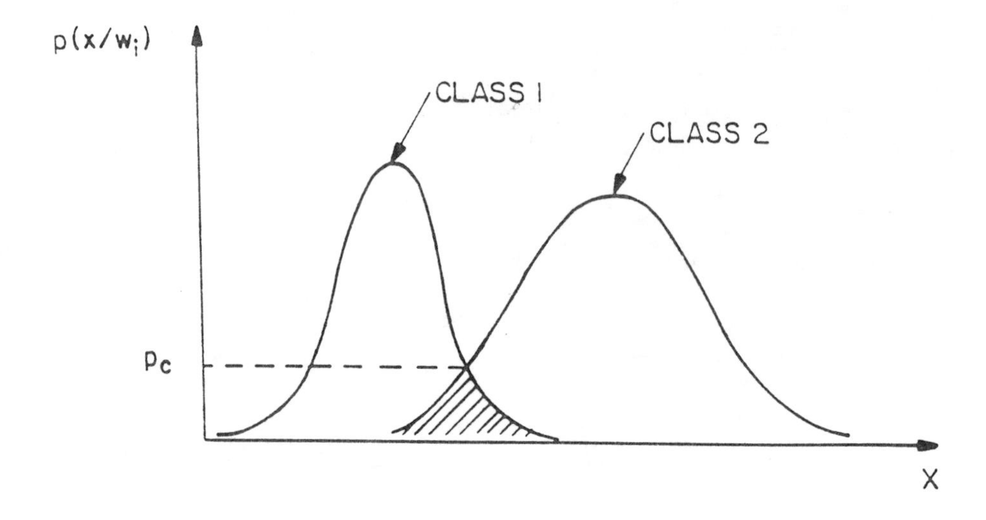

Figure 9: Overlapping probability density functions; symbol p_c denotes the critical value below which classification becomes ambiguous.

of the probability density functions. This is done by presenting the learning samples to TEXIS, processed using fuzzy pyramid linking and thresholding, and interactively identifying each of the flaws. Then, TEXIS performs the required measurements and updates the mean and standard deviation at each level of classification.

The probability density functions are generally overlapping (Figure 9) and the deterministic threshold P_t is determined so that $P_t > p_c$, where p_c is as shown in Figure 9 (for specific values see Table 1).

9.4 Conclusions

TEXIS is implemented on a VAX 11-785. The fuzzy pyramid linking is also implemented on an NCUBE with 8 processors. The latter implementation significantly reduces the processing time of the most computationally intensive processing step. By subdividing an image into 32×32 windows and submitting each of the regions to a separate processor, parallel implementation requires about 1/7 of the processing time required by the sequential implementation on a single processor.

With the chosen resolution and parameters shown in Table 1, the flaw detection rate (described in Section 2.2), both in the learning and testing phases, is 100%. The flaw recognition rate obtained by testing the system on 100 flaws is 81%, with the parameters shown in Table 1. An example of flaw clas-

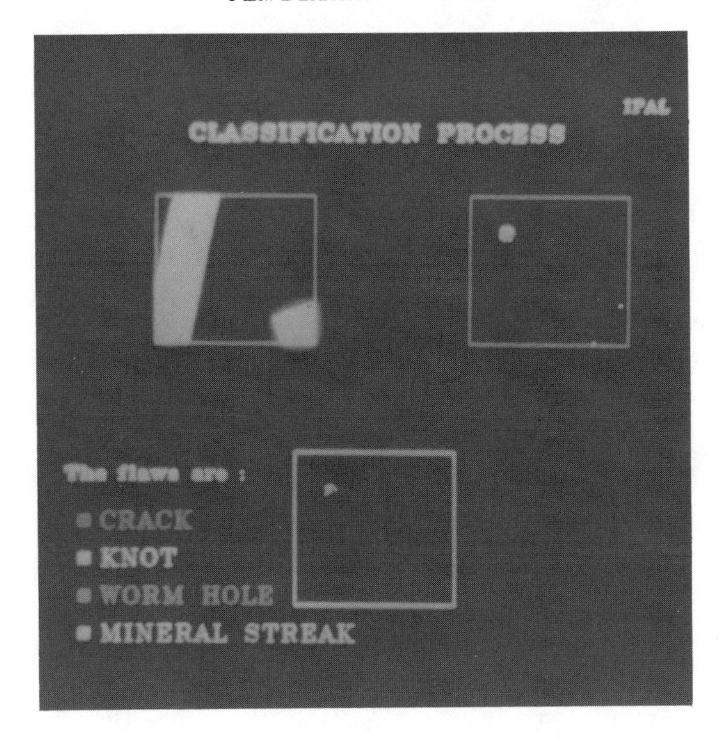

Figure 10: An examples of flaw classification.

sification is shown in Figure 10. The system does not classify flaws whose area is smaller than 16 pixels (which occurs with some worm holes) and has occasionally misclassified as worm holes small knots (12% of the knot population) that do not have well defined edges.

Once on-line, TEXIS would not only increase the quality of the manufactured product, but also increase the efficiency of the entire manufacturing process. The results would be a substantial savings in labor and materials cost, and a higher quality finished product. The resolution of the camera has proved to be the limiting factor in the system's performance. A higher resolution camera would allow the system to incorporate more textural information into the classification hierarchy and would permit more accurate classification of the flaws at earlier stages in the classification hierarchy, at the expense of increased computation time.

References

[1] Antonisse H.J., "Image Segmentation in Pyramids," *Computer Graphics and Image Processing*, vol. 19, pp. 367-383 (1982).

[2] Bezdek J.C., "A Convergence Theorem for Fuzzy ISODATA Clustering Algorithm," *IEEE Transactions on Pattern Analysis and Machine Intelligence*, vol. PAMI-2, no. 1, pp. 1-8 (1980).

[3] Borhesi, M., Cantoni, V., and Diani, M., "An Industrial Application of Texture Analysis," Proc. of the Seventh International Conference on Pattern Recognition, Montreal, Canada (1984).

[4] Brzakovic, D., Beck, H., and Sufi, N., "Defect Detection in Materials Characterized by Complex Textures," *Pattern Recognition*, vol. 23, no. 1/2, pp. 99-107 (1990).

[5] Brzakovic, D. and Khani, D., "Weld Pool Edge Detection for Automated Control of Welding," *IEEE Trans. on Robotics and Automation*, vol. 7, no. 3, pp. 397-403 (1991).

[6] Burt P. J., "The Pyramid as a Structure for Efficient Computation," *Multiresolution Image Processing and Analysis*, Rosenfield, A. (Ed.) pp. 6-35, Springer-Verlag, Berlin-Heidelberg (1984).

[7] Chatterji, B.N. "Fuzzy Set Theoretic Approach to Scene Analysis," in *Approximate Reasoning in Expert Systems*, Gupta, M.M, Kandel, A., Bandler,W. and Kiszka, J.B. (Eds.), North-Holland, New York, N.Y. (1985).

[8] Coggins, J.M. and Jain, A.K., "A Spatial Filtering Approach to Texture Analysis," *Pattern Recognition Letters*, pp. 195-203 (1985).

[9] Conners R.W., McMillin C.W., Lin K., and Vasquez-Espinosa R.E., "Identifying and Locating Surface Defects in Wood: Part of an Automated Lumber Processing System," *IEEE Transactions on Pattern Analysis and Machine Intelligence*, vol. PAMI-5, pp. 573-583 (1983).

[10] Gonzalez, R.C., and Wintz, P., *Digital Image Processing*, Addison-Wesley, Reading, Mass. (1987).

[11] Kasif, S. and Rosenfeld A., "Pyramid Linking is a Special Case of ISODATA," *IEEE Transactions on Systems, Man, and Cybernetics*, vol. SMC-13, no. 1, pp. 84-85 (1983).

[12] Marr D. and Hildreth, E.C., "Theory of Edge Detection," *Proc. of Royal Society London*, B-207, pp. 187-217 (1980).

[13] Mundy, J.L., "Visual Inspection of Metal Surfaces," Proc. of the Fifth International Conference on Pattern Recognition, Miami Beach, Fl. (1980).

[14] Sufi, N., Pyramid Based Segmentation of Texture Images, MS Thesis, University of Tennessee (1988).

[15] Zadeh, L.A. "Fuzzy Sets," *Information and Control*, vol. 8, pp. 338-353 (1965).

Appendix

This section describes a method for determining if the grain pattern follows the flaw. The method employs the following four steps: (i) coordinate transformation, (ii) directional filtering, (iii) edge detection, and (iv) counting. The proposed transformation is well suited for the particular class of images since it minimizes confusion between various concentric and intersecting edges. It has also been used for detection of weld pools as described in [5]. The effects of the transformation on the two classes of flaws (worm holes and knots) are illustrated in Figure 11.

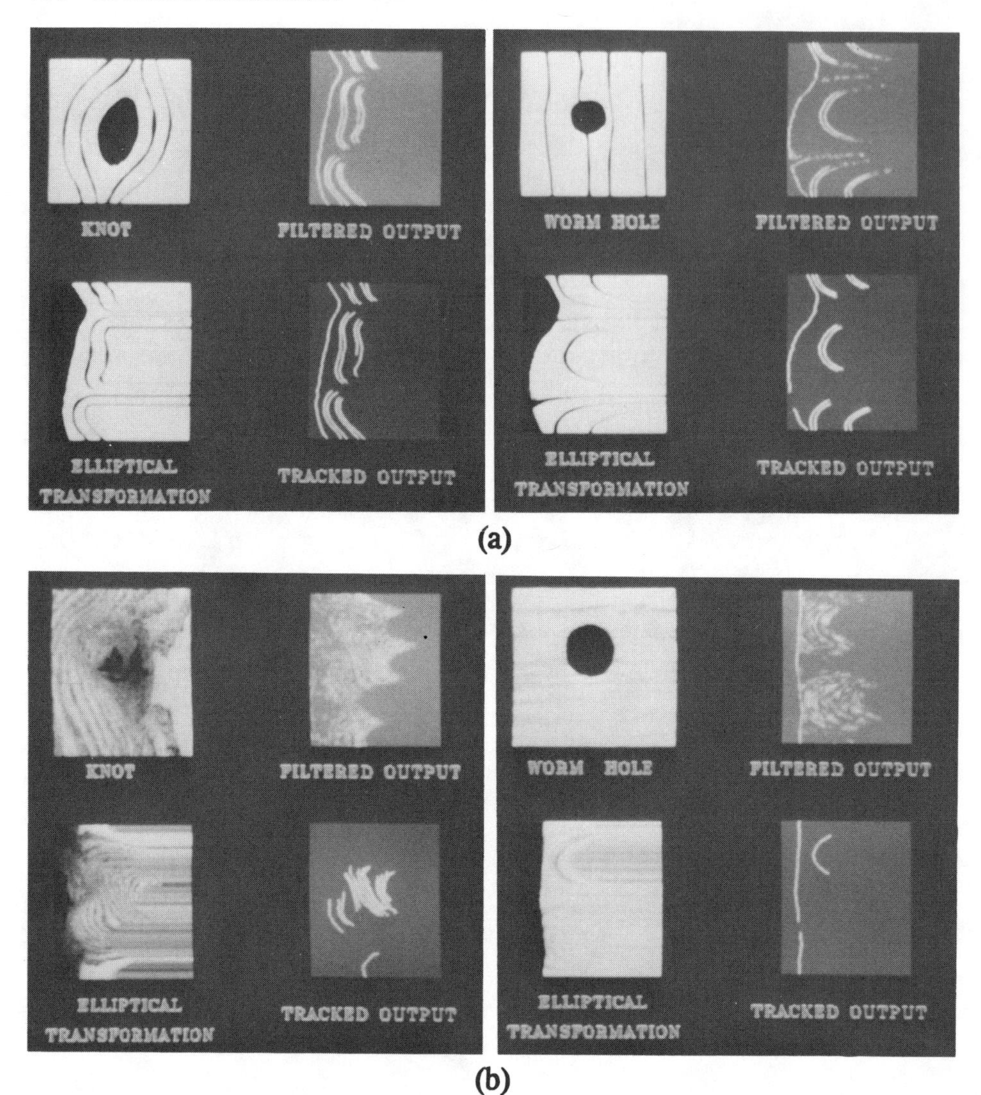

Figure 11: Examples of effects of transformation on worm holes and knots: (a) artificial knot and worm hole subjected to transformation and filtering showing that a number of edges is retained in the case of knot, (b) real knot and a worm hole subjected to transformation and filtering.

A1. Coordinate Transformation

The objective of this step is to simplify establishing the relationship between a flaw and the underlying grain pattern. This is accomplished by transforming a flaw edge having various orientations into a vertical line. In order to achieve this simplification, we model a flaw outline by an ellipse

$$\frac{(x-\zeta)^2}{\alpha^2} + \frac{(y-\eta)^2}{\beta^2} = 1, \tag{10}$$

where symbol (ζ, η) denotes the center of the ellipse and α and β are the half lengths of the major and minor axes. Furthermore, we employ what we shall call the (ρ, θ) transformation that maps points in the rectangular coordinate system (x, y) into the rectangular coordinate system (ρ, θ) (see also Figure 12). The (ρ, θ) coordinate transformation is defined as

$$\rho = \sqrt{\frac{(x-x_0)^2}{a^2} + \frac{(y-y_0)^2}{b^2}}, \tag{11}$$

$$\theta = \arctan\left(\frac{\frac{(y-y_0)}{b}}{\frac{(x-x_0)}{a}}\right), \tag{12}$$

where (x_0, y_0) is the center of transformation and a, b are constants. Given an image $F(x, y)$, the image in the transform domain, $E(\rho, \theta)$, is generated so that $E(\rho, \theta) = F(x, y)$. However, for a given integer coordinate pair (ρ, θ), there does not exist, in general, a corresponding integer coordinate pair (x, y). Consequently, the corresponding $F(x, y)$ is obtained by using bilinear interpolation in the (x, y) domain applied to the nearest four neighbours of (x, y) that have integer coordinates.

Using Equations (11) and (12) and considering a flaw outline modelled by Equation (10), for $x_0 = \zeta$, $y_0 = \eta$, $a = \alpha$, and $b = \beta$ this ellipse maps into a line $\rho = 1$, in the (ρ, θ) coordinate system. In order to increase resolution in the (ρ, θ) domain we multiply ρ by a factor $f \geq 1$. In this work we use $f = 40$, which we have experimentally found to be satisfactory for the images under consideration. It should be noted that the transformation from F to E space introduces smoothing, due to the bilinear interpolation in estimating pixel values; however, it does not change the basic image properties.

A2. Directional Filtering

The (ρ, θ) transformation maps an ellipse in the (x, y) coordinate system into a vertical line when correct values of parameters a, b, x_0 and y_0 are used. Assuming the presence of other intensity changes, directional filtering can be used to retain intensity changes only in the direction of interest. Also,

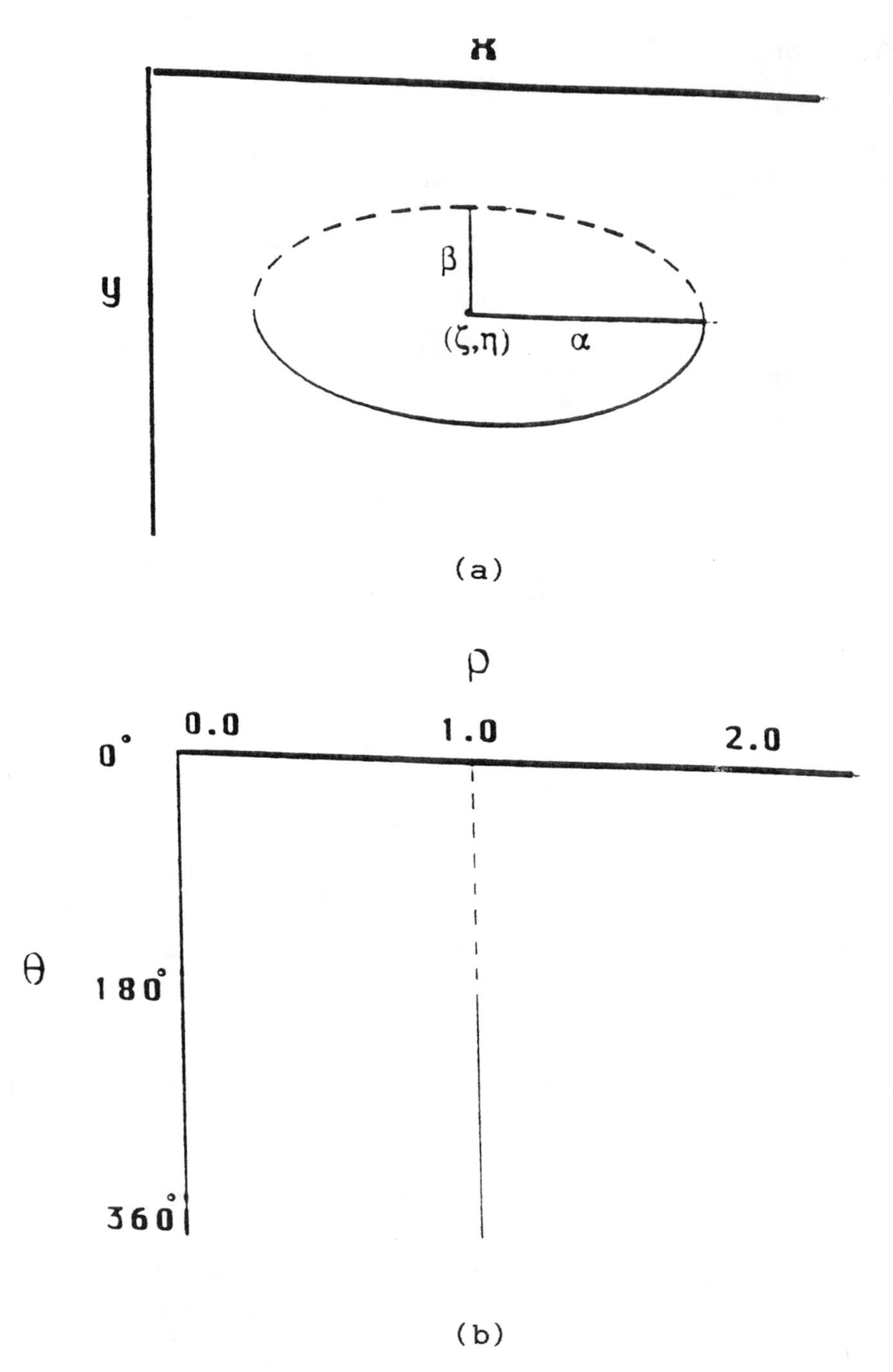

Figure 12: Effects of (ρ, θ) transformation on an ellipse: (a) original image, (b) transformed image (center of transformation was chosen to be the center of ellipse in (a) and half-lengths of major and minor axes were the transformation constants.)

directional filtering has a smoothing effect which decreases the amount of noise present in an image.

The transfer function of the directional filter, $G(u,v)$, used in this work, is defined by:

$$G(0,0) = \tfrac{1}{2}$$
$$[G(u,v)] = exp^{\left(-0.5\frac{\psi}{(17.5)^2}\right)} \qquad \text{for all}(u,v) \neq (0,0), \tag{13}$$

where

$$\psi = min\left[|\arctan(\frac{v}{u})|, |-180 - \arctan(\frac{v}{u})|\right], \tag{14}$$

as described in [8].

Filtering is performed in the Fourier domain, by first computing the Fourier transform of the image $E(\rho,\theta)$, $\mathcal{F}[E(\rho,\theta)]$. Next, $\mathcal{F}[E(\rho,\theta)]$ and $G(u,v)$ are multiplied. Finally, the the inverse Fourier transform, $\mathcal{F}^{-1}\{\mathcal{F}[E(\rho,\theta)G(u,v)]\}$, yields the filtered image.

A3. Edge Detection

This step employs the one-dimensional Marr-Hildreth edge detector [12]

$$\frac{d^2}{dx}G(x) = \frac{d^2}{dx}\left(-\frac{1}{\sqrt{2\pi}\sigma}e^{-\frac{x^2}{2\sigma^2}}\right) \tag{15}$$

to detect all vertical edges in the filtered image. The one-dimensional version of the edge detector is sufficient since the intensity changes exist only in a particular direction. It also offers significant computational advantage relative to the two-dimensional version. The advantage of this edge detector is that it has smoothing embedded in it and, thus, further reduces noise effects.

The localization of the detected edges and noise sensitivity are the function of parameter σ in Equation (15); in this work we use $\sigma = 2$. This σ value smooths an image and removes noise, thus simplifying the image.

A4. Counting

This step counts the number of edge segments remaining in the image that are longer than a prespecified edge length. In this case we use a length of 30 pixels.

A5. Transform Parameter Selection

In order to retain parallelism between the flaw and grain following its outline, we use the center of gravity of a flaw as the center of transformation and the half-lengths along its primary axes of symmetry as the parameters a and b in Equations (11) and (12). The thresholded output of fuzzy pyramid segmentation is used for these calculations. Examples of the effects of the transformation on grain surrounding worm holes and knots are shown in Figure 11.

Morphology

Chapter 10

Introduction to Binary Morphology†

R. C. Gonzalez, J. P. Basart

10.1 Introduction

The word *morphology* is commonly used to denote a branch of biology that deals with the form and structure of animals and plants. We use the same word in the present context to denote structural properties related to the shape of image components, such as skeletons, boundaries, and the convex hull of a region. Since automated visual identification of objects in an image is generally based on shape, morphology has become in the past few years a topic of considerable interest in areas such as computer vision, robotics, and medical image processing.

The language of mathematical morphology is set theory. As such, morphology offers a unified and powerful approach to a number of image description problems. Sets in mathematical morphology represent the shapes of objects in an image. For example, the set of all black pixels in a binary image is a complete description of the image. In binary images, the sets in question are members the 2-dimensional integer space Z^2, where each element of a set is a tuple (2-dimensional vector) whose coordinates are the (x, y) coordinates of a black (by convention) pixel in the image. Gray-scale digital images can be represented as sets whose components are in Z^3. In this case, two components of each element of the set refer to the coordinates of a pixel, and the third corresponds to its discrete intensity value. Sets in higher dimensional spaces can contain other image attributes, such as color and time-varying components.

In the following discussion, we develop and illustrate a number of important concepts in mathematical morphology. Many of these operations can be formulated in terms of n-dimensional Euclidean space, E^n. However, the focus in the sections that follow is on binary images whose components, as stated above, are elements of Z^2. Extensions to gray-scale images are discussed in Chapters 11 and 12.

10.2 Dilation and Erosion

We begin the discussion of morphological operations by treating in some detail two operations, *dilation* and *erosion*, which are the basis for most of the morphological operations discussed in later sections.

---

† The material in this chapter is based on a similar development in *Digital Image Processing*, by R.C. Gonzalez and R.E. Woods, ©1992, Addison-Wesley Publishing Co., Reading, Mass. Reprinted with permission of the publisher.

Some Basic Definitions

Let A and B be sets in Z^2 with components $a = (a_1, a_2)$ and $b = (b_1, b_2)$, respectively. The *translation* of A by $x = (x_1, x_2)$, denoted $(A)_x$, is defined as

$$(A)_x = \{ c \mid c = a + x, \text{ for } a \in A\} \tag{10.1}$$

The *reflection* of B, denoted by $\hat{B}$, is defined as

$$\hat{B} = \{x \mid x = -b, \text{ for } b \in B\} \tag{10.2}$$

The *complement* of set A is defined as

$$A^c = \{x \mid x \notin A\} \tag{10.3}$$

Finally, the *difference* of two sets A and B, denoted by $A - B$, is defined as

$$\begin{aligned} A - B &= \{x \mid x \in A, \ x \notin B\} \\ &= A \cap B^c \end{aligned} \tag{10.4}$$

Example: The definitions just discussed are illustrated in Fig. 10.1, where the black dot identifies the origin of each set. Part (a) of this figure shows a set A, and part (b) shows the translation of A by $x = (x_1, x_2)$. Note that translation is accomplished by adding (x_1, x_2) to every element of A.. Figure 10.1(c) shows a set B, and Fig, 10.1(d) shows its reflection about the origin. Finally, Fig. 10.1(e) shows a set A and its complement, and Fig. 10.1(f) shows the difference between the set A of Fig. 10.1(e) and the set B shown in Fig. 10.1(f).

Dilation

With the preceding discussion as background, let A and B be sets in Z^2. The *dilation* of A by B, denoted by $A \oplus B$, is defined as

$$A \oplus B = \{ x \mid (\hat{B})_x \cap A \neq \emptyset\} \tag{10.5}$$

We see that the dilation process consists of obtaining the reflection of B about its origin, and then shifting this reflection by x. The dilation of A by B is then the set of all x displacements such that $\hat{B}$ and A overlap by at least one nonzero element. This could also be stated by writing Eq. (10.5) as $A \oplus B = \{ x \mid [(\hat{B})_x \cap A] \subseteq A \}$. It is common terminology to refer to the set B as the *structuring element* in dilation, as well as in other morphological operations.

Equation (10.5) is not the only definition of dilation found in the current literature on morphology. However, this definition has a distinct advantage over other formulations in the sense that it is more

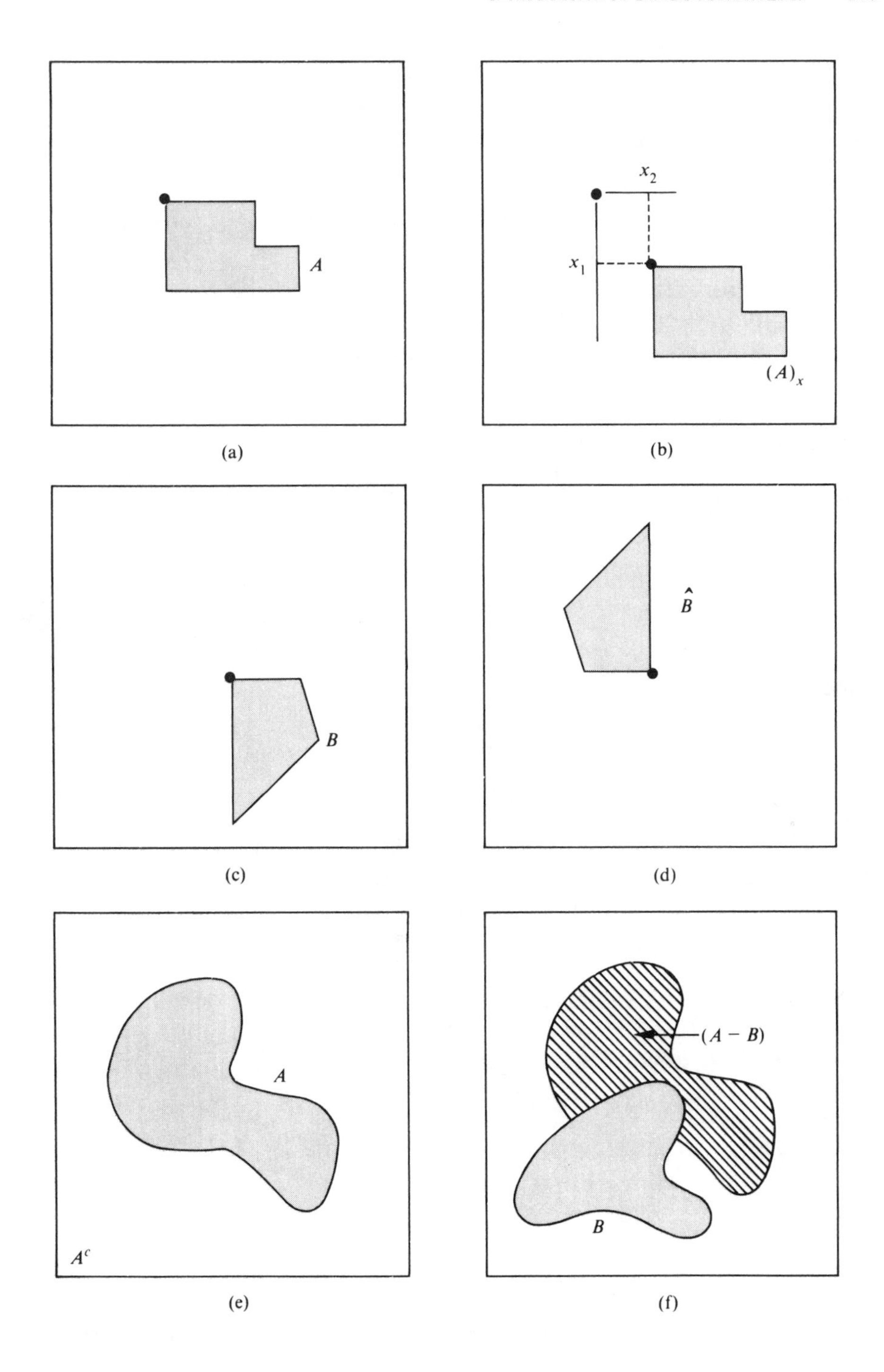

Figure 10.1. (a) Set A. (b) Set A translated by point x. (c) Set B. (d) Reflection of B. (e) Set A and its complement. (f) The difference of two sets (shown lined). The dots in each of the first four figures indicates the origin of the set.

intuitive when one views the structuring element B as a convolution mask. Although dilation is based on set operations while convolution is based on arithmetic operations, the basic process of "flipping" B about its origin and then successively displacing it so that it slides over set (image) A is analogous to the familiar convolution process in two dimensions.

Example: Figure 10.2(a) shows a simple set, and Fig. 10.2 shows a structuring element and its reflection. In this case the structuring element and its reflection are equal because B is symmetric with respect to its origin. The dashed line in Fig. 10.2(c) shows the original set for reference, and the solid line shows the limit beyond which any further displacements of the origin of $\hat{B}$ by x would cause the intersection of $\hat{B}$ and A to be empty. Thus, all points inside this boundary constitute the dilation of A by B. Continuing with the example, Fig. 10.2(d) shows a structuring element designed to achieve more dilation in the vertical than in the horizontal direction. The dilation achieved with this element is shown in Fig. 10.2(e).

Erosion

Given sets A and B in Z^2, the erosion of A by B, denoted by $A \ominus B$, is defined as

$$A \ominus B = \{x \mid (B)_x \subseteq A\} \tag{10.6}$$

which, in words, says that the erosion of A by B is the set of all points x such that B, translated by x, is contained in A. As in the case of dilation, Eq. (10.6) is not the only definition of erosion. However, Eq. (10.6) is usually favored in practical implementations of morphology for the same reasons stated earlier in connection with Eq. (10.5).

Example: Figure 10.3 shows an example similar to the one shown in Fig. 10.2. As before, the set A is shown dashed for reference, and the solid line shows the limit beyond which further displacement of the origin of B would cause this set to cease being completely contained in A. Thus, as shown in Fig. 10.3(c), the locus of points within this boundary constitutes the erosion of A by B. Continuing with the example, Fig. 10.3(d) shows an elongated structuring element, and Fig. 10.3(e) shows the erosion of A by this element. Note that the original set was eroded down to a line.

Before leaving this section, we note that dilation and erosion are duals of each other with respect to set complementation and reflection. That is,

$$(A \ominus B)^c = A^c \oplus \hat{B} \tag{10.7}$$

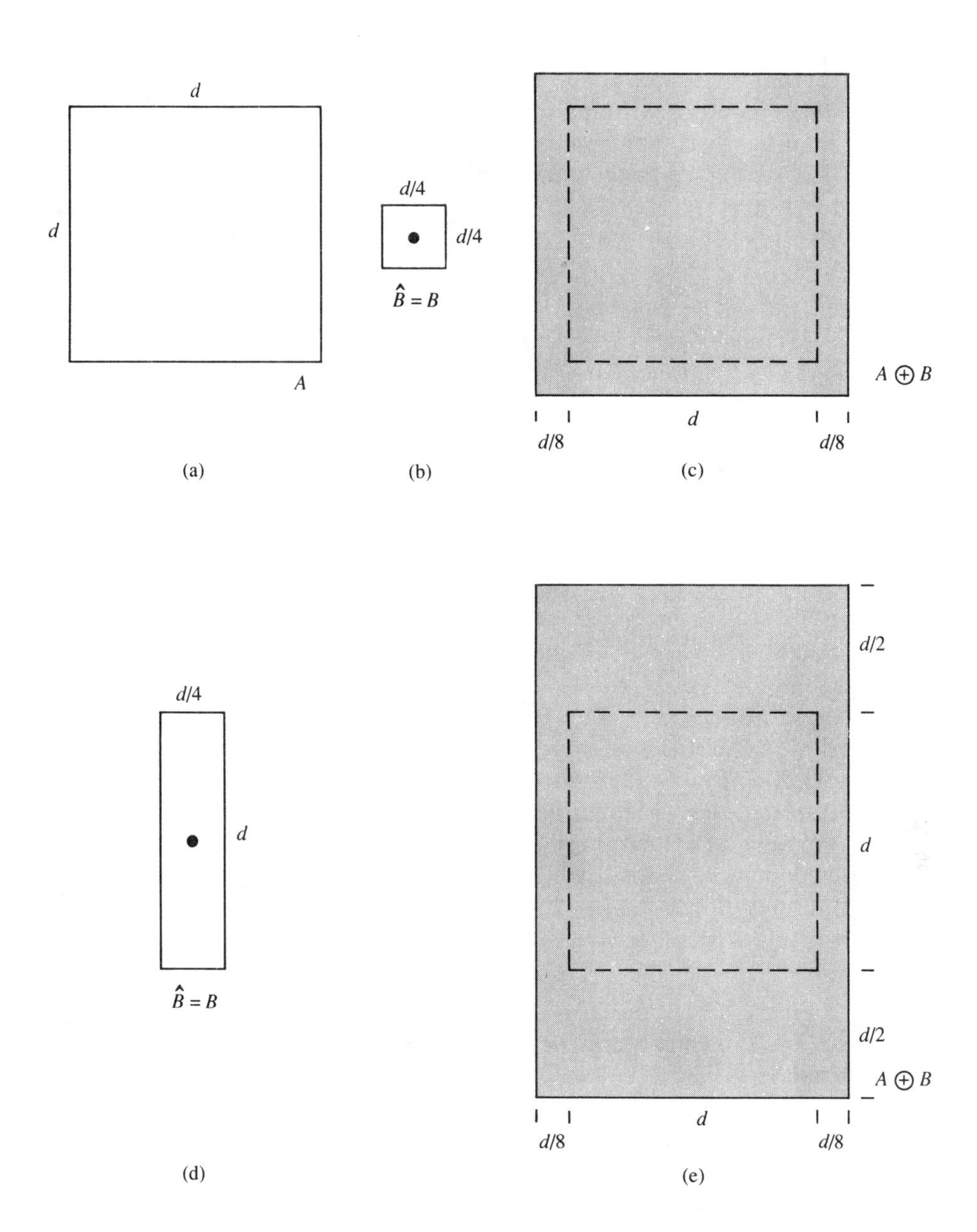

Figure 10.2. Two examples of dilation using different structuring elements.

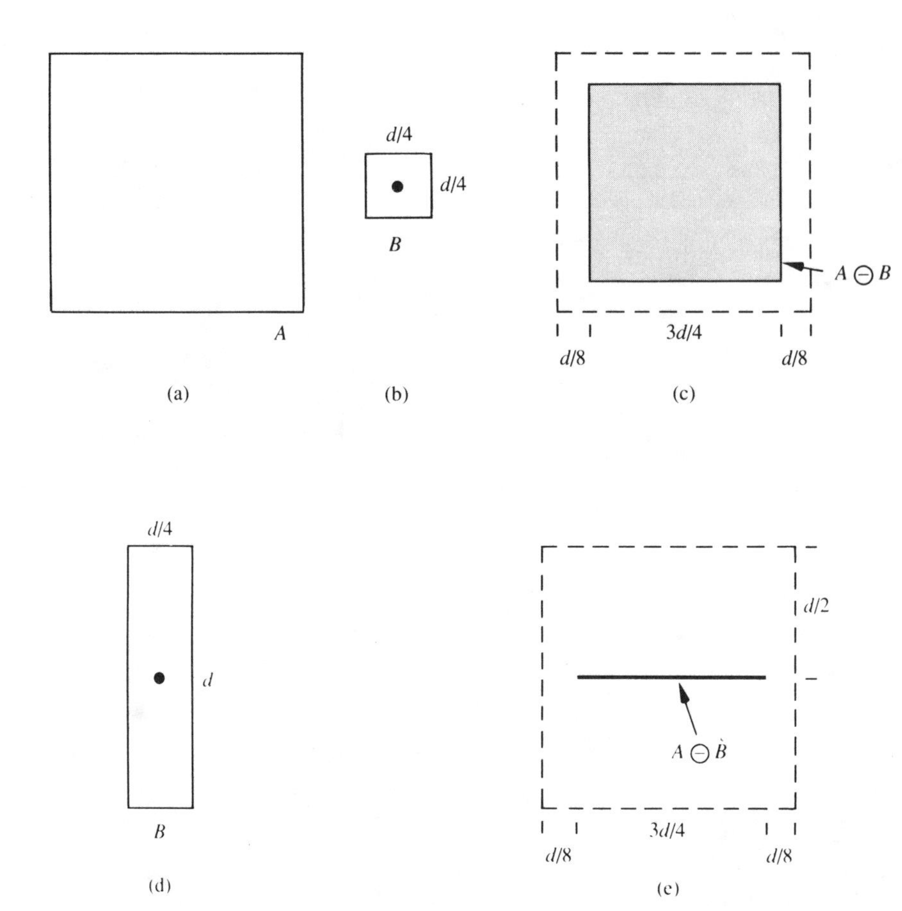

Figure 10.3. Two examples of erosion using different structuring elements.

We proceed to prove this result formally in order to illustrate a typical approach for establishing the validity of morphological expressions. Starting with the definition of erosion,

$$(A \ominus B)^c = \{x \mid (B)_x \subseteq A\}^c$$

If set $(B)_x$ is contained in set A, then it follows that $(B)_x \cap A^c = \varnothing$, in which case this equation becomes

$$(A \ominus B)^c = \{x \mid (B)_x \cap A^c = \varnothing\}^c$$

But, the complement of the set of x's that satisfy $(B)_x \cap A^c = \emptyset$ is the set of x's such that $(B)_x \cap A^c \neq \emptyset$. Thus, we have

$$\begin{aligned}(A \ominus B)^c &= \{ x \mid (B)_x \cap A^c \neq \emptyset \} \\ &= A^c \oplus \hat{B}\end{aligned}$$

where the last step follows from Eq. (10.5). This concludes the proof.

10.3 Opening and Closing

We saw in the last section that dilation expands an image and that erosion shrinks it. In this section we discuss two other important morphological operations, *opening* and *closing*. As will be seen in the following discussion, opening has the general effect of smoothing the contour of an image, breaking narrow isthmuses, and eliminating thin protrusions. Closing also tends to smooth sections of contours but, as opposed to opening, it has the general effect of fusing narrow breaks and long thin gulfs, eliminating small holes, and filling gaps in the contour.

The *opening* of set A by structuring element B, denoted by $A \circ B$, is defined as

$$A \circ B = (A \ominus B) \oplus B \tag{10.8}$$

which, in words, says that the opening of A by B is simply the erosion of A by B, followed by a dilation of the result by B.

The *closing* of set A by structuring element B, denoted by $A \bullet B$, is defined as

$$A \bullet B = (A \oplus B) \ominus B \tag{10.9}$$

We see that the closing of A by B is the dilation of A by B, followed by the erosion of the result by B.

Example: Figure 10.4 shows an example of opening and closing a set A with a disk structuring element. Figure 10.4 (a) shows the set in question, and Fig. 10.4(b) shows examples of various positions of the disk structuring element during the erosion process which, when completed, resulted in the disjoint figure shown in Fig. 10.4(c). Note that the bridge between the two main sections was eliminated as a result of its width being thin in relation to the diameter of the structuring element; that is, the structuring element could not be completely contained in this part of the set, thus violating the conditions of Eq. (10.6). This was also true of the two rightmost members of the object. The process of dilating the eroded set is shown in Fig. 10.4(d), and the final result of opening is shown in Fig. 10.4 (e). The results of closing A with the same structuring

Figure 10.4. Illustration of the opening and closing operations.

element are similarly shown in Figs. 10.4(f) through (i). Here we note that the result was to eliminate the small (in relation to B) bay on the left of the object. Note also the smoothing that resulted in parts of the object from both opening and closing the set A with a circular structuring element.

Opening and closing have a simple geometric interpretation. Suppose that, as an example, we view the disk structuring element B as a (flat) "rolling ball." The boundary of $A \circ B$ is then given by the points on the boundary of B that reach the *farthest* into the boundary of A as B is rolled around the *inside* of this boundary. It is easily verified that this interpretation yields Fig. 10.4(e) from Fig. 10.4(a). Note that all outward-pointing corners were rounded, while inward-pointing corners were not affected. Protruding elements where the ball did not fit were eliminated. This geometrical *fitting* property of the opening operation leads to a set-theoretic formulation which states that the opening of A by B is obtained by taking the union of all translates of B that fit into A. That is, opening can be expresses as a fitting process such that $A \circ B = \cup\{(B)_x \mid (B)_x \subset A\}$. Closing has a similar geometrical interpretation except that now, using again the rolling ball example, we roll B on the outside of the boundary (it is shown below that opening and closing are duals of each other, so it is not unexpected that we should now roll the ball on the outside). With this interpretation in mind, we see that Fig. 10.4(i) follows easily from Fig. 10.4(a). Note that the inward-pointing corners were rounded, while the outward-pointing corners remained unchanged. The leftmost intrusion on the boundary of A was reduced in size significantly because the ball did not fit there. Geometrically, we say that a point z is an element of $A \bullet B$ if and only if $(B)_x \cap A \neq \emptyset$ for any translate of $(B)_x$ that contains z.

As in the case of dilation and erosion, opening and closing are duals of each other with respect to set complementation and reflection. That is, it can be shown that

$$(A \bullet B)^c = (A^c \circ \hat{B}) \tag{10.10}$$

The opening operation satisfies the following important properties:

(*i*) $A \circ B$ is a subset (subimage) of A

(*ii*) If C is a subset of D, then $C \circ B$ is a subset of $D \circ B$

(*iii*) $(A \circ B) \circ B = A \circ B$

Similarly, we have that the closing operation satisfies:

(*i*) A is a subset (subimage) of $A \bullet B$

(*ii*) If C is a subset of D, then $C \bullet B$ is a subset of $D \bullet B$

(*iii*) $(A \bullet B) \bullet B = A \bullet B$

These properties play an important role in understanding the results obtained when the opening and closing operations are used for constructing morphological filters. For instance, if we construct a filter based on opening operations, we know that (*i*) the result will be a subset of the input; (*ii*) monotonicity will be preserved; and (*iii*) applying more than one opening operation has no effect on the result. This last property is sometimes called *idempotence*. Similar comments hold for the closing operation.

As an illustration, consider the simple binary image shown in Fig. 10.5(a), which consists of a rectangular object corrupted by noise. Here the noise manifests itself as dark elements (shown shaded) on a light background and as light voids on the dark object. Note that the set A consists of the object and the background noise, with the noise inside the object having created inner boundaries where the background shows through. The objective is to eliminate the noise and its effects on the object, while distorting the object as little as possible. We can use the morphological "filter" $(A \circ B) \bullet B$ to accomplish this. The result of opening A with a disk structuring element that is bigger than all noise components is shown in Fig. 10.5(c). We note that this operation took care of the background noise, but had no effect on the inner boundaries.

The background noise was eliminated in the erosion stage of opening because in this idealized example all noise components in the background are physically smaller than the structuring element (recall that erosion requires that the structuring element be completely contained in the set being eroded).

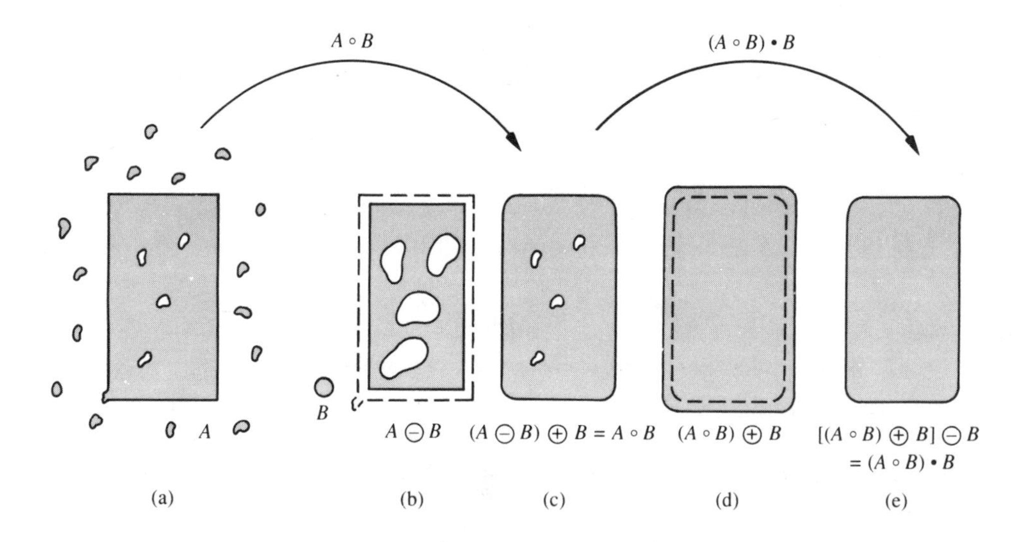

Figure 10.5. Example of morphological filtering of a noisy binary image.

It is noted that the size of the noise components inside the object increased in size (Fig. 10.5b). This is to be expected since the voids in the object actually are inner boundaries which should increase in size as the object is eroded. Finally, Fig. 10.5(e) shows the result of morphologically closing Fig. 10.5(c). The inner boundaries were eliminated as a result of the dilation stage of the closing operation, as shown in Fig. 10.5(d).

10.3 Hit-or-Miss Transform

The morphological hit-or-miss transform is a basic tool for shape detection. As a way of introduction to this concept, consider Fig. 10.6, which shows a set A consisting of three shapes (subsets) denoted by X, Y, and Z. The objective of the following discussion is to find the location of one of the shapes, say X.

Let the origin of each shape be located at its respective center of gravity. If we enclose X by a small window, W, then the *local background* of X with respect to W is the set difference $(W-X)$, as shown in Fig. 10.6(b). The complement of A, which will be needed below, is shown in Fig. 10.6(c). Figure 10.6(d) shows the erosion of A by X. Recall that the erosion of A by X is the set of locations of the origin of X such that X is completely contained in A; in this particular case, the set A is the union of the three subsets shown shaded in Fig. 10.6(a). Figure 10.6(e) shows the erosion of the complement of A by the local background set $(W-X)$. We see by studying figures (d) and (e) that the set of locations for which X *exactly* fits inside A is the *intersection* of the erosion of A by X, and the erosion of A^c by $(W-X)$, as shown in Fig. 10.6(f). In other words, if we let B denote the set composed of X and its background, then the match (or set of matches) of B in A, denoted by $A \circledast B$, is given by the relationship,

$$A \circledast B = (A \ominus X) \cap (A^c \ominus [W-X]) \tag{10.11}$$

We can generalize the notation a bit by letting $B = (B_1, B_2)$, where B_1 is the set formed from elements of B which are associated with an object, and B_2 is the set of elements of B which are associated with the corresponding background. In the example just discussed, we see that $B_1 = X$ and $B_2 = (W-X)$. Using this notation, we can write Eq. (10.11) as

$$A \circledast B = (A \ominus B_1) \cap (A^c \ominus B_2) \tag{10.12}$$

By using the definition of set differences, and the dual relationship between erosion and dilation, we can also write Eq. (10.12) in the following form:

$$A \circledast B = (A \ominus B_1) - (A \oplus \hat{B}_2) \tag{10.13}$$

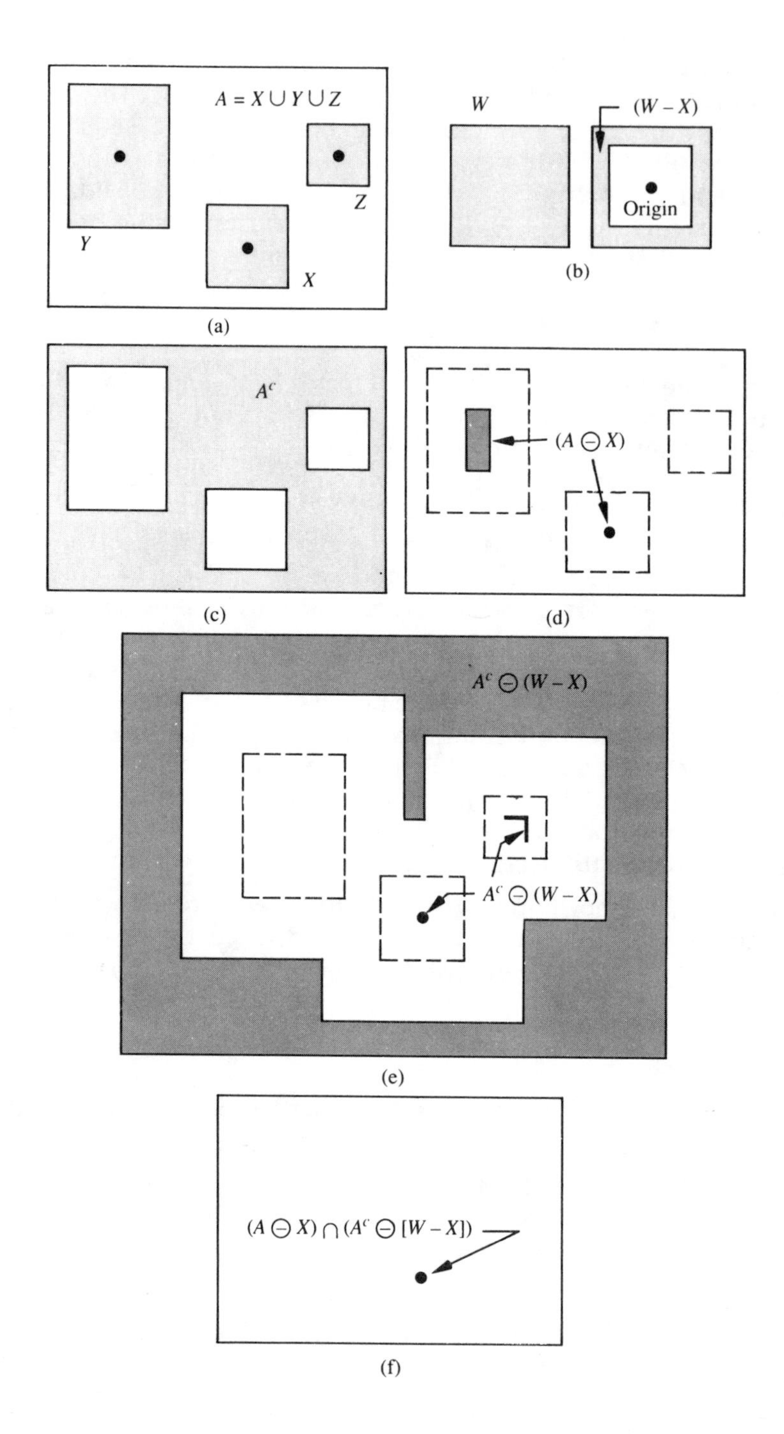

Figure 10.6. Illustration of the morphological Hit-or-Miss transform.

Summarizing the preceding discussion, we see that the set $A \circledast B$ contains all the points at which, simultaneously, B_1 found a match ("hit") in A, and B_2 found a match in A^c.

10.4 Some Basic Morphological Algorithms

In this section we use the concepts introduced thus far to develop and illustrate a set of important morphological algorithms. Unlike the illustrations used previously in this section, most of the figures used in the rest of the discussion are "mini-images," designed so that the reader can follow in a step-by-step fashion the mechanics of each of the morphological transforms as they are introduced.

Boundary Extraction

The boundary of a set A, denoted by $\beta(A)$, can be obtained by first eroding A by B, and then performing the set difference between A and its erosion. That is,

$$\beta(A) = A - (A \ominus B) \tag{10.14}$$

where B is a suitably chosen structuring element.

The mechanics of boundary extraction are illustrated in Fig. 10.7, which shows a simple binary object, a structuring element B, and the result of using Eq. (10.14). Although the structuring element shown in Fig. 10.7(b) is among the most-frequently used, it is by no means unique. For example, using a structuring element of size 5×5 would have resulted in a boundary whose thickness would have varied between two and three pixels. Note that, when the origin of B is on the border of the set, part of the structuring element lies outside the set. We normally treat this condition by implicitly assuming that values outside the boundary of the set are 0.

Region Filling

A simple algorithm for region filling based on set dilations, complementation, and intersections can be developed as follows. With reference to Fig. 10.8, let A denote a set containing a subset whose elements are 8-connected boundary points of a region. Given a point, p inside the boundary, the objective is to fill the entire region with 1's.

Since, by assumption, all non-boundary points are labeled 0, we assign a value of 1 to p to start the procedure. Based on this, we can use the following algorithm to fill the region with 1's:

$$X_k = (X_{k-1} \oplus B) \cap A^c \qquad k = 1, 2, 3, \ldots \tag{10.15}$$

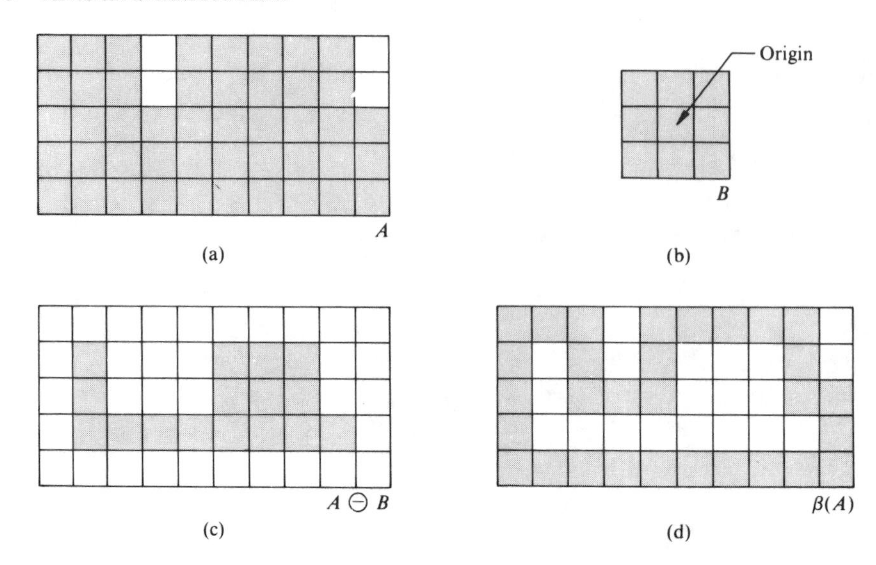

Figure 10.7. Example of boundary extraction.

where $X_0 = p$, and B is the symmetric structuring element shown in Fig. 10.8(c). The algorithm terminates at iteration step k if $X_k = X_{k-1}$. The set union of X_k and A contains the filled set and its boundary.

It is noted that the dilation process of Eq. (10.15) would fill the whole area if left unchecked. However, the intersection at each step with A^c limits the result to the inside of region in question (this type of delimiting process is sometimes called *conditional dilation*). The mechanics of Eq. (10.15) are illustrated further in the rest of Fig. 10.8. Although this example only has one subset, it is clear that the concept is applicable to any finite number of such subsets, as long as a point inside each boundary is given.

Extraction of Connected Components

The extraction of connected components in a binary image is central in many automated image analysis applications. Let Y represent a connected component contained in a set A, and assume that we know a point p of Y. Then, we can use the following iterative expression to find all the elements of Y:

$$X_k = (X_{k-1} \oplus B) \cap A \qquad k = 1,2,3,\ldots \tag{10.16}$$

where $X_0 = p$, and B is a suitable structuring element (see Fig. 10.9). If $X_k = X_{k-1}$ we say that the algorithm has converged, and we let $Y = X_k$.

It is noted that this equation is similar in form to Eq. (10.15). The only difference is that here we use A instead of its complement because all the elements we are seeking (i.e., the elements of the connected component) are labeled 1. The intersection with A at each iterative step

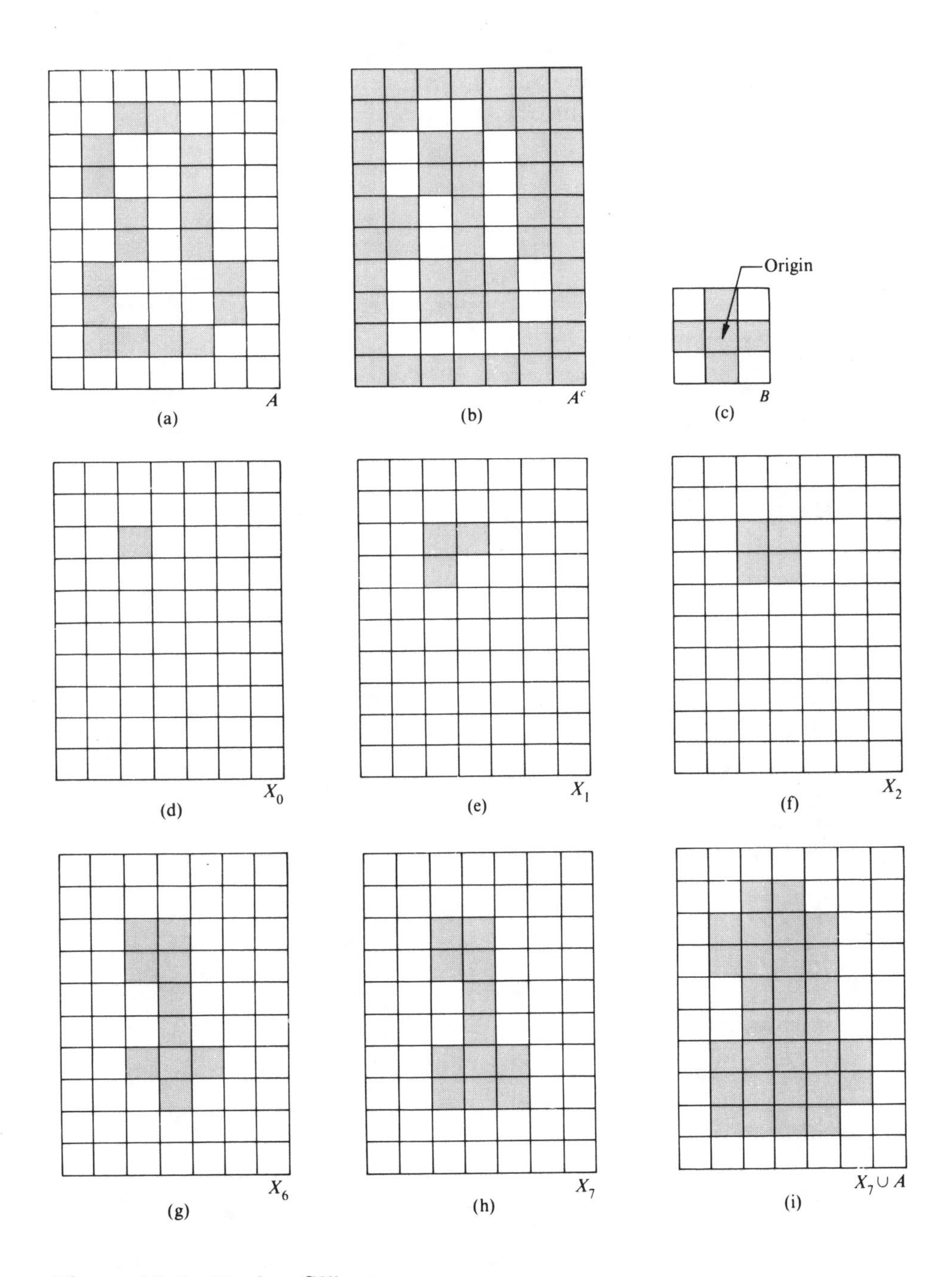

Figure 10.8. Region filling.

eliminates dilations that are centered about elements labeled 0. The mechanics of Eq. (10.16) are illustrated in Fig. 10.9. Note that the shape of the structuring element used assumes 8-connectivity between pixels. As in the region filling algorithm, the results just discussed are applicable to any finite number of sets of connected components contained in A.

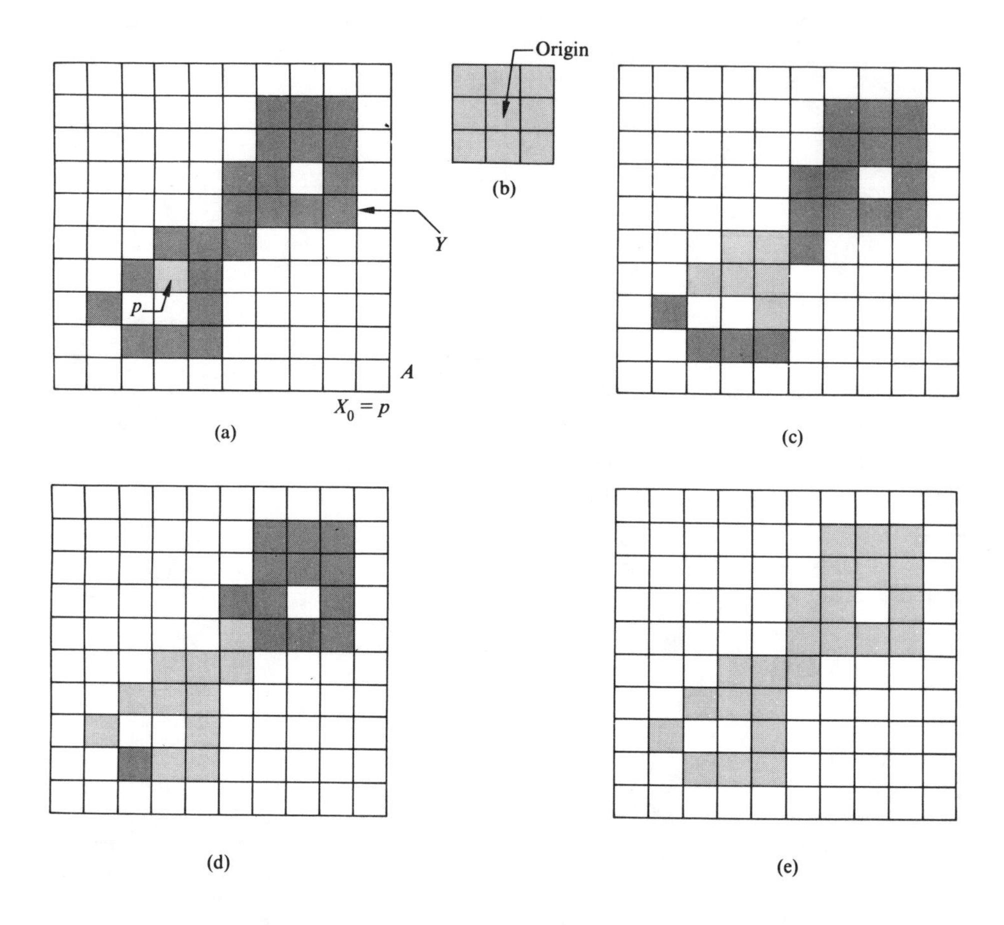

Figure 10.9. Extraction of connected component.

Convex Hull

In the following discussion, we present a simple morphological algorithm for obtaining the convex hull, $C(A)$, of a given set A. Letting B^i, $i = 1,2,3,4$, represent four structuring elements to be discussed below, the procedure consists of implementing the following equation:

$$X_k^i = (X \circledast B^i) \cup A \qquad i = 1, 2, 3, 4; \; k = 1, 2, 3, \ldots \qquad (10.17)$$

with $X_0^i = A$. If we let $D^i = X^i_{\text{conv}}$, where the subscript "conv" indicates convergence in the sense that $X_k^i = X_{k-1}^i$, then we can write the convex hull of A as

$$C(A) = \bigcup_{i=1}^{4} D^i \tag{10.18}$$

In other words, the procedure consists of iteratively applying the hit-or-miss transform to A with B^1; when no further changes occur, we perform the union with A and call the result D^1. Then we start with A again and repeat the procedure with B^2 until no further changes occur, and so on. The union of the four resulting D's constitutes the convex hull of A.

The procedure given in Eqs. (10.17) and (10.18) is illustrated in Fig. 10.10. Part (a) of this figure shows the structuring elements used in extracting the convex hull (the origin of each element is at its center). Figure 10.10(b) shows a set A for which we wish to find the convex hull. Starting with $X_0^1 = A$ resulted after four iterations of Eq. (10.17) in the set shown in Fig. 10.10(c). Then, letting $X_0^2 = A$ and again using Eq. (10.17) resulted in the set shown in Fig. 10.10(d) (note that convergence was achieved in only two steps). The next two results were obtained in the same way. Finally, forming the union of the sets in (c), (d), (e), and (f) resulted in the convex hull shown in Fig. 10.10(g). The contribution of each structuring element is high-lighted in the composite set shown in Fig. 10.10(h).

Thinning

The thinning of a set A by structuring element B, denoted by $A \otimes B$, can be defined in terms of the hit-or-miss transform, as follows:

$$\begin{aligned} A \otimes B &= A - (A \circledast B) \\ &= A \cap (A \circledast B)^c \end{aligned} \tag{10.19}$$

A more useful expression for thinning A symmetrically is based on a *sequence* of structuring elements, defined as

$$\{B\} = \{B^1, B^2, B^3, \ldots, B^n\} \tag{10.20}$$

where B^i is a rotated version of B^{i-1}. Using this concept, we now define thinning by a sequence of structuring elements, as follows:

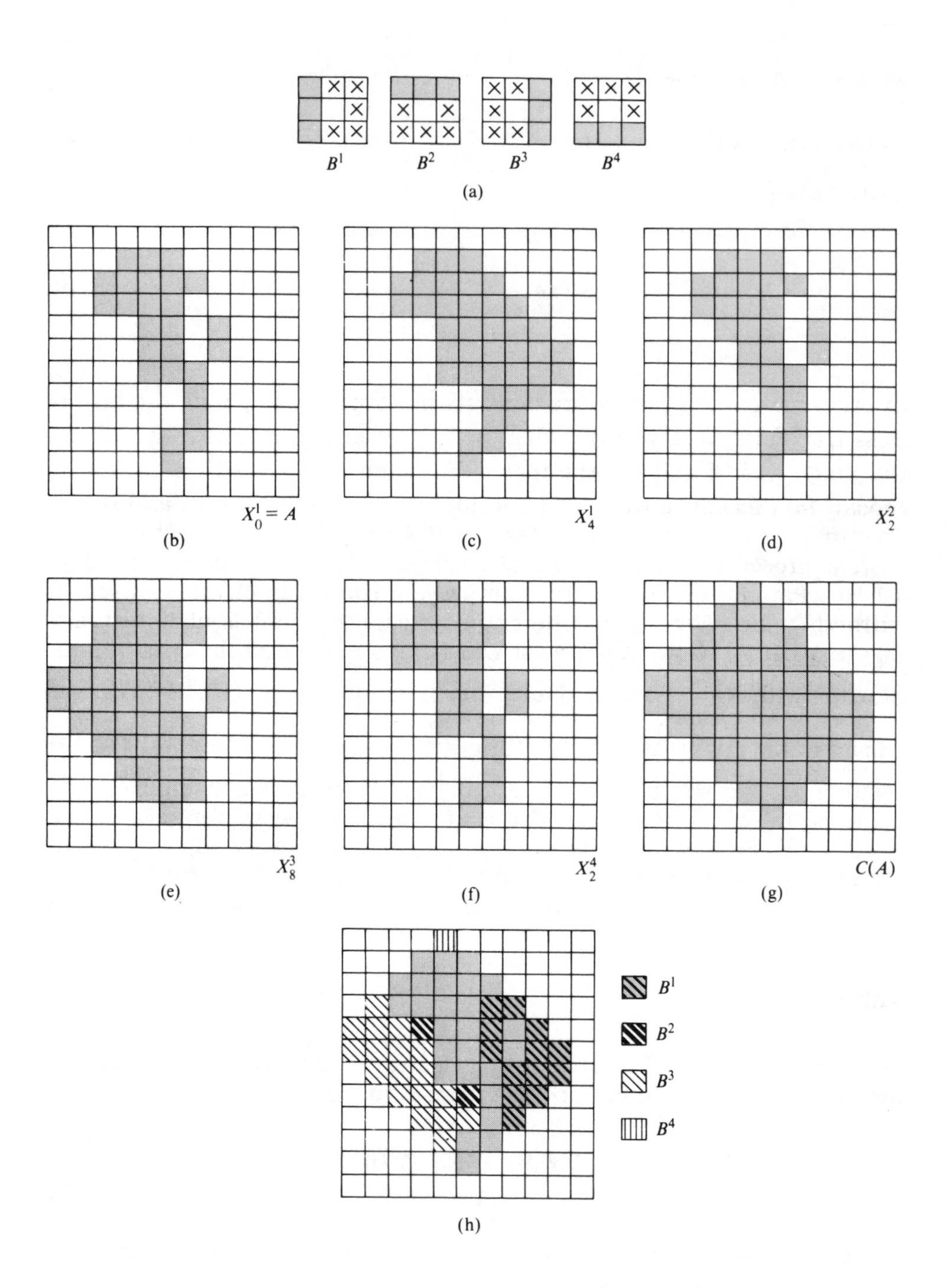

Figure 10.10. Computation of the convex hull.

$$A \otimes \{B\} = ((\ldots((A \otimes B^1) \otimes B^2) \ldots) \otimes B^n) \tag{10.21}$$

In other words, the process is to thin A by *one pass* with B^1, then thin the result with one pass of B^2, and so on, until A is thinned with one pass of B^n. The entire process is repeated until no further changes result.

Figure 10.11(a) shows a set of structuring elements commonly used for thinning, and Fig. 10.11(b) shows a set A we wish to thin using the procedure just discussed. The result of thinning with one raster pass of A with B^1 is shown in Fig. 10.11(c), and the results of passes with the other structuring elements are shown in Figs. 10.11(d) through (k). It is noted that convergence was achieved after the second pass of B^4. The thinned result is thus shown in Fig. 10.11(k). Finally, Fig. 10.11(l) shows the thinned set converted to *m*-connectivity to eliminate multiple paths.

Thickening

Thickening is the morphological dual of thinning, and is defined by the expression

$$A \odot B = A \cup (A \circledast B) \tag{10.22}$$

where B is a structuring element suitable for thickening. As above, we can define thickening as a sequential operation,

$$A \odot \{B\} = ((\ldots((A \odot B^1) \odot B^2) \ldots) \odot B^n) \tag{10.23}$$

The structuring elements used for thickening have the same form as those shown in Fig. 10.11(a) in connection with thinning, but with all 1's and 0's interchanged. However, a separate algorithm for thickening is seldom used in practice. Instead, the usual procedure is to thin the background of the set in question and then complement the result. In other words, if we wish to thicken a set A, we form $C = A^c$, thin C, and then form C^c. The procedure is illustrated in Fig. 10.12. Depending on the nature of A, it is not unusual for this procedure to result in some points that are disconnected, as Fig. 10.12(d) shows, so thickening by this method is usually followed by a simple post-processing step to remove disconnected points. Note from Fig. 10.12(c) that the thinned background forms a boundary for the thickening process. This is a useful feature not present in the direct implementation of thickening using Eq. (10.21), and it is one of the principal reasons why thickening is usually accomplished via thinning of the background.

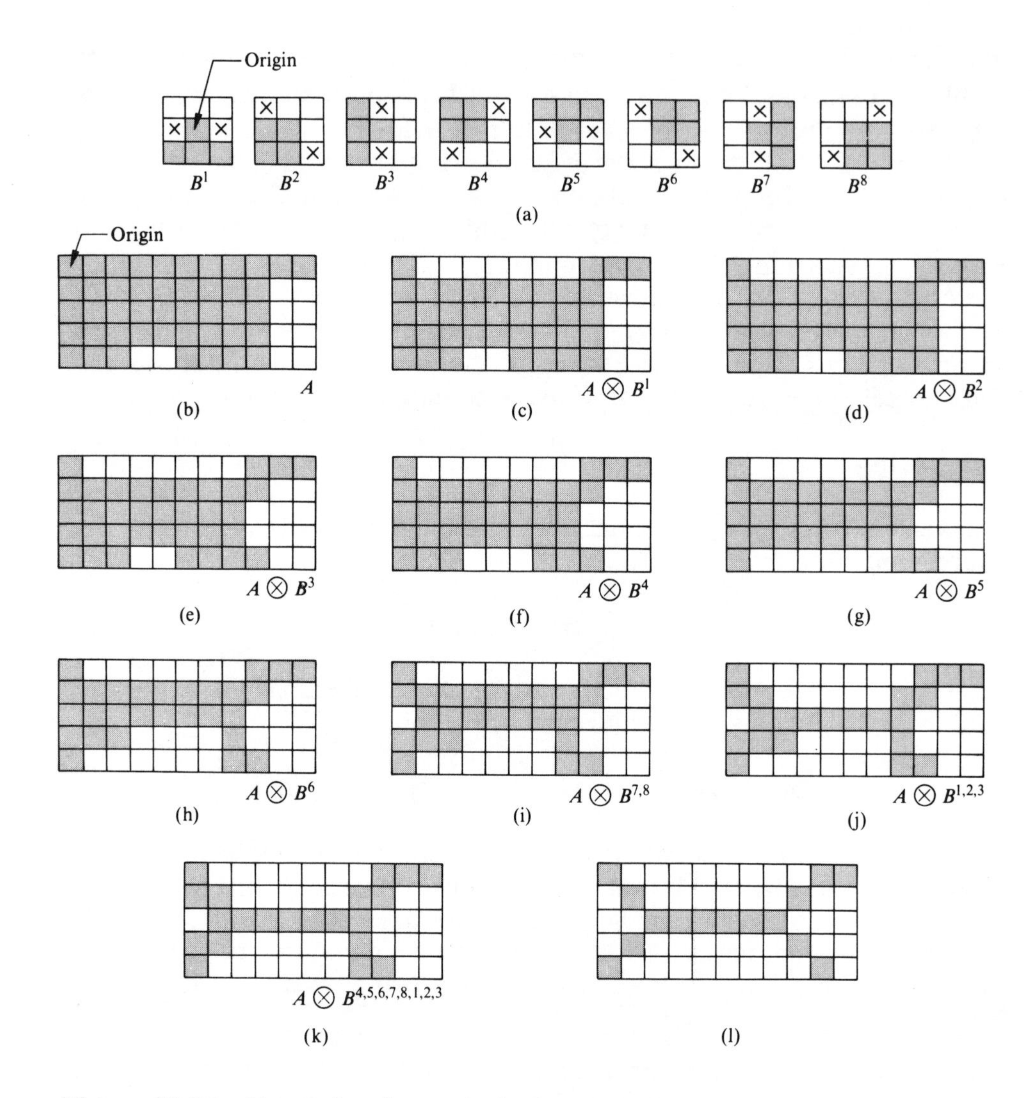

Figure 10.11. Example of morphological thinning.

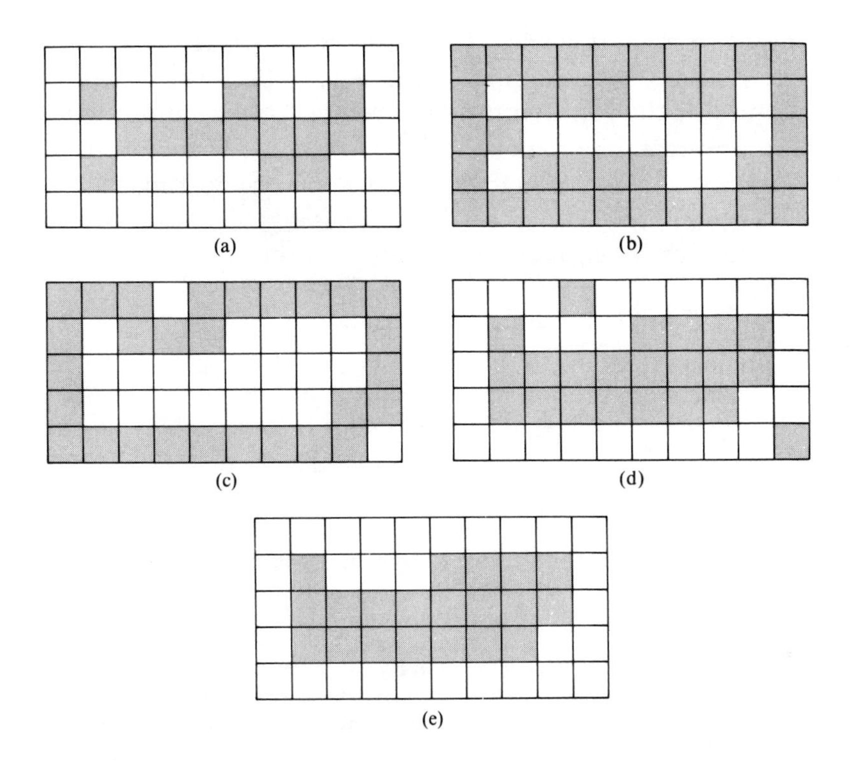

Figure 10.12. Example of thickening.

Skeletons

The skeleton of a set (region) A can be expressed in terms of erosions and openings. That is, letting $S(A)$ denote the skeleton of A, it can be shown that

$$S(A) = \bigcup_{k=0}^{K} S_k(A) \tag{10.24}$$

with

$$S_k(A) = \bigcup_{k=0}^{K} \{(A \ominus kB) - [(A \ominus kB) \circ B]\} \qquad (10.25)$$

where B is a structuring element to be defined below, $(A \ominus kB)$ indicates k successive erosions of A; that is $(A \ominus kB) = ((\ldots(A \ominus B) \ominus B) \ominus \ldots) \ominus B$, k times, and K is the last iterative step before A erodes down to an empty set. In other words, $K = \max\{k \mid (A \ominus kB) \neq \varnothing\}$. As indicated in Eq. (10.8), the symbol " $\circ$ " is used to denote the opening operation.

The formulation given in the two preceding equations states that, $S(A)$, the skeleton of A, can be obtained as the union of the *skeleton subsets* $S_k(A)$. It can also be shown that, given these subsets, it is possible to reconstruct A using the following equation:

$$A = \bigcup_{k=0}^{K} (S_k(A) \oplus kB) \qquad (10.26)$$

where $(S_k(A) \oplus kB)$ denotes k successive dilations of $S_k(A)$; that is $(S_k(A) \oplus kB) = ((\ldots(S_k(A) \oplus B) \oplus B) \oplus \ldots) \oplus B$, k times, and the limit of the summation, K, is as above.

As an example, consider Fig. 10.13(a), which shows a binary image with a variety of shapes of silicon carbide particles in a metal matrix composite material. Figure 10.13(b) shows the result of using the skeletonizing method just discussed. It can be seen that the skeletons form representations of the original objects. Note, however, that some of

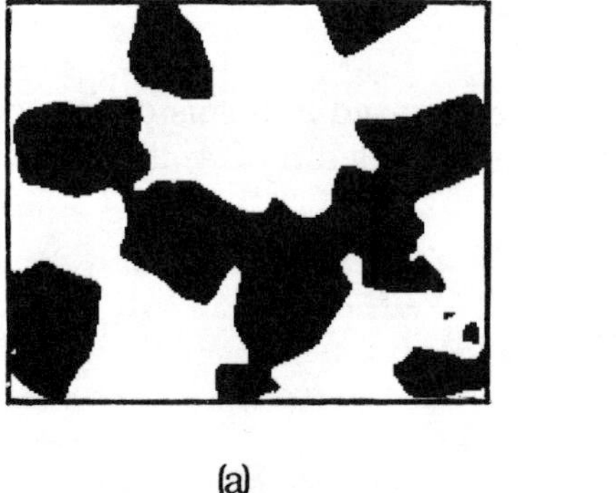

(a)

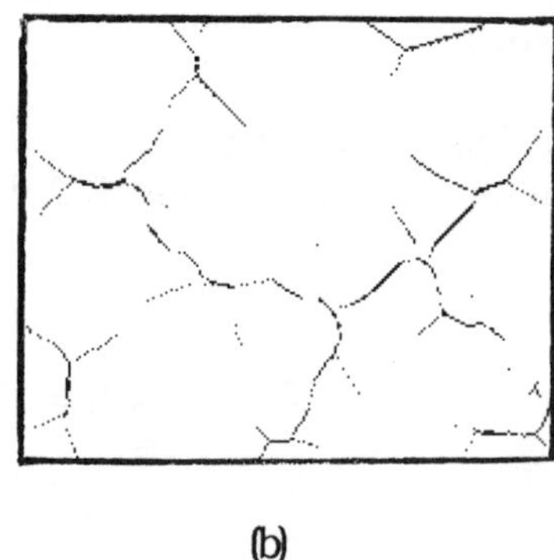

(b)

Figure 10.13. Illustration of skeletonizing. (a) Thresholded secondary electron micrograph of silicon particles embedded in an aluminum metal matrix composite material. (b) Result of skeletonizing. (Micrograph courtesy of Westinghouse.)

the skeletons are broken. This is not unexpected, since nothing in the above formulation of the morphological skeleton for discrete binary images guarantees connectivity. Thus, although morphology gives us an elegant formulation in terms of erosions and openings of the given set, one is led to heuristic formulations if we require, as is usually the case, that the skeleton be maximally thin, connected, and minimally eroded.

If two objects touch, (such as two silicon carbide particles) and it is desired to separate (segment) them, we can first find the skeletal segments, but then retain only portions of them in forming the skeleton. To do this, we let the lower limit in the union of Eq. (10.24) be a value $r > 0$, where r, selected based on the characteristics of a given problem, indicates how closely a line segment approaches the boundary. In other words, the larger we select r to be, the more thinned (and disconnected) the resulting composite skeleton will be. The result of this method of skeletonizing is called the *conditional skeleton.*

Pruning

Pruning methods are an essential complement of thinning and skeletonizing algorithms because these procedures tend to leave parasitic components that need to be cleaned up by post-processing. The following discussion starts with a pruning problem and develops a morphological solution based on the material introduced in the previous sections. Thus, we take advantage of what has been developed thus far to illustrate how one might go about solving a problem by combining several of the techniques discussed above.

A common approach to the automated recognition of hand-printed characters is to analyze the shape of the skeleton of each character. These skeletons are often characterized by "spurs" (i.e., parasitic components) caused during erosion by non-uniformities in the strokes composing the characters. We wish to develop a morphological technique for handling this problem, starting with the assumption that the length a parasitic component does not exceed three pixels.

Figure 10.14(a) shows the skeleton of a hand-printed "a." The parasitic component on the left-most part of the character is typical of what we are interested in removing. As a starting point in formulating a solution to this problem, we note that we can suppress a parasitic branch by successively eliminating its end point. Of course, this would also shorten (or could eliminate) other branches in the character but, in the absence of other structural information, the assumption is that any branch with three or less pixels is to be eliminated. Letting A denote the input set, we can obtain the desired result by thinning A with a sequence of structuring elements designed to detect only end points. That is, we form

$$X_1 = A \otimes \{B\} \qquad (10.27)$$

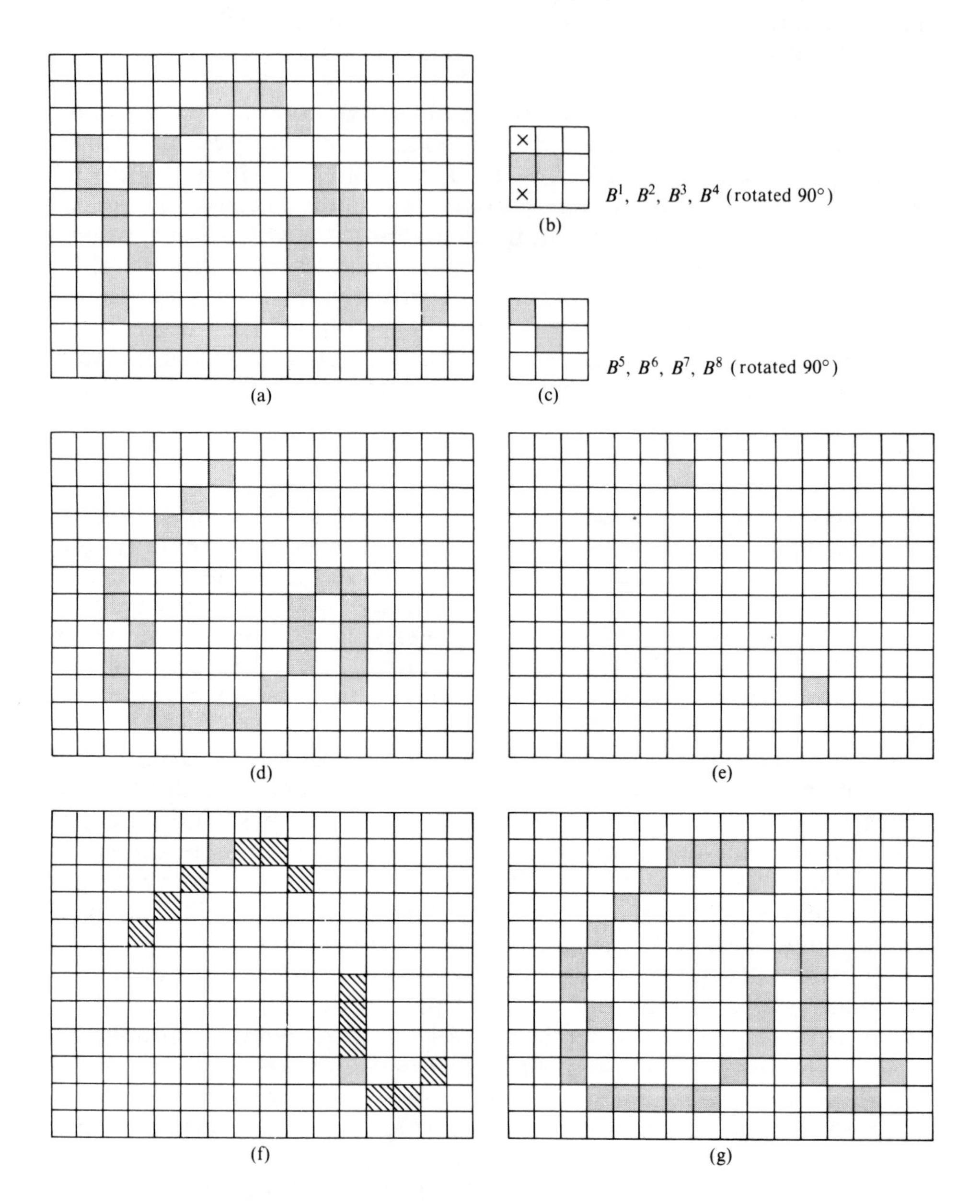

Figure 10.14. Example of pruning.

where $\{B\}$ denotes the sequence (see Eq. (10.20)) shown in Figs. 10.14(b) and (c). It is noted that the sequence of structuring elements consists of two different structures, each of which is rotated by 90° for a total of eight elements. One sometimes finds in the literature on morphology the use a single structuring element similar to the one shown in Fig. 10.14(b) but with "don't care" conditions along the entire first column. This is in error because, for example, this element would consider the point located in the eighth row, fourth column of Fig. 10.14(a) as an end point, thus eliminating it and breaking connectivity in the skeleton. Applying Eq. (10.27) to A three times yields the set X_1 shown in Fig. 10.14(b). The next step is to "restore" the character to its original form, but with the parasitic branches removed. To do this, we first form a set X_2 containing all end points in X_1 (Fig. 10.14(e)), as follows:

$$X_2 = \bigcup_{k=1}^{8} (X_1 \circledast B^k) \tag{10.28}$$

where the B^k are the same end-point detectors used above. This is followed by dilation of the end points three times, using set A as a delimiter, as follows:

$$X_3 = (X_2 \oplus H) \cap A \tag{10.29}$$

where H is a 3×3 structuring element of 1's. As in the case of region filling and extraction of connected components discussed earlier in this section, this type of conditional dilation prevents the creation of 1-valued elements outside the region of interest, as evidenced by the result shown in Fig. 10.14(f). Finally, we form the union of X_3 and X_1 to obtain the final result:

$$X_4 = X_1 \cup X_3 \tag{10.30}$$

as shown in Fig. 10.14(g).

In more complex scenarios, it is sometimes possible to pick up the "tips" of some parasitic branches when using Eq. (10.29). This can happen when the end points of these branches are near the skeleton. Although they may be eliminated by Eq. (10.27), they can be picked up again during dilation because they are valid points in A. Unless entire parasitic elements are picked up again (a rare case if these elements are short with respect to valid strokes), it is a simple matter to detect and eliminate them because they would be disconnected regions.

The alert reader may be thinking by now that there are easier ways to solve this problem. For example, we could have just kept track of all deleted points and simply reconnected the appropriate points to all end-points left after application of Eq. (10.27). While this is true, it is important to keep in mind that the advantage of the formulation we have just presented is that the entire problem was solved using simple morphological constructs. In practical situations where a set of such tools is available, the advantage would be that no new algorithms would have to be written. We would simply combine the necessary morphological functions into a sequence of operations.

Example: We conclude this section with a practical example illustrating the use of morphology in the preprocessing stage of a character recognition system capable of reading hand-written zip codes in U.S. mail. Figure 10.15(a) shows the address portion of an envelope after image thresholding. An early processing step after the address field is located consists of extracting all connected components in the area encompassing this field. Each connected component is then enclosed by the smallest box which completely contains that component. The boxes and their contents then form the basis for part of the logic that deals with the extraction of the region containing the zip code. Figure 10.15(b) is a close-up of the region containing the zip code in this particular example. We see three problems in this case: the first two characters (3 and 7) are joined, the first 1 is broken in the middle, and there is a break in the loop of the numeral 2.

Joined characters can be detected in a number of ways once the zip code has been found. For instance, if analysis of the bounding boxes reveals that there are less than five characters (or less than nine in the case of a "zip plus four"), we start looking for characters that are joined by measuring the relative width of the boxes enclosing the characters (which at this point are being treated as connected components). A box that is unusually wide with respect to the others typically corresponds to two or more joined characters. A morphological approach for separating the joined characters consists of eroding the contents of a box until separate "character-like" regions result. For instance, the problem of the touching 3 and 7 was solved by five iterations of erosion performed in the box containing these characters. The results showing character separation are highlighted in Fig. 10.15(c). Note that erosion was performed *only* in the area where touching characters were suspected.

The problem of broken characters can usually be handled by dilation. In preprocessing, broken characters are suspected when, for example, boxes enclosing some characters are small in relation to expected size, or when two or more boxes form an unusual arrangement, such as being stacked. This latter condition revealed the presence of a broken character in the case of the 1 shown in Fig. 10.15(b). If one assumes that the reason for breaks such as this is inconsistency in the width of the strokes, then it is natural to expect that other breaks might

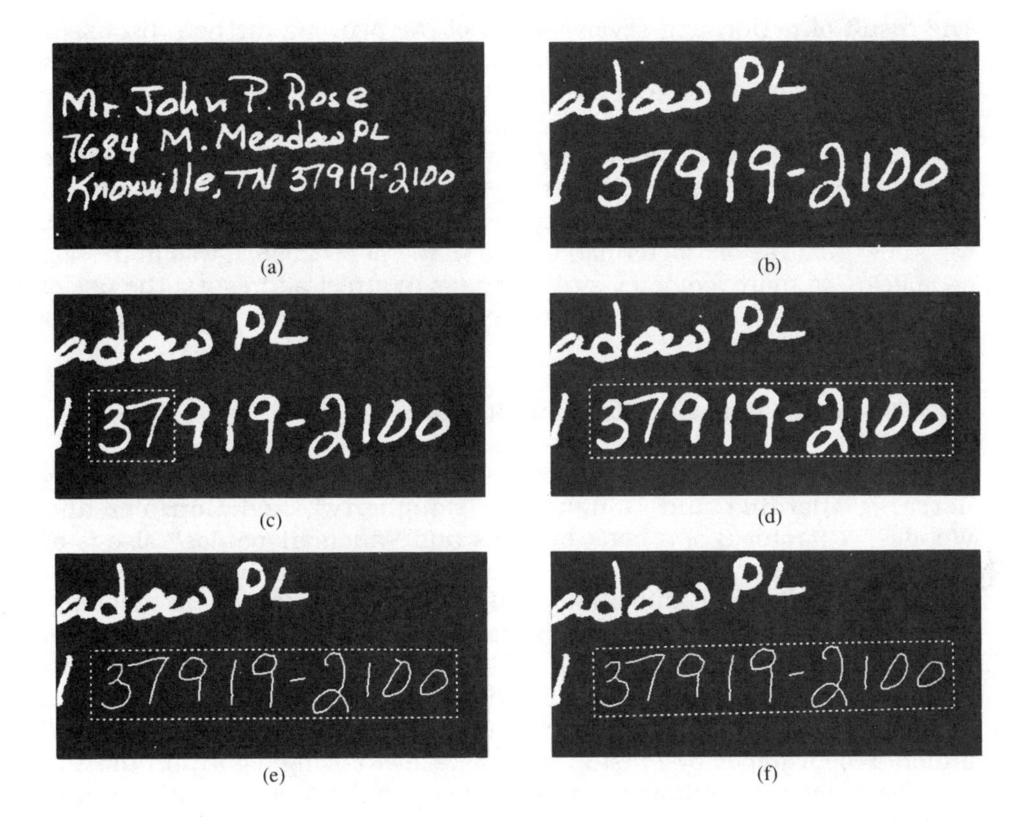

Figure 10.15. Example of character preprocessing using binary morphology.

be present in the zip code field, but which did not result in separate connected components (the break in the 2 is an example of this). Thus, it makes sense to perform dilation on all characters, monitoring to see that new characters, or characters that were separated earlier, are not joined by the dilation process. The result after three dilations performed on all the characters is shown in Fig. 10.15(d). Note that the gap in the middle of the broken 1 was bridged, as was the gap in the loop of the 2.

One of the principal approaches to structural character recognition is based on the analysis of the skeleton of each character. The skeletons of the zip code characters in Fig. 10.15(d) are shown in 10,16(e). Since connectivity and thinness of skeletons are essential elements in character recognition, and algorithm due to Zhang and Suen[11] was used. As noted in our earlier discussion on pruning, one of the problems with skeletons is the generation of parasitic branches which, incidentally, are a major source of error in character recognition if they are not handled properly. In the present example, we see a small branch in the corner of the 7, and a major branch on the top of one of the zeros.

The result of performing seven passes of the pruning method discussed above eliminated both parasitic branches, as shown in Fig. 8.42(f). As indicated earlier, the number of pruning iterations is usually a heuristic choice. For instance, if the branch on the zero had been on the bottom right side, the character could have been a Q, and completely deleting the branch would have caused an error. There is no sure way to get around this problem, other than to use contextual knowledge. In this example, we know that the character had to be a numeral because it was in the zip code field. In more complex situations (as in street addresses) the use of context involves correlating the zip code against street names valid for that code.

10.5 Bibliographical and Historical Remarks

Basic references for the discussion in this chapter are the books by Serra[1,2], Giardina and Dougherty[3], Dougherty[4], and Gonzalez and Woods[5]. Chapter 6 of a book by Pitas and Vanetsanopoulos[6] also is of interest. Papers by Haralick et al.[7] and by Maragos[8] provide a provide a tutorial overview of morphological methods in image processing. Although morphological methods have become a very active topic of research in the U.S. from the mid 1980's onward, it is of interest to know that the work of Golay back in the mid- and late 1960's already contained important elements of this subject matter (see, for example, Golay[9], and a more recent paper by Preston[10]). The skeletonizing algorithm used in the character recognition example in Section 10.4 is from Zhang and Suen[11].

A significant amount of work on binary and gray-scale morphology has been done in Europe since the early 1970's. The references in Serra[1,2] provide an excellent guide to that body of work. A more recent paper by Meyer and Beucher[12] gives an overview of the use of gray-scale morphology for solving segmentation problems. It is also of interest to note that a basic tie between binary and gray-scale morphology is provided by the so-called *umbra homomorphism theorem*. Although development of this topic is beyond the scope of the discussion in this chapter, the reader wishing a deeper understanding of this subject matter should consult the books by Serra[1] and by Giardina and Dougherty[3], as well as the paper by Haralick et al.[7]. See also Chapters 11 and 12 of this book for a discussion of gray-scale morphology and some of its applications.

References

[1] J. Serra, *Image Analysis and Mathematical Morphology*, Academic Press, New York, NY, 1982.

[2] J. Serra (ed.), *Image Analysis and Mathematical Morphology*, vol. 2, Academic Press, New York, NY, 1988.

[3] C.R. Giardina and E.R. Dougherty, *Morphological Methods in Image and Signal Processing*, Prentice-Hall, Englewood Cliffs, NJ, 1988.

[4] E.R. Dougherty, *An Introduction to Morphological Image Processing*, SPIE Press, Bellingham, WA, 1992.

[5] R.C. Gonzalez and R.E. Woods, *Digital Image Processing*, Addison-Wesley, Reading, MA, 1992.

[6] I. Pitas and A.N. Vanetsanopoulos, *Nonlinear Digital Filters: Principles and Applications*, Kluger Academic Publishers, Boston, MA, 1990.

[7] R.M. Haralick, S. R. Sternberg, and X. Zhuang, "Image Analysis Using Mathematical Morphology," *IEEE Trans. Pattern Anal. Machine Intell.*, vol. PAMI-9, no. 4, pp. 532-550, 1987.

[8] P. Maragos. "Tutorial on Advances in Morphological Image Processing and Analysis," Optical Engineering, vol. 26, no. 7, pp. 623-632, 1987.

[9] M.J.E. Golay, "Hexagonal Parallel Pattern Transformations," *IEEE Trans. Comput.* vol. C-18, pp. 733-740, 1969.

[11] T.Y. Zhang and C.Y. Suen, "A Fast Parallel Algorithm for Thinning Digital Patterns," *Comm. ACM*, vol. 27, no. 3, pp. 236-239, 1984.

[12] F. Meyer and S. Beucher, "Morphological Segmentation," *J. Visual Comm. and Image Representation*, vol. 1, no. 1, pp. 21-46, 1990.

Chapter 11

Introduction to Gray-Scale Morphology

J. P. Basart, M. S. Chackalackal, R. C. Gonzalez

11.1 Introduction

Morphological processing has proven to be a valuable tool in many image processing applications. One of the most recent areas to benefit from morphological processing is nondestructive evaluation (NDE). In this discipline, our goal is to detect, enhance, and measure flaws in materials. X-ray images of materials are often noisy and low in contrast; they have background trends, and contain geometric features of secondary interest which complicate information extraction about any flaws. An image processing task with these images often consists of removing unwanted features from the images and then enhancing the remaining desired features. Morphological image processing has been useful for a variety of tasks, such as background reduction, feature extraction, noise removal, and edge detection. In this chapter we give a general discussion of many morphological tools for gray-scale images, and illustrate their use on noisy x-ray images of materials. Our approach addresses the practitioner of morphology. Mathematical proofs of the concepts we discuss can be found in the references. We end the chapter with an introduction to image algebra. Morphological operations can be cast in this new algebra which has a wider set of operations than morphology and in the future may lead to new methods for processing images.

The mathematics of morphology is based on set theory as introduced by Matheron [1]. To a reader unacquainted with set theory the mathematics may obscure the relatively simple concepts being explained by the math. A beginner in morphology may benefit by reading Chapter 10 on binary morphology. Operations in mathematical morphology that occur in many procedures are opening and closing which in turn are related to the two most basic morphological operations, dilation and erosion. These fundamental concepts are explained in many tutorial sources such as Matheron [2], Serra [3], Giardina and Dougherty [4], Pratt [5], and Gonzalez and Woods [6]. In this chapter we will be primarily concerned with gray-scale operations in the first part, but will include a discussion on binary connectivity in the latter part of the chapter.

Initially, the growth of morphology as a discipline was handicapped by its incapability of handling multi-level intensities of images. Images had to be thresholded into two regions, bright and dark, before applying morphological processing. This narrowed the spectrum of images on which morphology could be applied. Gray-scale morphology began evolving in the late seventies and early eighties with major contributions from Sternberg [7] and [8] and Nakagawa and Rosenfeld [9]. The rate of contributions to morphological processing has continued to escalate. There is now an annual conference on morphology sponsored by the Society for Photo-Optical Instrumentation Engineers [10], [11].

11.2 Dilation and Erosion

A gray-scale image can be represented as a three-dimensional function with the x and y axes representing the spatial coordinates and z representing intensity. The binary morphological operations of dilation, erosion, opening, and closing naturally extend to gray-scale images by the use of *min* and *max* operators which were first discussed in a neighborhood sense by Nakagawa and Rosenfeld [9]. The general extension of the operators by Sternberg [7] and [8] strictly adhered to all the algebraic properties of binary morphology. Also in this general time period, Peleg and Rosenfeld [12] used gray-scale morphology to generalize the medial axis transform to gray scale imaging, Werman and Peleg [13] used gray scale morphology for texture feature extraction and, Coleman and Sampson [14] used gray scale morphology on range data imagery to help mate a robot to an object.

The principles of mathematical morphology are applicable to sets in Euclidean or digital spaces without regard to their dimension. The extension from binary images to gray-scale images took place with the introduction of the concepts of a three-dimensional binary image, umbra and top surface. However, with further development, it was found that the umbra and top surface could be bypassed in developing the gray scale counterparts of dilation, erosion, opening and closing. Consequently, for brevity, we will omit them here. The interested reader will find these concepts discussed in Serra [15], Sternberg [16], and Haralick, Sternberg, and Xinhua [17].

Throughout the discussions that follow, we adopt the notation that a capital bold-face letter, such as **A**, represents an entire image (or structuring element), and a small letter with functional dependence, such as *a(x,y)*, represents an element of that image (or structuring element).

11.2.1 Dilation

Dilation results in the smearing out of an image. The amount and direction of smearing is controlled by the structuring element which is a mini-image containing information on the morphology of interest in the main image.

The most basic explanations of gray-scale operations begin with the concept of an umbra and top surface. We omit these concepts and proceed directly to a working formula for dilation. The function defining the surface of an image **C**, obtained by dilating the image **A** by a structuring element **B** is given by

$$c(x,y) = \max\{a(x-i,y-j)+b(i,j) | (x-i),(y-j) \in D_a; (x,y) \in D_b\} \quad (11.1)$$

where D_a and D_b are the domains of **A** and **B**, respectively. In standard notation, dilation of an image **A** is written as

$$\mathbf{C} = \mathbf{A} \oplus \mathbf{B} \quad (11.2)$$

The operation is read as "circle plus." Both the image and the structuring element can be thought of as surfaces in the three-dimensional space of intensity vs. position. This is especially useful in thinking conceptually about various types of dilation.

The condition that the displacement parameters $(x-i)$ and $(y-j)$ have to be contained in the domain of a is analogous to the condition in the binary definition of dilation, where the two sets had to overlap by at least one element (see Chapter 10). Note also that the form of the above equation is like that of 2-D convolution with the max operation replacing the sums of convolution and the addition replacing the products of convolution.

We illustrate the notation and mechanics of the dilation expression by means of simple 1-D functions. For functions of one variable Eq. (11.1) reduces to the expression

$$\mathbf{A} \oplus \mathbf{B} = \max\{a(x-i) + b(i) | (x-i) \in D_a \textit{ and } x \in D_b\} \quad (11.3)$$

The conditions that the value of $(x - i)$ has to be in the domain of a and that the value of *i* has to be in the domain of *b*, imply that a and *b* overlap. These conditions are analogous to the requirement in the binary definition of dilation, where the two sets have to overlap by at least one element. Unlike the binary case, a, rather than the structuring element *b*, is shifted. Equation (11.1) could be written so that *b* undergoes translation instead of a. However, if D_b is smaller than D_a (a condition almost always found in practice), the form given in Eq. (11.1) is simpler in terms of indexing and achieves the same result. Conceptually, sliding a by b is really no different than sliding b by a.

Dilation is commutative, so the alternative approach of interchanging a and b and using (1) can be utilized to compute $\mathbf{A} \oplus \mathbf{B}$. The result is the same, and b now is the function translated. An example is shown in Fig. 11.1.

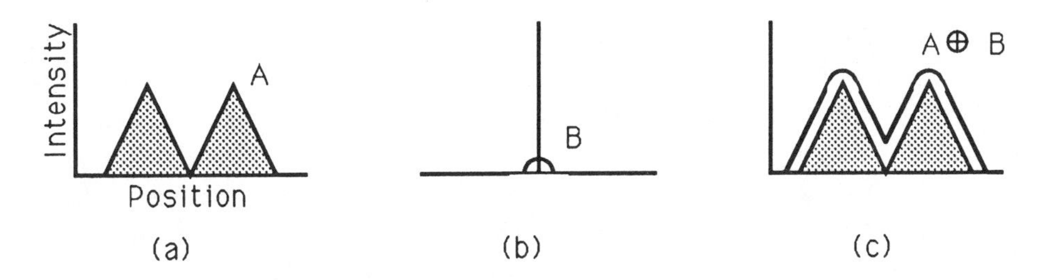

Figure 11.1: Example of dilation (a) one-dimensional slice through image, (b) 1D structuring element, and (c) dilation obtained by sliding b past a. The result is the upper trace.

Because dilation is based on choosing the maximum value of $a+b$ in a neighborhood defined by the shape of the structuring element, the general effect of performing dilation on a gray-scale image is two-fold: (1) if all the values of the structuring element are positive, the output image tends to be brighter than the input; and (2) dark details either are reduced or eliminated, depending on how their values and shapes relate to the structuring element used for dilation.

Algorithm for Dilation: We now give an algorithm for calculating dilation two dimensionally. Several steps are shown pictorially in Fig. 11.2. **A** represents a 5×5 image and **B** represents a 3×3 structuring element. The x,y plane is shown with the numbers representing the intensity at a particular x,y. The origin of **B** is represented by the circled number at the center in the square box. The origin of **A** is at the upper left corner. To start the algorithm the origin of **B** is superimposed on the center element of **A**. (Starting at this location is for convenience of illustration). Since **B** is a 3×3 mask, we ignore the boundary elements of **A** as we do not want the mask to fall outside **A**. Ignoring all the other elements in **A** for the moment (except for the nine elements coinciding with the structuring element), we translate the center element of **A** by all the elements in **B** as shown in Fig. 11.2c. Translating is accomplished by adding, one at a time, each of the elements in **B** to the center element in **A** and storing the results in their respective positions as shown in Fig. 11.2d. The origin of **B** is then shifted to the element to the right of the center element of **A** and the above translating operation is repeated as shown in Fig. 11.2e. The result of translating this element of **A** by **B** is repeated for the other seven elements in **A**, resulting in nine translates for the central pixel of **A**. The maximum intensity of those nine translates is kept as the result of dilation. The entire process is repeated for each pixel in **A** (except for the boundary) to give the final dilated image.

Dilating a gray-scale image causes the brighter regions in an image to grow. (Brighter is a relative term and represents regions brighter than the background.) At the same time it causes regions darker than the background to shrink. Fig. 11.3 illustrates an application of gray scale dilation. The picture on the top is a digitized radiograph of a composite material. The bright dot-like features along a vertical line near the center are flaws in the material. This image was dilated by a 7×7 hemispherical structuring element to obtain the image on the right. Notice how the flaws have grown with respect to the background. The flaws have been magnified while maintaining the image at the same size. The growth of the flaws depends on the size of the structuring element; the larger the size of the structuring element, the larger will be the growth of the bright regions.

11.2.2 Erosion

Erosion results in the shrinking of features in an image. As with dilation, we will omit the description of erosion using umbra and top surface, and go directly to a working definition of erosion. The function defining the surface of an image **C**, obtained by eroding **A** by **B** is given by

$$c(x,y) = \min\{a(x-i, y-j) - b(-i,-j) | (x-i) \in D_a \ and \ x \in D_b\} \quad (11.4)$$

where c(x,y) is the gray scale intensity at (x,y). The notation for erosion of **A** by **B** to give a result **C** is

$$\mathbf{C} = \mathbf{A} \ominus \mathbf{B}. \quad (11.5)$$

The notation $b(-i,-j)$ indicates that the reflection of $b(i,j)$ is taken. This is often notated as $\hat{b}(i,j) = b(-i,-j)$. As with binary morphology, dilation and erosion are duals with respect to function complementation and reflection. That is $[\mathbf{A} \ominus \mathbf{B}]^c = \mathbf{A}^c \oplus \hat{\mathbf{B}}$.

We illustrate the mechanics of Eq. (11.4) by eroding a simple 1-D function. For functions of one variable, the expression for erosion reduces to

$$\mathbf{A} \ominus \mathbf{B} = \min\{a(s+x) - b(x) | (s+x) \in D_a \ and \ x \in D_b\} \quad (11.6)$$

As in correlation, the function $a(s+x)$ moves to the left for positive s and to the right for negative s. The requirements that $(s+x) \in D_a$ and $x \in D_b$ imply that the range of b is completely contained within the range of the displaced a. These requirements are analogous to those in the binary definition of

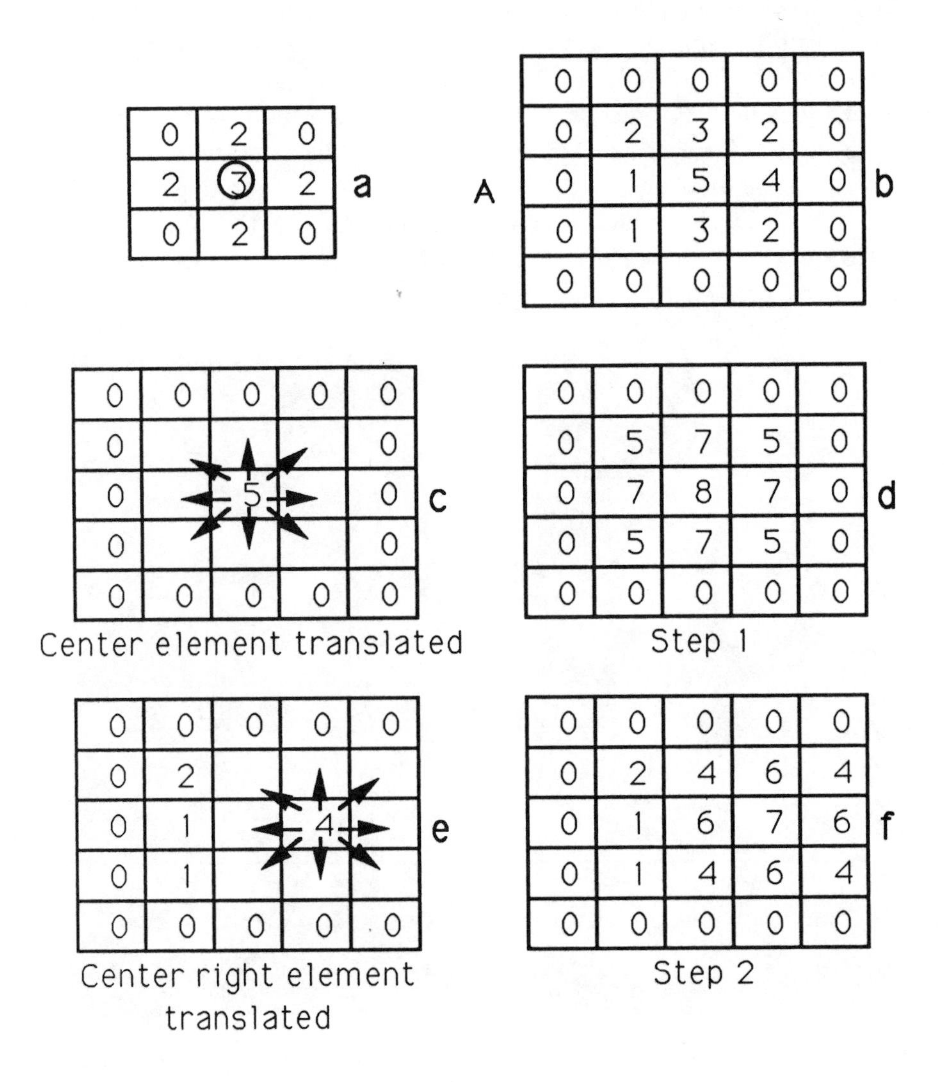

Figure 11.2: Algorithm for finding gray scale dilation: (a) 3×3 structuring element, (b) image, (c) translation of center image element, (d) sums of translation of center image element with each element of the structuring element, (e) translation of right center element in image, and (f) sums of translated element with structuring element.

erosion, where the structuring element has to be contained completely in the set being eroded.

Unlike in the binary definition of erosion, a, rather than the structuring element b, is often shifted. Equation (11.4) could be written so that b would be the function translated, resulting in a more complicated expression in terms of indexing. Because a sliding by b conceptually is the same as b sliding by a, the form of Eq. (11.4) is used for reasons stated at the end of the discussion on dilation. Fig. 11.4 shows the result of eroding the function of Fig. 11.1a by the structuring element of Fig. 11.1b. As Eq. (11.4) indicates, erosion is based on choosing the minimum value of $(a - b)$ in a neighborhood defined by the shape of the structuring element.

Figure 11.3: Application of gray scale dilation of x-ray image of a composite material. (a) original image and (b) dilated image. (Radiograph courtesy of Westinghouse).

Algorithm for Erosion: An algorithm that performs gray-scale erosion is shown pictorially in Fig. 11.5. **A** represents a 5×5 image and **B** represents a 3×3 structuring element. The origin of **B** is superimposed with the center element of **A** as shown in Fig. 11.5c. Ignoring all the other elements in **A** for the moment, we take the negative translates of the center element by the elements in **B**. Negative translating is done by vectorily subtracting each of the elements in **B** from the center element in **A** and storing the result at the corresponding location as shown in Fig. 11.5d. The process is repeated

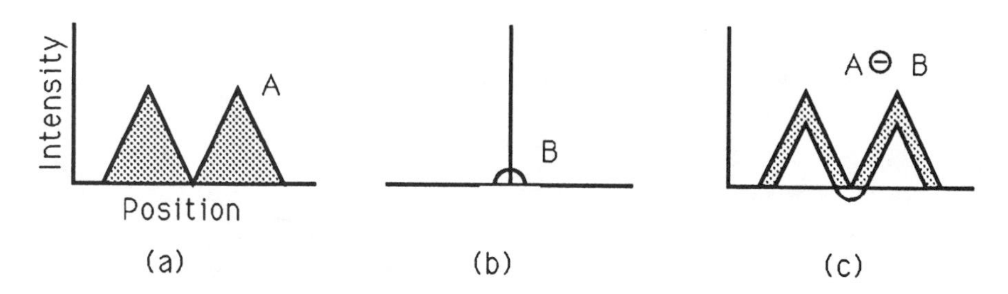

Figure 11.4: Example of erosion. (a) 1D slice through image, (b) structuring element, and (c) erosion of (a) by (b). The result is the lower trace.

for all other inner elements in **A** to give nine sets of negative translates. For each corresponding pixel location in the nine sets, the intensity values in the nine sets of negative translates are compared and the minimum intensity at each pixel is retained. The process can be initiated by placing the mask at any location in the image.

Eroding a gray scale image causes the regions darker than the background to grow. At the same time it causes regions brighter than the background to shrink. Fig. 11.6 illustrates an application of gray scale erosion. The picture on the top is a digitized radiograph of a pipe showing two transverse cracks in the image. The image was eroded by a 7×7 hemisphere. Notice in the eroded image how the dark horizontal flaws have grown with respect to the background.

The general effect of performing dilation on a gray-scale image is two-fold: (1) if all the elements of the structuring element are positive, the output image tends to be darker than the input image; and (2) the effect of bright details in the input image that are smaller in "area" than the structuring element is reduced, with the degree of reduction being determined by the gray-level values surrounding the bright detail and by the shape and amplitude values of the structuring element itself.

As with binary morphology, dilation and erosion are duals with respect to function complementation and reflection. That is

$$((a\ominus)b)^c(x,y) = (a^c \oplus \hat{b})(x,y) \tag{11.7}$$

vhere $a^c = -a(x,y)$ and $\hat{b} = b(-x,-y)$. Except as needed for clarity, we simplify the notation in the following discussions by omitting the arguments of all funcions.

11.3 Morphological Filters

Morphological filters are nonlinear signal transformations that locally modify geometric features of signals. Each signal is viewed as a set in a Eu-

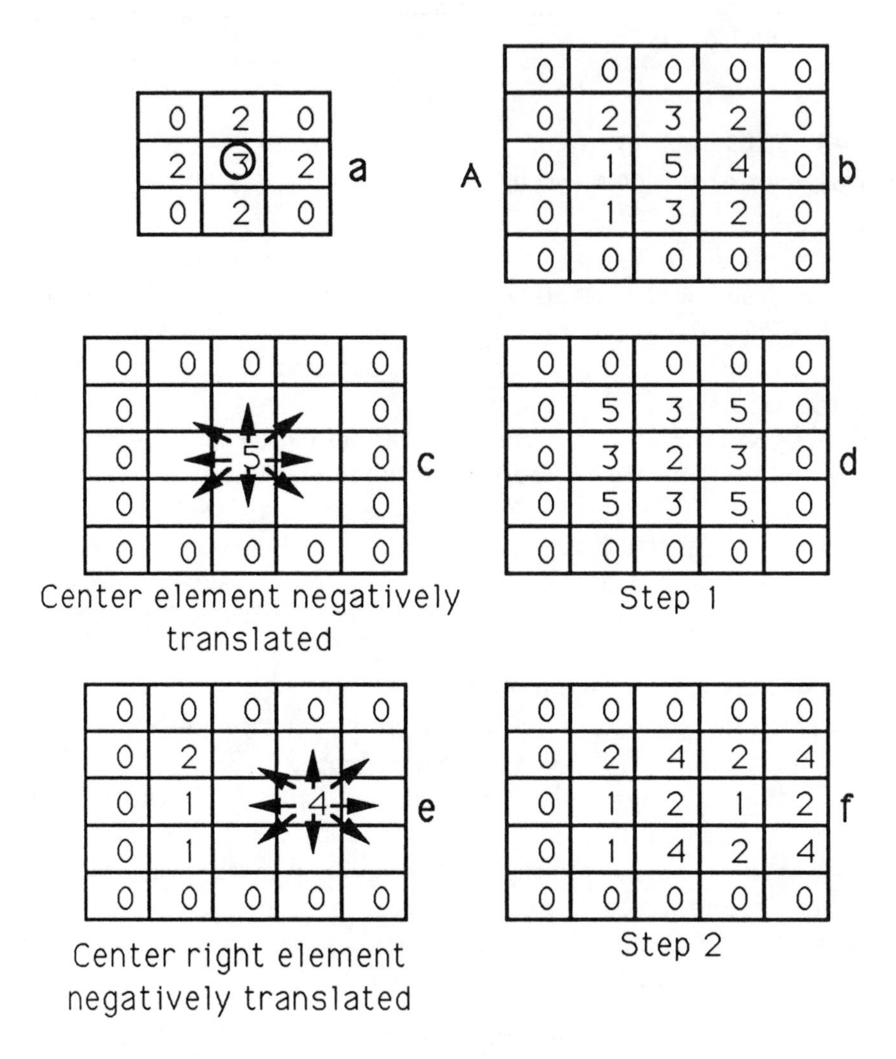

Figure 11.5: Algorithm for finding gray scale erosion: (a) 3×3 structuring element, (b) image, (c) translation of center image element, (d) differences of translation of center image element with each element of the structuring element, (e) translation of right center element in image, and (f) differences of translated element with structuring element.

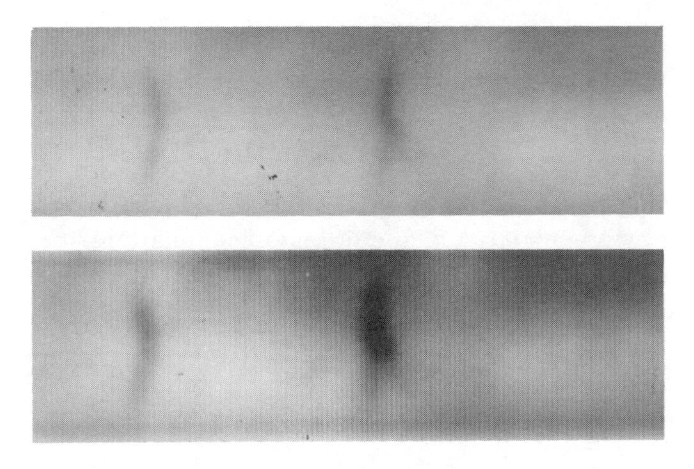

Figure 11.6: Application of gray scale erosion of x-ray image of a pipe. (a) original image and (b) eroded image. (Radiograph courtesy of ARCO)

clidean space. Morphological filters are set operations that transform the shape of the signal. Given a filter output and the filter operation one can obtain a quantitative description of the geometrical structure of the input signal that the filter has extracted. Serra [3] and Maragos and Schafer [18] discuss numerous applications of morphological filters in image processing. Areas of application include shape recognition, nonlinear filtering, edge detection, noise suppression, thinning, enhancement, representation and coding, texture analysis and shape smoothing. Developing morphological filters is an active area of current research by many investigators. Maragos and Schafer [19] introduced the representation of classical linear filters in terms of morphological operators, Chen and Yan [20] proved why mathematical morphology is more powerful in studying some vision problems than using derivatives of Gaussian-shaped filters of different sizes while Song and Delp [21] proposed a new class of morphological filters, known as the generalized morphological filter, for image enhancement.

11.3.1 Opening and Closing

Opening and closing are two morphological filters referred to as M-filters by Lantuejoul and Serra [22]. They consist of combinations of dilation and erosion which do not commute since dilation and erosion are not inverse operations. For example, information lost during erosion cannot be recovered from the eroded image by a dilation operation. Thus, erosion followed by dilation is not the same as dilation followed by erosion.

Opening: Gray-scale opening has the same definition as binary opening which is,

$$\mathbf{A} \circ \mathbf{B} = (\mathbf{A} \ominus \mathbf{B}) \oplus \mathbf{B} \tag{11.8}$$

where opening is denoted as $\mathbf{A} \circ \mathbf{B}$, $\mathbf{A}$ is the image, $\mathbf{B}$ is the structuring element, $\ominus$ represents erosion, and $\oplus$ represents dilation.

An alternate definition of opening [19] which is expressed directly in terms of set theory is

$$\mathbf{A} \circ \mathbf{B} = \cup(\mathbf{B})_y; \text{where}(\mathbf{B})_y \subset \mathbf{A} \tag{11.9}$$

where $\mathbf{B}_y$ is the translation of $\mathbf{B}$ by an element $y \in \mathbf{A}$. The result of morphological opening can be explained as the domain swept out by all the translations of $\mathbf{B}$ which are included in $\mathbf{A}$.

Opening is somewhat like a nonlinear low-pass filter in that it removes features brighter than the background and smaller than the structuring element. However, it is not like a low-pass *frequency* filter which would reject high spatial frequencies for both large and small structures. Opening passes large structure and deletes small structure (smaller than the structuring element), but both structures could have high spatial frequencies. The process of opening in one dimension is pictorially represented in Fig. 11.7. The ordinate is image intensity and the abscissa is position. Opening can be visualized as a process in which the structuring element is pushed apex up, under the top surface of the image and scanned along the image. The opened image consists of the highest points reached by the structuring element at each pixel as it is slid under the top surface of the image. Fig. 11.7 shows slices through the image $\mathbf{A}$ and the cylindrical structuring element $\mathbf{B}$. Note how all the peaks that had a base width smaller than the radius of the structuring element were removed from the image. The larger peaks were slightly clipped at the top. Opening an image breaks narrow isthmuses, and eliminates small islands and sharp peaks or capes.

As an example, we opened the image shown in Fig. 11.3a with a 11×11 cylinder. The largest flaw is less than 9×9 pixels in size. The result, shown in Fig. 11.8, has the bright flaws removed. The opening operation is very effective for removing bright objects from images.

Closing: Gray-scale closing has the same definition as binary closing. The *closing* of image $\mathbf{A}$ by structuring element $\mathbf{B}$ is denoted by $\mathbf{A} \bullet \mathbf{B}$ and defined as

$$\mathbf{A} \bullet \mathbf{B} = (\mathbf{A} \oplus \mathbf{B}) \ominus \mathbf{B} \tag{11.10}$$

Closing is to dark features as opening is to bright features in an image. It is a nonlinear filter that removes features darker than the background and smaller than the structuring element. The process of closing is pictorially represented in Fig. 11.9. Closing can be visualized as a process in which the

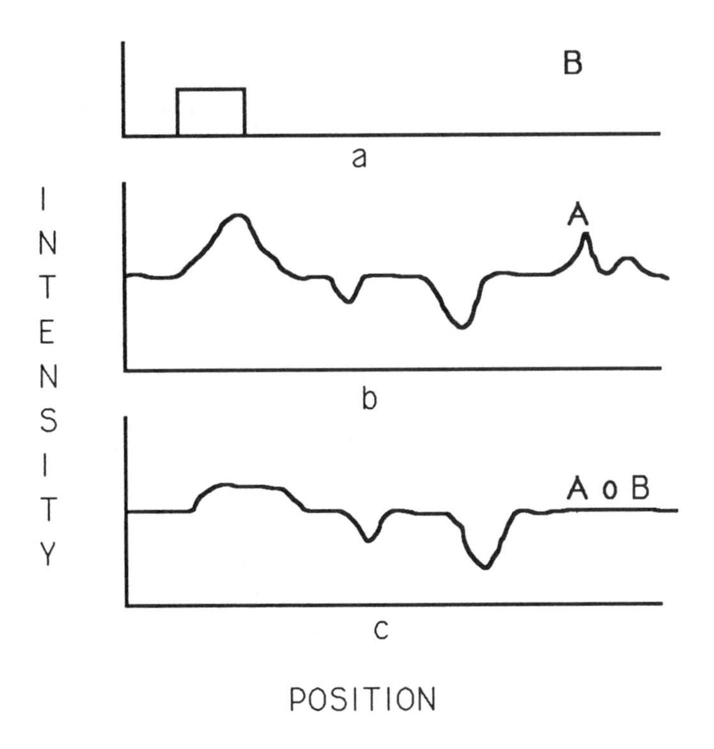

Figure 11.7: One-dimensional representation of gray-scale opening: (a) structuring element, (b) image, and (c) result of opening.

Figure 11.8: Result of opening image in Fig. 11.3a showing that the flaws have been removed.

structuring element is moved, apex down, over the top of the top surface of the image. The closed image consists of the lowest points reached by the structuring element at each pixel location. Fig. 11.9 shows slices (intensity vs. position) through the image **A** and the cylindrical structuring element. Note how all the pits that had an opening smaller than the diameter of the structuring element were removed from the image. Larger pits were retained to a great extent except for clipping due to the nature of the structuring element.

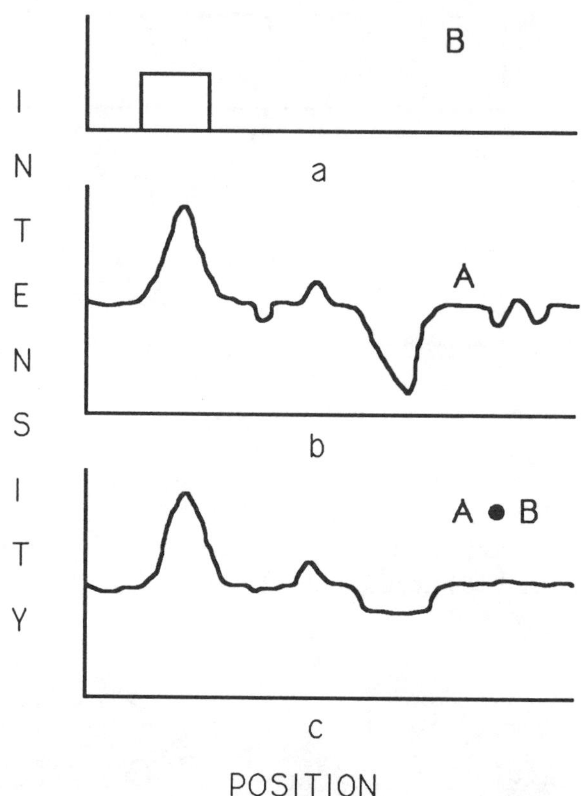

Figure 11.9: One-dimensional representation of closing: (a) structuring element, (b) image, and (c) result of closing.

Fig. 11.10a is the digitized image of a railroad track frog with shrinkage cracks in manganese steel which are the wispy structures in the image. This image was closed by a 25×25 cylinder resulting in the image in Fig. 11.10b. Much of the crack structure has been removed. Removing cracks is more difficult than removing roundish type structure since cracks are long and often larger than the size of the structuring element. If the orientation of a linear crack is known a priori, a planar structuring element could be used which is more effective for crack detection than a cylindrical structuring element.

Hybrid Filtering: A combination of opening and closing can be used

Figure 11.10: (a) Digitized x-ray image of frog in railroad track, and (b) result of closing (a) with a 25×25 cylinder showing removal of much of the crack structure. (Radiograph courtesy of the Association of American Railroads).

to eliminate noise-like features from the image. Thus, by opening and then closing an image with a small structuring element, it is possible to remove noise-like features smaller than the structuring element. Such a filter, called a hybrid filter, is illustrated in Fig. 11.11. A small hemisphere is frequently a useful choice for the structuring element in a hybrid filter. Fig. 11.12a shows a digitized radiograph of a weld in a fuel tank and a plot (Fig. 11.12b) giving intensity versus position of a horizontal slice through the center of the image. The image was hybrid filtered using a 5×5 hemisphere resulting in an image with a slice shown in Fig. 11.12c . The slice in Fig. 11.12c brings out the flaw (dip near center) much better than the one in Fig. 11.12b.

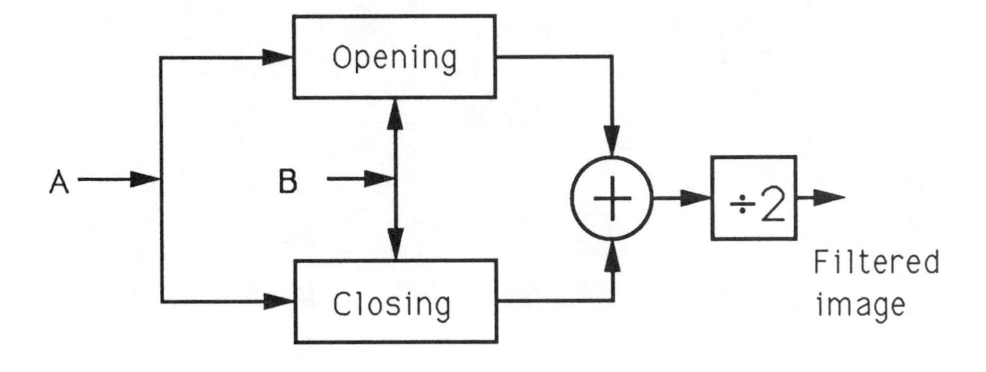

Figure 11.11: Hybrid filter which is a combination of opening and closing.

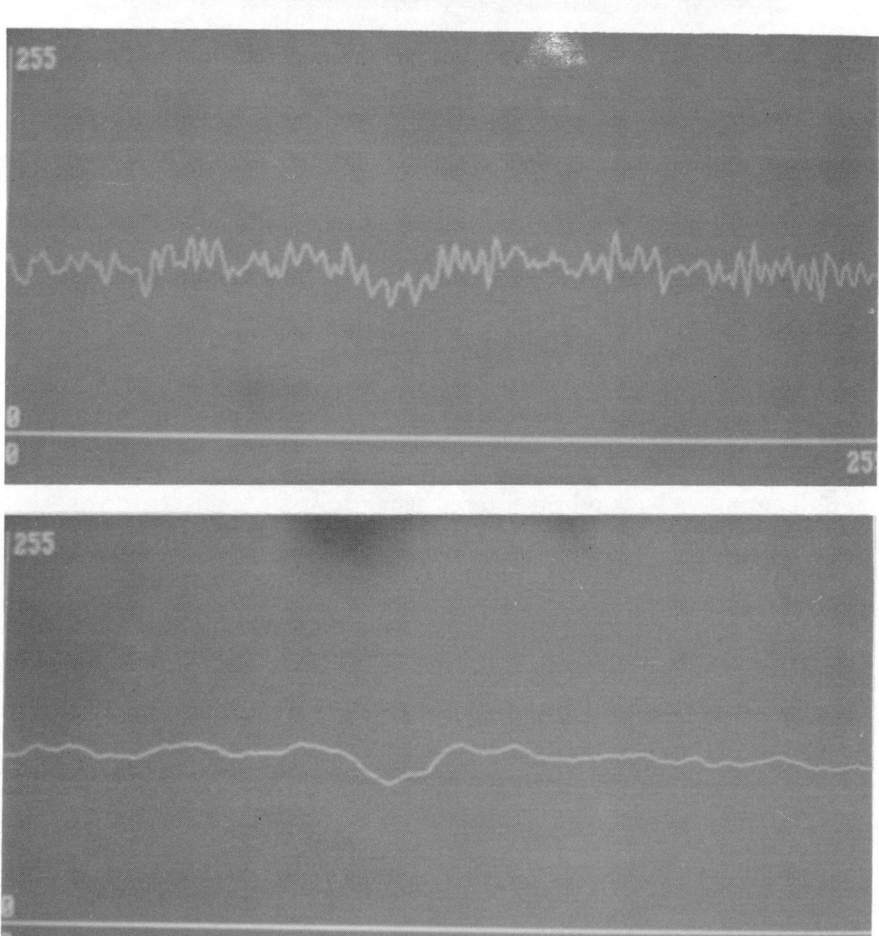

Figure 11.12: (a) Digitized x-ray radiograph of a flaw in a weld, and (b) plot of intensity vs. position for a horizontal slice through the flaw. (Radiograph courtesy of Martin Marietta)

Sieving: Sieving is a morphological filter for passing structures within a narrow range of sizes. For instance, bright dot-like flaws with diameters of n pixels (n is odd), can be extracted using

$$(\mathbf{A} \circ \mathbf{B}^{n \times n}) - (\mathbf{A} \circ \mathbf{B}^{(n-2)\times(n-2)}) \tag{11.11}$$

where the superscript stands for the size of the structuring element. Sieving is analogous to a bandpass frequency filter. The first term in Eq. (11.11) eliminates all bright structure whose size is smaller than $n \times n$. The second term in Eq. (11.11) eliminates all bright structure whose size is smaller than $(n-2) \times (n-2)$. Thus, subtracting the two terms leaves the structure whose size lies between $n \times n$ and $(n-2) \times (n-2)$. Sieving works best when the structure size to be filtered is on the order of a few pixels or larger.

An example of sieving is shown in Fig. 11.13. The original data in Fig. 11.13a shows an enlarged digitized image of raindrops on blotter paper. This data is not from the NDE area, but it well illustrates the concept of sieving. The scientific goal is to determine the size distribution of the drops. Applying the sieving operation to sort out drops of an intermediate size gives the result shown in Fig. 11.13b. The shape is squarish because of the quantization of the digitizing. Sieving very effectively extracted the medium-sized raindrops.

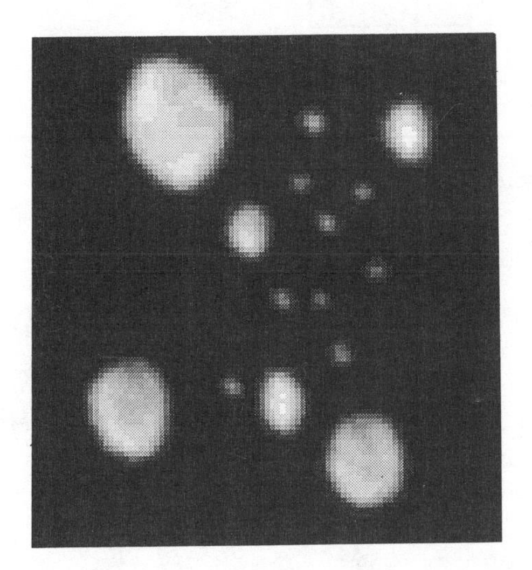

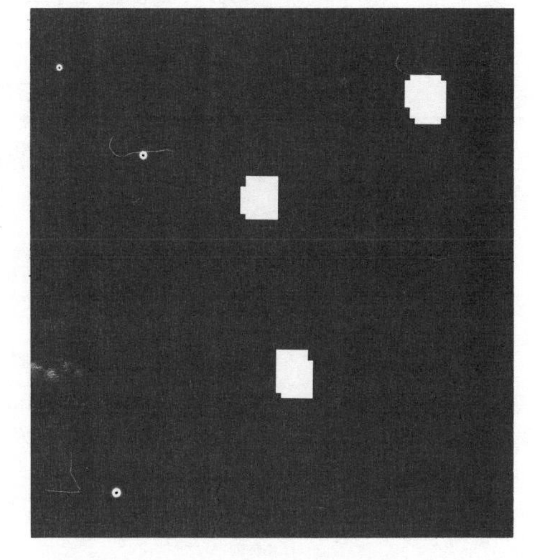

Figure 11.13: (a) Digitized image of raindrops on blotter paper, and (b) result of extracting intermediate size drops using sieving. The two structuring elements used for sieving were cylinders 7 pixels and 11 pixels in diameter. (Data courtesy of Harry Vaughan).

11.4 Structuring Elements

In morphological image processing, the image to be processed and the structuring element are an inseparable operational pair. The description of a morphological operation is not complete without specifying the structuring element. In gray-scale morphology, the structuring element can be any three-dimensional structure. Cones, cylinders, hemispheres and paraboloids are often useful for various images. The designation $n \times n$ (e.g. 9×9) for a hemispherical structuring element means that the spatial dimensions are $n \times n$ and the intensity over this region varies in a hemispherical manner. If the structuring element is a hemisphere, the center of the $n \times n$ mask corresponds to the maximum intensity of the hemisphere. A 9×9 mask is shown in two dimensions in Fig. 11.14, and in three dimensions in Fig. 11.15. Dilating an image with a hemispherical structuring element, for example, will cause bright spots to grow as the size of the mask increases.

<table>
<tr><td>0</td><td>0</td><td>0</td><td>0</td><td>0</td><td>0</td><td>0</td><td>0</td><td>0</td></tr>
<tr><td>0</td><td>0</td><td>4</td><td>6</td><td>6</td><td>6</td><td>4</td><td>0</td><td>0</td></tr>
<tr><td>0</td><td>4</td><td>6</td><td>7</td><td>8</td><td>7</td><td>6</td><td>4</td><td>0</td></tr>
<tr><td>0</td><td>6</td><td>7</td><td>8</td><td>9</td><td>8</td><td>7</td><td>6</td><td>0</td></tr>
<tr><td>0</td><td>6</td><td>8</td><td>9</td><td>9</td><td>9</td><td>8</td><td>6</td><td>0</td></tr>
<tr><td>0</td><td>6</td><td>7</td><td>8</td><td>9</td><td>8</td><td>7</td><td>6</td><td>0</td></tr>
<tr><td>0</td><td>4</td><td>6</td><td>7</td><td>8</td><td>7</td><td>6</td><td>4</td><td>0</td></tr>
<tr><td>0</td><td>0</td><td>4</td><td>6</td><td>6</td><td>6</td><td>4</td><td>0</td><td>0</td></tr>
<tr><td>0</td><td>0</td><td>0</td><td>0</td><td>0</td><td>0</td><td>0</td><td>0</td><td>0</td></tr>
</table>

Figure 11.14: Two-dimensional display of 9×9 hemispherical structuring element.

The expression for finding the elements in the $n \times n$ hemispherical mask is given by

$$w(x, y) = g^2 - (gx/k)^2 - (gy/k)^2 \tag{11.12}$$

where $w(x, y)$ is the intensity at location (x, y), g is the peak intensity at the center of the mask (0,0), x lies in the range $[-k, k]$ and y lies in the range $[-k, k]$ with $k = (n-1)/2$. The algorithm for finding the elements in an $n \times n$ cylindrical mask is given by:

$$\begin{aligned} if\ \ x^2 + y^2 &\le k^2 \\ then\ \ w(x, y) &= g \\ else\ \ w(x, y) &= 0 \end{aligned} \tag{11.13}$$

where g is the height of the cylinder. Note that the mask size is always an odd number so that the mask center lies on a pixel. The criteria for selecting a structuring elements is discussed later.

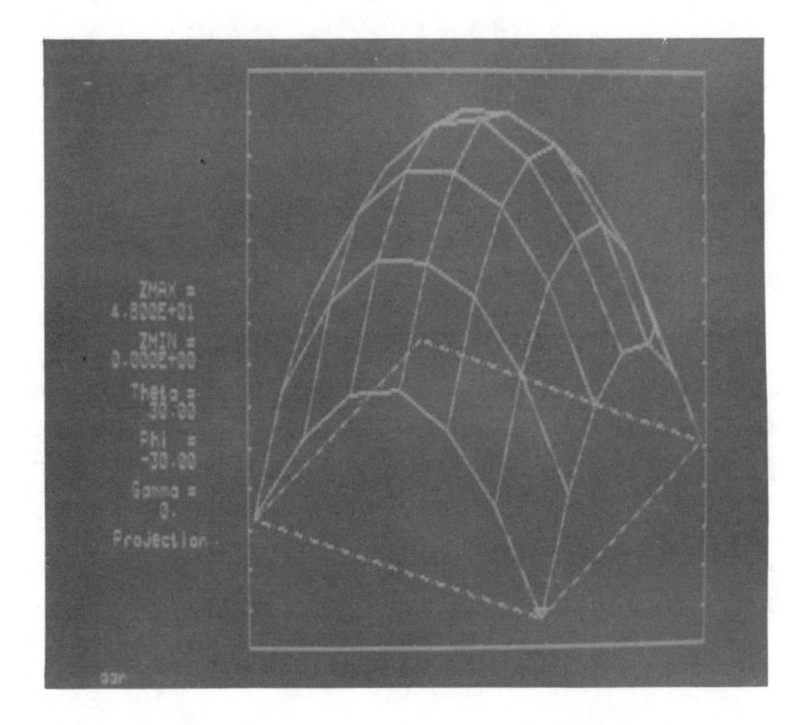

Figure 11.15: Three-dimensional display of 9×9 hemispherical structuring element.

11.4.1 Decomposition of Structuring Elements

The execution time of morphological routines depends on the size of the image processed and to a greater extent on the size of the structuring element. It can be quite large. For instance, if we want to dilate an image by a 3×3 structuring element, each pixel in the image generates nine translates. If the same image is dilated by a 15×15 structuring element, each pixel generates 225 translates. Thus, the computational time increases as the area of the structuring element.

Decomposition of structuring elements can be used to considerably reduce computational time. The theory underlying decomposition of structuring elements is given by the following theorem which is proved by Serra [3].

Decomposition Theorem: If the structuring element $\mathbf{B}$ has the decomposition $\mathbf{B} = \mathbf{B}_1 \oplus \mathbf{B}_2 \cdots \oplus \mathbf{B}_N$, then, the dilation and erosion of $\mathbf{A}$ by

B can be performed respectively as

$$
\begin{aligned}
\mathbf{A} \oplus \mathbf{B} &= \mathbf{A} \oplus (\mathbf{B}_1 \oplus \mathbf{B}_2 \cdots \oplus \mathbf{B}_N) \\
&= (((\mathbf{A} \oplus \mathbf{B}_1) \oplus \mathbf{B}_2) \cdots) \oplus \mathbf{B}_N, \qquad (11.14) \\
\mathbf{A} \ominus \mathbf{B} &= \mathbf{A} \ominus (\mathbf{B}_1 \oplus \mathbf{B}_2 \cdots \oplus \mathbf{B}_N) \\
&= (((\mathbf{A} \ominus \mathbf{B}_1) \ominus \mathbf{B}_2) \cdots) \ominus \mathbf{B}_N. \qquad (11.15)
\end{aligned}
$$

The major problem in decomposing a structuring element is determining the N smaller structuring elements which Zhuang and Haralick [23] discuss in detail. The structuring element we frequently use in our work with NDE images is a cylinder. A 5×5 cylinder can be expressed as the dilation of two 3×3 cylinders which implies that a 5×5 cylinder can be decomposed into two 3×3 cylinders as illustrated in Fig. 11.16. The two 3×3 cylinders contain a total of 10 nonzero pixels, whereas the 5×5 cylinder has 13 nonzero pixels indicating more computation time is required for the larger cylinder than for the two smaller cylinders. Although we call a 3×3 structuring element a cylinder, in digital form it appears as a cross. The reduction in computation time can be calculated by finding the difference between the area of the original structuring element and the sum of the areas of the N smaller structuring elements and dividing the difference by the area of the original structuring element. Thus, the fractional reduction in computation time going from a 5×5 cylinder to two 3×3 cylinders is $(25 - 18)/25$ or a $7/25$ reduction in time.

$$
\begin{array}{|ccc|}
- & 1 & - \\
1 & 1 & 1 \\
- & 1 & -
\end{array}
\oplus
\begin{array}{|ccc|}
- & 1 & - \\
1 & 1 & 1 \\
- & 1 & -
\end{array}
=
\begin{array}{|ccccc|}
- & - & 2 & - & - \\
- & 2 & 2 & 2 & - \\
2 & 2 & 2 & 2 & 2 \\
- & 2 & 2 & 2 & - \\
- & - & 2 & - & -
\end{array}
$$

Figure 11.16: Decomposition of a 5×5 structuring element of a cylinder into two 3×3 structuring elements.

Decomposition can be extended to a cylinder of any size. A 17×17 cylinder can be generated by eight repeated dilations with a 3×3 cylinder. Dilating by a 17×17 cylinder generates 289 translates for each pixel in the image, whereas repeated dilations by 3×3 cylinder generates 72 translates for each pixel. For any symmetrical structuring element, the number of repeated 3×3 dilations (or erosions) is given by the diameter of the original structuring element minus one, divided by two. As the structuring element increases in size, the fractional savings in computation time increases by decomposing it into smaller structuring elements.

11.5 Estimation of Background

One of the goals in NDE is to automatically detect flaws in a material. Automated detection of flaws is relatively simple when the flaws can be separated from the rest of the background. This can be done when the histogram of the image is bi-modal. That is, the background and the nonbackground intensities can be thresholded into distinct regions. Histograms of NDE x-ray images often tend to be uni-modal which prohibits thresholding. Many x-ray images have background trends in them that complicate automated detection of flaws and reduce the effectiveness of noise filters. So the first hurdle to be crossed towards automated detection is suppressing the background. One approach to background elimination is to estimate the background intensity levels using some form of low-pass filter (e.g., based upon a fast Fourier transformation of the digitized image). However, linear filtering techniques (based upon transforms into the frequency domain) alter image information in ways that can conflict with the need for precise measurement of the size and location of flaws that are of utmost importance in our work. On the other hand nonlinear filters such as opening and closing can suppress the background but still retain size and location information with a fair amount of accuracy [24]. Morphological filters alter the intensity values of images, but the geometric nature of the filters describes the manner in which the intensities are changed. Further, the extent to which the intensities are altered can be controlled depends on the nature of the structuring element.

11.5.1 Background Reduction

Features brighter than the background, but smaller than the structuring element, can be removed from an image with the opening operation. Thus, if the features of interest are brighter than the background, opening the image by a structuring element bigger than the largest feature will remove the features from the image leaving behind an estimate of the background. Subtracting the estimate of the background from the original image extracts the flaws. Structuring elements most commonly used are hemispheres and cylinders. If the flaws are bright, then

$$\text{Background estimate} = \mathbf{A} \circ \mathbf{B}, \quad (11.16)$$

$$\text{Background reduction} = \mathbf{A} - (\mathbf{A} \circ \mathbf{B}) \quad (11.17)$$

where $\mathbf{B}$ is larger than any of the bright features of interest. The location of the extracted flaws will be exactly the same as in the original image. The size also agrees with the original size if the structuring element exceeds the flaw size. As operations are never perfect, the background image may still contain a little of the intensity information.

Since opening removes all bright features smaller than the structuring element, the extracted flaws may contain noise-like features smaller than the structuring element. In most cases, there will be an intensity disparity between the flaws and the noise-like regions permitting noise removal by thresholding. If this is not the case, the best approach will be to remove the noise-like features first by opening the image by a small structuring element (say 5×5) and then using this image to estimate the background. The trade-off is that some of the smaller flaws will be lost. Alternatively, one could always use some preprocessing to remove noise before opening. Once the flaws are extracted and thresholded, there are many routines for locating and sizing the flaws.

Fig. 11.17 shows an example of background reduction. The largest flaw is roughly 9×9 pixels in size. The image shown in Fig. 11.3a was opened with an 11×11 hemisphere giving the background estimate shown in Fig. 11.17a. Subtracting the image in Fig. 11.17a from the one in Fig. 11.3a gives Fig. 11.17b with the flaws extracted. Noise-like features remain in the result, but can be easily removed by thresholding. The outer boundary of the image has been imperfectly processed. Boundaries often have to be accounted for on a case-by-case basis.

The closing operation removes features darker than the background but smaller than the structuring element from the image. Thus, if the features of interest are darker than the background, closing the image by a structuring element bigger than the largest feature will remove the features from the image leaving behind an estimate of the background. Subtracting the original image from the estimate of the background extracts the flaws. If the flaws are dark, then

$$\textit{Background estimate} = \mathbf{A} \bullet \mathbf{B}, \qquad (11.18)$$

$$\textit{Background reduction} = (\mathbf{A} \bullet \mathbf{B}) - \mathbf{A} \qquad (11.19)$$

where **B** is larger than any of the dark features of interest.

Fig. 11.18 illustrates the power of morphology to extract flaws that are hidden in background trends. Fig. 11.18a is the digitized x-ray radiograph of a casting. A flaw is hidden in the transition region from dark to bright which is caused by a change in the thickness of the casting. Since it is hardly visible, most image processing routines have difficulty detecting it. This image was closed by a 13×13 cylinder to obtain the background estimate, and then subtracted from the background estimate to pull out the flaw as shown by Fig. 11.18b. The size and location of the flaw remains the same, but the intensity information is inverted. Fig. 11.18c is an inversion of the center image.

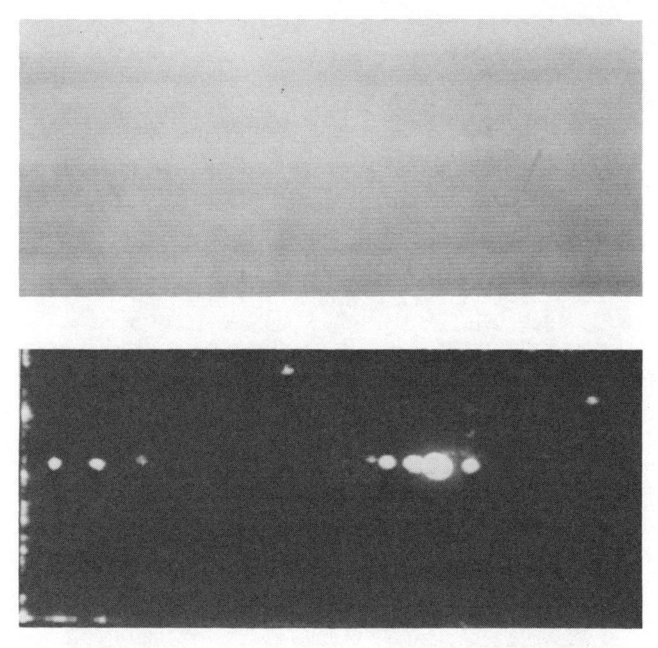

Figure 11.17: (a) Result of opening Fig. 11.3a with an 11×11 hemisphere which shows the flaws removed, and (b) removal of background by subtracting (a) from Fig. 11.3a.

11.5.2 Selection of Structuring Element

A variety of structuring elements have been tried on NDE images. Hemispheres and cylinders were found to be the most useful. For the purpose of background estimation, a cylinder seems to be the ideal structuring element. Fig. 11.19 illustrates the opening of a one-dimensional slice of **A** by a cylinder and a hemisphere of the same radius. The image opened by the cylinder is clearly a better estimate because it minimizes the residue of the flaw in the result. The top of the hemisphere may fit up into a flaw, resulting in a background surface that will not truly measure the background level. When the background surface is subtracted from the original spot intensities, the result will be a lowering of flaw intensities near the flaw peak (decreasing in effect as the flaw borders are approached). As seen in the figure, this problem is alleviated to a great extent by using a cylinder. A hemisphere of a larger radius can be comparable to a cylinder, but it will increase the computational time considerably.

For filtering purposes, rather than background removal, ahemisphere produces better results than a cylinder. Owing to the abrupt edges, a cylinder clips off a lot of useful intensity information, whereas a hemisphere with its rounded edges slides over (or under) the surface.

Figure 11.18: (a) Digitized image of flaw in casting, (b) result of closing (a) with a 13 × 13 cylinder and subtracting this from (a), and (c) inverted image of (b).

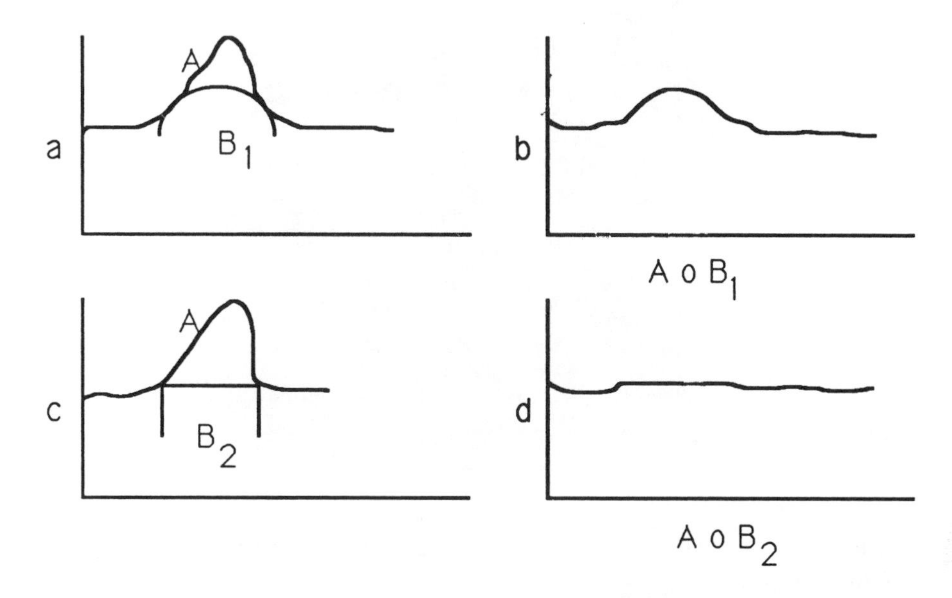

Figure 11.19: Comparison of one-dimensional openings with a hemisphere and a cylinder: (a) hemisphere under object, (b) result of opening (a), (c) cylinder under same object, and (d) result of opening.

11.5.3 Morphological Image Enhancement

For visual effects, closing can be used to produce images of very high contrast. It is simple to enhance an image by subtracting an extracted flaw from a white background. We choose a white background because the extracted flaws appear bright. The picture on the left in Fig. 11.20 shows a morphologically enhanced version of Fig. 11.10a. The flaws were extracted by closing with a 15 × 15 cylinder and then subtracting from a white background. The original image is of very low-contrast, but the enhanced image has considerably improved contrast and better defined features.

11.6 Morphological Edge Detection

Edges are probably the most reliable descriptors of an object's shape. For this reason edge detectors are commonly used in object recognition. Basically, the idea underlying most edge detection techniques is the computation of a local derivative operator. Such detectors are called gradient operators. Gradient operators are sensitive to noise and often tend to magnify it. NDE images often tend to be noisy and respond poorly to commonly used gradient operators. Though morphological edge detectors are simple, their performance is comparable to that of sophisticated edge focusing techniques in noisy conditions. Morphological routines are sensitive to noise, but unlike

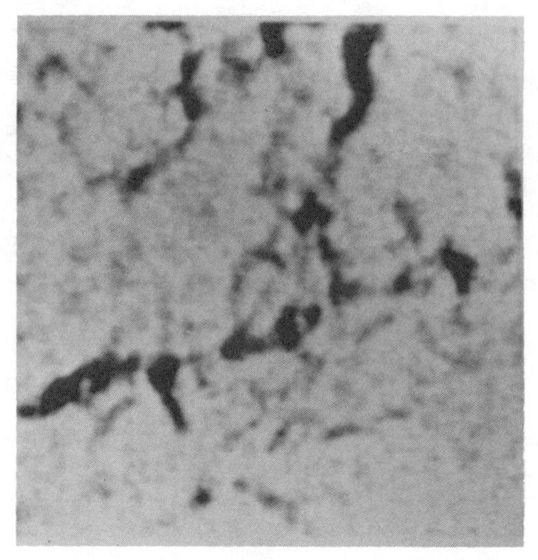

Figure 11.20: Enhanced image of Fig. 11.10a which was obtained by closing Fig. 11.10a with a 15×15 cylinder and subtracting this from a white background.

conventional edge detectors, they do not magnify noise. Furthermore, they are comparable in speed to a 3×3 convolution operation. In this section we discuss four different morphological edge detectors.

11.6.1 Morphological Gradient

Serra [3] and Meyer [25] define the gradient in terms of morphological operators as

$$Grad1 = (\mathbf{A} \oplus \mathbf{B}) - (\mathbf{A} \ominus \mathbf{B}) \tag{11.20}$$

where $\mathbf{B}$ is a 3×3 cylinder. Fig. 11.21 illustrates the use of this definition. $\mathbf{A} \oplus \mathbf{B}$ expands bright regions in $\mathbf{A}$ by a one-pixel width while $\mathbf{A} \ominus \mathbf{B}$ shrinks bright regions in $\mathbf{A}$ by a one-pixel width. Grad1 then gives a boundary two pixels wide. The two-pixel thick boundary might appear out of focus in some applications.

From experience, we found that a sharper boundary can be obtained by defining the gradient as

$$Grad2 = (\mathbf{A} \oplus \mathbf{B}) - \mathbf{A} \tag{11.21}$$

$$or \tag{11.22}$$

$$Grad2 = \mathbf{A} - (\mathbf{A} \ominus \mathbf{B}). \tag{11.23}$$

Fig. 11.22 illustrates the use of Grad2. In this case the boundary is one pixel wide. An NDE application of this edge detector is shown in Fig. 11.23. Fig. 11.23a is the digitized radiograph of a honeycomb structure and Fig. 11.23b was obtained by using Grad2 on the original. The objective of applying

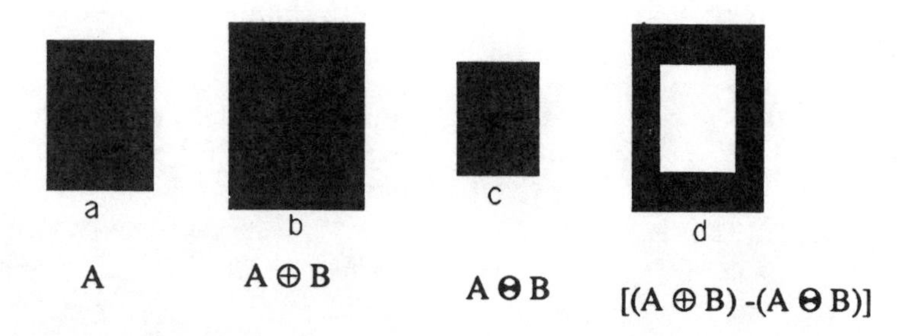

Figure 11.21: Illustration of Grad1: (a) original object, (b) (a) dilated with a 3×3 cylinder, (c) (a) eroded by a 3×3 cylinder, and (d) Grad1 result obtained from (b) minus (c) (exagerated edge thickness).

edge detection to the honeycomb was to detect the signature of crushed core, which appears as a halo around the hexagonal structure of the honeycomb. The arrow in Fig. 11.23a points to a region of interest. The image, as one can observe, is fairly noiseless. In the resulting image, the signature of crushed core appears as lines parallel to, but very close to, the hexagonal edges. Grad2 is comparable in performance, as well as computational time, to the Laplacian and other gradient operators. The results of Grad1 and Grad2 contain noise, but the noise has not been magnified.

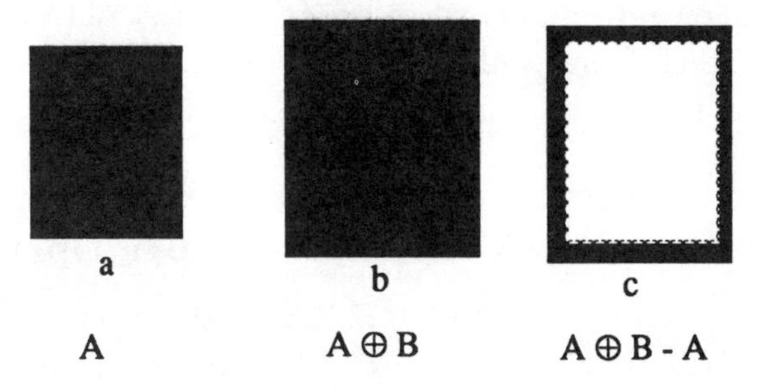

Figure 11.22: Illustration of Grad2: (a) original object, (b) (a) dilated by a 3×3 cylinder, (c) Grad2 result obtained from (b) minus (a).

A third morphological edge detector that is to a great extent less noise sensitive than the previous detectors is defined by

$$Grad3 = \min \{[(\mathbf{A} \oplus \mathbf{B}) - \mathbf{A}], [\mathbf{A} - (\mathbf{A} \ominus \mathbf{B}]\} \tag{11.24}$$

where the *min* operator gives the minimum of the two operators at each pixel. The results of this operator on ideal ramp edges are excellent. This operator is insensitive to isolated noise points, but, unfortunately, it is not able to detect ideal step edges. This is the motivation for the blur minimum morphological edge detector improvised by Lee et al. [26]. In this edge detector, the image is first blurred to convert the ideal step edges into ideal ramp edges, and then operated on by Grad3.

Figure 11.23: Application of Grad2 to honeycomb material: (a) digitized image of x-ray radiograph of honeycomb, and (b) result of applying Grad2 to (a). Arrows show region of crushed honeycomb (a) and two paralled lines (signature of crushed honeycomb) in edge detected image (b). (Radiograph courtesy of Joe Gray).

11.6.2 Blur Minimum Morphological Edge Operator:

As stated above, we can make the Grad3 operator sensitive to step edges by blurring the image before applying the Grad3 operator. One thing to note is that the domain of the blurring mask should be the same as the domain of **B** used for dilation and erosion. The domain of a 3×3 cylinder is $\{(0,1),(-1,1),(0,0),(1,1),(0,-1)\}$ and will be the domain of the blurring mask. Given an image **A**, its blurred version **I** is given by

$$I(i,j) = [A(i-1,j)+A(i,j)+A(i+1,j)+A(i,j+1)+A(i,j-1)]/5 \quad (11.25)$$

where $A(i,j)$ is the gray scale value at (i,j). Given the blurred image **I**, the modified gradient edge detector is defined by

$$Grad4 \;=\; \min \{[(\mathbf{I} \oplus \mathbf{B}) - \mathbf{I}], [\mathbf{I} - (\mathbf{I} \ominus \mathbf{B})]\}. \quad (11.26)$$

Due to the blurring operation, we lose some of the edge strength. Thus, if the image is not noisy to start with, it is better to use Grad3 without blurring the image. It is a trade-off between higher signal-to-noise ratio and sharper edges when we choose between Grad4 and Grad3. Grad4 has been successful in detecting edges in noisy images. Fig. 11.24 shows a real-time x-ray image of a honeycomb structure with a magnification of 6 times. Real-time x-ray images are much noisier than images digitized from x-ray films. Figs. 11.25a and 11.25b show the results of applying a Sobel operator and Grad4, respectively, to Fig. 11.24. As in the case of Fig. 11.23, the objective is to detect the crushed core which appears as lines parallel to the edges of the hexagonal pattern. The Sobel operator is successful in detecting the signature of the crushed core but, as can be seen in Fig. 11.25a, the image is too noisy. Grad4 detects the edges but maintains the noise level much lower than that in Fig. 11.25a.

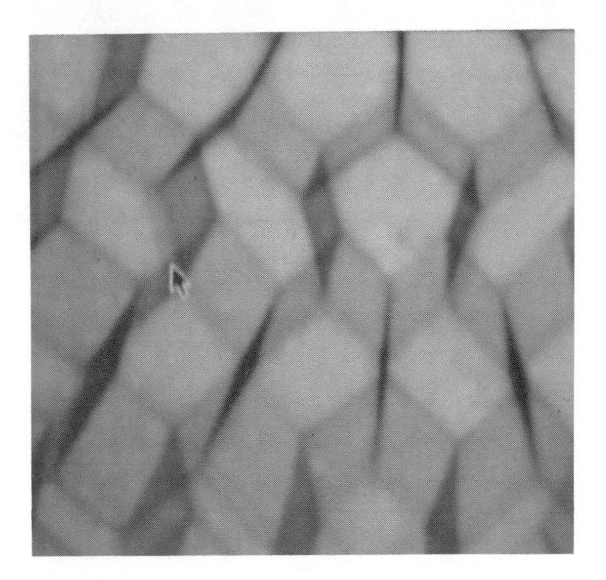

Figure 11.24: Digitized real-time x-ray radiograph of honeycomb material. Arrow shows region of crushing. (Radiograph courtesy of Joe Gray).

11.7 Segmentation

Frequently in image processing it is necessary to divide objects into segments which then may undergo additional processing. We illustrate segmentation by disconnecting particles in the image of a composite material. Fig. 11.26 illustrates a cross section of a metal matrix composite material with embedded silicon carbide particles. Many of the carbide particles appear to lie singly within the metal matrix, while other particles lie next to each other and appear connected. If we want to find statistics of particle size and orientation, we first have to disconnect the particles. We discuss two methods

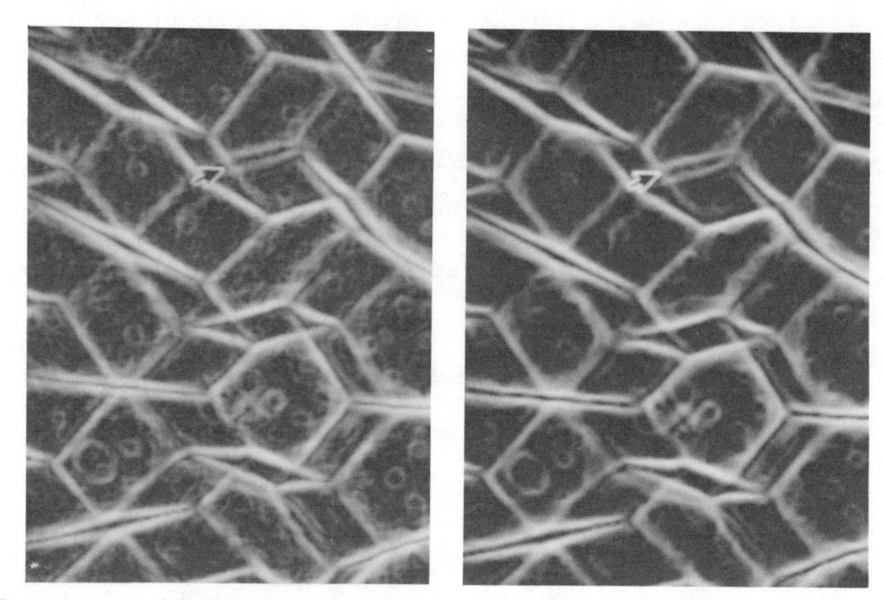

Figure 11.25: (a) Result of applying Sobel edge detector to Fig. 11.23, and (b) result of applying Grad4 edge detector to Fig. 11.23. The Grad4 result is less noisy than the Sobel result.

of segmentation: cluster fast segmentation and watershedding. But first we examine additional tools.

11.7.1 Conditonal Dilation

Two extensions to dilation are *conditional dilation* and *repeated conditional dilation.* Conditional dilation was discussed in Section 10.4 under the title of *Region Filling.* For convenience we repeat the definition here. Conditional dilation of **A** by **B** with respect to a condition **X** is denoted by $\mathbf{A} \oplus \mathbf{B}; \mathbf{X}$ and is defined by

$$\mathbf{A} \oplus \mathbf{B}; \mathbf{X} = (\mathbf{A} \oplus \mathbf{B}) \cap \mathbf{X}. \tag{11.27}$$

The result of dilating **A** by **B** contains only those regions common to the limiting set **X**.

Repeated conditional dilation is an extension of the above operation and is denoted by $\mathbf{A} \oplus \{\mathbf{B}\};\ \mathbf{X}$. The braces indicate a repeated operation. The definition of repeated conditional dilation is

$$\mathbf{A} \oplus \{\mathbf{B}\}; \mathbf{X} = \cdots [[[(\mathbf{A} \oplus \mathbf{B}) \cap \mathbf{X}] \oplus \mathbf{B}] \cap \mathbf{X}] \oplus \mathbf{B} \cdots. \tag{11.28}$$

A is repeatedly dilated by **B** until no further growth is observed in the set consisting of elements common to the limiting set **X** and the set obtained by repeated dilations.

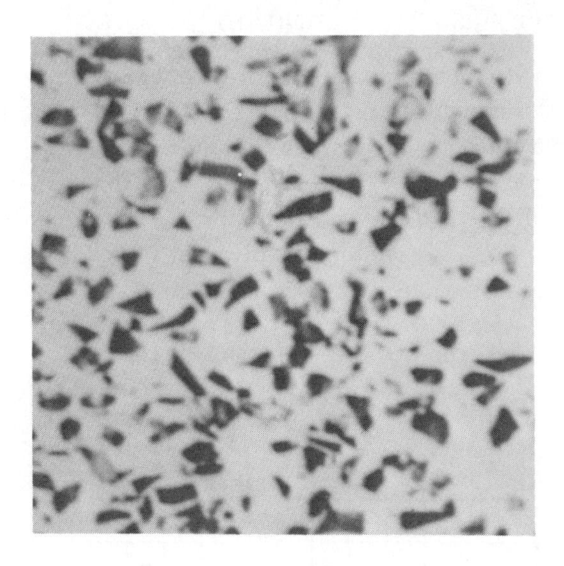

Figure 11.26: Secondary electron micrograph of composite material. (Micrograph courtesy of Westinghouse).

11.7.2 Ultimate Erosion

The principle of ultimate erosion is to repeatedly erode an object until it disappears, and then keep the result obtained one step before the disappearance. The final result is called a seed.

Let $\mathbf{A}_i = \mathbf{A} \ominus i\mathbf{B}$, where $\mathbf{B}$ is a unit circle and $i\mathbf{B}$ is a circle of radius i units. Then the *ultimate erosion* $\mathbf{Y}_i$ is defined to be the component of $\mathbf{A}_i$ which vanishes from any larger erosion $\mathbf{A}_j$ (j greater than i). The first step of ultimate erosion is

$$\mathbf{U}_i = (\mathbf{A}_{i+1} \oplus \{B\}); \mathbf{A}_i \tag{11.29}$$

which is a repeated conditonal dilation. The second step is to subtract the dilation from the erosion of $\mathbf{A}$:

$$\mathbf{Y}_i = \mathbf{A}_i - \mathbf{U}_i \tag{11.30}$$

The ultimate eroded sets of $\mathbf{A}$ are obtained by taking the union of all $\mathbf{Y}_i$s. Thus, the ultimate eroded image is

$$\mathbf{Y} = \cup_{i=1,m} \mathbf{Y}_i \tag{11.31}$$

where m is the number of stages of erosion. ($\mathbf{Y}_i$ represents the ultimate erosion of just one object in the image).

11.7.3 Cluster Fast Segmentation

We now procede with an explanation of how to separate particles in an image using cluster fast segmentation (CFS) approach [25]. The particles we are separating are assumed to have convex boundaries.

Two distint phases of CFS are: 1) To find markers for the zones to be separated, and 2) To draw the boundaries. Here, the markers are the ultimate-eroded sets $\mathbf{Y}_i$. The steps involved in CFS follow.

Step 1: Repeatedly erode the orignal image $\mathbf{A}_o$ with a unit disk:

$$\mathbf{A}_i = \mathbf{A} \ominus i\mathbf{B}, for\ i = 1, \cdots, m \quad where\ \{m : \mathbf{A}_m \neq \emptyset\} \tag{11.32}$$

where B is a unit circle, $\mathbf{A}_1 = \mathbf{A} \ominus \mathbf{B}$, $\mathbf{A}_2 = \mathbf{A} \ominus 2\mathbf{B}$, and so on until $\mathbf{A}_m = \mathbf{A} \ominus m\mathbf{B}$, and $\mathbf{A}_{m+1} = \emptyset$.

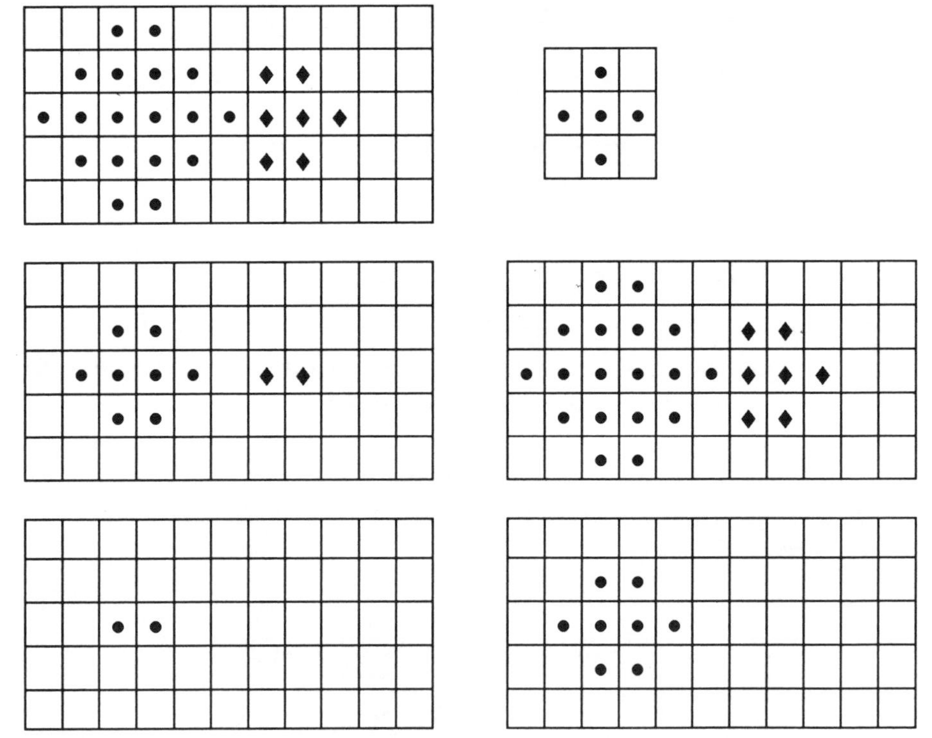

Figure 11.27: Steps of cluster fast segmentation. (a) original image, (b) structuring element, (c) first stage of erosion, (d) conditional dilation of (c) conditioned on (a), (e) second stage of erosion, and (f) conditional dilation of (e) conditioned on (c). The first seed is obtained from (a) minus (d), the second seed is obtained from (c) minus (f), and the third seed is shown in (e).

We continue eroding until everything is gone while keeping all intermediate results. Consider the example shown in Fig. 11.27a. This represents a binary image with the black pixels identified by black dots, diamonds and stars for simplicity of following the procedure. The white pixels are left black. The first stage of erosion, shown in Fig. 11.27c, eliminates the stars while shrinking the patches of dots and diamonds. Also, the diamonds are separated from the dots. The next stage of erosion creates Fig. 11.27e. The diamonds are gone and the dot patch has shrunk again. One more erosion step eliminates the dots. We are left with a null set.

Figure 11.28: Applicaton of CFS to one portion of the image shown in Fig. 11.26. (a) Original segment, and (b) result of applying CFS to (a). Image size in (b) was expanded by a factor of two to prevent particles from recombining. (particles were not expanded).

Step 2: Next, we ultimately erode each $\mathbf{A}_i$ and subtract the result from $\mathbf{A}_i$:

$$\mathbf{Y}_i = \mathbf{A}_i - (\mathbf{A}_{i+1} \oplus \{B\}; \mathbf{A}_i). \tag{11.33}$$

The $\mathbf{Y}_i$s are the ultimate eroded sets, or the "seeds" of the $\mathbf{A}$s.

To illustrate this step we return to the image in Fig. 11.27c and repeatedly dilate it by $\mathbf{B}$ while conditioning it with the original image, called $\mathbf{A}_0$. The result, shown in Fig. 11.27d, is the same as Fig. 11.27a except the stars are missing. To extract the stars only, we subtract Fig. 11.27d from Fig.

11.27a which leaves us with two stars. The result is the ultimately eroded $\mathbf{A}_0$, called $\mathbf{Y}_0$. This is our first "seed".

Next we repeat the process with $\mathbf{A}_2$ in Fig. 11.27e. We repeatedly dilate it with $\mathbf{B}$ conditioned on $\mathbf{A}_1$. This restores the dots, but does not restore the diamonds as shown in Fig. 11.27f. The result is subtracted from $\mathbf{A}_1$ in Fig. 11.27c giving the seed for the diamonds. Repeating the process once more give the seed for the dots.

Step 3: Finally, the seeds are grown back to the full size of their corresponding original particle using

$$\mathbf{U} = \cup \mathbf{Y}_i \oplus (i-1)B; \; for \; i = 1 \; to \; m. \tag{11.34}$$

We proportionally dilate each ultimate-eroded set to the size of its corresponding component.

The result of applying this process to one portion of Fig. 11.26 is shown in Fig. 11.28. Fig. 11.28a shows the original set of objects, and Fig. 11.28b shows the disconnected objects. An additional step was performed here. If we grew the seeds back to their original sizes the particles would again be connected. To circumvent this we placed the seeds on an image background which was twice as large as the original image. Then we grew the seeds back to their normal sizes.

One more refinement can be made which gives a truer reproduction of the original particles when the seeds are grown back. Instead of using a circularly symmetric structuring element we can use, for example, a thin oval. Then, we repeat the entire CFS process with this structuring element in each of four orientations: 0°, 45°, 90°, and 135°. We then take the union of the four results to get the final segmented image. The advantage of this approach is that the result gives separated particles that more closely resemble their connected counterparts.

11.7.4 Watershed

Another morphological method for segmenting connected objects in images is watershedding which was first proposed by Beucher and Lantuejoul [27]. The principle of this method is to create a relief map from the successive stages of eroding a binary image. In terms of physical terrain, the "watersheds" will be the domains of attraction of rain falling over the region [3]. Our procedure for executing the watershed segmentation follows the explanation by Russ [28]. The process consists of three steps.

Step 1: The first step in this technique is to create a so-called distance map in which the brightness of each pixel is a measure of its distance from the boundary of an object. Starting with a binary image, which can be created by thresholding a gray-scale image, pixels closer to the interior of an object are assigned increasing larger measures of distance.

To create the distance map morphologically, a binary image is repeatedly eroded, and after each stage of erosion, all remaining pixels have their intensities incremented by one. Consider the binary image in Fig. 11.29a. Each black pixel is labeled with a "1", and each white pixel is left blank. We erode this image with the binary structuring element shown in Fig. 11.29b which is an approximation to a unit disk. Each remaining pixel is re-labeled with a 2 as shown in Fig. 11.29c. Again we erode getting the results in Fig. 11.29d with each remaining pixel re-labeled with a 3. One more erosion eliminates all pixels which stops the process. Now we combine all previous maps while keeping the highest numerical label for each pixel. The result, called the distance map, is shown in Fig. 11.29e. Note that each erosion is executed as a binary erosion. The numerical labels are ignored during erosion.

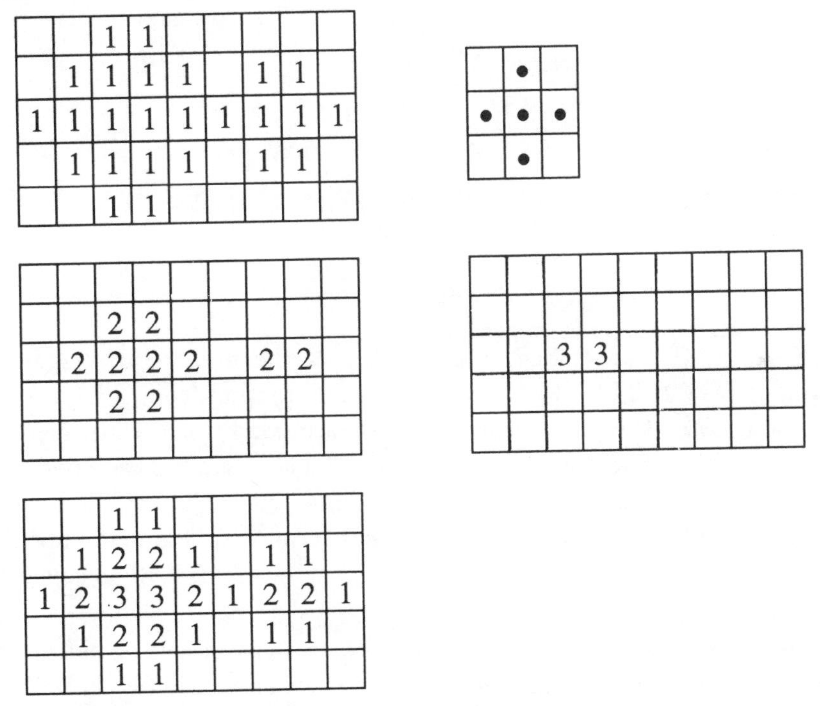

Figure 11.29: Steps of watershed. (a) orignal image, (b) structuring element, (c) relabeled pixels after erosion of (a) by (b), (d) second erosion with remaining pixels labeled with a 3, and (e) distance map which is a combination of erosion results and the original image.

In morphological notation the repeated erosion is given as

$$\mathbf{A}_i = \mathbf{A} \ominus i\mathbf{B}, \quad for \quad i = 1 \cdots m \quad where \ \{m : \mathbf{A}_m \neq 0\}. \qquad (11.35)$$

where m is the maximum number of nonnull maps. Note that the $\mathbf{A}_i$s for various "i"s are different stages in the repeated erosion.

Thinking topographically, the largest numbers in the distance map correspond to the peaks of mountains, and the smallest numbers correspond to valleys which are the watersheds. Segmentation occurs along the watersheds bridging the distance between the peaks.

Step 2: This step is the same as *Step 2* of cluster fast segmentation, which is the calculation of the ultimate eroded sets, the $\mathbf{Y}_i$s. As can be seen in Fig. 11.29e, the seeds will be the peak regions which can easily be identified because they are surrounded by pixels with a smaller distance measure.

Step 3: The last step is to grow the seeds back to their original size without allowing the various regions to reconnect. This step uses conditional thickening which is the significant difference between cluster fast segmentation and watershed. We show the algorithm for this step and then explain it:

$$\begin{aligned} Initialize\ \mathbf{W}_m &= \mathbf{Y}_m && (11.36)\\ Do\ n &= m-1\ \ to\ \ n=0 \\ \mathbf{W}_n &= \mathbf{Y}_n \cup \mathbf{W}_{(n+1)} \\ \mathbf{W}_n &= \mathbf{W}_n \odot \{\mathbf{T}^i\}; \mathbf{A}_m && (11.37)\\ n &= n-1 \\ end\ do \end{aligned}$$

where $\mathbf{W}_1$ is the watershed result and m is the number of stages in the erosion in *Step 1.* This algorithm states that starting from the final erosion stage (stage m), the ultimate-eroded sets are conditionally thickened with respect to the corresponding eroded set. Thus, $\mathbf{Y}_m$, will be conditionally thickened with respect to $\mathbf{A}_m$. The thickening process is regulated such that it prevents any of the particles from reconnecting. This is made possible by using $\mathbf{T}^i$, which consists of twelve structuring elements [28] as suggested in Fig. 11.30.

The process starts with the union of the last two seeds as shown in Fig. 11.31a. These two seeds are the same as that shown in Fig. 11.27. Next, Consider the first structuring element $\mathbf{T}^1$ shown in Fig. 11.30. We are going to apply the hit-or-miss transform as explained in Chapter 10. The center of $\mathbf{T}^1$ is superimposed on a pixel surrounding a seed in, say, $\mathbf{W}_n$. To grow this seed the elements in the structuring element must exactly match the seed region below it. That is, where the structuring element contains a "1" (black) the seed region must contain a "1". Where the structuring element contains a "0" (white) the seed region (outside the seed) must contain a "0". The unlabeled pixels in the structuring element are "don't care" pixels which could contain wither a "1" or a "0" in the seed region. If all required pixels match, a "1" is placed in $\mathbf{W}_n$ lying below the center pixel in the structuring element, thus growing the seed region in size by one pixel.

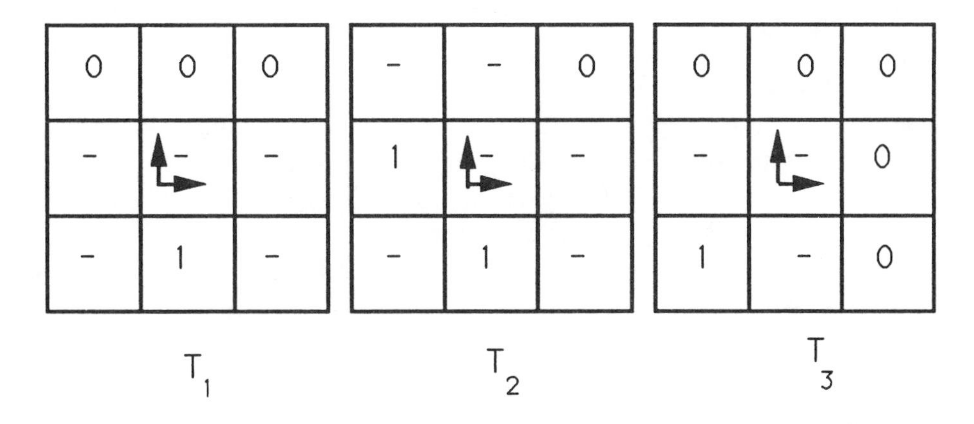

Figure 11.30: Three structuring elements for watershed. Three additional elements are formed from the first element shown by rotating it 90°, 180°, and 270°. Six more structuring elements are formed by rotating each of the other two structuring elements shown by 45°, 135°, and 225°.

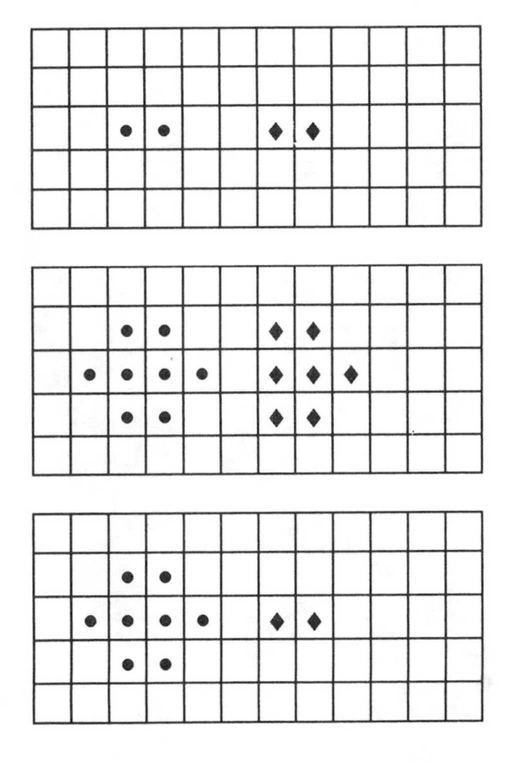

Figure 11.31: Growth of seeds in the watershed procedure. (a) union of the seeds from Fig. 11.27, (b) result of one iteration of thickening (a), (c) intersection of (b) with Fig. 11.27c.

This process is repeated with all of the 12 $\mathbf{T}^i$ structuring elements. Every $\mathbf{T}^i$ has zeros in it. It is the requirement that the zeros of $\mathbf{T}^i$ match $\mathbf{W}_n$ that keeps the grown regions from reconnecting. See Fig. 11.31b for the result of one iteration of thickening Fig. 11.31a. After all 12 $\mathbf{T}^i$s are used, $\mathbf{W}_n$ is intersected with a conditioning image. The result places a one-pixel thick region around the seed except where another seed region is nearby. Fig. 11.31c shows the result of intersecting Fig. 11.31b with Fig. 11.27c (recall Step 2 of watershed is the same as Step 2 of CFS).

The entire process is repeated starting with $\mathbf{T}^1$ again and continuing through the intersection step. The cycle keeps repeating until the result ceases to change.

Ultimate-eroded sets from the corresponding stage are added on at each stage while limiting the growth to those points contained in the corresponding eroded stage. It is to facilitate this that the distance map was created. The corresponding eroded stage can be tracked logistically using the brightness values in the distance map. The application of watershed segmentation to a portion of Fig. 11.26 is given in Fig. 11.32. Note how the particles were successfully separated along their watersheds. Although the watershed algorithm can successfully separate projects, it is computationally very intensive since it involves thickening by twelve structuring elements for each ultimate-eroded set, and we have to keep track of all the eroded stages.

Figure 11.32: Segmentation with the watershed technique. The connected objects in (a) were separated as shown in (b) in the region where rainwater would concentrate if the image intensity represented elevation of terrain.

11.7.5 Comments on CFS and Watershed

We have shown results of segmenting connected particles by two techniques. Comparing Figs. 11.28 and 11.32 we see two types of results. The watershed technique (Fig. 11.32) retained the original shapes of the particles very well. The boundaries inserted between the particles is clean, and appear to be logical. However, note that one particle in the bottom right has been erroneously divided into two pieces. This likely occured because of the concave nature of the boundary. From a study of silicon carbide particles we know that they do not have concave boundaries. If two particles overlap they can appear as one particle with a concave boundary. For our purposes we do not want the separation shown, but in other applications this separation is desireable.

On the other hand, CFS did not retain the overall shape of the particles very well, but was less subject to erroneous disconnection. The two techniques produced distinct results, neither of which is truely correct. The watershed technique would be superior when it is known that there is no particle overlap. That is, the particles are butted up to one another. If particle overlap occurs, CFS may be the better choice.

11.8 COMMENTS ON MORPHOLOGY

So far, we have discussed the mathematics of morphological image processing and illustrated its applications to NDE with many examples. We next give a few suggestions on how to use morphological signal processing. The basic tools, erosion and dilation, by themselves are seldom used. Opening and closing in various combinations are the most useful tools for analyzing the types of images discussed here. They could be used for filtering noise, but we found that the median, sigma and Kalman filters generally gave better results than morphological hybrid filtering. For suppressing the background, we have not found a technique as easy and effective as morphological processing. Its ability to pull out weak flaws is outstanding. If one's objective is to remove bright features from the image, the image should be opened by a cylinder of diameter greater than the size of the largest feature of interest. To remove dark flaws, the image should be closed by a cylinder of diameter greater than the size of the flaw. If one is interested in automated detection of flaws (or other features) in images with low contrast, background trends, or transition regions, morphology is an excellent tool.

Opening and closing can be used for quantitative studies of flaws and other geometrical features because they have very little effect on the intensity of features they remove or retain. In other words, opening and closing either mostly remove a feature, or mostly retain the feature. If the images are noisy, morphology tends to pull out some of the noise, but this can be minimized by preprocessing the image with a noise filter.

Using sieving, it is possible to extract features based on size. One can easily experiment with extraction by using various structuring elements. It is possible to pull out cracks (or long narrow objects) by opening or closing an image with line-like (planes in three dimensions) structuring elements [29].

Compared to other types of edge detectors, morphological edge detectors have the distinct advantage of not amplifying the noise. Noise can even be reduced by applying the blur minimum morphological operator although this will widen the edge somewhat.

Morphological processing clearly plays an important role in applied signal processing. Appropriate combinations of mathematical morphology and conventional image processing techniques give the practitioner a broad assembly of effective tools.

11.9 IMAGE ALGEBRA

Thus far we have expressed morphological processing in the standard notation for mathematical morphology. We now discuss a new type of formalism, image algebra, which is capable of incorporating all of mathematical morphology within it. In addition, image algebra incorporates linear processing techniques, such as convolution. We will discuss some of the basic operations of image algebra and write morphological processes in terms of this algebra, and give examples of the breadth of this algebra. The purpose of the presentation here is not to give the reader a working knowledge of image algebra, but rather to introduce the subject. The theory of image algebgra can be found in the references.

Image algebra is a high level mathematical language developed for representing image processing algorithms. The purpose of image algebra is to provide a common mathematical environment for the development of these algorithms. Image algebra can also considerably improve a programmer's efficiency since larger blocks of code are replaced by short algebraic statements. It also is considerably easier to debug programs. For example, gray-scale dilation, which requires about ten lines of code in Fortran, can be replaced by a single image algebra expression. A disadvantage of image algebra is that the notation may not aid ones' intuitive understanding of an algorithm.

In the mid 1980's, the U. S. Air Force Armament Lab (AFATL) requested the development of a highly structured mathematical foundation for image processing and image analysis with the intent that the fully developed structure would subsequently form the basis of a common image processing language. The goal of AFATL was to develop a complete, unified algebraic structure that provides a common mathematical environment for image processing algorithm development, optimization, comparison, coding, and performance evaluation. Several preprocessors have been written for image algebra including a Fortran package, a C package, and one for the parallel computer Maspar in parallel C. In addition, an image algebra ADA compiler is currently undergoing development as part of a software package to create an image processing workbench using image algebra. Several papers discussing the subsequently developed image algebra have been published. Ritter, Wilson and Davidson [30] give the various definitions of the image algebra accepted by the Air Force as a standard for their image processing work. The relationship between image algebra and mathematical morphology is described by Ritter, Wilson, and Davidson [30] and Davidson [32]. Ritter and Gader [33] and [34] discuss image algebra applications for parallel image processing. Applications of image algebra to image measurement and feature extraction are discussed by Ritter, Wilson, and Davidson [30].

Image algebra is inherently parallel and can be easily implemented on many parallel computers. It is an extension of morphological concepts developed by Serra and Sternberg of an algebraic theory specifically designed for image processing and image analysis. Sternberg [35] and [36] was also the first to use the phrase "image algebra" to describe the algebraic structure defined by mathematical morphology. Image algebra has been successfully used to perform all linear transforms, edge enhancement, local smoothing, morphological operations, Fourier-like transformations, image rotation, zooming, and image reduction. The inventors of image algebra have proven that it is theoretically possible to write any image processing routine in image algebra, although in practice it may be difficult to write a particular image processing routine in the form of image algebra.

11.9.1 IMAGES

In this discussion we consider only real valued images, which means that each pixel in the image takes on real values. Let $\mathbf{R}$ denote the set of real numbers and $\mathbf{X}$ denote the domain of the image. In terms of image algebra, a real valued image $\mathbf{a}$ (images are represented by lower case bold letters in image algebra) is defined as

$$\mathbf{a} = \{(\mathbf{x}, \mathbf{a}(\mathbf{x})) : \mathbf{x} \in \mathbf{X}\} \tag{11.38}$$

where $\mathbf{x}$ is the pixel location, $\mathbf{a}(\mathbf{x})$ is the pixel value (intensity which is real) at $\mathbf{x}$, and $(\mathbf{x}, \mathbf{a}(\mathbf{x}))$ is an element of image $\mathbf{a}$.

Pixel-by-pixel operations can be performed between images that reflect the arithmetic and logic operations on real numbers. Let $\mathbf{a}$ and $\mathbf{b}$ be two real valued images with the same domain $\mathbf{X}$. Then,

$$\mathbf{c} = \mathbf{a} + \mathbf{b} \;=\; \{(\mathbf{x}, \mathbf{c}(\mathbf{x})) : \mathbf{c}(\mathbf{x}) = \mathbf{a}(\mathbf{x}) + \mathbf{b}(\mathbf{x}), \mathbf{x} \in \mathbf{X}\} \tag{11.39}$$

$$\mathbf{c} = \mathbf{a} * \mathbf{b} \;=\; \{(\mathbf{x}, \mathbf{c}(\mathbf{x})) : \mathbf{c}(\mathbf{x}) = \mathbf{a}(\mathbf{x}) * \mathbf{b}(\mathbf{x}), \mathbf{x} \in \mathbf{X}\} \qquad (11.40)$$

$$\mathbf{c} = \mathbf{a} \vee \mathbf{b} \;=\; \{(\mathbf{x}, \mathbf{c}(\mathbf{x})) : \mathbf{c}(\mathbf{x}) = \mathbf{a}(\mathbf{x}) \vee \mathbf{b}(\mathbf{x}), \mathbf{x} \in \mathbf{X}\} \qquad (11.41)$$

where $\mathbf{c}$ is the resulting image and $(\mathbf{x}, \mathbf{c}(\mathbf{x}))$ is an element of $\mathbf{c}$. Further, '$*$' denotes multiplication and '$\vee$' denotes the maximum of the two numbers. Likewise, any other operation valid with real numbers can be performed on images. Note the parallel nature of these operations. Adding two images, for example, involves a set of independent additions of image intensities, all of which could be done in parallel.

Any function on $\mathbf{R}$ can be induced on a real valued image as given by

$$\mathbf{c} = f(\mathbf{a}) = \{(\mathbf{x}, \mathbf{c}(\mathbf{x})) : \mathbf{c}(\mathbf{x}) = f(\mathbf{a}(\mathbf{x})), \mathbf{x} \in \mathbf{X}\} \qquad (11.42)$$

For example:

$$\mathbf{c} = sin(\mathbf{a}) = \{(\mathbf{x}, \mathbf{c}(\mathbf{x})) : \mathbf{c}(\mathbf{x}) = sin(\mathbf{a}(\mathbf{x})), \mathbf{x} \in \mathbf{X}\} \qquad (11.43)$$

As can be seen in the definition and the example, an induced function is applied pointwise to the values in the image.

A special type of function called the characteristic function is useful in many image processing applications. Let $\mathbf{S} \subset \mathbf{R}$. The characteristic function applied to a real valued image produces a binary image (a thresholding operation). This is given by

$$\chi_S(\mathbf{a}) = \{(\mathbf{x}, \mathbf{c}(\mathbf{x})) : \mathbf{c}(\mathbf{x}) = 1 \;\; if \;\; \mathbf{a}(\mathbf{x}) \in \mathrm{S}, \;\; otherwise \;\; \mathbf{c}(\mathbf{x}) = 0\}. \qquad (11.44)$$

As an example, the set $\mathbf{S}$ might be all the values in $\mathbf{R}$ greater than some threshold k. This is denoted $\chi_{>k}$, and $\chi_{>k}(\mathbf{a})$ is a thresholded version of the image $\mathbf{a}$.

11.9.2 Templates

The most powerful tools of image algebra are templates and template operations. The template unifies the concepts of templates, masks, windows, and neighborhood functions used in image processing. The concept of templates is different from that of structuring elements used in mathematical morphology. The difference will become clear when we explain the principle of templates.

Let $\mathbf{X}$ be the domain of the original image, and $\mathbf{Y}$ be the domain of the resulting image. In morphological image processing the domains of the original and the resulting image are the same. This is no longer true in image algebra. The template is a collection of images that has as many images as there are points in $\mathbf{Y}$. Thus, for each $\mathbf{y} \in \mathbf{Y}$, there is a corresponding real valued image $\mathbf{t_y}$ in the template given by

$$\mathbf{t_y} = \{(\mathbf{x}, \mathbf{t_y}(\mathbf{x}) : \mathbf{x} \in \mathbf{X}\}. \qquad (11.45)$$

The point $\mathbf{y}$ is called the target point of the template $\mathbf{t}$, and the values $(\mathbf{t_y}(\mathbf{x}) : \mathbf{x} \in \mathbf{X})$ are called the weights of the template $\mathbf{t}$ at $\mathbf{y}$. Consider the 3 x 3 structuring element shown in Fig. 11.33a. For the point (25,25) in the resulting image, the corresponding template image $\mathbf{t}_{(25,25)}$ is given in Figs. 11.33b and 11.33c. As can be seen in Fig. 11.33c, the template image at any point consists of the structuring element translated to that point. The rest of the template image is filled with $-\infty$. This is an example of a template which corresponds to a morphological structuring element.

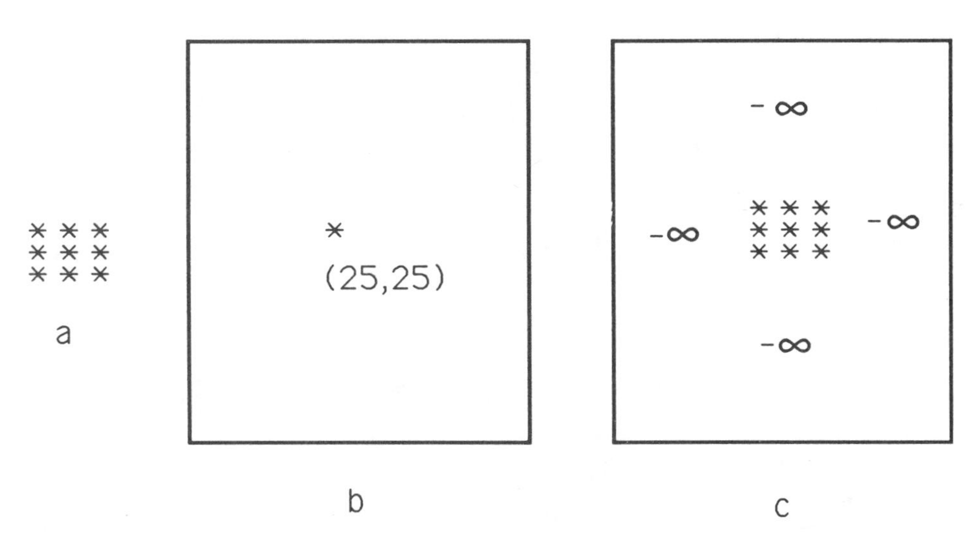

Figure 11.33: (a) 3×3 structuring element, (b) a one-point image, and (c) the template image corresponding to the one-point image. (c) was obtained by translating the structuring element by the image point and filling the background with $-\infty$.

The support of a real valued template is given by

$$\Im(\mathbf{t_y}) = \{\mathbf{x} \in \mathbf{X} : \mathbf{t_y}(\mathbf{x}) \neq 0\}, \tag{11.46}$$

while the infinite support of $\mathbf{t_y}$ is given as

$$\Im_{-\infty}(\mathbf{t_y}) = \{\mathbf{x} \in \mathbf{X} : \mathbf{t_y}(\mathbf{x}) \neq -\infty\}. \tag{11.47}$$

For the example in Fig. 11.33c, the nine pixels that are not $-\infty$ define the support of $\mathbf{t}_{(25,25)}$.

The transpose of $\mathbf{t_y}(\mathbf{x})$ is given by $\mathbf{t}'_\mathbf{y}(\mathbf{x}) = \mathbf{t_x}(\mathbf{y})$. The additive dual of the template $\mathbf{t}$ is the template $\mathbf{t}^*$, which is obtained by taking the transpose of $\mathbf{t}$ and changing the sign. Thus $\mathbf{t}^*_\mathbf{y}(\mathbf{x}) = -\mathbf{t_x}(\mathbf{y})$.

11.9.3 Operations between Images and Templates

The three basic operations between images and templates are denoted by $\oplus, \boxed{\vee}, \circledvee$, and called generalized convolution, additive maximum, and multiplicative maximum, respectively. These template operations transform each image point by pairing image and template values, performing some operation on the pairs, and then applying the basic operation of addition, maximum or multiplication to the resulting values.

The generalized backward convolution of image $\mathbf{a}$ by template $\mathbf{t}$ is defined by

$$\mathbf{a} \oplus \mathbf{t} = \{(\mathbf{y}, \mathbf{b}(\mathbf{y})) : \mathbf{b}(\mathbf{y}) = \sum_{\mathbf{x} \in \mathbf{X}} \mathbf{a}(\mathbf{x}) * \mathbf{t}_{\mathbf{y}}(\mathbf{x}), \mathbf{y} \in \mathbf{Y}\} \tag{11.48}$$

where $\mathbf{b}$ is the resulting image, $\mathbf{Y}$ is its domain, and $(\mathbf{y}, \mathbf{b}(\mathbf{y}))$ is an element in $\mathbf{b}$. Note that $\mathbf{t}_{\mathbf{y}}(\mathbf{x})$ is 0 outside its support. Thus, the convolution of $\mathbf{a}$ by $\mathbf{t}$ can be redefined as

$$\mathbf{a} \oplus \mathbf{t} = \{(\mathbf{y}, \mathbf{b}(\mathbf{y})) : \mathbf{b}(\mathbf{y}) = \sum_{\mathbf{x} \in \Im(\mathbf{t}_{\mathbf{y}})} \mathbf{a}(\mathbf{x}) * \mathbf{t}_{\mathbf{y}}(\mathbf{x}), \mathbf{y} \in \mathbf{Y}\}. \tag{11.49}$$

The backward additive maximum is defined as

$$\mathbf{a} \boxed{\vee} \mathbf{t} = \{(\mathbf{y}, \mathbf{b}(\mathbf{y})) : \mathbf{b}(\mathbf{y}) = \bigvee_{\mathbf{x} \in \Im(\mathbf{t}_{\mathbf{y}})} [\mathbf{a}(\mathbf{x}) + \mathbf{t}_{\mathbf{y}}(\mathbf{x})], \mathbf{y} \in \mathbf{Y}\} \tag{11.50}$$

where $\bigvee_{\mathbf{x} \in \Im(\mathbf{t}_{\mathbf{y}})}[(\mathbf{a}(\mathbf{x}) + \mathbf{t}_{\mathbf{y}}(\mathbf{x}))] = \max\{(\mathbf{a}(\mathbf{x}) + \mathbf{t}_{\mathbf{y}}(\mathbf{x})) : \mathbf{x} \in \mathbf{X}\}$.

The backward multiplicative maximum is defined as

$$\mathbf{a} \circledvee \mathbf{t} = \{(\mathbf{y}, \mathbf{b}(\mathbf{y})) : \mathbf{b}(\mathbf{y}) = \bigvee_{\mathbf{x} \in \Im(\mathbf{t}_{\mathbf{y}})} [\mathbf{a}(\mathbf{x}) * \mathbf{t}_{\mathbf{y}}(\mathbf{x})], \mathbf{y} \in \mathbf{Y}\}. \tag{11.51}$$

The generalized forward convolution of $\mathbf{a}$ by $\mathbf{t}$ is defined as

$$\mathbf{t} \oplus \mathbf{a} = \{(\mathbf{y}, \mathbf{b}(\mathbf{y})) : \mathbf{b}(\mathbf{y}) = \sum_{\mathbf{x} \in \Im(\mathbf{t}_{\mathbf{y}})} \mathbf{t}_{\mathbf{y}}(\mathbf{x}) * \mathbf{a}(\mathbf{x}), \mathbf{y} \in \mathbf{Y}\}. \tag{11.52}$$

The forward additive maximum is defined as

$$\mathbf{t} \boxed{\vee} \mathbf{a} = \{(\mathbf{y}, \mathbf{b}(\mathbf{y})) : \mathbf{b}(\mathbf{y}) = \bigvee_{\mathbf{x} \in \Im(\mathbf{t}_{\mathbf{y}})} [\mathbf{t}_{\mathbf{y}}(\mathbf{x}) + \mathbf{a}(\mathbf{x})], \mathbf{y} \in \mathbf{Y}\}. \tag{11.53}$$

The forward multiplicative maximum is defined as

$$\mathbf{t} \circledvee \mathbf{a} = \{(\mathbf{y}, \mathbf{b}(\mathbf{y})) : \mathbf{b}(\mathbf{y}) = \bigvee_{\mathbf{x} \in \Im(\mathbf{t}_{\mathbf{y}})} [\mathbf{t}_{\mathbf{y}}(\mathbf{x}) * \mathbf{a}(\mathbf{x})], \mathbf{y} \in \mathbf{Y}\}. \tag{11.54}$$

The operations $\boxed{\vee}$ and $\circledvee$ can be used to define the dual operations of additive minimum and multiplicative minimum. The additive minimum is defined as

$$\mathbf{a} \boxed{\wedge} \mathbf{t} = (\mathbf{t}^{*} \boxed{\vee} \mathbf{a}^{*})^{*}. \tag{11.55}$$

The multiplicative minimum is defined as

$$\mathbf{a} \,\textcircled{\wedge}\, \mathbf{t} = \overline{(\bar{\mathbf{t}} \,\textcircled{\vee}\, \bar{\mathbf{a}})} \tag{11.56}$$

where the overbar denotes the complement of the function or operaton below it.

A few examples of using image algebra for writing image processing algorithms are given below [37].

1. Local averaging on a 3 x 3 neighborhood: Let $\mathbf{a}$ be the image and $\mathbf{t}$ be the neighborhood template as given in Fig. 11.34. The new pixel value in the resulting image $\mathbf{B}$ is given by

$$\mathbf{c}(\mathbf{y}) = 1/9 \sum_{\mathbf{x} \in \Im(\mathbf{t_y})} \mathbf{a}(\mathbf{x}). \tag{11.57}$$

One has to code the above equation in some high level language which will take at least four to five lines of code. It can be executed using a single line of image algebra given by

$$(\mathbf{a} \oplus \mathbf{t}). \tag{11.58}$$

$\frac{1}{9}$	$\frac{1}{9}$	$\frac{1}{9}$
$\frac{1}{9}$	$\frac{1}{9}$	$\frac{1}{9}$
$\frac{1}{9}$	$\frac{1}{9}$	$\frac{1}{9}$

t

Figure 11.34: A 3 $\times$ 3 mask used for local averaging.

2. Dilation and erosion: The image algebra operators $\boxed{\vee}$ and $\boxed{\wedge}$ can be used to express the morphological operations of dilation and erosion for both binary and gray-scale images. This is based on the fact that dilation and erosion can be expressed in terms of local maxima and local minima, respectively. If $\mathbf{b}$ is the structuring element for dilation, then we determine the corresponding template $\mathbf{t}$ by setting $\Im(\mathbf{t_y}) = \mathbf{b}'_y$. Here $\mathbf{b_y}$ denotes the translation of $\mathbf{b}$ by the vector $\mathbf{y}$, where $\mathbf{y}$ is an element of $\mathbf{X}$. $\mathbf{X}$ is the domain of $\mathbf{c}$, the result of dilation, and $\mathbf{b}'_\mathbf{y}$ denotes the reflection of $\mathbf{b_y}$ about its origin. The template weights $\mathbf{t_y}(\mathbf{x})$ are defined to be the values assigned to $\mathbf{b}'_\mathbf{y}$ at location $\mathbf{x}$, and $\mathbf{t_y}(\mathbf{x}) = -\infty$ if $\mathbf{x}$ is not an element of $\mathbf{b}'_\mathbf{y}$. In image algebra terms the dilation of $\mathbf{a}$ by $\mathbf{b}$ can be expressed as one line of code

given by $\mathbf{a} \boxed{\vee} \mathbf{t}$. The erosion of $\mathbf{a}$ by $\mathbf{b}$ is given by $\mathbf{a} \boxed{\wedge} \mathbf{t}^*$. To write the dilation of $\mathbf{a}$ by $\mathbf{b}$ in Fortran would take at least ten lines of code.

3. Opening and Closing: Opening can be represented by a single line of code as given by $(\mathbf{a} \boxed{\wedge} \mathbf{t}^*) \boxed{\vee} \mathbf{t}$. Closing is given by $(\mathbf{a} \boxed{\vee} \mathbf{t}) \boxed{\wedge} \mathbf{t}^*$.

4. Edge Detection: Morphological edge detection is given by $(\mathbf{a} \boxed{\vee} \mathbf{t}) - \mathbf{a}$.

5. Hit or miss transform: The hit or miss transform is given by $(\mathbf{a} \boxed{\wedge} \mathbf{t}_1^*) * (\chi_0(\mathbf{a}) \boxed{\wedge} \mathbf{t}_2^*)$. Note that $\chi_0(\mathbf{a})$ represents the complement of $\mathbf{a}$.

6. Sobel edge detecton: The Sobel edge detector is given by $[(\mathbf{a} \oplus \mathbf{s})^2 + (\mathbf{a} \oplus \mathbf{t})^2]^{1/2}$ where the templates $\mathbf{s}$ and $\mathbf{t}$ are as given in Fig. 11.35.

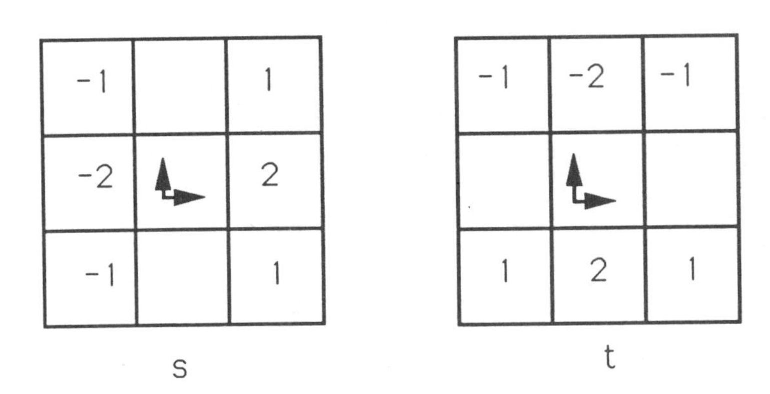

Figure 11.35: Two templates used for Sobel edge detection

11.10 COMMENTS ON IMAGE ALGEBRA

Previous authors have proven that the set of image algebra operations discussed in this section are sufficient to express any image-to-image transformation [31] and [38]. Image algebra contains structures such as linear algebra, mathematical morphology and recursive operations. It can also provides insight into solving image processing problems if one becomes familiar with the operations. One application has been to decompose templates into smaller templates [39], thereby providing a means for parallelizing morphological operations. Image algebra can be used to translate sequential-type algorithms to parallel-type algorithms [30]. Neural network algorithms can be written in image algebra and has led to the establishment of morphological neural networks [40]. Work is currently going on in the development of variant templates that can be used to filter noise [32].

11.11 Acknowledgments

The authors thank the Center for Nondestructive Evaluation and the Dept. of Electrical Engineering for support, and thank J. L. Davidson and Richard Wallingford for suggesting improvements to the manuscript.

References

[1] Matheron, G. *Elements Pour une Tiorre des Mulieux Poreux*, Masson, Paris, 1965.

[2] Matheron, G. *Random Sets and Integral Geometry*, Wiley, New York, 1975.

[3] Serra, J., *Image Analysis and Mathematical Morphology*, Academic Press, London, 1982.

[4] Giardina, C. R., and E. R. Dougherty, *Morphological Methods in Signal and Image Processing*, Prentice Hall, Englewood Cliffs, New Jersey, 1988.

[5] Pratt, W. K., *Digital Image Processing*, 2nd ed., Wiley, New York, 1991.

[6] Gonzalez, R. C., and R. E. Woods, *Digital Image Processing*, Addison-Wesley, Reading, Massachusetts, 1992.

[7] Sternberg, S. R., Pipeline architectures for image processing, in *Multi-computers and Image Processing*, Preston and L. Uhr, eds., Academic Press, New York, 291-305, 1982.

[8] Sternberg, S. R., Cellular computers and biomedical image processing, *Biomedical Images and Processing*, J. Sklansky, and J. C. Bisconte, eds. Springer-Verlag Berlin, 294-319, 1988.

[9] Nakagawa, Y., and A. Rosenfeld, A note on the use of local min and max operators in digital image processing, *IEEE Trans. Syst., Man, Cybern.*, **8**, 632-635, 1978.

[10] Gader, P. D., and C. R. Giardina, *Image Algebra and Morphological Image Processing*, SPIE Press, Bellingham, Washington, 1990.

[11] Gader, P. D., and C. R. Giardina, *Image Algebra and Morphological Image Processing*, SPIE Press, Bellingham, Washington, 1991.

[12] Peleg, S., and A. Rosenfeld, A min max medial axis transformation, *IEEE Trans. Pattern Anal. Machine Intell.*, **3**, 206-210, 1981.

[13] Werman, M., and S. Peleg, Min-max operators in texture analysis, *IEEE Trans. Pattern Anal. Machine Intell.*, **7**, 730-733, 1985.

[14] Coleman, E. N., and R. E. Sampson, Acquisition of Randomly Oriented Workpieces Through Structure Mating, *Proc. Computer Vision Pattern Recognition Conf.*, 350-357, 1982.

[15] Serra, J., Introduction to Mathematical Morphology, *Computer Vision, Graphics, and Image Processing*, **35**, 283-305, 1986.

[16] Sternberg, S. R., Grayscale Morphology, in *Computer Vision, Graphics, and Image Processing*, **35**, 333-355, 1986.

[17] Haralick, R. M., S. R. Sternberg, and X. Xinhua, Image Analysis Using Mathematical Morphology, *IEEE Transactions on PAMI*, **9**(4), 532-550, 1987.

[18] Maragos, P., and R. W. Schafer, Applications of Morphological Filtering to Image Processing and Analysis, *Proc. IEEE Int. Conf. ASSP*, 2067-2070, 1986.

[19] Maragos, P., and R. W. Schafer, Morphological Filters, *IEEE Trans. Acoust., Speech, Signal Processing*, **35**, 1153-1185, 1987.

[20] Chen, M., and P. Yan, A Multiscaling Approach Based on Morphological Filtering, *IEEE Transactions on PAMI*, **7**, 694-700, 1989.

[21] Song, J., and E. J. Delp, A generalization of morphological filters using multiple structuring elements, *Proc. of the 1989 IEEE International Symposium on Circuits and Systems*, 991-994, 1989.

[22] Lantuejoul, C., and J. Serra, M-Filters *Proc. IEEE Int. Conf. Acoust., Speech, Signal Processing*, 2063-2066, 1982.

[23] Zhuang, X. and R. M. Haralick, Morphological Structuring Element Decomposition, *Computer Vision, Graphics, and Image Processing*, **35**, 370-382 (1986).

[24] Meyer, F., Automatic Screening of Cytological Specimens, *Computer Vision, Graphics, and Image Processing*, **35**, 356-369, 1986.

[25] Meyer, F., Iterative image transformations on an automatic screening of cervical smears, *J. Histochem. Cytochem.*, **27**, 128-135, 1979.

[26] Lee, J. S. J., R. M. Haralick, and L. G. Shapiro, Morphologic Edge Detection, *Digital Image Processing in Industrial Applications*, 7-14, 1986.

[27] Beucher, S., and C. Lantejoul, *Use of Watersheds in Contour Dectection*, Proc. Int'l Workshop on Image Processing, CCETT, Rennes, France, 1979.

[28] Russ, J. C., *Computer-Assisted Microscopy*, Plenum Press, New York, 1990.

[29] Chackalackal, M. S., and J. P. Basart, *NDE X-Ray Image Analysis Using Mathematical Morphology, Review of Progress in Quantitative Nondestructive Evaluation*, D. O. Thompson and D. E. Chementi, eds. Plenum Press, New York, **9A**, 721-728, 1989.

[30] Ritter, G. X., J. N. Wilson, and J. L. Davidson, Image Algebra: An Overview, *Comp. Vision, Graphics, and Image Process.*, **49**, 297-331, 1990.

[31] Ritter, G. X., and J. N. Wilson, Image Algebra: A Unified Approach to Image Processing, *Proc. SPIE Medical Imaging Conference*, Newport Beach, CA, 1987.

[32] Davidson, J. L., Lattice Structures in the Image Algebra and Applications to Image Processing, *Ph. D. Thesis Univ. of Florida, Dept. of Math.*, Gainesville, FL, 1989.

[33] Ritter, G. X., and P. D. Gader, Image Algebra Implementation on Cellular Array Computers, *IEEE Computer Society Workshop on Computer Architecture for Pattern Analysis and Image Database Management*, Miami Beach, FL, 430-438, 1985.

[34] Ritter, G. X., and P. D. Gader, Image Algebra Techniques for Parallel Image Processing, *Parallel Distributed Computing*, **4**(5), 7-44, 1987.

[35] Sternberg, S. R., Language and Architecture for Parallel Image Processing, *Proc. Conf. on Pattern Recog. in Practice*, Amsterdam, 1980.

[36] Sternberg, S. R., Overview of Image Algebra and Related Issues, in *Integrated Technology for Parallel Image Processing*, S. Levialdi, ed., Academic Press, London, 1985.

[37] Ritter, G. X., J. N. Wilson, and J. L. Davidson, Image Algebra Application to Image Measurement and Feature Extraction, *Proc. of the 1989 SPIE OE/LASE 1989 Optics, Elec.-Optics, and Laser Appl. in Sci. and Egnr.*, Los Angeles, 1989.

[38] Ritter, G. X., M. A. Shrader-Frechette, and J. N. Wilson, Image Algebra: A Rigorous and Translucent Way of Approaching All Image Processing Operations, *Proc. 1987 SPIE Tech. Symp. Southeast on Optics, Elec.-Optics, and Sensors*, Orlando, FL, 1987.

[39] Davidson, J. L., Nonlinear Matrix Decompositions an Application to Parallel Processing, *J. of Math. Imaging and Vision*, submitted, 1991.

[40] Davidson, J. L., and G. X. Ritter, Theory of Morphological Neural Networks, *Proc. of the 1990 SPIE OE/LASE 1989 Optics, Elec.-Optics, and Laser Appl. in Sci. and Egnr.*, Los Angeles, **1215**, 378-388, 1990.

Chapter 12
Model-Based Morphology: The Opening Spectrum

R. M. Haralick, E. R. Dougherty, P. L. Katz

12.1 Introduction

Filtering by morphological operations is particularly suited for removal of clutter and noise objects which have been introduced into noiseless binary images. The morphological filtering is designed to exploit differences in the spatial nature (shape, size, orientation) of the objects (connected components) in the ideal noiseless images as compared to the noise/clutter objects.

Since the typical noise models (union, intersection set difference, etc.) for binary images are not additive, and the morphological processing is strongly nonlinear, optimal filtering results conventionally available for linear processing in the presence of additive noise are not directly applicable to morphological filtering of binary images.

In this paper we describe a morphological filtering analog to the classic Wiener filter, a preliminary account having been given in [1]. The discussion begins in Section 2 with a review of the Wiener filter and its extension to a Binary Wiener filter; in these the underlying model entails decomposing the signal and additive noise into spectral elements in terms of an orthogonal basis set. Classic Wiener optimal estimation weights the respective spectral elements in the noisy signal according to the expected values of signal and noise energy across the spectrum. Section 3 extracts the essence of the algebraic structure underlying the derivation of the Wiener filter, doing so in a way that retains the concepts of energy and spectral decomposition, but eliminates the assumptions of noise additivity, orthogonal bases, and even the concept of inner product. The stage is thus set for the subsequent morphological filtering results where those assumptions do not apply. Section 4 derives an optimal morphological filter for binary images composed of the union (not sum) of the signal and noise connected components. The spectral decomposition of signal and noise is in terms of an ordered basis of connected components where the ordering is based on the morphological opening operation. (Such a basis is, in a certain sense, a "nested" collection of sets.) Thus the underlying model is based upon that ordered basis (which provides prototypes of signal and noise objects scattered throughout the binary image) and upon a morphological spectrum derived from openings. Section 5 expands the results of Section 4 beyond allowing signal and noise objects to be taken from a single ordered basis (e.g. an ordered set of discs). In Section 5, the collection of prototypes can include any number of coordinated ordered bases (e.g. an ordered set of discs, as well as an ordered set of squares, as well as several ordered sets of lines each at different orientations.)

Whereas in the first five section we restrict ourselves to finite-component spectral representation, in Section 6 we treat the continuous case for a single ordered basis. Section 7 extends these results to multiple ordered bases. In

Section 8 we compare the opening-spectrum filter discussed herein to mean-square morphological-filter estimation.

12.2 The Wiener Filter

Regarding the discrete Wiener filter, let $b_1, \ldots, b_n$ be an orthonormal basis. The model for the ideal random signal f is that $f = \sum_{n=1}^{N} \alpha_n b_n$ where $E[\alpha_n] = 0, V[\alpha_n] = \sigma_{f_n}^2$, and $E[\alpha_m \alpha_n] = 0, m \neq n$. The variances $\sigma_{f_n}^2$ are taken to be known. The model for the random noise g is that $g = \sum_{n=1}^{N} \beta_n b_n$ where $E[\beta_n] = 0, V[\beta_n] = \sigma_{g_n}^2$, and $E[\beta_m \beta_n] = 0, m \neq n$. Noise and signal are uncorrelated so that $E[\alpha_n \beta_m] = 0$.

The observed noisy signal is $f + g = \sum_{n=1}^{N} (\alpha_n + \beta_n) b_n$. The Wiener filtering problem is to determine weights $w_1, \ldots, w_N$ to make the estimate $\hat{f}$ of f, $\hat{f} = \sum_{n=1}^{N} w_n(\alpha_n + \beta_n) b_n$ minimize $E[\rho(f, \hat{f})]$, where ρ is a metric. In the case of Euclidean distance for the metric ρ, $E[\rho(f, \hat{f})] = E[||f - \hat{f}||^2]$.

Now,

$$\begin{aligned} ||f - \hat{f}||^2 &= ||\sum_{n=1}^{N} \alpha_n b_n - \sum_{n=1}^{N} w_n(\alpha_n + \beta_n) b_n||^2 \\ &= \sum_{n=1}^{N} [w_n(\alpha_n + \beta_n) - \alpha_n]^2 \end{aligned} \tag{1}$$

And

$$\begin{aligned} E\left[||f - \hat{f}||^2\right] &= \sum_{n=1}^{N} E[(w_n(\alpha_n + \beta_n) - \alpha_n)^2] \\ &= \sum_{n=1}^{N} w_n^2(\sigma_{f_n}^2 + \sigma_{g_n}^2) - 2w_n \sigma_{f_n}^2 + \sigma_{f_n}^2 \end{aligned} \tag{2}$$

Hence, the minimizing weights are given by

$$w_n = \frac{\sigma_{f_n}^2}{\sigma_{f_n}^2 + \sigma_{g_n}^2}. \tag{3}$$

One can also define a binary Wiener filter, with weights restricted to 0 or 1. To determine the minimizing weights, we need just examine

$$w_n^2(\sigma_{f_n}^2 + \sigma_{g_n}^2) - 2w_n \sigma_{f_n}^2 + \sigma_{f_n}^2 = \begin{cases} \sigma_{f_n}^2 & \text{if } w_n = 0 \\ \sigma_{g_n}^2 & \text{if } w_n = 1 \end{cases} \tag{4}$$

Hence, under the constraint that the $w_n \in \{0, 1\}$, the minimizing weights are given by

$$w_n = \begin{cases} 0 & \text{if } \sigma_{f_n}^2 < \sigma_{g_n}^2 \\ 1 & \text{otherwise} \end{cases} \tag{5}$$

In this case the estimate $\hat{f} = \sum_{n \in S} (\alpha_n + \beta_n) b_n$, where $S = \{n | w_n = 1\}$. Thus the optimal binary Wiener filter retains that part of the spectrum where the expected signal energy exceeds the expected noise energy, and discards the rest.

12.3 Optimal Filtering in the Generalized Case

This section restates the binary Wiener filter results, retaining the classic algebraic structure under far less restrictive assumptions than those of Section 2. The new assumptions will in fact be consistent with the morphological filter we will develop in Section 4. Specifically we now relax the assumptions of additive noise, vector norms, inner products, and orthonormal bases, replacing them with more general assumptions on the nature of noise inclusion, distance, energy, and spectral decomposition, and the relationships between them.

Let f be any binary image in a set B of binary images and ψ be a mapping (a spectral decomposition) taking f into the N-tuple $(f_1, \ldots, f_N)$; that is $\psi : B \to B^N$. (In the case of the Wiener filter, the N-tuple $(f_1, \ldots, f_N)$ is $(\alpha_1 b_1, \ldots, \alpha_N b_N)$. Here, we incorporate into each f_n both the scalar and the basis elements.) Let ψ^{-1} be the inverse mapping re-assembling $(f_1, \ldots, f_N)$ back into f; that is $\psi^{-1} : B^N \to B$. The identity operator can be expressed as $\psi\psi^{-1}$ and $\psi^{-1}\psi$. For any two binary images f and g in B let there be defined a binary operation $<>$ such that $f <> g$ is also a binary image in B. When g is the noise, $f <> g$ corresponds to the observed noisy binary image. We require that $<>$ and ψ satisfy the relationship

$$\psi(f <> g) = (f_1 <> g_1, \ldots, f_N <> g_N). \tag{6}$$

Let ρ be the function evaluating the closeness of one image to another. Hence $\rho : B \times B \to [0, \infty)$. The function ρ must satisfy $\rho(f, h) = \sum_{n=1}^{N} \rho(f_n, h_n)$ where $\psi(f) = (f_1, \ldots, f_N)$ and $\psi(h) = (h_1, \ldots, h_N)$.

For any binary image g, we let $\#$ represent the operator which quantifies the energy in the binary image g; $\# : B \to [0, \infty)$. The operator $\#$ must satisfy $\#g = \sum_{n=1}^{N} \#g_n$, for spectral decomposition $\psi(g) = (g_1, \ldots, g_N)$. Finally, there is a relationship between ρ and $\#$: The distance between the binary image and the ideal image is just the energy in the noise image; $\rho(f <> g, f) = \#g$.

Let $w_n \in \{0, 1\}, n = 1, \ldots, N$ be binary weights and let the filtered binary image have a representation $(w_1(f_1 <> g_1), \ldots, w_N(f_N <> g_N))$ where

$$w_n(f_n <> g_n) = \begin{cases} f_n <> g_n & \text{if } w_n = 1 \\ \phi & \text{if } w_n = 0 \end{cases} \tag{7}$$

and ϕ is the binary image satisfying $f <> \phi = f$. The filtered binary image $\hat{f}$ itself can then be written as

$$\hat{f} = \psi^{-1}\left(w_1(f_1 <> g_1), \ldots, w_n(f_N, <> g_N)\right). \tag{8}$$

In essence the effect of the filtering is obtained by nulling spectral content of the observed noisy binary image.

The optimal filter parameters w_n are chosen to minimize

$$\begin{aligned} E[\rho(\hat{f}, f)] &= E\left[\sum_{n=1}^{N} \rho(\hat{f}_n, f_n)\right] = \sum_{n=1}^{N} E[\rho(w_n(f_n <> g_n), f_n)] \\ &= \sum_{n=1}^{N} E\left[\begin{cases} \#g_n & \text{if } w_n = 1 \\ \#f_n & \text{if } w_n = 0 \end{cases}\right]. \end{aligned} \tag{9}$$

Hence, the best value for w_n is given by

$$w_n = \begin{cases} 0 & \text{if } E[\#f_n] < E[\#g_n] \\ 1 & \text{otherwise.} \end{cases} \tag{10}$$

Then the index set S corresponding to the spectral content that will be included in the optimal filter output can be defined by $S = \{n | E[\#f_n] \geq E[\#g_n]\}$.

12.4 Optimal Binary Morphological Filter

To apply the foregoing algebraic filtering paradigm to mathematical morphology, we need to define the ideal random image model, the random noise model, the relationship of the observed image to the ideal random image and random noise, the formulation of representation operator ψ from morphological operators, the energy measure $\#$, and the closeness measure ρ. We begin with the representation operator ψ, which will be formulated relative to morphological opening, where the opening of binary image A by structuring element K is defined by

$$A \circ K = \bigcup \{K_x : K_x \subseteq A\} \tag{11}$$

where subscripts having names like x or y designate a translation of the set subscripted and where we assume all images are compact subsets of k-dimensional Euclidean space R^K. (See Haralick, Sternberg, and Zhuang [3], Dougherty and Giardina [4,5], or Serra [2] for the fundamental properties of the morphological opening.)

The representation operator ψ will be defined in a manner akin to the morphological granulometric pattern spectrum. To set up our definition for ψ in a way which relates to the ideal random image and noise models, we note that the opening operator has the following property: If $A = \bigcup_{i=1}^{I} A_i$, where each A_i is a connected component of A, and K is a connected structuring element, then

$$A \circ K = (\bigcup_{i=1}^{I} A_i) \circ K = \bigcup_{i=1}^{I} (A_i \circ K). \tag{12}$$

This property, that the opening of a union of connected components is the union of the openings, will be essential throughout our development. It is this property which motivates the following definition: Two sets A and B are said to not interfere with one another if and only if X, a connected component of $A \cup B$, implies that X is a connected component of A or of B but not both. It immediately follows that if A and B do not interfere with one another and K is a connected structuring element, then

$$(A \cup B) \circ K = (A \circ K) \cup (B \circ K). \tag{13}$$

The *opening-spectrum* operator ψ will be defined in terms of a set of openings. This set of openings will be based on the structuring elements in a naturally ordered morphological basis. We define a collection $\mathcal{K}$ of structuring elements to be an *opening spectrum basis* if and only if $K \in \mathcal{K}$ implies K is connected and $K, L \in \mathcal{K}$ implies $K \circ L = K$ or $K \circ L = \phi$. A opening-spectrum basis $\mathcal{K} = \{K(1), \ldots, K(M)\}$ is *naturally ordered* if and only if $K(1) = \{0\}$ and

$$K(i) \circ K(j) = \begin{cases} K(i) & j \leq i \\ \phi & j > i. \end{cases} \tag{14}$$

A simple example of an ordered opening-spectrum basis is a set of squares of increasing size, beginning with a square of one pixel.

Now we can define the operator ψ which produces a opening-spectrum with respect to a naturally ordered opening-spectrum basis $\mathcal{K} = \{K(1), \ldots, K(M)\}$. ψ is defined by $\psi(A) = (A_1, \ldots, A_M)$ where

$$A_m = A \circ K(m) - A \circ K(m+1) \tag{15}$$

for $m = 1, \ldots, M-1$, $A_M = A \circ K(M)$, and $K(1) = \{0\}$. A_m is that part of A which is open under $K(m)$ but not open under $K(m+1)$, except for A_M which is A opened by $K(M)$. A_M is the remainder. $K(1) = \{0\}$ assures that A_1 contains everything in A that does not fit any of the larger $K(M)$'s. It follows from this definition that for $i \neq j$, $A_i \cap A_j = \phi$. This happens because

$$\begin{aligned} A_i \cap A_j &= [A \circ K(i) - A \circ K(i+1)] \cap [A \circ K(j) - A \circ K(j+1)] \\ &= [A \circ K(i) \cap A \circ K(j)] \cap [A \circ K(i+1) \cup A \circ K(j+1)]^c \\ &= [A \circ K(\max\{i,j\})] \cap [A \circ K(\min\{i+1, j+1\})] \\ &= \phi \text{ since } \max\{i,j\} \geq \min\{i+1, j+1\} \text{ for any } i \neq j,\ i,j < M \end{aligned} \tag{16}$$

For the special case $j = M$ and for $i < M$, the derivation is

$$\begin{aligned} A_i \cap A_M &= [A \circ K(i) - A \circ K(i+1)] \cap A \circ K(M) \\ &= ([A \circ K(i) \cap [A \circ K(M)]) \cap [A \circ K(i+1)]^c \\ &= A \circ K(M) \cap [A \circ K(i+1)]^c \quad \text{since } A \circ K(i) \supseteq A \circ K(M) \\ &= \phi \quad \text{since } A \circ K(i+1) \supseteq A \circ K(M) \end{aligned} \tag{17}$$

It is easy to see that from the opening spectrum, $(A_1, \ldots, A_M)$, the original shape A can be exactly reconstructed since $\bigcup_{m=1}^{M} A_m = A$. This can be seen directly. Consider

$$\begin{aligned} \bigcup_{m=1}^{M} A_m = [A \circ K(1) - A \circ K(2)] \cup \ldots \\ \cup [A \circ K(M-1) - A \circ K(M)] \cup A \circ K(M) \end{aligned} \tag{18}$$

Since $K(i) \circ K(j) = K(i)$ for $i \geq j$, $A \circ K(j) \supseteq A \circ K(i)$ for $i \geq j$. (19)

Hence the sets $A \circ K(1), A \circ K(2), \ldots, A \circ K(M)$ are ordered in the sense that

$$A \circ K(1) \supseteq A \circ K(2) \supseteq \ldots \supseteq A \circ K(M) \tag{20}$$

From this it follows that for any $m \geq 2$,

$$[A \circ K(m-1) - A \circ K(m)] \cup A \circ K(m) = A \circ K(m-1) \tag{21}$$

Now by working from the right end of the union representation, taking two terms at a time, the entire union is seen to collapse to $A \circ K(1) = A$.

ψ^{-1} can then be defined by $\psi^{-1}(A_1, \ldots, A_M) = \bigcup_{m=1}^{M} A_m$. The existence of ψ^{-1} implies that the representation is unique in the sense that two different opening spectra must be associated with two different shapes and two different shapes must be associated with two different opening spectra. It implies, as well, that the representation is complete.

Next we discuss the spatial random process generation mechanism which produces binary image realizations. A spatial random process producing a set A is a non-interfering spatial Poisson process with respect to an ordered opening-spectrum basis $\mathcal{K}$ if and only if:

- For some Z, a Poisson distributed random number (with Poisson density parameter λ_A), which is the total connected component count of a binary image realization A;
- For some multinomial distributed numbers $L_1, \ldots, L_M$ with $\sum_{m=1}^{M} L_m = Z$ (with respective multinomial probabilities $p_1, \ldots, p_M$), which split the Z connected components into M subsets containing objects of the same type;
- For some randomly chosen translations $x_{mj}, m = 1, \ldots, M;\ j = 1, \ldots, L_m$;
- $A = \bigcup_{m=1}^{M} \bigcup_{j=1}^{L_m} K(m)_{x_{mj}}$, where the translated structuring elements do not interfere, i.e.,

$$K(i)_{x_{ij}} \bigcap K(m)_{x_{mn}} = \begin{cases} K(i)_{x_{ij}} & \text{if } i = m \text{ and } j = n \\ \phi & \text{otherwise.} \end{cases} \tag{22}$$

From this definition of a non-interfering random process, it follows that

$$\begin{aligned} A \circ K(\lambda) &= \left(\bigcup_{m=1}^{M} \bigcup_{j=1}^{L_m} K(m)_{x_{mj}} \right) \circ K(\lambda) \\ &= \bigcup_{m=1}^{M} \bigcup_{j=1}^{L_m} [K(m)_{x_{mj}} \circ K(\lambda)] \\ &= \bigcup_{m=\lambda}^{M} \bigcup_{j=1}^{L_m} K(m)_{x_{mj}} \end{aligned} \tag{23}$$

Moreover, if $\psi(A) = (A_1, \ldots, A_M)$, then

$$A_m = \bigcup_{j=1}^{L_m} K(m)_{x_{mj}} \tag{24}$$

for $m = 1, \ldots, M$. We interpret these results in the following manner: If A is opened by the λth basis structuring element, all components originating from "smaller" (lower-numbered) basis structuring elements are removed; the opening spectrum of A (with respect to the basis from which it was built) sorts A according to the index number of the underlying basis structuring elements, and leaves nothing out.

We consider both the ideal random image and the noise image to be generated by non-interfering random spatial processes. The observed noisy image is the union of the ideal image with a noise/clutter image. This motivates a definition of non-interfering spatial processes which here plays the role of the zero correlation between the coefficients of the image process and the coefficients of the noise process in the Wiener filter case. A random process generating realization D and a random process generating realization E are said to be non-interfering random processes if and only if D and E are always non-interfering sets for each realization.

We can now define an observed noisy image. Let A be a realization of a non-interfering spatial process (with respect to an ordered opening-spectrum basis $\mathcal{K}$) producing images of interest and let N be a realization of a non-interfering spatial process (with respect to the same $\mathcal{K}$) producing noise/clutter. We suppose that these processes do not interfere with one another. The observed noisy realization is defined as $A \cup N$. Let $\psi(A) = (A_1, \ldots, A_M), \psi(N) = (N_1, \ldots, N_M)$, and $\psi(A \cup N) = (B_1, \ldots, B_M)$. Then $B_m = A_m \cup N_m$. We reason as follows.

$$B_m = (A \cup N) \circ K(m) - (A \cup N) \circ K(m+1), \tag{25}$$

for $m = 1, \ldots, M-1$, and

$$B_M = (A \cup N) \circ K(M). \tag{26}$$

Because the processes do not interfere with one another,

$$\begin{aligned} B_m &= [A \circ K(m) \cup N \circ K(m)] - [A \circ K(m+1) \cup N \circ K(m+1)] \\ &= [A \circ K(m) - A \circ K(m+1)] \cup [N \circ K(m) - N \circ K(m+1)] \\ &= A_m \cup N_m \\ \text{and} \quad B_M &= A \circ K(m) \bigcup B \circ K(m) \\ &= A_M \bigcup N_M \end{aligned} \tag{27}$$

Thus we have just seen that

$$\psi(A \cup N) = (A_1 \cup N_1, \ldots, A_M \cup N_M). \tag{28}$$

The filtered image $\hat{A}$ will be based on selecting the most appropriate components from the opening-spectrum of $A \cup N$. Letting S be the set of components selected, we estimate A by $\hat{A}$ where

$$\hat{A} = \bigcup_{m \in S} (A_m \cup N_m) \text{ or } \hat{A} = \bigcup_{m \in S} B_m. \tag{29}$$

Thus by choosing the form of the estimation analogously to that of the binary Wiener filter, the estimation problem becomes one of choosing an appropriate index set S.

To determine S, we must first state our error criterion. For any two sets A and $\hat{A}$, we define the closeness (non-overlap) of A to $\hat{A}$ by $\rho(A, \hat{A}) = \#[(A-\hat{A}) \cup (\hat{A}-A)]$ where $\#$ is the set counting measure (pixel count, area). Our error criterion is then

$$E[\rho(A, \hat{A})] = E\left\{\#[(A - \hat{A}) \cup (\hat{A} - A)]\right\}. \tag{30}$$

To see how to choose S to minimize $E\left\{\#[(A - \hat{A}) \cup (\hat{A} - A)]\right\}$, first note that

$$\begin{aligned} A - \hat{A} &= \bigcup_{m=1}^{M} A_m - \bigcup_{m \in S} (A_m \cup N_m) = \bigcup_{\substack{m=1 \\ m \notin S}}^{M} A_m \\ \hat{A} - A &= \bigcup_{m \in S} A_m \cup N_m - \bigcup_{m=1}^{M} A_m = \bigcup_{m \in S} N_m. \end{aligned} \tag{31}$$

Hence,

$$\begin{aligned} \rho(A, \hat{A}) &= \#[(A - \hat{A}) \cup (\hat{A} - A)] \\ &= \#(A - \hat{A}) + \#(\hat{A} - A) \\ &= \# \bigcup_{\substack{m=1 \\ m \notin S}}^{M} A_m + \# \bigcup_{m \in S} N_m \\ &= \sum_{\substack{m=1 \\ m \notin S}}^{M} \#A_m + \sum_{m \in S} \#N_m \end{aligned} \tag{32}$$

The two summations above are respectively the area of the ideal image left out, plus the noise and clutter area left in. The individual terms decompose that area by spectral content.

Now, since each spectral component is built of translates of the same basis structuring elements, and since non-interference implies mutual exclusivity,

$$\begin{aligned} \#A_m &= \# \bigcup_{j=1}^{L_m} K(m)_{x_{mj}} \\ &= \sum_{j=1}^{L_m} \#K(m)_{x_{mj}} = L_m \#K(m) \end{aligned} \tag{33}$$

so that

$$E[\#A_m] = \#K(m) p_m \lambda_A \mathcal{A} \tag{34}$$

where p_m is the multinomial probability for the ideal image process, λ_A is the Poisson density parameter of the ideal image process, and $\mathcal{A}$ is the area of the image spatial domain. Likewise, $E[\#N_m] = \#K(m) q_m \lambda_N \mathcal{A}$, where q_m is the multinomial probability for the noise process and λ_N is the Poisson density parameter of the noise process.

To determine the index set S, we then have

$$E\left\{\#[(A-\hat{A})\cup(\hat{A}-A)]\right\} = E\left[\sum_{m=1}^{M}\begin{cases}\#A_m & m\notin S\\ \#N_m & m\in S\end{cases}\right] = \sum_{m=1}^{M}\begin{cases}E[\#A_m] & m\notin S\\ E[\#N_m] & m\in S\end{cases} \tag{35}$$

Hence, the best S is defined by

$$S = \{m|E[\#N_m] < E[\#A_m]\}, \tag{36}$$

or equivalently for the statistical assumptions made,

$$S = \{m|q_m\lambda_N < p_m\lambda_A\}. \tag{37}$$

A spectral component is retained according to the relative expectations of that component's "leave-out" of ideal image vs. "leave-in" of noise and clutter.

Figure 1 illustrates the concept of the filter. A is the ideal binary image; B is the observed noisy image. There are four structuring elements K(1), K(2), K(3), and K(4) which constitute an ordered basis. The four component images are given by

$$B1 = B\circ K(1) - B\circ K(2)$$
$$B2 = B\circ K(2) - B\circ K(3)$$
$$B3 = B\circ K(3) - B\circ K(4)$$
$$B4 = B\circ K(4)$$

Notice that all the binary-one pixels in B1 are noise. So the index set S, which selects which components constitute the filtered image, will not contain the index 1. The component images B2 and B3 contain more ideal image than noise so indices 2 and 3 are in S. Finally, the component image B4 has more noise than ideal image. Hence index 4 is not in S. The filtered image $\hat{A}$ is then defined by $\hat{A} = B2\cup B3$.

12.5 Extension to Generalized (Tau-)Openings

The results we have just obtained can be extended to where the opening operation is changed to a generalized opening operation. Recall that in the previous section, each basic structuring element was just a set K. In the generalized opening operation, each basic structuring element is a collection Q of sets. The generalized opening of an image I with Q is then defined by:

$$I\circ Q = \bigcup_{L'\in Q} I\circ L'. \tag{38}$$

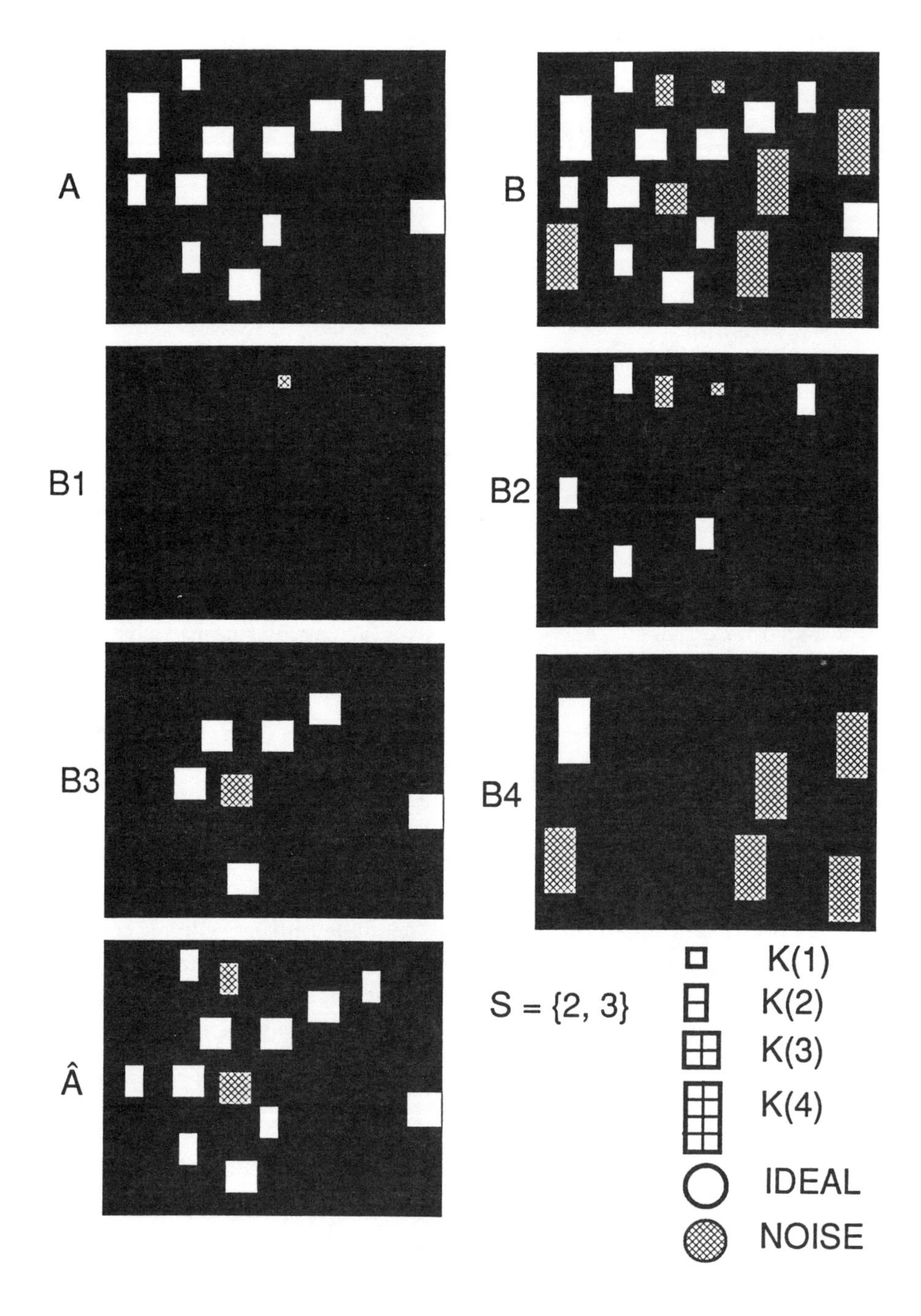

Figure 1 Figure 1 illustrates the filtering process. A is the ideal image; B is the observed noisy image. Using structuring elements K(1), K(2), K(3), and K(4) as the ordered basis produces component images B1, B2, B3, and B4. Component images B2 and B3 have more ideal image than noise, so the filtered image $\hat{A}$ is $B2 \cup B3$.

Regarding such generalized openings, Matheron [6] calls a filter Ψ a tau-opening if it satisfies four properties: it must be (1) anti-extensive, $\Psi(A) \subseteq A$; (2) translation invariant, $\Psi(A_x) = [\Psi(A)]_x$; (3) increasing, $A \subseteq B$ implies $\Psi(A) \subseteq \Psi(B)$; and (4) idempotent, $\Psi\Psi = \Psi$. The basic Matheron representation for tau-openings is that Ψ is a tau-opening if and only if there exists a collection Q such that Ψ is defined by eq. (38). Moreover, Q is a *base* for Inv[Ψ], the invariant class of Ψ; that is, the invariants for Ψ are unions of translations of elements in Q. For an elementary opening $A \circ K$, (K) is the base. The Matheron representation is discussed by Dougherty and Giardina [4,5], the gray-scale exension is given in [5], and both Serra [7] and Ronse and Heijmans [8] give lattice extensions.

The generalization is important because of the way it extends the underlying signal and noise spatial random process generation mechanism. For example, if the structuring elements were all line segments, the structuring element collection Q could consist of multiple orientation of line segments of the same length. The corresponding spatial random process would place non-interfering line segments at different orientations on the image. Or, the spatial random process could place non-interfering line segments, disks, or squares, on the image. For each size, the corresponding structuring element collection could be: line segments of the given size at a variety of orientations, a disk of the given size, and a square of the given size.

To see how the generalized opening can be used, we illustrate the case for which each structuring element collection contains exactly two structuring elements. Let $\mathcal{K} = \{K(1), \ldots, K(M)\}$ and $\mathcal{J} = \{J(1), \ldots, J(M)\}$ be naturally ordered opening bases. Define the collection $\mathcal{Q}$ by $\mathcal{Q} = \{Q(1), \ldots, Q(M)\}$ where $Q(m) = \{K(m), J(m)\}, m = 1, \ldots, M$. To make the ordering of the collection $\mathcal{K}$ and the collection $\mathcal{J}$ compatible, we require that

$$K(i) \circ J(j) = J(i) \circ K(j) = \phi \tag{39}$$

for $j > i$. Q is called a *generalized opening basis.*

Now, using the generalized opening operator, consider

$$\begin{aligned} K(i) \circ Q(j) &= K(i) \circ K(j) \cup K(i) \circ J(j) \\ &= \begin{cases} K(i) & i \geq j \\ \phi & \text{otherwise} \end{cases} \end{aligned} \tag{40}$$

Likewise,

$$\begin{aligned} J(i) \circ Q(j) &= J(i) \circ K(j) \cup J(i) \circ J(j) \\ &= \begin{cases} J(i) & i \geq j \\ \phi & \text{otherwise} \end{cases} \end{aligned} \tag{41}$$

Suppose that a realization A for a non-interfering process can be written as

$$A = \left[\bigcup_{m=1}^{M} \bigcup_{j=1}^{L_j^K} K(m)_{x_{mj}} \right] \bigcup \left[\bigcup_{m=1}^{M} \bigcup_{j=1}^{L_j^J} J(m)_{y_{mj}} \right] \tag{42}$$

where the sets in the collection

$$\{K(m)_{x_{mj}}, J(m)_{y_{mj}} : i = 1, \ldots, L_m^K, j = 1, \ldots, L_m^J\}_{m=1}^M \tag{43}$$

are naturally non-interfering. Then

$$\begin{aligned} A \circ Q(\lambda) &= \left[\bigcup_{m=1}^{M}\bigcup_{j=1}^{L_j^K} K(m)_{x_{mj}} \bigcup \bigcup_{m=1}^{M}\bigcup_{j=1}^{L_j^J} J(m)_{y_{mj}}\right] \circ Q(\lambda) \\ &= \bigcup_{m=1}^{M}\bigcup_{j=1}^{L_j^K} [K(m)_{x_{mj}} \circ Q(\lambda)] \bigcup \bigcup_{m=1}^{M}\bigcup_{j=1}^{L_j^J} [J(m)_{x_{mj}} \circ Q(\lambda)] \\ &= \bigcup_{m=\lambda}^{M}\bigcup_{j=1}^{L_j^K} K(m)_{x_{mj}} \bigcup \bigcup_{m=\lambda}^{M}\bigcup_{j=1}^{L_j^J} J(m)_{y_{mj}} \end{aligned} \tag{44}$$

Moreover, applying the spectrum definition of eq. (15) to the generalized opening Q yields

$$\begin{aligned} A_m &= A \circ Q(m) - A \circ Q(m+1) \\ &= \bigcup_{n=m}^{M}\bigcup_{j=1}^{L_j^K} K(n)_{x_{nj}} \bigcup \bigcup_{n=m}^{M}\bigcup_{j=1}^{L_j^J} J(n)_{y_{nj}} \\ &\qquad - \bigcup_{n=m+1}^{M}\bigcup_{j=1}^{L_j^K} K(n)_{x_{nj}} \bigcup \bigcup_{n=m+1}^{M}\bigcup_{j=1}^{L_j^J} J(n)_{y_{nj}} \\ &= \bigcup_{j=1}^{L_j^K} K(m)_{x_{nj}} \bigcup \bigcup_{j=1}^{L_j^J} J(m)_{y_{nj}} \end{aligned} \tag{45}$$

From this it is clear that the representation operator ψ based on Q has an inverse and $A = \bigcup_{m=1}^{M} A_m$. Furthermore, $A_i \bigcup A_j = \phi$ and $\#A = \sum_{m=1}^{M} \#A_m$. This fulfills the required conditions described in Section 3. Furthermore, results for Q containing collections of pairs of structuring elements are immediately generalizable to collections having any number of structuring elements.

To extend the optimal index set S given by eq. (28) to the situation where Q contains pairs, $Q(m) = \{K(m), J(m)\}$, we need only recognize that there are now four noninterferring processes to consider: (1) a signal process involving $\{K(m)\}$ with Poisson parameter λ_{AK} and multinomial probabilities p_{Km}, (2) a signal process involving $\{J(m)\}$ with Poisson parameter λ_{AJ} and multinomial probabilities p_{Jm}, (3) a noise process involving $\{K(m)\}$ with Poisson parameter λ_{NK} and multinomial probabilities q_{Km}, and (4) a noise process involving $\{J(m)\}$ with Poisson parameter λ_{NJ} and multinomial probabilities q_{Jm}. Since eq. (35) still applies, eq. (45) applied to both signal and noise yields

$$\begin{aligned} E[p(A, \hat{A})] = &\sum_{m \notin S} A\#K(m)[\lambda_{AK} p_{Km} + \lambda_{AJ} p_{Jm}] + \\ &\sum_{m \in S} A\#K(m)[\lambda_{NK} q_{Km} + \lambda_{NJ} q_{Jm}] \end{aligned} \tag{46}$$

Thus, the best S is defined by

$$S = \{m : \lambda_{NK} q_{Km} + \lambda_{NJ} q_{Jm} < \lambda_{AK} p_{Km} + \lambda_{AJ} p_{Jm} \tag{47}$$

Extension to more than two-structuring-element opening bases is straightforward.

12.6 Continuous Opening Spectra

In the present section we extend the preceding notions to the case of continuously parameterized openings, and in doing so relate the preset spectral theory to the granulometric theory of Matheron [6]. Because Euclidean granulometric theory does not apply to discrete space, it is at once recognized that the theory of the preceding sections is not rendered superfluous by the Euclidean approach: specifically, the theory of discrete opening spectra applies to both discrete and Euclidean space, whereas the continuous-spectra approach only applies to Euclidean space.

Matheron [6] defines a granulometry to be a family of binary-image operators $(\Psi_t), t \geq 0$, for which Ψ_t is antiextensive and monotonically increasing, $\Psi_t \Psi_r = \Psi_r \Psi_t = \Psi_{\max(t,r)}$ for all $t, r > 0$, and Ψ_0 is the identity. Here t is a generalized scale parameter. He further defines a Euclidean granulometry to be a granulometry for which Ψ_t is translation invariant and $\Psi_t(A) = t\Psi_t(A/t)$ for $t > 0$. If K is a convex, compact set, then the parameterized opening $\Psi_t(A) = A \circ tK$ is an Euclidean granulometry. Moreover, a deep theorem of Matheron [6] states that, for compact K, $A \circ tK$ is a granulometry if and only if K is convex. In particular, $tK \circ rK = tK$ whenever $t \geq r$ if and only if K is convex [clearly $tK \circ rK = \emptyset$ for $t < r$].

For continuous parameter $t \geq 0$, $\mathcal{K} = \{K(t)\}$ will be called for an *ordered opening basis* if and only if $K(t) \circ K(r) = K(t)$ for $r \leq t$ and $K(t) \circ K(r) = \emptyset$ for $r > t$. One way, but certainly not the only way, to generate such a class $\mathcal{K}$ is to consider a compact, conex set K, and define $K(t) = tK$.

The spectrum operator ψ can be adapted to the continuous setting by defining $\psi(A) = [A(t)]_{t \geq 0}$, where

$$A(t) = A \circ K(t) - \bigcup_{r>t} A \circ K(r) \tag{48}$$

For $t \neq t'$, $A(t) \cap A(t') = \emptyset$. To see this, suppose without loss of generality that $t' > t$. Then

$$\begin{aligned} A(t) \cap A(t') &= [A \circ K(t) \cap A \circ K(t')] \cap \\ &\quad \left\{ \left[\bigcup_{r>t} A \circ K(r) \right] \cup \left[\bigcup_{r>t'} A \circ K(r) \right] \right\}^c \\ &= A \circ K(t') \cap \left[\bigcup_{r>t} A \circ K(r) \right]^c \end{aligned} \tag{49}$$

which is null since the latter union includes $A \circ K(t')$.

In the present continuous setting we must adopt a more general view of the non-interfering spatial process. To do so we generalize the random grain model employed by Sand and Dougherty [9] in their analysis of the statistical distributions for granulometric pattern-spectrum moments. Specifically, we assume that to form a realization A, a component number Z is selected from a Poisson distribution with mean μ_A, parameters $t_1, t_2, \ldots, t_Z$ are independently selected from some distribution Π_A possessing density $f_A(t)$, translations $x_1, x_2, \ldots, x_Z$ are randomly chosen, and

$$A = \bigcup_{m=1}^{Z} K(t_m)_{x_m} \tag{50}$$

where the components are non-interfering. There are several salient points regarding this more general model:

1. It reduces to the former discrete model if the parameter class is finite.
2. Equation (22) holds.
3. Equation (23) holds, its new form being

$$A \circ K(\lambda) = \bigcup_{m=\lambda}^{Z} K(t_m)_{x_m} \tag{51}$$

4. Equation (24) holds, its new form being

$$A(t) = \bigcup_{m} \{K(t_m)_{x_m} : t_m = t\} \tag{52}$$

If we assume that noise realization N derives from a similar non-interfering process with Poisson mean μ_N and t_k selected from a distribution Π_N possessing density $f_N(t)$, then $\psi(A \cup N) = [A(t) \cup N(t)]$. The estimate $\hat{A}$ for A is given by eq. (29) with t_m in place of m; however, in the present context S is a subset of $[0, \infty)$ and is not a discrete set. The estimation problem is to find S for which $E[\rho(A, \hat{A})]$ is minimzed, with # now denoting area.

Similarly to eq. (32), it can be shown that

$$\rho(A, \hat{A}) = \sum_{t_m \notin S} \#A(t_m) + \sum_{t_k \in S} \#N(t_k) \tag{53}$$

Because the component counts for both signal and noise are random, $E[p(A, \hat{A})]$ does not easily reduce; however, if we make the simplifying assumption that the component counts are fixed, say at the respective means μ_A and μ_N, we then obtain

$$E[\rho(A, \hat{A})] = \mu_A \int_{S^c} \#K(t) f_A(t) dt + \mu_N \int_S \#K(t) f_N dt \tag{54}$$

To see the manner in which we arrive at eq. (54), let Λ denote the first summand in eq. (54) and let

$$\Lambda_m = \begin{cases} \#A(t_m), & \text{if } t_m \notin S \\ 0, & \text{otherwise} \end{cases} \tag{55}$$

Then

$$E[\Lambda] = \sum_{m=1}^{\mu_A} E[\Lambda_m] = \mu_A E[\Lambda_1] = \mu_A \int_{S^c} \#K(t)] f_A(t) dt \tag{56}$$

The second summand in eq. (54) is handled similarly. The best S is given by

$$S = \{t : \mu_N f_N(t) < \mu_A f_A(t)\} \tag{57}$$

Note the similarity to the discrete solution given in eq. (37).

12.7 Extension of Continuous Spectra to Tau-Openings

Generalization of the continuous theory to tau-openings with $Q(t) = \{K(t), J(t)\}$ proceeds along similar lines to the generalization in the discrete case, under the assumption that $K(t) \circ J(t') = J(t) \circ K(t') = \emptyset$ for $t' > t$. For instance, eq. (44) and (45) become

$$A \circ Q(\lambda) = \bigcup_{m=\lambda}^{Z} K(t_m)_{x_m} \bigcup \bigcup_{k=\lambda}^{W} J(t_k)_{x_k} \tag{58}$$

$$A(t) = \bigcup_{m} \{K(t_m)_{x_m} : t_m = t\} \bigcup \bigcup_{k} \{J(t_k)_{x_k} : t_k = t\} \tag{59}$$

where Z and W are the respective Poisson variables for $\{K(t)\}$ and $\{J(t)\}$, possessing respective means μ_{A_K} and μ_{A_J}, and it is assumed that the corresponding parameter sequences derive from the respective densities f_{A_K} and f_{A_J}. Generalization to more than two structuring-element sequences is immediate.

Like the signal, the noise too can be generated by both $\{K(t)\}$ and $\{J(t)\}$ with the $K(t)$ and $J(t)$ Poisson variables possessing means μ_{N_K} and μ_{N_J}, respectively, and the corresponding parameter sequences possessing probability densities f_{N_K} and f_{N_J}, respectively. Then the error equation takes the form

$$\begin{aligned} E[p(A, \hat{A})] = {} & \mu_{A_K} \int_{S^c} \#K(t) f_{A_K}(t) dt + \mu_{A_J} \int_{S^c} \#J(t) f_{A_J}(t) dt \\ & + \mu_{N_J} \int_{S} \#K(t) f_{N_J}(t) dt + \mu_{N_J} \int_{S} \#J(t) f_{N_J}(t) dt \end{aligned} \tag{60}$$

The preceding equation extends to any finite number of structuring-element sequences. In particular, if any of the Poisson means are zero, then the equation reduces to one in which the signal and noise are generated by different primitive shapes, which shows that our model allows signal and noise to be generated by different primitives.

As in the single-opening situation, there is a close connection between the present theory and the Matheron theory for Euclidean granulometries. Matheron

[6] calls a class of images $\mathbf{K}$ a generator of a Euclidean granulometry $\{\Psi_t\}$ if the invariant class of Ψ_1 consists of unions of translations of scalar multiples $tK, t \geq 1$, of elements $K \in \mathbf{K}$. If it happens that the images of $\mathbf{K}$ are convex, then

$$\Psi_t(A) = \bigcup\{A \circ tK : K \in \mathbf{K}\} \tag{61}$$

is a granulometry with generator $\mathbf{K}$. Now suppose $\mathbf{K} = \{K_1, K_2, \ldots, K_p\}$ is finite and $tK_1 \circ t'K_j = \emptyset$ for $t' > t$ and $i \neq j$. If for any K_i in $\mathbf{K}$ we define $K_i(t) = tK_i$, then $\{K_i(t)\}$ is a basis in our present spectral sense. Assuming each realization A of the spatial process is formed in the usual way from this basis, the spectral component $A(t)$ takes the form

$$A(t) = \Psi_t(A) - \bigcup_{r>t} \Psi_r(A) \tag{62}$$

Note that it has been demonstrated in [6] that $\Psi_r(A) < \Psi_t(A)$ for $r > t$, and that the invariant class of Ψ_r is a subset of the invariant class of Ψ_t.

12.8 Interpretation of the Optimal Estimator $\hat{A}$ in the context of Optimal Morphological Estimation

Morphological dilation and erosion operations are translation invariant and increasing. This motivates calling mappings which are increasing and translation invariant morphological filters. A general framework for the characterization of statistically optimal morphological filters has been developed by Dougherty [10, 11, 12, 13, 14]. An interesting question is how do we treat the problem of optimally estimating one random variable by a morphological funciton of a finite number of observations? Included in the discussions [10, 11] is the manner in which we apply constraints to the filter, so that the optimal estimator is a particular type of morphological filter, say tau-opening or linear operator. A key class of increasing, translation invariant mappings are the alternating sequential filters of Sternberg [15] and Lougheed [16] (see Serra [17]), and an optimization criterion for these has been developed by Schonfeld and Goutsias [18, 19]. In the present section, we wish to briefly investigate the relationship between the optimal filter based on the opening spectrum and the general problem of morphological estimation.

Returning again to the Wiener filter, the weights w_n of eq (3) provide the estimate $\hat{f}$ of f relative to an orthonormal basis $b_1, b_2, \ldots, b_n$, with the summation over this basis serving as the inversion back to the spatial domain. In the general algebriac paradigm of Section 3, f is found from the weighted representation by applying ψ^{-1}. When applying optimal estimation relative to the morphological representation in terms of $\mathcal{K}$, equation (29) provides the required inversion. An interesting and important question can be posed: Does the estimator $\hat{A}$ possess a morphological representation? That is, can we write $\hat{A} = \Omega(A \cup N)$, where Ω is a "morphological operation?" If by "morphological operation" we mean an increasing, translation invariant mapping, then $\hat{A}$ possesses no such representation. Indeed from the manner in which S is chosen, it can be seen that if $A \cup N'$ is obtained from $A \cup N$ by replacing a noise component $K(m)_x$ of N by a noise component $K(m')_y$ where $m' > m, m \in S, m' \notin S$, and $K(m')_y$ properly contains $K(m)_x$, then $A \cup N$ is a proper subset of $A \cup N'$, but, according to eq. (25), the filtered version of $A \cup N'$ is a proper subset of the filtered version of $A \cup N$. Thus, the optimal fitler determined by eq. (29) is not necessarily increasing (although it might be).

Whether we take the weak definition of a morphological filter adopted in [5, 10], that of being increasing and translation invariant, or the strong definition adopted by Serra [7], which includes idempotence (without assuming translation invariance because the definition lies in the context of lattice theory), the mapping $\Omega(A)$ defined by eq. (29) is not necessarily a morphological filter. Consequently, even though the measure $E[p(A, \hat{A})]$ can be interpreted as mean-square error in the binary setting, the operator Ω is not necessarily expressable in terms of the Matheron expansion as an union of erosions, and it is precisely this expansion in which the mean-square optimization theory of [10] is framed.

Nevertheless, the estimation operator is translation invariant and can be expressed "morphologically," where here we mean that it can be expressed using ordinary morphological operations in conjunction with set-theoretic operations. The desired expression is immediate from the definition of the spectrum operator ψ, and is imply eq. (25) applied to S. Rewritten, eq. (29) takes the form

$$A = \bigcup_{m \in S} (A \cup N) \circ K(m-1) - (A \cup N) \circ K(m) \tag{63}$$

12.9 Conclusion

For the problem of filtering corrupted binary images of the form $A \cup N$, we have chosen an appropriate morphological opening spectral decomposition, as well as distance and energy measures resulting in an appropriate measure of estimation error. Based upon these choices (which are quite different from the analogous choices for the additive noise/linear filter problem, and which eliminate the requirement for orthogonality or an inner product space) we have derived optimal filtering results analogous to conventional Weiner filtering results based on image and noise energy contents in each spectral bin.

The assumptions on the image and noise models in order for the results to be valid are presently fairly strong. The image and noise connected components are modeled as translated copies of objects from a single ordered opening basis set (Sections 4 and 6) or a collection of such basis sets (Sections 5 and 7). In addition there is a non-interference (non-overlap) condition so that all objects remain distinct and no objects are created that fail to arise directly from basis sets.

These conditions guarantee sufficiency. However, they are actually stronger than need be. They were sufficient to guarantee that $(A \cup B) \circ K = A \cup B$ and $\#(A \cup B) = \#A + \#B$. It is easy to create instances in which $(A \cup B) \circ K = A \cup B$ and A and B are not non-interfering sets. If A and B are not exclusive then $\#(A \cup B) \leq \#A + \#B$. So if the sets overlap, the quantities we have been computing will be strict upper bounds. However, in this case, the overlapping can be regarded as a random process and instead of computing $\#(A \cup B)$ a composition of $E[\#(A \cup B)] = k(\#A + \#B)$ for an appropriate $0 < k < 1$ can be made. Along these lines, the possibility of generalizing the results is quite strong.

In addition, in order to better handle irregular or ill-defined noise sets, as well as ideal (noise free) images comprised of families of objects for which no simple ordered opening basis is obvious, we are working on extending our results to instances where the assumptions on image and noise objects are relaxed. In particular, extension to the case where the objects are in some sense well-sorted by one or more bases is being sought in derivations and experiments.

12.10 Acknowledgement

This work was supported by the Office of Naval Research under its ARL Project program (Grant N0014-90-J-1369).

References

[1] R.M. Haralick, E.R. Dougherty, and P. Katz, "Model-Based Morphology," *Proc. SPIE,* Vol. 1472, Orlando, April 1991.

[2] J. Serra, *Image Analysis and Mathematical Morphology,* Academic Press, New York, 1983.

[3] R.M. Haralick, S. Sternberg, and X. Zhuang, "Image Analysis Using Mathematical Morphology," *IEEE Transactions on Pattern Analysis and Machine Intelligence,* Vol. 9, No. 4, 1987.

[4] E.R. Dougherty and C.R. Giardina, *Image Processing: Continuous to Discrete,* Prentice-Hall, Englewood Cliffs, 1987.

[5] C.R. Giardina and E.R. Dougherty, *Morphological Methods In Image and Signal Processing,* Prentice-hall, Englewood Cliffs, 1988.

[6] G. Matheron, *Random Sets and Integral Geometry,* John Wiley, New York, 1975.

[7] J. Serra, "Introduction to Morphological Filters," in *Image Analysis and Mathematical Morphology,* Vol. 2, ed. J. Serra, Academic Press, New York, 1988.

[8] C. Ronse and H.J. Heijmans, "The Algebraic Bass of Mathematical Morphology, Part II: Openings and Closings," Centrum voor Wiskunde en Informatica,

Report AM-R8904, 1989.

[9] F. Sand and E.R. Dougherty, "Statistics of the Morpholigical Pattern-Spectrun Moments for a Random-Grain Model," Morphological Imaging Laboratory Report MIL-91-02, Rochester Institute of Technology, Rochester, 1991 (submitted for publication).

[10] E.R. Dougherty, "Optimal Mean-Square N-Observation Digital Morphological Filters — Part I: Optimal Binary Filters," Morphological Imaging Laboratory Report MIL-90-02, Rochester Institute of Technology, Rochester, NY (to appear in *CVGIP: Image Understanding*).

[11] E.R. Dougherty, "Optimal Mean-Square N-Observation Digital Morphological Filters — Part II: Optimal Gray-Scale Filters," Morphological Imaging Laboratory Report MIL-90-03, Rochester Institute of Technology, Rochester, 1990 (to appear in *CVGIP: Image Understanding*).

[12] E.R. Dougherty, "The Optimal Mean-Square Digital Binary Morphological Filter," *SPSE 43d Annual Conference,* Rochester, May 1990.

[13] E.R. Dougherty and R.P. Loce, "Constrained Optimal Digital Morphological Filters," *Proc. 25th Annual Conference on Information Sciences and Systems,* Baltimore, March 1991.

[14] E.R. Dougherty, A. Mathew, and V. Swarnakar, "A Conditional Expectation Based Implementation of the Optimal Mean-Square Binary Morphological Filter, *Proc. SPIE,* Vol. 1451, San Hose, February 1991.

[15] S.R. Sternberg, "Morphology for Grey Tone Functions," *Computer Vision, Graphics, and Image Processing,* Vol. 35, 1986.

[16] R. Lougheed, "Lecture Notes for Summer Course in Mathematical Morphology," University of Michigan, Ann Arbor, 1983.

[17] J. Serra, "Alternating Sequential Filter," in *Image Analysis and Mathematical Morphology,* Vol. 2, ed. J. Serra, Academic Press, New York, 1988.

[18] D. Schonfeld and J. Goutsias, "Optimal Morphological Filters for Pattern Restoration," *Proc. SPIE,* Vol. 1199, Philadelphia, 1989.

[19] D. Schonfeld and J. Goutsias, "Optimal Morpholigical Pattern Recognition from Noisy Binary Images," *IEEE Transactions on Pattern Analysis and Machine Intelligence,* Vol. 13, No. 1, January 1991.

Motion

Chapter 13

Motion Analysis of Image Sequences

E. Salari

13.1 INTRODUCTION

The perception of visual motion plays a central role in biological as well as many emerging artificial vision systems. In the area of computer vision, motion perception and interpretation involves the analysis of a sequence of images from a changing world. This will allow the observer to determine the structure and motion of the moving objects, determine the observer's own motion (egomotion), and segment the changing visual field into moving versus non-moving areas. These tasks will in turn provide many important applications in industrial, medical, and military environments, such as autonomous vehicle navigation, image communication and digital TV, object tracking, computer animation, the study of heart and cell motion, etc.

Among the various tasks, three-dimensional structure and motion estimation is considered very important in computer vision and dynamic scene analysis. The general approach for the estimation of structure and motion parameters usually proceeds in two steps. In the first step, an intermediate representation of the original image sequence which can be related to three-dimensional structure and motion parameters is calculated. The second step provides algebraic equations to actually relate these intermediate representations to structure and motion parameters in the space and the solution for such parameters. The intermediate representations usually involve the calculation of optical flow, correspondences of various types of features, etc.

There have been a variety of algorithms proposed to solve for the structure and motion parameters of rigid objects from successive perspective views. These algorithms can be viewed as either nonlinear or linear algorithms. The nonlinear algorithms are generally solved by an iterative process requiring good initial guess values to converge to its actual solution. The linear algorithms involve solving for some intermediate parameters using linear equations. The motion parameters are then calculated from these intermediate parameters.

In this article, we briefly review some recent work relating to the estimation of two dimensional motion in an image plane (or the optical flow). These various techniques provide a diversity of approaches to tackle the important problem of calculating the optical flow which is essential in the estimation of structure and motion parameters in space. In the later portion of the article an overview of a variety of techniques used to estimate three-dimensional structure and motion from line correspondences is presented.

13.2 COMPUTING TWO-DIMENSIONAL MOTION

When an object moves relative to a sensor, the motion of its image in the image plane of the sensor produces an image flow field known as optical flow. The calculation of this two-dimensional motion involves obtaining a velocity vector at each pixel in the image plane. Optical flow can be used to segment time varying images into moving and stationary object areas, as well as an intermediate step in finding the structure and motion parameters of moving objects in the space.

Various schemes of calculating optical flow can be classified into three categories: correspondence based, spatio-temporal gradients, or techniques utilizing the measurements of the normal velocity components around the image contours. The correspondence based approach[1,2] provides a partial optical flow (i.e., flow velocities at feature points) directly from the displacement of features from two successive image frames divided by the time interval between them. The spatio-temporal gradient based methods, on the other hand, yield dense flow by considering some other constraints. In the following, we will review some methods to obtain the optical flow based on the spatio-temporal gradients and using the normal components of the velocity vector along the contours.

The spatio-temporal gradient based techniques take advantage of the following image flow constraint equation,

$$E_x v_x + E_y v_y + E_t = \nabla E \cdot V + E_t = 0 \qquad (2.1)$$

where, E_x, E_y are the components of spatial intensity gradient, v_x, v_y are the optical flow velocity components in the x and y directions, and E_t is the temporal intensity gradient. This image flow constraint equation is a single equation with two unknowns v_x, v_y. Assuming the image velocity is uniform, then the velocity components for a single moving object can be obtained using a pseudo-inverse optimization technique[3]. However, with multiple moving objects, a clustering technique[4,5] is used to estimate the motion of each object. The uniform velocity implies a restricted motion in which the object translates parallel to the image plane. Horn and Schunck[6] used a more general assumption that the flow velocity is not constant, rather it varies smoothly on the image plane. Using optimization techniques, they obtain the flow velocity from an iterative local operation process. This method provides a dense flow, but it is computationally intensive and applies to short range motion.

Yashida[7] proposed a velocity propagation technique in which the flow velocity is obtained by the estimation of the velocities at some prominent feature points and propagating them to neighboring points using the formulation of Horn and Schunck. The propagation process will be iterated until the velocities of all the points are calculated. Also, a scheme was devised to prevent the motion of a prominent feature point from one object to propogate to neighboring points which belong to other objects.

Davis, Wu, Sun[8] proposed a two-step technique also based on a propagation process. They first estimate the motion velocity vectors at image corner points and then propagate them along the image contour. In this method, the image flow constraint equation is rewritten as,

$$v_n = -\frac{E_t}{|\nabla E|} \tag{2.2}$$

Equation (2.2) provides a local measurement of the normal components of the velocity vectors. In the first step the velocity at a corner point is estimated using the normal components of the velocity vectors in its neighborhood along the contour. In the propagation step, an equation is developed in which the tangential component of the velocity at a point can be obtained from the velocity vector of the corner point and its normal velocity component. The reported propagation scheme works for a single moving object and it is not applicable to multiple moving objects with occlusion problems.

Hildreth[9], D'Haeyer[10] developed methods to calculate the motion along the contour. Equation (2.2) provides the normal component from the local computation, and by itself cannot provide a unique flow velocity (aperture problem). Hildreth adds a smoothness constraint along the contour and estimates the flow using optimization. D'Haeyer extended this idea and proposed the "minimum dilatation principle" constraint which can be identical to Hildreth's smoothness constraint in a special case. D'Haeyer also used the motion of a limited number of points on the curve in a minimization procedure from which the flow velocity is estimated.

Waxman and Wohn[11] modeled the components of the local flow velocity as a second order polynomial in terms of the Taylor expansion. The assumption of second order flow is true if the flow is generated from a moving planar surface (under perspective projection), however it is only a local approximation for a curved surface. By substituting the second order polynomial in a constraint equation $v_n = \mathbf{V} \cdot \mathbf{n}$, ($\mathbf{n}$ being the unit vector normal to the contour), the coefficients of the Taylor expansion are estimated from the measurements of the normal flow velocity v_n. Since the second order Taylor expansion of velocity components involves 12 unknowns this requires at least 12 measurements along the contour.

Nagel[12] examined relations between different methods exploiting the second partial derivatives of gray value functions in an attempt to find a common basis for the estimation of optical flow under various assumptions of being constant, changing linearly, or smoothly. Nagel[13] in earlier work presented a method to obtain the optical flow by minimization of the squared differences between the gray value structures observed from two frames. This led to the derivation of two nonlinear equations for the two unknown components of optical flow. A closed form solution is feasible when the gray value structures are considered to be corner points, otherwise the solution is obtained from an iterative process.

Wu, Brackett, and Wohn[14] proposed an iterative technique to estimate the two-dimensional motion parameters, which account for the transformation of one contour into another. Their method is based on the measurements of normal flow components involving the equation $v_n = \mathbf{V} \cdot \mathbf{n}$. Initially, v_n is estimated using a nearest point method. The predicted value of the full flow is then obtained using a least square approach involving the contour integral. The fact that the normal velocity components, v_n, cannot be measured accurately in real situations will lead to erroneous flow velocities. As a result, the normal flow components are re-estimated from the predited flow. This process is applied iteratively until its application does not provide any further significant improvements.

13.3 Structure and Motion from Line Correspondences

The accuracy of the three-dimensional motion parameter estimation relies heavily on the accuracy of the observed features in the image sequence. Various methods proposed for the determination of structure and motion can be based on either optical flow or correspondences of features. In the optical flow based approach[15-18], the estimation of the structure and motion parameters is based on the optical flow or velocity field in an image. The success of this approach depends on the quality of optical flow for which the calculation is difficult and highly sensitive to noise. The correspondence approach[19-30] assumes the features are extracted and matched between images; the features can be points, lines, or image contours. It appears that line features are more reliable and attractive than point features in the sense that their position and orientation can be determined to subpixel accuracy. In this section, we first provide a graph-theoretic approach for finding the line correspondences and then review several techniques to recover the three-dimensional motion and structure from the projection of lines in an image sequence. The number of lines, image frames, motion assumption and formulation varies for different approaches.

Salari and Balaji[33] developed an iterative graph-theoretic approach for the matching of line segments. This technique uses a line's local properties such as its length, width, orientation, contrast, steepness, along with its structural relationship with the other lines in the image to find matching pairs. Each image is considered as a relational graph, where each node represents a straight line and its properties. Two nodes in this graph are connected by the distance and angular relations between them. A general match between nodes from two relational structures and a one-to-one mapping between them that preserves the structural information, can be found using an auxiliary data structure called an association graph. Two nodes in the association graph are connected if they represent a compatible relation. The strength of the connection link between two nodes is indicated by a compatibility measure which depends on the preservation of the structural information. Such a compatibility measure will be refined through an iterative process using local information. The best match can be obtained from the largest totally connected set of nodes in the association graph called maximal clique. Figure 1 represents an office scene image pair and its extracted line features, and table 1 summarizes the matching process.

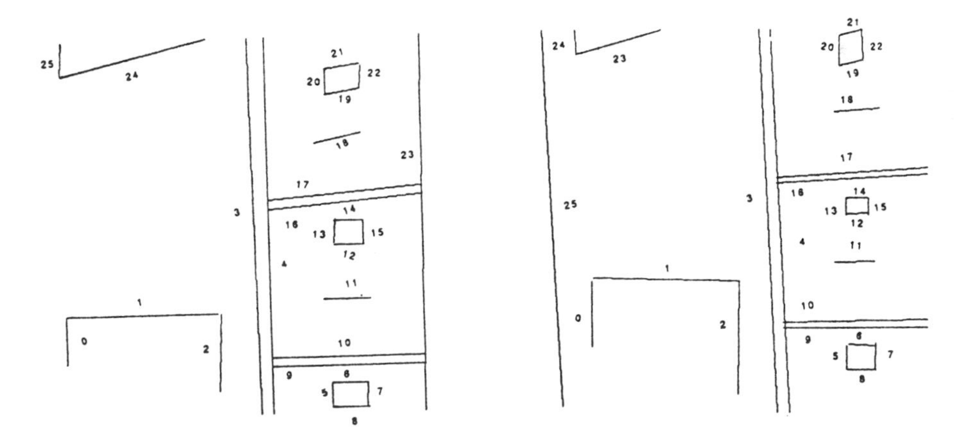

Figure 1. Office scene image pair and its extracted line features

To further explain the compatibility measure in the association graph, let (V_l, P, R) and (V_r, P, R) be the graph representations of the lines in the left and right images.

LINE LABELS OF LEFT IMAGE	LINE LABELS OF RIGHT IMAGE				
	MATCHING BASED ON PROPERTIES	MATCHING BEFORE REFINING ASSOC. GRAPH	MATCHING AFTER REFINING THE ASSOC. GRAPH		
			ITERATION 1	ITERATION 2	ITERATION 3
0	0	0	0	0	0
1	1	1	1	1	1
2	-	-	-	-	-
3	3, 4	-	-	-	3
4	4, 3	-	-	-	4
5	5, 7	5	5	5	5
6	6, 8, 11	-	-	6	6
7	5, 7	7	7	7	7
8	8, 11	8	8	8	8
9	9, 10	9	9	9	9
10	9, 10, 11	10	10	10	10
11	11, 18	11	11	11	11
12	6,8,11,12,14	12	12	12	12
13	5, 7, 13	13	13	13	13
14	8, 14	-	-	-	14
15	5, 15	-	-	15	15
16	9, 16, 17	-	-	16	16
17	10, 16, 17	-	-	-	17
18	18	-	18	18	18
19	-	-	-	-	-
20	-	-	-	-	-
21	-	-	-	-	-
22	22	22	22	22	22
23	-	-	-	-	-
24	23	-	23	23	23
25	24	24	24	24	24

Table 1. matching process of line features from left and right image pairs

V denotes the set of nodes (lines), P the properties of the lines, and R represents the structural relationships between two nodes. For each v_1 inV_l and v_2 in V_r, a node in the association graph G labeled (v_1, v_2) is assigned if v_1 and v_2 have the same properties. To define the compatibility measure between two nodes (v_i, v_p) and (v_j, v_q) in the association graph, the structural relations are used. The relation that we consider is the line's distance and angular relation with another line in the image. Let

$$K^{l}_{ij} = \alpha * \mathrm{Dist}\,(i,j) + \beta * \mathrm{Angle}\,(i,j)$$

$$K^{r}_{pq} = \alpha * \mathrm{Dist}\,(p,q) + \beta * \mathrm{Angle}\,(p,q)$$

where i, j are lines in the left ("l") image, p, q are lines in the right ("r") image, and α, β are weights (<1).

The compatibility measure between two nodes (v_i, v_p) and (v_j, v_q) in the association graph is defined as,

$$R_c' = \frac{\text{Min}\left(K_{ij}^{l}, K_{pq}^{r}\right)}{\text{Max}\left(K_{ij}^{l}, K_{pq}^{r}\right)}$$

This is modified as,

$$R_c = e^{\gamma d(i,j)} \,.\, R_c'$$

where d (i, j) is the distance between lines i and j, γ is a coefficient factor. The compatibility measure will determine the strength of the link between the nodes of the association graph, and a weak link will either be removed or changed to a regular link through an iterative process.

Liu and Huang[28] developed a two-stage method to estimate the motion parameters from line correspondences. The motion equation is assumed to be a rotation followed by translation. The rotation parameters, tilt, swing, and spin angles, as well as the three translational motion components in the x, y, z directions are all assumed to be varying from frame to frame. In the first stage, considering the correspondences of straight lines at three time instances t1, t2, t3, a nonlinear equation containing only rotation parameters is developed. This was possible by remodeling the motion equation as a translation followed by a rotation. The nonlinear equation involves six unknown rotational parameters (i.e. three parameters for motion between t1, t2 and three more for the motion between t2, t3). Each line correspondences over three frames provides one constraint equation. Consequently, it requires the correspondences of six lines over three frames to solve for the six unknowns. In the second stage, the rotational component of the motion is separated from the computation of total motion and then a linear equation is derived which involves only the six translational motion components. Since the translational motion parameters can be solved up to a scale factor, there remains only five unknowns to be estimated by fixing one of the translational motion components. The successful computation of this stage depends on how accurate the rotational parameters can be estimated from the first stage.

Mitiche, Seida and Aggrawal[29] proposed a method for structure and motion estimation based on the observation of four lines in three views. Their scheme uses the principle of invariances of angular configuration in rigid motion which states that the angle between any two lines in the space remains unchanged due to motion. If vector V1 on line l1 and V2 on line l2 represent the orientation of these lines with respect to the first view, and similarly V'1, V'2 represent the orientation of the same lines in the second view, then,

$$\text{Cos}^2\theta = \left(\frac{V_1 \cdot V_2}{|V_1||V_2|}\right)^2$$

and also,

$$\mathrm{Cos}^2\theta = \left(\frac{V_1' \cdot V_2'}{|V_1'||V_2'|}\right)^2$$

This implies

$$\left(\frac{V_1 \cdot V_2}{|V_1||V_2|}\right)^2 = \left(\frac{V_1' \cdot V_2'}{|V_1'||V_2'|}\right)^2 \qquad (3.1)$$

The orientation of each line can be expressed in terms of the coordinates of two points on its projection and one unknown parameter. Each pair of lines in two views provides one constraint as equation (3.1). They first obtained the orientation parameters of four lines (six possible pairs of lines) in three views which resulted in twelve equations with twelve unknowns. The rotation matrix is then obtained from these orientations, and finally the translational motion parameters are recovered after resolving the rotational motion.

Spetsakis and Aloimonos[27] presented a closed form solution to the structure and motion problem from line correspondences. They first show how to express the parameters of a line in three-dimensional space in terms of its motion parameters and the parameters of its images in a two frame sequence. This is done by considering only translational motion at first, which is then extended to the general motion involving both translation and rotation. The parameters of a line in space obtained from any two pairs of frames remains the same and from this fact they establish two linear equations by viewing one line in three frames. The two linear equations involve 27 unknowns. Using the correspondences of 13 lines, a 26x26 system of linear equations is developed from which the 27 unknowns are estimated (assuming one of the unknowns is unity). The estimated unknowns which are functions of motion parameters lead to the solution for the motion.

The remainder of this section will focus in more detail on the work of Salari and Jong[30]. They proposed a two-step method based on the correspondences of two lines over four frames to calculate the structure and motion parameters. Figure 2 represents the imaging configuration in which the images of two lines on the object in XYZ coordinates are shown in the image plane with xy coordinates. Initially, a set of nonlinear equations involving the structure and motion parameters is established. In the second step, a technique is introduced to obtain the initial guess values for the parameters of the nonlinear system from the existing closed form solution for planar surfaces.

Let $\vec{R}$ denote the position vector of a point (X,Y,Z) on a rigid object moving with a translational velocity $\vec{V} = [v_x, v_y, v_z]$, and a rotational velocity $\vec{\omega} = [\omega_x, \omega_y, \omega_z]$ as depicted in Figure 3, then the equation of motion is expressed as,

$$\vec{R}(t) = \vec{R}_0 + \vec{V}t + \left[S(\omega,t)\Omega + C(\omega,t)\Omega^2\right]\vec{R}_0 \qquad (3.2)$$

where

$$S(\omega,t) = \frac{\sin(|\omega|t))}{|\omega|}$$

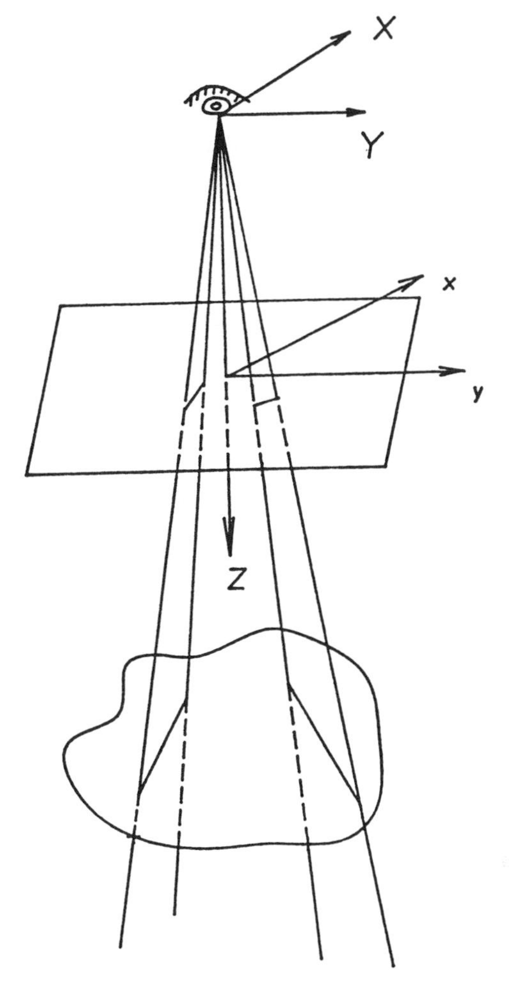

Figure 2. Imaging configuration.

$$C(\omega,t) = \frac{1-\cos(|\omega|t))}{|\omega|^2}$$

$$\Omega = \begin{bmatrix} 0 & -\omega_z & \omega_y \\ \omega_z & 0 & -\omega_x \\ -\omega_y & \omega_x & 0 \end{bmatrix}$$

and

$$|\omega| = \sqrt{\omega_x^2 + \omega_y^2 + \omega_z^2} \quad .$$

The position vector $\vec{R}(t)$ now is in terms of the initial position $\vec{R}_0$, the translational velocity $\vec{V}$, and the rotational velocity $\vec{\omega}$ associated with the functions $S(\omega,t)$, $C(\omega,t)$.

Given two lines **a** with equation $y = m_{a0} + b_{a0}$ and **b** with equation $y = m_{b0} + b_{b0}$ in image frame 0, select two points (x_{0i}, y_{0i}), i = 1,2 on line **a** and two points (x_{0i}, y_{0i}) i = 3,4 on line **b**. These points are projections of four points (X_{0i}, Y_{0i}, Z_{0i}), i = 1,2,3,4 in the space. It is well known that translational velocity and structure parameters can be determined up to a scale factor which is conveniently equal to Z_{01}. Therefore, the structural parameters h_is are defined as the following depth ratios,

$$h_i = \frac{Z_{0i}}{Z_{01}}, \; i = 1, 2, 3, 4 \quad (\text{note } h_1 = 1) \qquad (3.3)$$

From the perspective transformation, we have

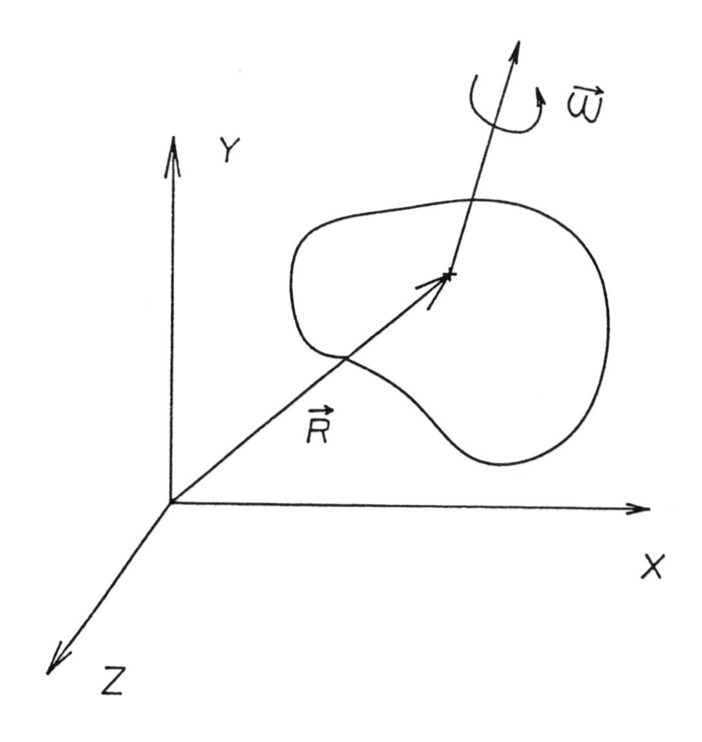

Figure 3. A moving object in 3-D space.

$$X_{0i} = \frac{1}{f} x_{0i} Z_{0i}, \quad Y_{0i} = \frac{1}{f} y_{0i} Z_{0i} \tag{3.4}$$

(f is the focal length of the lens)

Then,

$$\vec{R}_{0i} = (X_{0i}, Y_{0i}, Z_{0i}) = (\frac{1}{f} h_i Z_{01} x_{0i}, \frac{1}{f} h_i Z_{01} y_{0i}, h_i Z_{01}), \quad i = 1,2,3,4 \tag{3.5}$$

Assuming $f = Z01 = 1$, then

$$\vec{R}_{0i} = (h_i x_{0i}, h_i y_{0i}, h_i), \quad i = 1,2,3,4 \tag{3.6}$$

Substituting for Ω, Ω^2, and $\vec{R}_{0i}$ in equation 3.2, the components of $\vec{R}_i(t)$, $(X_i(t), Y_i(t), Z_i(t))$ can be obtained as,

$$X_i(t) = h_i x_{0i} + v_x t + (\omega_y h_i - \omega_z h_i y_{0i}) S(\omega,t) + \left[-\left(\omega_y^2 + \omega_z^2\right) h_i x_{0i} + \omega_x \omega_y h_i y_{0i} + \omega_x \omega_z h_i\right] C(\omega, t) \tag{3.7a}$$

$$Y_i(t) = h_i y_{oi} + v_y t + (\omega_z h_i x_{oi} - \omega_x h_i) S(\omega,t) + \left[\omega_y \omega_x h_i x_{0i} - \left(\omega_z^2 + \omega_x^2\right) h_i y_{0i} + \omega_y \omega_z h_i\right] C(\omega, t) \tag{3.7b}$$

$$Z_i(t) = h_i + v_z t + (\omega_x h_i y_{0i} - \omega_y h_i x_{0i}) S(\omega,t) + \left[\omega_z \omega_x h_i x_{0i} + \omega_z \omega_y h_i y_{0i} - \left(\omega_x^2 + \omega_y^2\right) h_i\right] C(\omega, t) \tag{3.7c}$$

$i = 1, 2, 3, 4.$

Now, the correspondences of two lines over four frames as shown in Figure 4 provides the necessary constraint equations to solve for unknown structures and motion parameters.

Let $(x_i(t_j), y_i(t_j))$ represent the coordinates of i-th point on j-th frame (note for $i = 1,2$, the points are located on line **a** and for $i = 3,4$, the points are on line **b**). It follows that,

$$f \frac{Y_i(t_j)}{Z_i(t_j)} = y_i(t_j) = m_{aj} x_i(t_j) + b_{aj} = f\, m_{aj} \frac{X_i(t_j)}{Z_i(t_j)} + b_{aj} \quad \text{for } i = 1,2$$

and

$$f\frac{Y_i(t_j)}{Z_i(t_j)} = y_i(t_j) = m_{bj}\, x_i\,(t_j) + b_{bj} = f\, m_{bj}\frac{X_i\,(t_j)}{Z_i\,(t_j)} + b_{bj} \quad \text{for } i = 3,4$$

or

$$fY_i(t_j) = f\, m_{aj}\, X_i\,(t_j) + b_{aj}\, Z_i(t_j), \quad i = 1,2 \tag{3.8a}$$

and

$$fY_i(t_j) = f\, m_{bj}\, X_i\,(t_j) + b_{bj}\, Z_i(t_j), \quad i = 3,4 \tag{3.8b}$$

$$j = 1,\ 2,\ 3$$

Substitution of equation (3.7a, b, c) into (3.8a, b) provides an over determined system of twelve nonlinear equations to solve for the three structure parameters h_2, h_3, h_4 and six motion parameters v_X, v_Y, v_Z, w_X, w_Y, w_Z. Since the equations are nonlinear, we do not expect any closed form solution, instead iterative procedure is used.

To find initial guess values for the iterative solutions of the simultaenous nonlinear equations, we use the existing solution for planar surfaces. Kanatani[15] uses the pseudo-orthographic approximation to obtain the structure and motion

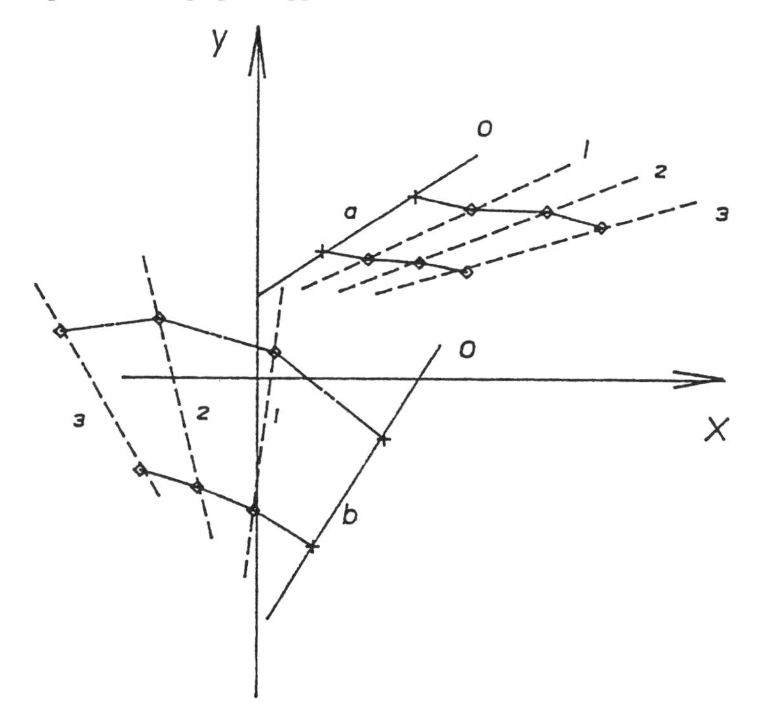

Figure 4. Correspondences of two lines over four frames.

parameters of a planar surface from its optical flow. This solution assumes that the optical flow of a planar surface which is specified by eight flow parameters a1, a2, ..., a8 is already provided. In fact considering two points on line **a** and one point on line **b** in frame 0, and knowing the equations of the correspondences of these two lines on frames 1, 2, and 3, as shown in Figure 5, there would be a set of nine linear equations from which the eight flow parameters a1, a2, ..., a8 are obtained.

13.4 CONCLUSION

This article presents an overview of some recent techniques for the calculation of two-dimensional motion in an image plane (or optical flow) and the three-dimensional structure and motion parameters using line correspondences. The motion of an object relative to a sensor can be obtained from the optical flow if the changes in the image sequence are indeed due to motion. However, difficulties arise when the object motion does not provide any change in the image or the changes in the image are not simply due to motion alone.

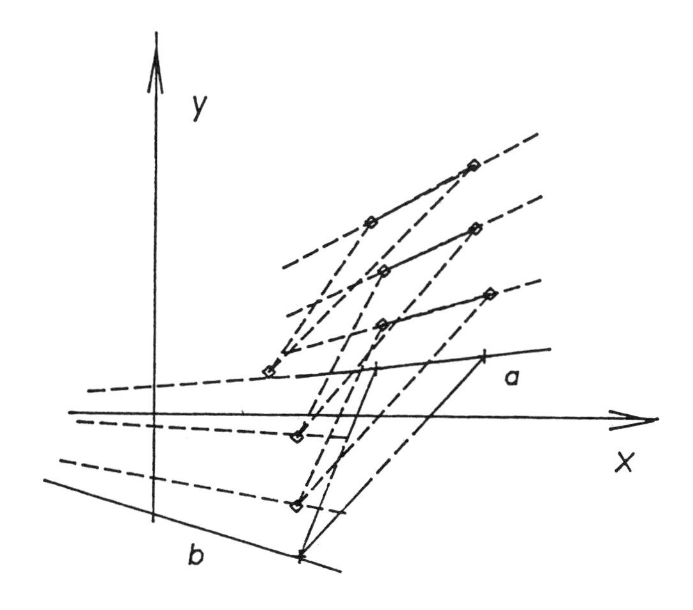

Figure 5. The motion of two points on line a and one point on line b over four frames.

Among the various methods introduced for optical flow calculation, the correspondence based methods are considered to be more immune to noise, although, finding the accurate correspondences of features are computationally difficult. The gradient based schemes, on the other hand, are highly susceptible to noise, but computationally attractive in the sense that real time implementation is feasible.

By establishing a relation between the observed flow on the image plane and the structure and motion parameters in three-dimensional space, a two-stage estimation procedure can be used to obtain the structure and motion parameters from optical flow. In the first stage, the optical flow or interframe correspondences is calculated from the input image sequence. The structure and motion is then estimated using some least-square or approaches involving nonlinear equations from the intermediate results of the first stage. It is possible to recover the structure and motion directly from the spatial and temporal gradients of image intensity without computing the difficult task of optical flow or solving the correspondence problem[31,32].

13.5 REFERENCES

[1] J. M. Prager and M. A. Arbib, "Computing the Optimal Flow: The Match Algorithm and Prediction," Comp. Vision, Graphics, and Image Processing, 24, 1983, pp. 271-314.

[2] S. T. Barnard and W. B. Thomson, "Disparity Analysis of Images,' IEEE Trans. PAMI, Vol. 2, 1980, pp. 333-340.

[3] W. B. Thomson and S. T. Barnard, "Lower Level Estimation and Interpretation of Visual Motion," Computer 14, Number 8, 1981, pp. 20-28.

[4] C. Cafforio and F. Rocca, "Methods for Measuring Small Displacements of Television Images," IEEE Trans. Inform. Theory, IT-22, 1976, pp. 573-579.

[5] C. L. Fennema and W. P. Thomson, "Velocity Determination in Scenes Containing Several Moving Objects," Comp. Graph. Image Proc., 9, 1979, pp. 301-315.

[6] B. K. P. Horn and B. G. Schunck, "Determining Optical Flow," Artif. Intell. 17, 1981, pp. 185-203.

[7] M. Yachida, "Determining Velocity Maps by Spatio-Temporal Neighborhoods from Image Sequences," Comp. Vision, Graphics, Image Proc. 21, 1983, pp. 262-279.

[8] L. S. Davis, Z. Wu, H. Sun, "Contour Based Motion Estimation," Comp. Vision, Graphics, Image Proc. 23, 1983, pp. 313-326.

[9] E. C. Hildreth, "Computations Underlying the Measurement of Visual Motion," Artif. Intell. 23, 1984, pp. 309-354.

[10] J. P. F. D'Haeyer, "Determining Motion of Image Curves from Local Pattern Changes," Comp. Vision, Graphics, Image Proc. 34, 1986, pp. 166-188.

[11] A. M. Waxman and K. Wohn, "Contour Evolution, Neighborhood Deformation and Global Image Flow: Planar Surfaces in Motion," Intl. J. of Robotics Research 4,

1985, pp. 95-108.

[12] H. H. Nagel, "On the Estimation of Optical Flow: Relations Between Different Approaches and Some New Results," Artif. Intell. 33, 1987, pp. 299-324.

[13] H. H. Nagel, "Displacement Vectors Derived from Second Order Intensity Variations in Image Sequences," Comp. Vision, Graphics, Image Proc. 21, 1983, pp. 85-117.

[14] J. Wu, R. Brockett, K. Wohn, "A Contour-Based Recovery of Image Flow: Iterative Method," IEEE Conf. on Comp. Vision and Pattern Recognition, 1989, pp. 124-129.

[15] K. Kanatani, "Structure and Motion from Optical Flow Under Perspective Projections," Comp. Vision, Graphics, Image Proc. 38, 1987, pp. 122-146.

[16] A. M. Waxman and S. Ullman, "Surface Structure and 3-D Motion from Image Flow: A Kinematic Analysis," Tech. Rep. 24, College Park, University of Maryland, Center for Automation Research, 1983.

[17] M. Subbarao and A. M. Waxman, "Closed Formm Solutions to Image Flow Equations for Planar Surface in Motion," Comp. Vision, Graphics, Image Proc. 36, 1986, pp. 208-228.

[18] K. Kanatani, "Structure from Motion Without Correspondence: General Principle," Proc. 9th Int. Joint Conf. Artif. Intell., Los Angeles, CA, 1985, pp. 886-888.

[19] J. W. Roach and J. K. Aggarwal, "Computer Tracking of Objects Moving in Space," IEEE Transactions PAMI, Vol. PAMI-1, No. 2, April 1979, pp. 127-135.

[20] J. W. Roach and J. K. Aggarwal, "Determining the Movement of Objects from a Sequence of Images," IEEE Transactions PAMI, Vol. PAMI-2, No. 6, November 1980, pp. 554-562.

[21] S. Ullman, The Interpretation of Visual Motion, MIT Press, Cambridge, 1979.

[22] R. Y. Tsai and T. S. Huang, "Estimating 3-D Motion Parameters of a Rigid Planar Patch I," IEEE Transactions ASSP, Vol. ASSP-29, No. 6, December 1981, pp. 1147-1152.

[23] R. Y. Tsai and T. S. Huang, "Uniqueness and Estimation of Three-Dimensional Motion Parameters of Rigid Objects with Curved Surface," IEEE Transactions PAMI, Vol. PAMI-6, No. 1, January 1984, pp. 13-26.

[24] H. C. Longuet-Higgins, "A Computer Algorithm for Reconstructing a Scene from Two Projections," Nature, Vol. 293, September 1981, pp. 133-135.

[25] I. Pavlin, "Motion from a Sequence of Images" SPIE Proc., Vol. 852, Nov. 1987, Cambridge, MA.

[26] H. Shariat, "The Motion Problem: How to Use More Than Two Frames," Ph.D. Dissertation, Univ. of Southern California, 1986.

[27] M. E. Spetsakis and Aloimonos, "Closed Form Solution to the Structure and Motion Problem from Line Correspondences," Proc. Six National Conf. on Artif. Intell. AAAI-87, Seattle, WA, July 1987, pp. 738-743.

[28] Y. Liu and T. S. Huang, "Estimation of Rigid Body motion Using Straight Line Correspondiences," IEEE Workshop on Motion: Representation and Analysis, Kiawah Island, SC, May 1986, pp. 47-51, also in CVGIP 43, pp. 37-52, 1988.

[29] A Mitiche, S. Seida, J. K. Aggarwal, "Line Based Computation of Structure and Motion Using Angular Invariance," IEEE Workshop on Motion: Representation and Analysis, Kiawah Island, SC, May 1986, pp. 175-180.

[30] E. Salari, C. M. Jong, "A Method to Calculate the Structure and Motion Parameters from Line Correspondences," Pattern Recognition, Vol. 23, No. 6, 1990, pp. 553-561.

[31] S. Negahdaripour and B.K.P. Horn, "Determining 3-D Motion of Planar Objects from Image Brightness Patterns," Proc. of the Intern. Joint Conf. on Artif. Intell., 1985, pp. 898-901.

[32] M. Yamamoto, "Direct Estimation of 3-D Motion Parameters from Image Sequence and Depth," Systems and Computers in Japan, Vol. 17, No. 2, 1986, pp. 59-68.

[33] E. Salari, S. Balaji, "Correspondences of Straight Lines Using Graph-Theoretic Approach," Proc. of the IEEE Intern. Conf. on Systems Eng., Pittsburgh, pp. 562-565, Aug. 9-11, 1990.

Chapter 14

Detection and Representation of Events in Motion Trajectories

K. Gould, K. Rangarajan, M. Shah

14.1 Introduction

The world we live in changes with time. Our visual system is capable of discovering these changes; in particular we are able to detect moving objects and recover structure from their motion. In our daily life we move our eyes, head and sometimes whole body in order to perceive the changing environment and to interact with the surroundings. We can recognize objects by looking at their shape only, however, recognition tremendously improves if motion information is incorporated as well. Conventional approaches to dynamic scene analysis attempt to recover structure of objects using a sequence of frames, under the assumption that the structure information will be used by a recognition system. However, motion itself has generally not been used explicitly for recognition. Moreover, most approaches to the *structure from motion* problem involve a number of assumptions regarding the objects and their motion, and can only deal with a restricted set of cases with a certain minimum number of points in some minimum number of frames. It is also necessary in these approaches to solve systems of non-linear equations using approximate methods which are very sensitive to noise.

We propose a *different* approach for the use of motion, in which the motion characteristics of moving objects are used without actually recovering the structure. In this approach, we consider extended trajectories followed by the objects. We believe that in many cases, where an object has a fixed and predefined motion, the trajectories of several points on the object may serve to uniquely identify the object itself. Therefore, it should be possible to recognize certain objects based on motion characteristics obtained from trajectories of representative points.

A group of trajectories carry information about the motion as well as the shape of the object they belong to. Therefore, a method which uses trajectory information for recognizing objects will be superior to the method using *only shape* information. Because it will be able to distinguish between objects having the same structure, but different motion, and between objects having the same motion, but different structure. One isolated trajectory does not carry any explicit information about the object shape, for instance a point on rotating cylinder and a cube will give rise to very similar trajectories. However, a translating cube and rotating cube can always be distinguished, because the spatial relationship between the points in sequential frames as well as the trajectories of points themselves will differ.

One domain of application for a system that recognizes objects based on their trajectories is in a controlled environment such as a factory, where the trajectories of objects can be used to distinguish between stationary and various moving obstacles. This information can then be used in planning a path for a moving piece of machinery. TPS can also be applied to track the motion of stars in the solar system, the trajectory followed by a military target, and chromosome motion in the human body.

In our approach, trajectories will be represented in a manner which will simplify the identification of changes in motion. The representation of the trajectories are analyzed at multiple scales in order to identify important *events* corresponding to discontinuities in direction, speed, and acceleration using scale-space. These important events are recorded in a representation called *Trajectory Primal Sketch* (TPS).

In Section 2, methods for representing trajectories and the changes in motion which occur in the trajectories will be discussed. In order to identify which of these changes are significant, the scale-space of the trajectory representation is calculated. This is discussed in Section 3. Section 4 deals with identifying the primitives of motion as represented by trajectories. We have found that the primitives of motion are the *straight line, circle, ellipse, cycloid, and projectile.* The exact behavior of each of these primitives in the trajectory representations and in scale space has also been determined so that areas of the trajectory which correspond to one of these primitives can easily be identified. Determining the primitive types of unknown trajectories is discussed in Section 5. Section 6 presents some of the results we have obtained. Finally, the composite TPS is discussed in section seven.

14.1.1 Related Work

A great deal of work has been done in the field of psychology to show that people can recognize objects from their trajectories [5, 11]. It has been theorized that humans can recognize an object based on the motion of several points on that object by inferring the three dimensional structure of the object from the transformations the two dimensional image undergoes.

Cutting [2] discusses two similar concepts to be used for recovering the structure of objects from their trajectories. The first concept, which is due to Johansson [4] is that the motion of an object can be separated into two parts, the *common motion* or the motion of the objects as a whole, and the *relative motion* or the motion of the individual parts of the object with respect to the entire object. Cutting defines the term *absolute motion* which is the path of a particular point on the object. The absolute motion of a point is equal to the sum of the common motion of the object and the relative motion of the point. The absolute motion of a point is also its trajectory.

The second concept Cutting discusses is due to Wallach [12] who says that there are two types of displacements an object can undergo, those relative to the *object* and those relative to the *observer.* These ideas are similar to those of Marr, whose *object centered coordinate system* corresponds to Wallach's displacements relative to the object and whose *viewer centered coordinate system* corresponds to Wallach's displacements relative to the observer. Cutting points out that the perceived center of the object centered coordinate system is critical to correctly identifying the motion of the object and the object itself.

Cutting gives examples of six different types of motion, *rolling wheels, walking people, swaying trees, aging faces, the rotating night sky* and *expanding flow fields.* From experiments with human observers, Cutting concludes that the type of motion determines which coordinate system, object centered or viewer centered, should be used. In the first four examples Cutting suggests that an object centered coordinate system is used by the observers since only one object in each image is moving. In the last two examples, expanding flow fields and the rotating night sky, a viewer centered coordinate system is more appropriate because the entire environment is changing rather than just one object.

Todd [11] is interested in distinguishing between rigid and several types of non-rigid motion such as bending, stretching, twisting and flowing. By displaying the trajectories of either rigid or non-rigid objects, Todd shows that human observers are able to distinguish between the two. Human observers are also able to visualize the three dimensional form of the rigidly moving objects from their trajectories.

Todd explains this by noting that the two dimensional projections of rotating rigid objects are elliptical trajectories, the minor axes of these ellipses lie along a single straight line, and the points must traverse these ellipses at the same frequencies. The purpose of Todd's experiments was to determine what would affect the observer's ability to distinguish between rigid and non-rigid motion, such as whether the axis of rotation is moving or stationary, the frame rate, and the speed of rotation, none of which affected performance significantly, and the number of frames, which did significantly affect the performance of the observers. He also found that some non-rigid motions are easier to detect than others. Non-rigid motions due to differences in relative frequency and orientation are easier to detect than those due to relative eccentricity.

14.1.2 Background - Primal Sketch

The term primal sketch has previously been used in shape representation. Marr introduced the term when he defined the *raw primal sketch* [6]. The raw primal sketch contains primitives which are *edges, bars, blobs* and *terminations.* Each primitive is further described by its orientation, contrast, length, width and position. These primitives represent the information from the zero-crossings of several channels. The raw primal sketch is used to create the *full primal sketch.* This is done by grouping the primitives in the raw primal sketch into tokens and finding the boundaries among sets of tokens. The main idea is to integrate the information from several channels of zero-crossings and identify primitives which correspond to significant intensity changes, and then recursively grouping these changes into boundaries.

A second example of the use of the term primal sketch is Asada and Brady's *curvature primal sketch* [1]. The curvature primal sketch is a method for representing the significant curvature changes on the boundaries of objects. The primitives are *corner* and *smooth join*, and the *crank, end*, and *bump* or *dent* which are combinations of corners.

We would like to define a new primal sketch, the trajectory primal sketch, which is used not in shape representation, but in motion representation. We will define a set of primitives which will represent the motion characteristics of trajectories, and show how unknown trajectories can be described using these primitives.

14.2 Trajectory Representations

Significant changes in motion refer to a segment of the trajectory where the direction of motion of the point, the speed of the point or both are changing rapidly. In order to identify the significant changes, a representation which contains all the information of the trajectory itself while making the motion analysis simpler is necessary. In other words changes in motion must be accurately represented and easy to identify. Specifically we would like to work with several 1-dimensional functions rather than the 2-dimensional projection of the trajectory. The approach we have taken to find an adequate trajectory representation is discussed below.

14.2.1 Trajectory $\Psi - S$ Curve Representation

Our first approach was to use a representation based on the $\Psi - S$ curve. The $\Psi - S$ curve is typically used in shape representation to define the boundaries of objects. In the case of trajectories, Ψ refers to the direction of motion of a point between two sequential time frames with respect to a horizontal line. S refers to the distance that a point moves between time t_i and t_{i-1}. This is a parametric one-dimensional function where $\sum_i S_i$ is the parameter. $\sum_n S_n$, where n is the number of frames in the trajectory, equals the total distance a point covers in moving from its initial position to its final position.

S and Ψ are calculated by applying the following equations to the trajectory points where (x_i, y_i) are the coordinates of a point in frame i.

$$S = \sqrt{(x_i - x_{i-1})^2 + (y_i - y_{i-1})^2} \tag{14.1}$$

$$\Psi = tan^{-1}\left(\frac{y_i - y_{i-1}}{x_i - x_{i-1}}\right) \tag{14.2}$$

The $\Psi - S$ curve accurately records the shape of the trajectory however two problems exist. First, $\sum_i S_i$ is a difficult parameter to work with. Second, the $\Psi - S$ curve itself does not consider the possible changes in speed of the point. This is a *serious* problem since the speed of a point, and therefore the time at which a significant change in motion occurs, is essential to the understanding of motion. This problem is illustrated in Figure 14.1.

Figure 14.1 shows the trajectories of two different rolling balls which cover the same amount of distance over the same path. The only difference between these two rolling balls is that the ball in Figure 14.1.(b) is moving faster than the ball in Figure 14.1.(a). It takes the ball in Figure 14.1.(a) 377 frames to cover the same distance that the ball in Figure 14.1.(b) covers in only 94 frames. As shown in Figure 14.1.(c) and (d), the $\Psi - S$ curves of the trajectories in Figure 14.1.(a) and (b), respectively, are virtually the same shape. In other words the significant changes in the shape of the two curves occur at the same position on the S axis.

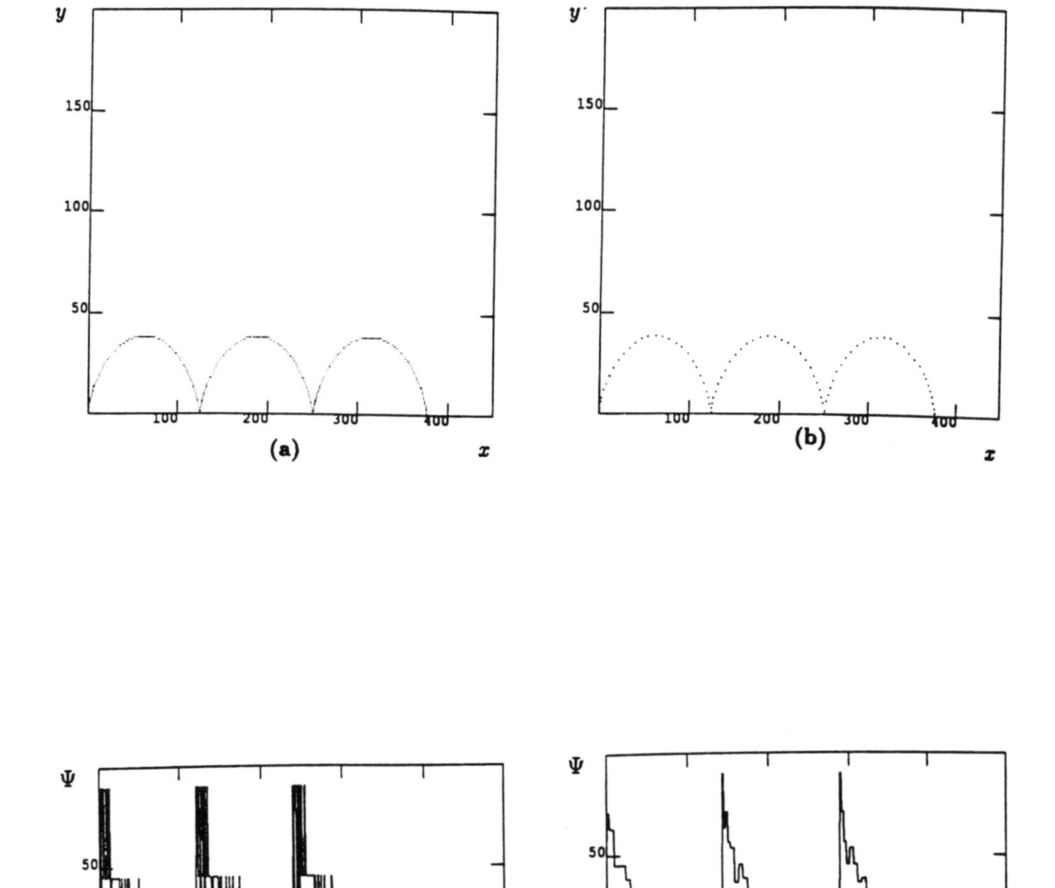

Figure 14.1: Trajectory of one point on (a) A rolling ball through 377 frames, (b) A second rolling ball through 94 frames, (c) $\Psi - S$ curve of ball in (a), (d) $\Psi - S$ curve of ball in (b).

•	•	• •	•		•	• •	•	•
1	2	3 4	5		1	2 3	4	5
		(a)				(b)		

Figure 14.2: A point on a translating object. (a) Case a, (b) Case b. Even though the two motions are significantly different, since there is no change in the direction in both cases, the $\Psi - S$ like representation will not be able to distinguish between them.

Therefore the $\Psi - S$ curve representation is not adequate to distinguish between the two trajectories since a very valuable piece of information is lost, that is time. Another simple example is shown in Figure 14.2. Here the locations of a point on the translating object in five frames is shown for two cases. Even though the two motions are significantly different, since there is no change in the direction in both cases, the $\Psi - S$ like representation will not be able to distinguish between them.

14.2.2 Trajectory Direction and Speed Representations

When dealing with shape, the only relevant information is the direction and length of a line segment on the boundary. However, when dealing with motion, time is an essential piece of information to record. Therefore, instead of considering Ψ as a function of s, as is done in shape representation, two graphs are used. The first one plots Ψ, or the direction of motion, as a function of time. This is known as the *trajectory direction representation.* The second graph plots S, or distance, as a function of time and is known as the *trajectory speed representation.*

$$\Psi = \frac{tan^{-1}\left(\frac{y_i - y_{i-1}}{x_i - x_{i-1}}\right)}{\Delta t} \tag{14.3}$$

$$S = \frac{\sqrt{(x_i - x_{i-1})^2 + (y_i - y_{i-1})^2}}{\Delta t} \tag{14.4}$$

To simplify these equations, if t refers to the frame number rather than the actual time, then Δt is always equal to one, and two divisions are eliminated. The trajectory direction and speed representations make the changes in direction and speed very obvious to the human observer. They also make a strong distinction between changes in speed versus changes in direction.

Figure 14.3.(a) shows the direction curve for the trajectory in Figure 1.(a). Its shape is very similar to the $\Psi - S$ curve of that trajectory, except that it is not as long. This is because Ψ, or the direction, is plotted as a function of time rather than distance. If the object moved exactly one pixel each time frame, the $\Psi - S$ curve and the direction curve of that trajectory would be exactly the same since the point would be moving one unit of distance every unit of time. Figure 14.3.(b) shows the speed curve of the trajectory in Figure 14.1.(a). The small peaks in the speed curve are the areas of the trajectory where the ball is moving faster. By comparing the speed curve with the direction curve it is seen that the increase in speed occurs at the same time as the ball passes over the peaks in its trajectory. The ball is moving faster in these areas because the points in the trajectory are closer together, which means more distance is traveled in that time frame. The direction and speed curves for the rolling ball in Figure 14.1 .(b) are shown in Figure 14.4. These curves have similar shape but the elapsed time is much shorter.

14.2.3 Trajectory Velocity Representations

The trajectory velocity representations are another way to incorporate time into the $\Psi - S$ information. In this case there are again two graphs, the first one called v_x plots the velocity in the positive x direction against the time, the second graph called v_y plots the velocity in the positive y direction against time.

v_x and v_y are calculated from the following equations:

$$v_x = \frac{x_i - x_{i-1}}{\Delta t} \tag{14.5}$$

$$v_y = \frac{y_i - y_{i-1}}{\Delta t} \tag{14.6}$$

As with previous method, if we let t be the time between frames Δt becomes 1, simplifying the equations. Examples of the trajectory velocity representations for the two rolling balls in Figure 14.1 are shown in Figures 14.3 and 14.4. The v_x curves for both balls are cosine curves plus some constant which raises the curve above zero. The v_y curves for both balls are sine curves. Although v_x and v_y for the two different balls have the same general form, the amplitude and the frequency of these two sets of curves are very different.

The trajectory velocity representations record all the information available in the trajectory. Changes in motion are also easily identified from this trajectory representation. Segments of the curve which are fairly horizontal correspond to times when the motion of the point is fairly constant. Segments of the curve where the slope is not zero correspond to times when the motion of the point is changing. The greater the magnitude of the slope the more rapidly the motion is changing.

14.3 Trajectory Primal Sketch

This section describes a method for converting the trajectory velocity representations into the Trajectory Primal Sketch. The TPS must be a compact representation of the significant changes in motion. We create the first level of this compact representation by identifying the changes at various scales. This results in a set of contours known as *TPS contours*, where each contour corresponds to a change in motion. The important information contained in the TPS contours is the position or frame number at which a contour occurs, the height or strength of the TPS contour and the shape of the contour. Calculating the TPS contours, and extracting these important values from the contours are explained in the next two sections.

14.3.1 Calculating TPS Contours

Once the trajectory representations have been calculated, the changes in motion which appear as discontinuities in these representations need to be identified. This

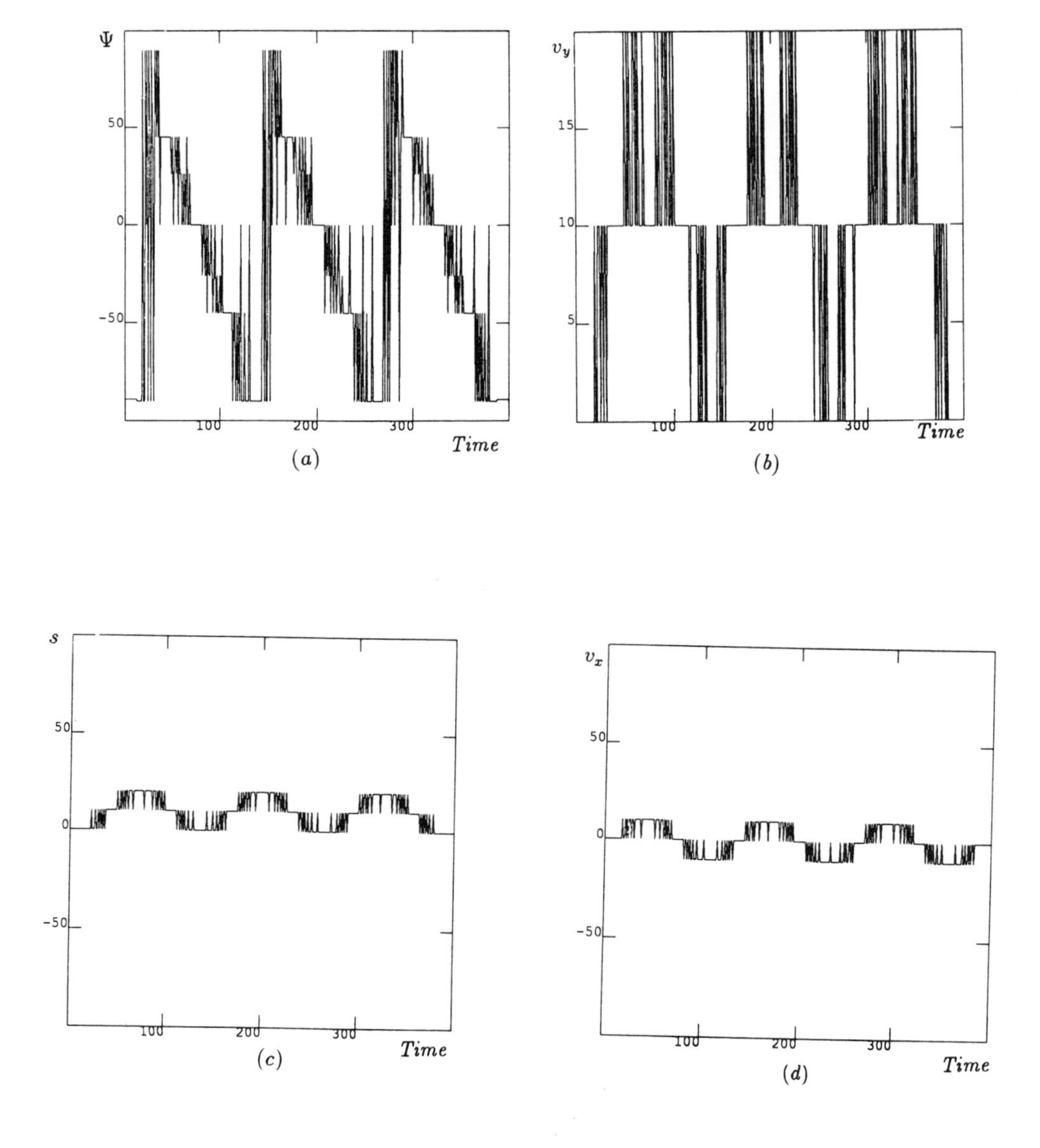

Figure 14.3: For rolling ball of Figure 1.a (a) Direction curve. (b) Speed curve. (c) v_x curve. (d) v_y curve.

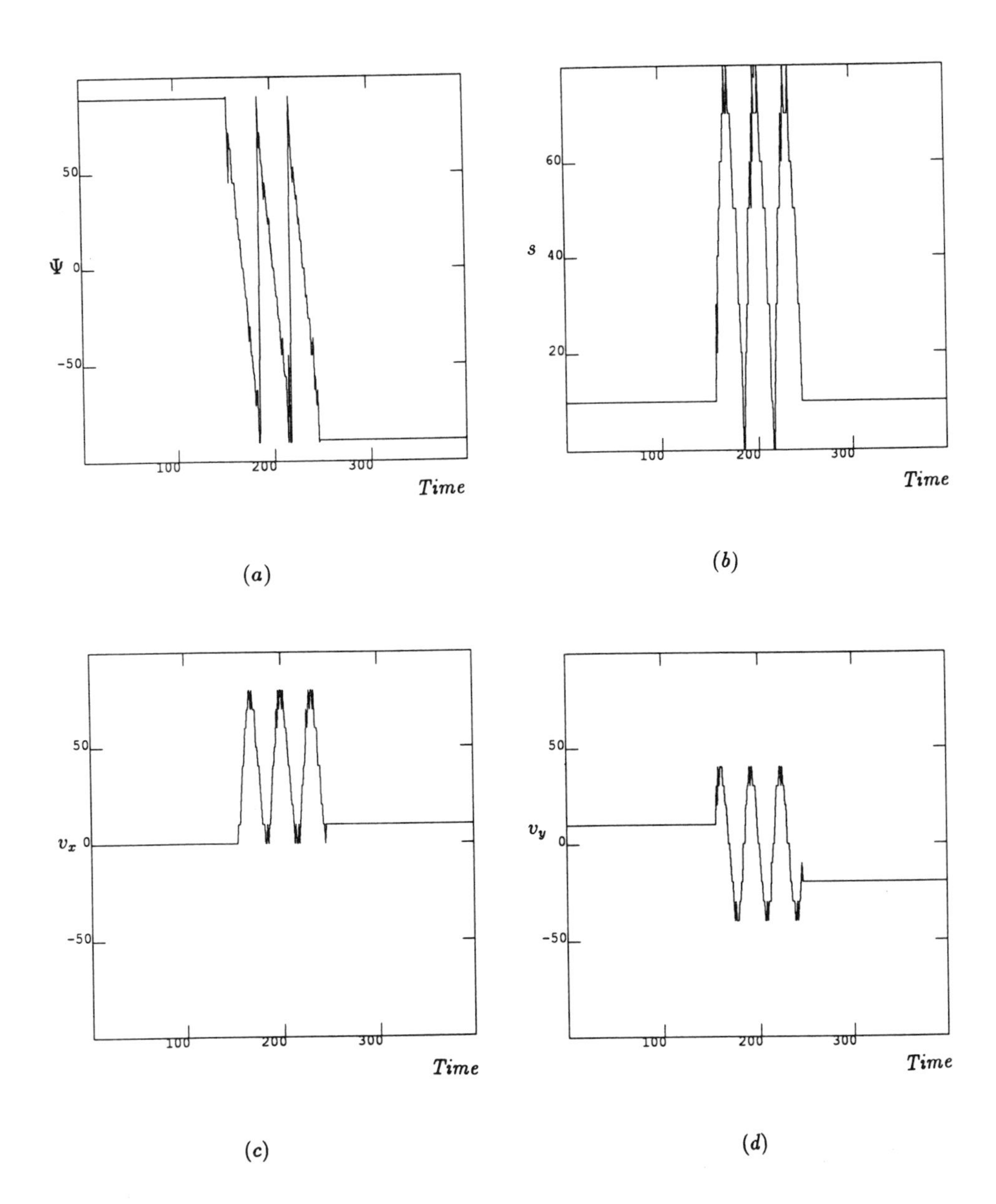

Figure 14.4: For rolling ball of Figure 1.b (a) Direction curve. (b) Speed curve. (c) v_x curve. (d) v_y curve.

is done by studying the scale-space of the trajectory representation [14, 10] which we call *TPS contours.* Scale space is used because the discontinuities may appear at various scales depending on the physical motion of the point.

The *TPS contours* are calculated by applying a mask to the input signal. This mask is created using the Gaussian and its derivatives, where the value of σ can vary between one and fifteen. The size of the mask is dependent on σ. Since the Gaussian approaches zero after 3σ, the size of the mask should be approximately $2 * (3 * \sigma)$. We have used a mask size which is equal to $6 * \sigma + 1$ to insure the size of the mask is odd. The results of applying this mask are then checked for zero-crossings which correspond to discontinuities at a particular scale. TPS contours are the curves which result from plotting the position of a zero-crossing, or the frame at which a zero-crossing occurred, on the horizontal axis and the value of σ on the vertical axis. An example of a typical trajectory and scalespace contours related to its v_x, and v_y are shown in Figure 14.5. It is clear from this Figure that nature of the contours is complex, there are large number of contours at the lower scale, which do not survive at higher scales. Therefore a method is needed to identify contours corresponding to important events.

14.3.2 Parsing TPS Contours

The TPS contours referred to in the previous section were represented as a simple list of coordinates, $(frame, \sigma)$, which correspond to the frame number and the value of σ at which a zero-crossing occurred. This list does not show any relation between the various coordinates, such as which zero-crossings lie on the same contour. In order to use this data to characterize motion we would like to link these unrelated zero-crossings and determine a representative location, strength and shape for each contour. Witkin refers to this process as Coarse-to-Fine tracking [14].

We begin by creating a two dimensional array in which elements that correspond to zero-crossings will have a value of one, all other elements will have a value of zero. This array will be used to link the zero-crossings into contours by tracking relatively adjacent elements of the two dimensional array with a value of one.

Tracking begins at the smallest σ value rather than at the largest σ value as in coarse-to-fine tracking. We have found that in some cases it is impossible to track a contour entirely from one endpoint to the other. Therefore we will start tracking at the smallest scale since the location of the zero-crossing is most accurate at this scale, and the accurate location of the zero-crossing is extremely important. After the two dimensional matrix is created with the frame number on its horizontal axis and σ on its vertical axis, the first zero-crossing is located. Next, we begin to track the contour which may begin with this zero-crossing by checking a neighborhood around this element for another zero-crossing. This neighborhood is shown in Figure 14.6. The current zero-crossing is marked by an $*$ in this Figure. The numbers refer to the order in which the adjacent elements are checked for the next zero-crossing. This tracking process continues until there are no zero-crossing in the neighborhood of the current zero-crossing. Then we return to the smallest value of σ and search for the next zero-crossing which may mark the beginning of another contour.

While performing this tracking process, three values are calculated which describe the contours *location, strength* and *shape.* The first value, the *location* of the contour, is simply the frame number where the contour originated. The *strength*

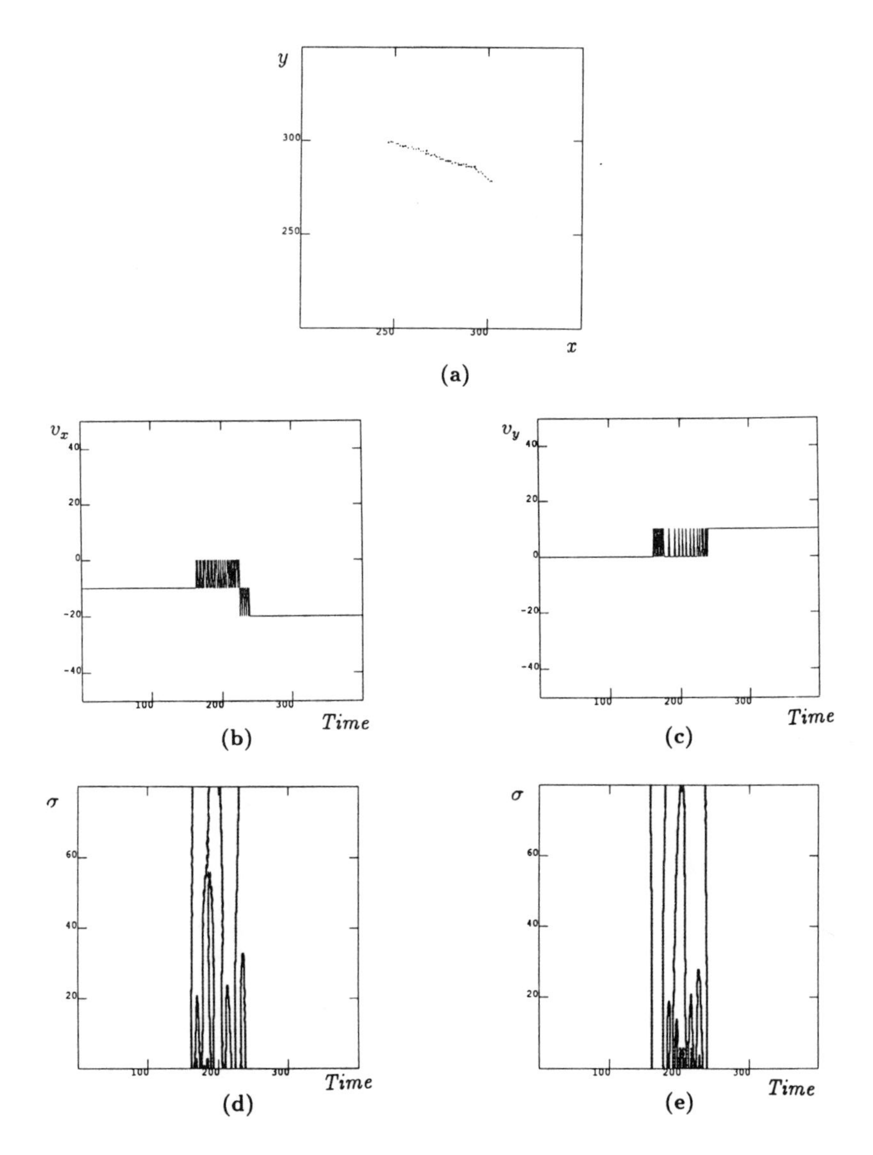

Figure 14.5: A typical trajectory and its representations. (a) Trajectory, (b) v_x, (c) v_y, (d) scalespace of v_x, (e) scalespace of v_y.

7	5	4	6	8
	2	1	3	
		*		

Figure 14.6: Neighborhood for tracking contours.

of the contour is the number of zero-crossings that belong to that contour. The value which represents the *shape*, or the *straightness*, of the contour is calculated by summing the distance between each zero-crossing as it is linked to the next zero crossing. For example if the next zero-crossing is in region one, then the distance equals one, or if the next zero-crossing is in region seven, then the distance equals $\sqrt{8}$. After the entire contour has been linked this sum is divided by the $strength - 1$. A contour whose next zero-crossing was always found in region one would have a *shape* value equal to one. The greater the shape value is the more curved and irregular the contour is.

Only the contours which survive over a large percentage of the range of σ should be considered to correspond to significant changes in motion. For our experiments we required that the contours survive over 60% of the σ values. The shape value could also be used to pick contours that represent significant changes in motion, since drastic changes in motion result in trajectory representation segments which are similar to step edges, and the scale-space model of a step edge is known to be a straight line [10]. The TPS contains these three values for all contours which survive.

14.4 Primitive Trajectories

In this section, we will present a number of *primitive* trajectories which can be written as analytical expressions. We will compute the expressions for their v_x, and v_y, and the *trajectory primal sketch contours.* For each primitive trajectory, we will identify important *events* in its TPS. The aim is to express an arbitrary trajectory as a composition of these primitives. We will consider four main types of motion: translation, rotation, projectile and cycloid.

14.4.1 Translation

The trajectory corresponding to translation can be expressed as a sum of straight lines. We know that the equation of a straight line is given by:

$$y = mx + c \tag{14.7}$$

where m, and c are the slope and y-intercept respectively. Now, incorporating the *time* in the above equation we can rewrite it as:

$$x = at \tag{14.8}$$

$$y = mat + c \tag{14.9}$$

Differentiating x, y with respect to t we get the expressions for v_x and v_y:

$$v_x = a \quad (14.10)$$

$$v_y = ma. \quad (14.11)$$

The sum of n such straight lines for a translation trajectory are given by:

$$x = \sum_{i=1}^{n} a_i t \left(U(t - t_i) - U(t - t_{i+1})\right) \quad (14.12)$$

$$y = \sum_{i=1}^{n} (m_i a_i t + c_i)\left(U(t - t_i) - U(t - t_{i+1})\right) \quad (14.13)$$

where $U(t)$ is the unit step function, defined such that $U(t) = 1$ for $t > 0$ and $U(t) = 0$ otherwise. Now, v_x, v_y are given by:

$$v_x = \sum_{i=1}^{n} a_i t \left(\delta(t - t_i) - \delta(t - t_{i+1})\right) + \sum_{i=1}^{n} a_i \left(U(t - t_i) - U(t - t_{i+1})\right) \quad (14.14)$$

$$v_y = \sum_{i=1}^{n} (m_i a_i t + c)\left(\delta(t - t_i) - \delta(t - t_{i+1})\right) + \sum_{i=1}^{n} (m_i a_i)\left(U(t - t_i) - U(t - t_{i+1})\right) \quad (14.15)$$

where $\delta(t)$ is the impulse function. Now, the TPS contours are the loci of zero-crossings of the following expression:

$$g_{tt}^{\sigma} * v_x = g_{tt}^{\sigma} * \sum_{i=1}^{n} a_i t \left(\delta(t - t_i) - \delta(t - t_{i+1})\right) + \sum_{i=1}^{n} a_i \left(U(t - t_i) - U(t - t_{i+1})\right) \quad (14.16)$$

$$= \sum_{i=1}^{n} a_i \left(t_i\, g_{tt}^{\sigma}(t_i) - t_{i+1}\, g_{tt}^{\sigma}(t_{i+1})\right) + \sum_{i=1}^{n} a_i \left(g_t^{\sigma}(t_i) - g_t^{\sigma}(t_{i+1})\right) \quad (14.17)$$

where $g_t{}^{\sigma}$, g_{tt}^{σ} are the respectively the first and second derivatives of Gaussian with zero mean and standard deviation σ ($g^{\sigma}(t) = e^{-\frac{t^2}{2\sigma^2}}$). And the TPS contours for v_y is given by:

$$g_{tt}^{\sigma} * v_y = g_{tt}^{\sigma} * \sum_{i=1}^{n} (m_i a_i t + c)\left(\delta(t - t_i) - \delta(t - t_{i+1})\right) + \sum_{i=1}^{n} (m_i a_i \left(U(t - t_i) - U(t - t_{i+1})\right) \quad (14.18)$$

$$= \sum_{i=1}^{n} (m_i a_i\, t_i + c)\, g_{tt}^{\sigma}(t_i)) - (m_i t_{i+1} + c)\, g_{tt}^{\sigma}(t_{i+1})$$

$$+ \sum_{i=1}^{n} m_i a_i \left(g_t^\sigma(t_i) - g_t^\sigma(t_{i+1})\right) \quad (14.19)$$

In Figure 14.7.a we have shown an example of translation motion of a point which is moving from location A to E in time $t_E - t_A$. Between locations A, and B the point is moving with the constant speed in the same direction. At location B the speed is changed instantaneously, but the direction remains the same, the point continues to move with the same speed and direction up to location C where the direction changes instantaneously but the speed remains the same. The point continues with the constant speed and in the same direction up to location D, where there is a sudden change in the speed as well as in the direction. The TPS for this trajectory contains the location, strength and shape of the TPS contours which correspond to significant changes in motion. The locations of these significant changes in motion are is shown in Figure 14.7.a . We have indicated the discontinuities in v_x by '+', and the discontinuities in v_y by 'X'. It is clear that the points B, C, and D are identified as events in the trajectory. At B we observe the discontinuity in v_x, while at C and D we have discontinuities in both v_x and v_y.

14.4.2 Rotation

The trajectory corresponding to the rotation around a *fixed* axis can be expressed by an *ellipse*. The ellipse is defined as follow:

$$\frac{x^2}{a^2} + \frac{y^2}{b^2} = 1 \quad (14.20)$$

where a, and b are the major and minor axes respectively. By incorporating time and writing this equation separately for v_x and v_y we get:

$$x = -a * \cos(\omega * t) \quad (14.21)$$

$$y = b * \sin(\omega * t) \quad (14.22)$$

where ω is frequency. Figure 14.8, shows the parametric representation of ellipse. The angle of rotation $\theta = \omega * t$. Notice, that for $a = b = r$ the above equations reduce to equations for a *circle* of radius r around the origin. The TPS contours of this trajectory can be obtained by convolving the above equations with g_{tt}^σ:

$$g_{tt}^\sigma * v_x = -g_{tt}^\sigma * (-a\omega) \sin \omega t \quad (14.23)$$

$$= -a\omega \sin \omega t \quad (14.24)$$

since there is no effect of convolving Gaussian with the sine function. Similarly, we get the following for v_y:

$$g_{tt}^\sigma * v_y = g_{tt}^\sigma * b\omega * \cos \omega t \quad (14.25)$$

$$= b\omega \cos \omega t \quad (14.26)$$

Therefore, in the interval 0— 2π the TPS contours of v_x will be three straight lines one each at $0, \pi, 2\pi$ for ωt. While the TPS contours of v_y will be two straight lines one each at $\frac{\pi}{2}, \frac{3\pi}{2}$. One example trajectory of a point rotating about a fixed axis is shown in Figure 14.7.b. Four events corresponding to this trajectory are also shown. The endpoints of the major axis are identified as significant changes in v_x.

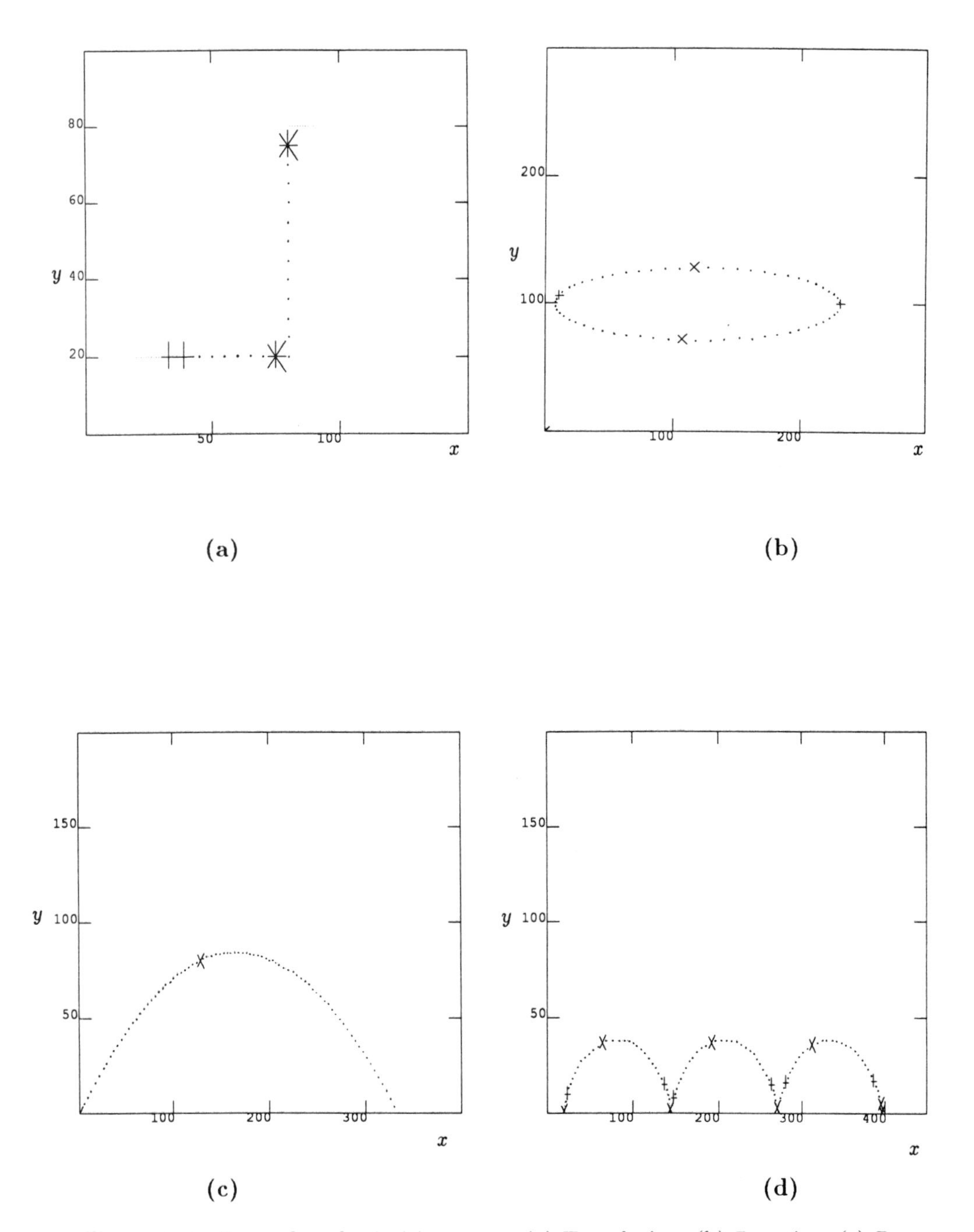

Figure 14.7: Examples of primitive types. (a) Translation, (b) Rotation, (c) Projectile, (d) Cycloid.

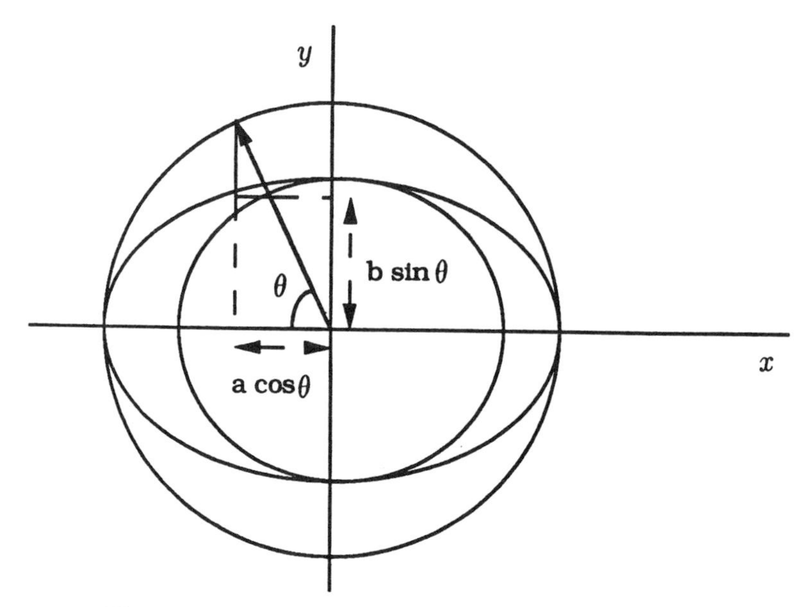

Figure 14.8: Parametric representation of an ellipse.

These are the points where, due to the direction of rotation (counter-clockwise), v_x makes the transition from positive values to negative on the right side of the ellipse and from negative to positive values on the left side of the ellipse. Similarly, at the endpoints of the minor axis, v_y changes from positive to negative values on the top and from negative to positive on the bottom. If the object were to rotate in the clockwise direction, the positions of the events would remain the same, but the positive to negative and negative to positive transitions would be exchanged.

14.4.3 Projectile

The trajectory followed by an object in the space due to *gravity* is called projectile motion, and it is defined as follows:

$$x = v_0(\cos\alpha)\,t \tag{14.27}$$

$$y = v_0\sin\alpha\, t + \mathcal{G}\frac{t^2}{2} \tag{14.28}$$

where v_0 is initial velocity, $\mathcal{G}$ is the acceleration due to gravity, and α is the angle. Differentiating above equations with respect to t we get:

$$v_x = -v_0\cos\alpha \tag{14.29}$$

$$v_y = v_0\sin\alpha + \mathcal{G}\,t \tag{14.30}$$

Figure 14.7.c shows a synthetic trajectory and its TPS for projectile. A sole event in this trajectory is a change in v_y which is indicated by an 'X'. This event occurs at the position where the values of v_y shift from positive changes to negative changes.

14.4.4 Cycloid

The trajectory followed by the object which is rotating around a translating axis is defined by a cycloid. The cycloid is defined as:

$$x = a(\omega t - \sin \omega t) \quad (14.31)$$

$$y = a(1 - \cos \omega t) \quad (14.32)$$

where a is constant, and ω is the frequency. The expressions for v_x, and v_y are:

$$v_x = a(\omega - \omega \cos \omega t) \quad (14.33)$$

$$v_y = a\omega \sin \omega t \quad (14.34)$$

We have shown in Figure 14.7.d a trajectory corresponding to cycloid motion. This trajectories might be obtained from a point on the rim of a rolling wheel. This trajectory contains both types of discontinuities. The changes in v_y, indicated by an 'X', occur at the top of each peak and in between peaks. These are the positions where v_y changes from positive to negative or negative to positive. The changes in v_x occur between the peaks on both sides of the v_y event. This is due to a change in speed as each point approaches the bottom of the peak. The first '+' in each pair marks a slowing down in the positive x direction, while the second '+' marks a speeding up of the point in the positive x direction.

14.5 Determining Primitive Type

The *trajectory primal sketch* contains the location, strength, and shape of the TPS contours for the discontinuities in velocity as well as the discontinuities in the first derivative of velocity i.e. the discontinuities in acceleration. From the analysis and examples in section 4, it is clear that the first derivative discontinuities of both the rotation and cycloid have a sine and cosine relationship to each other. Therefore the first step in identifying primitive types is to separate all the trajectories into two categories. The first category or the *rotation/cycloid group* will contain all trajectories which exhibit a sine/cosine relationship in the first derivative. Everything else will be placed into the *translation group*.

The rotation/cycloid group can be broken down further into either rotation or cycloid motion by examining the discontinuities in velocity as well as the discontinuities in the first derivative of velocity. As predicted in the analysis of cycloid motion, the v_x graph for cycloid motion will be shifted some value above or below the zero axis. So when the velocity discontinuities for v_x are calculated, the scale space contours will not look like a cosine curve as they did with the acceleration discontinuities. Therefore v_x and v_y will not have a sine/cosine relationship. However, the scale space of v_x and v_y of a rotating trajectory will have a sine/cosine relationship. Rotation and cycloid motion can be differentiated by checking for a sine/cosine relationship in the velocity discontinuities. If it exists, then the trajectory is an example of rotation, otherwise it is a cycloid.

The trajectories placed into the translation group can also be further classified. The trajectories themselves will be broken down into segments, and each of these segments will be classified as either *straight line translation* or *curved translation*. The value of the slope of the velocity curve is the same as the value of the acceleration of the point within that segment. When a point is moving in a straight line, the acceleration of v_x and v_y must be the same. However, when a point is turning steadily, i.e., moving in a curved line, then the acceleration of v_x and v_y will be different. The slope of v_x and v_y within a segment are compared to see if they are similar to each other within a reasonable bound; if they are then the corresponding segment of the trajectory is labeled as straight line translation. If the values of the slopes are significantly different from each other, then the segment of the trajectory is labeled as curved translation.

The segmentation is accomplished by using the locations of the TPS contours of both the v_x and v_y graphs of a trajectory as the end points of each segment. The slope of v_x and v_y are calculated within each segment using the values of the velocity graphs at each of the end points of the segment. The slope of v_x and v_y are then compared to determine if the translation is straight line or curved.

Using the locations of significant changes in motion found in the TPS and this method, the primitive type of all the trajectories in this paper have been correctly determined.

14.6 Examples

In this section we will present results analyzing the TPS for a number of trajectories obtained from real scenes. Since the trajectories from the real scenes were given for a small number of frames, we used interpolation to explode the original trajectories to a large number of frames. We assumed that the motion between any two consecutive frames was in a straight line. In fact, one can compute the extended trajectories with a large number of frames from a moving sequence without using any assumptions. Here, we do not consider that to be any significant factor in our results.

Figure 14.9 shows four trajectories from the Superman sequence which was used by Sethi and Jain [9]. The TPS for one of the trajectories is shown in Figure 14.9.(d). This particular trajectory is made by tracking a point on the head of the leftmost man in the scene. Note that all important events, i.e. the places where the direction or speed of the man changes, in this trajectory are captured by the TPS. The changes occur as the man moves both toward the camera and slightly to the right. The changes in v_x occur as the man makes small changes in direction and changes in speed. The changes in direction in v_y correspond to the man's head bobbing up and down as he runs toward the camera. There are also changes in speed. Figure 14.10 shows the v_x and v_y and corresponding scalespace contours for this trajectory.

Next, the results for the Blocks scene are shown in Figure 14.11. In this scene four different blocks are moving towards the center of the image. Trajectories of points on two of these block are shown in Figure 14.11.(a). These two block are a rectangular shaped block which travels from left to right across the image, and a triangular shaped block which moves from the upper right corner of the image to the center of the image. The TPS of a point on the rectangle is shown in Figure 14.11.(b). The two blocks whose trajectories are not shown are a rectangle which does not move and a triangle which moves from the bottom center of the image to the top center. The Figure 14.12 shows the results for Object scene. This scene consists of three rectangular blocks, one begins at the lower left corner of the image, the second begins in the lower right, and the third begins at the top center of the

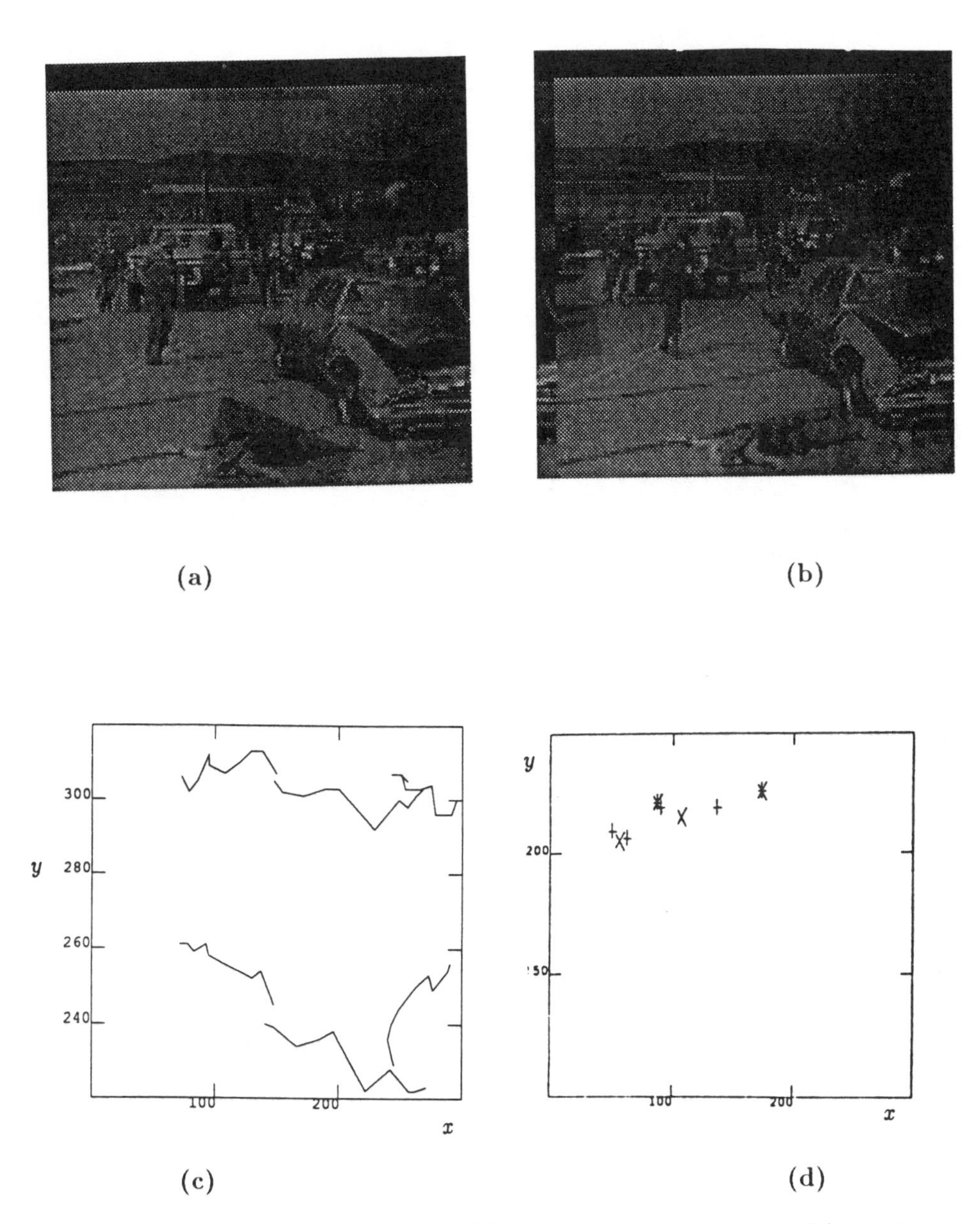

Figure 14.9: Superman Sequence (a)-(b). Two frames of sequence, (c). Trajectories, (d). TPS of S1 trajectory.

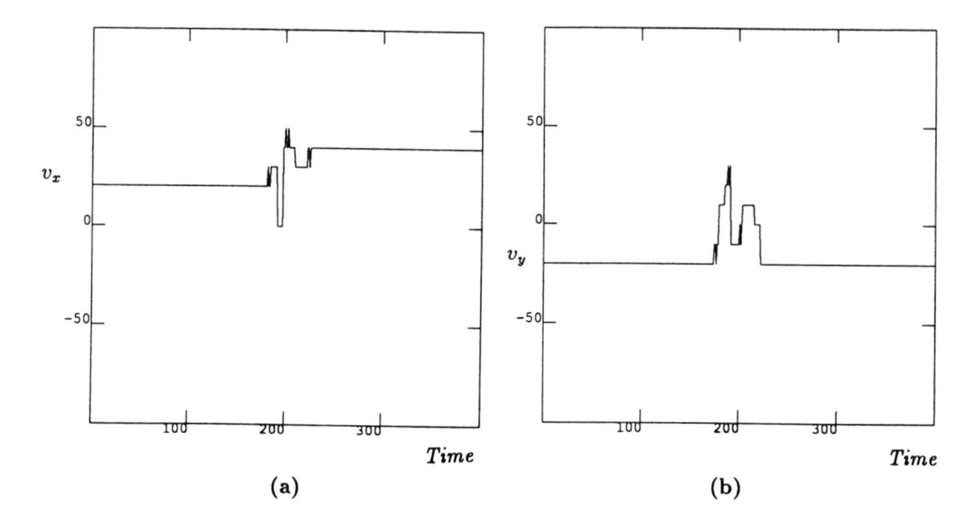

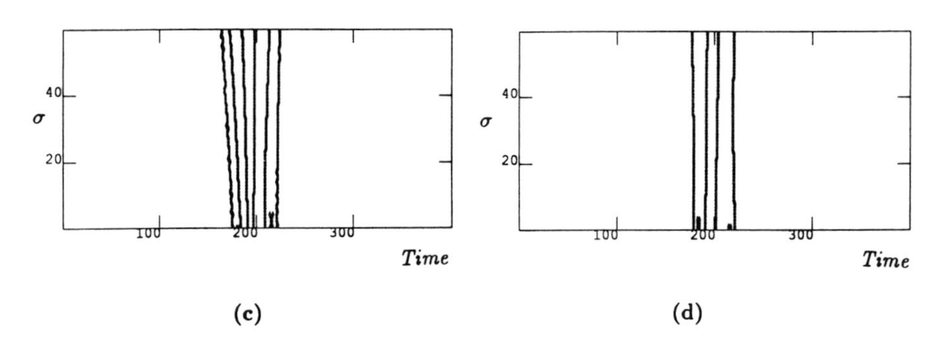

Figure 14.10: Trajectory Velocities of S1 and their scalespaces. (a). v_x, (b). v_y, (c). Scalespace of v_x, (d). Scalespace of v_y.

image. All three of the blocks move toward the center of the image in a straight line, they meet in the middle and then continue away from each other. Trajectories of three points on the block which begins at the lower left corner of the image are shown in Figure 14.12.(a). The TPS of one of these trajectories is shown in Figure 14.12.(b).

Figure 14.13 contains the nine trajectories of the Card sequence and three images from this sequence. This sequence consists of two objects moving from right to left and slightly upwards. Figure 14.13.(e) shows the TPS of one trajectory on the top object, and (f) is the TPS of a trajectory on the lowest object. Both these objects are translating, but each has several velocity changes in both x and y.

Figure 14.14 shows the trajectories obtained from the *Walker* sequence. This sequence was obtained from a program reported by Cutting [3]. In this sequence a person is shown walking. Eleven points representing the head, right shoulder, left and right knees, left and right elbows, right hip, left and right wrists, and left and right ankles of a person are tracked through ten frames. The trajectory is then expanded to obtain 99 frames using the interpolation method described earlier. The entire body moves up and down in a slight bouncing manner. The movements of the shoulder and hip are ellipsoidal and the movement of arms and legs are pendular. Figure 14.14.(c) shows the TPS for one foot of the walker while (d) show the TPS for an elbow. The trajectory of the foot changes velocity in both the x and y direction. The velocity of the elbow changes in the x direction with only one change in the y direction. Figure 14.14.(e) shows the TPS for one wrist of the walker. This trajectory has several velocity changes in the x direction, and two changes in the y direction where the wrist move up slightly and then down again.

The primitive type of all the trajectories in this section is translation, and based on the information in the TPS, they are classified as translation by our procedure for determining primitive types.

14.7 Composite Trajectory Primal Sketch

So for we have been dealing with individual trajectories. There can be several trajectories belonging to a single object, we would like to create a composite representation which captures the commonalities between trajectories belonging to the same object. This representation, we shall refer to as *CTPS*, *Composite Trajectory Primal Sketch*. A representation of a set of data is complete, if the data can be regenerated from the representation with a desired accuracy. In the case of CTPS, the input data is the coordinates of the feature points in the frames taken at different instants. Therefore, we will also present a reconstruction scheme for translation and rotation cases.

14.7.1 Translation

When the objects are quite far away from the camera, orthographic projection can be assumed. Under orthographic projection, trajectories of points on an object that undergoes translation only are identical and hence have identical sets of events in their TPS. The events could be either in v_x or v_y or both. The CTPS representation stores the events on one of the trajectories and the spatial coordi-

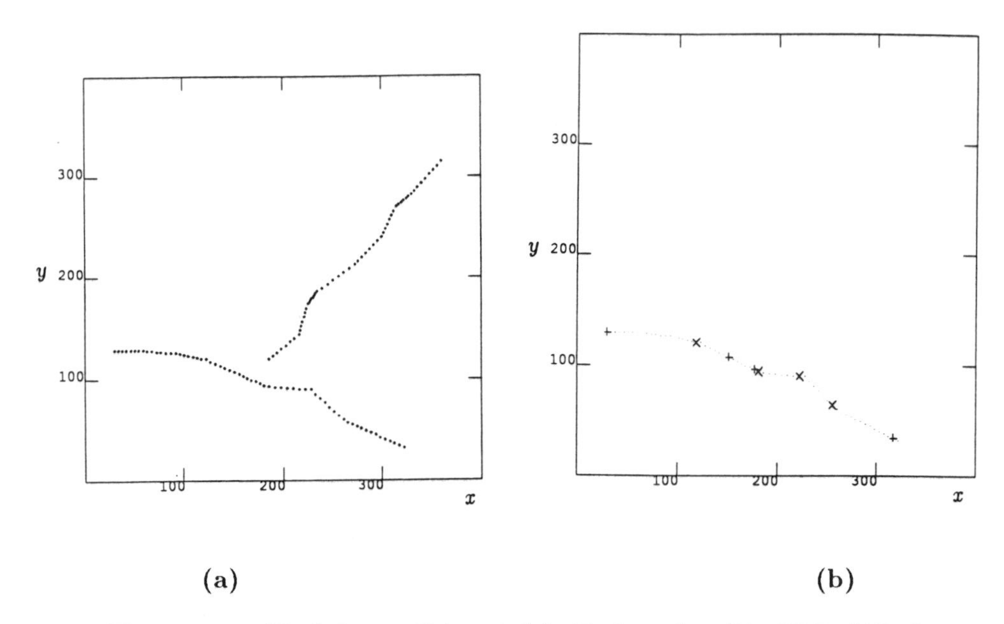

Figure 14.11: Block Scene Object-A (a). Trajectories, (b). TPS of Block1

nates of all the tracked points in the first frame. Each event is characterized by its location i.e the frame number of its occurrence, and average v_x and v_y at that instant. The average v_x at the instance of an event is calculated by dividing the displacement in x between this event and the immediate next event by the time interval between them. The average v_y at the instance of an event is calculated by dividing the displacement in y between this event and the immediate next event by the time interval between them. The CTPS representation also stores an initial event located in the first frame, in addition to the observed events. With this information, we will be able to recreate the entire sequence for all the points on the object.

Figure 14.15 shows the CTPS structure for the translation case. Figure 14.16.a shows one of the trajectories with the TPS events marked on it. The trajectory of the Cube has been chosen so as to include all possible combinations of events in v_x and v_y. Initially the Cube is traveling along the x direction with a velocity of $v_x = 3$ and $v_y = 0$, and in frame 21 it changes its direction and moves along the y axis with $v_x = 0$ and $v_y = 2$. This is a speed change in both x and y directions and is accompanied by a direction change. This change is registered as an event in both v_x and v_y in TPS. In frame 51, cube increases its speed alone i.e. $v_x = 0$, $v_y = 4$, without changing its direction. This shows up as an event in v_y alone. In frame 81 the Cube changes its velocity to $v_x = 2$, $v_y = 4$ with a direction change. This is registered as an event in v_x only. Next, in frame 111 the Cube changes its velocity to $v_x = 4$, $v_y = 0$ with a direction change, this shows up an event both in v_x and v_y. In frame 146 it changes its velocity to $v_x = 6$, $v_y = 0$, which is an event

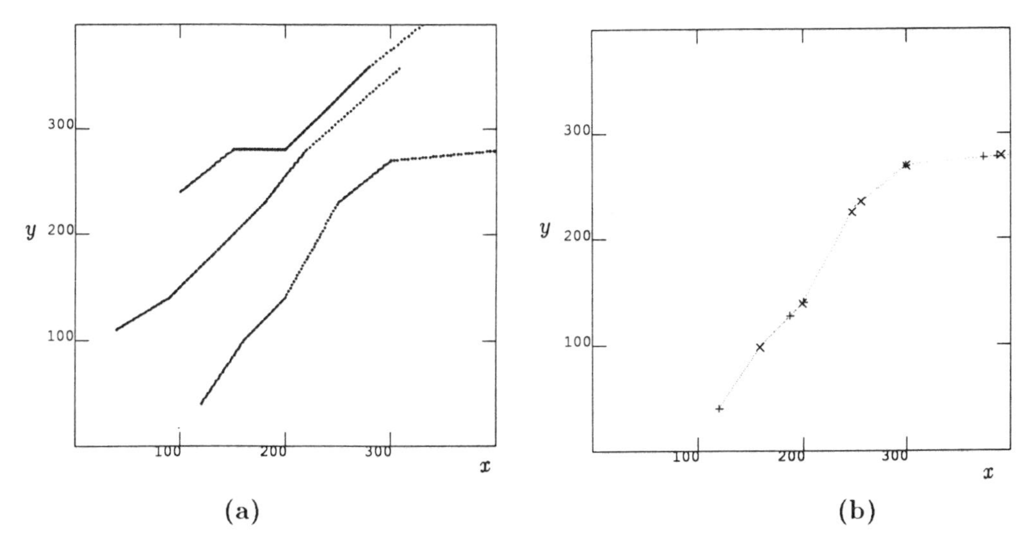

Figure 14.12: Block Scene Object-B (a). Trajectories, (b). TPS of OA1

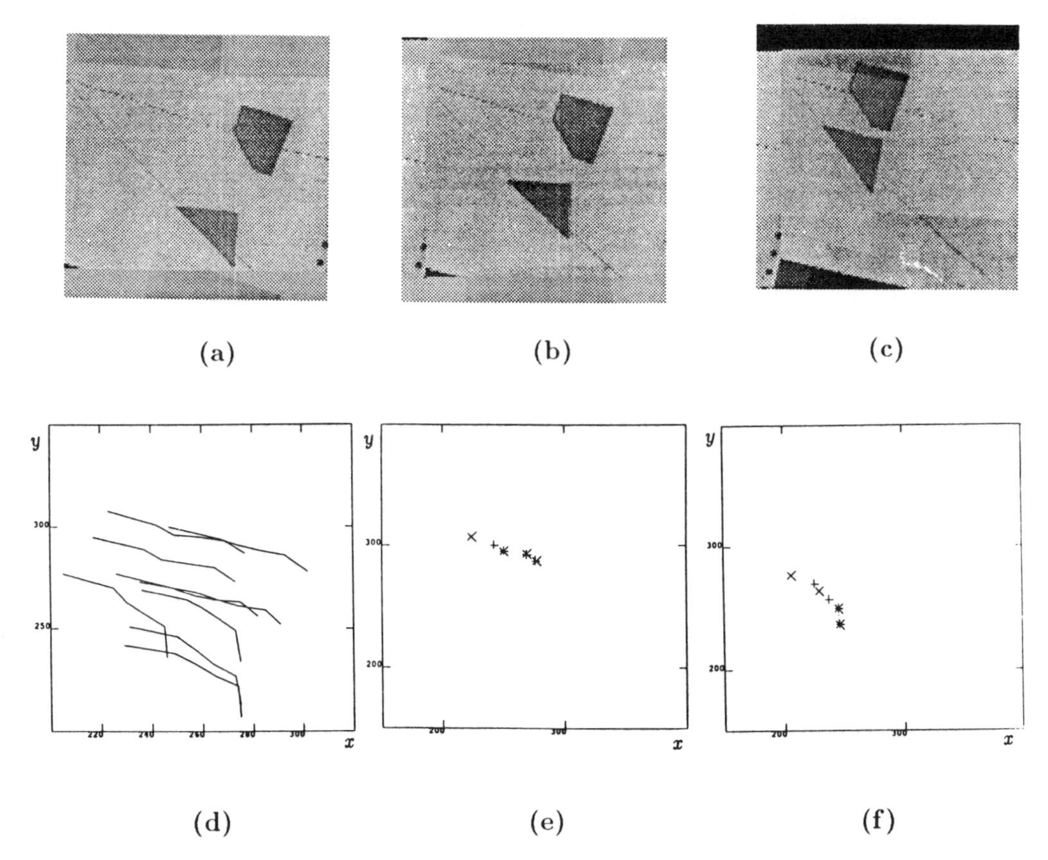

Figure 14.13: Card Sequence. (a) Frame-1, (b) Frame-3, (c) Frame-5, (d) Trajectories, (e). TPS of Block1, (f) TPS of Block2.

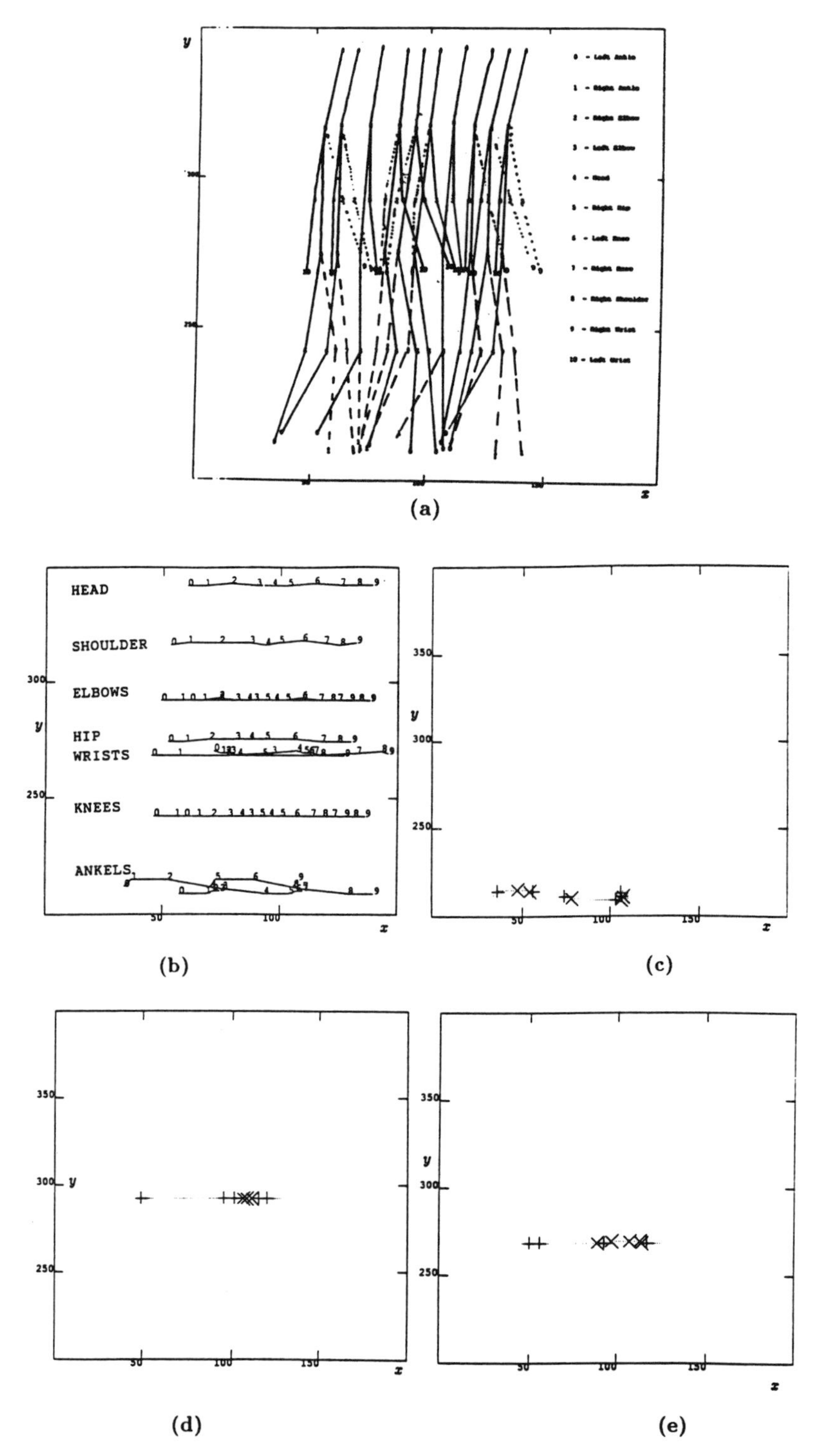

Figure 14.14: Results for Walker Scene. (a) Walker Sequence, (b) Trajectories, (c) TPS of Right Foot, (d) Left Elbow, (e) Wrist.

in x alone without direction change. In frame 176 it changes its velocity to $v_x = 6$, $v_y = -2$ which is an event in v_y alone without a direction change. In frame 206 it changes its velocity to $v_x = 12$, $v_y = -4$ which is an event in both v_x and v_y without a direction change. Finally, in frame 241 it changes its velocity to $v_x = 0$, $v_y = -4$ which is an event in v_x alone and it involves a direction change. Figure 14.16.b shows the CTPS representation for the Cube. Figure 14.16.c shows the reconstructed trajectories from the representation.

Figures 14.17.a-b and 14.17.c-d show shows respectively the first and last two frames in a 15 frame sequence. We applied the Moravec interest operator [7] to this sequence of images and selected interesting points by setting a threshold. The interest points in the first frame were then edited to choose two points on the walking man, one on his head and another on his shoulder. The interest points selected in the first frame are shown in Figure 14.17.e. The correspondence method [8], with minor modifications was used to compute the trajectory of these two points. The generated trajectories of these two points are almost parallel, as expected and are shown in figure 14.17.f. The ctps representation of this trajectory is shown in figure 14.17.g. The reconstructed trajectories, by choosing events which survive over 5% of the σ values are shown in figure 14.17.h. The number of events picked up is nearly equal to the number of frames in the trajectory. One reason being with a low threshold of 5%, even weak events survive. Therefore, the number of events can be varied depending on the application by changing the threshold. The other reason being the number of frames considered is not large. We had problems in generating a long sequence with a stationary camera, as the object was moving out of view in a small interval of time.

14.7.2 Rotation

As noted earlier trajectories corresponding to the rotation around a fixed axis can be represented by an ellipse. An ellipse is characterized by its phase, frequency, eccentricity, orientation, size, x-intercept and the distance between the x-intercept and the center of ellipse [11]. Storing the spatial coordinates of the end points of its major and minor axis along with the frequency and phase information also completely specifies an ellipse. The line joining the end points of the minor axis is extended to obtain the x-intercept, the orientation of this line is the orientation of the ellipse, also the lengths of the major and minor axis are used to compute the size and eccentricity. The point of intersection between the major and the minor axis marks the center of the ellipse and hence the distance between the $x-$intercept and the center of the ellipse is computed. Trajectories of points lying on the same rotating object are ellipses with the same frequency, orientation and x-intercept [11]. The fixed axis assumption [13] makes an equivalent statement that the minor axis of the ellipses generated by the points on the same rotating object will all be collinear. Figure 14.18 shows our CTPS for trajectories of rotating objects. The representation stores the frequency of rotation of the object and the component trajectories of the points on the object which are all ellipses. Each component trajectory is represented by the spatial coordinates of the end points of the major and minor axis of that ellipse along with the phase information.

Consider a simple case in which the major and minor axis of the ellipse are aligned respectively with the x and y axis. Let the origin of the $x - y$ coordinate system be shifted to (x_c, y_c), the center of the ellipse. Then, parametric equation

Translation CTPS			
Number Of Points On the Object		:: *npoints*	
Number Of Events In the Trajectory		:: *nevents*	
Location			
Point		x	y
1		..	..
2		..	..
..		..	..
..		..	..
..		..	..
npoints		..	..
Events			
No	frame	v_x	v_y
1	..	..	..
2	..	..	..
..	..	..	..
..	..	..	..
..	..	..	..
nevents	..	..	..

Figure 14.15: Translation CTPS. The information regarding the locations of points in the first frame, and the events is recorded. Each event is characterized by its location i.e the frame number of its occurrence, and the average velocities at that instant.

of the ellipse with respect to the origin at (x_c, y_c) can be written as:

$$x = -a * \cos\theta \quad (14.35)$$

$$y = b * \sin\theta \quad (14.36)$$

Figure 14.8 shows the notation used. The frequency of rotation of the arm OP is the same as that of the corresponding point that is rotating in 3D. Also, $\theta = \alpha + \omega * t$, where α is the phase angle, and ω the frequency of rotation. Hence, if we know ω, the frequency of rotation, the parameters a, b, x_c, y_c of the ellipse, and the phase angle α of the trajectory, we will be able to determine the position of the point at any instant of time t.

The orientation of the ellipse is decided by the axis about which the object rotates. The decomposition of a trajectory into v_x, and v_y makes it sensitive to orientation. When the ellipse is oriented such that the major and minor axis respectively are along the x-axis and y-axis, the two events in the v_x and v_y respectively appear at the end points on the major and minor axes. As the ellipse gets reoriented by an angle θ, the events are offset by θ and hence don't appear at the end points of the major and minor axes. On the other hand we find that the direction and speed representation is orientation insensitive. However, the observed events do not appear at the end points of the minor axis of the ellipse. The events in speed appear at angles $\pi/4$, $3 * \pi/4$, $5 * \pi/4$ and $7 * \pi/4$, and the events in direction are at angles 0, π. Since the distance between points doesn't change with the change of axis, events in speed are orientation independent. Similarly, change in direction is orientation independent as change in direction doesn't change with the change

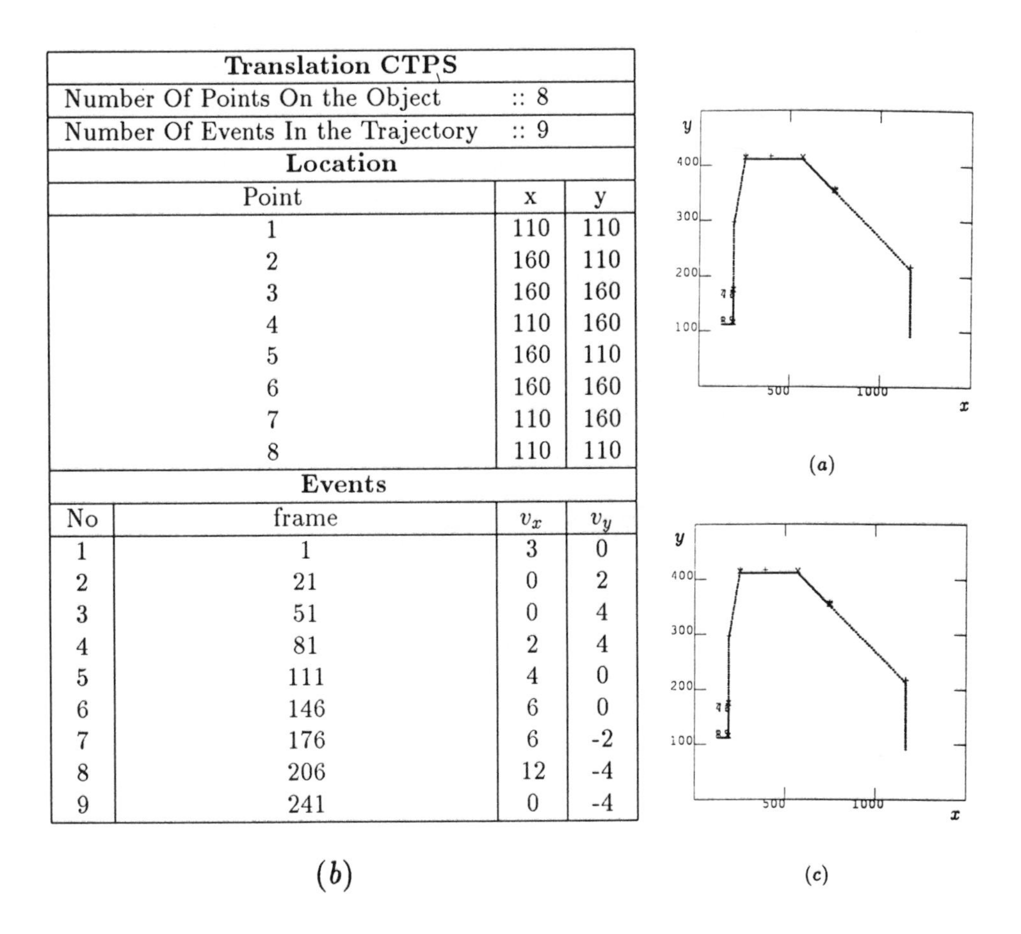

Translation CTPS			
Number Of Points On the Object	:: 8		
Number Of Events In the Trajectory	:: 9		
Location			
Point		x	y
1		110	110
2		160	110
3		160	160
4		110	160
5		160	110
6		160	160
7		110	160
8		110	110
Events			
No	frame	v_x	v_y
1	1	3	0
2	21	0	2
3	51	0	4
4	81	2	4
5	111	4	0
6	146	6	0
7	176	6	-2
8	206	12	-4
9	241	0	-4

Figure 14.16: (a) One of the trajectories with the TPS events marked on it. (b) The CTPS representation for this translating cube. (c) The reconstructed trajectories from the representation.

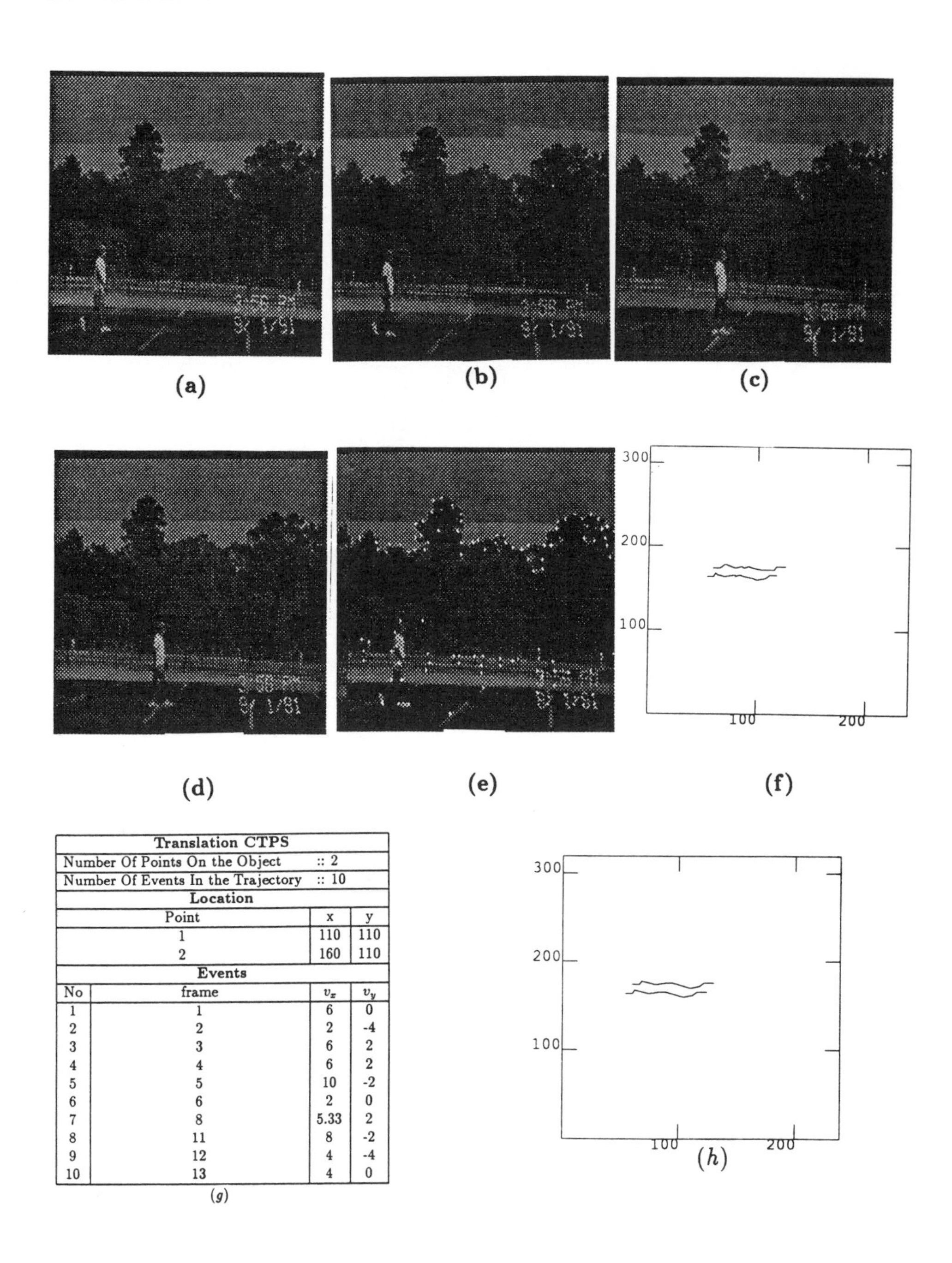

Translation CTPS			
Number Of Points On the Object	:: 2		
Number Of Events In the Trajectory	:: 10		
Location			
Point		x	y
1		110	110
2		160	110
Events			
No	frame	v_x	v_y
1	1	6	0
2	2	2	-4
3	3	6	2
4	4	6	2
5	5	10	-2
6	6	2	0
7	8	5.33	2
8	11	8	-2
9	12	4	-4
10	13	4	0

(g)

Figure 14.17: (a)-(b). The first two frames in a 15 frame real sequence. (c)-(d). The last two frames in the sequence. (e). The interest points detected in the first frame. (f). The generated trajectories of a point on the head and a point on the shoulder. The trajectories of these two points are almost parallel, as expected. (g). The ctps for these trajectories. (h). The reconstructed trajectories, by choosing events which survive over 5% of the σ.

Rotation CTPS									
Number Of Points				:: npoints					
Frequency Of Rotation				:: ω					
Point	Major Axis				Minor Axis				Phase
	x1	y1	x2	y2	x3	y3	x4	y4	
1	..	..	..	..	..	..	..	..	..
2	..	..	..	..	..	..	..	..	..
..	..	..	..	..	..	..	..	..	..
..	..	..	..	..	..	..	..	..	..
..	..	..	..	..	..	..	..	..	..
..	..	..	..	..	..	..	..	..	..
npoints	..	..	..	..	..	..	..	..	..

Figure 14.18: Rotation CTPS. The representation stores the frequency of rotation of the object and the component trajectories of the points on the object which are all ellipses. Each elliptical trajectory is represented by the spatial coordinates of the end points of the major and minor axis of that ellipse along with the phase information.

of axis. The events in direction are at the end points of the major axis. The four events in speed will mark the end points of the major and minor axis if they are shifted by 45°. In our implementation we use the direction events in identifying the end points of the major axis of the ellipse and the speed events for identifying the endpoints of the minor axis. Points belonging to the same object will have the same frequency of rotation. The frequency of rotation ω can be determined from the TPS of the trajectories, as follows $\omega = \frac{1}{2.\Delta_\tau}$, where $\Delta\tau$ is the number of frames elapsed between two consecutive events in direction. The point of intersection between the major and minor axis is the center (x_c, y_c) of the ellipse, a is the half length of the major axis of the ellipse, and b the half length of the minor axis. Ideally, the major and minor axis should be perpendicular to each other and intersect at their mid points. However, due to delocalization of the events this is not the always the case. We have noticed that the delocalization of the end points of the major axis is negligibly small as the movement near these end points is very small. On the other hand the movement near the end points of the minor axis is large, and even a delocalization by only one frame makes a significant change in the orientation of the minor axis. The difference between delocalization of the events at the end point of major and minor axis will be more evident in an ellipse with a high eccentricity value. Hence, we use the following procedure to compute the parameters for reconstructing the ellipse. The spatial coordinates of the end points of the major and minor axis are computed from the direction and speed events. The point of intersection and the average length of the half segments of the minor axis is computed first. The mid point of the major axis gives (x_c, y_c). Thus the parameters x_c, y_c, a and b are computed consistently. Next, the phase angle α of a trajectory is computed as $\alpha = 2\pi - \omega.t^x$, where t^x is the frame number at which the direction event at the left end of the major axis is observed.

Figure 14.19.b shows the ellipse generated by the corner-1 of a Cube shown

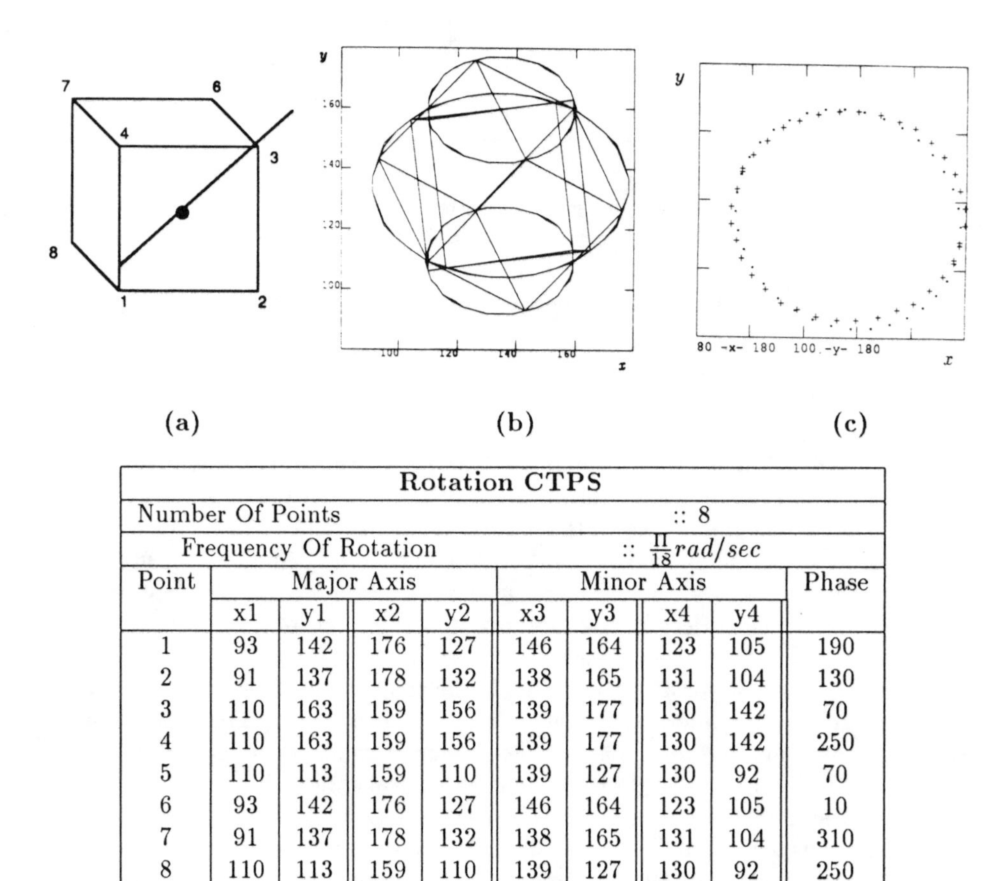

Rotation CTPS									
Number Of Points						:: 8			
Frequency Of Rotation						:: $\frac{\Pi}{18} rad/sec$			
Point	Major Axis				Minor Axis				Phase
	x1	y1	x2	y2	x3	y3	x4	y4	
1	93	142	176	127	146	164	123	105	190
2	91	137	178	132	138	165	131	104	130
3	110	163	159	156	139	177	130	142	70
4	110	163	159	156	139	177	130	142	250
5	110	113	159	110	139	127	130	92	70
6	93	142	176	127	146	164	123	105	10
7	91	137	178	132	138	165	131	104	310
8	110	113	159	110	139	127	130	92	250

(d)

Figure 14.19: (a) A Cube rotating about an axis with direction *(0,1,1)*, passing through its centroid at (135, 135, 135). (b) The elliptic trajectories traced out by the corners of the Cube. (c) The reconstructed trajectory of corner 1, superimposed on the original trajectory shown in b. Points on the original trajectory are marked by '+' and on the reconstructed trajectory by '.' (d) The rotation CTPS of the Cube.

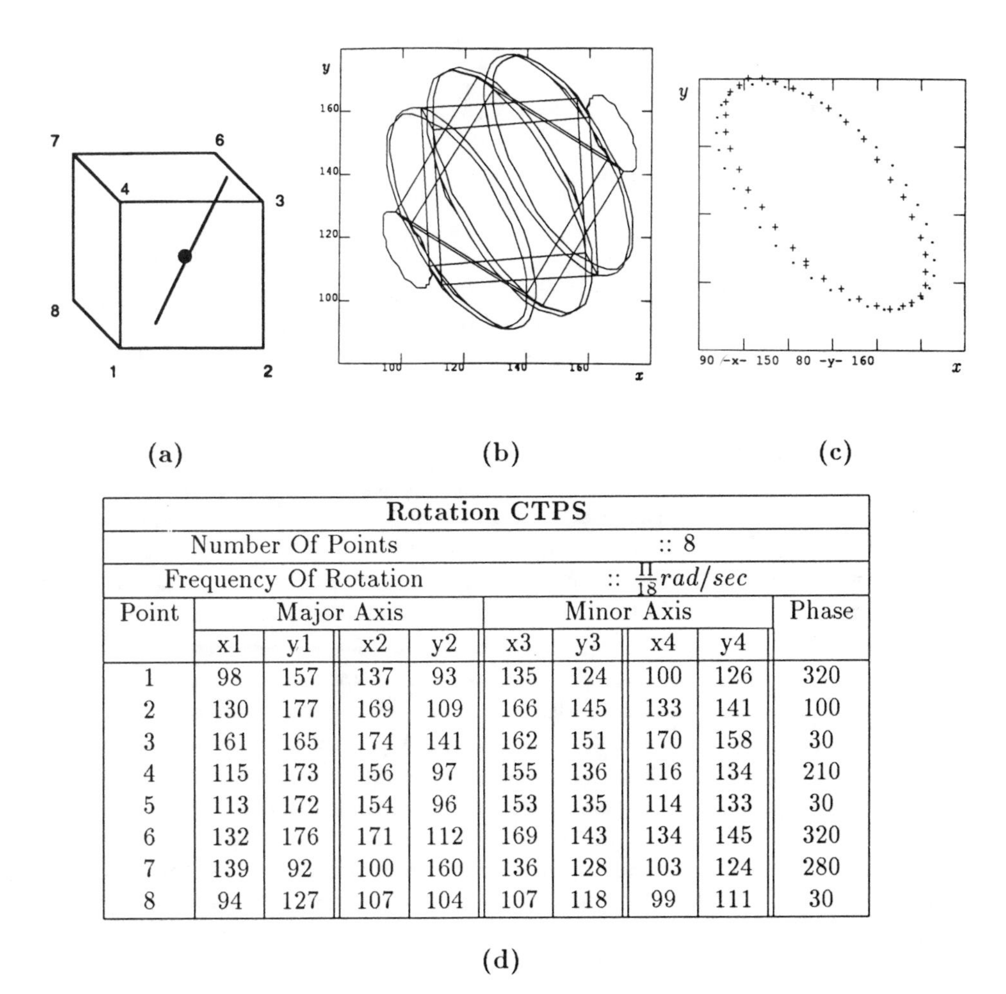

Rotation CTPS									
Number Of Points					:: 8				
Frequency Of Rotation					:: $\frac{\Pi}{18} rad/sec$				
Point	Major Axis				Minor Axis				Phase
	x1	y1	x2	y2	x3	y3	x4	y4	
1	98	157	137	93	135	124	100	126	320
2	130	177	169	109	166	145	133	141	100
3	161	165	174	141	162	151	170	158	30
4	115	173	156	97	155	136	116	134	210
5	113	172	154	96	153	135	114	133	30
6	132	176	171	112	169	143	134	145	320
7	139	92	100	160	136	128	103	124	280
8	94	127	107	104	107	118	99	111	30

Figure 14.20: (a) A Cube rotating about an axis with direction *(2,1,1)*, passing through its centroid (135, 135, 135). (b) The elliptic trajectories traced out by the corners of the Cube. (c) The reconstructed trajectory of corner 1, superimposed on the original trajectory shown in b. Points on the original trajectory are marked by '+' and on the reconstructed trajectory by '.' (d) The rotation CTPS of the cube.

#	Max	Min	Av
1	6.11	0	3.77
2	2.03	0	1.69
3	2.06	0	1.28
4	2.06	0	1.28
5	4.72	0	3.03
6	6.11	0	3.77
7	2.03	0	1.69
8	4.72	0	3.03

(a)

#	Max	Min	Av
1	10.99	0	8.33
2	6.62	0	4.89
3	3.57	0	1.58
4	8.99	0	6.23
5	8.99	0	6.22
6	10.99	0	8.335
7	6.62	0	4.894
8	3.94	0	2.59

(b)

Figure 14.21: Error Tables for (a) Figure 19, (b) Figure 20.

in figure 14.19.a rotating about an axis with direction *(0,1,1)*, passing through (135, 135, 135). Orthographic projection was used to generate the trajectories. The Cube was rotating at a frequency of $\frac{1}{36}$ rotation per second i.e. 10° per second. The observed events in direction which mark respectively the end points of the major and minor axis are separated by 18 frames. Figure 14.19.c shows the reconstructed trajectory of corner-1, superimposed on the original trajectory. The small discrepancy between the original and the reconstructed trajectory is due to the error in detecting the end points of major and minor axis from scale space.

The Table in figure 14.21.a shows the maximum, minimum and the average error in reconstructing the trajectories of the rotating Cube shown in figure 14.19. The Euclidean distance between a point on the original trajectory and the position of the point on the reconstructed trajectory at the same time instant is considered as the error measure. The minimum error is always 0, since the original trajectory and the reconstructed trajectory are aligned at the top end of the minor axis.

Figure 14.20.b shows the ellipses traced out by the corners of a Cube shown in Figure 14.20.a rotating about an axis with direction *(2,1,1)*, passing through (135, 135, 135). In this case also, orthographic projection was used to generate the trajectories, and it was assumed that the Cube was rotating at a frequency of $\frac{1}{36}$ rotation per second. The observed events in direction and speed respectively were used to find the end points of the major and minor axes. Figure 14.20.c shows the reconstructed trajectory of corner-1, superimposed on the original trajectory. The small discrepancy between the original and the reconstructed trajectory is due to the error in detecting the end points of the major and minor axis from scale space. The Table in Figure 14.21.b shows the maximum, minimum and the average error in reconstructing the trajectories of the rotating Cube shown in Figure 14.20.

14.8 Conclusion

In this paper, we proposed a new approach for use of motion in a computer vision system. In our approach, we use motion characteristics of objects without actually recovering the structure. We outlined a multi-scale scheme for representing the important events in the motion trajectories. These important events correspond to the discontinuities in speed, direction and acceleration of the objects. Our method consists of converting the 2-D trajectory into two 1-D parametric functions, v_x and v_y. These functions are then analyzed at multiple scales to identify the significant changes in motion. The results of the multi-scale analysis are then used to determine the primitive type of the trajectory based on a relationship between the significant changes in motion in v_x and v_y. From experimental results with both real and synthetic trajectories, the method is quite promising. Further, we showed how a set of trajectories belonging to a single object can be compactly represented in a composite trajectory primal sketch representation. We also presented a method for reconstructing a trajectory from its CTPS.

References

[1] Asada, H., and Brady, M. The curvature primal sketch. Technical report, MIT AI memo 758, Cambridge: MIT, 1984.

[2] J.E. Cutting. *Motion representation and perception*, chapter Perceiving and recovering structure from events, pages 264–270. North Holland, New York, 1986.

[3] Cutting, J.E. A program to generate synthetic walkers as dynamic point-light displays. *Behaviour Research Methods and Instrumentation*, 10(1):91–94, 1977.

[4] Johansson, G. *Configurations in event perception.* Almqvist and Wiskell, Uppsala, Sweden, 1950.

[5] Johansson, G. Visual perception of biological motion. *Scientific American*, 232:76–89, June, 1975.

[6] Marr, D. *Vision.* Freeman, San Francisco, CA, 1982.

[7] Moravec, H.P. Towards automatic visual obstacle avoidance. In *Proceedings of International Joint Conference on Artificial Intelligence-5*, page 584, MIT, Cambridge, Masachussets, 1977.

[8] Rangarajan, K., and Shah, M. Establishing motion correspondence. Technical Report CS-TR-88-26, University of Central Florida, Computer Science Department, November, 1988.

[9] Sethi, I.K., and Jain, R. Finding trajectories of points in a monocular image sequence. Technical Report RSD-TR-3-85, University of Michigan Center for Research on Integrated Manufacturing, April, 1985.

[10] Shah, M. and Sood, A. and Jain, R. Pulse and staircase edge models. *Computer Vision, Graphics, and Image Processing*, 34:321–341, June, 1986.

[11] Todd, J.T. Visual information about rigid and nonrigid motion: A geometric analysis. *J. Experimental Psychology: Human Perception and Performance*, 8:238–252, 1982.

[12] Wallach, H. *The nature and art of motion*, chapter Visual perception of motion. George Braziller, New York, 1965.

[13] Webb, J. A. , Aggarwal, J.K. Visually interpretting the motion of objects in space. *Computer*, 14(8):40–46, August, 1981.

[14] Witkin, A. Scale-space filtering. In *Proceedings Eighth International Joint Conference on Artificial Intelligence*, pages 1019–1021, Karlsruhe, W.Germany: IEEE Computer Society, 1983.

Applications

Chapter 15

Generating Structure Hypotheses in Cerebral Magnetic Resonance Images Using Segment-Based Focusing and Graph Theoretic Cycle Enumeration

K. L. Boyer, S. V. Raman, S. Sarkar

15.1. Introduction

15.1.1 Motivation

A great deal of work has been done on low-level processing of medical images as well as on the imaging process itself [1]. Higher level processing methods, however, have often suffered from a combination of strict domain dependency and a lack of full automation [2, 3, 4]. Clearly, one useful step in developing a medical image analysis package will be to design some method of extracting descriptions of specific structures, greatly facilitating any subsequent mensuration for statistical purposes or diagnostic assistance [5, 6, 7].

Images from modalities as varied as magnetic resonance imaging (MRI), computed tomography (CT), and even positron emmission tomography (PET), share several underlying characteristics. For instance, the orientations of the objects of interest are mutually constrained. Of course, variations within a population produce minor fluctuations in the sizes and shapes of anatomical structures; other variables such as age, weight, and environmental factors also contribute to a broad spectrum of individual characteristics. Nevertheless, the general *patterns* remain fairly consistent. In addition, the relative positions of the structures are quite invariant. These and other factors suggest model based computer vision as a natural approach to the problem of understanding medical images [8].

The subject of this chapter is closed structure hypothesis generation. We do *not* describe a complete vision system. That goal is some time from fruition. We also should point out that our aim is to develop autonomous techniques applicable to a broad range of problem domains. As such, we present some fairly fundamental work on a vision system component with wide application (in medical image understanding) as opposed to a complete system needing human intervention while solving only a highly specific problem. This should not be taken as a pejorative comment regarding such efforts, it is just an observation that our goals are different. As a nice example of the complete system philosophy, we refer the reader to [7].

In our approach, the spatial relationships among segments are represented in the form of a directed graph. This allows us to extract geometric structures by various graph theoretic operations. We construct our representation so that well-developed cycle enumeration algorithms for directed graphs enable us to form structure hypotheses. Though we demonstrate the algorithm on medical images, it is applicable in other domains as a process assisting a perceptual organization module. Perceptual organization is a process of assembling features into groups which are perceptually significant based on various cues, and is used to reduce the combinatorics of model based object recognition [9, 10]. One of the principles of organization is the *enclosure* property, i.e., a set of features which encloses an area is favored over other sets that do not.

15.1.2 Prior Work

In [11], Bergholm suggests a pixel based edge focusing algorithm based on the premise that edge points (corresponding to LoG zero crossings) move no more than two pixels per step increment in the scale parameter. However, this assumption is valid only under large σ conditions. Bergholm first obtains a coarse set of edges and then applies the edge detector at successively finer scales. In each step, edge detection is performed only within fixed windows around those edge pixels obtained at the previous scale, thus *focusing* edges. The resulting contours at each stage represent a refinement of the previous image within 1-pixel windows around each of its edge points. This method leads to unnecessary noise in the final image (as Tihanyi and Barron have also observed [12]) because all edge segments near old edges are kept, regardless of whether or not they actually correspond to refinements of old edge segments. One major difficulty with the assumption of a maximum two-pixel migration per step increment of the scale parameter is that it breaks down at very fine levels of resolution: pixels move more rapidly at finer scales than at coarser scales, relatively speaking. Although Bergholm sets $\Delta\sigma = 0.7$ for $\sigma > 2$ and $\Delta\sigma = 0.3$ for $\sigma < 2$, he does not employ a rigorously defined schedule. We do.

Canny [13] applies variable blurring to edge refinement. This technique blurs different parts of the image to different degrees, based on a measure of local noise.

Babaud, *et al.* [14] justify the concept of scale space in Gaussian filtering, but only in one dimension. Yuille and Poggio extend this discussion to 2-D; in addition proving that zero-crossing contours obtained from Gaussian filtering may not exist at coarser scales, but cannot vanish at finer scales [15, 16, 17]. In [14], the authors recognize the "split-and-merge" effect in two dimensions.

In [18], Rake presents a technique for delineating parallel structures using a ribbon-finding process. This yields, for example, an outline of the scalp from a transverse cranial MRI. Two limitations in this method exist: (1) as in many other edge detection based schemes, the process involves a manual selection of the scale parameter, and (2) imposing the parallel condition restricts the problem to finding locally straight features, and would probably not succeed in finding more convoluted structures like the cerebrum or cerebellum.

Amini *et al.* [19] hypothesize closed boundaries of objects by grouping edge segments in a polygonal model with the vertices of the polygons being the centroids of the edge segments. The edges are grouped by best first search using a heuristic suitable for convex, polygonal structures. Unfortunately, this method is inappropriate for our problem because few, if any, of the features of interest (cerebrum, etc.) are convex.

We also refer the reader to work by Lu and Jain [20] for a theoretical treatment of the behavior of edges in scale space. Although their analysis focuses on linear edges, it is impressive in its rigor. They intend to use this analysis to construct a rule-based system for scale space analysis, including focusing. Our approach is more direct.

As an overview, our steps for generating feature hypotheses are:

1. Use edge detection and then segment-based edge focusing to obtain a set of primitives (edge segments) which accurately and concisely describe all significant features in the image.
2. Identify associations among primitives based on the proximity of their endpoints. The associations and the segments are represented as the adjacency matrix of a proximity graph.
3. Generate feature hypotheses by enumerating cycles in this graph.

15.2. Segment-Based Edge Focusing

We use either the Laplacian-of-Gaussian (LoG) edge detector [21] or the optimal zero crossing operator (OZCO) developed by Sarkar and Boyer [22] to outline the features of interest in our image by detecting photometric changes. The notion of a "scale space" arises from the edge detectors' scale parameter which determines both the edge localization as well as the error rate[1]. At coarse scales (large values of the scale parameter), edge accuracy is poor, but false edges rarely occur. As the scale parameter decreases, localization improves, but these more accurate edges are buried within an increasingly noisy response. Bomans *et al.* [23] deal with this problem by choosing a particular scale to yield moderate results.

In [24], we introduced a superior, whole-contour based edge focusing scheme, with particular attention given to optimizing the traversal of scale space. We have since enhanced this method to make it even more efficient, while retaining the notion of a theoretically sound focusing schedule. To keep this discussion reasonably self-contained, we will first briefly summarize the prior result.

15.2.1 Review of Contour Based Focusing

Two shortcomings of Bergholm's method are: (1) there is unneccessary noise in the final image because all edge points near old edges are kept, including bifurcations and so on; and (2) the arbitrary selection of step size(s) during the focusing process leads to a suboptimal traversal of scale space (see [12] and [24]). We address the

[1] σ serves as the scale parameter for the LoG, and γ is the corresponding variable for the OZCO.

first problem, in part, by focusing whole contours rather than individual pixels, enabling us to gain robustness against unexpected large single edge pixel movements by evaluating the average movement over the whole contour. By mathematically determining the appropriate step size for a desired *similarity* between outputs at different scales, we eliminate the second problem, as well. What follows is a discussion of these two concepts.

Since the edges are derived from real images, successively refined edge representations in scale space correspond to increasingly accurate depictions of the actual contour. So for a given contour, the edge description at one level of resolution is not dramatically different from a description of the same contour at a slightly finer scale. Although any particular point may fluctuate rapidly, the average effect is small. In fact, we can derive bounds on edge pixel migration for various edge operators by considering a few canonical edge structures (see [24]).

Coarser regions of the scale space produce smoother contours, which are locally more nearly straight, while finer scales give more tortuous contours. Following individual pixels through scale space is impractical because there is no one-to-one correspondence of pixels between any two discrete levels of scale. In view of this, we choose to follow sets of points, or contours, instead of individual pixels. The contour selection procedure is based on the average pixel migration over the contour. To recognize the instance of a coarse scale contour in a finer scale (as discussed below) we search among the contours at the finer scale and require that the average pixel migration be less than the bounds mentioned above. To increase the efficiency of the algorithm, we exit the calculation of the average displacement once we exceed a threshold set by the bound on expected edge pixel migration.

15.2.2 The Similarity Functional

In edge focusing we wish to go through the scale space of an edge operator, from a coarse scale starting point to a fine scale ending point, as quickly as possible with the fewest possible errors. For matching, one must choose a next scale of the edge operator such that the contour gross shape is relatively stable and individual edge point migration is not excessive. If we take very small steps then the contours will not move much, but focusing will take a long time. A very large step can introduce large changes in the contour, requiring a complicated matching process.

Our matcher, while accommodating splits and merges, does nonetheless assume that the degree of individual edge point migration from scale to scale is limited. Now if the edge detectors at two scales are quite similar, their responses, i.e. the edge contours, will also be quite similar, and *vice versa.* So we define the *similarity* parameter, (Σ), as a functional which measures the expected degree of similarity in the output of the edge detector operating at two different scales. It is based on the cross spectral density of the edge detector response for two different scales, which measures the frequency interrelationship between two processes. There also exists a counterpart relationship in the time (or space) domain which is an equivalent measure of the filter similarity. In the discussion which follows, we confine our attention to the linear filtering portion of the edge detection operation; the edge decisions are assumed to be based on zero crossings or local maxima detection.

Let the edge operator impulse response at two different scales, σ_1 and σ_2 ($\sigma_1 > \sigma_2$) have Fourier transforms given by $H_{\sigma_1}(f)$ and $H_{\sigma_2}(f)$ respectively. The cross spectral density of the outputs of the two operators at two scales (or any two filters), when driven by a white noise source, is given by:

$$S_{H_{\sigma_2}H_{\sigma_1}}(f) = H_{\sigma_2}(f)H^*_{\sigma_1}(f) \tag{2.1}$$

where the $*$ superscript denotes complex conjugation. We define similarity by:

$$\Sigma(H, \sigma_2, \sigma_1) = \frac{\int_{-\infty}^{\infty} S_{H_{\sigma_2}H_{\sigma_1}}(f)df}{\sqrt{\int_{-\infty}^{\infty} S_{H_{\sigma_2}H_{\sigma_2}}(f)df \int_{-\infty}^{\infty} S_{H_{\sigma_1}H_{\sigma_1}}(f)df}} \tag{2.2}$$

$\Sigma(\bullet, \bullet, \bullet)$ is the integral of the cross spectral density, normalized by the square root of the product of the spectral densities of each of the filters. Note that when $\sigma_2 = \sigma_1$, $\Sigma = 1.0$, implying identical responses, the limiting case of similarity. With the same input image, there is no new information available. When the frequency response of the two edge operators are such that that they do not overlap at all, then their cross spectral density is zero and so is the similarity. The two responses are completely orthogonal with each contributing totally unique information.

Our schedule for reducing σ through scale space assumes constant similarity between successive scale space parameters. The similarity must be prudently chosen; a small similarity results in a large step size and a rapid traversal of the scale space, but between scales the contours will differ greatly so the matching strategy may not succeed.

15.2.2.1 LoG Similarity

The Laplacian-of-Gaussian edge detector is expressed mathematically as:

$$\nabla^2 g(x, y) = \frac{1}{2\pi\sigma^4}(2 - (\frac{x^2 + y^2}{\sigma^2}))e^{-\frac{x^2+y^2}{2\sigma^2}} \tag{2.3}$$

The LoG is circularly symmetric in both space and frequency. The similarity parameter for such a 2D filter in polar coordinates is given by:

$$\Sigma = \frac{\int_{-\infty}^{\infty} S_{H_{\sigma_2}H_{\sigma_1}}(r)dr}{\sqrt{\int_{-\infty}^{\infty} S_{H_{\sigma_2}H_{\sigma_2}}(r)dr \int_{-\infty}^{\infty} S_{H_{\sigma_1}H_{\sigma_1}}(r)dr}} \tag{2.4}$$

The frequency response of the LoG operator is given by:

$$H_\sigma = r^2 e^{-\frac{r^2\sigma^2}{2}} \tag{2.5}$$

The numerator of the similarity functional becomes:

$$\int_{-\infty}^{\infty} S_{H_{\sigma_2}H_{\sigma_1}}(r)dr = \int_{-\infty}^{\infty} r^4 \exp\left[\frac{-r^2(\sigma_2^2 + \sigma_1^2)}{2}\right]dr = \frac{3\sqrt{2\pi}}{(\sigma_2^2 + \sigma_1^2)^{\frac{5}{2}}}$$

and

$$\int_{-\infty}^{\infty} S_{H_\sigma H_\sigma}(r)dr = \frac{3\sqrt{\pi}}{4\sigma^5}$$

Hence the similarity functional between two LoG's of σ_1 and σ_2 is:

$$\Sigma = \frac{4\sqrt{2}}{(\frac{\sigma_2}{\sigma_1} + \frac{\sigma_1}{\sigma_2})^{\frac{5}{2}}} \tag{2.6}$$

Setting Σ to a constant value, say S, we arrive at the following formula:

$$\sigma_2 = \sigma_1 \left(\frac{k_{LoG} - \sqrt{k_{LoG}^2 - 4}}{2} \right) \quad \text{where} \quad k_{LoG} = (2/S^{\frac{2}{5}}) \quad \text{and} \quad \sigma_1 > \sigma_2 \tag{2.7}$$

If we denote $(\sigma_1 - \sigma_2)$ by $\Delta\sigma$ and σ_1 by σ, the value of the current scale, we get:

$$\frac{\Delta\sigma}{\sigma} = \left(1 - \frac{k_{LoG} - \sqrt{k_{LoG}^2 - 4}}{2} \right) \tag{2.8}$$

Equation (2.8) gives the relationship among three parameters: the present scale, σ, the next scale step to be taken, $\Delta\sigma$, and the value of the similarity functional, S. Given the value of the similarity determined by the amount of change in the contour we can tolerate[2], we select the ratio $\frac{\Delta\sigma}{\sigma}$. Note that the step size is proportional to the present σ.

15.2.2.2 OZCO Similarity

We follow a development similar to that for the the LoG operator for the optimal edge detection operator suggested by Sarkar and Boyer [22]. The operator is derived by maximizing three criteria first formalized by Canny [25] for FIR peak responding operators and later extended to IIR and zero crossing responding operators by Sarkar and Boyer [26]. For zero crossing operators these criteria are the slope ratio at the edge location, the localization precision of the detector, and a criterion based on spurious response frequency. The details can be found in [27, 22, 28]. This operator has another advantage in that it has a very fast (real time) recursive implementation whose computational and memory requirements are independent of scale. Though fast implementations of the LoG exist [29], the complexity still depends on the scale.

The optimal zero crossing operator is directional, operating perpendicular to the local edge; therefore, a 1D analysis will hold. The impulse response is:

$$h_\beta(x) = A\left(1 + \alpha\beta|x| - \frac{\alpha+1}{2}\beta^2x^2\right)e^{-\beta|x|} \qquad -\infty < x < \infty \tag{2.9}$$

[2] A similarity functional of value around 0.8 works well.

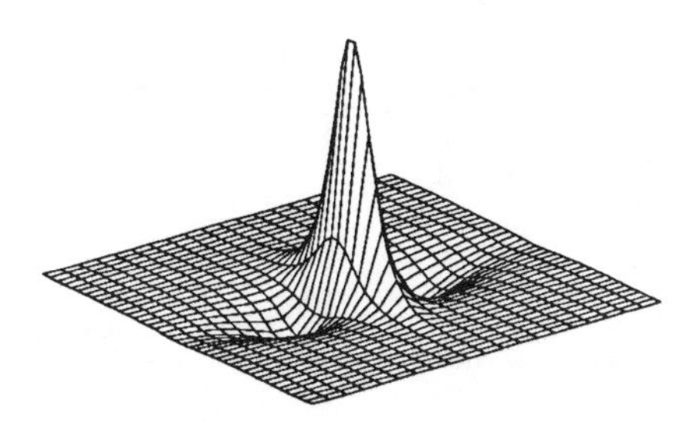

Figure 2.1: Plot of the optimal zero crossing operator (OZCO) of Sarkar and Boyer

The plot of the operator in 2D is shown in Fig. 2.1, for $\alpha = -0.999466$ and $\beta = 0.2274$. The extention to 2D entails a lowpass noise-reducing projection function, orthogonal to the detection direction. Two such mutually orthogonal 2D filters are applied and their outputs combined. The details are beyond the scope of this paper, but [22] contains a complete treatment of this topic. β is a scaling parameter analogous to σ for the LoG, but behaves in the opposite sense. A is an arbitrary gain constant.

For this operator it is more convenient to perform the analysis in the space domain rather than in the frequency domain. The similarity functional in the space domain is given by:

$$\Sigma = \frac{\int_{-\infty}^{\infty} h_{\beta_1} h_{\beta_2}^*(x)dx}{\sqrt{\int_{-\infty}^{\infty} |h_{\beta_1}|^2(x)dx \int_{-\infty}^{\infty} |h_{\beta_2}|^2(x)dx}} \tag{2.10}$$

where β is the scale of the edge detection filter. As β is decreased the spatial extent of the filter increases resulting in fewer spurious responses and a loss of detail and fine edge structure. For comparative purposes, we work with $1/\beta = \gamma$, which has the same qualitative behavior for this operator as does σ for the LoG. To derive the formula above for Σ we used the following identity:

$$\int_{-\infty}^{\infty} S_{H_{\beta_1} H_{\beta_2}}(f)df = R_{h_{\beta_1} h_{\beta_2}}(0) = \int_{-\infty}^{\infty} h_{\beta_1} h_{\beta_2}^*(x)dx$$

where $R_{h_1 h_2}$ denotes the cross correlation of the signals h_1 and h_2. Using Equations (2.10) and (2.9) we get the following form for Σ for this operator:

$$\Sigma = \frac{8}{(\sqrt{\frac{\gamma_1}{\gamma_2}} + \sqrt{\frac{\gamma_2}{\gamma_1}})^{\frac{3}{2}}} \tag{2.11}$$

If we fix the similarity at say, $\Sigma = S$, then

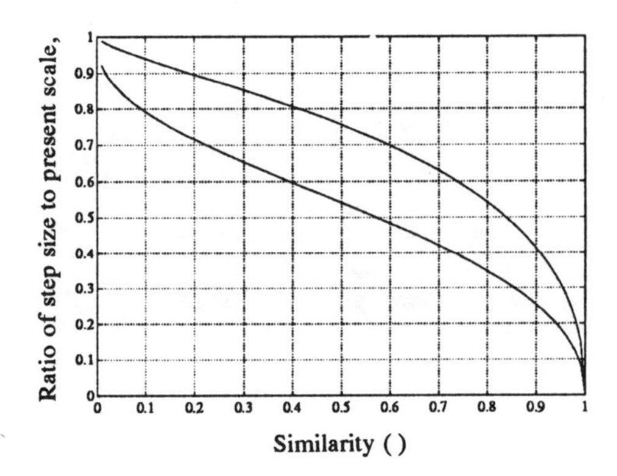

Figure 2.2: Comparison of the Ratio of the step size and the present (σ or γ) vs. the similarity functional for the LoG and the OZCO.

$$\gamma_2 = \gamma_1 \left(\frac{k_{SB} - \sqrt{k_{SB}^2 - 4}}{2} \right)^2 \quad \text{where} \quad k_{SB} = \frac{2}{S^{\frac{1}{3}}} \quad \text{and} \quad \gamma_1 > \gamma_2$$

As before, if we denote the change in step size by $\Delta\gamma = \gamma_1 - \gamma_2$, and γ_1 by γ, indicating the current scale, then we have:

$$\frac{\Delta\gamma}{\gamma} = \left(1 - \left(\frac{k_{SB} - \sqrt{k_{SB}^2 - 4}}{2} \right)^2 \right) \tag{2.12}$$

Fig. 2.2 plots the ratio of the step size to the present scale against the similarity functional for each operator. Note that the curve for the OZCO lies above that of the LoG for all values of the similarity functional. This means that *one can take larger steps across the scale space for the OZCO than for the LoG.* This effect is verified by our experimental results.

15.2.3 Segment Based Focusing

We decompose the contours into segments and focus these instead of focusing whole contours to reduce computation. With contour-based focusing, especially when the LoG is used, the lengths of the contours can slow the algorithm considerably. For instance, when two long contours lie close together for some distance but then diverge significantly, many calculations may be performed before the disparity is discovered. With short segments, however, such situations do not arise, since a few computations quickly reveal whether or not a given segment at the finer scale matches a particular coarse scale segment and so we can effectively make use of the early exit condition.

Segment Based Boundary Refinement Algorithm

```
I1 = image of edge segments at resolution 1
I2 = image of edge segments at (finer) resolution 2
loop over I1 segments
      loop over I2 segments
            let C1 = shorter of the two segments being compared
            let C2 = longer segment
            loop over pixels of C1
                  loop over pixels of C2
                        find d8 = smallest eight-distance between
                        the C1 pixel being considered and any C2 pixel
                  end loop over C2 pixels
                  min-d = sum of d8's for all C1 pixels thus far
                  if min-d > dmax
                     then terminate the calculation for this C1-C2 pair
                  endif
            end loop over C1 pixels
            match-factor = min-d / l(C1)
      end loop over I2 segments
end loop over I1 segments
keep all segments from the fine scale image with high match-factors
```

Figure 2.3: The segment-based focusing algorithm.

We choose to segment the contours into constant curvature segments because the boundaries of features of interest can, in most cases, be described compactly in this way. Wuescher and Boyer have developed a robust contour decomposition technique which produces segments of (nearly) constant curvature [30]. Using this, we can quickly break long contours into more manageable components and proceed with edge focusing in the same manner as before. Fig. 2.3 summarizes the algorithm for matching segments in a finer scale edge image to segments from a coarser scale representation[3]. This procedure is repeated at successively finer scales until an edge image of sufficient precision is obtained.

Segment based focusing has the added advantage of being more robust to noise effects while generating feature hypotheses. A long connected contour may suggest a single underlying feature. However, because of nearby features or noise, contours corresponding to multiple features can merge at some scales to form a single continuous contour. These mergings generally produce curvature changes. Thus, partitioning the contours into constant curvature segments will break them at these points. Building structure hypotheses as discussed in the next section is easier under these conditions.

---

[3] The threshold for match-factors is, at this point, arbitrary. For more details regarding the rest of the algorithm the reader is referred to [24]. We have found that 0.7 works well.

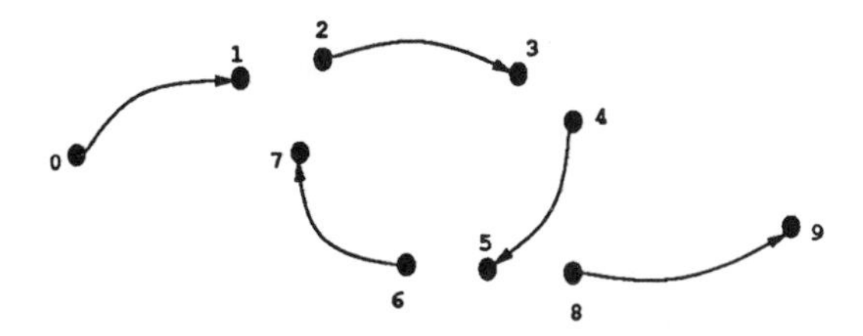

Figure 3.1: The graphical representation of edge segments.

15.3. Graph-Theoretic Cycle Enumeration

In this section we outline the feature hypothesis generation process. This is done using graphical representations of the focused edge segments. In the domain of cranial MRI most features of interest, like ventricles, cerebellum, and cerebrum, have *closed* boundaries. We exploit this closedness property in our algorithm.

15.3.1 Graphical Representation

We first create a graphical representation of the focused segments. The nodes of this graph are the segment endpoints while the links are the segments themselves. We associate a direction with each link corresponding to the traversing direction along the edge segment, defined so that the brighter gray level is to the right. We use this to prune false connections, as explained below. To increase the efficiency of the algorithm, we also follow a particular node labelling scheme. The starting point (with respect to the given traversing scheme) is labelled with an *even* number and corresponding endpoint is marked with (*even* +1). So all links corresponding to possible edge segments go from a node labelled with an even number to a node labelled with an odd number. This scheme is depicted in Fig. 3.1[1].

The next step connects segment endpoints which are close together and so might be possible continuation links between segments. This is needed to reconstruct boundaries broken by noise or other perturbations. One method to do this would be a highly inefficient brute force search over all endpoints, looking for nearby endpoints. To circumvent this, we use voting methods. The theoretical development of voting methods as a highly efficient computational architecture for primitive perceptual organization is beyond the scope of this chapter; see [31].

In voting methods, global concensus is built gradually and begins with a definition of a compatibility relation for perceptual grouping. The compatibility relation between segments may, in general, be based on attributes of the endpoints (tokens) like proximity, similarity in average gray level along the segments, and so on. It is also possible to include attributes inherited from ancestral segments lower in the organizational hierarchy. A voting space is created spanned by the attributes under consideration. Each endpoint token votes, independently of all others, for all points

[1] We connect all endpoints (startpoints) near the border of the image to a startpoint (endpoint) of a dummy segment. This is done to handle features which cross the boundary, like the skull.

in the voting space which satisfy the compatibility relation with itself. After all the votes are cast, we scan this space for regions which are compatible with multiple tokens. This produces the associations of interest. Sarkar and Boyer [31] analyze the time complexity of such a method and show its advantage over traditional search procedures.

In the current context, we use the voting method to associate endpoints in close proximity *only*. We could consider other geometric attributes such as the slope at the endpoint, curvature, or photometric attributes like average gray level, or average gradient along the contour. Although useful in other domains, we did not find them useful here. These endpoint associations form additional links in the graphical representation denoting possible endpoint extensions.

Correct associations are far more likely to preserve photometric polarity than not. Correct, polarity non-preserving associations should be inferred in a higher level process to limit the combinatorics of the current problem. That is, it is much simpler to go back and find the relatively few missed associations of this type afterward (if needed for the structures of interest) than it is to delete the many false associations of this type which would otherwise result. To avoid these "improper" associations, when we join two segments the sense of the photometric polarity across the edge must be preserved. This means that all valid links should be from an odd node to an even node, as depicted in Fig. 3.2(a). Thus, we delete all odd-odd and even-even associations and set the direction of the remainder according to the polarity consistency constraint; they go from odd to even nodes to preserve the sense of traversing the associated segments (see Fig. 3.2(a)). We then have a graphical representation of the edge structure with nodes representing segment endpoints, directed links from even nodes to odd nodes representing segments, and proposed links from odd to even nodes representing edge join hypotheses.

15.3.2 Cycle Enumeration

Generating boundary hypotheses for closed features corresponds to enumerating cycles in the directed graph. This is illustrated in Fig. 3.2(b). Various graph theoretic techniques exist to solve this problem. The first step in all such algorithms is to break the graph into blocks. By blocks we mean a set of subgraphs, no two of which share a cycle. The steps are enumerated below. For more details the reader is referred to any of a number of textbooks in graph theory ([32] and [33] are very good).

- First, break the underlying non-directed graph into connected components by depth first search. The connected components of a graph are the maximum number of subgraphs which have no edge connecting them. Thus they can be treated independently of others.
- In each component identify fundamental cycles [2] by first constructing a spanning tree and then adding the chords.

[2] These constitute a sort of basis for all the cycles in a graph.

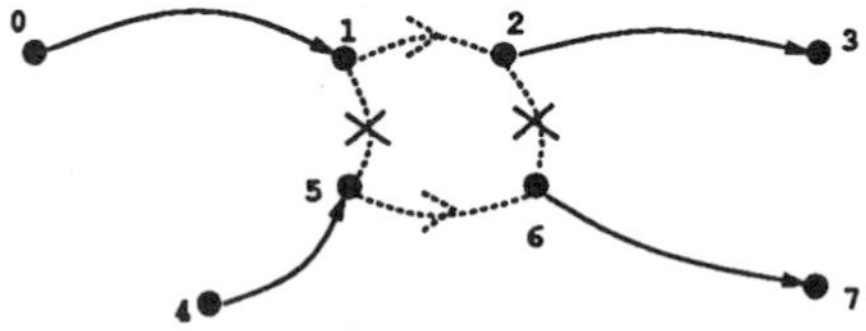

Figure 3.2: Example Graphs (a) depicts the valid and the invalid associations (b) graph corresponding to a typical closed feature plus a "dangling" edge.

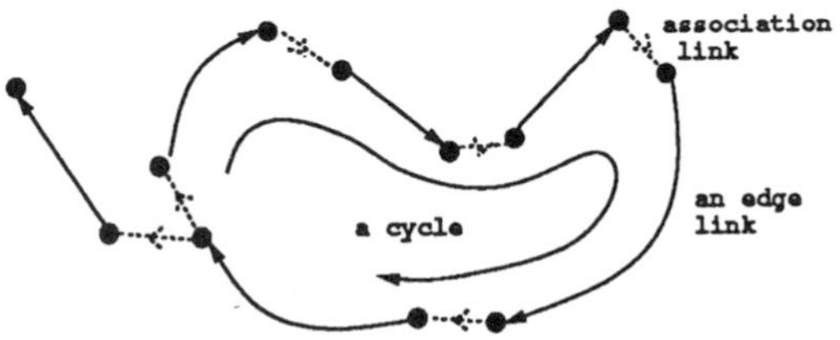

- Partion the fundamental cycles into non-intersecting groups (no edges in common). The nodes of each partition correspond to the blocks.

Once we have the blocks, we could proceed by considering the fundamental cycles and various subsets of them. However, we avoid this approach because:

- The directed nature of the graph cannot be used, and many spurious cycles will be generated. In effect, we would not use all the information stored in the graph.
- Not all combinations of fundamental cycles form cycles, and pruning them is time consuming. Even the algorithm outlined in [34], which orders the fundamental circuits in a particular way to avoid generating spurious cycles, took more than 3 days to run on a typical image in our domain, using a TI Explorer II$^+$ LISP machine.

The execution time is reduced by using the directed nature of the graph. The features of interest are bounded by segments having consistent polarity. Therefore, many cycles can be rejected out of hand. We used the algorithm outlined in [35, pages 348–353], which has a time complexity of $\mathcal{O}((|V|+|E|)(c+1))$, where $|V|$ is the number of vertices or nodes, $|E|$ is the number of edges or links, and c is the number of cycles in the directed graph. This is clearly near optimal, since the time taken just to list the cycles must be $\bar{l}c$, where $\bar{l}$ is the average cycle length, and clearly, $\bar{l} = \mathcal{O}(|V|)$.

The cycles are generated by a depth-first search in which edges are added to the path until a cycle is produced. To avoid duplicating cycles, we order the vertices from 1 to $|V|$, and consider each cycle to be rooted at its lowest-numbered vertex. We begin the search at vertex s and build a directed path $(s, v_1, v_2, \cdots, v_k)$, such that $v_i > s$, $1 \leq i \leq k$. To prevent traversing cycles that originate at a vertex v_i during the search for cycles rooted at s, it is necessary to indicate that all vertices on the current path (except s) are unavailable as extensions of that path. A cycle is reported only when we come back to the starting vertex, $v_{k+1} = s$. After generating the cycle $(s, v_1, v_2, \cdots, v_k, s)$, we explore the next edge leading out from v_k. If all edges departing from v_k have been explored, we back up to the previous vertex v_{k-1} and try to extend the path from that point, and so on until we backtrack past s. The vertices are unmarked when we back up past them to the previous vertex on the current path. If the current path up to vertex v did not lead to a cycle rooted at s, v remains unavailable for any future path beginning from the same root, s, after we back up past it. This prevents searching for cycles in parts of the graph on which such searches have proven unsuccessful. The process is repeated for $s = 1, 2, \cdots, |V|$. For more details the reader is referred to the text [35].

This algorithm executes significantly faster than that using fundamental cycles, typically requiring 15-20 minutes, on the same LISP machine. Most of that time is devoted to partitioning the graph into its strongly connected components. Greater speed could be achieved by more efficient coding. An added advantage of this algorithm is that the cycles as generated have their segments already ordered as necessary to calculate geometric attributes; this is not the case for algorithms using fundamental cycles.

15.4. Experimental Results

Fig. 4.2(a) shows the gray-level MRI of a slightly posterior section of the brain. The LoG contours obtained at $\sigma = 5$ are shown in Fig. 4.2(b), and those at $\sigma = 2$ in Fig. 4.2(c). The image at $\sigma = 5$ seems to contain at least a coarse representation of most of the significant structures, such as the skull and cerebrum. Starting with these contours, both contour-based and segment-based focusing was performed to $\sigma = 2$. These results are shown in Figs. 4.2(d) and 4.2(e), respectively. The same value of similarity was used in both runs, $\Sigma = 0.8$, giving the same two-step schedules through scale space: σ was decreased from 5 to 3.3, and then from 3.3 to 2. The outputs in both cases are quite similar overall. Fig. 4.2(f) represents the difference between Fig. 4.2(d) and Fig. 4.2(e). For the most part, the contours omitted by segment-based focusing do not contribute significantly to descriptions of structural phenomena. Although some parts of the inner skull boundary have not been kept, their presence is not essential to a gross description of the skull (this can be seen in Fig.4.2(f)). What *does* significantly differ is the time required for focusing: focusing whole contours from $\sigma = 5$ to $\sigma = 2$ took approximately *ten hours*, whereas the same focusing routine performed with segmentation required only *ten minutes*. This comparison has been performed on several other images, with very similar results.

Cycles were generated from the segmentally focused image in Fig. 4.2(e) by bridging gaps fewer than 4 pixels wide[1]. Since only two gray levels are used (black and white), it is impossible to see individual cycles in this image. Some of the anatomically significant cycles have been isolated in Figs. 4.2(g) and 4.2(h). Note that we have drawn only the detected segments participating in the cycles, not the hypothesized connections between disjoint segments. Fig. 4.2(g) shows the cycle which most closely outlines the skull. Some local discontinuities are present; these arise because in the original edge image, there are two contours of consistent polarity (one representing the skull and the other encircling the surface of the head) which lie in close proximity to one another. After segmenting, associations are formed not only between endpoints on the same contour but also between endpoints on both contours because they are so close. So the resulting cycle occasionally jumps between contours, but this could be smoothed out if desired.

The cycles generated form our hypotheses for various structures in the brain. The hypotheses can be ranked according to the values of attributes pertinent for the identification of various structures. We calculate the following feature vector to describe each hypothesis:

- **Area:** We estimate a cycle's area (in units of $pixels^2$) by connecting disjoint segments with a straight line. Also, if a cycle's starting and ending segments meet the boundary of the image, they are connected along the boundary.
- **Perimeter:** The length of the closed boundary pixels.
- **Compactness:** Defined to be $2\sqrt{\pi \; Area}/Perimeter$, it ranges between 0 and 1 (for a circle).
- **Centroid.**
- **Moments:** Second order central moments $(\mu_{20}, \mu_{02}, \mu_{11})$, these estimate the spread of the boundary along the x and the y axes. We also estimate the minimum and maximum moments of inertia ($I_{\min}$ and $I_{\max}$, respectively).
- **Orientation:** This is defined to be the axis of minimum moment, or the principle axis.
- **Best Fitting Ellipse:** The major axis and minor axis of the best fitting ellipse to the boundary.
- **Enclosing Rectangle:** Defined to be the smallest upright rectangle enclosing the boundary, it is characterized by its upper left corner and lower right corners.

The feature vectors for the four cycles corresponding to the ventricles and skull (Figs. 4.2(h) and (g)) are shown in Fig. 4.1. Note that we calculate the feature vector for all the cycles and here we have simply listed those corresponding to some interesting cycles.

---

[1] This correspond to a proximity quantization index of 8 pixels (twice the gap one wants to bridge) used in the voting method. Selection of this has not yet been rigorously defined. In the results presented here, it is chosen to be large enough to find the significant cycles, and small enough to minimize the number of trivial cycles.

CYCLE FEATURE VECTORS: Fig. 7					
		Ventricles			
		Upper Left	**Upper Right**	**Lower**	**Skull**
Area		160.5	266.5	273.0	20482.5
Perimeter		53.11	101.8	86.32	812.7
Compactness		0.85	0.57	0.68	0.62
Centroid		(87 62)	(86 111)	(130 89)	(102 90)
Moment	μ_{20}	1163.9	3670.3	1893.9	1581700.0
	μ_{02}	1629.1	5031.6	5583.0	2002302.5
	μ_{11}	-748.9	2494.5	247.1	100621.0
	I_{min}	612.3	1765.3	1877.4	1558867.7
	I_{max}	2180.7	6936.7	5599.5	2025134.5
Orientation		126.4	52.6	86.2	77.2
Ellipse Axes	*Major*	8.5	11.5	10.5	41.4
	Minor	4.5	5.8	6.1	36.3
Rectangle		(77 55) (96 69)	(71 98) (98 123)	(117 80) (145 98)	(7 13) (173 159)

Figure 4.1: Feature vectors corresponding to the cycles shown in Fig. 7 (g) and (h)

The next trial used the top portion of another posterior MRI brain section. Fig. 4.4(a) presents the gray-level image. For this image the OZCO was used to generate edges at $\gamma = 3$, 1.5, and 1. Σ was set to 0.9, giving a two-step refinement schedule going from $\gamma = 3$ to 1.5 and then from $\gamma = 1.5$ to 1. The resulting edge image after segment-based focusing is given in Fig. 4.4(b). The cycles were generated by bridging 7 pixel gaps. Some of the interesting cycles are shown in Fig. 4.4. The cycle corresponding to the ventricle is shown in Fig. 4.4c. In Fig. 4.4(d), a cycle depicting the skull has been isolated, and the cerebrum is represented by the cycle shown in Fig. 4.4(e). The feature vectors corresponding to these cycles are shown in Fig. 4.3.

A much more anterior MRI section was used in the third example; this is evident by the presence of the eyes in Fig. 4.5(a). Using the LoG, edges were detected at $\sigma = 5$, 3.3, and 2. These edges were then segmentally focused and the resulting image is given in Fig. 4.5(b). Fig. 4.5(c) shows all the cycles generated by bridging gaps of 5 pixels in the association voting. Finally, one cycle which outlines the skull is given in Fig. 4.5(d).

In the fourth and final set of results, a transverse section through the brain was used, and the MR image is shown in Fig. 4.6(a). The edge detector used here is the OZCO, and segment-based focusing was done from $\gamma = 3$ to 1.5 to 1. The results from this operation are shown in Fig. 4.6(b). Bridging 9 pixel gaps, the algorithm found 86 cycles in the focused image, and all of these are presented together in Fig. 4.6(c). Fig. 4.6(d) presents the cycle circumnavigating the cerebellum.

We now compare the performance of our algorithm with manually estimated parameters for various structures in the brain. To calculate the feature vectors, we manually traced the structures of interest and used the resulting boundary contour. These are compared with the feature vector calculated using the boundary hypothesized by our algorithm (see Fig. 4.1 and Fig. 4.3). We connect the breaks with straight line segments; a more sophisticated method of joining (e.g., splines) would give better estimates for the geometric properties. However, even this simple

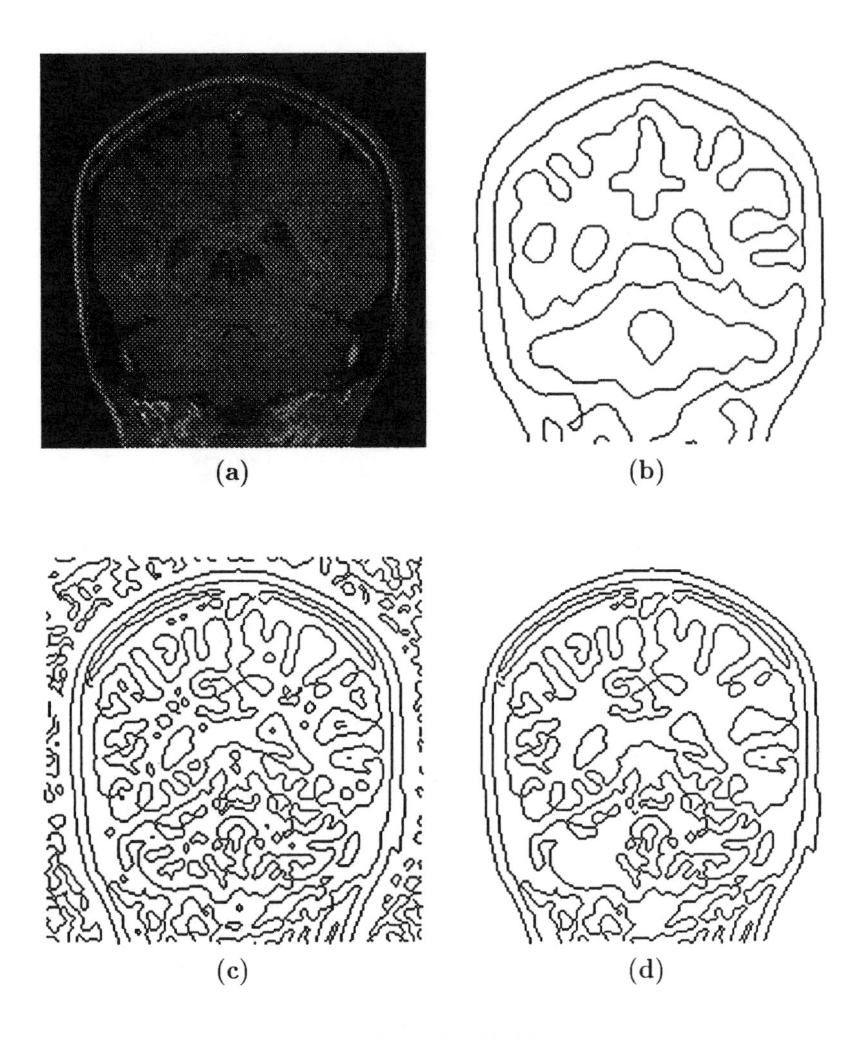

Figure 4.2 (a)-(d)

scheme gives us results which are comparable to those obtained manually, without the tedium.

For comparison we picked the upper left and right ventricles[2] of Fig. 4.2 and the ventricles in Fig. 4.4. The estimates obtained manually appear in Fig. 4.8. The manual outlines are shown in Fig. 4.7. Note that except for the ventricle on the right in Fig. 4.7(a), the other ventricles have outlines similar to that generated by the edge detector. The similarities are reflected in the feature vectors. The corresponding automatic estimates are shown in columns 2 and 3 of Fig. 4.1 and in column 2 in Fig. 4.3. Note that the ellipse parameters are very consistent even for the ventricle which was not outlined properly.

[2]...with respect to the image plane orientation. For the anatomically inclined, the correct terminology is "right lateral" and "left lateral."

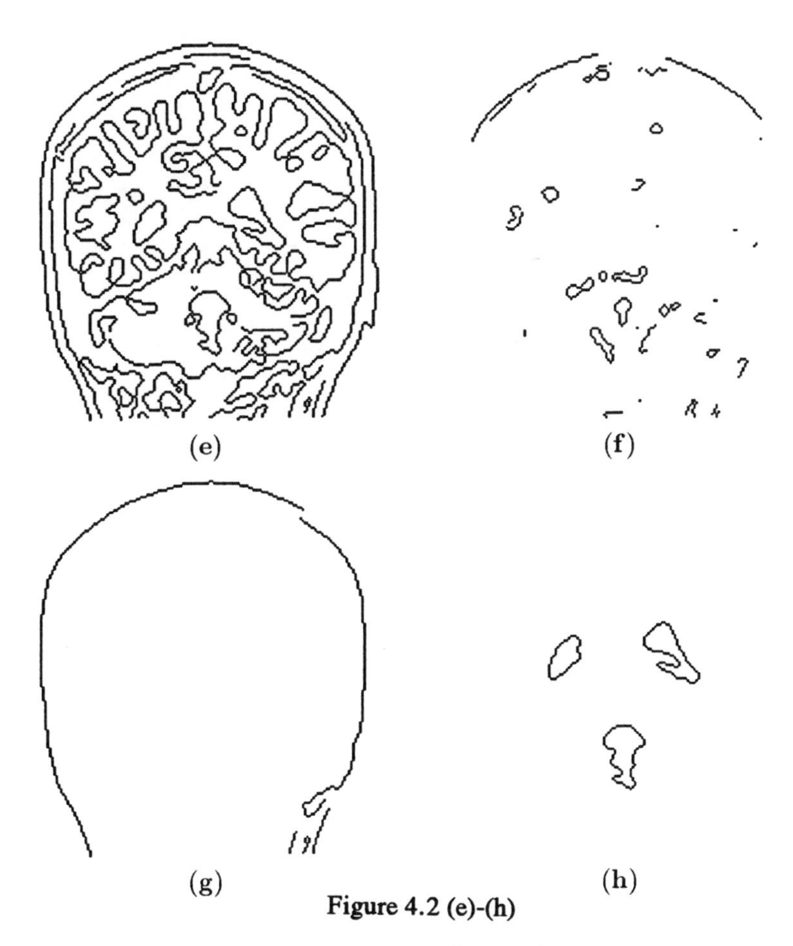

Figure 4.2 (e)-(h)

Figure 4.2: (a) Gray-level image of a posterior frontal MRI section of the brain. (b) Edges detected with the LoG at $\sigma = 5$. (c) LoG contours at $\sigma = 2$. (d) Traced edges after contour-based focusing from $\sigma = 5$ to $\sigma = 2$. (e) Traced edges after segment-based focusing from $\sigma = 5$ to $\sigma = 2$. (f) Difference between (d) and (e). (g) Cycle corresponding to the skull. (h) The three cycles which describe the ventricles.

The manual and automatically generated estimates are close for these cases. We should recall that the manual estimates have errors of their own and should not necessarily be taken as ground truth. The accuracy of the automatic estimates can be increased by focusing to a finer scale, according to our focusing schedule. The problem is not in the mensuration of the structures, it lies in the automatic identification of them. Once these structures are recognized, their boundaries can be refined using various local methods or dynamic algorithms as in [36].

CYCLE FEATURE VECTORS: Fig. 9				
		Ventricle	**Skull**	**Cerebrum**
Area		151.0	18636.5	9813.5
Perimeter		86.7	555.8	808.0
Compactness		0.5	0.87	0.43
Centroid		(73 91)	(90 91)	(85 89)
Moment	μ_{20}	2563.5	1672877.2	832885.0
	μ_{02}	1497.5	1364233.7	832857.5
	μ_{11}	169.8	20641.0	-31329.0
	$I_{\min}$	1471.1	1362859.5	801542.25
	$I_{\max}$	2589.9	1674251.5	864200.3
Orientation		8.8	3.8	-45.0
Ellipse Axes	*Major*	8.13	39.2	32.7
	Minor	6.13	35.4	31.49
Rectangle		(66 83) (81 102)	(6 12) (148 169)	(25 26) (135 152)

Figure 4.3: Feature vectors corresponding to the cycles shown in Fig. 9 (c)-(e)

15.5. Final Remarks

The next step is to identify the structurally significant cycles by some sort of hypothesis ranking based on geometric and photometric attributes. For example, the skull can be easily identified since it is often the longest cycle generated, has a central axis of symmetry and encloses a large area. The expected areas and shapes of the structures of interest can thus be used to form matchpools for various objects of interest. The final matches are selected based on feature vectors and relational constraints, that is, by the use of the positions of various structures in the image plane relative to one another. Various "atlases" for tomography provide extensive illustrations of a variety of brain slices (Matsui and Hirano [37], for example). Using the fact that each anatomical structure has a characteristic appearance in each 2D slice, a flexible topologically structured model base can be developed. Evaluating a structure hypothesis will entail comparison with models in various slices about the current (estimated) slice position.

The reader may note that the cross-sections of biological structures, which may be rather convoluted, do not necessarily appear as *single* closed contours. Also, some structures such as the Caudate Nucleus will not have corresponding hypotheses generated directly owing to the photometric consistency constraint. While these observations are certainly correct, they do not represent major obstacles since we can recognize anatomical structures as collections of modeled contours, and other collections of segments, as needed. The important point is that the vast majority of structures of interest can be found through photometrically consistent cycle enumeration. This reduces the computational load significantly, not only by efficient recognition of most structures, but also by introducing constraints on the location and appearance of the "special cases."

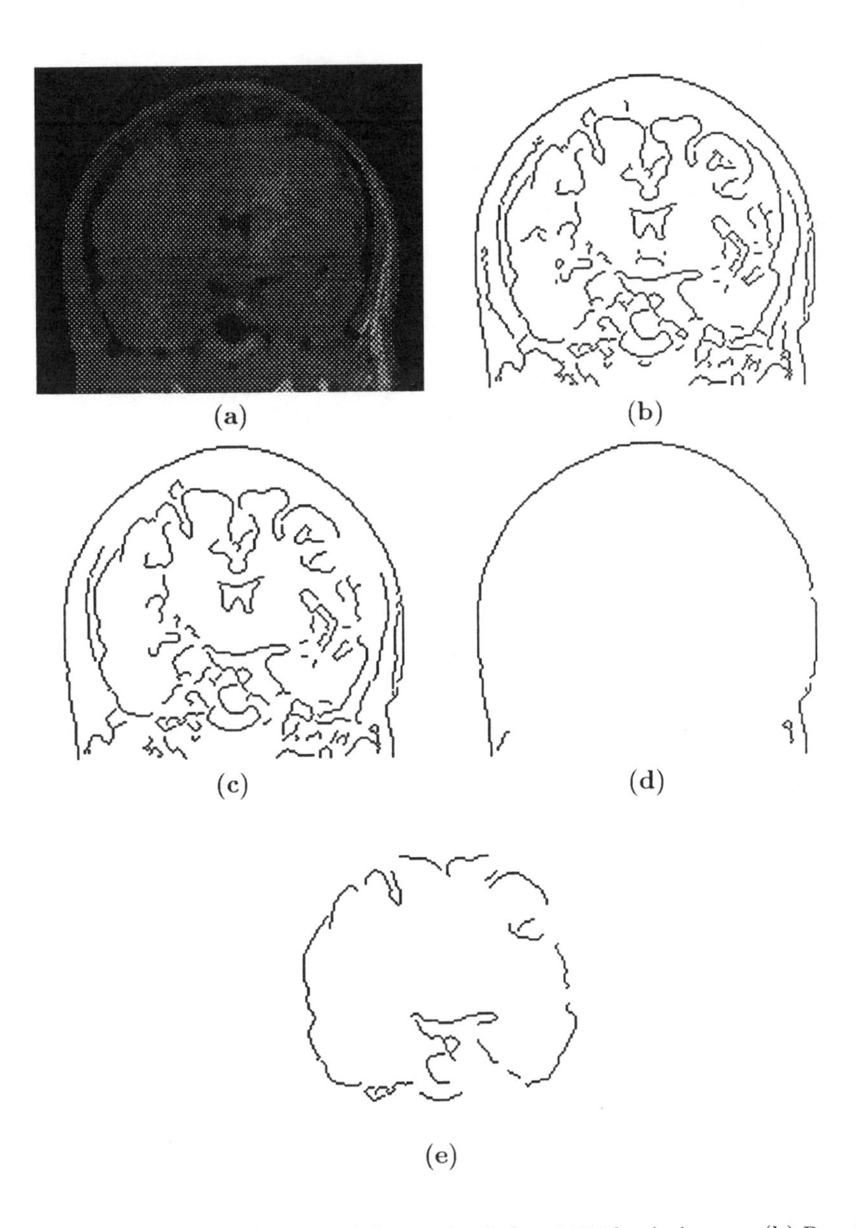

Figure 4.4: (a) Gray-level image of the top half of an MRI brain image. (b) Resulting edges after segment-based focusing. (c) Cycles generated brigding gaps of 7 pixels. (d) Cycle which outlines the skull. (e) A cycle depicting the cerebrum.

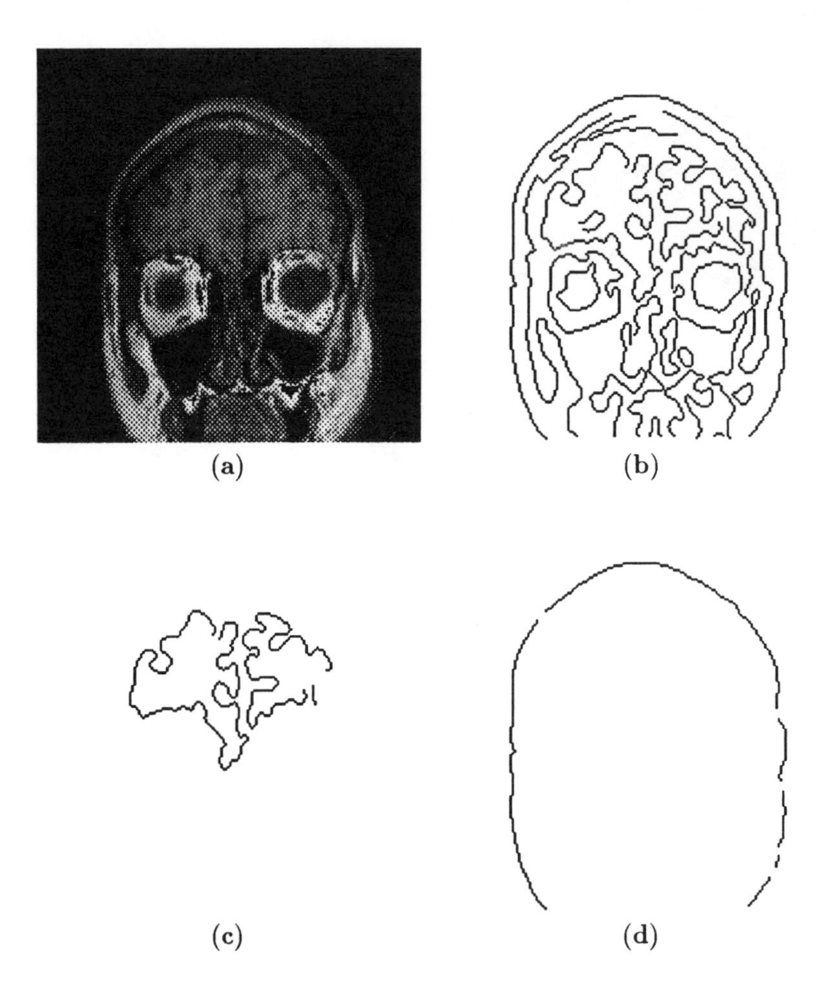

Figure 4.5: (a) Gray-level image of an anterior MRI brain section. (b) Resulting edges after segment-based focusing. (c) Cycles generated corresponding to right and left hemispheres. (d) Cycle which outlines the skull.

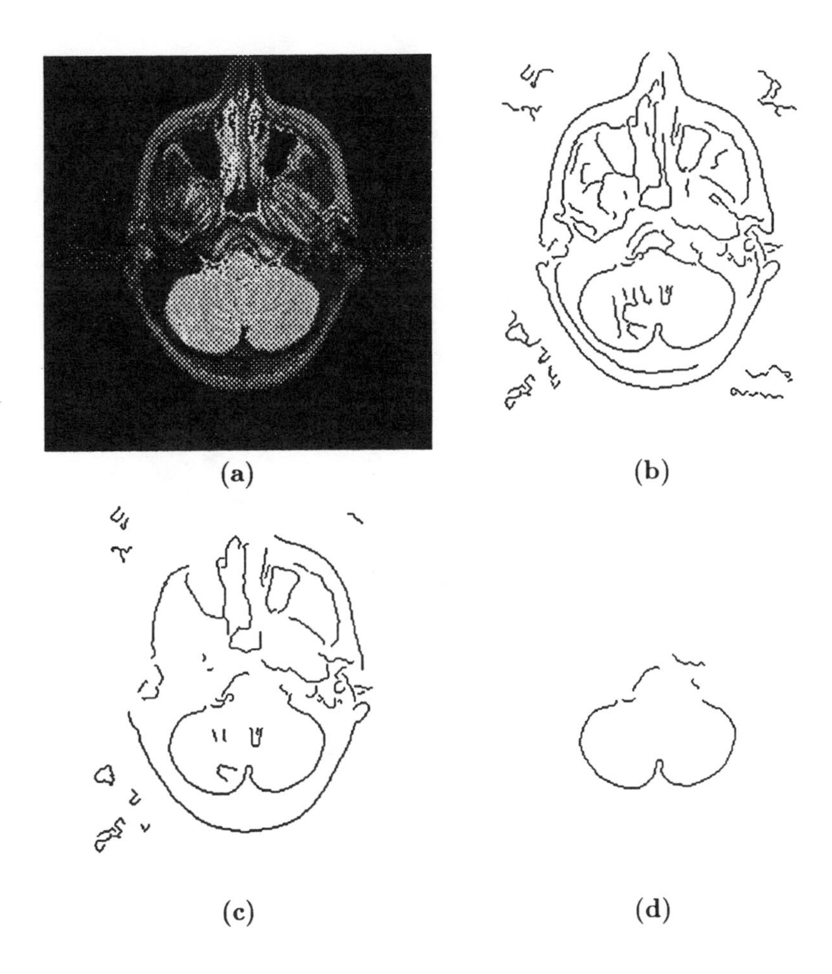

Figure 4.6: (a) Gray-level image of a transverse MRI brain section, note scanner noise. (b) Resulting edges after segment-based focusing. (c) Cycles generated by bridging gaps of 9 pixels. (d) Cycle which outlines the cerebellum.

(a) (b)

Figure 4.7: Manually traced outlines of the ventricles. (a) Corresponds to Fig. 7. (b) corresponds to Fig. 9.

MANUALLY CALCULATED FEATURE VECTORS				
		Upper Left	**Upper Right**	**Central**
Area		154.0	221.0	192.0
Perimeter		51.7	81.8	84.6
Compactness		0.85	0.64	0.58
Centroid		(87 63)	(86 112)	(73 93)
Moment	μ_{20}	1067.6	3748.6	3308.7
	μ_{02}	1459.5	4156.0	2338.0
	μ_{11}	-578.7	2803.0	-500.0
	$I_{\min}$	652.6	1142	2126.5
	$I_{\max}$	1874.6	6762.7	3520.1
Orientation		125.7	47.1	-22.9
Ellipse Axes	*Major*	8.0	12.0	8.7
	Minor	4.7	4.9	6.8
Rectangle		(79 56) (96 71)	(73 99) (99 124)	(64 82) (83 104)

Figure 4.8: Manually calculated feature vectors corresponding to the ventricles shown in Fig. 7 (columns 2 and 3) and in Fig. 9 (column 4)

15.6. References

[1] S. P. Raya, "Low-level segmentation of 3-d magnetic resonance brain images – a rule-based system," *IEEE Transactions on Medical Imaging*, vol. 9, pp. 327–337, Sept. 1990.

[2] W. E. Higgins, N. Chung, and E. L. Ritman, "Extraction of left-ventricular chamber from 3-d ct images of the heart," *IEEE Transactions on Medical Imaging*, vol. 9, pp. 384–395, Dec. 1990.

[3] T. M. Hertzberg, G. F. Tremblay, and C. F. Lam, "Computer assisted localization of nervous system injuries," *Computers and Biomedical Research*, vol. 20, pp. 489–496, 1987.

[4] T. L. Faber and E. M. Stokely, "Feature detection in 3-d medical images using shape information," *IEEE Transactions on Medical Imaging*, vol. MI-6, pp. 8–13, Mar. 1987.

[5] I. Kapouleas, "Segmentation and feature extraction for magnetic resonance brain image analysis," in *International Conference on Pattern Recognition*, pp. 583–590, 1990.

[6] D. Y. Amamoto, R. Kasturi, and A. Mamourian, "Tissue-type discrimination in magnetic resonance images," in *International Conference on Pattern Recognition*, pp. 603–607, 1990.

[7] D. N. Kennedy, P. A. Filipek, and J. V. S. Caviness, "Anatomic segmentation and volumetric calculations in nuclear magnetic resonance imaging," *IEEE Transactions on Medical Imaging*, vol. 8, pp. 1–7, Mar. 1989.

[8] N. Kassemeijer, L. J. Van Erning, and G. J. Eijkman, "Recognition of organs in CT image sequences: A model guided approach," *Computers and Biomedical Research*, vol. 21, pp. 434–448, 1988.

[9] D. G. Lowe, *Perceptual Organization and Visual Recognition*. Boston: Kluwer Academic Publishers, 1985.

[10] D. G. Lowe, "Three - dimensional object recognition from single two - dimensional images," *Artificial Intelligence*, vol. 31, pp. 355–395, 1987.

[11] F. Bergholm, "Edge focusing," *IEEE Transactions on Pattern Analysis and Machine Intelligence*, vol. PAMI-9, pp. 726–741, Nov. 1987.

[12] E. Z. Tihanyi and J. L. Barron, "Spatio-temporal edge focusing," in *International Conference on Pattern Recognition*, pp. 213–216, 1990.

[13] J. Canny, "Finding edges and lines in images," Tech. Rep. AI-TR-720, MIT Artificial Intelligence Laboratory, June 1983.

[14] J. Babaud, A. P. Witkin, M. Baudin, and R. O. Duda, "Uniqueness of the Gaussian kernel for scale-space filtering," *IEEE Transactions on Pattern Analysis and Machine Intelligence*, vol. PAMI-8, no. 1, pp. 26–33, 1986.

[15] A. Yuille and T. Poggio, "Fingerprint theorems," in *Proc. AAAI*, pp. 362–365, 1984.

[16] A. Yuille and T. Poggio, "Scaling theorems for zero crossings," *IEEE Transactions on Pattern Analysis and Machine Intelligence*, vol. PAMI-8, no. 1, pp. 15–25, 1986.

[17] A. Yuille and T. Poggio, "Scaling and fingerprint theorems for zero-crossings," in *Advances in Computer Vision* (C. Brown, ed.), pp. 47–78, Lawrence Erlbaum, 1988.

[18] S. T. Rake, "Finding parallel structures in medical images," in *Computer Applications to Assist Radiology (Proceedings of SCAR '90)* (R. L. Arenson and R. M. Friedenberg, eds.), pp. 646–652, Symposia Foundation, 1990.

[19] A. Amini, T. Weymouth, and D. Anderson, "A parallel algorithm for determining two-dimensional object positions using incomplete information about their boundaries," *Pattern Recognition*, vol. 22, no. 1, pp. 21–28, 1989.

[20] Y. Lu and R. Jain, "Behavior of edges in scale space," *IEEE Transactions on Pattern Analysis and Machine Intelligence*, vol. 11, pp. 337–356, Apr. 1989.

[21] D. Marr and E. Hildreth, "Theory of edge detection," *Proceedings of the Royal Society of London*, vol. 207, pp. 187–217, 1980.

[22] S. Sarkar and K. L. Boyer, "Optimal infinite impulse response zero crossing based edge detectors," *Computer Vision, Graphics, and Image Processing: Image Understanding*, vol. 54, pp. 224–243, Sept. 1991.

[23] M. Bomans, K. Hohne, U. Tiede, and M. Riemer, "3-D segmentation of MR images of the head for 3-D display," *IEEE Transactions on Medical Imaging*, vol. 9, pp. 177–183, June 1990.

[24] S. V. Raman, S. Sarkar, and K. L. Boyer, "Tissue boundaary refinement in magnetic resonance images using contour-based scale space matching," *IEEE Transactions on Medical Imaging*, vol. 10, pp. 109–121, June 1991.

[25] J. Canny, "A computational approach to edge detection," *IEEE Transactions on Pattern Analysis and Machine Intelligence*, vol. PAMI-8, pp. 679–714, Nov. 1986.

[26] S. Sarkar and K. L. Boyer, "Optimal, efficient, recursive edge detection filters," in *International Conference on Pattern Recognition*, pp. 931–936, June 1990.

[27] S. Sarkar and K. L. Boyer, "On optimal infinite impulse response edge detection filters." Accepted to *IEEE Transactions on Pattern Analysis and Machine Intelligence* Aug, 1989.

[28] S. Sarkar, "Optimal, efficient detection and low level perceptual organization of image edge features," Master's thesis, The Ohio State University, 1990.

[29] G. E. Sotak and K. L. Boyer, "The Laplacian-of-Gaussian kernel: A formal analysis and design procedure for fast, accurate convolution and full-frame output," *Computer Vision, Graphics, and Image Processing*, vol. 48, no. 2, pp. 147–189, 1989.

[30] D. M. Wuescher and K. L. Boyer, "Robust contour decomposition using a constant curvature criterion," *IEEE Transactions on Pattern Analysis and Machine Intelligence*, vol. 13, pp. 41–51, Jan. 1991.

[31] S. Sarkar and K. L. Boyer, "A highly efficient computational structure for perceptual organization," Tech. Rep. SAMPL-90-06, SAMP-Lab, Dept. of EE, OSU, November 1990. Submitted to *IEEE Transactions on Systems, Man, and Cybernetics.*

[32] V. Chachra, P. M. Ghare, and J. M. Moore, *Applications of Graph Theory Algorithms.* New York: Elsevier North Holland, Inc., 1979.

[33] F. Harary, *Graph Theory.* Addison-Wesley, 1969.

[34] J. Welch, Jr., "A mechanical analysis of the cyclic structure of undirected linear graphs," *Journal of the Association for Computing Machinery*, vol. 13, pp. 205–210, Apr. 1966.

[35] E. M. Reingold, *Combinatorial Algorithms.* Englewood Cliffs, N.J.: Prentice Hall, 1977.

[36] A. A. Amini, T. E. Weymouth, and R. C. Jain, "Using dynamic programming for solving variational problems in vision," *IEEE Transactions on Pattern Analysis and Machine Intelligence*, vol. 12, pp. 855–867, Sept. 1990.

[37] T. Matsui and A. Hirano, *An Atlas of the Human Brain for Computerized Tomography.* New York: Igaku-Shoin, 1978.

Chapter 16

Knowledge-Guided Boundary Detection for Medical Images

S. Tehrani, T. E. Weymouth

16.1 Introduction

The construction of complete boundaries of objects and the analysis of their motion in an image sequence are two important and difficult problems in Computer Vision. Although many researchers have attempted to solve these two problems separately, they are not disjoint problems and a solution to one can help in finding the other. A general solution to these problems which would be applicable to all cases is very difficult to achieve. They become even more difficult when dealing with low contrast images and general, non-rigid object motion. Therefore, we have attempted to analyze these problems and have proposed a solution for low-contrast boundaries and non-rigid motion of a specific object. One domain that requires such a solution is Ventriculography, analyzing X-ray motion pictures of a heart chamber.

We have taken advantage of a such restricted domain while analyzing this complex problem. Firstly, any solution must address such complications in feature extraction for our restricted domain. Secondly, expert knowledge in the form of diagnostic models of the heart boundary and motion has to be applied to guide the system in object detection and recognition. Finally, since our image analysis technique combines both data-directed (bottom-up), and goal-guided (top-down) approaches, some issues concerning control must be addressed. To control both bottom-up and top-down processes, a system that offers opportunistic problem-solving techniques has been employed.

16.1.1 Low-level Processing

Boundary detection is an essential part of many Computer Vision related tasks. One way of defining boundaries between objects or between an object and the background is the determination of points where the gray values change abruptly. By proper selection of these points, the boundary can be formed using one of a variety of interpolation or approximation techniques. The process of boundary detection consists of the following three major and distinct steps: edge detection, edge point selection, and boundary formation. Edge detection is the process of defining points with an abrupt change in the intensity. This is based on the assumption that different objects have different intensity values.

In general, boundary determination is a challenging problem. However, it would not be a very interesting problem in the case where simple man-made objects are illuminated with laboratory controlled lighting because under controlled conditions the objects present high contrast at their boundaries with predictable shapes and image characteristics. In such situations, a simple edge linking algorithm suffices. However, medical image processing has long been plagued with the problem of extracting clear boundaries of objects from noisy and low contrast images. Most medical images such as X-rays, microscope slides, or CT scans are low contrast by nature or design. In addition, the material of the objects in question is frequently self-occluded or partially transparent (Figure 1) with uncertain position, size, orientation, shape, motion, etc. Moreover, there are uncertainties related to image characteristics such as the type of noise and amount of the image brightness or contrast. Therefore, the precise boundary characteristics of these objects cannot be efficiently described by mathematical models, useful for image analysis.

These conditions cause difficulties in the interpretation of such images by the computer (Figure 2). However, medical experts routinely perform interpretation of medical image sequences which are precise enough for diagnoses; thus, there must be enough information in the images and enough expert knowledge to extract the correct boundaries of a sequence. Various sources of knowledge must be acquired and encoded into flexible program modules to be used by the system. Once the edge points are found, the boundary can be formed using one of many interpolated methods described in [11].

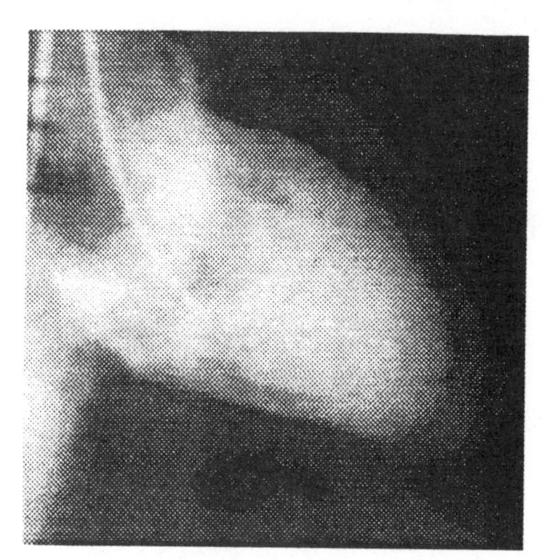

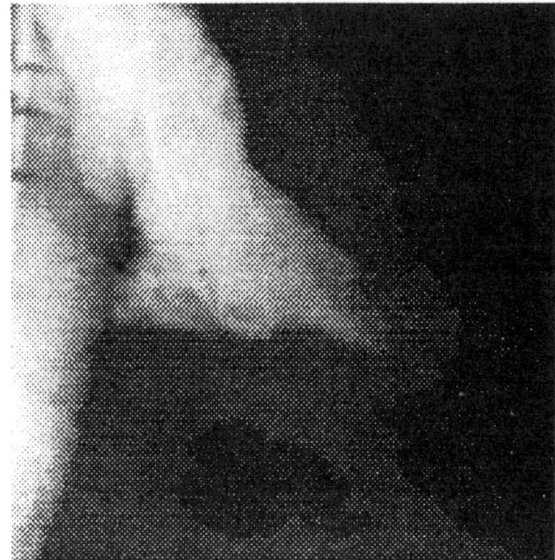

Figure 1: The end-diastolic and end-systolic frames (frames 1 and 12) of an unprocessed, digitized cineventriculogram.

Another way of looking at an image sequence of a beating heart is to view it as an elastic, non-rigid body in motion. Nevertheless, there has been very little research on the motion analysis of elastic bodies in Computer Vision. There are two reasons for this. First, the analysis of rigid motion, translation, rotation and observer motion, is complex enough that it discourages researchers from becoming involved in a more general and difficult problem concerning the motion of non-rigid objects. The second reason is the lack of available knowledge and mathematical models for formulating non-rigid movement of a vast variety of objects. The problem, however, becomes manageable if the scope is confined to the motion of a specific object in a narrow domain such as the motion of the left ventricular boundary.

Ascertaining the motion of non-rigid objects is particularly important in the field of Ventriculography, as the analysis of ventricular wall motion helps in understanding the behavior of the heart function and discovering the cause of cardiac disease symptoms [6]. Incorporating the temporal information as well as spatial shape information can lead to better object detection, recognition and motion understanding. Since the images are taken at 30 or 60 frames per second and the heart beat rate is about one beat per second, we can assume that the objects in the image sequence are moving slowly over time. By this assumption, spurious edges that appear and disappear within a short period of time would be considered noise and would be filtered out.

In current clinical practice, since no viable automatic method exists, the correct ventricular boundaries are manually traced by an expert technician or physician. It is important to notice how and where the human experts incorporate various types of knowledge in their decisions. For example, in tracing the left ventricular shape, the experts must distinguish the heart shape from other objects in the X-ray image based on their experience. They may also connect parts of the boundary that are not very clear and confirm their judgement by utilizing the position of an edge from images before or after the current image in the sequence. The following steps are given as an example of a manual tracing procedure and diagnosis routinely performed by the human expert.

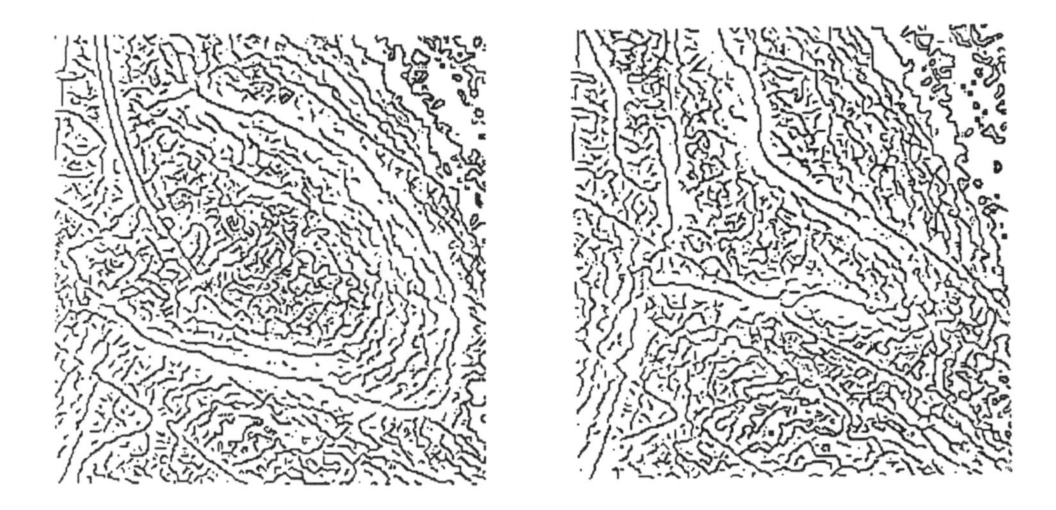

Figure 2: The results of simple edge detection applied to unprocessed, digitized cineventriculograms at end-diastolic and end-systolic frame.

1- Extract the cycle of interest from many cycles of a beating heart sequence.

2- Envision the movement and the location of the ventricle in the entire cycle, and if possible, identify any other non-ventricular objects in the image (both moving and stationary).

3- Start from the end-diastolic image due to the higher contrast of this image.

4- Assign the initial boundary by tracking the boundary from the anterior aortic root area, moving clockwise along the anterior aspect, around the apex, and along the inferior aspect of the ventricle.

5- Identify the mitral valve region where the boundary can be confusing due to the low image contrast. Use the shape knowledge to trace the correct boundary, terminating at the inferior aortic root.

6- If there are multiple co-centric partial boundaries (due to the dye mixing, noise, or other artifacts), take the most outer one which has "enough" contrast.

7- If a part of the boundary is not very clear because it is fading or partially occluded, look at previous and subsequent images to interpolate the missing segments of the boundary. Using the motion of the ventricle is very helpful in identifying obscure segments of the boundary.

8- Edit parts of the boundary that are not smooth or that are not consistent with the general shape of the ventricle.

9- Use the accumulated information about the ventricular boundary in the sequence to interpret the rest of the images more efficiently.

10- If no further boundary editing is required, advance to the next image (go to step 4).

11- Look through the extracted boundaries of the cycle. If there are any inconsistencies in the motion of sections of the boundaries, edit the corresponding sections.

12- Determine dysfunctions by comparing the shape of normal and abnormal ventricles with that of the extracted boundaries.

The process of manual tracing is time consuming, requires a high level of training, and is subject to observer error. To relieve operator tedium, and remove observer bias or error, the goal of our system is to automate as much of the task as possible.

16.1.2 Overview of the Solution

The boundary determination of the left ventricle and analysis of its non-rigid motion requires expert knowledge in terms of diagnostic models of the heart in motion to correctly interpret the image sequence. Since the shape and motion of the left ventricular boundary has been under investigation for many years, the knowledge required for this analysis can be acquired from an expert in radiography or the current cardiology literature.

Imperfect models and noisy data can produce ambiguous partial solutions. To resolve erroneous partial solutions, diverse sources of information must be exploited. That is, multiple sources of information need to be incorporated in the system to overcome the noise and unreliable knowledge. These sources of knowledge are in the form of cooperating and competing knowledge sources (KSs) that advance partial solutions in a non-deterministic manner. Since these KSs are not applied in any predefined order during the problem solving, a system is desired which permits the opportunistic control of processing.

A blackboard architecture [12] was employed as a basis for image interpretation in the system design. Although this architecture has been used in similar domains [7], it has not yet been applied to this complex problem. We have used the blackboard architecture because it is powerful and modular for our knowledge-based application. This is due to the partitioning of the domain knowledge into a set of functionally independent knowledge sources (KSs), the uniformity of the knowledge interaction, and the choice of domain dependent control strategies. In this architecture, KSs interact with each other through a single blackboard data-base while they are being controlled by domain-dependent control strategies that are capable of handling such a knowledge-intensive task.

Each KS functions independently performing a particular test against the input data or against solutions found on the blackboard, the global data structure. They take partial solutions (hypotheses) as input and produce a more complete solution using the knowledge embedded in them. These new hypotheses may combine other partial solutions and will search for additional supporting data. Therefore, solutions at the lower levels of the hierarchy (more detailed levels of abstraction) are used to promote solutions at higher levels. Also, higher-level KSs can define goals for the lower ones. These goals can be used to direct and control subsequent processing, leading to more focused problem solving. Each KS tends to solve the problem from a different angle. The aim is to have a cooperative competition among KSs that are operating at various levels of abstraction. The cooperative operations among KSs propose advances in the solution. By defining the terms of cooperation and by controlling the activation of KSs, the system will come up with a consistent solution at the top level, the highest level of abstraction.

The following are some of the features of our proposed solution.

1- Ventricular boundaries are identified by the application of general knowledge as well as domain knowledge to the images in the sequence. An example of general knowledge is that the consistency in the motion of objects can be used to separate the objects from noise. An example of domain knowledge is the expertise of a physician or a trained technician for recognizing the shape and motion of the left ventricle in an X-ray image sequence.

2- The expertise of the technician or physician is also incorporated in the control structure of the system. For instance, an expert would start by first outlining higher contrast regions of the left ventricular boundary, and then joining the boundary pieces and filling the gaps.

3- Although the use of local information in a single image produces uncertain and erroneous results, the uncertainty and error can be reduced by combining the information in multiple images or by combining other sources of information. For instance, missing segments of the boundary may be identified by finding its associated segments in the preceding or following images.

4- The available experimentally derived models of heart shapes are used to determine how well the extracted boundary fits the models. The shape models play an important role in determining the quality of the results.

5- The multi-frame sequences enable expectations as to shape and location of the boundary of the object of interest in the subsequent images. These expectations are essential for efficiency and performance of the system.

Four important implementation aspects of this system are: First, local features such as edges are grouped to build a complete description of the moving heart. Second, descriptions of objects are organized in a hierarchy with various levels of abstraction from coarse (top) to fine (bottom). Third, knowledge is organized in a hierarchy with KSs (procedural knowledge) that interact between various levels of abstraction. That is, KSs can be activated in both top-down and bottom-up orders. These KSs cooperate to advance the solution until they arrive at a solution consistent with the diagnostic model of the heart. Fourth, opportunistic problem-solving techniques are used to control the order of activation of both data-directed and goal-driven KSs.

In series of examples, we show how edge points are extracted and linked in our system to form boundary fragments, how adjacent or overlapping fragments are collected and connected, how boundary fragments are tracked, how they are matched against heart models, how experimental models of the LV boundaries are derived, how uncertainties are dealt with, how the KSs interact, and finally how KS activations are organized by the control structure.

The system was evaluated based on the performance of each KS, individually, as well as its interaction with other KSs. The system was run on many image sequences and the results were compared with manual tracings, confirming the correctness of the boundaries obtained by this approach. Overall, this system results in robust image interpretation which is required in Medicine and many other applications of Computer Vision.

16.2 Image interpretation

Image understanding requires the detection of objects in a particular scene and the establishments of their relationships in space and/or in time. To establish the relationships, two kinds of knowledge can be used in an image understanding task. The first is global or domain-independent knowledge, such as assumptions about the smoothness of object surfaces or the consistency in the motion of objects. The second is domain-specific knowledge, in our case the knowledge used in Ventriculography, such as the shape of the ventricle and the relationships between the objects in the X-ray image. Examples of domain knowledge are the amount of expansion or contraction of a beating heart and the maximum amount of rotation of the long axis of the left ventricular boundary in an image sequence. These, in turn, will define the approximate size, position and orientation of the heart boundaries throughout the image sequence.

Our system groups local features, in this case edges, to build a specific description of a moving heart in the image sequence. By the application of global and domain knowledge, the true edges, which are consistent in time and satisfy specific features of the heart shape, are emphasized over spurious edges which do not conform to these conditions, but which may exhibit stronger intensity gradients.

To handle such a complex problem, the following important issues were considered in the engineering of our system.

1- How to Build a Modular System. Which architecture easily permits the addition or removal of some knowledge or information without the need to change the entire design of the system?

2- How to Organize Knowledge. Which organization will allow both spatial and temporal relationships among objects to be easily defined and manipulated?

3- How to Represent the Global and Domain Knowledge. What shape and temporal models are flexible enough to capture the variance in shape of the ventricle with its corresponding motion, and yet specific enough to be distinguishable from the other objects? What is the procedure for matching the boundaries against those models? What is the best grain size of input to be passed to the high-level interpreter (i.e., gray level images, edge points with corresponding directions, or edge segments with their features)?

4- How to Deal with Uncertainty. What are robust methods that will perform gracefully in the absence of certain information or in the presence of noise or unwanted structures? Can it perform satisfactorily when there are uncertainties in the description of models?

5- How to Choose a Proper Control Strategy. Which architecture permits a domain-specific control strategy? What type of control strategy is simple to understand and easy to implement, and yet powerful enough to handle various sources of information?

6- How to Build a System Incrementally. Which architecture permits the incremental design? Which characteristic of an architecture allows it to pursue its goals and not collapse while including additional knowledge or removing obsolete modules?

16.2.1 The Blackboard Architecture

A system which is well suited for dealing with the above issues is the blackboard architecture [7]. Typical characteristics of blackboard systems are organizing knowledge into a hierarchical global data structure, partitioning knowledge into a collection of knowledge sources (KSs), generating alternative hypotheses, solving the problem opportunistically, allowing domain specific control strategies, and providing an environment for the incremental design. The hierarchical global data structure, the blackboard, contains a collection of KSs operating on various levels of abstraction. The blackboard facilitates interactions between KSs while reducing redundant low-level operations. Alternative hypotheses allow similar units with various confidences to be created on the blackboard. This way, alternative partial solutions can be generated on the blackboard while a partial solution can in fact comprise the final solution. The opportunistic problem-solving approach combines data-directed hypotheses (bottom-up approach) with model-driven matching (top-down approach). User-defined control structures provide a set of domain-dependent control strategies possibly with various feedback loops. These loops can reduce the effect of noise and erroneous isolated points on the output of the system. The incremental design permits the knowledge engineer to incorporate more KSs into the system as they become available without the need to modify the underlying architecture.

Each KS has a pre-condition and an action similar to the rule base systems. The pre-condition function returns a measure (importance factor) for the applicability of the KS to the state of the problem, and a list of the specific units that activated it. The action procedure performs operations to advance the solution which in turn may change the state of the problem by producing more hypotheses with various confidences. Within each KS, there are input levels and output levels that determine which units can activate the KS and what type of hypotheses may be produced. The determination of confidence and importance measures and the control of activation of KSs using those measures are important for performance reasons (see section 16.3.8). The levels of abstraction in our specific domain and the corresponding KSs that operate on or between these levels will be described in the next section.

16.2.2 Hierarchical Representation and I/O Description

The system has two kinds of input: i) a sequence of X-ray images obtained from a cardiac cycle and ii) the experimentally derived models of ventricular shapes determined from a statistical summary of manually traced boundaries of many normal and abnormal ventricles [5]. The output of the system is a set of left ventricular boundaries to be used for diagnosis.

The description of units is represented in the hierarchy at various levels of abstraction from fine (bottom) to coarse (top). The hierarchical representation of the blackboard consists of three layers. The middle layer of the blackboard has two sides: STATIC which corresponds to frame by frame information and DYNAMIC which corresponds to moving objects (Figure 3). The levels of the static side from bottom to top of the hierarchy are: Edge Point, Boundary Fragment, Curve, Boundary and Heart Description. The levels of the dynamic side are: Edge Sequence, Boundary Fragment Sequence, Curve Sequence, Boundary Sequence, and finally Heart Sequence. There are two other layers, a layer below and a layer above the hierarchy. The layer below the hierarchy is a gray level image sequence, and the layer above is the diagnostic model of the heart. The abstractions on the static side of the blackboard summarize the information in each frame, whereas the abstractions on the dynamic side unify the motion of objects over the entire X-ray sequence. The description of the blackboard levels from bottom to top is as follows:

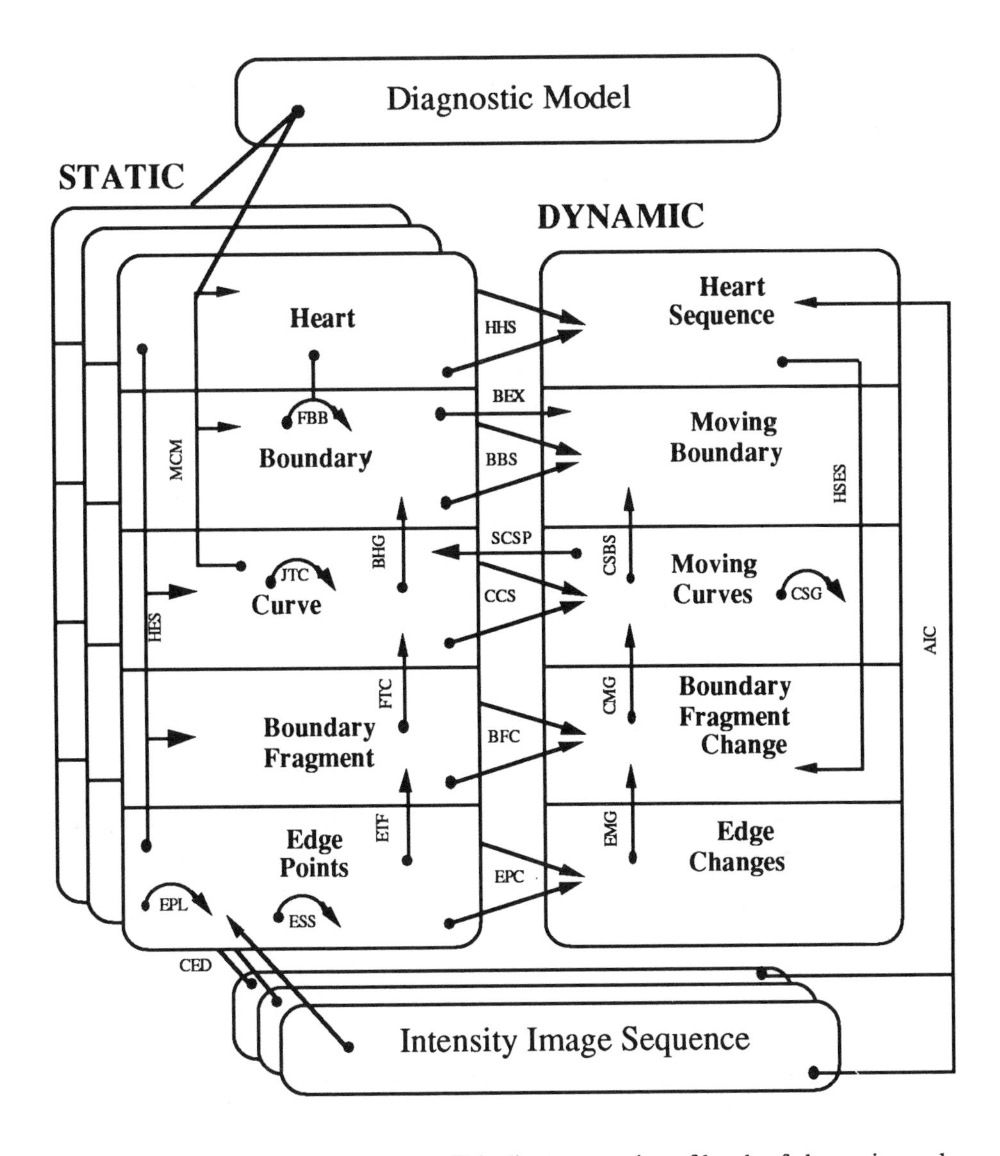

Figure 3: Diagram of our blackboard. This diagram consists of levels of abstraction and KSs that are interacting between levels.

1- Gray Level Image Sequence: a sequence of X-ray images digitized at 30 frames per second. Images of the left ventricle were digitized from 35 mm cineangiographic film in the 30 degree right anterior oblique (RAO) projection because a large number of studies are available in this form. The digitized images are 256 by 256 pixels with 8 bits of gray-level data.

2- Edge Point: points of abrupt change in the intensity image. A subset of these points is the set of points that have a significant change in the intensity across the boundary of objects. In our system, edge points are derived by the application of the Canny edge operator [2] to the intensity image.

3- Edge Sequence: edge points that are changing position in the sequence. Consistent motion of edge points corresponds to the motion of an object, whereas inconsistency in the changing position is assumed to be noise and must be discarded.

4- Boundary Fragment: a set of linked edge points that are adjacent in space. A boundary fragment forms a part of the boundary of an object in the X-ray image. A unit in this level contains statistical information about the intensity, gradient, gradient direction along the boundary fragment as well as the position of the end points and the length of the fragment. At this level, boundary fragments are simple units and cannot be connected; hence, there is no composite boundary fragment unit.

5- Boundary Fragment Sequence: moving boundary fragments collected either from consistent motion of edge points that are adjacent in space or from boundary fragments that are moving closely in time.

6- Curve: a polyline representation of the boundary fragment. A unit at this level contains the shape of the fragment which can be used to match against the left ventricular (LV) models. The polyline representation contains line segments that are used for tracking curves in the image sequence. The curves are also joined at this level to construct larger composite curves. There are also links between the boundary fragments and curves to distinguish composite curves from simple curve units.

7- Curve Sequence: a collection of moving curves. A unit at this level contains the relationship between curves in subsequent frames and the amount of consistency in their motion. There are four types of Curve Sequence (CS) units. 1) A CS is a basic unit consisting of two curve units, one from each of the two adjacent frames. 2) A Space-CS combines two CS units with a common curve. Thus, it contains three curves, two of which are from one frame and the third (common) is from the next or the previous frame. 3) A Time-CS is a curve sequence which extends in time only. This unit can be obtained by grouping the CS units over time which may have as many curves as there are frames in the sequence, but no two curves can belong to the same frame. 4) A General-CS is a unit which may be constructed from any of the above CS units.

8- Boundary: boundaries of objects obtained by a model-guided linking of the curve units. These boundaries specify structures that are present in the X-ray image sequence. The left ventricle is one of the structures in the X-ray image, so its boundary is included in this set. Note that the boundary which best matches a heart model is considered to be the solution for that frame at that time.

9- Boundary Sequence: a class of boundaries that are moving in time. This class is generated by grouping either the curve sequences that are spatially adjacent or the LV boundaries in successive frames. One such element of the class is the motion of the ventricle; thus, the final solution lies at this level.

10- Heart: a specific description of the left ventricular (LV) shape. This description, called a model instance of the LV boundary, is generated during partial or complete boundary matching. The shape of the model instance is obtained from the LV shape data-base contained in the diagnostic models of the heart and the parameters are derived from the matching. When an identical or a close match is generated by joining a new piece to the curves, a new heart model will not be instantiated; instead, the confidence of the previous instantiation will be increased. This increase in the confidence affects the determination of the best boundary unit.

11- Heart Sequence: a sequence of left ventricular model instances. This sequence contains model instances that vary slowly in time. Since the parameters of a model instance (position, orientation and size) cannot change rapidly from frame to frame, consistency in the parameters is used to influence the confidence of the heart sequence. In addition, if there is a missing model instance, it could be interpolated using the parameters of the adjacent models.

12- Diagnostic Model: a data structure containing normal and abnormal models of the heart sequence with statistical information about each of the three types of abnormality (inferior, anterior, and both inferior & anterior). In addition, it contains the average, maximum and minimum of the position, orientation and size of the ventricular shapes for every frame of the sequence.

Each unit of the blackboard contains a confidence factor which helps in the control decisions and correct object interpretation. More specific description of the confidence factors can be found in section 16.3.8. In addition to the three layers, there is another space defined on the blackboard. This space (called OBJECT space) contains two important units:

1- Endpoint Unit: the (x,y) coordinates of the endpoint of a boundary fragment with the gradient direction at that point. The coordinates are used in retrieving spatially adjacent boundary fragments for the connection operation, and the direction is used to ignore boundary fragments which have opposite gradient directions at the joining endpoints.

2- Line Segment Unit: a segment of the polyline representation of a curve unit. A unit in this space contains the (x,y) coordinates and the gradient direction at the center of the line in addition to the orientation of the line. The orientation of these units for a given curve comprises the Theta-S representation of the curve. The orientation of these units is used for model matching (Section 16.7.2) and the position of these units is used for tracking the curve units in the sequence (Section 16.3.5).

16.2.3 Description of Knowledge Sources

In our system, the procedural knowledge is embedded in knowledge sources (KSs) that interact between units in the same or different levels of the hierarchy (Figure 3). KSs access the relationships between units represented by bi-directional links (pointers). They use object relationships and the embedded knowledge to improve the solution. They take a partial solution as input and produce a more complete solution or take a partial solution and search for more supporting data. In order to test and evaluate the system, many KSs have been designed, implemented and tested. The following is a list of KSs that have been suggested for both image feature extraction and interpretation. The implemented KSs are marked by a star and will be discussed in depth in the respective sections.

1- Canny Edge Detection * (CED): a bottom-up process which extracts edge points from the X-ray input image, and returns a binary edge mask image along with the magnitude and direction of the gradient at the edge points.

2- Edge Point Linking * (EPL): connects the neighboring edge points in an edge image to form an initial set of edge segments. A data structure is also generated for each edge segment which contains information about the segment, such as: intensity, position, gradient and chain code. The data structures of all edge groups are kept in a linked list for every frame and sorted by decreasing order of the edge segment strength (the length of the edge segment times the sum of the gradient magnitudes along the segment).

3- Edge Segment Splitting * (ESS): disconnects the edge segments that are incorrectly linked and produces smaller edge segments. It splits an edge segment either at the point of high curvature or at a point which is near the end point of another edge fragment .

4- Edge to Fragment * (ETF): takes the top N (e.g., N = 4) edge segments from the linked list and hypothesizes them at the Boundary Fragment level of the blackboard. If there are no more edge segment left in the link list, the system will ignore the remaining activities on the blackboard and will halt. Thus, it recognizes the termination condition of the problem solving.

5- Fragment to Curve * (FTC): generates curves out of relatively long boundary fragments (at least 5 line segments long – about 35 pixels). This KS constructs the polyline segments of the curve units and computes the information required for filling the slots of the line segments. It also computes the Theta-S shape representation required for the model matching.

6- Join Two Curves * (JTC): connects two neighboring curves in space, and forms a new hypothesis for a larger portion of the boundary. This also includes joining overlapping curves using a linear connection or a smooth transition between the two overlapping parts.

7- Matching Curves against Models * (MCM): takes a curve shape description and matches it with the available models of the heart. This KS is activated when the curve is long enough for matching. It is also capable of matching the curves that are longer than the models and finding their acceptable parts as complete boundaries. The result of this matching is a heart unit containing the parameters and the score of the matching. The parameters of a heart model are the type, translation, rotation and scale. Using these parameters, a Heart unit can be instantiated.

8- Boundary Hypotheses Generating * (BHG): generates hypotheses for plausible boundaries, especially for the left ventricular boundary, using the most promising curve candidates. The left ventricular boundary hypotheses are created using a partial match between the curve hypothesis and the heart model.

9- Find the Best Boundary * (FBB): selects the boundary with the highest confidence which is also closest to the description of the ventricular shape. That is, not only must the boundary have a high confidence but the heart unit that matched it must also have the highest confidence. This boundary represents the best LV boundary interpretation found so far for a particular image.

10- Heart to Edge Segment * (HES): finds supporting edge segments in an image that are close to the hypothesized heart unit and satisfy certain conditions with respect to the model. The selected edge segments can be used to guide the refinement of the model, which in turn can be used to select more fragments. Although these supporting edge segments may be very small and have low confidence, they may solve the puzzle by filling the gaps of the boundary. Therefore, they are given high priority to be promoted to the Boundary Fragment level and then to the Curve level. In addition, the distance constraints for filling the gaps are more relaxed for these segments.

11- Edge Point Changes (EPC): groups the edge points that are adjacent in time. Those points that exhibit a consistent motion though the image sequence are preferred over the random motion of noise in the background.

12- Edge Movements Grouping (EMG): groups the edge changes that are spatial neighbors into fragment changes.

13- Boundary Fragment Changes (BFC): groups boundary fragments that are adjacent within two frames.

14- Curve Movements Grouping (CMG): groups the boundary fragment changes that are neighbors in space to produce a curve sequence unit.

15- Curve to Curve Sequence * (CCS): takes a curve unit and finds other neighboring curves in the adjacent frames. This KS builds the basic Curve Sequence unit (CS) by matching the line segments of the curve against that of the curves in the adjacent frames.

16- Curve Sequence Grouping * (CSG): takes the curve description of moving objects and constructs a more abstract description of the curve movements. That is, this KS combines the basic CS units and makes more complex CS units such as Space-CS, Time-CS and General-CS. It also checks the consistency or redundancy of the new hypothesis.

17- Space Curve Sequence Patching * (SCSP): takes a space curve sequence and by using the common curve, it fills the gap (patches) between the other two curves.

18- Curve Sequence to Boundary Sequence (CSBS): takes a time curve sequence description (Time-CS) and converts it into a boundary sequence if the curves are long enough and can represent complete left ventricular boundaries.

19- Boundary to Boundary Sequence * (BBS): groups the boundary of objects in time. This grouping would be used to analyze the motion of objects. The complete solution is identified by this KS when the complete left ventricular boundaries of all frames are collected.

20- Single Boundary Extension * (BEX): take a complete boundary and extends it throughout the sequence. Once a complete boundary is found, it can be extended throughout as much of the sequence as possible using the exact position of the boundary points. This means that once the complete boundary in one frame is identified, it can be extended throughout the sequence, which would be a much faster and less expensive KS for finding the solution. This KS was designed and implemented as a stand-alone program. With minimal user interaction to select the initial boundary fragments, the program was able to find all other boundaries between the ED and ES frames. It was used to test the performance of this type of boundary extraction for the available medical images [9].

21- Heart to Heart Sequence * (HHS): builds a motion description of the ventricular model instance using the individual heart descriptions. This KS employs the consistencies of the parameters of the heart descriptions (one description per frame) to construct a heart sequence unit.

22- Heart Sequence to Edge Sequence (HSES): imposes temporal constraints on the moving edge points such as the range or direction of movements of the edge points. For instance, if the heart is in the contracting phase, the edge segments should move toward the inside of the ventricle with a certain speed.

23- Average Intensity Changes * (AIC): collects relative changes in the average intensity of the images in the cardiac cycle, and adds them to the description of the heart sequence. This information is a rough estimate for the contraction or expansion of the beating heart and can be used to restrict the search for the position of the boundary in the subsequent images.

Since the system allows the generation of alternate hypotheses, one of the most difficult problems is that they may generate many identical hypothesis. Identical hypotheses are those with identical sub-parts (symbolically identical) or with different sub-parts but occupying the same locations on the plane (physically identical). The generation of identical hypotheses must be prevented during the design and implementation of the KSs because sometimes the system can fall in an infinite loop of producing the same unit over and over again. For more in-depth analysis see [8].

To have a working system, it is not necessary to implement all of the KSs. Nevertheless, enough of them have been implemented to reach the solution from at least two different paths. This allows us to test various feedback loops and to evaluate the control parameters. Since the blackboard architecture permits the incremental building of the system, more specialized KSs could be added to this list to take care of unusual cases.

16.3 Discussion

An important task in the design and implementation of a blackboard system is to define complete specifications of each KS. These specifications consist of the kinds of input and output of the KS, the reasons for its activation, and the operations that are performed when the KS is actually executed. For each implemented KS, we describe how relatively important it is to be activated (using importance measures), what conditions must be satisfied for its activation, what objects would be produced when executed, what types of techniques are employed, what parameters are used, and what type of effect each parameter would have on the behavior of the system or the final output. We start with detection of edges and evaluation of relevant edge information, and we proceed by addressing problems concerning curves, boundaries and models. We will close the discussion with confidence measures of the blackboard units, importance measures of the KSs, and finally the components of the control structure.

16.3.1 Edge Detection and Related KSs

Given a sequence of left ventricular images, the first step in boundary construction involves the use of some edge detector. Several approaches have been proposed for detecting edge elements in an image. One of the edge detection techniques which recently has become very popular is the Canny edge operator [2]. We chose the Canny edge detector also because it uses an optimal filter that minimizes noise and maximizes the localization while producing thin edge segments suitable for our boundary representation. Therefore, it is an appropriate edge detector for the kind of low contrast X-ray images we are dealing with. In the next section, we will discuss the implementation of the Canny edge detector and address its required parameters.

16.3.1.1 Canny Edge Detection (CED)

The Canny edge detector starts by smoothing the intensity image using the Gaussian filter [2]. The smoothing filter is a two dimensional Gaussian filter with a single parameter sigma that defines the degree of smoothness. A high value for the sigma tends to remove weak edges, but smooths out sharp corners and introduces a localization error in the position of edge segments . On the other hand, a low sigma value produces sharper corners and more accurate edge position, but does not significantly reduce the amount of noise. A value of sigma equal to 2.0, corresponding to the kernel-size of 11, was used in our experiments. Experiments showed that the system is not very sensitive to the exact selection of the sigma parameter (see [8]).

The 2-D Gaussian filter is applied by cascading two 1-D Gaussian filters which produce two directional derivatives. These derivatives are used to compute the magnitude and direction of the gradient. The magnitude values for all pixels in the image comprise a magnitude image. The magnitude image is thinned by the non-maximal suppression process. Then, two thresholds are applied: a high threshold and a low threshold. The high threshold is for detecting high contrast edge points that are most likely a part of the object boundaries, and the low threshold is for discriminating noisy edges from the rest of the image. Specifically, those edge points whose magnitudes of the gradient are above the high threshold are marked strong edges, and the ones with magnitudes below the low threshold are assumed to be noise and are eliminated. Edge points with magnitudes in between the two thresholds are included only if they are connected to a previously marked edge point. In our implementation, the two thresholds are given in the form of percentiles of the edge points whose gradient magnitudes are above certain values. The low percentile is defined as a percentage of the high percentile. Given the two percentiles, the two thresholds are computed by means of the histogram of the gradient magnitude image. This technique is referred to as double thresholding.

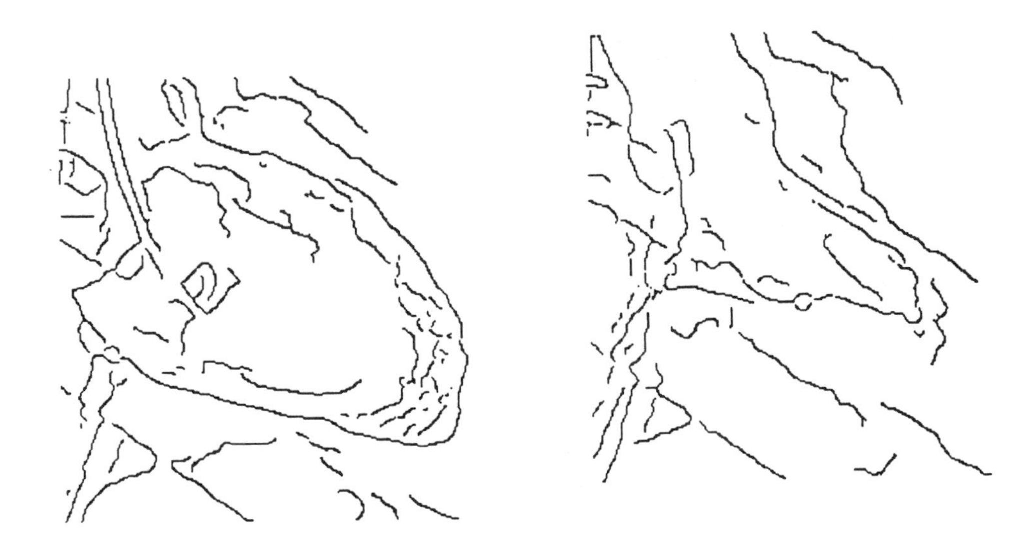

Figure 4: The binary output of the Canny edge operator at frames 1 and 12 (sigma = 2.0, high percentile is 70%, and low percentile is 40%).

The result of double thresholding is influenced by the value of the high percentile. When the value is too high (e.g. above 95%), even significant edges may be lost whereas when the value is too low (e.g., below 50%), a large number of false edges will be included. The low percentile determines how much noise is tolerable. A low percentile below 40% (of the high percentile) introduces too many noisy edges which slows down the high level processes. Edges with magnitudes below the low percentile must be considered noise and must be discarded. Due to the low contrast of the X-ray images, the values of these percentiles were selected to be as small as possible so that all correct edges would be included. By choosing sufficiently low percentile values, there would be no need to further search in the edge image for more edge elements. In our system, the high and low threshold values are chosen to be the value of 70th percentile and the value of 28th percentile (40% of the 70%), respectively (Figure 4). These values are low enough so that even many weak edges can be included.

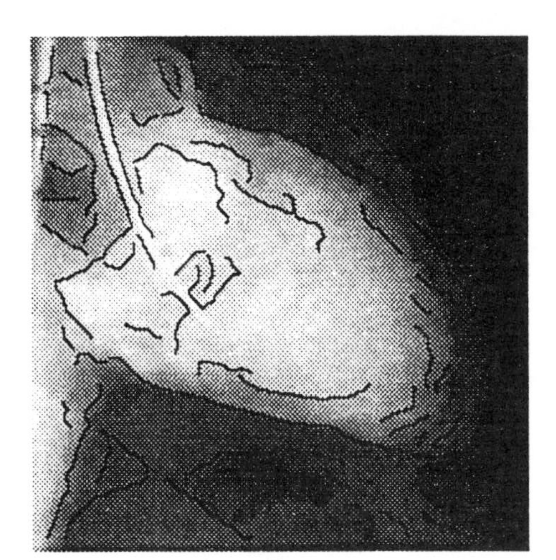

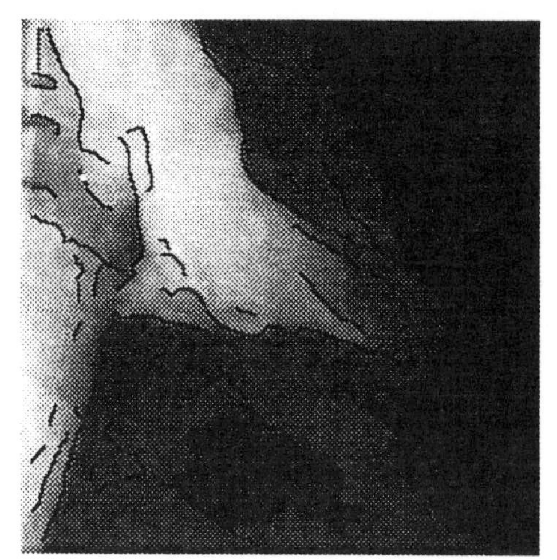

Figure 5: Edge segments of frames 1 and 12 after edge linking. Small edge segments are removed and the rest are overlaid on the images for better visualization.

16.3.1.2 Edge Point Linking (EPL)

The EPL KS performs double thresholding on the magnitude image. Then by choosing a point on the binary mask image with a gradient above the high gradient threshold, it traces the edge elements in all directions using the binary and the magnitude images. Note that there might be several edge segments branching from the main edge segment. In this case, small branches are trimmed. Edge segments that are shorter than a threshold (7 pixels) are also assumed to be noise and are filtered out.

By considering only thin edges that are outcomes of non-maximal suppression, double thresholding, and the above filtering operations, there will be a drastic data reduction. This can be realized through the following example: the number of discrete data points for a 256x256 image is 65536 points. This number would be reduced to less than 2000 edge points corresponding to about only 50 thinned edge segments (Figure 5).

Each edge segment is represented by a data structure. Encapsulating such information into a data structure permits the edges to be easily interpreted and manipulated by more sophisticated high level image understanding techniques. The contents of the data structure will be explained in the next section.

Edge Segment Data Structure

There is a data structure associated with each edge segment containing positional and gradient information. The intention for collecting such information in a data structure is to avoid any further referencing to the intensity and gradient images. The following is a list of edge segment slots:

Index	Slot	Value	Comment
1	NAME	"EDGE-0389"	;Name.
2	SIZE	5	;Number of the points.
3	LENGTH	5.4142137	;Sum of Euclidean distances.
4	HEAD	(156 116)	;Coord. of the first point.
5	TAIL	(154 113)	;Coord. of the last point.
6	CHAIN CODE	(3 4 2 4)	;Eight-connected chain-code.
7	MIN-DIST	29.529646	;Positional distances.
8	MAX-DIST	30.463093	;to the center of the image.
9	MEAN-DIST	29.549965	;Centroid.
10	MBR	(154 113 156 116)	;Minimum Bounding Box.
11	MIN	56	;Intensity information.
12	MAX	62	
13	VARIANCE	23.699247	
14	MEAN	59.2	
15	MIN-GRD	43	;Gradient information.
16	MAX-GRD	254	
17	VARIANCE-GRD	1548.03	
18	MEAN-GRD	103.697365	
19	POLY-LINE	((156 116) ...)	;Polyline representation.
20	THETA-S	(1.57 ...)	;Slope angle.
21	SUB-EDGE	nil	;List of the connected edges.
22	STRENGTH	2805	;Importance measure.
23	HEART	HEART-0001	;Image data structure.

Table 1: An example of an edge segment data structure.

1- Name: a unique name identifying the edge segment.

2- Size: number of points in an edge segment.

3- Length: the sum of the interpixel Euclidian distances between every two points.

4- Positional Information: the location of the beginning (head), the end (tail), the eight-connected chain code of the edge segment describing its shape between the two ends, the minimum, maximum and mean distances to the center of the image, and finally its bounding rectangle.

5- Intensity and Gradient: the maximum, minimum, average and variance of both the intensity and the gradient magnitude along the edge segment.

6- Polyline and Slope Angle Representations: a linked list of *x*-*y* coordinates of points on an edge segment that are a constant distance apart, and a linked list of angles between every two such points. These linked lists comprise the shape information required for curve analysis and matching between curves and respective models.

7- Sub-Segment Lists: a linked list of sub-segments. This is a list of smaller edge segments that are connected to produce a larger segment. If the linked list is empty, the edge segment is original and not made by any other sub-segments.

8- Strength: the importance of the edge segment which is proportional to the gradient magnitude and the length of the edge segment.

9- Image Data Structure Pointer: a pointer to the image data structure containing the edge segment.

The data structures of the edge segments found in an image are kept in a linked list sorted according to their strength (importance factor). More important edge segments (stronger edges) are usually consumed from the top of the linked list by the high level processes. Less important edges (weaker edges) are used upon a specific request by the high level processes. Since weaker edges show up at the end of the list, they usually do not have much influence on boundary interpretation by themselves. Weak or low confidence edges are usually retrieved when they are known to be missing parts of the boundary. The retrieval of weak edges is guided by the model matching of the heart boundary or by their distance to the complete boundaries of adjacent images. There are two KSs that fetch edge segments based on the adjacency of the segments to a model or to a complete boundary (boundary template). The first one is the model-guided matching of the edge segments performed by Heart to Edge Segment KS (HES). The second is Single Boundary Extension KS (BEX) which utilizes the boundary templates.

Image Data Structure

The image data structure contains a list of pointers to all edge segments of that image. The information about edge segments in an image, in addition to some global information about the image itself, constitutes a data structure for that image. This image data structure is used when spatial or temporal information is needed. It is also used as a reference for determining whether two edge segments belong to the same image, or whether they are adjacent in time. Image data structures are kept in a linked-list according to their position in the image sequence. They contain the following information:

1- Name: a unique name for the image data structure.

2- Sigma of the Gaussian: the sigma of the Gaussian filter used in the Canny edge detector.

3- Kernel Size: the corresponding window size used in the Canny edge detector.

4- High and Low Percentiles: the high and low percentiles used in the double thresholding operations.

5- Image Pointers: four slots are allocated for the pointers to the intensity and gradient images which are an 8-bit intensity image, a 1-bit binary edge image, a 16-bit (unsigned) magnitude image, and an 8-bit direction image. The direction image quantizes 2π directions into 180 steps (i.e., 2 degrees per quantization step).

6- Average Intensity: the average intensity of the input, intensity image within a region of interest. This is an estimate of relative changes in the ventricular volumes which can be used to predict the state (contraction/expansion) of the ventricle within the image sequence in addition to the iso-volumic contraction or relaxation period where the volume is almost constant (i.e., average intensity would be almost constant).

7- Edge Segment Lists: a linked list of all edge segments.

8- Available Segments: a linked list of available edge segments not being used by the blackboard.

9- The number of edges: the number of edge segments in the above list.

```
Index Slot         Value           Comment
---------------------------------------------------------------
 1 NAME            "HEART-0001"   ;Name.
 2 SEQUENCE        1              ;Frame number.
 3 SIGMA           2.0            ;Sigma of the Gaussian.
 4 WINDOW-SIZE     11             ;Window size of the Gaussian.
 5 HIGH THRESH     70%
 6 LOW THRESH      40%
 7 IMAGE           #<IMAGE:  heart_001.256>
 8 EDGE-IMAGE      #<IMAGE:  heart_map_sig2.256>
 9 MAG-IMAGE       #<IMAGE:  heart_mag_sig2.256>
 10 DIR-IMAGE      #<IMAGE:  heart_dir_sig2.256>
 11 AVR-INTENSITY 130.78765   ;Average image intensity.
 12 NUM-OF-EDGES 40           ;Number of images.
 13 EDGE-LIST (EDGE-0009 EDGE-0005 EDGE-0004 ...) ;All
 14 AVAIL-EDGES  (EDGE-0005 EDGE-0004 ...) ; Available ones
---------------------------------------------------------------
```

Table 2: An example of an image data structure.

16.3.2 Joining Edge Segment

A pair of edge segments are identified and prepared for joining by Join Two Curves KS (JTC). When two edge segments are designated to be joined, the two ends that are going to be connected must be identified. To find the joining ends, the Euclidean distances between the four combinations of the endpoints are measured. The four combinations are $(head_1, head_2)$, $(head_1, tail_2)$, $(tail_1, head_2)$ and $(tail_1, tail_2)$, where $head_i$ and $tail_i$ are the starting and ending points of edge segment i. The endpoint pair with the minimum distance is chosen for joining. At this point, only adjacent edge segments are considered whose minimum distance between their endpoints are within a certain threshold (20 pixels for 256x256 images). We will explain the connection of these edge segments, shortly. More complex relations between edge segments and their connecting procedures will be explained in section 16.3.4.4 in terms of curve representation.

Two edge segments (E_1 and E_2) are joined using a small, straight line connecting the two closest endpoints. The two closest endpoints (joining endpoints) are removed and the other two endpoints are announced to be the *head* and the *tail* of the new edge segment (E). Depending on which endpoints are close to each other, one of the edge segments may have to be reversed. The edge segment reversing will be explained in the next section. There are four combinations consisting of two pairs of symmetric cases:

1- If the joining endpoints are in the form of $(head_1, tail_2)$, then $head_2$ and $tail_1$ will be the endpoints of the new edge segment. The new edge segment is formed by concatenation of these three chain code lists: the chain code of E_2, the chain code of the connecting line segment and the chain code of E_1 in that order. The chain code of the connecting line is obtained by selecting colinear points on the image array between $tail_2$ and $head_1$.

2- If the joining endpoints are in the form of $(head_1, head_2)$, the smaller edge segment will be reversed. Once the edge segment is reversed, the rest of the procedure is similar to case 1.

3- The case of $(tail_1, head_2)$, is similar to case 1 with the order of two edge segments being interchanged.

4- The case of $(tail_1, tail_2)$ is similar to case 2.

After the chain code of the new edge segments is formed, a new edge segment data structure will be created and filled. All of the slots of the new edge segment can be efficiently computed from the data structure of the two edge segments directly without referring to the corresponding intensity and gradient images (except for a few points filling the gap between two edge segments). Some examples of such direct computations are given below:

$$S_E = S_{E_1} + S_{gap} + S_{E_2} \tag{16.1}$$

$$L_E = L_{E_1} + L_{gap} + L_{E_2}$$

$$\left|\nabla G_E(x, y)\right| = \frac{S_{E_1}\left|\nabla G_{E_1}\right| + S_{gap}\left|\nabla G_{gap}\right| + S_{E_2}\left|\nabla G_{E_2}\right|}{S_E}$$

$$Min(x_E) = Min\,[Min(x_{E_1}), Min(x_{gap}), Min(x_{E_2})]$$

$$\overline{x_E} = \frac{S_{E_1}\overline{x_{E_1}} + S_{gap}\overline{x_{gap}} + S_{E_2}\overline{x_{E_2}}}{S_E}$$

$$\Gamma(E) = \frac{1}{\Gamma_{max}} L_E S_E \left|\nabla G_E\right|$$

where S, L, G(x,y), Min(x), Γ are the size, the length, the gradient, the minimum of x, and the strength of the edge segment, respectively. The polyline and the Theta-S slots will not be filled until the edge segment is promoted to the Curve level.

The SUB-EDGE slot is filled with a linked list of the two original edge segments. The linked list of sub-edges keeps track of how the edge segment is produced. If a list of more than two edge segments are to be connected, the chain code is formed recursively based on successive pairs of edge segments in that list (the ordering is important among the edge segments). Finally, when the new edge segment is formed, the SUB-EDGE slot points to the list of edges that formed it.

16.3.2.1 Edge Segment Reversing

Sometimes the direction in which an edge segment is traced has to be reversed, for instance, when two edge segments are to be connected as discussed in the previous section (cases 2 and 4). In these cases, since most of the slots in the edge segment are independent of the tracing direction, a copy of the data structure is created and then, a few slots are modified. Obviously, the head and tail must be switched. The eight-connected chain code, which is a linked list of numbers between 0 to 7, has to be reversed. In addition, at every point, 180° must be added to the direction of the code in the chain code.

For an eight-connected chain code, this is simply done by adding number 4 modulo 8 to each code. The polyline, which is a linked list of polygon vertices in the form of x-y coordinate pairs, also has to be reversed. The Theta-S is reversed similar to the chain code; that is, first the linked list is reversed and then π is added to each of the slope angles. (The polyline and the Theta-S representation will be described later in section 16.3.4.1).

16.3.2.2 Edge Segment Splitting (ESS)

One of the problems with edge linking is that the extracted edge segments sometimes contain extraneous parts which must be trimmed. In summary, to trim a significant edge segment (longer than 50 pixels), the positions where the extraneous parts meet the rest of the edge segment are identified, and then the extraneous parts are eliminated. Edge segments that are shorter then 50 pixels are not considered for this process because they are too short and do not contain enough useful information for further processing.

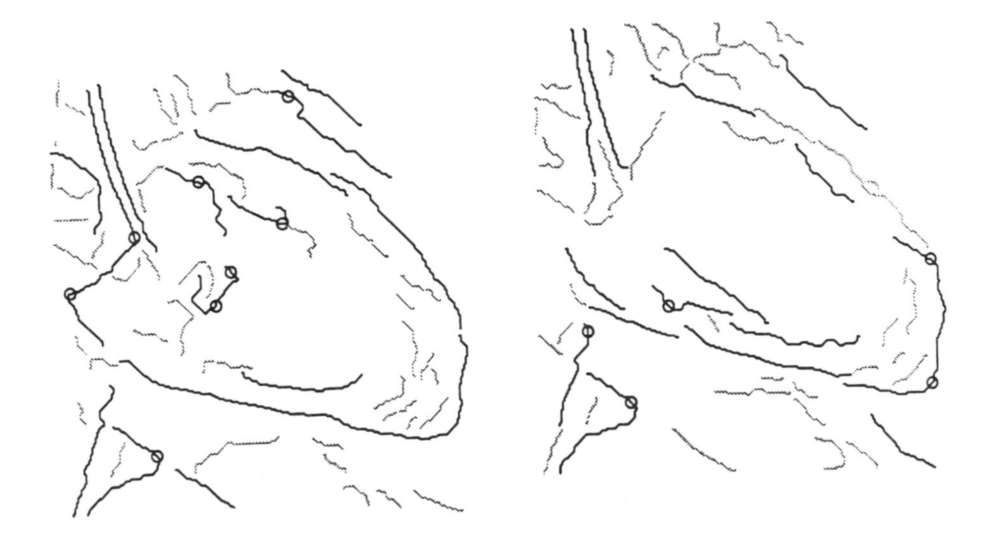

Figure 6: For these two images, 50 pixel boundary fragments (dark) are disconnected at the points of high curvature indicated by a circle. The threshold for distinguishing high curvature from low curvature points is 2.3.

The positions to split the edge segment are identified either from its relationships to other objects or from the characteristics of the edge segment itself. Such objects may be, for instance, another edge segment, a template, or a model. One of the characteristics of an edge segment is that it may contain sharp corners, identifiable from the positions of high curvature. Since we assume that left ventricular boundaries are smooth curves, there should not be any corner or high curvature point on the edge segment. Due to the smoothness assumption, corners usually relate to locations where two boundary pieces were incorrectly connected. Edge segment regions with curvature values greater than the experimentally defined value of 2.3 are considered as corners (Figure 6). We split such edge segments at the corners due to the undesired high curvature characteristics. Another characteristic of an edge segment is the intensity and gradient probability distribution along the segment. For instance, if the intensity or gradient variance along the edge segment is high, it can be concluded that the edge segment consists of more than one part. The position where edge segments would be incorrectly connected could be obtained by a simple histogram technique. Edge segment splitting does not have any dramatic effect on the interpretation process because the original edge segment will remain on the blackboard as an alternative hypothesis. Examples of relationships among edge segments are given in section 16.3.4.6 for joining overlapping curves, and examples of relationships to a template are given in section 16.3.7.4.

When an edge segment is split, new edge segments are produced by creating and filling a new data structure for each split segment. Except for the head, tail and chain code, other slots of the original edge segment are not useful. Thus, the rest of the slots in the edge segment data structure have to be re-computed from the intensity and gradient images. As opposed to joining edge segments where we have to be careful about the direction of the chain code and whether it has to be reversed or not, the chain code for the new edge segment is simply a copy of the corresponding chain code portion of the original edge segment. The positional information is computed based on the chain code and the rest of the slots are filled, accordingly. Finally, the importance measure of each new edge segments is computed from its data structure.

16.3.3 Edge to Fragment (ETF)

The ETF brings edge segments from the edge point level into the Boundary Fragment level of the blackboard. To accomplish this, the KS converts edge segments to boundary fragment units by retrieving them from the top of an appropriate edge segment linked list. This KS is activated when there is a need to process more edge segments (low level data). However, it would be inefficient if the KS becomes activated for every edge segment. On the other hand, if all edge segments within one image are instantiated at the Boundary Fragment level, all of the problem solving attention would be focused on that image. Most edge segments that are at the end of the link list are probably noise and unimportant; thus, their instantaneous instantiations would be unnecessary.

The number of simultaneously instantiated edge segments determines the amount of problem solving that is taking place in the current image versus problem solving throughout the sequence. That is, if the number is high, more activities will be created for the current image, whereas, if the number is low, other images of the sequence will be involved more rapidly. Experiments show that a number between 4 and 10 (we chose 4) is suitable for this process.

In fact, instantiating a few boundary fragments is a kind of focus of attention mechanism which allows the problem solver to focus on a smaller set of edge segments before moving on to another set or to another image. This focusing mechanism uses the idea of an "island of certainty" by concentrating the processing effort on a smaller set of edge segments and a smaller range of images rather than on all edge segments and all images. It also prevents the processing of images in a random order.

This KS does not have any precondition. It becomes activated when there are no more KSs scheduled on the blackboard or the scheduled activities have very low priorities. Every time the KS is executed, it schedules itself on the scheduling queue using a proper priority value. When the KS is executed for the first time, the priority value does not matter because it is the only KS on the queue. While the priorities of other KSs are defined through the importance factors, the priority of this KS is defined as a function of the maximum and minimum importance factor (strength) associated with the group of edge segments that are simultaneously hypothesized at the Boundary Fragment level of the blackboard. If the priority is set too high (as high as or higher than the maximum in that group), the problem solver quickly asks for more edge segments to process before the current group has been adequately processed (too greedy!), and if the priority is set too low (as low as or lower than the minimum), the problem solver tries to finish all activities regarding the current group of edges before turning to another frame (too conservative and lazy!). In the latter case, the inter-frame activities are not mixed very well, either. In our implementation, we chose the midpoint between the maximum and the minimum (i.e., the ratio is 0.5). Experiments may be conducted to find better ratios between the minimum and maximum priorities, or even to dynamically change the ratio with time.

This KS also determines the condition for termination of the interpretation process. That is, the system stops when this KS is activated and there are no more edge segments left in all of the link lists. The rest of the activities scheduled on the blackboard are assumed to be unimportant and are ignored.

16.3.4 Curve Representations and Operations

Curve units, which are more abstract objects than the edge segments and boundary fragments, reside on a higher level of the blackboard. Using such units, most operations can be applied more efficiently. This makes curve units very significant. Curves are also important because they are the intermediate representation that bridges between edges (at a lower level of abstraction) and models (at a higher level of abstraction). Therefore, we need a simple and efficient representation for this kind of intermediate unit. In the following sections, we will address the representations that are being used at the Curve level of the blackboard as well as the KSs that are operating on this level using such representations.

16.3.4.1 Polyline and Slope-angle Representations

The polyline representation is employed for tracking curve units in the sequence, and the polyline slope angles are used for matching a curve to a given model. One way of constructing the polyline of a curve is by connecting every two adjacent points on the corresponding edge segment. (This is merely the x-y coordinate representation of the chain code.) There are two problems with this approach regarding the slopes of the polyline. First, since these points lie on a regular grid specified by the image array, there are only eight possible directions on the grid for the neighboring points. The slopes of such a polyline are heavily corrupted by the quantization noise; thus, the polyline slopes require a substantial amount of low pass filtering. By inspection, if a low pass filter is applied to the x-y coordinates of a curve, a smoother curve is produced, but the produced curve becomes smaller. Secondly and more importantly, since we are dealing with the discrete spatial domain, more specifically, eight-connected curves, the spacing between the points is not uniform. The irregular spacing of a curve results in an inaccurate arc length, as the length of the curve is not the number of points on the corresponding edge segment; and filtering requires uniform spacing. In order to achieve an accurate arc length and correct filtering, the curve must be resampled uniformly.

Resampling of a curve with regular spacing alleviates all of the above problems. One way of resampling is to assume that the curve is piece-wise linear. That is, the curve is approximated by small constant-size lines (polylines), d units long. Small values of d cause too much quantization noise in the slopes and large values of d cause an undersampling of the curve. The resampling interval (d) also affects the efficiency of the system because small d values make too many linear segments which slow down the curve matching and tracking process. Intuitively, for the same smoothness, the value of d should be linearly proportional to the resolution of the image. Visually, a number between 5 and 10 is suitable for left ventricular boundaries in 256x256 images (Figure 7). We chose $d = 7$ pixels to minimize the error for straight lines in the 45 and 135 degree directions because every 5 points in these directions is 7 pixels long. Note that the sampling interval (d) does not have to be an integer number, and in fact, it is not for the polylines that describe the left ventricular models (i.e., $d = l/100$, where l is the length of the boundary model).

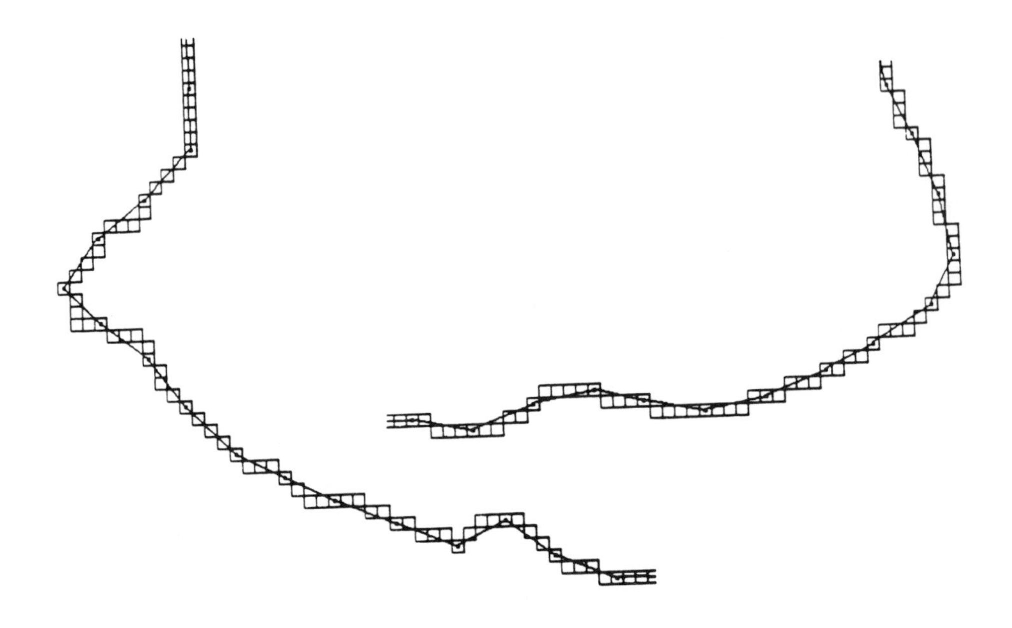

Figure 7: Two examples of the piece-wise linear approximation. In this approximation, points that are 5 pixels apart are connected by a line.

16.3.4.2 Fragment to Curve (FTC)

This KS converts a relatively long boundary fragment unit to a curve unit – at least 5 linear segments long (35 pixels). This way, the converted boundary fragments can extend themselves by seeking other neighboring boundary fragments. After the curve unit is formed, the KS constructs the polyline and slope angle representations of the curve and computes the information required for filling the slots of the linear segment units. Finally, it establishes the links between the curve and the boundary fragment units. The polyline will be used for tracking the curve units in the image sequence, and the slope angle (Theta-S) shape representation will be used for matching the curve to the heart models. Finally, the KS fills the rest of the slots of the curve unit.

16.3.4.3 Joining Two Curves (JTC)

The KS for joining two curves (JTC) is activated when its pre-condition detects boundary fragments that are near each other. All boundary fragment endpoints are searched that are inside two rectangles centered at the two curve endpoints. Not all nearby boundary fragment endpoints are necessarily suitable for joining. For example, endpoints whose gradient orientations are opposite to one another are assumed to belong to two parallel structures and therefore should not be joined. In addition, the intensity values near the ventricular boundary change continuously and smoothly (not like a checker board); thus, the gradient direction cannot change abruptly. Note that there may be overlapping curves that are not detected by the distance of their endpoints. These overlapping curves can be identified through their positions with respect to a curve from another frame (Section

16.3.5.3), a boundary template (Section 16.3.6.4), or a heart unit (Section 16.3.7.4). Note that it is important to make sure that the two curves have not been previously connected by another KS. After curves are joined through their edge segments, a composite curve will be generated and its slots will be filled the same way as those of the combined edge segment.

16.3.4.4 Curve Relationships

The relationships between two curves can be categorized into three cases: adjacent curves, overlapping curves, and enclosing curves (Figure 8). The curve relationships can be determined using minimum distances between the endpoints of one curve and those of the other curve. Before we define these three relationships, we need to define the relationships between a point with respect to a curve.

Definition 1: Curve Projection. *The projection of a point onto a curve is the closest point on the curve to that point.*

This definition is clearly an extension of the projection of a point onto a line; however, the projection may not be unique (e.g., consider the projection of the center of a circular arc onto the arc). To make the projection unique when a point has two or more disjoint projection points, the one closest to the beginning of the curve (*head*) is considered to be the projection point. The uniqueness of the projection point provides unambiguous relationships among edge segments or curves. The uniqueness in interpreting the curve relationships is vital for the reproducibility of the results required by the system evaluation.

Definition 2: Distance to a Curve. *The distance of a point to a curve is the minimum distance between the point and all of the points on the curve.*

The distance of a point to a curve can also be defined in terms of the distance of the point to its projection. Note that the minimum distance does not require the uniqueness property of the projection; thus, it may be found more efficiently.

Definition 3: Adjacent Curves. *Two curves are called adjacent iff the projections of both endpoints of one curve are one of the endpoints on the other curve.*

This means that none of the endpoints fall in between the other curve. There are four combinations of endpoints and their projections. These combinations make four pairs of endpoints for adjacent curves. Among the four pairs, there is one pair with the minimum distance. This pair is referred to as "joining endpoints" because adjacent curves will be connected through these two endpoints. The distance between the two joining endpoints (joining distance) further classifies the adjacent curves into "far curves", "near curves" and "touching curves". Far curves are two curves with the joining distance greater than a threshold (20 pixels). Near curves are those with the joining distance less than the threshold. If the joining distance between two curves is less than or equal to the square root of 2, the two curves are touching at their joining endpoints; hence, touching curves are a subset of near curves.

Definition 4: Overlapping Curves. *Two curves are called overlapping iff the projection of an endpoint of one curve is an endpoint on the other curve, but the projection of the other endpoint of the first curve is not an endpoint of the second curve, but is within a distance threshold.*

That is, the projection of one of the endpoints is an endpoint on the other curve because the endpoint is outside of the other curve, and the projection of the other endpoint is not an endpoint because it falls inside the curve (in between the two endpoints). Also, the distances between the endpoint that falls inside of the curve and its projection must be within a limit (40 pixels). Otherwise, the two curves will be considered as far curves.

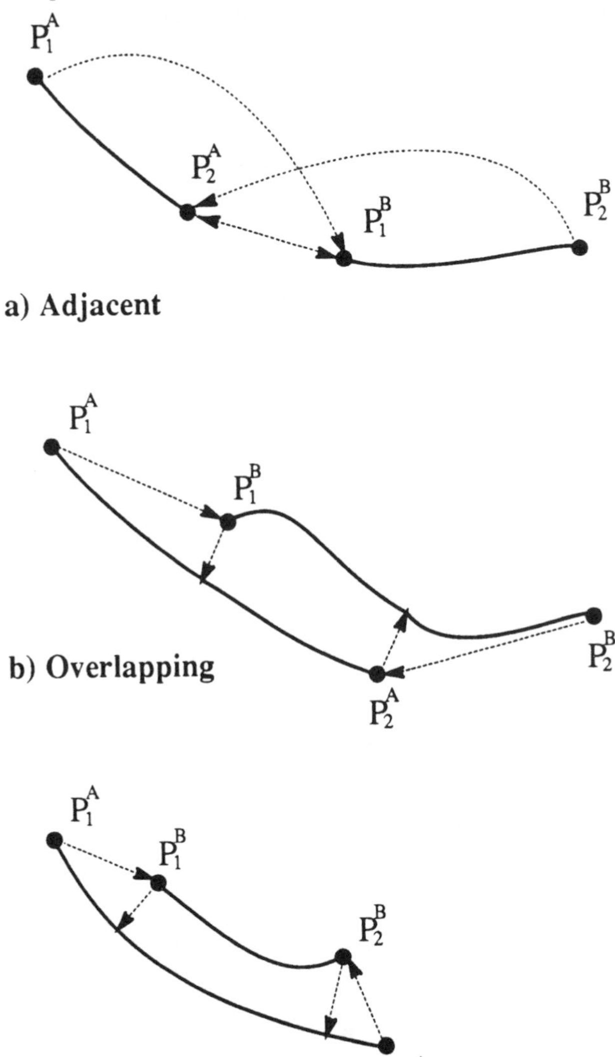

Figure 8: a) Curve A is adjacent to curve B because the projection of its endpoints is one of the endpoints of B. b) Curve A is overlapping with curve B because the projection of one endpoint of one curve falls in the middle of the other curve (see $P_1{}^B$ and $P_2{}^A$). Of course, the projections of the other endpoints are endpoints. c) Curve A is enclosing curve B (or B is enclosed in A) because the projections of both endpoints of B fall between the endpoints of A.

Definition 5: Enclosed Curve. *A curve is enclosed within another curve iff the projections of both of its endpoints are not any of the endpoints of the other curve, and the distances between the endpoints to the other curve are less than a threshold. That is, both endpoints of the enclosed curve fall inside of the enclosing curve.*

Usually, the enclosing curve is the larger one and both of its endpoint projections are the endpoints of the enclosed curve. If both distances between the endpoints of the enclosed curve to the other curve are greater than another threshold (40 pixels), the two curves are considered as far curves, and if only one of the distances is more than the threshold, the two curves are overlapping. Far and enclosed curves are not considered for connecting by the JTC KS; however, far curves can be connected using a third curve (see section 16.3.5.3.).

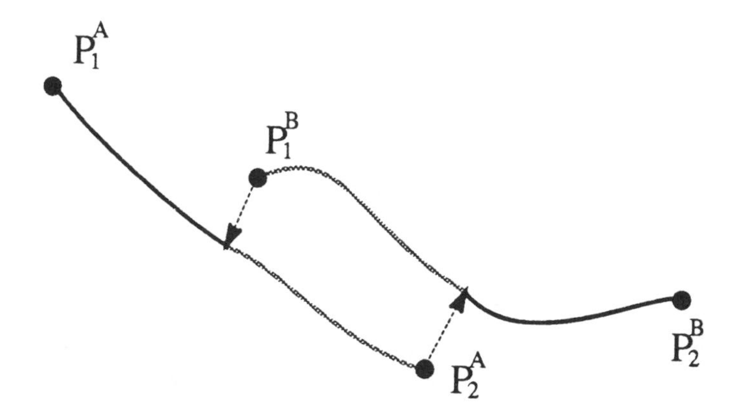

Figure 9: The overlapping portion is identified by the projection of the endpoints. These overlapping sections will be removed during the connection operation.

16.3.4.5 Joining Near Curves

Two near adjacent curves are connected by a straight line. A straight line connects the tail of one curve to the head of the other curve. The operation is identical to the connection of edge segments. Since touching curves are a degenerate case of near curves with no gaps, the connection is similar but there will be no line segment added. Note that not all curve connections are acceptable. For example, if the joint of the two curves produces a corner (with the same curvature threshold required by the curve splitting KS), the two curves will not be joined.

16.3.4.6 Joining Overlapping Curves

For joining overlapping curves, first the portion of overlap for each curve has to be determined. The overlapping portions are removed and replaced by a straight line segment for small overlaps and a curve for large overlaps. The overlapping portion of the first curve is precisely defined by the portion of the curve that lies between the projections of the two endpoints of the second curve onto the first curve. Note that one of the endpoints of the second curve falls on one of the endpoints of the first curve (Figure 9).

The new curve is obtained by combining three touching curves: the two curves without the overlap and the transitional curve. Since the produced transitional curve is not necessarily uniformly spaced, first, the edge segments of the three curves are produced, and then it is uniformly resampled (Figure 10). The rest of the slots of the new edge segment and the new curve unit are filled directly from the intensity and edge images (the information in the original edge segments cannot be used in this case). Finally, the links are established between the new composite curve and the boundary fragments of the overlapping curves. This process produces much better overall results than using a straight line for the overlapping portion.

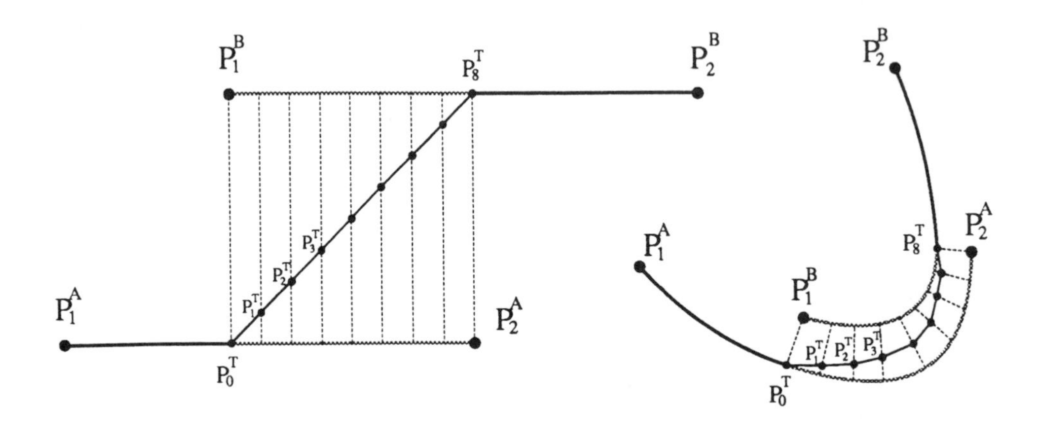

Figure 10: Chords are represented by dashed lines between the two overlapping portions. The transitional curve connects the intermediate points (P_i^T) of the chords by a piece-wise linear curve. a) The transitional curve is a line for linear overlaps. b) The transitional curve is a curve connecting two overlapping curves.

16.3.5 Curve Tracking in the Image Sequence

The information in the sequence of images is very valuable for object motion understanding. Due to the relatively high frame rate, objects in the image sequence are assumed to move slowly over time. That is, within two subsequent frames, segments of the boundary cannot move more than a certain number of pixels. The same is true for the orientation and gradient direction of a segment. By this temporal continuity assumption, spurious edges that appear and disappear within a short period of time are most likely noise and need to be filtered out. By this assumption, basic curve sequences are produced using the movements of curve polylines in the adjacent frames. Then, the basic units are combined to obtain more complex curve sequences.

16.3.5.1 Curve to Curve Sequence (CCS)

The Curve to Curve Sequence (CCS) KS takes a curve unit and finds other neighboring curves in the adjacent frames. The KS utilizes the polyline representation of a curve to retrieve the neighboring line units in the adjacent frames. Given the above smoothness assumption about the motion of boundary fragments in successive frames, the linear segments of the curve polyline whose distance, orientation or gradient direction changes are less than a set of predefined thresholds are included and the rest are discarded.

The included linear segments are scored according to the distance, orientation, and average gradient direction differences. The thresholds are 20 pixels for the distance and 30 degrees for angular changes. It should be noted that the thresholds are solely used to reduce the amount of computation because their values are large enough to capture all correct linear segment candidates. Furthermore, those discarded linear segments that do not conform to the above thresholds would not affect the interpretation because they receive very low confidence values anyway. Also, two adjacent curves are not considered as a curve sequence if they do not overlap enough (e.g., the number of linear segments that matched is less than 5), or if the confidence of the matching was below a threshold (below 5%). (See section 16.3.8 for the confidence and importance measures.)

When the neighboring curves in the adjacent frames are found, they will be combined into a basic Curve Sequence unit (CS). Basic curve sequence units are then grouped for further analysis of more complex curve movements in time.

16.3.5.2 Curve Sequence Grouping (CSG)

A unit at this level contains relationships between curves in adjacent frames. More complex units at this level, which are obtained by combining basic curve sequence units (CS), contain temporal information about the image sequence. Using such units, temporal information can be extended to more than two frames.

This KS primarily combines basic CS units and constructs a more abstract description of curve movements such as Space-CS, Time-CS and General-CS units. It also examines the redundancy of the new hypothesis through the links to the original curves and boundary fragments in order to avoid multiple identical hypotheses. There are four types of curve sequence units (Figure 11).

1- A CS is a basic unit consisting of two curve units, one from each of two adjacent frames. The two curves in this simple CS unit are related through the tracking constraints imposed by the polyline representation of curve units.

2- A Space-CS relates two curves in an image through a common adjacent curve in time. This unit is directly formed by combining two basic curve sequences. There are two cases when two basic CS units with a common curve are considered. The other two curves belong either to the same image or to images that are two frames apart. The former case produces a Space-CS unit and the latter produces a simple version of a Time-CS unit which will be defined next. A Space-CS unit may be used for filling the gap between two curves in one frame using the common curve in another frame.

3- A Time-CS is a curve sequence which can only be extended in time. This unit can be built by incrementally grouping the basic CS units over time, or by combining two or more smaller Time-CS units. (In a restricted sense, a basic CS is also a Time-CS). Conceptually, a Time-CS may contain as many curves as there are frames in the sequence, but none of the two curves can belong to the same frame. Note that, when curves of this unit are complete boundaries, the unit can potentially be promoted to the boundary sequence level. This is yet another path to the final solution. A Time-CS unit may be utilized to analyze the motion of a curve throughout the sequence. However, we did not thoroughly examine these types of curve sequences during the motion analysis for an image sequence.

4- A General-CS is a unit which may be constructed from any of the above CS units.. Thus, this unit is the most general and also the most complex curve sequence of all. The most useful unit of this kind would be the combination of two Time-CS units with some overlapping units, which may be used to conclude some relationships between curves of the same frame. The unit can be promoted to the boundary sequence level.

When a unit is complex, it contains a great deal of information, but it is more difficult to analyze. It is also more difficult to understand the complex relationships among the subparts. In fact, the whole blackboard can be considered as one giant unit. However, without dividing it into various levels of abstraction, it would be impossible to understand the activities that are taking place on the blackboard. In addition, when a unit consists of many sub-parts, it takes longer to create, it requires more effort to examine its uniqueness, and it is more time-consuming to construct the relationships between the sub-parts. In this research, we have been able to analyze CS and Space-CS units and to draw conclusions about missing gaps between curves of the same image and to fill the gaps using Space-CS units.

16.3.5.3 Space Curve Sequence Patching (SCSP)

When a space curve sequence (Space-CS) is built, the two curves that are in the same frame can be joined using the common curve in the other frame. This is especially suitable for joining curves with a large gap between them, and for detecting overlapping curves with endpoints that are far from each other. In the former case, the large gap is filled by a part of the common curve, whereas, in the latter case, the overlapping curves are joined by themselves without the use of the common curve. Composite curves are not considered for these processes at the moment because they can be joined later on, when the large gap is filled (although this may not be very efficient). This is mainly due to the complications that arise in the detection of multiple identical hypotheses for Space-CS units.

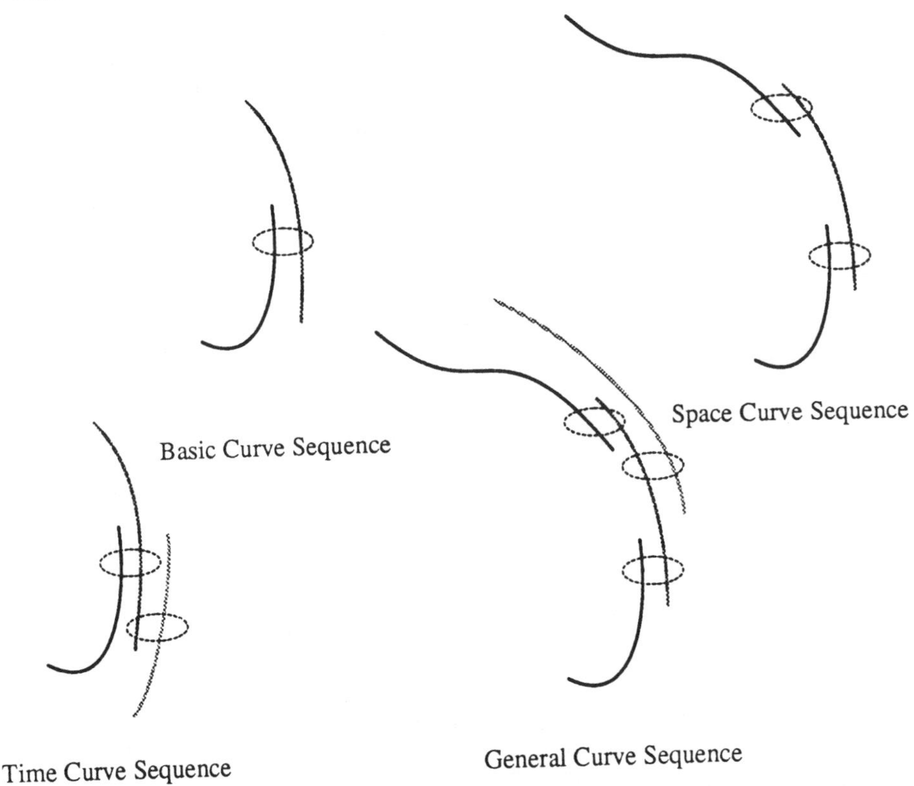

Figure 11: Examples of the four types of curve sequence units.

Before joining the two curves, we have to make sure that they are not already connected. This is performed through the link between the curve and its corresponding boundary fragments. That is, if their boundary fragments point to the same curve, that curve is the joint of the two curves on the blackboard. If there is a link to such a curve, the two curves will not be joined again. For composite curves using their boundary fragments, these relationships become more complex to analyze. This is the main reason that composite curves are not used in Space-CS units. An alternative solution is that the two curves can be joined and can be saved as alternative hypotheses on the blackboard. In this fashion, the quality of the joined curve can determine which curve sequence to use.

There are four cases: adjacent, overlap, enclosed and far curves. The first three cases are similar to joining two edge segments. The joining process for far curves is as follows. Since the two curves that are in one frame have to have some overlap with the common curve (due to the tracking conditions), the common curve and the other two curves will be joined the same way that two overlapping curves in one frame would. The resulting curve belongs to the frame that contains the two joining curves (not to the frame with the common curve). Overlapping curves are joined the same way as was described in section 16.3.2. Recall that there may be overlapping curves that cannot be detected by themselves because the distance between their endpoints is greater than the threshold (20 pixels). Now, however, they can be considered for joining. Enclosing curves are not considered for joining because they produce sharp bends if joined.

16.3.6 Boundary Operations

Boundaries are the most important units of the blackboard because they form a boundary sequence which is the output of our system. Boundary sequences can be generated in many ways. They can be generated by collecting a single boundary from every frame (BBS), by extending a complete boundary throughout the sequence (BEX), or by converting a time curve sequence unit (Time-CS) to a boundary sequence (CSBS). The first case involves three KSs: the one that promotes long curves to boundaries (BHG), the one that finds the most promising left ventricular boundary in each frame using particular left ventricular models (FBB), and the one that combines the most promising, individual boundaries into a boundary sequence (BBS). In the second case, a single, complete boundary of a frame (a boundary template) is extended throughout the sequence. The last case suggests that Time-CS units can potentially be converted to boundary sequences. However, the implementation of this case is left for the future.

Boundaries have a format similar to curves. The difference is the type of operations that can be performed on them. Curves can be extended in time and space, and can be matched against models, whereas, boundaries can only be extended in time. More importantly, boundaries are the representations used in the final solution.

16.3.6.1 Boundary Hypotheses Generating (BHG)

This KS hypothesizes a boundary unit on the Boundary level of the blackboard by promoting a significantly long curve that well matches a heart model. Small curves (smaller that 250 pixels) are not considered for this process because they do not carry enough features for the matching. In fact, very short curves can match a part of any model with minimal error because, at the extreme, a linear segment of a curve polyline can perfectly match (with zero error) a linear segment of a model.

As processing increases, many curves are extended which causes improvements in the partial solutions; hence, longer boundaries with higher quality will be generated. The quality of a boundary is determined by the confidence measure associated with the curve and the error in the matching to the model. We assume a confidence of 95% is high enough for accepting a boundary. (See section 16.3.8 for the discussion of the confidence measures.) At any time, the best boundary of a frame (the highest confidence boundary) is reported as the best solution for that frame at that time. The best boundaries can be improved over time, which requires constantly updating the set of best boundaries in the sequence.

16.3.6.2 Find the Best Boundary (FBB)

This KS is responsible for providing the best boundary candidate found for all frames at any particular time. The task is performed by selecting the boundary with the highest confidence (see section 16.3.8 for the confidence factor of a boundary unit) which is also related to the description of the heart unit with the highest confidence, one boundary per frame. That is, the boundary not only must have a high confidence, but the heart unit that matched it must also have the highest confidence. During the interpretation process, similar boundaries vote for identical or indistinguishable heart models (i.e., the same shapes with similar matching parameters). Note that very similar heart models do not become instantiated over and over on the blackboard; rather, the confidence of the first instantiation of the heart unit will be raised and the parameters will be adjusted. Usually, the confidence of a boundary is the same as that of the heart model, especially at the beginning of the interpretation process. But as the interpretation process proceeds, the heart units receive higher and higher confidence values when an identical or a very close match is generated.

Therefore, the following process is used for finding the best boundary. First, the heart unit with the highest confidence in a frame is chosen and then, through the link between the heart unit and the list of associated boundary units, the highest ranked boundary is selected. This boundary represents the best left ventricular boundary interpretation found so far for that particular frame. When all boundaries with sufficiently high quality are formed for a sequence, the system reports these boundaries in the form of a boundary sequence unit as the final solution and halts. This type of halting condition may only occur for good quality images at this stage.

16.3.6.3 Boundary to Boundary Sequence (BBS)

This KS is intended to group the boundaries of objects in the image sequence. This is a more specific KS than the Curve Sequence Grouping in which the units have to be identified as complete boundaries. This grouping would be useful in analysis of object motion. However, we have solely used it for identification of the left ventricular boundary movements. This KS finally creates a hypothesis that contains the complete solution. This is when the complete left ventricular boundaries of all frames are identified using the FBB knowledge source.

16.3.6.4 Single Boundary Extension (BEX)

The automatic boundary detection in a left ventriculogram can be facilitated by taking advantage of the consistencies between frames in the sequence of images. This is especially important to assist in the edge detection at end-systole which is typically problematic when the single end-systolic image is analyzed. This section describes an approach for the extraction of the boundary of the left ventricle throughout a sequence which takes advantage of the consistency of the heart position and shape from frame to frame. The BEX knowledge source uses this approach to derive the placement of the boundaries within a sequence when the complete boundary of a frame is available.

This approach involves the selection of a number of candidate edge segments, filtering the candidates by removing those that do not satisfy certain conditions with respect to the template, sorting them and trimming their extraneous parts using the template, and finally linking the sorted and trimmed edge segments. Once the edge segments are linked, they are smoothed to form a new boundary template. The new template will be used in the subsequent or the previous frame depending on the direction that the boundary sequence is growing. For more details on this KS, see [8].

16.3.7 Heart Model Generation and Model Matching

The principal problem with methods based on a model of the heart is that models which are general enough to encompass all heart shapes are too indefinite to be effectively matched to the details of the boundary shape. It is especially difficult to match data points to the model features since there are not enough strong feature points on the left ventricular boundary due to the smoothness of the anatomic structures, Thus, matching techniques based on the feature characteristic of objects cannot be applied to this domain.

In addition, the boundaries of normal hearts can have a vast variety of shapes. When hearts with abnormalities are considered, as would be needed for any diagnostic system, each class of abnormality has a distinct, characteristic shape [5,6]. Thus, the construction of a reasonable model of the heart shape is not a simple task. The problem of matching such a model to data is further complicated by the fact that heart position, orientation and size can vary widely for various patient studies.

16.3.7.1 A Model for the Left Ventricular Boundary

In this section, we propose a method for generating left ventricular boundary models of both normal and abnormal shapes, including both anterior and inferior abnormalities. The method is based on a general notion of the average shape, size and orientation of the left ventricular boundaries obtained from a clinical data set. Ideally, this model should be invariant to rotation, translation and scale within certain limits. This is because the heart appears neither in a certain location in the image nor in a particular orientation. In addition, the heart size varies widely from patient to patient. However, there are bounds on the above measures, illustrated by the following facts: the position of the ventricle is usually closer to the center of the image; there are only a range of possible orientations; all parts of the ventricular boundary must be visible in the image. The model description contains the mean and the limits of the size and the orientation of the heart boundaries as well as descriptors for different shapes. The shape descriptor is invariant to translation, and the rotational component is represented by an offset. The model descriptors could be very precise if a few boundary samples with similar shapes are used, or it could be general when a large data set with a variety of shapes is used.

Our technique to achieve this model is the representation of contours in Theta-S space (Figure 12). In this technique, a two-dimensional curve (e.g. $f(x,y)=0$) is transformed into a one-dimensional function such as $\theta = \Theta(s)$ where Θ is a function describing the tangent slope angles ($tan^{-1}\, dy/dx$) and s is the arc length, which is the length of the curve from its starting point. This function is invariant to translation in the image plane because all quantities are measured with respect to a reference point on the curve. Rotation of the contour in the Cartesian space is the same as adding an offset to the $\Theta(s)$ function. It can be concluded that straight lines in the image plane corresponds to zero-slope lines in Θ-s space, inflection points to extrema, and circles to constant-slope lines.

Polyline and slope angle representations, described for curve units of the blackboard, are employed here to approximate the Θ-s function using the angles of linear segments of the polyline representation (i.e., $\tan^{-1} (y_2-y_1)/(x_2-x_1)$). Note that to achieve a continuous representation, the value of 2π needs to be added or subtracted from the above function.

It should be noted that given the starting point, the curve can be reconstructed up to a scale factor (Figure 13). That is, a change in the location of the starting point (*head*), in the offset to the tangent angles, and in the length of the linear segments (d) reproduces curves that are translated, rotated and scaled, respectively. By varying such parameters, the curves and models can be compared and models can be instantiated on the blackboard. This model instantiation is used to fetch small and low confidence edge segments into the Boundary Fragment level. This increases the speed of generating boundaries with missing fragments.

The curvature of a curve, the first derivative of the tangent angle at each point with respect to the arc length, has been studied and extensively used in shape analysis of objects [1,4]. This measure is more suitable for emphasizing sharp corners and for objects with high curvature features, because high curvature features can dominate the amount of noise and slow variation of the boundaries in such objects. These types of features, however, cannot be found on the ventricular boundary due to its smooth shape, low curvature, and small variation along its boundary. Furthermore, the curvature function totally precludes the use of the orientation limits of the left ventricular boundaries (e.g., the left ventricular boundary is never displayed upside down, but the curvature remains the same). Hence, the curvature may not be appropriate for the kind of matching we are looking for.

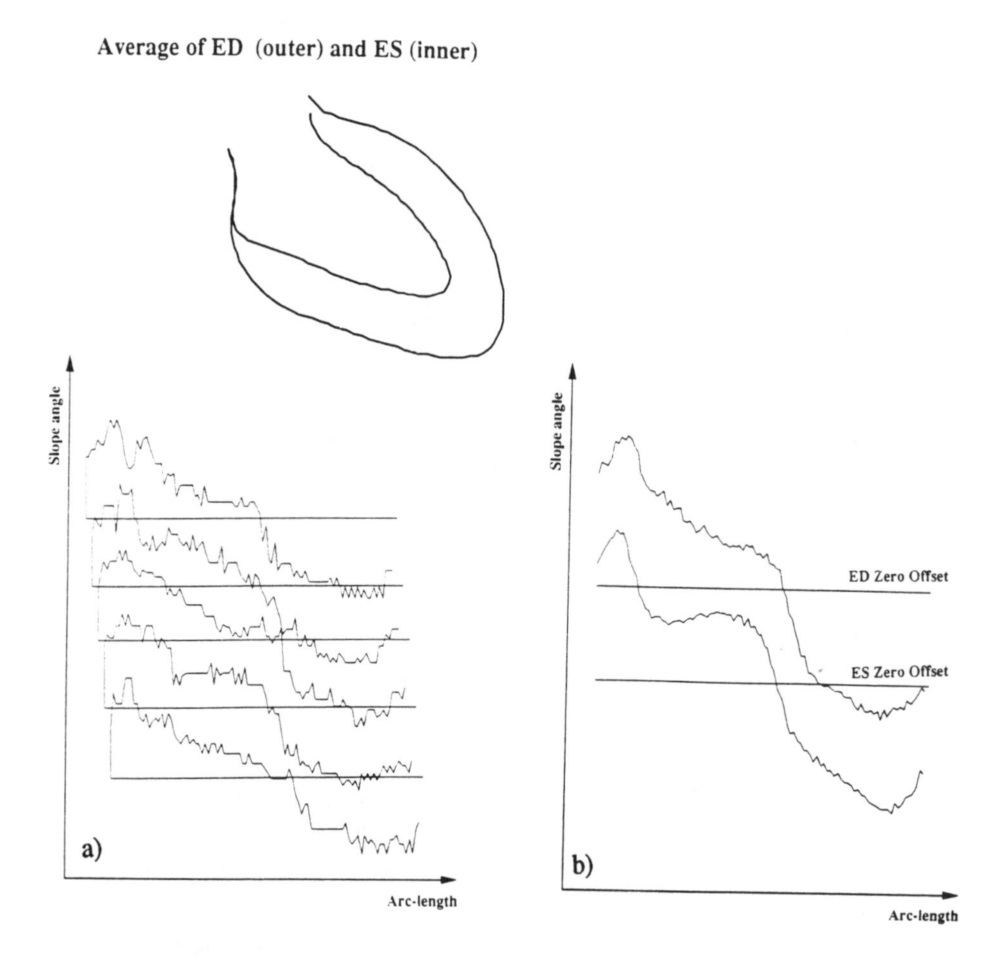

Figure 12: a) Slope angle representation of normal boundaries at end-diastolic (ED) and end-systolic frame for five patients. b) Average shape descriptor of ED and ES frames in the Θ-s and x-y spaces. Notice how smooth the slope angle functions and the boundaries are.The vertical axis is the slope angle and the horizontal axis is the arc-length of the curve from one of the endpoints. The center lines are the zero offsets.

Four classes of ventricular shapes have been identified: normal, inferior, anterior, and both inferior & anterior abnormalities which can be used to produce four sets of models, one for each class. We will explain this in terms of one frame, and then we will show how to expand it to all frames. To find the Θ-s model for a class of patients, the manually traced boundaries are divided into K (e.g., K = 100) uniform polylines. Then, for each class, the average slope of each linear segment of the polyline is computed, which results an average model for that class (Figure 14). Note that all ventricular boundaries are traced in the same direction to make their Θ-s functions compatible. In our system, in addition to the average shape descriptors, the models include the average and the range of the model parameters. The statistical values are obtained from the manual tracings of many patients' boundaries of the same class.

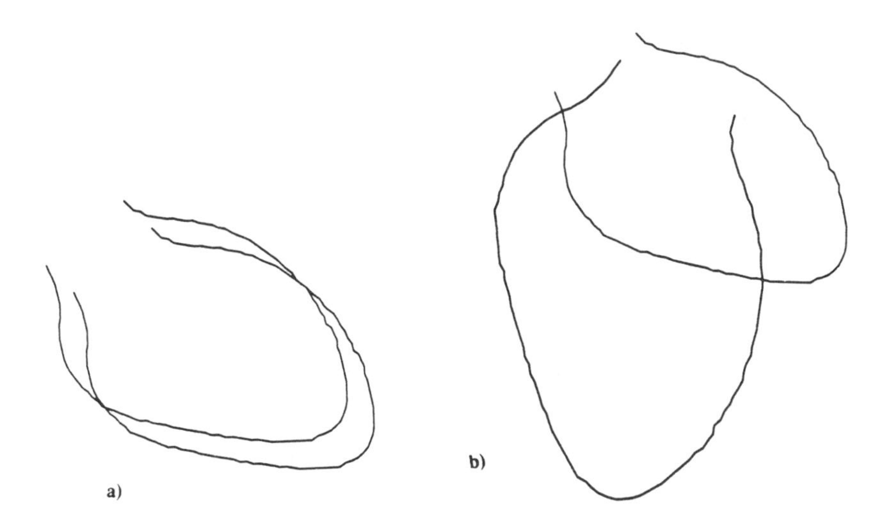

Figure 13: Reconstruction of the boundary using the shape descriptor and the starting point. a) Average: head = (100,100), d = 7 and θ_0 = 0.0. b) Enlarged and rotated: head = (50,50), d = 9 and θ_0 = 0.5.

The models are utilized for partial matching against curve units of the blackboard. The matching determines the unknown parameters of the model. Once the parameters are found, the model can be instantiated as a left ventricular boundary model instance on the image. These models are matched against the polyline representation of curves or boundaries to distinguish the ventricular shape from other objects. The current version of the system does not perform the diagnostic analysis since the type of the model is assumed to be known. However, if all classes of models are available, the matching can be used in the same way to determine the type of abnormality.

16.3.7.2 Matching Curves against Models (MCM)

In order to determine whether a curve is a part of the left ventricular boundary, we make use of the particular models. A particular model is derived from the existing global data-base with the known class, sequence number and number of frames in the cycle. Then the particular model is accurately matched against the curve or the boundary of interest. By changing the parameters of the model, boundary models with various positions, orientations and sizes can be generated. The model that best matches a curve will be instantiated as a heart unit on the Heart level of the blackboard. Heart units have the following slots: a pointer to the heart model descriptor, a pointer to the list of boundaries that matched it, the list of matching parameters, and the confidence and importance measures. (See section 16.3.8 for the confidence and importance measures.)

This matching process uses a cost function which is defined in terms of the mean square error between the slope angle (shape descriptor) of a model and that of a curve or a boundary. The matching can be used for ranking the curves or complete boundaries that are smaller, equal or larger than the model. The best match corresponds to the minimum value of the cost function. The minimum value is obtained by varying the size of the model and the relative offset between the beginning of the model and the boundary descriptor. For a particular size of the model, orientation of the model instance is directly determined by minimizing the cost function. Once the size and the orientation of the model instance are determined, the model will be placed in the x-y plane by a translation vector which is the average of the distance vectors between the curve and the corresponding portion of the model. (See [8,10] for more details). This matching is specially useful for open contours with preferences on their size and/or on their orientation, or even bounds on those values.

The generation of heart hypotheses serves two purposes. First, it is used as a focus of attention mechanism for extracting other edge segments in the image that are near the model (to be discussed in section 16.3.7.4). Second, it serves as a standard for determining the quality of the output (the boundary hypotheses). The output quality is determined by the confidence of the heart hypothesis and the confidence of the boundary that matched it (see section 16.3.8), and both of them depend on how well the boundary fits the model. More specifically, the quality depends on the score of the match expressed by the error between the boundary and the model.

16.3.7.3 Procedure for Generating Heart Hypotheses

Heart hypotheses are only generated when an identical or a similar one does not exist for the same frame, and are reinforced when such a unit exists. This is an important remark for the heart hypotheses because it enforces a higher confidence for the heart hypotheses than the boundary hypotheses. (Note that heart hypotheses are the units of the Heart level of the blackboard.) Theoretically, all parts of the left ventricular boundary should vote for the same heart model (the same parameters of match); however, due to the insufficient information (features) in the small boundary parts, the parameters may be slightly off. If each partial matching with small differences in the parameters produces a different heart unit, it would result in an overwhelming amount of overhead for the system in terms of future activities. Moreover, the additional heart units are usually so close in the parameter space that they are visually indistinguishable when displayed on the image plane. In order to increase the efficiency by preventing the generation of indistinguishable heart units, the matching parameters have to differ by certain thresholds. The thresholds in our system are 5° for the orientation differences and 10 pixels for the positional differences, which is the distance between the starting position of the new and old heart instances. Since the size is already quantized, the two sets of parameters must have the same size. Potentially, one can use a threshold on a weighted sum of the parameter differences (a vector difference in the parameter space).

The procedure for generating a new heart hypothesis or updating an old hypothesis is as follows. When a new match is generated, the matching parameters are compared to all of the heart hypotheses of the same size in the same image. If there is no heart unit with similar parameters in that image a new heart unit is produced. If the parameters are close, a new heart unit is not generated, instead, the confidence and the parameters of the old heart unit are modified. The confidence of the old heart unit will be increased using the confidence of the curve and that of the new match (see section 16.3.8). The updating of the parameters is based on a weighted sum of the new and the old parameters with the weights being the confidences of the new hypothesis and old heart unit. This way, the new heart hypothesis is merged into the old heart unit.

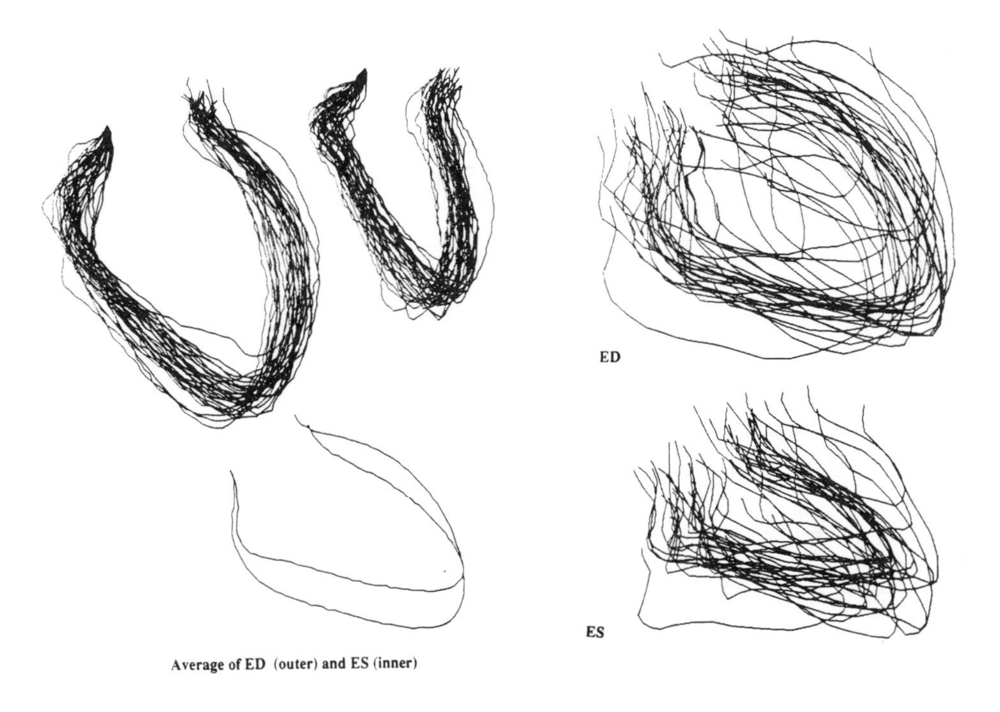

Figure 14: Manual tracings of 30 patients' left ventricular boundaries at end-diastolic and end-systolic frames. The 30 manual tracings of the ED and ES frames are normalized with respect to size and orientation. Normalized average boundaries at ED and ES are drawn with a fixed starting point using the average size and the average orientation.

16.3.7.4 Heart to Edge Segment (HES)

A particular left ventricular model is used to select edge segments that are clearly supported by data in the image. Once a particular shape descriptor is matched against a curve and a heart unit is hypothesized on the blackboard, the HES KS will be activated so that the problem solving can pay more attention to the edge points that are near the heart unit. This is also considered as a focus of attention mechanism for the problem solver because it focuses on fewer edge segments, only those near the model. The KS finds supporting edge segments in an image that are close to the hypothesized heart unit and satisfy certain conditions with respect to the heart model. The conditions are the same as the conditions explained for the templates (see section 16.3.6.4). The selected edge segments can be used to guide the refinement of the model, which in turn can be used to select more fragments. These supporting edge segments may be very small and have low confidence; however, they may play a pivotal role by filling the gaps between the boundary fragments. Therefore, despite the fact that they may be small and low confidence, they are given high importance to be converted to boundary fragments and to be joined to the original curve that activated the KS. In addition, the distance threshold for filling the gaps is relaxed for these fragments (40 pixels) because there is a higher confidence in joining them. The order in which the boundary fragments are joined is determined by the model. These boundary fragments are joined using their relationships in terms of adjacent, overlapping and enclosed as discussed before.

16.3.7.5 Heart to Heart Sequence (HHS)

This KS builds a motion description of the ventricular model instances using the consistent heart units. This KS employs the consistencies between the parameters of the heart model descriptions (one heart hypothesis per frame) to construct a heart sequence unit. The sequence of heart units can be used to hypothesize heart units for the frames that lack such units. This hypothesizing of pseudo heart units, which can be obtained by interpolating the matching parameters, would be influential in selecting supporting edge segments and guiding the search.

16.3.8 Confidence and Importance Measures

Confidence and importance measures are the means for handling the uncertainty of blackboard hypotheses. Each hypothesis is assigned a confidence factor (belief) which determines how reliable the hypothesis is. For instance, the belief of a boundary fragment hypothesis is initialized to some measure of *edginess* and is updated by matching the hypothesis against a ventricular model or by examining its movement in the subsequent frames. These confidence measures also influence the importance measures that the pre-condition of each KS returns. Therefore, they must be carefully defined to establish a partial ordering among blackboard units as well as KS activations. If these measures are not precisely defined, the system would still function but with lower efficiency. If they are incorrectly defined, however, the behavior of the system would become unpredictable.

The confidence factor of all hypotheses (units) must be normalized to numbers between 0 and 1 to permit a correct comparison between various units on the blackboard. To fulfill this requirement, the confidence factors for a combination of two or more hypotheses cannot be increased simply by adding up the confidences of the individual ones. This is because, it should not be possible to combine two hypotheses with high confidences and obtain a confidence factor greater than one for the combined one. For instance, suppose two units have confidence values of 80%. It does not make sense to combine them by just adding the two confidence values and obtaining a confidence value of 160% (i.e., a number greater than one!). Instead, it makes sense to raise the remaining 20% of the confidence value of one of them to the 80% confidence value of the other one (i.e., 16%). The total confidence of the combined unit becomes 96%. The restricted confidence addition of two confidence factors β_1, β_2 can be formulated as:

$$\beta = \beta_1 \oplus \beta_2 = \beta_1 + \beta_2 - \beta_1\beta_2 \qquad (16.2)$$

Note that this operation is commutative and associative so it does not matter how and in what order we combine two units.

The importance of a hypothesis does not have to be the same as its confidence measures nor does it have to grow at the same rate because there are situations where it is very crucial to activate a KS but the data is not very reliable. Unlike certainty factors, the importance factors do not have to be between 0 and 1. However, they have to be somewhat uniform for all units used by the KSs. Examples of certainty factors and importance measures are as follows:

- Edge segment confidence and importance measures: The confidence factor of an edge segment is basically the sum of the gradient magnitude along the segment, which means there is a higher confidence for a longer edge segment and for an edge segment with a higher contrast across the edge. The importance factor (edge segment strength) is influenced by the length of the edge segment even more because longer edges contain more shape information, which is more suitable for matching against models. The two measures are:

$$\beta(E) = \frac{1}{2\beta_{max}} \sum_{x,y \in E} \left| \nabla G(x,y) \right| = \frac{S_E \left| \nabla G_E \right|}{2\beta_{max}} \tag{16.3}$$

$$\Gamma(E) = \frac{L_E}{\Gamma_{max}} \sum_{x,y \in E} \left| \nabla G(x,y) \right| = \frac{2\beta_{max} L_E}{\Gamma_{max}} \beta(E) = \frac{L_E S_E \left| \nabla G_E \right|}{\Gamma_{max}}$$

where β, Γ and $G(x,y)$ are the confidence factor, the importance factor, and the gradient of the Gaussian image, respectively. Similarly, L_E and L_{max} are the length of the edge segment and the length of the edge segment with the maximum confidence in the entire sequence. β_{max} is the normalizing factor which is the maximum of the gradient sum of all edge segments in the sequence. This makes the maximum belief of an edge segment equal to 0.5. Γ_{max} is the normalizing factor for the importance factors (i.e., the importance factor for the edge segment with highest confidence is equal one. The reason that the maximum confidence of an edge segment is chosen to be 0.5 is that edge segments are probably not complete boundaries. Therefore, we would like boundaries with higher confidence to be generated by the combination of other edge segments. This allows the new, combined units to have confidence values greater than the maximum confidence of unprocessed edge segments.

- Boundary Fragment confidence and importance factors: The confidence and importance values are the same as those of the original edge segments because they represent the same entities in the image and contain the same information. That is,

$$\begin{aligned} \beta(F) &= \beta(E) \\ \Gamma(F) &= \Gamma(E) \end{aligned} \tag{16.4}$$

- Curve confidence and importance factors: The confidence and importance of an unprocessed curve are the same as those of the associated boundary fragment. That is,

$$\begin{aligned} \beta(C) &= \beta(F) \\ \Gamma(C) &= \Gamma(F) \end{aligned} \tag{16.5}$$

However, since curves can be combined, the confidence of a composite curve is the restricted confidence sum of its sub-parts normalized by their lengths to compensate for the length of the gaps between the sub-parts. In this case, a gap between curves reduces the confidence factor of the composite curves. The importance factor of a composite curve is the product of its confidence and its length which is not the same as the sum of importance factors of the sub-parts. These measures for combining two curves are:

$$\beta(C_1C_2) = (\beta(C_1) \oplus \beta(C_2)) \times \frac{L_{C_1} + L_{C_2}}{L_{C_1C_2}}$$

$$\Gamma(C_1C_2) = \frac{2\beta_{max} L_{C_1C_2}}{\Gamma_{max}} \beta(C_1C_2) \tag{16.6}$$

where $L_{C1C2} = L_{C1} + L_{C2} + L_{gap}$ is the length of the composite curve.

- Boundary confidence and importance factors: Basically, the confidence of a boundary hypothesis is determined by the confidence of its generating curve hypothesis and how well it fits a heart model. The importance of a boundary unit is determined by its confidence and its length. That is,

$$\beta(B) = \beta(C) \oplus MATCH(M, C)$$
$$\Gamma(B) = \frac{2\beta_{max} L_B}{\Gamma_{max}} \beta(B) \tag{16.7}$$

where *MATCH(M,C)* is the measure of the matching score which corresponds to the normalized least mean square error between the curve and the model. Thus, the confidence of a boundary unit depends only on the curve and the score of the match.

- Heart confidence and importance factors: The measures are the same as those of the boundary when the heart unit is newly created. That is,

$$\beta(H) = \beta(B) \tag{16.8}$$
$$\Gamma(H) = \frac{2\beta_{max} L_H}{\Gamma_{max}} \beta(H)$$

where L_H is the length of the model instance ($L_H = 100\ d_H$). Recall that, d_H is the size of the line segments of the model, one of the parameters of the matching. The only difference between the confidence of a heart unit and the confidence of a boundary unit is that the confidence of a heart unit can be increased when an identical or very similar match (similar set of heart model parameters) is generated. More specifically, the confidence of the existing heart unit (H_{old}) will be increased by the confidence on the new boundary. The confidence of boundary units will not be increased by an identical match because a new boundary unit is generated for every match. These measures for a heart unit are modified by:

$$\beta(H) = \beta(H_{old}) \oplus \beta(B)$$
$$\Gamma(B) = \frac{2\beta_{max} L_H}{\Gamma_{max}} \beta(H) \tag{16.9}$$

- The confidence and importance factors for a moving line segment: The confidence factor for matching two linear segments of a curve polyline depends on the orientation and the gradient direction differences, and the distance between the two linear segments. That is,

$$\beta(S_1, S_2) = \left(1 - \frac{|\theta_i - \theta_j|}{\theta_0}\right) \times \left(1 - \frac{|\alpha_i - \alpha_j|}{\alpha_0}\right) \times \left(1 - \frac{Dist(S_1, S_2)}{\delta_0}\right)$$
$$\Gamma(C_1 C_2) = \frac{2\beta_{max} d}{\Gamma_{max}} \beta(S_1, S_2) \tag{16.10}$$

where θ_i, α_i and $Dist(S_i,S_j)$ are the orientation, gradient direction and the Euclidian distance between the center of the two linear segments, respectively. Also, θ_0, α_0 and δ_0 are similarly the normalization factors for the orientation, and the gradient direction and the distance. ($d = 7$ is the length of the linear segment of the curve polyline.)

- The confidence and importance of a basic curve sequence unit: The confidence of a curve sequence unit depends on the sum of the moving line segment confidences in addition to the confidence values of the two curves, themselves. That is:

$$\beta(C_1, C_2) = \left[\underset{\forall S_i \in C_i, \forall S_j \in C_j}{\oplus} \beta(S_1, S_2) \right] \oplus \beta(C_1) \oplus \beta(C_2)$$

$$\Gamma(C_1, C_2) = \frac{2\beta_{max} L_{overlap}}{\Gamma_{max}} \beta(C_1, C_2) \qquad (16.11)$$

where the first term in the bracket is the restricted confidence sum of the linear segment movement confidences and $\beta(C_i)$ is the confidence of the curve C_i. $L_{overlap}$ is the length of the overlapping portion which is the number of acceptable moving linear segments, n, times the constant length of each segment, d. Also, $\beta(C_i, C_j)$ and $\Gamma(C_i, C_j)$ are the confidence and importance factors of a basic curve sequence obtained from the two adjacent curves in time.

The confidence factors of other units are computed based on the restricted confidence sum of their sub-parts. For example, the confidence of a Space-CS is a restricted confidence sum of the two basic curve sequences that created it (not the confidences of the original curves). That is, $\beta_{Space\text{-}CS} = \beta_{CS1} \oplus \beta_{CS2}$.

16.3.9 Control Strategy

Since the sequence of activation of each KS cannot be preprogrammed, we need an opportunistic control mechanism to be responsible for the dynamic activation of KSs. The Generic Blackboard system (GBB) allows the design of a flexible control strategy for the domain specific problem. It also comes with a set of control structures such as a simple control shell and BB1. We have used the simple control shell and modified it to allow debugging and visual inspection capabilities to be included.

The simple control shell is a priority event scheduler. That is, given a set of KSs and the conditions of their activations, the control shell of GBB schedules the sequence of execution of KSs based on the priority values generated by the KS pre-condition.

The control shell is interfaced to the blackboard data-base by means of a set of blackboard events. These events signal the control shell; the corresponding signals are the activities that are taking place on the blackboard. For example, an event is reported any time a hypothesis is generated. At this time, every KS that is applicable to the state of the problem is stored as a KS instantiation record on a queue. A KS is applicable when its pre-condition returns a positive value corresponding to the importance factor. The importance factors also define the ranking among the scheduled KSs. The instantiation records contain the name of the KS, the importance factor, the reasons for activation and the parameters required by the action part of the KS. The records are merged into the scheduling queue which is sorted by the priority (importance) values. Therefore, the controller performs a cycle of operations which consists of choosing a KS, executing the KS to produce some hypotheses, taking its output hypotheses and collecting all applicable KSs that use such hypotheses as input, ranking the new KSs, and finally scheduling them for the next cycle of operations (Figure 15).

For every cycle in a simple control strategy, the highest ranked (the most important) KS instantiation record is retrieved from the queue to be executed. The execution of KSs, in turn, produces more events to be handled by the scheduler. The control cycle can be altered to permit KSs to create instantiation records or to permit the user to monitor, test, or modify the contents of the blackboard while the system is running. One of the modifications that we have made to the structure of the simple control shell is that KSs are allowed to place a KS instantiation record on the queue with the supervision of the scheduler. An example of such interaction between a KS and the scheduler is when the ETF (Edge to Fragment) KS places itself on the queue for the next execution (see section 16.3.3). That is, the KS requests a KS instantiation record, fills the slots and hands it along with the proper priority value to the scheduler. Then, the scheduler inserts the record into the proper place in the scheduling queue. Another modification is that the control cycle is altered so that debugging facilities can be incorporated in the system. Examples of such facilities are: setting break points, stepping through the cycle, and recovering from an unexpected system error. The last one is specially important for saving the system implementer's time because in the old version of the controller, if any problem occurs during the execution of the KSs, the system halts and must be restarted. This causes all of the problem solving activities to be wasted. After the error is corrected and the problem is resolved, this modification to the controller allows the system to resume its course of operations from a cycle before the time that the error occurred. This way only activities within a cycle of execution may be lost. Finally, the event handler is modified so that newly generated hypotheses can be examined and displayed on the terminal. These facilities play an important role in the debugging necessary for system development.

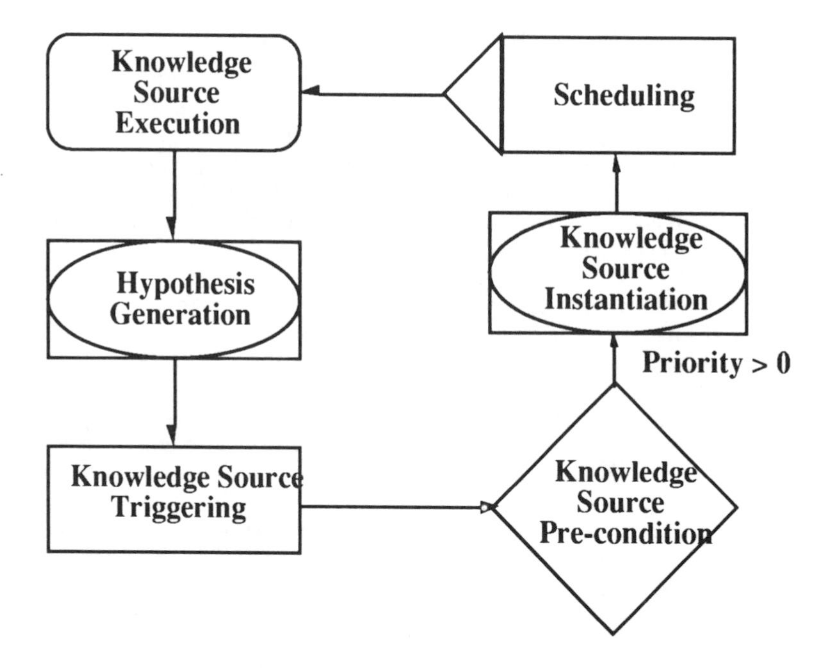

Figure 15: Activities that are taking place in a cycle of the simple control shell.

16.4 System Integration and Evaluation

In this section, we describe sub-parts of the system and the tools needed for building and testing them. The system was implemented predominantly in Common Lisp. To gain efficiency, some of its computationally intensive functions were written in C. The system consists of two major sub-systems: The Vision System (TVS) and the Generic Blackboard (GBB). TVS [13] is an environment for building knowledge-based vision systems based on a sophisticated interactive window interface for displaying images and color graphics. We designed and implemented TVS in such a way that it is capable of performing symbolic manipulations using Lisp as well as efficient image-based, graphical, and scale-invariant printing operations using the C language, the Apollo graphics routines (GPR) and the Postscript language. GBB [12] is a well structured, portable, flexible, skeletal system written in Common Lisp. GBB was designed to unify many characteristics of blackboard systems proposed to date. It was developed with the goal of rapid implementation and prototyping in various application domains and efficient execution of such implementations. This generic system provides software tools for assisting a knowledge engineer in constructing systems that make use of a blackboard framework. Once the elements of the system are defined, the system can be tested by incrementally adding the KSs. In the next section, we will explain the format of KSs and blackboard units in terms of the Generic Blackboard (GBB) with examples describing unit representations, KS definitions, and some of the blackboard operations.

16.4.1 The Generic Blackboard (GBB)

GBB consists of two distinct, modular subsystems: a control shell and a blackboard data-base development sub-system. It allows the implementation of various control strategies and allows changes to the blackboard data-base without the need to modify the control shell and vice-versa. The knowledge engineer has to define the format of the blackboard units, write code for KSs, define the conditions of their activations, properly set their priorities, and finally choose one of the predefined control structures from the GBB repertoire of control shells or design and implement a more competent, domain-dependent control strategy.

The control shell monitors the blackboard activities and schedules KSs for execution. With GBB comes a set of control structures such as the simple control shell and the BB1. We have chosen the simple control shell because it is simple and efficient. We have modified this control to accept debugging commands and to display various blackboard units on the specific graphical windows (see [8]).

The data-base development sub-system is implemented using two specification languages: one for defining the blackboard and its objects, and the other for the object insertion/retrieval structure. The blackboard is a hierarchical data structure with very powerful pattern matching which permits efficient insertion, retrieval and deletion of objects in the data-base. Typical examples of objects or units in the blackboard are hypotheses, goals and KS activation records. The application implementer writes domain-specific code to define the blackboard and the corresponding objects, and GBB defines the proper strategy for the efficient storage and retrieval of these objects. The implementer is also responsible for writing the KSs, defining the conditions of their invocations, and assigning their priorities.

16.4.1.1 Pattern Matching Operation

The key to efficiency in GBB is the rapid insertion and retrieval of blackboard units, which is facilitated by an efficient pattern matching language. The pattern matcher stores and retrieves blackboard units based on their characteristics such as their locations in space or in time. It performs these operations efficiently because it partitions the storage and provides access functions based on the characteristics of the unit. Other facilities in the language allow the filtering of units before or after unit retrieval. GBB also allows the creation of an arbitrary number of sub-blackboards, spaces or levels on the main blackboard or any other sub-blackboard. In addition, facilities are provided for the automatic linking and ordering of the blackboard units which permits the pattern matcher to focus on a certain part of each level.

One of the most frequently used operations defined in the pattern matching language is the Find-Units operation. Find-Units is a primitive function for retrieving candidate units from spaces based on the unit names, types, or specific patterns. Patterns can be quite complex when dealing with composite, overlapping units. These patterns can also specify units in certain locations or within an area of the image consisting of several overlapping rectangles. Thus, the Find-Units function can be efficiently employed to retrieve edge segments based on their bounding rectangles. We have used this function to retrieve endpoint units and line-segment units that reside in the neighboring area of a certain point. These operations are used in retrieving neighboring curves in space (JTC KS) or tracing a curve in time (CCS KS).

16.4.2 Implementation of the Blackboard

The blackboard in our application is made of three spaces: STATIC, DYNAMIC and OBJECT (Figure 16). STATIC space consists of as many sub-blackboards as there are images in the sequence. Each sub-blackboard is a hierarchical structure containing all the information about one image. The information about one image is encoded in the blackboard units and in the edge segment and image data structures described in section 16.3.1.2. The links between the units are bi-directional links for a homogeneous representation of the relationships among blackboard units. In our system, these links are defined only between units of different levels, thus allowing the system to efficiently detect multiple identical hypotheses that may be created at the same level by decomposing the object into its subparts.

DYNAMIC space is a single hierarchical structure with the same number of levels as there are in a STATIC sub-blackboard. This space contains units relating STATIC sub-blackboard units that are adjacent both in space and in time. Relating such units provides declarative, temporal knowledge of objects in the image sequence.

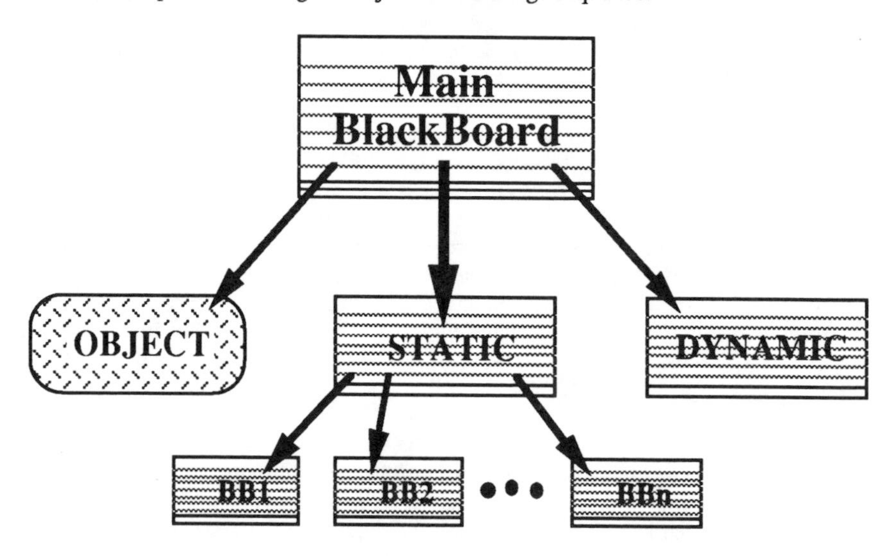

Figure 16: The blackboard structure and the related spaces.

The last space is the OBJECT space which contains two types of units: endpoints and line segments. An endpoint unit is created for every end of a boundary fragment. This enables the system to use the Find-Units operation to quickly retrieve boundary fragments whose endpoints are within a certain distance of a specific location in the image. Similarly, line segment units are indexed by the position of their mid-point. The Find-Units operator is applied again to collect all line segments that are in the two adjacent frames of the curve unit, and whose mid-points are within a certain distance to the line segment mid-points of other curves. These units are efficiently retrieved by the Find-Units function and stored into two separate lists, one for each adjacent frame. Once these line segments are collected in the two linked lists, more constraints will be imposed on them for further filtering and ranking. Examples of such constraints are the orientation and gradient direction difference thresholds described in section 16.3.5.2. These lists are used to identify the curve portions that are closely moving in time while tracking a curve in the image sequence.

16.4.3 Examining the Behavior of the System

The system was tested on several image sequences. To better understand the behavior of the system, the testing was performed in several stages. In the first stage, we compared the results of the system when most of the KSs were inhibited. Inhibiting some KSs enabled us to analyze solutions derived by other KSs and to isolate problems. There are two ways that we can inhibit a KS: by changing the parameters and by temporarily changing its pre-condition to make it always return zero. The exclusion of models was achieved by increasing the size of the acceptable curves for matching to a very large number. This way there would be no curve large enough to satisfy the conditions for matching. In the case of curve sequences, the CCS (Curve to Curve Sequence) KS pre-condition was changed to return an importance factor of zero. In this case, the KS was not activated because zero importance means that the KS is not applicable to the state of the problem. Inhibition of CCS stopped all other curve sequence related KSs from activation. To compare the results of different stages, the system was run for only 100 cycles. Normally, the first few cycles of all stages were similar, but once sufficiently long curves were produced, the behavior of the system changed depending on whether model matching or temporal information was available.

We conducted four experiments by inhibiting different KSs. Each experiment showed the effect of a certain kind of KS on the system. In the first experiment, we did not incorporate models and temporal information; thus the processing became completely bottom-up. In the second one, we added models only. In the third, we included curve sequences. The last one which is the combination of all produced better results.

In the first experiment, important edge segments were promoted to the Boundary Fragment level and then to the Curve level. In the meantime, some curves were connected to their adjacent boundary fragments and created longer curves. However, large gaps between curves were not filled, and boundary units were not instantiated. Instead, the system tried to expand itself throughout the sequence while connecting every possible adjacent boundary fragment. In general, it wandered like a nomad and did not accomplish much.

By including the models in the second experiment, the behavior of the system improved substantially. It became more focused, due to the participation of the HES (Heart to Edge Segment) KS. Once a model was generated, it sought more supporting edge segments and quickly instantiated them on the higher levels of the blackboard. Boundary pieces were also connected more rapidly. Even some of the larger gaps were filled using the small edge segments that were near the heart model – edge segments which would have never been brought up to the Boundary Fragment level, or would have been brought up very late without the help of the model. However, some of the gaps still remained unfilled, and the boundaries were not perfect.

In the third experiment, the temporal information came into play. In this stage, simple curve sequences were generated by CCS and then Space-CS units, more complex units, were formed by CSG (Curve Sequence Grouping). Although the impact of the temporal information was not as great as that of the models, some more curves, which were probably far away and could not be connected before, were connected by SCSP (Space Curve Sequence Patching) using curves of the adjacent frames.

Finally, models and temporal information were incorporated at the same time which resulted in better and longer boundaries. In this experiment, most of the gaps were filled either using small supporting edge segments or using curve sequences. Unfortunately, even when both models and temporal information were combined, we could not achieve a complete sequence of boundaries. However, once a complete boundary was generated for one frame, it was passed to the BEX (Single Boundary Extension) KS which forced the production of a boundary sequence. Note that, to compare the quality of complete solutions obtained from various paths that lead to boundary sequences, more KSs need to be incorporated. Also, the system would be capable of handling unusual or unpredictable cases by incorporating special purpose KSs when such cases arise.

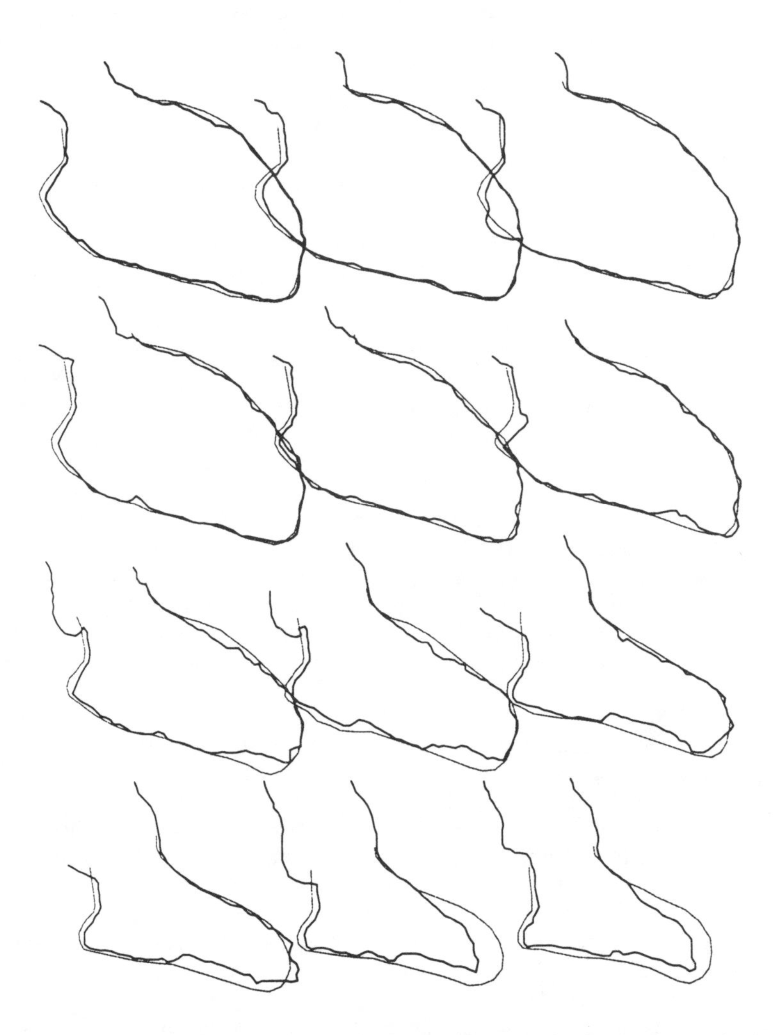

Figure 17: The system provides a set of complete boundaries in the form of a boundary sequence unit. (Darker boundaries are the computer generated boundaries, whereas lighter ones are the manual tracings.)

Since it is difficult to show the results of all image sequences, we illustrate the complete boundaries throughout the sequence for one image sequence and compare them to the corresponding manual tracings (Figure 17). For a complete medical comparison of the results of many studies with their corresponding manual tracings see [8,9].

16.4.4 Sensitivity

Sensitivity of the system to some parameters was qualitatively explained in the Section 16.3. Quantitative measurements were also obtained for the Canny edge detection parameters in [8]. Also, the system was run for a certain number of cycles while specific KSs were enabled or disabled. Thus, the behavior of the system was analyzed by changing parameters and changing the type of knowledge which was present in the system. The sensitivity analysis suggests that more methods should be developed to provide quantitative measures of solutions. Quantitative measures would tell the system developer how much a change in the system parameters or incorporating a new KS improves the results. (See [8] for complete sensitivity analysis of various parameters of the system.)

16.5 Summary and Conclusion

A system has been developed that automatically extracts the left ventricular boundary guided by existing experimental shape models and by the motion of such boundaries through the image sequence. It is shown how such information is used by the system and how the pieces are put together to construct a reliable, working system. Many issues such as system integration, feature extraction and knowledge representation have been addressed with examples of system execution and the testing process. We hope that the techniques used in our system as well as the evaluation of the results will be valuable and contribute to Cardiology, Medical Imaging, and Computer Vision.

The motion analysis of non-rigid objects is a very interesting and useful area in Computer Vision. The difficulties in the analysis of non-rigid motion have been addressed and illustrated through the use of X-ray motion pictures of the heart, which show it translating, rotating and deforming as it beats. Furthermore, the interpretation of cineventriculograms of the left ventricle is not only problematic because of the elastic motion of the heart, but is also more complicated due to the low contrast images we are dealing with and non-homogeneous contrasts around the heart boundary. The solution to this sophisticated problem would be applicable to any other domain that involves low contrast, noisy images, or involves complex non-rigid motion.

We chose the blackboard architecture for our knowledge-guided task while developing both proper low-level and high-level operators. We have defined various levels of abstraction on the blackboard knowledge base and procedural KSs that operate between these levels. Many low-level and high-level KSs have been designed, implemented, and tested on several images. Examples of such KSs are edge linking, grouping of the boundary fragments and curves both in space and in time, connecting curves and matching them against experimental models of the heart shapes. The system has been designed with the provision that more specialized KSs can be incorporated to handle specific cases as the knowledge becomes available. As more KSs are incorporated in the system, the system becomes more robust against noise and confounding, non-cardiac structures.

The analysis begins with automated ventricular border recognition throughout the entire image sequence. This task demands the integration of information extracted from images in a sequence as well as model-based object recognition, given uncertainties in both data and models. We have employed edge information extracted from the image sequence using the Canny edge operator. We have developed a method for linking the extracted edge points in a certain order so that extraneous edge points can be removed. Also, edge segment branches are identified and disconnected while coherent edge points are linked. Linking of edge points led to the construction of edge segments and boundary fragments. These boundary fragments needed to be connected to form a more complete boundary fragment and finally a complete boundary. To connect such boundary pieces we had to introduce several relationships between them via their endpoints. For clarity and computational efficiency, these relationships, which determine whether two boundary fragments are joinable or not, were precisely expressed in terms of logical expressions based on the equality of endpoints and projections of other endpoints only.

Using the location of boundary fragment endpoints, we defined three types of relationships between two curves: enclosed, adjacent and overlapping. We also developed procedures for connecting such curves based on those relationships. Enclosed curves were not joined because sharp corners were produced. Two adjacent curves that were very close were joined by a straight line while other adjacent curves were connected using a template or a third curve. Overlapping curves which had a small overlapping portion were connected by a straight line after removing the overlapping portions of the two curves. Those overlapping curves which had a larger overlapping region were connected using a linear transitioning curve instead of a straight line. Although these relationships may involve one or two parameters that are dependent on the image resolution, the method used in describing the relationships and the techniques used in connecting such edge segments can be employed in any application of Computer Vision.

Edge segments were represented by a global data structure containing positional and gradient information. Such data structures were designed to encapsulate all necessary information about an edge segment in order to reduce the amount of interaction between the interpretation processes and the underlying data (i.e., the image sequence). Edge segments in an image were kept in a linked list sorted by their strength. This way, all small and noisy edge segments were kept at the end of the list to make the system independent of unreliable edges and the exact values of the thresholds used in edge detection. The edge segment linked list, along with some other information about the image, were kept in a global image data structure for ease of data manipulation.

A technique was developed that uniformly re-samples the edge segments into polylines, necessary for filtering and comparing curves. The uniform polyline representation produces curves that are smoother and have fewer points. We used the polyline representation for estimating the slope angle function of a curve. The slope angle function, in turn, was implemented to derive the curvature function which identifies corners and sharp turns corresponding to incorrectly linked edge segments. We split edge segments at the corners specified by the location of high curvature. The polyline representation which is a simple and efficient means for representing partial and complete boundaries has constantly been exploited in many places in the system. We believe that this type of polyline representation suits many other areas of Computer Vision involving edge points and boundaries.

We have devised several methods for shape representation to describe normal and various abnormal shaped ventricles. As we have shown, a proper choice of model is crucial for achieving the correct interpretation of the images. Thus, we employed models for heart shapes to rate the quality of a partial interpretation and to recognize acceptable complete boundaries.

We have shown how the models are derived from the left ventricular manual tracings of many patients. Similar types of models based on our technique have been developed for other research projects dealing with anatomic structures in medical images. For the left ventricle, four classes of models have been identified based on normal and abnormal heart shapes. We have obtained a sequence of models for each class by averaging the normalized slope angle functions derived from manual tracings of many left ventricular boundaries of the same type. The models were employed for matching against boundaries and partial boundaries.

The heart models were precisely matched against curves and boundaries to determine the unknown position, orientation and size of the model. Once the parameters of the models were computed, they were instantiated as a heart unit on the blackboard. The placement of a heart unit on the image plane promoted more supporting edge segments to the Curve level. During the matching, more promising curves (long curves with relatively high confidence) were hypothesized as boundaries. The best boundaries of all images were grouped into a sequence of boundaries that would eventually represent the final solution. Single boundaries were also forced to extended throughout the sequence as an alternative way for finding the final boundary sequence. This is particularly useful when all boundaries may not be collected by the other parts of the system.

In order to evaluate the goodness of a solution or the confidence of any blackboard unit, a confidence factor was defined for each unit. To keep these factors uniform, they were normalized to a range of 0.0 to 1.0. A new addition operator was defined for increasing the confidence factors to keep them within that range. Importance factors were defined based on the confidence factors of the same units in order to produce priorities required by scheduling. Finally, we have addressed the role of the importance factors in the scheduling of the KSs.

We explained how the system was built on top of two pre-existing subsystems: TVS and GBB. We wrote TVS to provide capabilities for processing images and displaying color graphics as well as generating Postscript files for resolution-independent printing. GBB was the blackboard architecture implementation employed in our image understanding task. We defined the blackboard, sub-blackboards, and spaces in GBB and represented declarative knowledge using the blackboard units and the relationships between them. We specified three spaces: 1) STATIC space for storing frame by frame information, 2) DYNAMIC space for keeping track of temporal information, 3) OBJECT space for holding two elementary units. The units stored in the OBJECT space were rapidly retrieved using the pattern matching capabilities of GBB. We also defined procedural knowledge in terms of KSs and conditions of their activations. The KSs were incrementally incorporated and tested within GBB.

It was important to build a flexible system that allowed many modifications without the need to change the underlying architecture. This was important because new knowledge is constantly incorporated into the system causing it to evolve through many modifications. To handle such rapid evolution, we provided extensions to the control structure which facilitated debugging the blackboard program and devised a means for resuming the program when a system error occurred. We also provided the user with visualization aids that graphically display the blackboard units on several windows. The debugging facilities and the visualization aids were tremendously helpful during the analysis and modification of the system behavior. We urge that these capabilities be incorporated in all image understanding systems, in particular knowledge-guided systems with non-deterministic program flow.

In summary, the aim of this effort has been to have the computer analyze cardiac X-ray images with a bare minimum of human intervention. The interpretation of low-contrast images of a moving non-rigid body is a complex and difficult problem for the computer. However, significant progress has been made because it is set up in a narrow domain. We have developed a Blackboard system that automatically extracts the left ventricular boundary using global and domain specific knowledge. This allows the physicians to spend their valuable time on diagnostic analysis, leaving the time-consuming manual tracing job to the computer. We believe our system will have a value in daily patient care as well as in teaching and research.

References

[1] H. Asada and M. Brady, "The curvature primal sketch," IEEE Transactions on Pattern Analysis and Machine Intelligence, Vol. 8, No. 1, January 1986.

[2] J.F. Canny, "A Computational Approach to Edge Detection," IEEE Transactions on Pattern Analysis and Machine Intelligence, Vol. 8, No. 6, November 1986.

[3] D.D. Corkill, K.Q. Gallagher and K. E. Murry, "GBB: A generic Blackboard development system," Proceedings of National Conference on Artificial Intelligence, pp. 1008-1014, 1987.

[4] P.G. Gottschalk, J.L. Turney and T.N. Mudge, "Two-dimensional partially visible object recognition using efficient multidimensional range queries," IEEE International Conference on Robotics and Automation, pp. 1582-1589, IEEE 87CH2413-3, in Raleigh, North Carolina, 1987.

[5] G.B.J. Mancini, S.F. Deboe, E. Anselmo, M.T. Lefree,"A Comparison of Traditional Wall Motion Assessment of Quantitative Shape Analysis: A New Method for Characterizing Left Ventricular Function in Humans," American Heart Journal, Vol. 114, No.5, pp. 1183-1191, November 1987.

[6] G.B.J. Mancini, E. Anselmo, S.B. Simon, M.T. Lefree, R.A. Vogel, "Quantitative Regional Analysis: An Application of Shape Determination for the Assessment of Segmental Left Ventricular Function in Man," American Heart Journal, Vol. 113, No. 2, pp. 326-334, February 1987.

[7] Penny H. Nii, "Blackboard Systems," The Artificial Intelligence Magazine, Vol. 7, part I: No.2, pp. 38-53 and part II: No.3, pp. 82-106, 1986.

[8] Saeid Tehrani, "Knowledge-Guided Boundary Determination in Low Contrast Imagery: An Application to Medical Images," Ph.D. Dissertation, The University of Michigan, Ann Arbor, May 1991.

[9] S. Tehrani, T.E. Weymouth, F. Luk, K. DePaulis, P.R. Williamson and G.B.J. Mancini, "Automatic Extension of Left Ventricular Boundary Description Throughout an Image Sequence," Accepted for publication in IEEE Transactions on Medical Imaging.

[10] S. Tehrani, T.E. Weymouth and G.B.J. Mancini, "Model Generation and Partial Matching to Left Ventricular Boundaries," Proceedings of SPIE 4th Conference on Medical Imaging, March 1990.

[11] S. Tehrani, T.E. Weymouth and B. Schunck, "Optimum Boundary Interpolation Using Piecewise Cubic Polynomials with Tangent Slopes," Accepted for publication to Computer Vision Graphics and Image Processing.

[12] T.E. Weymouth and A.A. Amini, "A framework for knowledge-based computer vision: Using a blackboard architecture," VISION-87 Conference Proceedings, June 1987.

[13] T.E. Weymouth, A.A. Amini, S. Tehrani, "TVS: An Environment for Building Knowledge-Based Vision Systems," Proceedings of Applications of Artificial Intelligence VII, Orlando, Florida, March 1989.

Chapter 17
Combining Edge Pixels into Parameterized Curve Segments Using the MDL Principle and the Hough Transform

J. Sheinvald, B. Dom, W. Niblack, S. Banerjee

17.1 Introduction

Edge detectors often produce a set of individual edge pixels, or "edgels", from the original pixel data. This chapter describes a method for grouping the edgels into parameterized curve segments. The goal is to produce a set of, say, line segments from the set of edgels. The method is based on the Minimum Description Length (MDL) principle from information theory. One of the main advantages of MDL methods is that they remove (or reduce) the use of thresholds and adjustable parameters from the algorithms, and the result is often a method which is quite robust. On the other hand, a problem sometimes associated with MDL methods is that they require a minimization over a very large and irregular search space. For the problem at hand, we show how the Hough transform (HT) may be used to drastically reduce this search space, yielding an extremely efficient (although suboptimal) search. The result is an algorithm in which MDL overcomes standard problems with the HT – when to stop searching for peaks in the Hough array, what are the line segment endpoints – while the HT overcomes problems with MDL – the large search space – and which produces a pleasing set of line segments.

The technique is applicable to a variety of parameterized curves (lines, circles, ellipses, triangles, etc.), and naturally handles a multiple, unknown number of curves. An extension using the magnitude and direction of the gradient is also presented. Examples are given detecting straight line segments in simulated and real images. Edge detection is a basic operation in image processing and analysis, typically producing a set of "edgels" in an image. A subsequent step is the identification of parameterized curves or curve segments from the edgels, such as line segments, and circular or elliptic arc segments. Such an operation is necessary in scene analysis, path planning, model-based vision, and related forms of image interpretation. This paper describes a method of identifying the number of and parameters for the curve segments from the edgels.

We assume an image representing some scene in which there are curves (e.g. the natural boundaries of objects), and an edge detector that operates on the image to produce a set of edgels. Two common classes of edgel detectors are (1) the combination of a gradient operator plus thresholding of the gradient magnitude, and (2) operators such as the Marr-Hildreth[1] and Canny operators[2], which tend to produce connected, thinned set of edgels. In this chapter, we consider the first class, and in particular the case where the edgels have not been thinned. We assume the output of the edge detector is a rectangular grid of pixels, where each pixel takes a binary value "black" (edgel) or "white" (non-edgel). This will be the primary input to our algorithm. In addition, the edge detector may produce information such as the gradient direction and magnitude at each pixel, and we will show how these may be used as well.

Regardless of the form of edge detector, there will in general be noise in the image as well as spatial and gray level quantization effects that result in the following:

1. Detected real edge points may be displaced from their true locations.
2. The edgels will include spurious points not associated with any real edge. We shall refer to these points as "background noise points".
3. The detected edgels will not include all real edge points, giving gaps and missing points along the true object boundaries.

Our objective is, given these effects, to find a robust method of detecting curve segments from the edgels.

Various authors have treated this problem. Nevatia and Babu [3] determine line segments by first linking edgels into sets based on their (thinned) gradient directions, and then approximating each linked set by a set of straight line segments that give a good polygonal approximation to the linked set. Both McKeown et. al. [4] and Nazif and Levine [5] use a combination of gradient-based procedures to combine edgels into short segments, and rules to link short segments into longer ones. These methods use a variety of empirically set thresholds in the rules to perform the linking. Burns, et. al. [6] presents a clever method that groups edgels into "line support" regions based on the gradient direction, and within each region determines the plane of the edge by a gradient-weighted fit. The edge is then found as the intersection of this plane with the horizontal plane of average pixel intensities. One result of this method is that parameters of the line segment (such as its endpoints) may be found from the line support region. Rosin and West [7] and West and Rosin [8] describe methods for segmenting 8-connected sets of thin edgels (e.g. from a Marr-Hildreth operator) into parameterized curves consisting of straight line segments and circular arcs. They use a polygonal approximation method similar to [3], but avoid a fixed error threshold in their approximation by defining a "significance measure" of a line (or circular arc) segment as the ratio of the segment length divided by the maximum deviation of the actual curve from the approximating segment. Thus longer segments are allowed to have larger deviations, giving a form of scale independence. Boldt et. al. [9] use a hierarchical approach, linking edgels into tokens, and tokens into successively longer tokens to obtain line segments. The linking rules require a number of thresholds, similar to those in [4] and [5].

The method we propose does not perform any explicit linking of the edgels. Rather it hypothesizes different sets of curve segments to "explain" the given edgels, and then evaluates each hypothesis. The evaluation is based on the MDL principle and fundamentally says that the best hypothesis is the one which allows the encoding of the edgel data with the shortest codelength.

In our case, each hypothesis is in fact a parameterized model of all points in the image. A model consists of (1) a set of (parameterized) curve segments, and (2) a noise probability model describing how edgels get spread about the given curve segments, and a probability model for background noise. The heart of the MDL approach is to select that model that would give the shortest codelength for encoding both the model and the data (in a hypothetical but well-defined encoding scheme based on principles from information theory). The models have adjustable parameters. These parameter values affect the codelength and instead of being manually set or adjusted, they are computed to be those values giving the minimum codelength. The search for the codelength minimizing values is not necessarily easy, and among the results of our analysis will be procedures for automatically finding the (nearly) optimal, codelength minimizing values.

A significant advantage of this criterion is the fact that it provides a universal yardstick (the encoding length, measured for example in bits) for comparing the performance of a wide variety of models, thus enabling us to choose the "best" curve set as our estimate. For example, the method can directly compare models using only line segments versus those including line segments plus higher order curves.

The MDL principle has been successfully applied in various pattern recognition areas: classification [10], clustering [11], feature selection [12, 13], deriving image descriptions [14, 15], image segmentation [16, 17], and signal detection in sensor arrays [18]. It is an alternative to traditional statistical methods such as the likelihood-ratio criterion for hypothesis testing, reducing subjective decisions (such as selecting the significance level in the likelihood-ratio criterion) to a minimization problem. It often yields simpler criteria and better results [19, 20].

A potential disadvantage of MDL methods is that the codelength minimization may be over a very large search space[1] and hence computationally expensive. The algorithm we suggest for finding the optimal parameters in our application uses the Hough transform (HT) to greatly reduce this search space and make the application of MDL feasible, even efficient. Further, this combination of MDL and HT overcomes two familiar problems associated with the HT: (1) detecting the endpoints of located lines, and (2) determining the threshold level that defines a "peak" in the Hough array (i.e. a value that enables the detection of all the curves on one hand, while rejecting spurious curves on the other). As we show, MDL offers a natural

[1] In fact, this is not a problem with MDL, but a fact of modelling. The point is, there are many models to consider.

solution to both of these problems.

The method derived can also be applied to the more general problem of fitting multiple parameterized curves to a given set of data, where the number of curves and their parameters is initially unknown. In such an application, the method can be regarded as an extension of robust single-curve fitting methods (as described in [21], for instance).

The remainder of this chapter is organized as follows. After introducing the MDL criterion in Section 17.2, two general families of probability models suitable for digital "edgel images" are described in Section 17.3. These families, when used in conjunction with the MDL criterion, enable us to estimate both the number of curves and their parameters from a given set of edgels. In Section 17.4 we summarize the Hough transform, and in Section 17.5 we describe an efficient algorithm combining MDL and the HT for finding straight line segments. In Section 17.6 we extend the method, enabling it to handle gradient information (using both the magnitude and the direction information). Section 17.7 contains results on simulated and real images, Section 17.8 discussions, and Section 17.8 conclusions.

17.2 The MDL criterion

17.2.1 Introduction

The MDL criterion for model selection [22] is concerned with the following general problem: Given a set of N observations $\mathbf{U} = \{u_1, \ldots, u_N\}$ and a family of candidate models[2] $\{M^{(k)}\}_{k=1,2,\ldots}$ "explaining" $\mathbf{U}$, determine the best model. Model $M^{(k)}$ is typically written as the pair $(\theta^{(k)}, k)$, consisting of a "structure parameter" k, specifying the form of the model, plus a set of parameters $\theta^{(k)}$. As an example, in the model class of polynomials, k might specify the order of polynomial and $\theta^{(k)}$ the polynomial coefficients. To be precise, MDL usually considers each model to be a parameterized probability function

$$p(\mathbf{U}|M^{(k)}) \triangleq p(\mathbf{U}|\theta^{(k)}, k), \quad k = 1, 2, \ldots$$

giving the probability of the observed data, where $\theta^{(k)} \in \Theta^{(k)}$ is the parameter vector associated with the model $M^{(k)}$ (it may be a different length for each model), and $\Theta^{(k)}$ is the domain of $\theta^{(k)}$.

The MDL approach to selecting the "best" model is based on information theory arguments, and can be viewed as a formalization of the physicists' Ockham's razor principle: the simplest model explaining the observations is the best. In particular,

[2] We use the term *model* to refer to a functional form for describing the data. In this view the model includes two kinds a variables, those representing the data, $\mathbf{U}$, and those representing parameters, $\theta^{(k)}$. Using this terminology, *fitting* the model $M^{(k)}$ to the data $\mathbf{U}$ consists of determining optimal values for the parameters $\theta^{(k)}$. We will also use the term *model class* to refer to this family of models.

MDL asserts that the best model is the one that yields the shortest prefix code[3] for the combination of the observations $\mathbf{U}$ and the model $M^{(k)}$. Strictly speaking, we are only concerned with encoding the data and the model is simply a device to be used in performing this encoding. This is done by first encoding the model and then encoding the data using the model.

If we have probability densities for k and $\theta^{(k)}$, the prefix codelength for the observations and the model, which we write as $L(\mathbf{U}, M^{(k)})$ or $L(\mathbf{U}, \theta^{(k)}, k)$, is, according to Shannon, [4]

$$\begin{aligned} L(\mathbf{U}, \theta^{(k)}, k) &= -\log p(\mathbf{U}, \hat{\theta}^{(k)}, k) \\ &= -\log p(\mathbf{U}|\hat{\theta}^{(k)}, k) - \log p(\hat{\theta}^{(k)}|k) - \log p(k) \end{aligned} \tag{17.1}$$

where $\hat{\theta}^{(k)}$ is the maximum likelihood estimator of $\theta^{(k)}$. Thus MDL states that the best model is the one corresponding to

$$\tilde{k} = \arg\min_k \{-\log p(\mathbf{U}|\hat{\theta}^{(k)}, k) - \log p(\hat{\theta}^{(k)}|k) - \log p(k)\} \tag{17.2}$$

The three terms on the right correspond to the length of the codewords that describe (in order, from right back to left) what model is being used (i.e. the number k), the parameter vector $\hat{\theta}^{(k)}$ associated with this model, and the observations $\mathbf{U}$ encoded using the model.

The term $p(k)$, called the *prior* on k, reflects our prior knowledge about the probability of having model $M^{(k)}$ as the underlying machinery producing the data. In the following sections (and in most applications of MDL), we assume this prior is uniform, contributing identically for all the models, (i.e. $p(i) = p(j);\ \forall i, j$) so that it can be omitted from the criterion.

The term $p(\hat{\theta}^{(k)}|k)$ (also refered to as a *prior* on $\theta^{(k)}$) is the probability of having specific parameter values in model k, and the second term in Equation (17.1), $-\log p(\hat{\theta}^{(k)}|k)$, is the codelength necessary to encode these parameters. For real-valued parameters, it is in this term that one of the key differences between MDL and other methods, such as maximum likelihood (ML) and maximum a posteriori (MAP), occurs.

To understand this difference consider the fact that there is actually a subtle problem involved with using Equation (17.1) to perform the encoding mentioned. If the possible values of $\theta^{(k)}$ form a countable (discrete) set, then $p(\hat{\theta}^{(k)}|k)$ is a probability corresponding to one of those values and the encoding can be performed using (17.1) as is. However, in the case we are describing (which is the usual case), $\theta^{(k)}$ is real-valued (i.e. its values are taken from a continuum) and infinite precision is therefore required to specify them. In this case, $p(\hat{\theta}^{(k)}|k)$ is a probability *density*, which must be multiplied by a parameter-space volume element $d\theta^{(k)}$, to obtain a probability, and it is this probability whose logarithm is the codelength for the

[3] A prefix code is defined as a code in which no codeword is a prefix of another codeword. It is also called *instantaneous* code since it enables unique decoding of a stream of codewords as they arrive, without the need for a comma sign between the codewords. see [23], for example.

[4] We shall use the natural logarithm in this paper (unless stated otherwise).

parameters. The size of $d\theta^{(k)}$ is implicitly the precision to which $\theta^{(k)}$ is specified. Note that in the limit $d\theta^{(k)} \rightarrow 0$ the codelength for the parameters will approach infinity. It should be clear from this that it is possible, in principle, to obtain an optimum (total-codelength-minimizing) value for this precision. This problem is explored by Rissanen in [12]. The result of his investigation is an expression that is the codelength of the optimal-precision (i.e.truncated) parameters, plus the extra codelength for encoding the data with these truncated rather than exact parameter values. This extra codelength is combined with the second term in Equation (17.1), which is then written as:

$$L(\hat{\theta}^{(k)}|k) = -\log p(\hat{\theta}^{(k)}) + \tfrac{1}{2}K^{(k)}\log N \tag{17.3}$$

when a prior is available, and

$$L(\hat{\theta}^{(k)}|k) = \tfrac{1}{2}K^{(k)}\log N \tag{17.4}$$

when it is not (where $K^{(k)}$ is the number of "free" components in $\theta^{(k)}$). In the former case, $\hat{\theta}^{(k)}$ is the MAP estimate for $\theta^{(k)}$, while in the latter, it is the ML estimate. It is these (untruncated[5]) values that are used to evaluate $-\log p(\mathbf{U}, \hat{\theta}^{(k)}, k)$ in Equation (17.1). These are asymptotic expressions, valid for $N \rightarrow \infty$ (in practice, for $N \gg k$). In many practical cases, $p(\hat{\theta}^{(k)})$ is not known (or is assumed uniform), and the second form is used. Very importantly, and in contrast with ML and many uses of MAP methods, this expression is a function of $K^{(k)}$, and, in particular, an increasing function of $K^{(k)}$. This means that complex, higher order models are given a longer codelength, i.e. penalized, and this is a natural and intuitively appealing property. When used in Equation (17.1), this term is usually called the "penalty term", because it penalizes models with many parameters.

The net effect is that MDL provides a "cost function" or yardstick to measure each candidate model, that cost being the codelength necessary to encode the model and the given data using the model. The place of MDL in the overall algorithm is shown in the diagram of Figure 17.1. Note that MDL does not provide a searching procedure, and given a model class (which may be extremely large), some searching technique such as branch-and-bound or a greedy algorithm must be used. Devising the search strategy is often an important component of an MDL solution. A major aspect of the algorithm described in this chapter is the search technique based on the Hough transform that is applicable to an important class of problems in machine vision.

17.2.2 Applying the MDL criterion

For the problem at hand, let u_i represent the binary value of pixel i:

$$u_i = \begin{cases} 1 & \text{if pixel } i \text{ is black} \\ 0 & \text{if pixel } i \text{ is white} \end{cases}$$

[5] The implicit practical definition of "untruncated" is: specified to the precision of the particular computer floating-point representation being used.

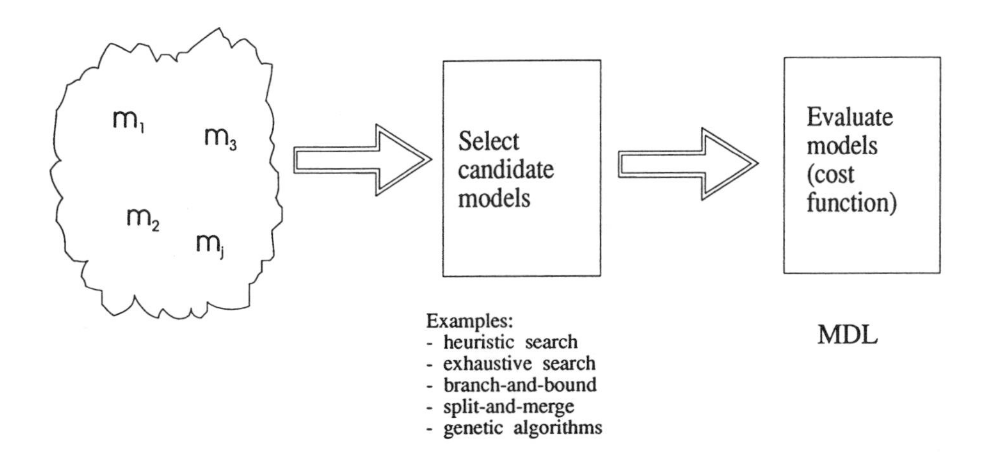

Figure 17.1: Selecting and evaluating models from a model class.

with $i = 1, \ldots, N$ being some indexing of the pixels, and N representing the total number of pixels in the image. What we need is a model class that "explains" the u_i.

We propose the following. Let $\mathcal{C}*$ be a set of curve segments, for example segments of polynomial curves up to order two. Let $\mathcal{C}$ be the family of all sets of curve segments from $\mathcal{C}*$ that can occur in the image. For a given set of curve segments $C^{(k)} \in \mathcal{C}$, let $\theta_c^{(k)}$ be the parameters necessary to specify them. For example, if $C^{(k)}$ specifies straight line segments, $\theta_c^{(k)}$ requires four free parameters for each segment, the x and y of the endpoints; in case of a (complete) circle, three parameters are needed, the center point, and radius. Further, assume that edge points are spread about each curve segment with some distribution (due to noise), and also that there are background noise points not associated with any curve segment. Let $\theta_p^{(k)}$ contain the parameters necessary to represent these distributions. The complete parameter set for model $M^{(k)}$ is $\theta^{(k)} = (\theta_c^{(k)}, \theta_p^{(k)})$ and with these we are able to write an expression for $p(\mathbf{U} \mid \theta^{(k)}, k)$.

It follows from Equation (17.1) that the minimum description length of the image, using model $M^{(k)}$ is given by:

$$MDL(k) \;=\; \min_{\theta^{(k)} \in \Theta^{(k)}} \left\{ -\log p(\mathbf{U} \mid \theta^{(k)}, k) + \; L(\theta_c^{(k)}|k) + L(\theta_p^{(k)}|k) \right\}$$

where $L(\theta_c^{(k)}|k)$ denotes the description length of the curves, and $L(\theta_p^{(k)}|k)$ denotes the description length of the parameters of the probability model. For example, if $M^{(k)}$ specifies one straight line segment and one circular arc segment, the above equation says that the best particular set of one line segment and one circular arc segment is the one that minimizes the expression in braces.

The minimum description length of the set of edgels over the whole family of models is given by:

$$\begin{aligned} MDL &= \min_k\{MDL(k)\} \\ &= \min_{k,\theta^{(k)}\in\Theta^{(k)}} \left\{-\log p(\mathbf{U} \mid \theta^{(k)}, k) + L(\theta_c^{(k)}|k) + L(\theta_p^{(k)}|k)\right\} \end{aligned} \tag{17.5}$$

and the best model is the one for which this minimum is obtained. Thus this best model is the one giving the minimum over all model forms – such as all sets of one line segment, all sets of two line segments, all sets of one line segment and one circular arc segment, and so on.

If we assume that the pixels are independent, the first term in the braces of Equation (17.5) can be written as:

$$p(\mathbf{U}|k,\theta^{(k)}) = \prod_{i\in I} p(u_i|\theta^{(k)}, k) \tag{17.6}$$

where I denotes the pixel index set $\{1,\cdots,N\}$. The MDL criterion can then be written as:

$$MDL = \min_{k,\theta^{(k)}\in\Theta^{(k)}} \left\{\left[\sum_{i\in I} -\log p(u_i \mid \theta^{(k)}, k)\right] + L(\theta_c^{(k)}|k) + L(\theta_p^{(k)}|k)\right\} \tag{17.7}$$

Equation (17.7) is the key equation from which our method is developed. We must now derive specific expressions for each term in the equation, and also find a reasonable way to perform the minimization, which is over a large space. It includes the set of all possible sets of curve segments in the image, as well as all possible values of the noise parameters.

The term $L(\theta_c^{(k)}|k)$ gives the length needed to specify the parameters of the curves, and may be represented using Equation (17.4). Assuming it takes K_c free parameters to specify the curves in model k, $L(\theta_c^{(k)}|k)$ is given by $(K_c/2)\log N$. Notice that in the particular case of straight line segments, where it takes four parameters to specify each segment, we get $(4/2)\log N = 2\log N$ per segment. This happens to be the code length needed to specify two grid-quantized endpoints; i.e. on a grid of N pixels, it takes $\log N$ bits to specify one of the grid points assuming a uniform distribution, so $2\log N$ bits to specify two endpoints. Thus, Equation (17.4) implicitly assumes pixel-size resolution for the end-points coordinates[6]. The same codelength was used to describe line segments on a grid in [24].

We are now ready to consider expressions for $p(u_i \mid \theta^{(k)}, k)$ given a specific noise probability model.

[6] [22] derived an optimal resolution for the parameters, based on optimizing the code-length. As shown here, this optimal resolution coincides with the grid resolution.

17.3 Probability models

Due to the wide variety of real-world pictures, it is difficult or impossible to find a general model of the distribution of edgels in an image, given a set of curve segments, that will fit all possible pictures. The properties of a rural landscape picture taken by a remote sensing radar, for example, are different from those of a picture of a printed circuit board taken by a frame grabber. Here we consider the "uniform probability about curves of width w" model. This model is defined as follows: the probability that a pixel is black is P_n if its distance from every curve exceeds $w/2$, and P_l otherwise. This model is suitable for a gradient-magnitude edge detector applied to a picture with homogenous noise and linear decrease of intensity along the normal to the curves. Figure 17.2 shows this case in one dimension. Part (a) shows the intensity measured along a cross-sectional line passing from a high-intensity zone (on the left side), through a transitional zone representing the curve width (pixels location 20-30), to a low-intensity zone (on the right side). Part (b) shows the absolute value of the intensity difference between adjacent pixels, along with some arbitrary threshold level. A pixel becomes black if the absolute value of the intensity difference is above the threshold level. Since the noise has uniform distribution, and the average intensity decrease across the curve is also uniform, the resulting probability of having a black pixel is uniformly distributed, as shown in part (c).

The parameters associated with this noise probability model are $\theta_p \triangleq (P_n, P_l, w)$. Using this model, Equation (17.7) becomes:

$$\begin{aligned} MDL &= \min_{C^{(k)} \in \mathcal{C}, \theta_p} \{-n_n \log P_n - \bar{n}_n \log(1 - P_n) \\ &\quad -n_l \log P_l - \bar{n}_l \log(1 - P_l) + \tfrac{1}{2} K_c \log N\} \end{aligned} \tag{17.8}$$

where K_c is the number of free parameters needed to specify the curves in $C^{(k)}$; n_n and $\bar{n}_n$ are the number of black pixels and the number of white pixels, respectively, whose distance from the curve set $C^{(k)}$ is greater than $w/2$; and n_l and $\bar{n}_l$ are the number of black pixels and white pixels (respectively) whose distance from the curve set is less than or equal to $w/2$. We have omitted $L(\theta_p^{(k)}|k)$ since its contribution is identical for all the parameter sets.

The minimizing values for P_l and P_n can be obtained by differentiating the above function:

$$\hat{P}_l = \frac{n_l}{n_l + \bar{n}_l} \qquad \hat{P}_n = \frac{n_n}{n_n + \bar{n}_n}$$

Thus the (globally) best values of $\hat{P}_l$ and $\hat{P}_n$ can be computed once n_l and n_n are known, and these can be computed for any given set of curve segments and segment width w by counting black and white pixels on the curves and in the background.

The remaining parameters are those specifying the curve segments and w. The minimizing value for w is found by exhaustive search. The minimizing values for the curves' parameters can, in principle, also be obtained by exhaustive search,

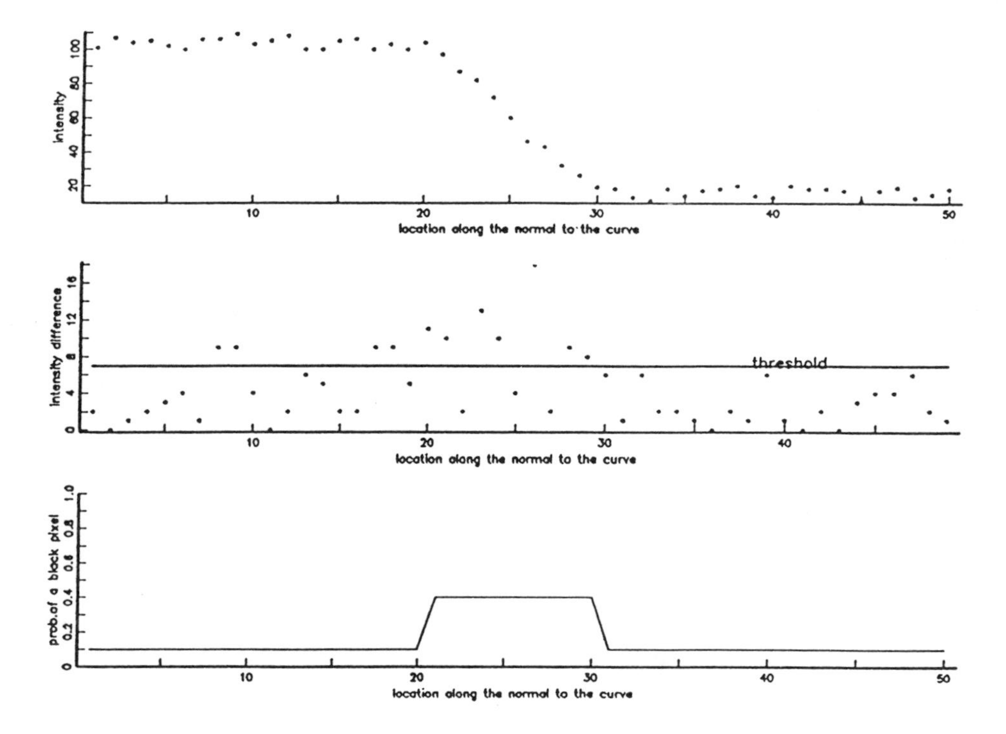

Figure 17.2: Simple edge detection. Top to bottom: (a) The cross sectional intensity. (b) Absolute value of adjacent pixel differences. (c) The probability of crossing the threshold.

but this is infeasible practically – we would have to consider every possible set of combinations of curve parameter. In the next sections, we propose a sub-optimal minimization algorithm that makes use of the Hough transform(HT) to find these parameters. We begin with a brief introduction to the HT.

Remark: For the sake of simplicity we have assumed identical probability P_l and influence distance, w, for all the curves. One may assume different parameters for each curve, but in this case the $L(\theta_p^{(k)}|k)$ term can not be dropped from (17.8) and consequently the code length of the curve's parameters must be increased[7]. Then, the optimal probabilities of each curve need to be computed from the pixels "belonging" to that curve only (assuming that the intersection area of curve i with the other curves is negligible relative to the area of the curve):

$$\hat{P}_{l_i} = \frac{n_{l_i}}{n_{l_i} + \bar{n}_{l_i}} \tag{17.9}$$

where $P_{l_i}, n_{l_i}, \bar{n}_{l_i}$ are the probability parameter and the number of the black and white pixels (respectively) in the "influence area" of curve i.

17.4 The Hough transform

The Hough transform (see [25] for an extensive survey) provides a means for detecting parameterized curves in an image. Suppose that the image consists of a set of points $\{z_j\}_{j=1,\ldots,J}$ lying on a curve c characterized by the equation:

$$c: \quad f(z;\psi) = 0 \tag{17.10}$$

where $\psi \in \Psi$ is a vector of parameters $\psi = (\psi_1, \ldots, \psi_r)$, with Ψ being the domain of ψ. An r-dimensional grid is formed in the parameter domain, with some pre-determined resolution. For each grid point ψ^i there is a corresponding curve c^i in the image plane defined by: $f(z;\psi^i) = 0$ The HT is an r-dimensional array of cells, with each cell corresponding to a grid point. Each cell contains an integer[8] $h(i)$ that represent the number of votes that the corresponding grid point receives. Each point in the image votes for all possible curves of the form (17.10) that it can lie on, with following voting procedure:

1. Set $h(i) = 0 \; \forall i$
2. For $j = 1, 2, \ldots, J$:

   increment by 1 all[9] the HT cells for which the corresponding grid points "distance" from the $(r-1)$-dimensional parameter-space surface $S_j : \; f(z_j;\psi) = 0$ is less than some pre-determined value δ_0.

[7] In case the domain of w is limited to a value much smaller than the image dimensions, the code length needed for describing w can be neglected. Similarly, if the resolution needed for $\hat{P}_{l_i}$ is coarse enough, its code length can be neglected. Notice that the resolution of $\hat{P}_{l_i}$ can not be higher than $\frac{1}{n_{l_i}+\bar{n}_{l_i}}$.

[8] See [26] for extension to a real valued array obtained by "spreading" each vote over some neighboring HT cells, and [27] for extension to a continuous HT.

[9] Better results, as well as significant reduction in the amount of computation, can be achieved by using the gradient information. The gradient direction information can be used to increment

The "distance" $\delta(i,j)$ of a grid point ψ^i from the surface $\mathcal{S}_j$ is usually measured along one of the parameter space coordinates, say ψ_r . That is, if

$$f(z_j, \psi_1^i, \ldots, \psi_{r-1}^i; \psi_r) = 0$$

has a number of solutions $\psi_r = \{\psi_{r1}, \psi_{r2}, \ldots\}$ then $\delta(i,j) = Min_k \quad | \psi_{rk} - \psi_r^i |$. In the case of straight lines, a convenient parameterization is $\psi = (\rho, \phi)$ for $0 \leq \phi < \pi$, where ρ is the (perpendicular) distance of the origin from the line, and ϕ is the angle a normal to the line forms with the positive x-axis. The equation of a line l using this parameterization is:

$$l: \quad f(z; \psi) = \rho - x \cos\phi - y \sin\phi = 0$$

for $z = (x, y)$. The distance of a grid point $\psi^i = (\rho^i, \phi^i)$ from the parameter-space sinusoid $\mathcal{S}_j$

$$\mathcal{S}_j: \quad f(z_j, \psi) = \rho - x_j \cos\phi - y_j \sin\phi = 0$$

is usually measured along the ρ-axis: $\delta(i,j) = | \rho^i - x_j \cos\phi^i - y_j \sin\phi^i |$, so that $h(i)$ represents the number of the image points in a swath with width $2\delta_0$ and center line l_i:

$$l_i: \quad \rho^i - x \cos\phi^i - y \sin\phi^i \; = \; 0$$

In the case of a circle parameterized by its center point and its radius R, the distance in the parameter space is usually measured along R, so that $h(i)$ represents the number of image points contained in an annulus.

In general, we shall call the set of all points that can contribute votes to cell i the *domain* of cell i; i.e. $domain(i) = \{z_j \quad | \quad \delta(i,j) < \delta_0\}$. δ_0 determines the size of the cell domains, and consequently the amount of overlap between adjacent cell domains. Notice that the domains of two different cells are not necessarily mutually exclusive.

17.4.1 The effects of the background noise

Suppose that the image consists only of background noise points created according to the uniform model described in Section 17.3. Let us define the location of a pixel as the coordinates z of its center point. Then for a given family of curves, associated with cell i there is a number H_i that represents the total number of pixels located in the domain of this cell. (In the case of lines, H_i is the number of pixels located within the swath of cell i.) The actual count of cell i, $h(i)$, is a binomially distributed random number, since each pixel in the domain has a fixed probability (P_n) of being black. The expected value (mean) of the cell count is given by $h_i \triangleq E\{h(i)\} = H_i P_n$. If $h_i >> 1$, the binomial distribution can be approximated (using DeMoivre-Laplace

---

only those cells that represent curves (approximately) perpendicular to that direction. The gradient magnitude information can be used to increment the cells by a number proportional to the magnitude, see Ballard(1982).

theorem, see [28]) by a Gaussian distribution with the same mean, and a variance given by:

$$\nu_i^2 \triangleq E\{(h(i) - h_i)^2\} = H_i P_n (1 - P_n)$$

However, in case there is a curve in the image, and some of the pixels of the domain of cell i are under the influence of the curve, $h(i)$ will have a higher mean and a higher variance. In the absence of noise one usually estimates the curve parameters by picking those associated with the maximum count cell. However, this seems to unfairly prefer cells with large H_i. A more reasonable criterion is:

$$CR(i) = \frac{h(i) - h_i}{\nu_i} = \frac{h(i) - H_i P_n}{\sqrt{H_i P_n (1 - P_n)}} \tag{17.11}$$

This criterion has the same distribution for every cell in the absence of curves, namely zero mean, unity variance Gaussian distribution. It happens to be the log-likelihood ratio criterion for testing the hypothesis that $H_i P_n$ is the mean of $h(i)$. A similar criterion was used in [29].

17.4.2 Considerations in choosing the grid resolution and δ_0

The resolution of the grid is usually dictated by the accuracy needed from the curve parameters estimates (see [26]), and the amount of available memory. The choice of δ_0 determines the width of the cell domain swaths (in the case of lines). In case the grid resolution is higher than the width (w) of the curves, one should choose $2\delta_0 \approx w$ since choosing $2\delta_0 \gg w$ will cause several of the cells to contain all the votes of the curve points, thus creating ambiguity in picking the right cell, and in addition, the "signal to noise ratio" of the cells will be smaller. On the other hand, choosing $2\delta_0 \ll w$ will divide the votes of the curve points among several cells, again causing ambiguity.

17.5 An algorithm for finding line segments

We now describe an algorithm that finds straight line segments in an image. We assume the uniform model, using the same edge-point probability P_l and line width w for all the lines, and we try to minimize the cost function (17.8). The HT is utilized as a means of indicating the most probable swath to contain a line segment. The decision whether the swath indeed contains a line segment, and the determination of its location, are based on the cost function. Once a line segment has been detected, its parameters (endpoints and width w) are adjusted with a fine tuning procedure, the edge-points associated with it are deleted from the image, the HT of the thinned image (i.e. the image with associated edge points deleted) is computed, and the whole process is repeated again. The algorithm is sub-optimal in the sense that we are not guaranteed to have reached the optimal (codelength minimizing) parameters at the end, but simulations show quite satisfactory results.

The main steps of the algorithm are:

1. Choose initial estimates for w, P_l, and P_n . These values will be recomputed in the algorithm and results are not so sensitive to initial values. The initial estimate for w requires some prior knowledge about the possible range of w. The initial estimate for P_n can be set to some fraction of $\frac{N_b}{N}$, where N_b represents the total number of black pixels in the image, and the initial estimate for P_l can be set to some multiple (> 1) of the initial P_n.

2. Perform the Hough transform, using $2\delta_0 = w$, and pick the cell with the greatest likelihood to contain a line segment, using criterion (17.11). Since the location of the line segments is fine tuned in step (4), the HT grid can be set coarse. (However, it should be chosen fine enough to ensure that every line lies wholly in some cell domain).

3. Detect all line segments along the swath associated with this cell, according to the swath segmentation algorithm, described below. This divides the selected swath, along its longer dimension, into line segments and gaps. If no line-segments are detected go to (6).

4. Perform "fine-tuning" of the parameters of the detected line segments (i.e. w, and the end points) by locally minimizing the cost function (the fine-tuning procedure is described below).

5. Delete the points of the detected line segments from the image, and go to (2).

6. Estimate $\hat{P}_l$ and $\hat{P}_n$ according to 17.9, and iterate steps (2)-(5) until there is no significant change in $\hat{P}_l$ and $\hat{P}_n$.

To save computation time, the HT updating following the detected segments points deletion (step (2)) can be done by: (1) computing the HT of an image that consists of the deleted points only, and (2) subtracting this HT array from the current array. Furthermore, both savings in computation time and better results can be achieved if the gradient information is used in forming the HT, as discussed in [30].

17.5.1 The swath segmentation algorithm

Let T denote the length of the swath, w being its width. Let $t \in [0, T]$ be the longitudinal axis of the swath. We define a segment $s(t, \tau)$ to be the set of all swath pixels whose center points have longitudinal coordinates in the range $[t, t+\tau]$. The aim of the swath segmentation is to divide the swath along the longitudinal axis into line-segments, with gaps between them, in such a manner that the cost function of the swath will be minimized.

The segmentation of a swath is performed by sowing seeds, enlarging the seeds, and merging them, in a manner illustrated for a horizontal swath in Figure 17.3.

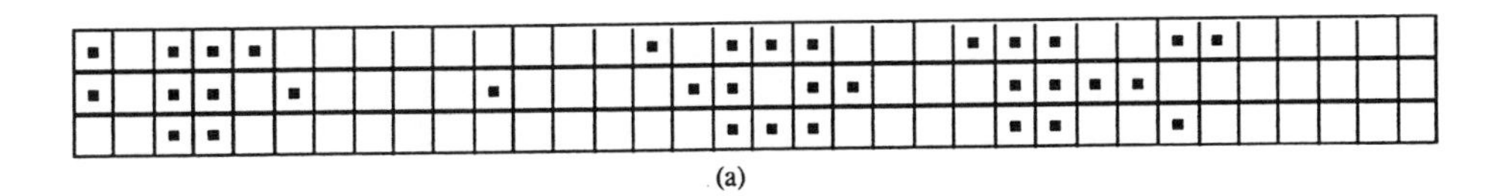
(a)

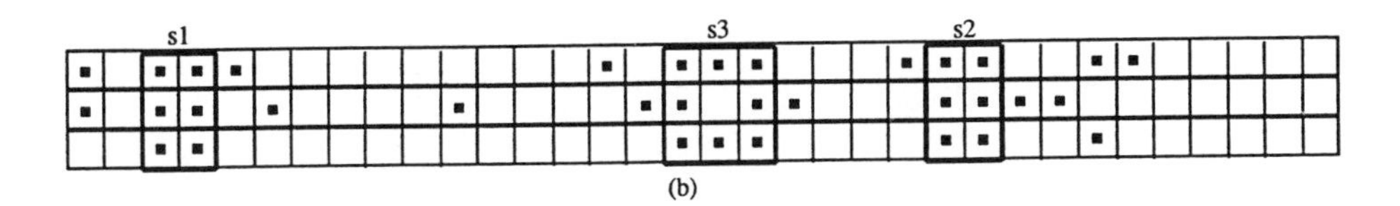

(b)

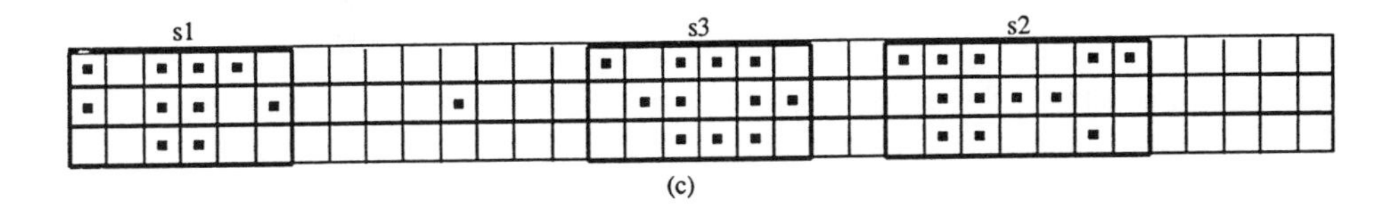

(c)

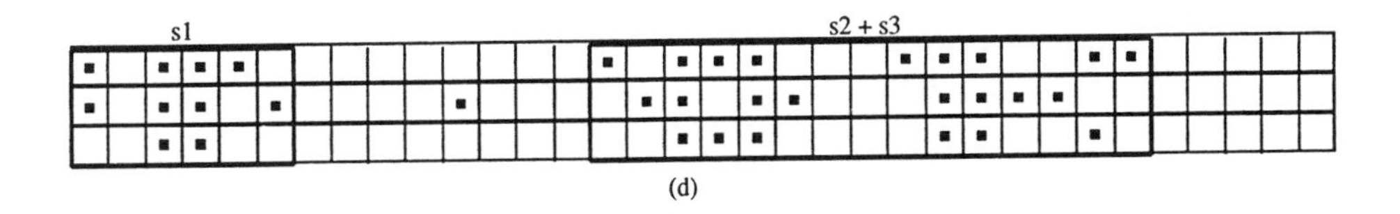

(d)

Figure 17.3: Swath segmentation. Top to bottom: (a) The swath. (b) The detected seeds. (c) Seed expansion. (d) Merging the seeds.

The pixels belonging to the swath are represented in part (a), with dots marking the black pixels. A segment of the swath becomes a seed if it costs less to encode as a line segment than it costs to encode as noise, that is if:

$$\Delta(s) \geq 2 \log N \tag{17.12}$$

where we define the Δ function to be the difference between the code-length obtained by encoding the segment's pixel-values (denoted by s) as curve-pixels and the code-length obtained by encoding them as background noise:

$$\begin{aligned} \Delta(s) &\triangleq [n_s \log P_l + \bar{n}_s \log(1 - P_l)] - [n_s \log P_n + \bar{n}_s \log(1 - P_n)] \\ &= a n_s - b \bar{n}_s \end{aligned} \tag{17.13}$$

where n_s, and $\bar{n}_s$ are the number of black and white pixels (respectively) in the segment, and where a and b are positive numbers defined by:

$$a \triangleq \log \frac{P_l}{P_n} \qquad b \triangleq \log \frac{1 - P_n}{1 - P_l}$$

Thus the Δ function is just a linear combination of the number of the black and the number of the white pixels contained in its argument.

We search exhaustively for all possible non-overlapping seeds, starting the search with the smallest possible seeds, and then gradually increasing the size. Each time the whole swath is searched. Figure 17.3(b) shows the seeds s1, s2, s3 (detected in this order) detected in the swath shown in Figure 17.3(a).

After all possible non-overlapping seeds have been formed, each seed is enlarged if the cost decreases by this enlargement (notice that this time we do not have to pay the cost of encoding the segment end-points, since we have already paid it when we created the seed). That is, if:

$$\Delta(e) \geq 0 \tag{17.14}$$

where e represents the segment added to the seed. Each seed is made as large as possible by trying all possible non-overlapping expansions on either side of the seed, starting with the smallest possible expansions. Every time a valid expansion e is detected (i.e. eq. 17.14 is valid for e), the seed is enlarged and we begin the process again.

In the final step, every two adjacent segments are merged into one long segment (thus saving the code length of 2 end-points) if $2 \log N \geq -\Delta(g)$ where g represents the gap between the two segments.

We can sum up the segmentation algorithm as follows:

1. Set $\tau = 1$
   (a) For $t = 1, 2, \ldots, T$ try to convert the swath-segment $s(t, \tau)$ into a seed, provided that this segment does not overlap any already existing seeds (the swath-segment becomes a seed if 17.12 is valid for this segment. If a seed is formed at, say t_0, then the search is continued at $t = t_0 + \tau$).

   (b) Repeat 1a for $\tau = 2, \ldots, T$.

2. (a) Enlarge the first seed by an additional segment of length $l = 1$ (on either side) if 17.14 is true, and if the addition does not overlap any already existing seeds.
   If the seed is enlarged then $l \leftarrow 0$.
   (b) Unless all the neighboring seeds or the swath ends have been reached, set $l \leftarrow l + 1$, and go to 2a
   (c) Repeat 2a and 2b for the next seed.

3. Try to combine every 2 adjacent segments.

This algorithm leads to an optimal segmentation of the swath, in the sense that the cost of the swath is minimized.

Remarks:

- The right hand side of Equation (17.12) serves as a barrier against forming new line segments. At first, it seems surprising that this barrier is a function of the image size: a set of points that is considered as a line segment in a small-sized image, could be ignored as background noise in a larger image. But a second thought reveals that our eye is prone to making the same judgement: in a big image, that contains many lines and many noise points, small-sized groups of points will usually be ignored as noise. The reason for this is that the larger the image is, the more likely is the possibility that, somewhere in the image, the background noise points will cluster up to form a pattern looking like a small line-segment. Furthermore, the larger the image is, the more likely is the possibility that some noisy swath will be picked up (mistakenly) in the HT instead of the swath containing the small line-segment (as the cells variance ν_i becomes comparable to the number of the line points).

- In practical implementations it is more convenient to choose the t-axis as the x-axis for "horizontal' swaths (and as the y-axis for "vertical" swaths), where a swath is called "horizontal" (or "vertical") if the absolute value of the angle its center line creates with the positive x-axis (or positive y-axis) is less than $\pi/4$. In our simulations we used this convention, and we approximated the areas of the segments as parallelograms (rather than rectangles) ending with sides parallel to the x-axis (y-axis for "vertical" segments), as shown in Figure 17.4. A pixel "belongs" to the segment if its center point is included in the parallelogram. The number of pixels per column (row) in a "horizontal" ("vertical") may vary, but the formulation of the swath-segmentation algorithm is capable of coping with it.

- The detected segments can be used as a starting point for searching for more complex structures (such as triangles, squares, etc.) using the same objective cost function. For instance, combining the end points can save the description length of one end point. Further investigation is needed in this subject.

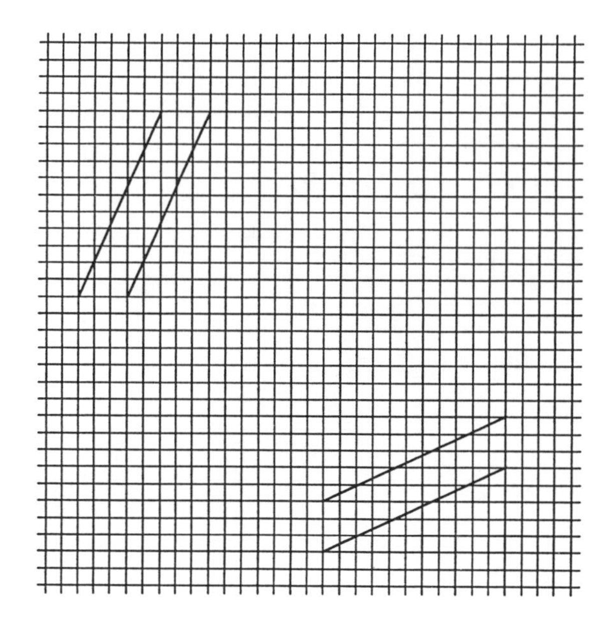

Figure 17.4: Horizontal and vertical swaths as used in the implementation.

17.5.2 The fine tuning procedure

To achieve greater accuracy in the line-segment locations we use a fine-tuning procedure. The procedure is needed since quantization effects, background noise, and the presence of multi-lines (several nearly co-linear line segments) in the image tend to divert the maximum cell from its true location. In addition, the optimal width of each segment has to be estimated to enable the elimination of all the points associated with the segment. The parameters of each detected line-segment (i.e. its end-points and its width) are varied locally over a small range so as to locally minimize the cost function, Equation (17.8). Any local minimization procedure can be used.

The procedure used in our simulations was based on Hough-transforming an image that included only a window around the detected line segment (the window was just a broadened segment). Higher grid resolution was used, and only a portion of the HT array, in the vicinity of the current parameters estimates, was computed (to save computation time). The maximal count cell domain was then picked as the up-dated line segment, and the cost of the window computed. Repeating this process for various values of δ_0, we chose our estimate for the line width as $2\hat{\delta}_0$, where $\hat{\delta}_0$ is the minimizing value for the cost of the window. (Notice that implicit in this procedure is the assumption that only one line is present in the window).

17.6 Using the gradient information

In real pictures, the gradient (both its magnitude and its direction) provides useful evidence for the existence (or non-existence) of a curve and its direction. If the "signal to noise ratio" in the vicinity of the curve is high enough, the gradient vector points in a direction normal to the curve (provided that the gradient is not measured in an irregular point of the curve, such as a corner). Utilizing the gradient direction information can improve the performance of our curve detector when applied to real pictures. The gradient information has been widely used in edge-detectors, see e.g. [2], where the gradient direction served as an estimator of the local normal direction, while the local maximum of the magnitude of the gradient component in that direction was thresholded to determine the existence and location of an edge point.

17.6.1 The probability model

To incorporate the gradient information (both magnitude and direction) into our curve detector, we change our probability model, attaching to each pixel two values: m^i which represents the gradient magnitude measured at pixel i (or some function of the gradient magnitude such as the signal to noise ratio at the gradient operator output), and $\varphi_g^i (0 \leq \varphi_g^i < 2\pi)$ which represents the direction of the gradient vector[10]. We replace the probability $p(u_i \mid k, \theta^{(k)})$ in our MDL criterion, Equation (17.7) by the following distribution, which gives the probability of pixel i having those two values given the location of the curves:

$$p(m^i, \varphi_g^i \mid \theta^{(k)}, k) = p(m^i \mid \theta^{(k)}, k) \cdot p(\varphi_g^i \mid \theta^{(k)}, k, m^i)$$

Assuming independency of the pixels we obtain our general curve detection formula:

$$\begin{aligned} MDL &= \min_{k,\theta^{(k)} \in \Theta^{(k)}} \left[\left(\sum_{i \in I} [-\log p(m^i \mid k, \theta^{(k)}) - \log p(\varphi_g^i \mid k, \theta^{(k)}, m^i)] \right) \right. \\ &\quad \left. + L(\theta_c^{(k)}|k) + L(\theta_p^{(k)}|k) \right] \qquad (17.15) \end{aligned}$$

17.6.2 Uniform pdfs

We shall now proceed to demonstrate the use of this formula using simple pdfs that will facilitate the computations, while permitting the application to a wide enough variety of pictures. In the following sections we shall assume that the curves are continuous, smooth, and well separated (thus avoiding curve end and intersection

[10] Using the range $[0, 2\pi)$ (as opposed to using the $[0, \pi)$ range) enables us to identify which side of the curve has a higher intensity. It also improves the immunity to the background noise points by reducing (by a factor of 2) the probability that they will affect the HT cells count (as explained below), and (more importantly) by reducing their effect on the swaths segmentation. But, in principle, one may as well use the range $[0, \pi]$ (using the direction modulu π).

effects, where the gradient direction is irregular), and we shall use the following terminology: the distance $d(i;C)$ of pixel i from the curve set C will be defined as the distance between the center of pixel i and the nearest point belonging to the curve set. If the distance of pixel i from a curve is less or equal to $w/2$, we shall say that pixel i lies "on the curve" (or "belongs to the curve"). If in addition, the absolute value of the angle between the gradient direction at pixel i and the direction of the normal to the curve is less than some small angle α (we shall define α more explicitly later) we shall call the pixel "perpendicular".

We choose the magnitude information to be a binary value, thus enabling both the use of the outputs of sophisticated edge detectors (such as [2]) that make use of additional local information (such as the local noise level, the local magnitude maximum, etc.)[11], and a computationally simpler algorithm. The probability of m^i being "black" will be assumed to be uniform[12]:

$$p(m^i = black \mid \theta) = \begin{cases} P_l & \text{if pixel } i \text{ is on the curves} \\ P_n & \text{otherwise} \end{cases}$$

If pixel i is located on a curve, the function $p(\varphi_g^i \mid \theta, m^i)$ will have its main bulk concentrated near the normal direction. For the sake of simplicity we shall assume that φ_g^i is uniformly distributed:

$$p(\varphi_g^i \mid \theta, \text{black}) = \begin{cases} p_{gb} & \text{if } |\varphi_g^i - \varphi_c^i| \le \alpha \\ \tilde{p}_{gb} & \text{otherwise} \end{cases}$$

$$p(\varphi_g^i \mid \theta, \text{white}) = \begin{cases} p_{gw} & \text{if } |\varphi_g^i - \varphi_c^i| \le \alpha \\ \tilde{p}_{gw} & \text{otherwise} \end{cases}$$

where p_{gb} and p_{gw} are parameters that must be estimated, φ_c^i is the normal direction at pixel i (pointing towards the greater intensity area), α is some pre-determined (small) angle that reflects our prior estimate about the deviation of the gradient direction from the normal direction (in our simulations we used $\alpha = \pi/18$), and $\tilde{p}_{gb}$, $\tilde{p}_{gw}$ are given by:

$$\tilde{p}_{gb} = \frac{1 - 2p_{gb}\alpha}{2\pi - 2\alpha} \qquad \tilde{p}_{gw} = \frac{1 - 2p_{gw}\alpha}{2\pi - 2\alpha}$$

In case pixel i is not located on any curve, we shall assume that the gradient direction has an omni-directional uniform distribution $p(\varphi_g^i \mid \theta, m^i) = 1/(2\pi)$.

[11] Due to the use of the local information, the pixel values at the output of such detectors are usually correlated (for instance, the probability of having two adjacent black pixels located in a direction normal to the curve is lower than the product of their individual probabilities, due to local non-maximum suppression), thus violating our independency assumption. We shall neglect the effect of this correlation, but one can use a different probability model that takes account of this correlation (attributing, for instance, smaller probabilities to the case of more than one black pixel located in a normal direction on a curve), at the cost of increasing the amount of computations.

[12] For the sake of simplicity we shall omit the superscript ^{k} from our following expressions.

17.6.3 The MDL criterion

Using the above uniform pdfs, we can rewrite Equation (17.15) as:

$$\begin{aligned} MDL \;=\; & \min_{C^{(k)} \in C, \theta_p} \{ -n_n \log P_n - \bar{n}_n \log(1 - P_n) \\ & -n_l \log P_l - \bar{n}_l \log(1 - P_l) \\ & -n_{lg} \log p_{gb} - (n_l - n_{lg}) \log \tilde{p}_{gb} - \bar{n}_{lg} \log p_{gw} - (\bar{n}_l - \bar{n}_{lg}) \log \tilde{p}_{gw} \\ & -(n_n + \bar{n}_n) \log(\frac{1}{2\pi}) + \tfrac{1}{2} K_c \log N \; \} \end{aligned} \tag{17.16}$$

where n_n and $\bar{n}_n$ are the number of black pixels and the number of white pixels, respectively, not located on the curve set $C^{(k)}$, n_l and $\bar{n}_l$ represent the number of black pixels and white pixels (respectively) located on the curve set $C^{(k)}$, n_{lg} and $\bar{n}_{lg}$ represent the number of perpendicular black pixels and perpendicular white pixels, respectively. K_c is the number of free parameters required to specify the curves.

Notice that since the number of the perpendicular pixels influences the cost function, we expect that using the criterion (17.16) will yield better results than using (17.8) as our criterion (both in locating the curves' end points and in aligning the curves).

The minimizing values for P_l,P_n,p_{gb}, and p_{gw} can be easily obtained by differentiating the above function (17.16):

$$\hat{P}_l = \frac{n_l}{n_l + \bar{n}_l} \qquad \hat{P}_n = \frac{n_n}{n_n + \bar{n}_n}$$

$$\hat{p}_{gb} = \frac{n_{lg}}{2\alpha n_l} \qquad \hat{p}_{gw} = \frac{\bar{n}_{lg}}{2\alpha \bar{n}_l}$$

The minimizing values of the rest of the parameters will be found by the algorithm given below.

Remark: For the sake of simplicity we have assumed identical probabilities P_l,p_{gb}, and p_{gw}, and influence distance w for all the curves. One can assume different parameters for each curve, but the $L(\theta_p^{(k)}|k)$ term in Equation (17.15) can not be dropped in this case, and consequently the code length of the curves parameters must be increased[13]. Besides, the optimal probabilities of each curve have to be computed from the pixels "belonging" to that curve only:

$$\hat{P}_{l_i} = \frac{n_{l_i}}{n_{l_i} + \bar{n}_{l_i}} \qquad \hat{p}_{gb_i} = \frac{n_{lg_i}}{2\alpha n_{l_i}} \qquad \hat{p}_{gw_i} = \frac{\bar{n}_{lg_i}}{2\alpha \bar{n}_{l_i}}$$

where $\hat{P}_{l_i}$, $\hat{p}_{gb_i}$, $\hat{p}_{gw_i}$, n_{l_i}, $\bar{n}_{l_i}$, n_{lg_i}, and $\bar{n}_{lg_i}$ are the estimated probability parameters, the number of the black and white pixels, and the number of perpendicular black and perpendicular white pixels (respectively) in the "influence" area of curve i.

[13] In case the domain of w is limited to a value much smaller than N, the code length needed for describing w can be neglected. Similarly, if the resolution of $\hat{P}_{l_i}$, $\hat{p}_{gb_i}$, $\hat{p}_{gw_i}$ is coarse enough, their code length can be neglected.

17.6.4 The algorithm

The algorithm we use is identical to the algorithm described in Section 17.5, with the following modifications:

- While performing the HT, we increment for each black pixel, only the "perpendicular" cells, i.e. those cells that represent curves with a normal deviating no more than α from the gradient direction at that pixel. By doing this we are reducing the amount of computations, and we are also reducing the contribution of the background noise points (by an average factor of $\frac{2\alpha}{2\pi}$, assuming that gradient direction is uniformly distributed in those points).
- Due to the fact that the probability that a noise point located within a cell domain will contribute a vote to the cell is $\frac{2\alpha}{2\pi}$, we have to modify the expression for the candidacy criterion (17.11), replacing P_n by $(P_n\alpha/\pi)$.
- We use the following Δ function in the swath segmentation algorithm:

$$\Delta(s) = a_g n_s - b_g \bar{n}_s + c_g n_{sg} + d_g \bar{n}_{sg}$$

where:

$$a_g \triangleq \log\left[\frac{2\pi\tilde{p}_{gb}P_l}{P_n}\right] \quad b_g \triangleq \log\left[\frac{1-P_n}{2\pi\tilde{p}_{gw}(1-P_l)}\right] \quad c_g \triangleq \log\left[\frac{p_{gb}}{\tilde{p}_{gb}}\right] \quad d_g \triangleq \log\left[\frac{p_{gw}}{\tilde{p}_{gw}}\right]$$

17.7 Examples

17.7.1 A synthetic image

To assess the method described in Section 5, we created a set of 100×100 pixel synthetic images, using a Gaussian cross-sectional pdf for the lines:

$$p(u_i = 1 \mid d) = P_n + P_l \exp -(\frac{d^2}{2\sigma^2})$$

where d is the distance of the center of the i-th pixel from the nearest line. Notice that this model deviates from the uniform model. The true lines are shown in 17.5(a), and the synthetic image is shown in 17.5(b). The parameters used for creating this image were:

$P_l = (0.4, 0.2, 0.4, 0.8, 0.3, 0.5, 0.4)$ for lines 1-7, respectively; $P_n = 0.04$; and $\sigma = 3$.

The probability model we used for detecting the lines was the uniform model (not taking advantage of our knowledge about the true (Gaussian) model used to generate the images). The algorithm described in Section 5 was implemented with a slight modification: we estimated P_l for each line separately, dividing the number

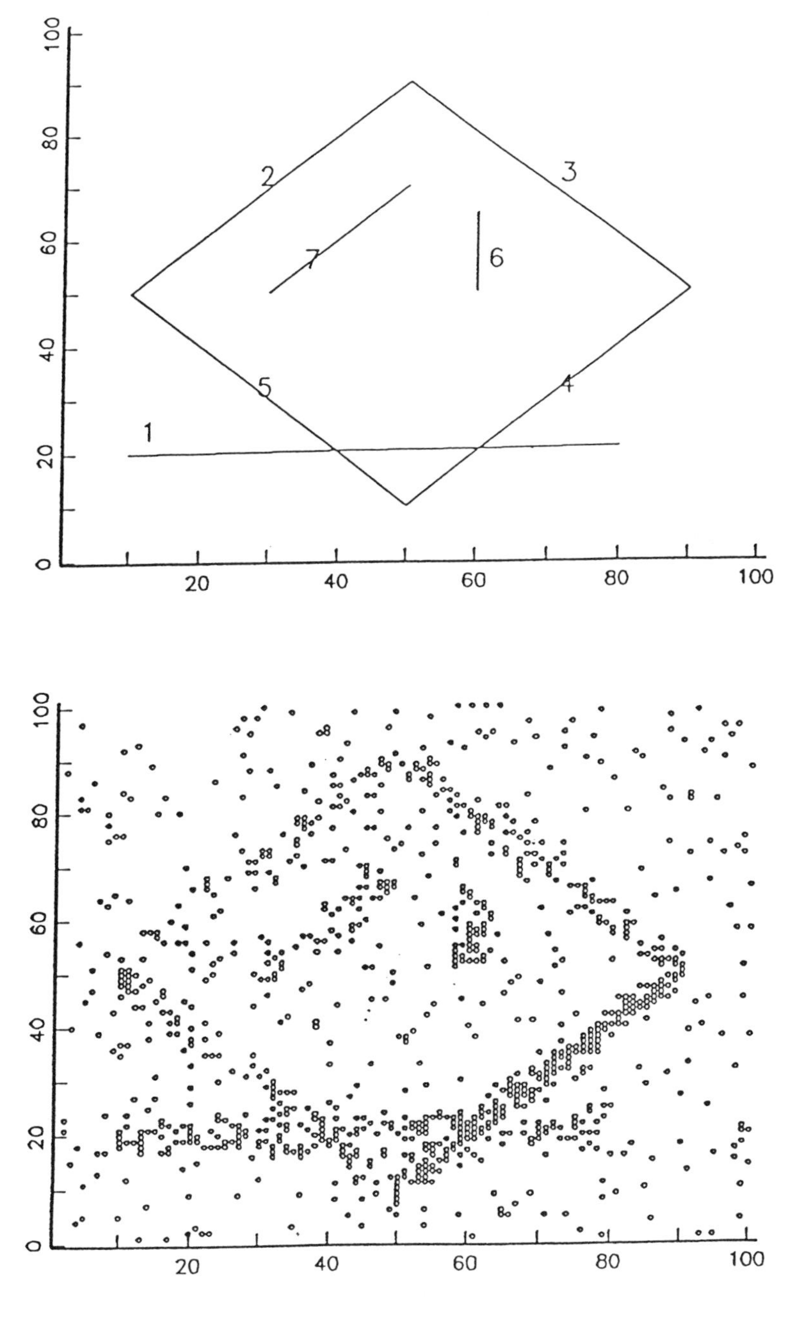

Figure 17.5: The synthetic image test case. (a) The true lines. (b) The (noisy) generated edgels.

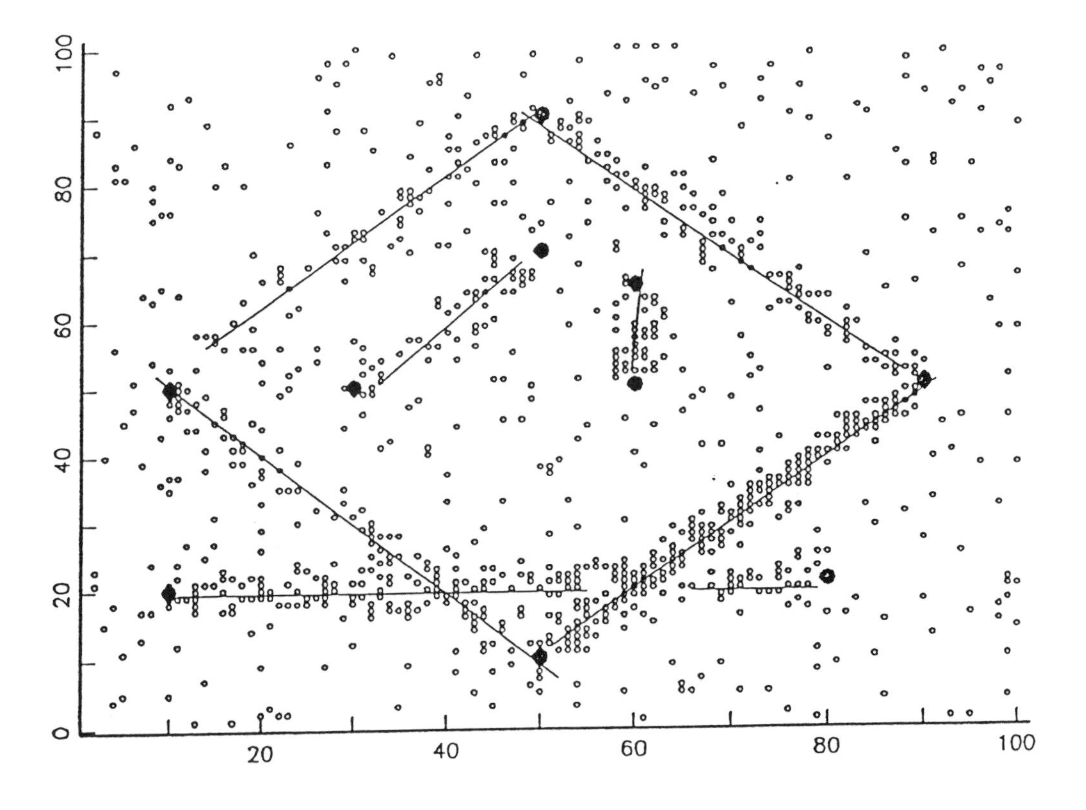

Figure 17.5: (Continued) The synthetic image test case. (c) The located lines. The heavy dots show the true line segment endpoints.

of the black pixels by the total number of the pixels in the fine-tuned line-segment. The resolution of the HT grid was: $\Delta\phi = 2$ degrees, $\Delta\rho = 2$, $2\delta_0 = 4$. The initial estimates were:

$$\hat{w} = 3; \quad \hat{P}_n = 0.5N_b/N; \quad \hat{P}_l = 2\hat{P}_n$$

where N_b is the total number of black pixels in the given image. The fine tuning range for $\hat{w}$ was [3,4,5,6].

The simulation was run numerous times, the difference being the random noise that was added. A typical result is shown in 17.5(c). Only 2 iterations (step (6) in the main algorithm) were needed to get the results shown, where the large black dots denote the true end-points.

The elimination of the detected line points (step (5) in the algorithm) can unduly create gaps in new lines intersecting the already detected lines, as can be seen in the lower horizontal line of 17.5(c). This phenomenon can be avoided by adding a procedure that will perform the swath segmentation algorithm on the original image and compare the results with the results obtained with the dwindled image, filling up gaps caused by the elimination step.

17.7.2 Real images

The method that uses the gradient direction was applied to the 8-bit per pixel 106×106[14] digital picture shown in Figure 17.6a. A simple thresholded gradient magnitude edge detection scheme was used, where the gradient was computed by convolving the picture with the following (Sobel like) masks:

$$G_x = \begin{bmatrix} 0.5 & 1 & 0.5 \\ 1 & 2 & 1 \\ 0 & 0 & 0 \\ -1 & -2 & -1 \\ -0.5 & -1 & -0.5 \end{bmatrix} \qquad G_y = G_x^T$$

The points shown in Figure 17.6b designate pixels in which the gradient magnitude exceeded a threshold level. The line segments shown in Figure 17.6b were detected by the algorithm described in Section 6 with the following modifications:

- The range of the gradient direction was limited to $[0, \pi]$ (by modulo π operation).
- We assumed that both black pixels and white pixels located on a line segment have the same gradient direction distribution. (In other words, we constrained[15] $p_{gb} = p_{gw}$).

[14] The reason for this strange number is that the boundaries of the convolution output are useless, yielding a 100×100 image when omitted.

[15] The reason for this constraint is the fact that the number of white pixels on each line segment is not large enough to enable reliable estimation of p_{gw}.

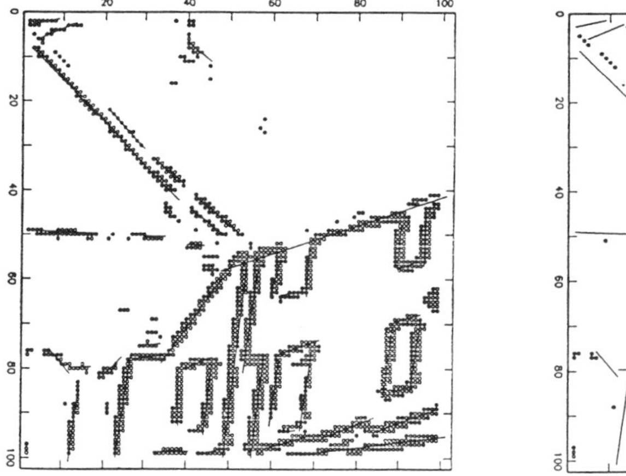

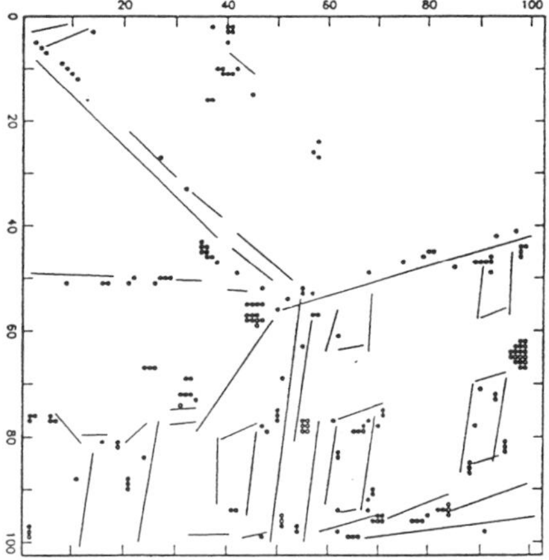

Figure 17.6: (a) Test image of a house. (b) The detected edgels with located line segments overlaid. (c) The detected segments and noise edgels.

- The search for additional line segments was continued even if no line segment had been detected (by the swath-segmentation algorithm) in the current swath. The search was stopped the first time a cell with a count less than the average background noise count (i.e. $CR(i) \leq 0$) had been selected by the algorithm as the most likely to contain a line segment. Every time a barren swath was encountered, we set to zero the cell associated with it and its closest neighbors in order to prevent a repeated selection of this swath by the algorithm. This modification enabled us to detect some of the small line segments shown in Figure 17.6b.

We used $\alpha = \pi/18$ and the following initial parameters:

$$\hat{w}_i = 1 \ , \ \hat{P}_n = 0.03 \ , \ \hat{P}_{li} = 0.8 \ , \ \hat{p}_{gb_i} = 5/\pi \quad (\forall i).$$

The HT resolution was: $\Delta\phi = 1$ degree, $\Delta\rho = 1$, $2\delta_0 = 2$, and we estimated the parameters of each curve separately, with the fine-tuning range for $\hat{w}_i$ being $[1, 2, 3]$.

The results shown in Figure 17.6c are substantially better than what could have been achieved without using the gradient direction (i.e. using (17.8) as our criterion). The improvement is expressed both in (1) better location of the lines' end-points (without the gradient direction some of the lines extended to neighboring edge pixels when the gap between the true end-points and the neighbors was small) and (2) better orientation of some of the short segments. Also, exploiting the white pixels gradient direction helps the algorithm in deciding whether to create a gap in a line: if the majority of the white pixels are perpendicular, a gap is not formed in spite of the lack of black pixels (as manifested in the horizontal (lower) boundary of the main roof).

Figure 17.6c shows the detected lines along with the background noise points (i.e. points not associated with any line). This last figure suggests that in case the background noise is not homogenous, a non-constant probability function $p_n(z)$ can be estimated.

Figures 17.7, 17.8, and 17.9 show three additional examples. In each case, the original image, the computed edgels, and the detected line segments are shown. All are run with the identical algorithm.

The original in Figure 17.7 is a 256x256 image of a house. Gaps exist in the edgels (not visible at the scale shown) but the detected line segments cover many of these and match well the set of edgels. The optimal width w was found to be 1. Figure 17.8, of an airplane, is 100x100. In this example, cases occur where two parallel edges are visible in the image, but the algorithm found three, such as along the front edges of the wings. This is because the same value of the width w is used to find all segments in the image, and is not currently adjusted on a segment by segment basis. (The value of w is adjusted for each segment in the fine tuning procedure, but this is after the segment is found.) The triple lines were correctly found as doubles during the seach over larger w, but the result shown ($w = 3$) gave the shorter codelength over the entire image. The printed circuit board image is 300x300. The detected segments include essentially all of the pattern boundaries in

Figure 17.7: Test image of a house. The original grey level image, the computed edgels, and the detected line segments are shown.

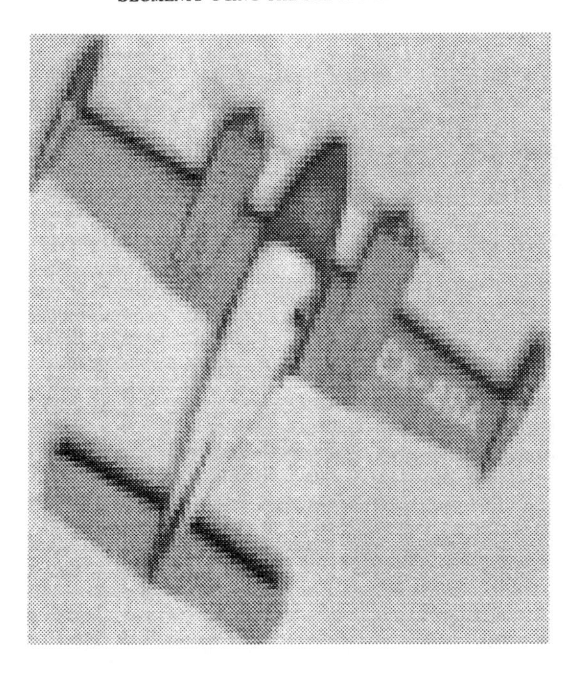

Figure 17.8: Test image of an airplane. The original grey level image, the computed edgels, and the detected line segments are shown.

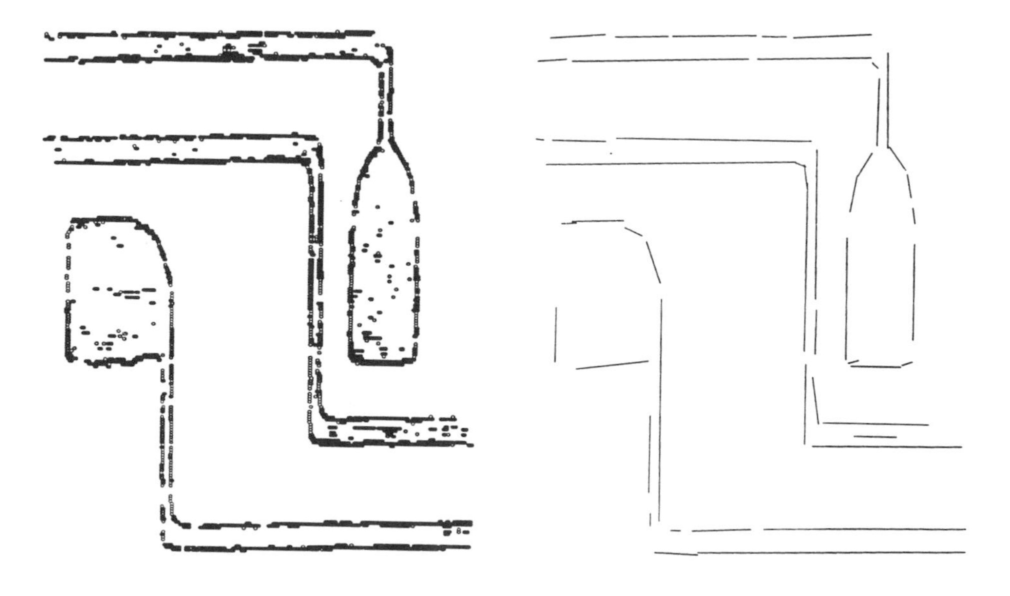

Figure 17.9: Test image of a printed circuit board. The original grey level image, the computed edgels, and the detected line segments are shown.

the image, excluding the noise edgels. Here the optimal value of w is 2.

17.8 Discussion

We have described an algorithm that combines the Hough transform, MDL, and various models of noise probability (both about the line segments and in the background) to find line segments in an image. Notice that a full model of all the data was necessary – everything was described, even the background noise points, and there is no data that is rejected or ignored. This is true in general with MDL methods, and thus they are strongly model based. To the extent that the model class can explain the data, the methods will work well. Otherwise they will not. It is up to the algorithm designer to define a "good" model class, so the issue becomes one of careful modelling. This may be difficult – for example, maybe the noise isn't Gaussian after all. However, similar to a use of MAP methods in which an attempt is made to determine real prior distributions, using MDL forces the designer to study the fundamental physical problem being addressed.

Secondly, MDL methods provide a way of avoiding certain thresholds. As an example, in the case considered in this chapter, we did not have a threshold k in some linking rule: "Link together two sets of edgels that are separated by a gap of k pixels". If the codelength is shorter when the two sets are considered as one segment, they are " linked". Otherwise they are not. No explicit rule and associated threshold is necessary. This is not to say all arbitrariness is removed. However, in MDL it is in the selection of the form of the various models (i.e. the set of possible curve types and the functional forms of the probability models used) to consider. This is at a higher level than selecting thresholds and the results obtained are less sensitive to such choices than they are to the values of parameters (thresholds). Also, of course, the model class, $\mathcal{M}$, may include as many functional forms as one wishes to consider. Though the price to be paid in computation for exercising this option may be considerable.

Thirdly, in the case where parameters are used, they are naturally set to their codelength-minimizing values, i.e. there is a fixed, algorithmic way to establish parameter values. Such was the case with our line segment parameters and the segment width parameter w. The disadvantage is that there may be no analytic way (e.g. taking derivatives, gradient descent) to find the minimizing values. If no better technique can be found, they must be searched for by (typically expensive) exhaustive searching. But, as for the parameters of the line segments in our application, often a suboptimal but useful search technique can be found.

Another property of an MDL derived solution is that it satisfies an optimality criterion, namely minimal codelength (within the model class). For many algorithms, the result is not optimal in any meaningful sense, it is only the result of the algorithm. One can argue that an optimality criterion is not necessary, or, if so, that minimal codelength is not the best measure. However, we suggest it as one valuable criterion (perhaps among many), and it has both a strong intuitive basis, and increasing experimental evidence of providing useful results.

Concerning methods with adjustable thresholds, they are valuable and appropriate in many cases. Practical industrial machine vision systems, for example, almost always use some forms of thresholds. Given a stable set of images (which may cover a very broad range), methods using carefully set thresholds work well. (We would guess, in fact, that a threshold value that works is near the codelength minimizing value of the problem when posed using MDL.) However, given the current interest and need in computer vision for general robust methods, and the limitations of fixed threshold algorithms, MDL techniques provide one approach to improved robustness.

17.9 Conclusion

We have described a method to detect multiple parameterized curve segments — determine the number of curves, the parameters of each curve, and their endpoints — from the set of edgels in an image. We have combined MDL with the Hough transform, each complementing the other, to provide a fast and robust method. The segments produced are very pleasing, and well-suited to subsequent processing such as high-level scene interpretation.

The method may be extended in numerous ways – to allow parameters w and P_l to be computed for each segment, to handle higher order curve segments, etc. One promising extension is to model thin edges such as produces by a Canny or Marr-Hildreth operators. Finally, the general methods of MDL can find applications in many other important problems in machine vision such as image segmentation, model based vision, shape descriptors, and motion analysis.

References

[1] D. Marr and E. Hildreth. Theory of edge detection. *Proc. Royal Society of London*, B207:187–217, 1980.

[2] John Canny. A computational approach to edge detection. *IEEE PAMI*, 8(6):679–698, November 1986.

[3] Ramakant Nevatia and K. Ramesh Babu. Linear feature extraction and detection. *Computer Graphics and Image Processing*, 13:257–269, 1980.

[4] D. M. McKeown, W. A. Harvey, and J. McDermott. Rule based interpretation of aerial imagery. *IEEE PAMI*, 7(5):570–585, September 1985.

[5] A. M. Nazif and M. D. Levine. Low level image segmentation: An expert system. *IEEE PAMI*, 6:555–577, 1984.

[6] J. Brian Burns, Allen Hanson, and Edward Riseman. Extracting straight lines. *IEEE PAMI*, 8(4):425–455, 1986.

[7] P. L. Rosin and G. A. W. West. Segmentation of edges into lines and arcs. *Image and Vision Computing*, 7:109–114, 1989.

[8] G. A. W. West and P. L. Rosin. Techniques for segmenting image curves into meaningful lines. *Pattern Recognition*, 24(7):643–652, 1991.

[9] Michael Boldt, Richard Weiss, and Edward Riseman. Token-based extraction of straight lines. *IEEE T-SMC*, 19(6):1581–1594, 1989.

[10] C. S. Wallace and D. M. Boulton. An information measure for classification. *Computer Journal*, 11(2):185–194, 1968.

[11] J. Segen and A. C. Anderson. A minimal representation criterion for clustering. In *Proc. 12th ann Comp Sci and Stat Symp*, pages 332–334, 1979.

[12] J. Rissanen. *Stochastic Complexity in Statistical Inquiry*, volume 15. World Scientific Series in Computer Science, 1989.

[13] B. Dom, W. Niblack, and J. Sheinvald. Feature selection with stochastic complexity. In *Proceedings of the IEEE Conference on Computer Vision and Pattern Recognition (CVPR) 1989*, pages 241–248, 1989.

[14] Trevor Darrell, Stan Sclaroff, and Alex Pentland. Segmentation by minimal description. In *Proceedings of the IEEE Third International Conference on Computer Vision (ICCV) 1990*, pages 112–116, Osaka, Japan, December 1990.

[15] Trevor Darrell and Alex Pentland. Recovery of minimal descriptions using parallel robust estimation. Technical Report 163, Vision and Modelling Group, Media Lab, MIT, February 1991.

[16] Y. G. Leclerc. Constructing simple stable descriptions for image partitioning. *International Journal of Computer Vision*, 3(1):73–102, May 1989.

[17] P. Fua and A. J. Hanson. Extracting generic shapes using model driven optimization. In *Proceedings of the Image Understanding Workshop*, pages 994–1004, Boston, 1988.

[18] M. Max and T. Kailath. Detection of signals by information theoretic criteria. *IEEE ASSP*, 33(2), April 1985.

[19] J. Sheinvald, B. Dom, and W. Niblack. Feature selection for classification using the mdl principle. *IBM Research Report RJ 7117*, 1989.

[20] J. Sheinvald, B. Dom, and W. Niblack. A modeling approach to feature selection. In *Proceedings of the 10th International Conference on Pattern Recognition (ICPR)*, pages 535–539, Atlantic City, NJ, June 1990.

[21] I. Weiss. Line fitting in a noisy image. *IEEE PAMI*, 11(3), March 1989.

[22] J. Rissanen. Modelling by shortest data description. *Automatica*, 14:465–471, 1978.

[23] R. W. Hamming. *Coding and Information Theory.* Prentice-Hall, New York, 1980.

[24] Grahame B. Smith. Image-to-image correspondence: Linear structure mapping. Technical Report Technical Note 331, SRI International, July 1984.

[25] J. Illingworth and J. Kittler. A survey of the hough transform. *Computer Vision, Graphics, and Image Processing*, 44:87–116, 1988.

[26] W. Niblack and D. Petkovic. On improving the accuracy of the hough transform. *Machine Vision and Applications*, 3(2):87–106, 1990.

[27] N. Kiryati and A. M. Bruckstein. Anti-aliasing the hough transform. Technical Report EE Publication No. 697, Technion, December 1988.

[28] A. Papoulis. *Probability, Random Variables, and Stochastic Processes.* McGraw-Hill, 1965.

[29] Melvin Cohen and Godfried Toussaint. On the detection of structures in noisy pictures. *Pattern Recognition*, 9:95–98, 1977.

[30] D. H. Ballard and C. M. Brown. *Computer Vision.* Prentice-Hall, 1982.

Chapter 18

Estimating Potato Acreage and Yield in the Columbia Basin Using Landsat

G. R. Waddington, C.-F. Chen, L. Mann

18.1 INTRODUCTION

18.1.1 Overview

Accurate and timely regional potato acreage and yield information is valuable to growers and processors for use in marketing decisions. Cropix, Inc. uses remotely sensed satellite data to monitor potato crops, thereby providing early indications of market conditions and selling the information to growers and processors in the Columbia River Basin. The identification and analysis of potato fields is based on multiple acquisitions of Landsat Multispectral Scanner (MSS) digital data used in an unsupervised clustering approach with masking of multitemporal data sets. The same techniques have been tested using Landsat Thematic Mapper (TM) digital data in anticipation of the eventual retirement of the MSS sensor. Yield prediction is based on a weather driven model with the addition of vegetative indices, derived from satellite data, to approximate planting and die-back dates for yield estimates of each field. Experience has demonstrated that, in an agricultural market, data timeliness is the single most limiting factor when operating a commercial service using Landsat satellite data.

18.1.2 The Cropix service

In 1984, Cropix Inc. was established to provide Columbia River Basin potato growers and processors with acreage estimates derived from Landsat satellite data. Currently, Cropix provides customers with potato market information through a series of reports issued periodically during the growing season. Acreage estimates by county are published in July, followed by acreage accuracy assessments and yield estimates as more satellite data is acquired. The contents of the report include tabular acreage and yield estimates, an accuracy assessment, prints of enhanced Landsat satellite data for the survey area, crop maps generated from classified MSS data, color-coded yield maps showing expected yield for all potato fields, and historical USDA state and national potato statistics. Observations and brief explanations of the results are also included to enhance and clarify report findings.

18.1.3 Value of market information

Potatoes are a high value crop which can be profitable but also risky to grow, requiring daily attention to details such as irrigation, fertilizer application, and disease control. Potato consumption varies little from year to year, resulting in wide price swings relative to small changes in production. Growers face a very significant financial risk as a result of potato price volatility. In 1983, for example, potato prices went from $80 per ton to $130 per ton in 90 days. For a grower who held back 1,000 acres for better markets, the profit margin would approach $1,500,000, assuming a yield of 30 tons per acre. Most potatoes are sold on preseason contracts with processors, the balance of the crop is sold on the "open" market for either processing or fresh produce.

Potato market information is available through the United States Department of Agriculture (USDA), grower's association surveys, potato processor field surveys, and the coffee shop rumor mill. The time of availability for this information is variable and the accuracy can be suspect, leading to incorrect market assumptions. Satellite remote sensing provides an alternative method to estimating crop acreage and yield potential, offering an additional source of market information.

18.1.4 The survey area

The Pacific Northwest accounts for roughly 50% of the nation's potato crop and over 80% of the potato processing. Washington and Oregon are second to Idaho as the largest potato producing states. The survey area, shown in Figure 18.1, covers the irrigated farmland in the Columbia River Basin of Oregon and Washington where approximately 20% of the total US crop is grown. The area is characterized by extensive center pivot irrigation systems drawing water from the Columbia and Snake Rivers and applying it to otherwise dry, desert rangeland. As a result, the landscape is dotted with circular fields which, from the air, appear as a polkadot pattern. Two Landsat MSS scenes cover the 44,000 square kilometer survey area.

18.1.5 Remote sensing in a commercial environment

Potato market information is of greatest value when it is available in a timely manner, since market conditions can change quickly. Cropix focuses on receiving Landsat data as quickly as possible after the satellite passes over, performing the necessary image processing to generate production statistics, and distributing the report to customers in as little time as possible. For the potato market, and other agricultural markets, rapid data turnaround is the only way to provide a commercially viable information service based on satellite data. As pointed out in papers by Ryerson, Dobbins, and Thibault[1], Lo, Scarpace, and Lillesand[2], Hall and Badhwar[3], and Williams[4], remote sensing technology can be used as a tool in agricultural applications; however, its potential for commercial use has not been fully realized. Waddington and Lamb[5] have noted that inadequate data delivery has been the greatest factor limiting the commercial use of remote sensing by the private sector.

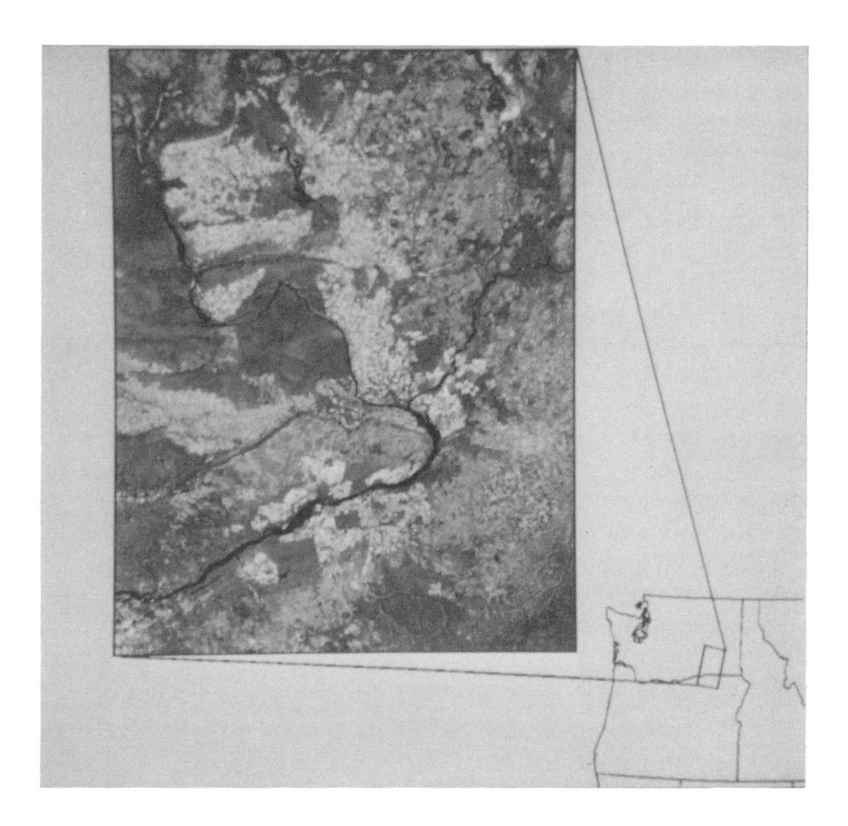

Figure 18.1. The Cropix survey area covering the Columbia River Basin in Oregon and Washington. The majority of the irrigated agriculture is adjacent to rivers and lakes.

Due to delays in satellite image delivery, Cropix has been forced to streamline image processing techniques and report generation in order to deliver market information while it is still fresh. Under funding from NASA's Earth Observation Commercialization Application Program 1 (EOCAP), Cropix has been able to speed image processing time through hardware and software upgrades, and straight forward, accurate, processing techniques. With assistance from NASA Ames Research Center at Moffett Field, California, an easy-to-use, fast, and flexible processing strategy was developed to allow Cropix to get information to customers when it is most useful, and to handle a variety of image data availability scenarios.

The focus of the chapter is to describe techniques established under EOCAP 1 and currently used by Cropix to provide potato acreage and yield estimates from satellite data. A discussion of issues that Cropix has faced using remote sensing and image processing to provide a commercial agricultural information service is also included.

18.2 IMAGE PROCESSING METHODS

18.2.1 Advances under EOCAP 1

The main objective under EOCAP was to develop an easy-to-use, timely image processing procedure, affordable by small business, to estimate potato market statistics using Landsat data. The project team consisted of NASA Ames Research Center, which provided image processing technical support, Oregon State University, which searched for, selected, and implemented a potato yield model, and Cropix, which maintaining the existing commercial service while identifying customer needs. Prior to EOCAP, Cropix procedures were labor intensive and inefficient. Classification of image data required extensive analyst involvement and results were usually unacceptable.

The procedure developed under EOCAP combines the use of unsupervised classification (clustering) with multitemporal masking which reduces analyst involvement, speeds processing time, and generates accurate results. Currently under investigation is the use of a neural network classification algorithm that would take advantage of textural patterns, in addition to spectral characteristics, to identify potato fields and features within fields with a higher degree of accuracy than current image processing techniques.

18.2.2 Multiple Landsat MSS acquisitions

To take advantage of the different crop growing cycles for improved crop identification, Cropix acquires multiple Landsat MSS scenes during the growing season. A single acquisition does not provide enough information to accurately identify potatoes. In the months of April and May, the main crops which have a green canopy are alfalfa, wheat, and pasture. Corn and potatoes are still underground or barely emerging. An MSS acquisition during this time period allows for identification of these crops. By early June, the majority of potato fields have a large enough canopy to be identified with the MSS data. Satellite data at this time, or within a month, is used for locating and counting potato acres. Later season satellite data acquisitions are useful for separating out some of the fresh vegetable crops; however, these crops make up only a small percentage of all other crops different from potatoes. Satellite data throughout the growing season are also used for tracking potato field growth and estimating planting and die-back dates, critical to accurate yield prediction using the yield model.

The Landsat MSS sensor records electromagnetic energy reflected from the earth's surface in four distinct bands. These are MSS band 1, recording energy in the region from 0.5-0.6μm, MSS band 2, recording in the region from 0.6-0.7μm, MSS band 3, recording in the region from 0.7-0.8μm, and MSS band 4, recording in the region from 0.8-1.1μm. These band passes are suited to identifying different types of ground features such as urban area, roads, surface water, geological structure, and particularly, the vegetation.

18.2.3 Masking and combining multiple MSS acquisitions

In order to improve the classification of potatoes, other confusion crops are eliminated through the use of masking and combining multiple image data sets. In addition, a digitized non-irrigated land mask is applied to all acquisitions, since these areas do not contain any irrigated agriculture. Masking also speeds processing time. Using an early season MSS scene, wheat, alfalfa, and pasture are identified and masked out. The image data is first combined with the non-irrigated land mask, then run through a euclidean distance clustering algorithm to generate spectral classes for assigning to crop types. Wheat, alfalfa, and pasture fields have a full green canopy by April, and, as a result, have a high infrared (IR) reflectance. Potato fields, at this time, are bare soil with no above soil growth until May. By using large separability distances for clusters and large sampling intervals, 10 to 15 spectral classes are generated. The resulting spectral classes have large differences in IR reflectance.

Spectral class clusters are identified by examining spectral plots, generated from the statistics output of the clustering algorithm. Further verification is made by comparing the location and type of crop for a sampling of fields observed from the ground (commonly termed "ground truth") with what the classified data shows. An example of the spectral class plots for a May 8, 1989 MSS scene are shown in Figure 18.2, all ten resulting classes are shown. This type of two dimensional graph allows for the evaluation of curve shapes for initial separation. Interpretation of spectral classes to mask involves observing the pattern of the spectral curves, specifically comparing values from both IR bands, MSS 3 and 4 with the red band, MSS 2, and looking for large increases between MSS 2 versus MSS 3 and MSS 4. This is the characteristic spectral pattern for green foliage.

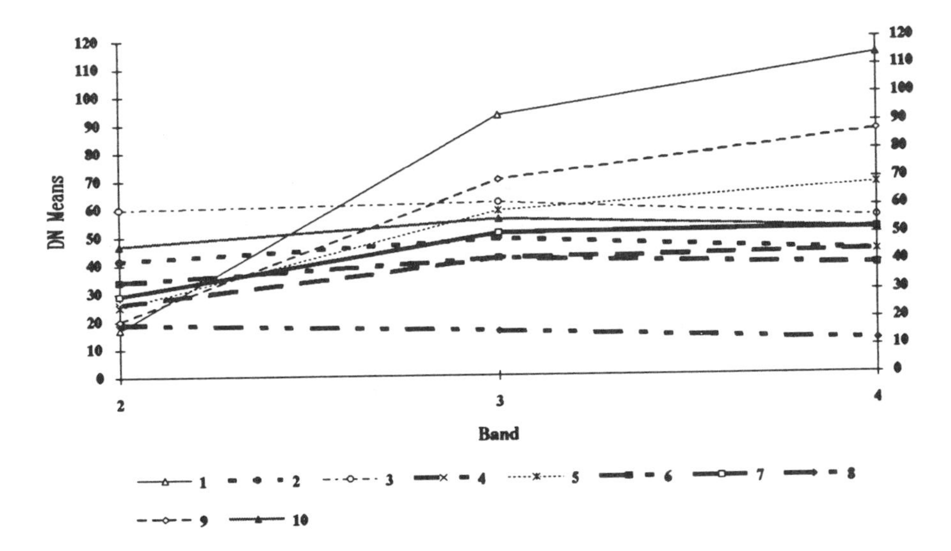

Figure 18.2. Spectral plots of classes resulting from clustering a May 8, 1989 MSS scene. Classes 1, 5 and 9 are probable alfalfa, wheat, and pasture.

Spectral classes with high IR and low red reflectance in the May image data are verified, with the aid of available ground truth, to be crops other than potatoes. These classes are renumbered to 0 and all other classes to 1, creating a mask image. Masking is used to reduce the confusion between potatoes and non-potatoes when later MSS data is processed.

The next stage in the process involves the combination of the wheat and alfalfa mask with a June or July acquisition (mid-season) for use in locating potato fields. The mask is registered to the mid-season image data, instead of registering the mid-season image data to the mask, in order to avoid re-sampling spectral data and further degrading spectral quality. Difficulties encountered in using this process are discussed in a later section on image data files. Once registered, the mid-season image data is multiplied by the mask, effectively removing all wheat, alfalfa, and pasture fields. An example of the result is shown in Plate 18.1a (see page 544), where a 1024x1024 pixel window has been masked by both the digitized sage/range mask and the wheat/alfalfa mask.

The masked mid-season image data is run through the cluster algorithm to generate spectral classes for subsequent categorizing into potato, corn, other crop, and sage/range crop classes. Plotting the output statistics from the cluster algorithm allows for initial identification of probable potato spectral classes. Figure 18.3 shows plots of spectral class means for a June 25, 1989 MSS scene which has been masked. Classes with a corresponding low red/high IR spectral response are labeled as potential potato classes. With the addition of ground truth information, further differentiation between corn and potatoes is accomplished. Frequently, a few small regions in the survey area need the addition of supervised training sites to get better separation between corn and potato fields. Some spectral classes generated from clustering straddle potato and corn clusters, making it impossible to separate the crops. Since separability distances within the cluster algorithm are set for finding spectral classes with large differences in IR reflectance, smaller differences are sometimes lost. The finer distinctions between corn and potatoes for these regions can be restored by using additional supervised spectral classes.

Using a preliminary accuracy spot check, the classified image data are assessed to determine whether or not an acceptable level of accuracy has been achieved. Typically, if potato fields are located correctly 90 to 95% of the time with commission and omission errors of less than 15% for either, then the classified image data is considered acceptable and acres of potatoes can be tabulated. An attempt is made to reach this condition for all areas in the survey area. When this is not possible, the best possible accuracy is achieved with the available data and refinement is accomplished with later satellite data acquisitions.

18.2.4 Acreage tabulation with digitized field boundaries

The procedure of acreage tabulation begins with the final classified image data files. Plate 18.1b (see page 544) shows an example of a 1024x1024 pixel window within a classified image data file. Field boundaries have been digitized for approximately 7,000 fields in the survey area. With each field boundary, there is a unique center point coordinate and acreage attribute, which was calculated when the field was first digitized. The acreage is based on the number of pixels within the boundary. Landsat TM data is used as a guide when digitizing, since the increased resolution (30mx30m pixel versus 60mx60m MSS pixel) minimizes the guesswork involved in locating the edge of the field.

The center point coordinate acts as a database record key for each field. Within the database, information for each field is stored and used to assess various features characteristic to the field such as previous year's crop, ownership, MSS band means and various vegetative indices calculated for each satellite data acquisition. Using automated techniques, the classified image data file is analyzed and the center point coordinates for fields identified as potatoes are stored in an output file. This file of potato field center points is imported to the database where acreage tabulation occurs. Within the database, each field is referenced to geographic location, such as the county within which it belongs. This allows for acreage estimates to be presented as county totals, as well as state and Columbia Basin totals. Potato acreage broken down by county is available through the USDA in November of the following year.

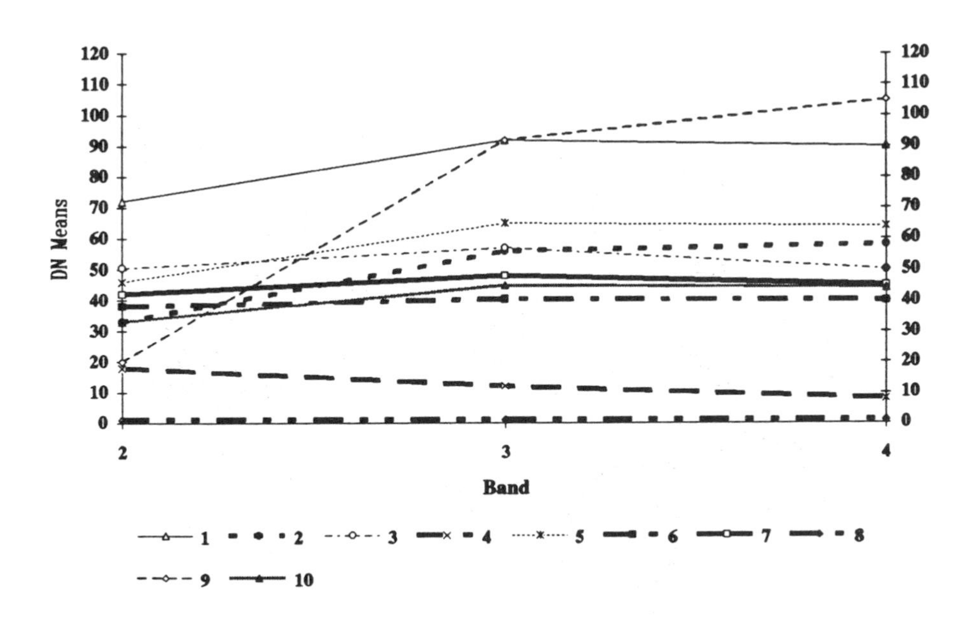

Figure 18.3. Spectral plots of classes resulting from clustering a masked June 25, 1989 MSS scene. Classes 5 is the mask and Classes 1 and 9 are probable potatoes.

Plate 18.1a. An example of the non-irrigated land and wheat/alfalfa masks applied to a mid-season MSS image for input to the clustering algorithm.

Plate 18.1b. A final crop map used for counting acres of potatoes. Potato fields are color-coded red, alfalfa fields are green, corn fields are cyan, wheat fields are yellow, white is rangeland, and blue is water.

18.2.5 Image data files

The entire survey area is covered by two Landsat MSS scenes, Path 44 Row 27 and Path 44 Row 28, each roughly 3,000 scan lines by 3,500 pixels. The full scenes are subset into two sets of image data files 2,500 pixels by 1,200 and 2,500 scan lines, which cover completely the major potato growing areas. Image processing is performed on these large files to speed processing time and limit the amount of analyst intervention. The 1024x1024 pixel window, set by the resolution of the graphics card, is used for evaluating image processing results, and printing enhanced satellite data and crop classification maps.

Experience with Landsat MSS data has shown a deterioration of geometric quality within the data, requiring more effort to register successive image dates. By selecting numerous ground control points, one image data file can be rubber-sheeted to register with a second image data file. Purchasing Landsat data already corrected to a map projection would make registration easy; however, the processing time required by the Earth Observation Satellite Corporation (EOSAT) to generate and deliver the product would jeopardize the commercial viability of the Cropix product.

18.2.6 Flexible procedures for varying conditions

Although the processing steps appear fairly straight forward, there are needs to have some flexibility built into the techniques and strategies in order to handle situations when timely data is not available or too cloudy, or when crop conditions due to seasonal variations result in modified crop calendars. To demonstrate this situation, the following example has been provided.

More frequent cloud cover in the spring months can limit the ability to generate a complete wheat/alfalfa mask. This has been a common occurrence for the last 4 years. For the 1991 growing season, the early spring MSS acquisition (April 20) was not sufficient for complete wheat masking since there had been a substantial number of fields which were obscured by cloud, and other fields which had suffered winter wheat kill and been replanted to spring wheat. The spring wheat was not far enough in development to have a high IR/low red reflectance. The winter wheat kill was more of a problem in the northern half of the survey area where planting dates for all crops tend to trail the southern half by about 1 to 2 weeks. Cloud cover was widespread in the south. As a result, it was necessary to use two spring MSS dates to create a more thorough wheat/alfalfa mask.

The two MSS data sets were combined in the same way that the wheat/alfalfa mask is combined with the mid-season image data acquisition. Clustering the masked second spring image data set was aimed at deriving spectral classes with a high IR/low red reflectance, without picking up any potato fields, which were beginning to show a partial canopy at this time in the season. After identifying spectral classes that represent spring wheat, the final wheat/alfalfa mask was created by assigning all pixels classified as spring wheat to 0 and all else to 1, with the exception of the already masked area, which was left unchanged.

Image processing procedures are performed in a way to optimize the identification of potato fields given any combination of available satellite data. The estimated acreage for potatoes needs to be as accurate as possible, even at the expense of the correct identification of other crops. An effort is made to get a 70% correct location on the other main crops (alfalfa, wheat, corn), but the focus is on finding potato fields correctly 90 to 95% of the time. These levels of accuracy are excellent in the remote sensing field, but a 10% error in estimated acreage can be very significant to the customer who has thousands of dollars invested in a crop.

18.2.7 Neural Networks Classifier for Crop and Feature Detection

Using remotely sensed data for production management is another key component that has recently been added to Cropix existing services. The production management factors include irrigation hardware problem detection, plant growth uniformity, nutrient, and water stresses detection. Features to be detected for production management purposes are far more complex in nature than those used in land use/cover classification due to temporal and spatial variations in spectral signatures. Conventional classification algorithms use minimum distance to means or maximum likelihood decision rules are not always appropriate when the features of interest are not well-defined. Figure 18.4 shows a schematic diagram outlining the operation of the conventional and neural network classifiers.

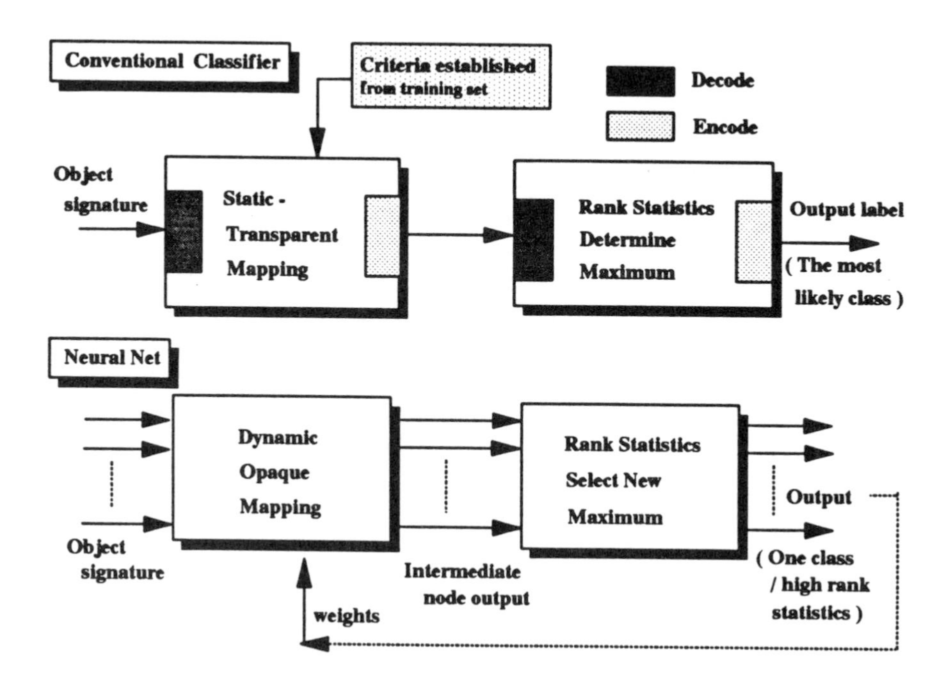

Figure 18.4. Comparison of the conventional statistical classifier algorithm and the neural networks algorithm.

Image processing procedures combining neural networks, texture analysis, and fuzzy set theory are being adopted as a tool for production management. The classifier is designed and configured as a fully interconnected back propagation network (with 3 layers including a hidden layer) as shown in Figure 18.5. The designed network is capable of handling *N* multispectral band inputs. The structure of this network configuration is summarized in the following paragraphs.

The first layer is the input layer which includes *Nx3x3* neurons, where *N* is the number of spectral bands used in the classification. The typical *3x3* convolution window is implemented to handle texture information during training process.

The second layer makes up a hidden layer. The optimal choice of the number of ***layer units*** remains a debatable issue. The previous experience indicated that the classification error of an ideally trained neural network classifier does not increase by introducing new hidden layer elements. Generally, too many neurons in this layer could trap the network within a localized minima. Too few neurons in this layer would cause the network fail to generate an internal crop type representation during the input signal partition process. In a typical growing season, when 9 to 12 different crops and ground cover types are generally identified, a hidden layer with 15 to 20 layer units should be appropriate.

The third and final layer is the output layer. The output layer is composed of ***P*** units (neurons), where ***P*** is the desired number of crop/ground cover types.

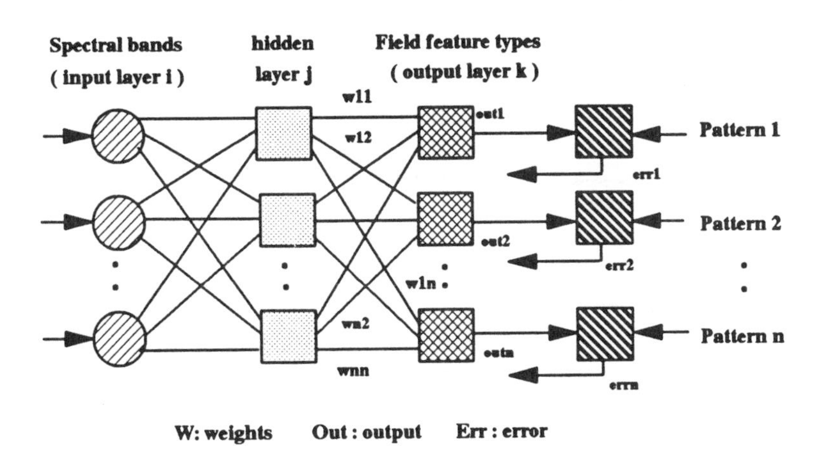

Figure 18.5. Schematic diagram of the Back Propagation Network for field pattern recognition.

The accuracy of the back propagation neural network classifier (BPNN) was compared to the minimum distance to means and the maximum likelihood classifier, with the results shown in Table 18.1. The comparison was performed using May 10, 1988 SPOT HRV satellite image data.

Table 18.1. Comparison of accuracies achieved using the minimum distance, maximum likelihood, and neural network classifiers.

Classification Algorithm	Accuracy Bounds	Confidence Level
Minimum Distance	< 0.868,0.943 >	95%
Maximum Likelihood	< 0.849,0.912 >	95%
Neural Networks	< 0.911,0.933 >	95%

The properly trained neural network classifier demonstrates reasonable accuracy when compared to conventional classifiers. The narrow accuracy bounds also indicate the neural network's capability to resolve spectral signatures from different confusion crops.

18.3 CLASSIFICATION ACCURACY

18.3.1 Ground truth collection

In order to verify the location and crop types found through the analysis of satellite data, known areas on the ground are used for comparison with the crop classification. Cropix collects ground truth during the growing season by driving the public roads and using a combination of maps, derived from the satellite data and field boundary files, and a GPS (Global Positioning System) locator, to verify the ground truth collectors location on the ground.

The GPS receiver uses signals from NAVSTAR, a constellation of satellites designed by the U.S Defense Department, to calculate its position on the earth's surface to within 15 meters. This tool helps the ground truth collector to align the satellite-derived maps with conditions on the ground, since changes can occur between the current season and previous season which are not reflected in maps created from previous year's satellite data. The readings stored in the GPS receiver are downloaded to a personal computer where they are translated into a common reference frame and displayed on the satellite data. Then the ground truth information can be entered into the database through the use of the digitized field boundary files with the addition of GPS waypoints for verification.

The sampling scheme involves the use of a stratified random sample in order to limit bias in the accuracy computation. This is important since the accuracy results are used to adjust acreage estimates. By sampling a number of fields for each crop in an amount proportional to the distribution of these crops in the entire population, representative accuracies are achieved. The ground truth collector travels transects, designed from the existing road network, to collect information in a well distributed manner throughout the survey area. From the information brought back by the ground truth collector, random selection is made, since it is easier for the person in the field to collect as much information as possible instead of randomly selecting fields to drive to and noting the type of crop grown.

On the average, roughly 280 potato fields are identified on the ground for the entire survey area. The accuracy analysis is performed in the database for ease of computation and the results are used to modify final potato acreage estimates. By comparing the omission and commission errors, an offset is found which is used to adjust the acreage estimate up or down according to the classification accuracy.

18.3.2 Accuracies for 1991

The overall accuracy for the 1991 season, as summarized in Table 18.2, was a 95% correct identification of potato fields. This represents the column accuracy. More specifically, of 265 ground truth potato fields, 252 were correctly located on the classifications. This means that only 5% of the ground truth potato fields were classified as another crop (5% omission error). The row accuracy for potatoes was 93%, or 7% of other crop fields were classified as potatoes (7% commission error). The resulting offset of omission and commission errors was roughly a 2% overestimation of potato fields, and the associated acreage. For the customer using the classified image data maps, 95% of the potato fields have been correctly identified on the map, but only 93% of those fields classified as potatoes are actually potato fields on the ground.

The accuracy for the survey area is also broken down by county to provide an indication of where the classification is more or less accurate. Generally, the northern part of the survey area has lower accuracies than the rest of the area. The northern part is characterized by smaller fields and smaller farms with more varied management practices. There are also greater variations in soil types and topography, which contribute to lower levels of success mapping potato fields. The percentage of the total acreage for the survey area found in the northern part is small, so that lower accuracies are accepted.

Table 18.2. Classification accuracy for the entire survey area in 1991.

	TRUTH					
CLASSIFICATION	Potatoes	Corn	Wheat/alfalfa	Other	Total	Row Accuracy
Potatoes	252	4	13	4	273	92%
Corn	9	125	42	5	181	69%
Wheat/Alfalfa	3	26	307	28	364	84%
Other	1	31	17	30	79	38%
Total	265	186	379	67	714	
Column Accuracy	95%	67%	81%	45%		80%

18.3.3 Results using Landsat TM

Under the EOCAP study, comparisons between using Landsat TM and MSS data were undertaken since MSS data may not be available in the near future. Although different spectral bands exist between TM and MSS, the same image processing procedures were used to generate crop classifications. The comparison was done using two subscenes covering a portion of the northern and southern basin from satellite data recorded in 1989. This year was selected since Cropix was able to acquire both TM and MSS data for three dates during the season.

The classification accuracies for the TM data were much more varied than with the MSS data. Tables 18.3-18.6 show the error matrices for the classified subscenes. These accuracies were derived using techniques outlined in a paper by Story and Congalton[6]. Overall map accuracy was 54% for the southern subscene and 51% for the northern subscene using MSS (Table 18.3 and 18.4). For potatoes, the southern subscene had a column accuracy (accuracy of mapped classes) of 93% and a row accuracy of 94%. This translates into an 7% error in omission, the percent of potato field identified as non-potatoes, and 6% error in commission, the percent of non-potato fields identified as potatoes. For potatoes in the northern subscene, the column accuracy was 81% and the row accuracy was 73%. These lower accuracies are similar to those achieved in 1991.

For the TM data, overall map accuracy for the southern subscene was 65%, as shown in Table 18.5. The accuracy for potatoes was not as high as with the MSS data. The column accuracy was only 71% while the row accuracy was 94%. This means that while only 71% of the potato fields were correct, 94% of the potatoes were correctly identified. Table 18.6 summarizes the accuracy achieved with the TM data in the north. The northern subscene had an overall accuracy of 29% with a column accuracy of 24% and a row accuracy of 16% for potatoes. This result is substantially worse than what was found using the MSS data. In a paper by Mann, Salute, and Waddington[7], more details about this comparison are provided.

Table 18.3. Error matrix for the southern area MSS data.

	TRUTH						
CLASSIFICATION	Potatoes	Corn	Wheat	Alfalfa	Other	Total	Row Accuracy
Potatoes	272	5	4	4	3	288	94%
Corn	9	96	1	47	18	171	56%
Wheat	0	0	0	0	0	0	0%
Alfalfa	4	4	2	56	1	67	84%
Other	8	13	277	37	81	416	19%
Total	293	118	284	144	103	505	
Column Accuracy	93%	81%	0%	39%	79%		54%

Table 18.4. Error matrix for the northern area MSS data.

CLASSIFICATION	TRUTH						
	Potatoes	Corn	Wheat	Alfalfa	Other	Total	Row Accuracy
Potatoes	29	3	0	7	1	40	73%
Corn	3	13	1	9	2	28	46%
Wheat	3	5	52	5	1	66	79%
Alfalfa	0	0	10	26	7	43	60%
Other	1	55	4	6	10	76	13%
Total	36	76	67	53	21	130	
Column Accuracy	81%	17%	78%	49%	48%		51%

Table 18.5. Error matrix for the southern area TM data.

CLASSIFICATION	TRUTH						
	Potatoes	Corn	Wheat	Alfalfa	Other	Total	Row Accuracy
Potatoes	78	1	1	1	2	83	94%
Corn	0	0	0	0	0	0	0%
Wheat	5	0	122	5	5	136	90%
Alfalfa	19	3	5	82	82	117	70%
Other	8	65	2	33	17	125	14%
Total	110	69	130	121	31	299	
Column Accuracy	71%	0%	94%	68%	55%		65%

Table 18.6. Error matrix for the northern area TM data.

CLASSIFICATION	TRUTH						
	Potatoes	Corn	Wheat	Alfalfa	Other	Total	Row Accuracy
Potatoes	4	0	1	7	13	25	16%
Corn	0	0	3	2	0	5	0%
Wheat	1	1	20	0	1	23	87%
Alfalfa	1	2	0	4	3	10	40%
Other	11	39	2	5	9	66	14%
Total	17	42	26	18	26	37	
Column Accuracy	24%	0%	77%	22%	35%		29%

18.4 POTATO YIELD ESTIMATION

18.4.1 The yield model

In addition to providing estimates of potato acreage, Cropix is able to estimate potato yield with a combination of an empirical yield model, driven primarily by weather, and information derived from satellite data. Of all the models available, the Fishman Model was selected because of its ability to simulate several basic processes that occur in the potato plant and its suitability for use in the survey area. The Fishman Model was developed at the Volcani Institute in Israel by a team of seven scientists led by Dr. Svetlana Fishman.

The model was revised and calibrated, by Oregon State University, to conditions in the Columbia Basin using data collected over a two year period. Two large farms located in the southern part of the survey area were chosen as test sites. The data included farm records on crop treatment, dry weights of plant components, ground cover measurements, in particular, leaf area index (LAI), and spectral data recorded from a spectrometer mounted on a boom truck. Over 34,000 pieces of data were recorded and used to adjust the model and develop relationships between satellite observations and yield model input parameters.

Weather is the major input and has the largest effect on resulting yields. Other variables, such as fertilizer application, irrigation rates, and factors relating to field management, are set to an average value for the Columbia Basin. Weather data is collected from a weather station located in the southern portion of the survey area, weather data from other stations within the Columbia Basin can be used to account for variations in the microclimate across the region.

For reliable yield estimates, the planting and harvest dates for a field or fields has to be known. For growers interested in their own farms, these dates can be provided by the grower. This is not possible to do for all growers in the Columbia Basin, since the number of farms is large, making it impractical to survey growers, and frequently this type of information is proprietary. In order to estimate yield for the Columbia Basin, satellite data is used to approximate planting and harvest dates.

18.4.2 Using satellite data with the model

Acquiring satellite data throughout the growing season provides a means for monitoring potato fields and tracking their development. In order to estimate planting and harvest dates, early and late season Landsat MSS overpasses are used. For the potato fields located by the crop classification, the ratio of IR divided by red reflectance is calculated for pixels extracted from the image data within a sample box centered in each field. With the use of a field spectrometer and field samples, relationships have been derived between the leaf area index and IR/red reflectance. Based on the leaf area index and growing degree days, the emergence date can be estimated and planting date projected back from there.

The harvest date is more difficult to find. For the model, the critical date is the end of dieback, not harvest, since the final yield is not influenced by the length of time from dieback to harvest. Using the ratio IR/red from July and August MSS overpasses, dieback date can be estimated by comparing the ratio found in the different data sets. The stage of dieback can be estimated from the shape of the ratio curve plotted over time.

18.4.3 Yield model output formats

The model output can be presented in the form of a look up table or 3 dimensional graphics plot. The model estimates yield for a given range of planting and harvest dates. An example of the 3 dimensional model output is shown in Figure 18.6, where the x and y axes show harvest date and planting date, respectively, and the z axis shows tons per acre yield. The date is displayed in days of the year format.

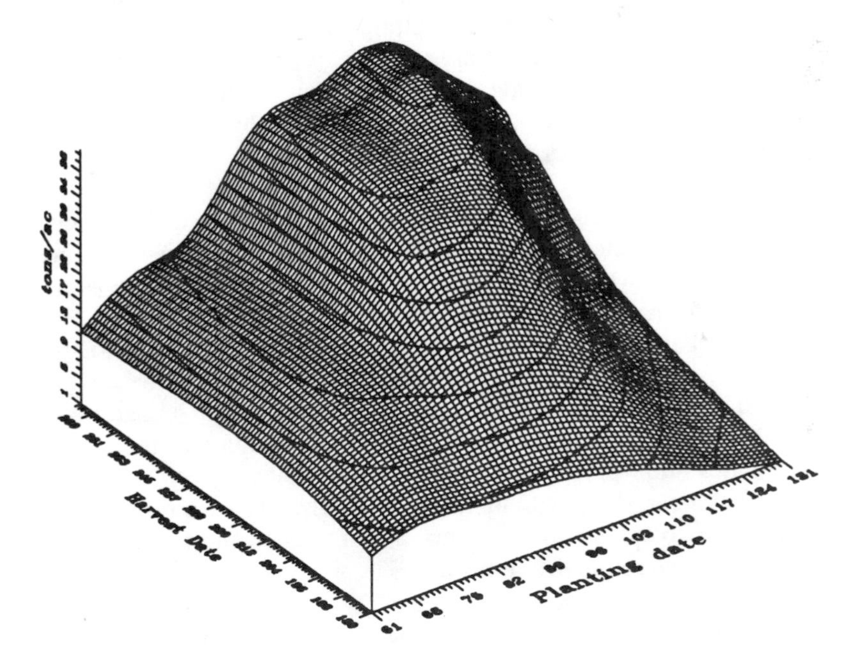

Figure 18.6. Output data from the potato yield model shown in three dimensional as a "yield potential surface".

To utilize the yield output in the form of look up table, a matrix is constructed with planting dates as row heading and harvest dates as column heading. The entries in the matrix represent potato yield for each combination of dates. Within the database, the percentage of potato fields with each possible combination of dates is computed and multiplied by the yield matrix for a final weighted yield estimate of the entire survey area. Yield estimates are also provided by county and state designations.

In addition to graphical and tabular yield results, color-coded yield potential maps can be created. These maps show which fields can be expected to yield high, average, and low. The yield is calculated for each potato field in the database and placed into categories of high to low depending on the range of values.

Yield potential can be estimated throughout the growing season by using the existing weather data and using 10 year average weather data for the balance of the season. Planting date can be found with the early season acquisition and harvest date can be projected using historical trends. This provides an early indication of how the yield is shaping up for the current growing season.

18.5 LEARNING FROM EXPERIENCE

18.5.1 Issues limiting commercial viability

Using remote sensing data collected from satellites to provide a basis for a commercial business serving the agricultural community imposes limitations on providing to a large market. There are several issues which are responsible for these limitations, the first being data turnaround time, and the second being data availability. With improvements in satellite sensor technology and data processing systems, both of these issues can be resolved.

In agriculture, timing is critical since crop conditions and markets are very dynamic. Currently, satellite data is available anywhere from one to four weeks after the satellite passes over. This delay in data delivery limits its use as a source of agricultural information in a rapidly changing environment. The Cropix potato survey can use Landsat MSS data received two weeks after overpass for acreage and yield prediction, but a three to five week delay is debilitating to the survey. In order to get accurate potato acreage estimates, satellite data has to be acquired no earlier than the beginning of June, when the potato plant is approaching canopy closure. This translates into a mid- to late June date for data delivery, which allows for a potential first acreage estimate by the first of July. Acreage estimates within this time frame are acceptable to customers, a month later and the information is not as helpful with marketing decisions.

The availability of Landsat MSS data is controlled by numerous factors including weather and the satellite orbit. The satellite passes over the same location every 16 days. The opportunity for data availability is improved since currently two satellites, Landsat-4 and Landsat-5, both collecting MSS data, have staggered orbits to allow for repeat coverage every 8 days. Even with four chances a month for clear skies, cloud free data in the month of June (in particular, early June) has been limited. Satellite data recorded in mid- to late June or early July has been used, but reports issued in the second half of July have discouraged customers and limited interest in subscribing to the service. Cloud cover problems have also created the need for flexible image processing techniques, as developed with assistance from NASA.

These two factors, particularly data turnaround time, prevent satellite data from being used as a farm management tool, a potentially large market. With an additional grant from NASA under EOCAP 2, Cropix will investigate the utility of rapid data turnaround for field problem detection. Using satellite data received 24 to 48 hours after satellite overpass, Cropix will monitor fields for irrigation and fertility problems, providing the information to the grower so corrective action can be taken before any substantial loss in yield occurs. This type of information will form an additional service Cropix offers to customers.

18.5.2 Meeting market needs

The agricultural information market has a need for a reliable source of acreage and yield estimates to create a more stable market. Providing this type of information using satellite data is limited by the previously mentioned factors. With the current satellite systems, the expansion of the existing Cropix service is limited. Future alternatives might include the ability to subscribe to the satellite data stream in a way similar to subscribing to cable television. Another alternative might be the use of a geostationary satellite, which can be controlled from the Cropix office, allowing for satellite data when skies are clear. Alternatives such as these would enhance the ability to provide agricultural market information using satellite data.

18.5.3 Conclusion

Satellite remote sensing has great utility as an information source in agriculture; however, current data delivery systems prevent widespread use. To counteract the limits imposed by data availability, image processing techniques need to be simple but effective to allow for fast data processing. Taking advantage of the varied crop growing patterns by using multiple satellite data acquisitions allows for accurate potato crop acreage estimates. Landsat data has proven its utility in agriculture and other satellite platforms, such as SPOT (Satellite Pour l'Observation de la Terre, operated by the French company SPOT Image), provide data with varied abilities for providing alternate types of agricultural information. Uses of other satellite data types will allow Cropix to expand its current services, given adequate data availability.

Alternate data sources are necessary for Cropix to maintain an information service. In light of this fact and the eventual retirement of Landsat MSS, Landsat TM satellite data was compared with MSS data to measure the suitability of TM data as a replacement. The map accuracies achieved using Landsat TM data were not as high as those found using MSS data, especially for the northern subscene. There are several speculations as to why accuracies were lower in the north with both the TM and MSS data. The greatest suspicion relates to difference in ground truth sample sizes. Typically, more samples are collected in the southern region than the north. Ideally, sample sizes should reflect the proportion of each crop grown in the area. Geographically, the north and south exhibit differences in topography, elevation, soil types, microclimates, weather, and planting dates. These differences directly influence the ability to identify potatoes using Landsat and limit the validity of the comparison. Further investigation is needed to fully examine the utility of Landsat TM data for locating potatoes.

With improvements in timely data delivery, Cropix will be able to provide a valuable information source to the agricultural community using Landsat satellite data. Alternate services, such as field monitoring for crop problems, based on the interpretation of satellite data, will be investigated under EOCAP 2. Future plans also include expansion of the potato survey to other major potato growing states, and surveys of other types of crops.

Acknowledgements

Portions of this research have been made available under National Aeronautics and Space Administration grant number NCC2-569. Thanks to everyone involved in reviewing the manuscript; their comments and suggestions were greatly appreciated.

REFERENCES

1. R. Ryerson, R. Dobbins, and C. Thibault, "Timely crop area estimates from Landsat", *Photogrammetric Engineering and Remote Sensing*, 51, 1735-1743 (1985).

2. T. Lo, F. Scarpace, and T. Lillesand, "Use of multitemporal spectral profiles in agricultural land-cover classification", *Photogrammetric Engineering and Remote Sensing*, 52, 535-544 (1986).

3. F. Hall and G. Badhwar, "Signature-Extendable Technology: Global space-based crop recognition", *IEEE Transactions on Geoscience and Remote Sensing*, GE-25, 93-103 (1987).

4. H. Williamson, "The discrimination of irrigated orchard and vine crops using remotely sensed data", *Photogrammetric Engineering and Remote Sensing*, 55, 77-83 (1989).

5. G. Waddington and F. Lamb, "Using remote sensing images in commercial agriculture", *Advanced Imaging*, 5, 46-49 (1990).

6. M. Story and R. Congalton, "Accuracy assessment: A user's perspective", *Photogrammetric Engineering and Remote Sensing*, 52, 397-399 (1986).

7. L. Mann, J. Salute, and G. Waddington, "Commercial application of remote sensing for Columbia Basin potato crop estimation", In the *Proceedings of the 1991 International Geoscience and Remote Sensing Symposium*, Helsinki, Finland. In press.

About the Editors

Yaghoub Mahdavieh received the Bachelor's degree in mechanical engineering from the University of London in 1978, the Master's degree in automatic control engineering, and the Doctorate in computer vision from the University of Manchester Institute of Science and Technology, UK, in 1979 and 1983, respectively. In 1983 he joined Evans and Sutherland Computer Corporation, Cambridge, England, where he was involved in research and development of computer-generated 3-D images and analysis. In 1985 he joined Automatix International UK Ltd. as a senior engineer. He designed, developed, and implemented several practical image analysis projects such as advanced automated character recognition and expert dimensional measurements of industrial parts. He was involved with teaching and consulting activities in the areas of machine vision and image analysis. Since 1988 he has been with General Electric Aircraft Engines, where he has been engaged in research and development activities in the field of advanced automated image analysis for commercial and military applications. He received GE's achievement award in 1989. Dr. Mahdavieh is author or co-author of several articles related to image analysis and computer vision.

Rafael C. Gonzalez received the B.S.E.E. degree from the University of Miami in 1965 and the M.E. and Ph.D. degrees in electrical engineering from the University of Florida, Gainesville, in 1967 and 1970, respectively. He has been affiliated with GT&E, the Center for Information Research at the University of Florida, NASA, and is presently Distinguished Service Professor of Electrical and Computer Engineering at the University of Tennessee, Knoxville. He founded Perceptics Corporation in 1982 and was its president for the following ten years. The last three years of this term were spent under an employment agreement with Westinghouse, who acquired the company in 1989. Dr. Gonzalez is a frequent consultant to industry and government in the areas of pattern recognition, image processing, and machine learning. He received the 1978 UTK Chancellor's Research Scholar Award, the 1980 Magnavox Engineering Professor Award, and the 1980 M.E. Brooks Distinguished Professor Award for his work in these fields. He became a Distinguished Service Professor at the University of Tennessee in 1984. He was awarded the University of Miami's Distinguished Alumnus Award in 1985, the 1987 IEEE Outstanding Engineer Award for Commercial Development in Tennessee, and the 1988 Albert Rose National Award for Excellence in Commercial Image Processing. He is also the recipient of the 1989 B. Otto Wheeley Award for Excellence in Technology Transfer, the 1989 Coopers and Lybrand Entrepreneur of the Year Award, and the 1992 IEEE Region 3 Outstanding Engineer Award. Dr. Gonzalez is author or co-author of over 100 articles and four books: *Pattern Recognition Principles, Digital Image Processing, Syntactic Pattern Recognition: An Introduction* (Addison-Wesley), and *Robotics: Control, Sensing, Vision and Intelligence* (McGraw-Hill). He is also a co-holder of two U.S. patents, and has been an associate editor for *IEEE Trans. on Systems, Man and Cybernetics* and the *International Journal of Computer and Information Sciences.* He is a member of several professional and honorary societies, including Tau Beta Pi, Phi Kappa Phi, Eta Kappa Nu, and Sigma Xi. He is a Fellow of the IEEE.